Implementing GAAS 2016–17

Implementing GAAS 2016–17

**A Practical Guide
to Auditing and Reporting**

Ian Connon
Helen MacNeill
BDO LLP

 Wolters Kluwer

Disclaimer

This publication is sold with the understanding that neither the publisher nor the authors, with regard to this publication, are engaged in rendering legal or professional services. The material contained in this publication neither purports, nor is intended to be, advice on any particular matter.

Although this publication incorporates a considerable degree of standardisation, subjective judgment by the user, based on individual circumstances, is indispensable.This publication is an 'aid' and cannot be expected to replace such judgment.

Neither the publisher nor the authors can accept any responsibility or liability to any person, whether a purchaser of this publication or not, in respect of anything done oromitted to be done by any such person in reliance, whether sole or partial, upon the whole or any part of the contents of this publication.

© Financial Reporting Council Ltd (FRC). Adapted and reproduced with the kind permission of the Financial Reporting Council. All rights reserved. For further information, please visit www.frc.org.uk or call +44 (0) 20 7492 2300.

ISBN 978-1-78540-255-5

British Library Cataloguing-in-Publication Data

A catalogue record for this book is available from the British Library.

Typeset by Innodata Inc., India.

Printed by Gutenberg Press Ltd, Malta.

CONTENTS

Contents

Contents

Contents

Contents

Contents

PREFACE

Although the full impact has yet to be felt, one of the major features of the past year has been the efforts of various bodies involved in the implementation of the EU Audit Directive and Regulation, and the efforts of the profession and other interested parties to ensure that the requirements are applied in the UK in a sensible and proportionate manner. The Directive amends the EU's 2006 Statutory Audit Directive which governs statutory audits throughout the EU and on which our current auditing regime is partially based. The Regulation only applies to the audits of public interest entities (PIEs), i.e. entities with securities listed on a regulated market, banks, building societies and insurers. Both the Directive and the Regulation are the outcome of a long process to reform and regulate the audit market with a view to improving quality, competition and consistency across the single market of the EU. Many of the more outrageous proposals originally put forward by the European Commission have been significantly watered down over the years, others have already, in effect, been adopted by regulators and standards setters in the UK. The result, nevertheless, is a significant package of changes, due to come into effect on 17 June 2016 (although at the time of writing, the legislation required to enable this to happen had not been enacted).

Changes arising from the implementation of the Directive and Regulation are widespread and include:

- revised and restructured ethical standards issued by the FRC – primarily affecting audits of PIEs with more onerous restrictions and rules regarding independence and the provision of non-audit services, but also widening the scope of the revised ethical standard to cover other assurance services as well as audit;
- revised auditing standards incorporating detailed requirements of the Directive and Regulation;
- changes to the UK Corporate Governance Code;
- changes to FCA and PRA Rules for regulated entities; and
- changes in the role of the FRC which will become the designated 'competent authority' for oversight and regulation of the audit profession. As part of this, the FRC has redefined the role of its AQR team and the ICAEW's QAD such that many smaller firms with listed company clients or unlisted entities now designated as PIEs will find themselves falling within the scope of AQR inspection for the first time.

At the same time, the FRC has taken the opportunity to update and revise ISAs (UK and Ireland) to reflect a number of changes made recently to International Standards on Auditing by the International Auditing and Assurance Standards Board (IAASB). These include changes to emphasise the auditor's responsibilities in relation to disclosures in the financial statements, new requirements in relation to 'other information' in the annual report and adoption of the IAASB's revised auditor reporting standards. This latter change will have a big impact on the format and wording of auditor's reports – although in most cases, the new standards will first apply for June 2018 year ends. Another key change in the audit report is the introduction of a new ISA 701 dealing with reporting of 'Key Audit Matters' (KAMs). This follows the same sort of approach to enhanced reporting as has been used recently in the UK for listed companies and others following the UK Corporate Governance Code but envisages the possibility of voluntary reporting of KAMs by auditors of other entities.

Given that the changes referred to above are intended to apply for audits of financial periods commencing on or after 17 June 2016, and given that much of the detail has now been published at least in 'final draft' form, we have tried where possible to reflect the new requirements in this book. Unfortunately we have not been able to provide all the practical examples we would have liked and will need to see to how practice develops in certain areas, such as audit reporting, and whether further guidance is forthcoming from the FRC or elsewhere. This is something we will revisit in future editions of the book.

Other significant developments in the year include changes to UK GAAP following the introduction of FRS 102 and accompanying standards. Application of these standards continues to pose significant challenges for some companies and their auditors. Small companies, of course, continue to be able to apply the FRSSE for another year before being forced to switch to the new section 1A of FRS 102, although some will have chosen to early adopt the new requirements. Micro-entities may also early adopt FRS 105. For both small companies and micro-entities, this adds a further layer of complication as early adoption automatically triggers other requirements of the *Companies, Partnerships and Groups (Accounts and Reports) Regulations* 2015 such as the new small companies filing regime (under which abbreviated accounts, as such, no longer exist) and the requirement for the auditor (if there is one) to report further on the directors' report. Further complications arise where companies choose to prepare abridged accounts or choose not to file elements of the annual report. New regulations have also recently been issued to extend these new rules to LLPs and qualifying partnerships which were scoped out from the original legislative changes. All of this has significant implications for preparers of accounts and, where applicable, auditors, who may also have issues with the adequacy of disclosures in the context of a true and fair view. This is another area in which it will be interesting to see how practice develops.

For solicitors, the SRA has revised the requirements for reporting accountants, relaxing the reporting requirements but at the same time introducing much more judgment into the accountant's role. For entities holding client money or assets, the FRC has issued a new standard covering the auditor's responsibilities when providing assurance reports to the FRC under the CASS rules. These changes are covered in **Chapters 45** and **9** respectively.

Simplifications to the auditor cessation rules in the Companies Act, which were introduced by some fairly complicated wording in the *Deregulation Act* 2015, came into force in October 2015 and are reflected in **Chapter 38**.

Audit exemption thresholds continue to rise with the Government confirming that exemption thresholds would change to line up with the new (increased) small company size limits for accounting purposes. This means that for periods commencing on or after 1 January 2016, companies with turnover up to £10.2m may be able to claim audit exemption. This puts the UK, along with Germany and the Netherlands, at the top of the permitted range for audit exemption under EU legislation. Good news for deregulation enthusiasts and for companies perhaps, not so good for auditors, although there is still considerable scope for the development of other assurance services.

On the international front the IAASB remains busy with projects looking at ISA 540 (estimates), ISA 600 (group audits) and ISA 315 (understanding and risk assessment) along with wider projects considering quality control procedures for audit and the application of professional scepticism by auditors, which has been flagged as an area of concern by global audit regulators. An invitation to comment (ITC) Enhancing Audit Quality in the Public Interest: A Focus on Professional Skepticism, Quality Control and Group Audits was issued in December 2015 inviting views in these and other areas.

As regards scepticism, the IAASB is exploring key questions like what is it, what skills and competencies are needed of auditors, what are the impediments to exercising professional scepticism and how should it be documented? On quality control, it notes that existing standards such as ISQC 1 and ISA 220 may be seen as a bit reactive, given the focus on compliance with standards and programs. It asks whether, as in other industries, more could be done to adopt a more proactive 'right first time' or 'quality management' approach so that when audits are done, the result is automatically of a high quality and it is not necessary to double check that this is the case. These projects are at an early stage and concrete proposals will no doubt take some time to develop.

Other matters under consideration are the growing use of data analytics and the possibility of new audit techniques being developed as a result of changing business practices and developments in technology. Auditing needs to move with the times and auditing standards should not be seen as a barrier to innovation.

For those entities where audit is still required, audit quality remains a key area of focus for regulators. In recently published reports both AQR and QAD include some positive comments in this respect. However, whilst they note improvements in some areas, they also list a number of common failings and areas where further improvement is still required. Keeping up with ever changing requirements and the increasing expectations of regulators and, at the same time meeting the demands of clients, remains a challenge for firms of all sizes, with no sign that this is going to diminish in the near future. This book does not provide all the answers but we hope that it will help to guide both the novice and the experienced practitioner through the maze of standards and guidance with which they are now expected to be familiar.

We are grateful to the many people who have contributed over the years to the material in this book. In particular, we should like to acknowledge the contributions of Don Bawtree, Jenny Bennett, Ros Brickman, Nick Carter-Pegg, Chris Kirton, Peter Lewis, Nigel Read and Philip Rego whose help in updating the book this year has been invaluable.

As usual, any suggestions as to how the book could be further improved would be welcome. Please e-mail your views to uk-contentqueries@wolterskluwer.com.

Ian Connon

Helen MacNeill

BDO LLP
June 2016

1 THE NATURE OF AUDITING STANDARDS

1.1 Introduction

For the purpose of this book, Generally Accepted Auditing Standards (GAAS) are the rules which are acknowledged as those by which auditors can measure their performance and by which others can measure them. In the widest sense, these standards are set by a variety of groups:

- government, in the form of legislation;
- officially designated or generally recognised standard setting bodies, in the form of pronouncements of varying authority;
- professional bodies, in the form of guidance for members;
- courts in judgments on cases involving auditors;
- practitioners whose 'internal' standards may become a generally accepted 'norm' especially in areas where there are no public pronouncements; and
- regulators, whose interpretation of standards effectively determines what is or is not generally accepted.

1.2 Limitations of standards

Because of the nature of auditing, the development of a framework of auditing standards which will provide answers to all the questions and problems faced by auditors is not feasible. There will always be judgments over questions – such as how much evidence is enough in a given case? – to which auditing standards will not provide a solution. This is aggravated by the relationship between auditing and accounting. Auditors form opinions on financial statements, the preparation of which involves, amongst other things, appraisals of the likely outcome of uncertain future events. Auditing standards are also constrained by this uncertainty. As business practices and financial reporting practices evolve and adapt to changing circumstances, the auditor must also be able to adapt his approach. Whilst auditing standards aim to establish a principles-based set of requirements to which auditors must adhere, this can only be a framework to assist the auditor in making judgments and forming opinions, not a rigid system of rules.

1.3 Authoritative bodies

In the main, GAAS emanates from the pronouncements of authoritative bodies which have been granted the legal status to issue standards or which are accepted by audit practitioners and the bodies which regulate them as having the authority to issue guidance. From the point of view of this book, GAAS encompasses not only the standards issued by those bodies but also any guidance on their application.

What constitutes GAAS, in practice, is subject to evolution and change. Auditors in the UK must have regard to a large number of pronouncements issued by various bodies in order to ascertain what actually constitutes GAAS. The main bodies which either issue, or have issued, audit requirements, standards or related guidance are:

- the European Union, which issues Directives regarding the statutory audit of companies that must be incorporated into national law by Member States, and Regulations that have direct application for specific groups of entities;
- the UK government which issues legislation governing the audit of companies and other legally constituted entities within the framework and context of EU legislation;
- International Federation of Accountants (IFAC) and its standard setting boards the International Auditing and Assurance Standards Board (IAASB) and the International Ethical Standards Board for Accountants (IESBA);
- the Financial Reporting Council (FRC);
- professional accountancy bodies, for example, the Institute of Chartered Accountants in England and Wales (ICAEW) which issues guidance through its Audit and Assurance Faculty and other committees.

1.4 International Auditing and Assurance Standards Board

1.4.1 Background

The International Auditing and Assurance Standards Board ('the IAASB') is an independent standard-setting board within the International Federation of Accountants (IFAC). It was formed as the International Auditing Practices Committee in 1978, and develops auditing and assurance standards, guidance and other pronouncements used by professional accountants worldwide.

The initial Auditing Guidelines were first published as International Standards on Auditing (ISAs) in 1991 and have been extensively revised, reviewed and enhanced since that date. As a result, IFAC has established itself as an internationally accepted standard setter with the aim of setting high quality standards for audit, assurance and quality control that strengthen public confidence in the global profession, thus supporting credibility and trust in financial markets. According to IFAC's website, over 111 jurisdictions worldwide, including the UK, have committeed to using the IAASB's clarified auditing standards (see **1.6**).

1.4.2   Structure and processes

The Public Interest Oversight Board (PIOB) oversees the public interest activities of the whole of IFAC including the IAASB. The PIOB's objective is to increase confidence of investors and others by ensuring that the processes of IFAC are responsive to the public interest. This includes the setting of standards by the IAASB.

When setting standards and guidance, the IAASB gains input from its own Consultative Advisory Group, national auditing standard setters, IFAC member bodies and their members, and the general public. The Consultative Advisory Group (CAG) is comprised of representatives of regulators, business and international organisations, and users and preparers of financial statements who are interested in the development and maintenance of high quality international standards on auditing.

1.4.3   IAASB pronouncements

As well as the ISAs, the IAASB issues other guidance which is of relevance to UK auditors. IAASB pronouncements comprise:

- International Standards on Auditing (ISAs);
- International Standards on Assurance Engagements (ISAEs);
- International Standards on Review Engagements (ISREs);
- International Standards on Related Services (ISRSs);
- International Standards on Quality Control (ISQCs); and
- International Auditing Practice Statements (IAPSs).

In addition, the IAASB staff occasionally issue guidance notes such as practice alerts and bulletins. These are for information purposes only and have no authoritative status.

IAASB pronouncements have no direct authority in the UK, although the UK is committed to supporting IFAC and the FRC has largely adopted the auditing and quality control standards as the basis for its own standards. Through their membership of IFAC, professional accountancy bodies in the UK are also committed to using their best endeavours to promote IFAC standards.

1.5   The Financial Reporting Council and the Auditing Practices Board

The FRC is now the main standard-setting body, replacing the former Auditing Practices Board (APB), which was responsible for many of the extant standards. The FRC Board is supported by three Committees:

- the Codes and Standards Committee;
- the Conduct Committee; and
- the Executive Committee.

The Codes and Standards Committee advises the FRC Board on matters relating to codes, standard-setting and policy questions, through its Accounting, Actuarial and Audit and Assurance Councils.

The Conduct Committee advises the Board on matters relating to conduct activities to promote high-quality corporate reporting, including monitoring, oversight, investigative and disciplinary functions through its Monitoring and Case Management Committees.

The Executive Committee supports the Board by advising on strategic issues and providing day-to day oversight of the work of the FRC.

The FRC's Scope and Authority of Pronouncements statement sets out:

- an overview of the types of document issued by the FRC;
- the level of authority associated with each type of document; and
- the regulatory regime supporting FRC pronouncements derived from legislation and the rules of the accountancy bodies.

The Statement includes the *Auditors' Code* which sets out the principles that the FRC expects to guide the conduct of auditors, as well as underlying its own guidance and the ethical standards of the professional bodies. The code is set out in **Table 1**.

TABLE 1: The Auditors' Code

Accountability

Auditors act in the interests of primary stakeholders, whilst having regard to the wider public interest. The identity of primary stakeholders is determined by reference to the statute or agreement requiring an audit: in the case of companies, the primary stakeholder is the general body of shareholders.

Integrity

Auditors act with integrity, fulfilling their responsibilities with honesty, fairness, candour, courage and confidentiality. Confidential information obtained in the course of the audit is disclosed only when required in the public interest, or by operation of law.

Objectivity and independence

Auditors are objective and provide impartial opinions unaffected by bias, prejudice and compromise and conflicts of interest. Auditors are also independent, this requires them to be free from situations and relationships which would make it probable that a reasonable and informed third party would conclude that the auditors' objectivity either is impaired or could be impaired.

Competence

Auditors act with professional skill, derived from their qualification, training and practical experience. This demands an understanding of financial reporting and business issues, together with expertise in accumulating and assessing the evidence necessary to form an opinion.

Rigour

Auditors approach their work with thoroughness and with an attitude of professional scepticism. They assess critically the information and explanations obtained in the course of their work and such additional evidence as they consider necessary for the purposes of their audit.

Judgment

Auditors apply professional judgment taking account of materiality in the context of the matter on which they are reporting.

Clear, complete and effective communication

Auditors' reports contain clear expressions of opinion and set out information necessary for a proper understanding of that opinion. Auditors communicate audit matters of governance interest arising from the audit of financial statements with those charged with governance of an entity.

Association

Auditors allow their reports to be included in documents containing other information only if they consider that the additional information is not in conflict with the matters covered by their report and they have no cause to believe it to be misleading.

Providing value

Auditors add to the reliability and quality of financial reporting; they provide to directors and officers constructive observations arising from the audit process; and thereby contribute to the effective operation of business, capital markets and the public sector.

1.6 Development of International Standards on Auditing (UK and Ireland)

International Standards on Auditing (ISAs) are issued by the International Auditing and Assurance Standards Board (IAASB).

1.6.1   Original ISAs (UK and Ireland)

In May 2004, the APB announced its intention to adopt the ISAs issued by the IAASB for use in the UK and Ireland, first reviewing all of the existing Statements of Auditing Standards (SASs) to identify instances where they contained higher standards than those contained in the equivalent ISAs, and supplementing the ISAs accordingly. The resultant International Standards of Auditing (UK and Ireland) ('ISAs (UK and Ireland)') were effective for the audit of financial statements for periods commencing on or after 15 December 2004.

1.6.2   IAASB's clarity project

At the same time the IAASB began a comprehensive project aimed at improving the clarity of its ISAs. The IAASB also took the opportunity to update and improve a number of the ISAs and the project was completed in March 2009 when 36 newly updated and clarified ISAs were issued. They were effective internationally for the audits of financial statements for periods commencing on or after 15 December 2009.

1.6.3   UK adoption of clarified ISAs

In the UK, the APB revised ISAs (UK and Ireland) on the basis of the new IAASB standards. The new 'clarified' ISAs (UK and Ireland) contained some additional paragraphs of supplementary material (grey-shaded paragraphs) which:

- addressed specific UK and Irish legal and regulatory requirements; and
- maintained a small number of other existing FRC/APB requirements and guidance considered necessary to prevent changes in audit practice to the detriment of audit quality. With improvements made to the underlying ISAs, the number of UK 'add-ons' was considerably reduced.

These new ISAs (UK and Ireland) were effective for audits of financial statements for periods ending on or after 15 December 2010.

One exception was ISA 700 *Forming an Opinion and Reporting on Financial Statements* which was not adopted by the APB. The APB instead issued ISA (UK and Ireland) 700 *The independent auditor's report on financial statements* which addressed the requirements of company law and also provided for a more concise auditor's report, addressing issues raised in the consultation process.

1.6.4   EU Audit Directive and Regulation

In April 2014, after a long and tortuous consultation process, the European Parliament and the Council of the European Union issued Regulation

EU/537/2014 covering specific requirements regarding the statutory audit of public interest entities[1] (PIEs) (referred to as the Audit Regulation), and Directive 2014/56/EU which amended Directive 2006/43/EC covering the statutory audit of annual accounts and consolidated accounts (the Audit Directive). Both apply with effect from 17 June 2016. The Audit Regulation has the direct effect of law and EU member states are required to adopt appropriate provisions to ensure its effective application. The Audit Directive does not have a direct effect in law and EU member states are required to adopt and publish the measures necessary to comply with it.

The Audit Regulation and Audit Directive together require revisions to both the Ethical and Auditing Standards as well as changes to the UK Corporate Governance Code and amendments to UK law.

In the UK, the government and the FRC decided to incorporate many of the detailed provisions of the Regulation and Directive directly into Auditing Standards, rather than as new requirements of the Companies Act and an exposure draft of revised standards to incorporate these amendments was published for comment in September 2015. This approach has the advantage of keeping detailed requirements for statutory audit in one place as well as providing greater flexibility for maintenance in the future given the difficulty involved in changing primary legislation. The downside is that the standards themselves will contain much more UK specific material than previously, much more material that is applicable only to PIEs and some that is apparently duplicated where EU requirements and IAASB standards overlap. Requirements deriving from the Regulation and Directive are distinguished in the draft revised ISAs by being grey shaded material and by inclusion of 'R' or 'D' respectively in the paragraph number.

In April 2016, the FRC released these changes as final draft ISAs. Subject to legislative changes in progress at the time of writing, it is expected that the ISAs will be applicable for the audit of financial statements for periods commencing on or after 17 June 2016. Unless noted otherwise, this book has been updated to reflect the changes contained in the final draft ISAs. For earlier periods, the previous versions of ISAs (UK and Ireland) are applicable.

A number of the amendments relate only to PIEs. These are reflected in the appropriate chapters and also listed in a new **Appendix 2** for ease of reference.

1.6.5   *Other changes to ISAs*

As well as incorporating changes resulting from the Audit Directive and the Regulation, the revised standards will also include a number of recent changes to the IAASB's standards resulting from recent projects relating to the audit of other information and disclosures in the financial statements and to auditor

---

[1] Public interest entities are defined in ISQC 1 as those whose transferable securities are admitted to trading on a regulated market, credit institutions and insurance undertakings. This includes fully listed entities in the UK, but not those listed on AIM.

reporting. These changes are widely spread throughout the suite of ISAs (UK and Ireland) but are not separately identified in the draft revised standards.

Reporting standards

In the April 2016 ISAs, the FRC has also taken the opportunity to adopt the IAASB's ISA 700. Previously, the FRC had concerns that introducing the 2008 version of ISA 700 would perpetuate the use of 'boiler plate' language in auditor reports and as such preferred to issue a UK specific standard instead. However, over recent years, the FRC has worked closely with the IAASB to address their concerns and has agreed to adopt the IAASB's ISA 700 (Revised) and also the new ISA 701, subject to including additional UK 'pluses' to retain some requirements already incorporated into the UK's extant standard.

The resulting changes are noted in the reporting chapters of this book, however, the example audit reports have not yet been updated to reflect the changes as it is not yet clear how the revised standard will be applied in a UK context.

1.6.6   Application of ISAs (UK and Ireland)

ISA (UK and Ireland) 200 (Revised June 2016) *Objective and General Principles Governing an Audit of Financial Statements* is a 'grandfather standard' and sets out a number of basic principles and assumptions on which all other standards are based.

Each ISA sets out an objective for the auditor and specifies a number of requirements with which the auditor must comply, where relevant, in order to meet his objective. In order to meet the objective, it may be necessary for the auditor to carry out further procedures in addition to those required by ISAs. In exceptional circumstances, it may be necessary for the auditor to depart from a relevant requirement in which case he will need to perform other procedures in order to achieve his objective. An example of such a situation may be where the ISA requires the auditor to carry out a specific procedure which, in the specific circumstances, would not be effective in achieving its aim. The ISAs also contain application and other explanatory material which is intended to assist auditors in interpreting and applying the standards but which is not prescriptive. The auditor is, however, required to have an understanding of the full text of an ISA, including the application and other explanatory material, in order to apply its requirements properly.

ISA (UK and Ireland) 200 (Revised June 2016) requires auditors to conduct their audits in accordance with ISAs (UK and Ireland) and with an attitude of professional scepticism throughout. Auditors are to recognise the possibility of a material misstatement due to facts or behaviour indicating irregularities, including fraud or error, notwithstanding the auditor's past experience of the honesty and integrity of the entity's management and of those charged with governance. This means that the audit should be approached with a questioning mind, with auditors making critical assessments of the evidence obtained, remaining alert for contradictions or evidence which makes them question the reliability of documents or management representations.

Auditors should also comply with the FRC's Ethical Standard (see **Chapter 2**) and other ethical pronouncements issued by their professional body.

ISA (UK and Ireland) 200 (Revised June 2016) requires auditors to plan and perform their work in order to reduce audit risk to an acceptably low level, having regard to the requirements of the ISAs (UK and Ireland), their professional body, legislation and the terms of the engagement. Auditors must make an assessment of the audit risk, but are not responsible for the detection of misstatements that are not material to the financial statements taken as a whole.

ISAs (UK and Ireland) that have been substantively changed as a result of the the above changes or the requirements of the EU Regulations and Directive are identified in the FRC's final draft by inclusion of the words '(Revised 2016)' in the title and this is used to indicate these standards throughout the book, where applicable. For a full list of extant ISAs, please refer to **Appendix 1**.

1.7   Other FRC guidance

1.7.1   *Practice Notes*

The FRC also issues Practice Notes to assist auditors in applying auditing standards to particular circumstances in specific industries. Practice Notes are persuasive rather than prescriptive although they are indicative of good practice. Most Practice Notes have been updated following the adoption of clarified ISAs (see **1.6.3**).

1.7.2   *Bulletins*

Bulletins have the same status as Practice Notes and are issued to provide auditors with timely guidance on new and emerging issues.

1.7.3   *Standards*

The FRC has also issued one new assurance standard, *Providing assurance on client assets to the Financial Conduct Authority*, which applies to work carried out by auditors under Client Asset (CASS) Rules of the Financial Conduct Authority.

1.7.4 Statements of Recommended Practice (SORPs)

In 2016, the FRC issued a revised policy for the development and approval of SORPs. Until now, SORPs have been issued to provide industry specific guidance primarily on financial reporting issues but the new policy extends to all FRC pronouncements and will permit approved SORP making bodies to issue industry specific auditing guidance. To be effective, any such pronouncements will require formal endorsement by the FRC.

1.8 Other guidance

Since its formation in 1995, guidance on auditing matters has been issued by the Audit and Assurance Faculty of the ICAEW in the form of Technical Releases, many of which are referred to throughout this publication. Technical Releases are listed in **Appendix 1**.

1.9 Conventions

The reader should note that throughout this book, the male pronoun is used to cover references to both the male and female.

1.10 Accounting framework

Accounting standards FRSs 101, 102, 103, 104 and 105 replaced previous UK accounting standards (other than the FRSSE) for accounting periods commencing on or after 1 January 2015, but may be adopted early. Where this publication refers to the financial reporting framework, this should be taken to refer to the current relevant standards applicable to the engagement. The applicable financial reporting framework also includes the requirements of applicable law.

2 AUDIT REGULATION AND ETHICS

2.1 Introduction

Only registered auditors may accept appointment as company auditors in the UK. This has been the case since the relevant provisions of the *Companies Act 1989* became effective on 1 October 1991 and this requirement is retained in the *Companies Act* 2006. In addition, where audits of other entities are required by law or regulations (e.g. certain charities and pension schemes), the auditor is required to be a registered auditor. Audit firms and individual audit engagement partners must be registered with a Recognised Supervisory Body (RSB). In order to qualify as an RSB, an organisation must have rules to ensure that its members, who are therefore qualified to accept appointments as company auditors, are properly regulated and monitored. To date the Institute of Chartered Accountants in England and Wales (ICAEW), the Institute of Chartered Accountants of Scotland (ICAS), the Institute of Chartered Accountants in Ireland (ICAI) (now operating as Chartered Accountants Ireland) and the Association of Chartered Certified Accountants (ACCA) have become RSBs for this purpose. In order to maintain registered auditor status, auditors registered with ICAEW, ICAS or ICAI must comply with Audit Regulations issued jointly by these bodies.

The definition of 'audit' includes audits of financial statements where required by law and any other function in respect of any of these entities that is required by law to be discharged by a registered auditor (for example, the report on the transfer of non-cash assets to a public company).

This publication is written with the presumption that the reader's audit firm is registered with the ICAEW as its RSB. Where this is not the case, and the firm is registered with an alternative RSB, this should be taken in account when reading example letters, for example those in **Chapter 38** which are addressed to the ICAEW.

The RSB's regulations must cover the following areas:

- qualification of auditors;
- control of audit firms by qualified individuals;
- fit and proper persons;
- professional integrity and independence;
- technical standards (see **2.8**);
- procedures to maintain competence (see **2.9**); and
- meeting claims (see **2.10**).

The rules must also provide for monitoring and enforcement (see **2.12** and **2.13**), membership eligibility (see **2.11**), investigation of complaints and discipline.

2.1.1   Ethical standards for auditors

Each RSB has its own Code of Ethics but in 2003, the responsibility for setting standards for independence, objectivity and integrity in respect of audit activities was transferred to the APB who published five Ethical Standards in October 2004 and an Ethical Standard, *Provisions Available for Small Entities* in December 2004 ('ES – PASE'). These are discussed in **2.6** and **2.7** below.

A number of reviews of Ethical Standards have taken place since then, with the most recent finalised updates to Ethical Standards 1 and 5 being published in December 2011, to Ethical Standards 2, 4 and the PASE in December 2010 and to Ethical Standard 3 in October 2009.

Responsibility for the issue of ethical standards for auditors now lies with the Financial Reporting Council ('FRC') who took over the functions of the APB and is now designated as the competent authority for the regulation of the auditing profession.

In April 2016, the FRC issued a final draft of a proposed Revised Ethical Standard 2016 which, subject to legislation, is due to take effect for audit and assurance engagements relating to periods commencing on or after 17 June 2016 and which will replace the existing Ethical Standards for Auditors and the Provisions available for small entities ('ES-PASE'). This latest review incorporates the requirements of the EU Audit Directive and EU Regulation and largely affects auditors of public interest entities ('PIEs'). A summary of the proposed changes is noted in **2.6.1** but these have not been integrated into this publication. When released, the revision will result in one Ethical Standard divided into sections. The scope of the standard is also widened to cover 'all public assurance engagements' and as a result, the new standard will apply to all audit and assurance engagements performed under the FRC's standards, including Standards for Investment Reporting ('SIRs') and the recently issued standard for CASS reporting (see **Chapter 9**), although not all requirements will apply equally to all types of engagement.

In July 2006, the ICAEW updated ethical guidance for its members in its Code of Ethics. Further details are given in **2.5** below.

2.1.2   Audit regulations

Audit Regulations are issued by the RSBs to govern the conduct of registered auditors. First issued in 1991, they have been subject to many changes and updates with the latest amendment being in November 2013. In addition to the matters outlined above, the regulations stipulate how audit reports must be signed (see **2.14**) and include requirements concerning working papers (see **2.15**).

2.1.3 Competition

In recent years, there have been a number of proposals to increase audit competition – this is covered in **2.16**.

2.2 Qualification

The *Companies Act* states that for a qualification to be recognised, it must, among other things, involve:

- a course of theoretical instruction;
- examinations; and
- three years' practical training.

2.3 Control of audit firms

A firm may not be recognised as a registered auditor unless it is controlled by qualified persons. In simple terms, this means that a majority of the members of the firm are qualified persons although certain of the RSBs have in fact imposed more stringent requirements than this.

2.4 Fit and proper person

An RSB must have adequate rules and practices designed to ensure that persons eligible under its rules are fit and proper persons to be so appointed. This will normally involve ensuring that there is a suitable procedure for notification, both to the firm by partners and employees and to the RSB by the firms, of matters relating to partners and employees in respect of:

- financial integrity and reliability;
- convictions or civil liabilities; and
- good reputation or character – including previous disciplinary procedures with professional bodies or other regulatory organisations.

2.5 ICAEW Code of Ethics

2.5.1 Background

In July 2006, the ICAEW issued its own *Code of Ethics* ('the Code') to assist its members in meeting the highest standards of professional conduct and replacing the previous *Guide to Professional Ethics*. It has subsequently been updated and the current version was effective from 1 January 2011. The Code applies to all ICAEW members (including students), affiliates, employees of member firms and member firms themselves (together 'professional accountants'). It is applicable to all professional and business activities, whether remunerated or voluntary.

The Code was derived from the International Ethics Standards Board of Accountants' (IESBA) Code of Ethics issued in July 2009 by the International Federation of Accountants (IFAC), supplemented with additional requirements and guidance where this was considered appropriate by the ICAEW. It adopts a principles-based approach, with threats to the fundamental principles and related safeguards illustrated by a series of case studies. **Table 1** below sets out the independence requirements to be adopted for different types of assurance engagement.

TABLE 1: Independence requirements for different types of assurance engagements

Type of assurance requirement	Independence requirements to be followed
Audit engagements in accordance with ISAs (UK and Ireland)	The FRC's Ethical Standards for Auditors[1]
Audit engagements performed in accordance with other standards	Section 290 of the ICAEW's Code or if more convenient to apply, the independence requirements of the FRC's Ethical Standards for Auditors[1]
Review engagement	Section 290 of the ICAEW's Code or if more convenient to apply, the independence requirements of the FRC's Ethical Standards for Auditors[1]
Other types of assurance engagements	Section 291 of the ICAEW's Code[2]
Reports in accordance with Statements of Investment Circular Reporting Standards (SIRS)	The FRC's Ethical Standard for Reporting Accountants (ESRA)[1]

[1]Expected to be withdrawn in 2016 and replaced by the FRC's Revised Ethical Standard 2016.
[2]The FRC's new Ethical Standard will apply from 2016 for assurance engagements carried out under FRC assurance standards.

The Code is split into four sections dealing with:

- issues of general application to all members; and
- issues of specific interest to:

  - members in practice;
  - members in business; and
  - members undertaking insolvency work.

2.5.2 The fundamental principles

The Code sets out five fundamental principles that must be complied with at all times. These are set out in **Table 2** below.

TABLE 2: Five fundamental principles in the ICAEW Code of Ethics

Integrity

A professional accountant should be straightforward and honest in all professional and business relationships.

Objectivity

A professional accountant should not allow bias, conflict of interest or undue influence of others to override professional or business judgments.

Professional Competence and Due Care

A professional accountant should maintain professional knowledge and skill at the level required to ensure that a client or employer receives competent professional services based on current developments in practice, legislation and techniques and should act diligently and in accordance with applicable technical and professional standards.

Confidentiality

A professional accountant should respect the confidentiality of information acquired as a result of professional and business relationships and, therefore, should not disclose any such information to third parties without proper and specific authority, unless there is a legal or professional right or duty to disclose, nor use the information for the personal advantage of the professional accountant or third parties.

Professional Behaviour

A professional accountant should comply with relevant laws and regulations and should avoid any action that discredits the profession.

The environment in which professional accountants operate may lead to specific threats to these fundamental principles. As it is impossible to envisage every possible threat that may occur, the Code sets out a conceptual framework which requires professional accountants to identify, evaluate and address these threats individually rather than just comply with a predetermined set of rules. Where professional accountants identify significant threats they should apply suitable safeguards to eliminate them or reduce them to an acceptable level.

When considering whether a threat is significant, professional accountants should consider both quantitative and qualitative factors. Where suitable safeguards cannot be applied, the professional accountant should not accept, or should resign, from the engagement.

2.5.3   Threats and safeguards

The Code sets out the following types of threats to the fundamental principles:

- self-interest threats, as a result of the financial or other interests of a professional accountant or of an immediate or close family member;
- self-review threats, when a previous judgment needs to be re-evaluated by the professional accountant responsible for that judgment;
- advocacy threats, when a professional accountant promotes a position or opinion to the point that subsequent objectivity may be compromised;
- familiarity threats, when, because of a close relationship, a professional accountant becomes too sympathetic to the interests of others; and
- intimidation threats, when a professional accountant may be deterred from acting objectively by actual or perceived threats.

Each type of threat may arise in relation to the professional accountant themselves or in relation to a connected person such as a close family member, a fellow partner or other professional associate.

There are two main types of safeguard set out in the Code:

- safeguards created by the profession, legislation or regulation; and
- safeguards in the work environment.

The first category includes, but is not restricted to:

- educational, training and experience requirements for entry into the profession;
- continuing professional development requirements;
- corporate governance regulations;
- professional standards;
- professional or regulatory monitoring and disciplinary procedures; and
- external review by a legally empowered third party of the reports, returns, communications or information produced by a professional accountant.

The actual safeguards used will depend on the circumstances. In assessing whether the safeguards are reasonable, professional accountants should consider what a reasonable and informed third party would consider to be acceptable.

2.5.4   Conflict resolution

When applying the fundamental principles, conflicts may arise. The Code states that it is preferable for such conflicts to be resolved within the organisation before obtaining advice from the Institute or legal advisors. Where necessary, professional accountants should consult with other appropriate persons within the organisation.

When conflicts occur, professional accountants should consider:

- relevant facts;
- relevant parties;
- ethical issues involved;
- fundamental principles related to the matter in question;
- established internal procedures; and
- alternative courses of action.

If, having exhausted all possibilities, the conflict remains unresolved, the professional accountant should refuse to remain associated with the matter creating the conflict. This may involve a firm resignation from an engagement or an individual withdrawing from an engagement team or resigning from a firm.

2.5.5 Conflicts of interest and confidentiality

In January 2000, the ICAEW's Business Law Committee issued TECH 4/00 *Conflicts of interest and confidentiality* to provide guidance for accountants on the implications of the decision in the case of *Prince Jefri Bolkiah v KPMG*. The guidance was intended to be read in conjunction with the ICAEW's Guide to professional Ethics (now the Code of Ethics).

The judgment stresses that where an accountant is acting as a fiduciary, he cannot act for clients with conflicting interests without their informed consent. Since the law is unclear about when accountants act as fiduciaries, consent should be obtained whenever there is potential conflict. Such conflicts of interest could be wide ranging and could extend to audit clients who are competitors with one another in a particular market. This requirement does not apply to former clients, although duties of confidentiality will continue.

The guidance suggests additional paragraphs to be included in the engagement letter to deal with these issues. The paragraphs are set out in **Table 3**.

TABLE 3: Paragraphs to be included in an engagement letter where potential conflict of interest exists

Conflict and Confidentiality

You agree that we may reserve the right to act during this engagement for other clients whose interests are or may be adverse to yours, subject to the confidentiality requirements detailed here.

We confirm that where you give us confidential information, we shall at all times keep it confidential, except as required by law or as provided for in regulatory, ethical or other professional pronouncements applicable to our engagement.

You agree that it will be sufficient compliance with our duty of confidence for us to take such steps as we in good faith think fit to preserve confidential information both during and after termination of this engagement.

Although these paragraphs leave accountants potentially liable for any actual breach of confidence, this is only where they do not take appropriate steps to keep confidential information secure. This means that the erection of 'Chinese Walls' may be avoided.

Chinese Walls

Where an accountant is not able to obtain consent from his client in line with the paragraphs in **Table 3**, it is possible for a Chinese Wall to be effective within a firm. The Prince Jefri ruling states that the Chinese Wall must have the characteristics noted in **Table 4** to be effective.

TABLE 4: Characteristics of an effective Chinese Wall

- The physical separation of the various departments in order to insulate them from each other (this may include details such as separate dining arrangements).
- Training to emphasise the importance of not divulging confidential information.
- Strict and defined procedures for when it is felt that the wall should be crossed and the maintaining of proper records where this occurs.
- Monitoring of the effectiveness of the wall by compliance officers.
- Disciplinary sanctions where there has been a breach of the wall.

In addition, an effective Chinese Wall needs to be an established part of an organisation, not created on an ad hoc basis. Physical segregation would not create an effective barrier within a single department.

2.5.6   Control of confidentiality and independence

A firm must have procedures to ensure that staff are aware of confidentiality and independence issues. Confidentiality applies to the information obtained during the course of professional work and the obligation not to disclose or use it. Firms need to be able to demonstrate that they have procedures to ensure that such issues have been brought to the attention of staff. This can be demonstrated by having staff certify their awareness of the procedures. Additionally, as regards independence, the firm should circulate details of listed companies of which it is the auditor to both partners and employees to enable them to identify any potential conflicts.

2.5.7   Receipt of information in confidence by auditors

In addition to the professional guidance found in the Code on the ethics of the disclosure and use of confidential information, guidance can also be found in the ICAEW's Technical Release TECH 10/14AAF *Receipt of information in confidence by auditors*. TECH 10/14AAF provides additional assistance in the resolution of ethical problems that may arise where auditors receive information from a source other than their client, with a request or the implication that the information or its source should be kept confidential. Such circumstances may arise in relation to information received from regulators, from employees or from third parties such as trading partners. In these circumstances, auditors should always act with integrity; take into account their legal obligations including potential duties to report to regulators or to report suspicions of money laundering; use best endeavours to protect the identity of informants; and consider the significance of any such matters raised in relation to the audit.

2.6   Ethical Standards for Auditors

In October 2004, the APB issued its *Ethical Standards for Auditors* covering integrity, objectivity and independence.

- Ethical Standard 1, *Integrity, Objectivity and Independence*;
- Ethical Standard 2, *Financial, Business, Employment and Personal Relationships*;
- Ethical Standard 3, *Long Association with the Audit Engagement*;
- Ethical Standard 4, *Fees, Remuneration and Evaluation Policies, Litigation, Gifts and Hospitality*; and
- Ethical Standard 5, *Non-audit Services Provided to Audit Clients*.

Certain exemptions in respect of audits of small entities were set out in the Ethical Standard – Provisions Available for Small Entities (PASE).

A number of revisions have been made to these Ethical Standards. Ethical Standard 3 (Revised) was last revised in October 2009. Ethical Standards 1, 2, 4 and 5 (Revised) were issued in December 2010 along with the PASE (Revised). Further minor amendments to Ethical Standards 1 and 5 (Revised) were published in December 2011.

The Ethical Standards also incorporate the requirements set out in:

- the EC Recommendation on 'Statutory auditors' independence in the EU: a set of the fundamental principles'; and
- the International Ethics Standards Board for Accountants ('IESBA') *Code of Ethics for Professional Accountants*,

so that when auditors follow the FRC standards, they will also largely have complied with the principles set out in the international guidance. The Revised Ethical Standard 2016 will also include requirements of the EU Audit Directive and EU Audit Regulation. The Audit Directive establishes specific requirements concerning the statutory audit of annual and consolidated financial statements. The Audit Regulation establishes further specific requirements regarding the statutory audit of 'public interest entities'.

2.6.1   The proposed Revised Ethical Standard 2016

The proposed Revised Ethical Standard 2016, when finalised, will consist of one standard to replace the five individual Ethical Standards and comprises a number of sections:

- Part A: Overarching Principles and Supporting Ethical Provisions; and
- Part B:

    - Section 1, *General Requirements and Guidance*;
    - Section 2, *Financial, Business, Employment and Personal Relationships*;
    - Section 3, *Long Association with Engagements and with Entities Relevant to Engagements*;
    - Section 4, *Fees, Remuneration and Evaluation Policies, Gifts and Hospitality, Litigation*;
    - Section 5, *Non-audit/Additional Services*; and
    - Section 6, *Provisions Available for Audits of Small Entities*.

The main changes in the proposed 2016 standard, other than the presentation and formatting changes, are set out below.

General requirements

An audit firm will be required to establish appropriate and effective operational and administrative arrangements to identify and manage threats to independence and to deal with and record incidents that may affect the integrity of its audit activities and be able to demonstrate to the competent authority (FRC) that the arrangements are appropriate given the complexity and size of the firm.

Where a firm is a member of a network, management of the UK firm will have a responsibility to make arrangements for ensuring that appropriate ethical policies are applied across the network and that policies, procedures and quality control systems are implemented and operating effectively.

A firm's policy on resolving differences of opinion should include differences of opinion between the Ethics Partner and those consulting him. The Ethics Partner also should not take on any role that would conflict with the role of Ethics Partner.

New provisions relate to identification of threats to independence where an audit client merges with or is acquired by another entity.

For public interest entities and other listed entities, specific requirements have been introduced to assess and document in the engagement working papers various matters including all significant threats to integrity or objectivity, and safeguards to mitigate them, compliance with the Ethical Standard, competence and adequacy of resources.

Relationships

Stricter requirements will apply to the holding of direct and indirect financial interests in clients by partners and persons in a position to influence the outcome, which will extend to 'persons closely associated' with the partner or other person, not just immediate family members.

Stricter procedures and restrictions will apply where partners or staff leave the firm to join audit clients or entities that subsequently wish to become audit clients.

Long association

For audits of public interest entities, Key Audit Partners involved in the audit will need to rotate after five years (previously seven). Firms will also be required to introduce policies of gradual rotation of senior personnel involved in public interest entity audits.

Fees, remuneration and gifts

For audits of public interest entities, a cap (based on a 70% of the average audit fee) will be imposed for the provision of certain non-audit services.

A new requirement is that in evaluating an individual's performance and considering promotions a primary criterion will be the individual's contribution to the quality of the engagement.

Gifts or hospitality should not be accepted by the firm, its partners, others in a position to affect the conduct of the audit or those closely associated with them unless a reasonable third party would regard them as trivial and inconsequential. This is a change of emphasis and a simplification of current rules.

Non-audit services

Contingent fees will not be allowed for tax services to public interest entities or other listed entities with market capitalisation exceeding 200m euros.

The Ethical Standard includes a long list of prohibited non-audit services for public interest entities derived from the EU Audit Regulation. The auditor of a public interest entity will also need to consider the implications for his independence if any such services are provided to entities controlled by the audited entity by other firms in the same network.

The following sections are based on the standards as revised in 2009–11 and may not fully reflect changes to be introduced by the proposed 2016 FRC Ethical Standard, which will apply for audit and assurance engagements for periods commencing on or after 17 June 2016.

2.6.2 Ethical Standard 1 (Revised): Integrity, Objectivity and Independence

Ethical Standard 1 (Revised) (ES1) states:

'Public confidence in the operation of the capital markets and in the conduct of public interest entities depends, in part, upon the credibility of the opinions and reports issued by the auditors in connection with the audit of the financial statements. Such credibility depends on beliefs concerning the integrity, objectivity and independence of the auditors and the quality of audit work they perform.'

It defines each of the terms integrity, objectivity and independence as follows:

- 'integrity requires not only honesty but a broad range of related qualities such as fairness, candour, courage, intellectual honesty and confidentiality';
- 'objectivity is a state of mind that excludes bias, prejudice and compromise and that gives fair and impartial consideration to all matters that are relevant to the task in hand, disregarding those that are not. Objectivity requires that the auditors' judgment is not affected by conflicts of interests'; and
- 'independence is freedom from situations and relationships which make it probable that a reasonable and informed third party would conclude that objectivity is either impaired or could be impaired'.

The Standard requires firms to establish formal and written policies and procedures to ensure that those in a position to influence the conduct and outcome of an audit act with integrity, objectivity and independence. This should involve the leadership of the firm engendering an environment where ethics are considered more important than commercial considerations, and designating an 'ethics partner' to have overall responsibility for the firm's policies and procedures.

The policies and procedures in place should include those set out in **Table 5**.

TABLE 5: Ethical policies and procedures

- Requirements for partners and staff to report where applicable:

    - family and other personal relationships involving an audit client of the firm;
    - financial interests in an audit client of the firm; and
    - decisions to join an audit client.

- Monitoring of compliance with the firm's policies and procedures relating to integrity, objectivity and independence. Such monitoring procedures include, on a test basis, periodic review of the audit engagement partners' documentation of their consideration of the auditors' objectivity and independence, addressing, for example:

    - financial interests in audit clients;
    - economic dependency on audit clients;
    - the performance of non-audit services; and
    - audit partner rotation.

- Prompt communication of identified breaches of the firm's policies and procedures to the relevant audit engagement partners.
- Evaluation by audit engagement partners of the implications of any identified breaches of the firm's policies and procedures that are reported to them.
- Reporting by audit engagement partners of particular circumstances or relationships as required by the FRC Ethical Standards (Revised).
- Prohibiting members of the audit team from being involved in the decision making of the audited entity, or assuming responsibility for, management decisions for the audit client.
- Operation of a disciplinary mechanism to promote compliance with policies and procedures.
- Empowerment of staff to communicate to senior levels within the firm any issue of objectivity and independence that concerns them; this includes establishing clear communication channels open to staff, encouraging staff to use these channels and ensuring that staff who use these channels are not subject to disciplinary proceedings as a result.

All firms of more than three partners who are responsible individuals should designate a partner in the firm as 'ethics partner'. The ethics partner will have responsibility for:

- the adequacy of the firm's policies and procedures relating to integrity, objectivity and independence, their compliance with the Ethical Standards, and the effectiveness of their communications to partners and staff within the firm; and
- providing related guidance to individual partners to ensure a consistent approach to the application of the Ethical Standards.

The ethics partner should be suitably experienced and hold sufficient authority within a firm.

Firms with three or less partners where it is not practicable to designate an ethics partner should ensure that the relevant issues are regularly discussed by all partners. Sole practitioners should discuss with the ethics helpline of their professional body any matters where a difficult or objective judgment must be made.

The auditor should identify and assess threats to his objectivity and apply safeguards that will either eliminate or reduce the threat to an acceptable level. The principal types of threat are set out in **Table 6**.

TABLE 6: Types of threat to objectivity

- Self-interest threat – the auditor has financial or other interest that would affect his decision making.
- Self-review threat – if auditing his own non-audit work.
- Management threat – the firm has made judgments or taken decisions that are the responsibility of management.
- Advocacy threat – the auditor has acted as an advocate and has supported a position taken by management in an adversarial context.
- Familiarity (or trust) threat – the auditor has a close personal relationship with the client.
- Intimidation threat – the auditor is influenced by fear or threats.

The significance of threats should be considered throughout the audit both individually and on a cumulative basis, but at least when:

- considering whether to accept or retain an audit engagement;
- planning the audit;
- forming an opinion on the financial statements;
- considering whether to accept or retain an engagement to provide non-audit services to an audit client; and
- potential threats are reported to the audit engagement partner.

This assessment of threats should be documented, together with details of actions taken as a result of identified threats. The firm should have procedures in place to ensure that any possible threats are reported to the audit engagement partner or the ethics partner. The audit engagement partner should not accept or continue an audit engagement if it is concluded that a threat to objectivity and independence cannot be reduced to an acceptable level.

A threat to independence may also arise from providing non-audit services to a third party who is connected to an audited entity and the outcome of that service has a material impact on the financial statements of the audited entity. Such arrangements should also be considered when assessing objectivity. Examples include providing actuarial advice to the pension scheme of an audited entity.

At the end of the audit process, but prior to issuing the audit report, the audit engagement partner should reach an overall conclusion on whether any threats to objectivity and independence have been properly addressed. If they are unable to conclude that this is the case, the audit report should not be issued, and the firm should resign.

In the case of listed companies and other public interest entities, the assessment and documentation of the assessment, should be reviewed by an independent partner and those charged with governance should be informed of any significant facts and matters that bear on the auditor's objectivity and independence on a timely basis.

For all clients, the key elements of the audit engagement partner's consideration of objectivity and independence should be communicated to those charged with governance. These may include:

- the principal threats, if any, to objectivity and independence identified by the auditor, including consideration of all relationships between the audit client, its affiliates and directors and the audit firm;
- any safeguards adopted and the reasons why they are considered to be effective;
- any independent partner review;
- the overall assessment of threats and safeguards; and
- information about the general policies and processes within the audit firm for maintaining objectivity and independence.

The minimum requirements for listed companies are set out in **Table 7**.

- where the client makes the loan or guarantee to the audit firm, it is neither material to the audit firm or the client, or where the client makes the loan or guarantee to a person able to influence the audit or his immediate family members it is not material to that individual.

Business relationships

Audit firms and persons able to influence audits (and their immediate family members) should not enter into business relationships with audit clients except for the purchase of goods or services in the normal course of business where the transaction is not material to either party.

Examples of business relationships that may create self-interest, advocacy or intimidation threats include:

- joint ventures with the audit client or with a director, officer or other senior management;
- arrangements to combine services or products and market them with reference to both parties;
- acting as a distributor or marketer of any of the audit client's products or services; or
- other commercial transactions such as the audit firm leasing office space from the audit client.

Employment relationships

Audit staff should not:

- be employed by both audit firm and audit client;
- be loaned by the firm to the client, except if it is for a short period of time and does not involve staff or partners performing non-audit services which would not have been permitted under ES5. Also, the audit client must agree that the member of staff will not hold a management position and will not have responsibility for management decisions or preparing or recording accounting entries; or
- be involved in auditing any work they performed whilst on loan with the client.

If a former partner of the firm joins an audit client, the firm must ensure that all connections with the partner are severed before any further audit work is performed for that client. This includes settling outstanding financial interests and ensuring that the partner does not participate or appear to participate in the firm's business or professional activities.

Firms should have procedures to ensure that partners or senior audit team members are required to notify the firm as soon as there is a potential for them to become employed by an audit client. Other members of the team should notify the firm as soon as their employment by an audit client becomes probable. Any such person must be removed from the audit team immediately and the work they performed on the current and most recent audit should be reviewed.

When a partner becomes a director, including a non-executive director, or enters a key management position with an audit client within two years of acting as an engagement partner, EQCR partner, key audit partner or partner in the chain of command for that client, the firm must resign as auditor. Reappointment cannot take place until a two-year 'cooling off' period has elapsed. If any other audit team member joins the client as a director or in a key management position within two years of leaving, the firm should consider whether the composition of the current audit team remains appropriate.

Similarly, a partner or an employee of an audit firm should not accept a governance role with an audit client. A prohibited governance role would be appointment to the board of directors or any subcommittee of that board or to any position in any entity which holds directly or indirectly, more than 20% of the voting rights of the audit client. Where a governance role is accepted by an immediate or close family member, or another partner or employee in the office, safeguards can usually be put in place to mitigate any threats.

When a director or a person able to exercise significant influence over the preparation of the financial statements transfers from audit client to audit firm, he should not be involved in the audit of that client for a period of at least two years from leaving the audit client, although a longer exclusion period may be appropriate depending on the auditor's assessment of threats and safeguards.

Family and other personal relationships

The Standard states that:

'a relationship between a person who is in a position to influence the conduct and outcome of the audit and another party does not generally affect the consideration of the auditor's objectivity'.

However, this may not be the case where a family relationship exists and that family member also has a financial, business or employment relationship with the audit client. The significance of any threat will depend on:

- the relevant person's involvement in the audit;
- the nature of the relationship between the relevant person and his or her family member; and
- the family member's relationship with the audit client.

Therefore partners and professional staff should report any immediate family (i.e. spouse and dependents), close family (i.e. parents, non-dependent children and siblings) and other personal relationships involving an audit client, to their firm where they consider it might create a threat to independence or objectivity. Such information should be passed to the engagement partner who will be able to assess the threat to independence and objectivity and apply appropriate safeguards.

The audit engagement partner should also consider whether any external consultant involved in the audit will be objective, and document the rationale for their conclusion.

2.6.4   Ethical Standard 3 (Revised): Long Association with the Audit Engagement

The Standard states that firms should monitor the length of time that audit engagement partners, key audit partners and staff in senior positions serve as members of the engagement team for each audit.

The Standard suggests rotating the audit partners and senior members of the audit team after a period of time. For listed and public interest entities, the maximum period is determined as five years. A suggested maximum of ten years is given for non-listed clients, although this is not mandatory and alternative safeguards could be applied. Where the individual is not rotated from the audit after ten years, the reasons for this should be documented and these facts communicated to those charged with governance.

For listed and public interest entities, the Standard states that partner rotation is the only permissible safeguard. **Table 8** sets out the time limits for rotation.

TABLE 8: Time limits for partner rotation for listed and public interest entities

In the case of listed companies and other public interest entities, the audit firm should establish policies and procedures to ensure that:

- no one should act as audit engagement partner or as independent partner for a continuous period longer than five years;[1,2]
- where an independent partner becomes the audit engagement partner, the combined period of service in these positions should not exceed five years; and
- anyone who has acted as the audit engagement partner or the independent partner, or held a combination of such positions, for a particular audit client for a period of five years should not hold any position of responsibility in relation to the audit engagement until a further period of five years has elapsed.

[1] The revision to ES3 published in October 2009 allows the five year rule to be extended to seven years where the audit committee (or equivalent) of the entity decide that such an extension is necessary to safeguard the quality of the audit and this is agreed by the audit firm involved. This may be where substantial change has recently been made or will be made to the nature or structure of the entity's business or there are unexpected changes in the senior management of the audited entity. In such circumstances, alternative safeguards should be put in place to reduce any threats to an acceptable level. Disclosure of the extension must be made to the shareholders as soon as possible and again in each of the subsequent years.
[2] Where an audit client becomes listed or public interest the period before the listing etc. will be taken into account when calculating the five years elapsed. However, if on listing the partner has served four years or more, he can serve up to two further years.

A seven-year limit is imposed for rotation of key audit partners. A key audit partner is an audit partner, or other person performing the function of an audit partner, of the engagement team (other than the audit engagement partner) who is involved at the group level and is responsible for key decisions or judgments on significant matters, such as on significant subsidiaries or divisions, or on significant risk factors that relate to the audit of that client. Additionally, the seven-year limit applies when the key audit partner becomes the engagement partner. The 'cooling off' period before the key audit partner can assume any responsibility in relation to this client is two years.

The same seven-year limit is relevant to other partners and staff in senior positions after which time a review of the threats and safeguards relevant to objectivity and independence must be made. Where there are threats identified a suitable safeguard may be to remove the member of staff from the audit team.

2.6.5 Ethical Standard 4 (Revised): Fees, Remuneration and Evaluation Policies, Litigation, Gifts and Hospitality

Fees

The Standard sets out the following requirements in relation to fees:

- sufficient partners and staff with appropriate skills must be used on an audit, irrespective of fees charged;
- an audit should not be undertaken on a contingent fee basis;
- a firm should not undertake an engagement to provide non-audit services in respect of an audited entity on a contingent fee basis where the:
  - contingent fee is material to the audit firm, or that part of the firm by reference to which the audit engagement partner's profit share is calculated;
  - the non-audit service is a tax service; or
  - the outcome of those non-audit services (and, therefore, the amount of the fee) is dependent on a future or contemporary audit judgment relating to a material matter in the financial statements of the audited entity;
- for listed companies, the audit engagement partner should disclose to the audit committee in writing any contingent fee arrangements for non-audit services;
- fees and payment arrangements should be agreed with the client prior to the audit firm being appointed for the following period; and
- where overdue fees arise, the audit engagement partner, together with the ethics partner, should consider whether it is necessary to resign.

Remuneration and evaluation policies

The Standard states that the audit team should not include in its objectives the selling of non-audit services to the audit client, and team members should not be evaluated or remunerated based on their success in selling non-audit services.

Gifts and hospitality

The Standard states that the audit firm and those in a position to influence the conduct and outcome of the audit (and their immediate family) should not accept gifts from an audit client other than low-value items of a promotional or commemorative nature. Neither should they accept hospitality unless it is reasonable in terms of its frequency, nature and cost.

The audit firm should establish policies on the nature and value of gifts and hospitality that may be accepted from and offered to audit clients, their directors, officers and employees.

Litigation

Unless insignificant, the audit firm should not continue or accept an audit engagement where litigation is in progress or is probable.

2.6.6   Ethical Standard 5 (Revised): Non-Audit Services Provided to Audited Entities

Ethical Standard 5 was revised in 2011 following a consultation in response to the Treasury Select Committee's report *Banking Crisis: reforming corporate governance and pay in the City*. The Treasury Select Committee's report called for a review of the appropriateness of auditors providing non-audit services to their audit clients, stating:

> 'We strongly believe that investor confidence, and trust in audit would be enhanced by a prohibition on audit firms conducting non-audit work for the same company.'

Ethical Standard 5 (Revised) states that a firm must consider whether acceptance of a non-audit service engagement may give rise to threats to objectivity. The test stated in the Standard is whether a reasonable and informed third party would regard the objectives of the proposed engagement as being inconsistent with the objectives of the audit of the financial statements. If this is the case, they must either not accept the non-audit service engagement or provide the non-audit service having resigned their position as auditor. Procedures should be in place to ensure that the possible provision of non-audit services is notified to the audit engagement partner prior to accepting the work.

The audit engagement partner should ensure that those charged with governance of the audit client are informed of all significant facts relating to non-audit services that may have a bearing on the auditor's objectivity and independence. For listed clients, they should also be informed where their policy on obtaining non-audit services from their auditor is inconsistent with the requirements of the FRC's Ethical Standards (Revised), and if their own policy has been breached.

The Standard then details risks to objectivity that may arise from the provision of the following services:

- internal audit;
- information technology;
- valuation;
- actuarial valuation;
- litigation support;
- taxation;
- legal;

- recruitment and remuneration;
- corporate finance;
- transaction-related services; and
- accounting.

It also suggests safeguards which could be put in place, if any, to allow the auditor to continue his work in an independent and objective manner.

2.6.7   Revised Ethical Standard 2016

Threats to the independence and objectivity of the auditor arising from the provision of non-audit services has been one of the key themes of the EU audit reform project which culminated in changes to the Audit Directive and the Audit Regulation. As a result, the Revised Ethical Standard 2016 includes an extensive list of prohibited non-audit services that may not be provided by auditors of public interest entities – although many of these were effectively prohibited under existing ethical standards.

In addition, the revised standard introduces a complex capping formula restricting, for such entities, the total value of non-audit services (where permitted) in comparison with audit fees, averaged over a three-year period. This cap applies on a group wide basis and includes consideration of non-audit services provided by other firms in the auditor's network – whether or not those firms are involved in the audit of the group accounts.

Although the most restrictive requirements derive from the EU Audit Regulation and therefore apply only to the audits of public interest entities, the FRC has decided to retain many of its existing restrictions in relation to listed companies that are not PIEs (for example companies traded on the AIM market). However, some of these restrictions have been relaxed so as not to apply to smaller listed non-PIE entities. Such 'SME listed' entities will, in general, be companies with equity shares with a market capitalisation of less than €200m or listed debt with a value of less than €200m, traded on a market that is not an EU regulated market.

The new rules are complex and auditors of public interest entities and other listed entities should give careful consideration to the requirements of the Revised Ethical Standard 2016 which will apply to audits of financial reporting periods commencing on or after 17 June 2016.

2.7   Ethical Standard – Provisions Available for Small Entities

2.7.1   Background

The FRC is aware that a limited number of the requirements in the Ethical Standard are difficult for certain audit firms to comply with, particularly when auditing a small entity. Whilst the FRC is clear that the ES is appropriate in the interests of establishing the integrity, objectivity and independence of auditors, it accepts that certain dispensations are appropriate to facilitate the cost effective audit of the financial statements of small entities which are not public interest entities.

The Ethical Standard – *Provisions Available for Small Entities* (ES – PASE) sets out these dispensations.

The ES – PASE was revised in December 2010 at the same time as Ethical Standards 1, 2, 4 and 5. The current version is effective from 30 April 2011. For purposes of the ES – PASE, a Small Entity client is defined in **Table 9**.

TABLE 9: Definition of a Small Entity client

For the purposes of the ES – PASE, in the UK[1] a 'Small Entity' is:

- not a listed company, or an affiliate thereof;
- any company that qualifies as a small company under the *Companies Act* 2006 (or, where group accounts are prepared, any group that qualifies as a small group);
- any charity with an income of less than the turnover threshold applicable to small companies as defined in the *Companies Act* 2006 (currently £6.5m);
- any pension fund with less than 100 members including active, deferred and pensioner members (but excluding schemes in wind up that formerly had more than 100 members);
- any firm, bank and building society, regulated by the FSA, or its successors (including any mortgage firm or insurance broker), which is not required to appoint an auditor by the relevant regulator;
- any credit union which is a mutually owned financial cooperative established under the *Credit Unions Act* 1979 and the *Industrial and Provident Societies Act* 1965 (or equivalent legislation);
- any entity registered under the *Industrial and Provident Societies Act* 1965, incorporated under the *Friendly Societies Act* 1992 or registered under the *Friendly Societies Act* 1974 (or equivalent legislation), which meets the *Companies Act* 2006 definition of a small company, set out above;
- any registered social landlord with less than 250 units; and
- any other entity, such as a club, which would be a Small Entity if it were a company.

Where an entity falls into more than one of the above categories, it will only be a Small Entity if it meets the criteria for all relevant categories.

[1]Different definitions apply in the Republic of Ireland.

2.7.2   Non-audit services

The ES – PASE exempts the auditor of a Small Entity client, from adhering to the requirements in paragraph 38, 104 and 145(b) of ES 5.

Paragraph 38 of ES 5 (Revised) requires that where an audit firm provides non-audit services to an audited entity where there is no 'informed management', it is unlikely that any other safeguards can eliminate a management threat or reduce it to an acceptable level such that the non-audit service may be provided to the client.

When undertaking non-audit services for a Small Entity, the audit firm is not required to adhere to the same prohibitions in ES 5 (Revised) provided that:

- it discusses objectivity and independence issues related to the provision of non-audit services with those charged with governance, confirming that management accept responsibility for any decisions taken; and
- it discloses the fact that it has applied the standard (see **2.7.5**).

In addition, the auditor of a Small Entity will have exemption from the requirements of paragraphs 104 and 145(b) of ES 5 (Revised) which prevent the audit firm from undertaking an engagement to provide tax services or restructuring services to an audit client where this would involve acting as an advocate for the audit client, before an appeals tribunal or court in the resolution of an issue:

- that is material to the financial statements; or
- where the outcome of the tax issue is dependent on a future or contemporary audit judgment.

See **2.7.5** for implications for the audit report and financial statements disclosures where advantage is taken of any of these exemptions.

2.7.3   Economic dependence

Where total audit and non-audit fees for a small entity client will regularly exceed 10% of the fee income of the firm (or the part of the firm by reference to which the audit partner's profit share is calculated) but will not regularly exceed 15%, the ES – PASE provides an exemption from the requirement in Ethical Standard 4 that an external independent quality control review be performed. The exemption is available as long as the expectation that fees will amount to between 10 and 15% is disclosed to the ethics partner and to those charged with governance of the client.

2.7.4   Partners joining an audit client

Paragraph 44 of ES 2 (Revised) requires an audit firm to resign from an engagement for a two-year 'cooling off' period if a former partner of that firm is appointed as a director or in a key management position at the client, if that partner had acted as audit engagement partner, independent partner, key audit partner or partner in the chain of command at any time in the two years prior to this appointment.

An audit firm of a Small Entity is exempt from this requirement as long as the firm takes appropriate steps to ensure that there have been no significant threats to the audit team's integrity, objectivity and independence and discloses the fact that it has taken advantage of the exemption in its audit report. Example steps for a Small Audit Firm to take are set out in **Table 10**.

Where this exemption is used, the fact must be disclosed in the auditor's report and further disclosures in line with the example in **Table 12** should be made in the financial statements or the auditor's report.

TABLE 10: Possible steps for a firm to take to guard against threats to independence relating to paragraph 44 of ES 2 (Revised)

- Assess significance of the self-interest, familiarity or intimidation threats having regard to:
  - the position the individual has taken at the audit client;
  - the nature and amount of any involvement the individual will have with the audit team or the audit process;
  - the length of time that has passed since the individual was a member of the audit team or firm; and
  - the former position of the individual within the audit team or firm.

- If that threat is anything other than clearly insignificant, apply safeguards such as:
  - considering the appropriateness or necessity of modifying the audit plan for the audit engagement;
  - assigning an audit team to the subsequent audit engagement that is of sufficient experience in relation to the individual who has joined the audit client;
  - involving an audit partner or senior staff member with appropriate expertise, who was not a member of the audit team, to review the work done or otherwise advise as necessary; or
  - perform a quality control review of the audit engagement.

2.7.5 Audit report wording

Where advantage has been taken of one or more of the exemptions in the ES – PASE relating to non-audit services or a former partner joining the client, the auditor's report must disclose this fact and either the financial statements or the auditor's report must give details.

The ES – PASE gives example wording for the disclosure required in the audit report.

This is reproduced in **Table 11**.

TABLE 11: Example[2] audit report wording where an ES – PASE exemption has been used

Respective responsibilities of directors and auditor

As explained more fully in the Directors' Responsibility Statement [set out on page ...], the directors are responsible for the preparation of the financial statements and for being satisfied that they give a true and fair view.

Our responsibility is to audit and express an opinion on the financial statements in accordance with applicable law and International Standards on Auditing (UK and Ireland).

Those standards require us to comply with Ethical Standards issued by the Financial Reporting Council (FRC), including *Ethical Standard – Provisions Available for Small Entities*, in the circumstances set out in note x to the financial statements.

[2] This example is based on existing ISAs and has not been updated to reflect changes to audit reporting ISAs which will take effect for periods commencing 17 June 2016.

Examples of the disclosures in the financial statements referred to in the example in **Table 11** are also provided by the ES – PASE. These are reproduced in **Table 12**.

TABLE 12: Example disclosures in the financial statements where exemptions are used

Management threat/self-review threat in relation to non-audit services (2.6.2 above)

Note [x]: In common with many other businesses of our size and nature, we use our auditor to prepare and submit returns to the tax authorities and assist with the preparation of the financial statements.

Advocacy threat – tax services (2.6.2 above)

Note [x]: In common with many other businesses of our size and nature, we use our auditor to provide tax advice and to represent us, as necessary, at tax tribunals.

Partners joining an audit client (2.6.4 above)

Note [x]: XYZ, a former partner of [audit firm] joined [audit client] as [a director] on [date].

2.8   Technical standards

The body must have rules and practices as to the technical standards to be applied in company audit work and the manner in which they are to be applied. In practice, the UK bodies have adopted the ISAs (UK and Ireland) and registered auditors must be able to demonstrate compliance with these.

In practice, to comply with audit regulations, firms are required to have procedures covering, in addition to the areas mentioned above:

- acceptance of appointment and reappointments; and
- quality control and ISQC (UK and Ireland) 1 (Revised June 2016).

2.8.1   Acceptance of appointment and reappointment

A firm will normally be expected to have procedures which ensure that before accepting an appointment, and also in considering whether to accept reappointment as auditor of a company, issues of the firm's independence and those of its competence to act are addressed. In addressing competence to act, the firm must assess whether or not the partners and employees have the necessary skills and training for the particular type of appointment.

2.8.2   Quality control

There must be an adequate system of quality control (see **Chapter 3**). This will involve not only ensuring adequate review procedures but also some measure of quality assurance procedures, for example, 'hot' review of work by independent partners before the opinion is signed off and also 'cold' review procedures to ensure that work has been properly carried out in accordance with the firm's procedures. Quality control will also ensure that the various procedures necessary to ensure compliance with the regulations of the RSB have been carried out.

2.9   Maintaining competence

There must be adequate arrangements to ensure that persons eligible for appointment as a company auditor continue to maintain an appropriate level of competence in the conduct of company audits. This is done by ensuring that there are satisfactory arrangements for training and continuing professional education (CPE) for members of bodies – the levels of desired CPE are normally set out in the rules of the various RSBs.

Although an audit firm's ability to audit rests with its partners and staff, these may change over time. As a result, to demonstrate its competence a firm must use audit manuals, audit programmes, checklists and standard procedures.

The amount of formal documentation and procedures will depend on the size of the firm and its clients. Even the smallest firm is likely to need some documentation such as audit programmes, but as it grows in size, or as its clients become more complex in their nature, procedures may need to be developed further to assist staff to carry out audit work in accordance with audit regulations.

2.10 Meeting of claims

There must be adequate rules to ensure that any registered auditor has adequate professional indemnity insurance (PII) cover to secure them against claims arising out of company audit work. In order to become a registered auditor, a firm must demonstrate that there is sufficient PII cover in place.

2.11 Other areas

In addition to the above, each RSB must have rules relating to eligibility for membership, disciplinary arrangements, investigation of complaints and keeping a published register of members. It must also take into account the costs of any rules it makes in terms of the benefit to be obtained and be involved in the promotion and maintenance of auditing standards.

In particular, audit regulations:

- explicitly state that a firm or member of an Institute must be registered by a RSB before accepting an audit appointment;
- require firms to formally apply before appointing a new Responsible Individual (RI), rather than just informing the registering Institute of the new RI; and
- clarify that the Regulations apply to all charities, not just those registered under the Charities Acts in England and Wales.

2.12 Oversight of the profession

Responsibility for oversight of the auditing profession was transferred from the Professional Oversight Board for Accountancy (POBA) to the FRC in 2012.

The FRC's Conduct Committee is now responsible for overseeing the Conduct Division in its work promoting high quality corporate reporting. Its responsibilities include overseeing:

- monitoring of recognised supervisory and recognised qualifying bodies;
- audit quality reviews;
- corporate reporting reviews;
- professional discipline; and
- oversight of the regulation of accountants and actuaries.

2.13   Audit quality monitoring

The FRC's Audit Quality Review (AQR) team monitors the quality of the audits of listed and other major public interest entities and the policies and procedures supporting audit quality at the major audit firms in the UK. The overall objective of its work is to monitor and promote improvements in the quality of auditing of listed and other major public interest entities.

The FRC publishes annually details of the scope of the AQR team's work, which includes the audits of all UK incorporated entities with listed securities (both equity and debt). From 2016–17, it is intended that AQR scope will be extended to include all public interest entities but will no longer include large non-PIE entities. For firms not previously included in AQR scope, this will apply from the 2017–18 cycle of inspections.

In addition, each RSB must have in place arrangements for monitoring the quality of audits carried out by its members, other than those that fall within the remit of the AQR team's review. The ICAEW does this through its Quality Assurance Directorate (QAD), which is responsible for monitoring all other statutory audits conducted by ICAEW registered firms on a six-year cycle. Firms with listed clients are selected on a three-year cycle and the QAD aims to visit the largest audit firms every year.

Both the Financial Reporting Council and the QAD report their visit results and findings to the ICAEW's Audit Registration Committee.

2.14   Reports by registered auditors

The Audit Regulations apply to audits of companies, LLPs, building societies, credit unions, registered charities, friendly and industrial and provident societies, and persons authorised under the *Financial Services and Markets Act* 2000. They also apply to audits of pension schemes, certain partnerships, OEICs and unit trusts.

Where the auditor issues a report in respect of an audit of financial statements, or any other function to which the regulations apply, the report must be signed in the name of the firm, together with the phrase 'Statutory auditor(s)'.

2.15   Other international developments

In February 2016, the IESBA released an exposure draft called *Limited Re-exposure of Proposed Changes to the Code Addressing the Long Association of Personnel with an Audit Client*. The exposure draft broadly covers the following areas:

- strengthening the general provisions that apply to all audit engagements;
- increasing the mandatory cooling-off period from two to five years for the engagement partner on the audit of a client that is a public interest entity;
- strengthening the restrictions on the type of activities that can be undertaken by any former key audit partner during the cooling-off period;
- ensuring the concurrence of those charged with governance with respect to the application of certain exception paragraphs; and
- increasing the cooling-off period from two to five years for the EQCR on a listed entity and to three years on a public interest entity.

The IESBA will consider comments on the exposure draft following the comment period which ran to May 2016. Some of these issues are already covered by UK standards (e.g. the cooling off period for engagement partners on listed entities) but any further implications for the UK will be considered in due course.

3 QUALITY CONTROL FOR AUDIT WORK

3.1 Introduction

This chapter examines the area of quality control relating both to audit firms and to individual audits.

Under audit regulation, each Recognised Supervisory Body (RSB) must ensure that its members have an adequate system of quality control (see **Chapter 2**).

The chapter has been updated to reflect the changes contained in final draft ISAs issued by the FRC in April 2016. Subject to legislative changes in progress at the time of writing, it is expected that International Standard on Quality Control (ISQC) (UK and Ireland) 1 (Revised June 2016), *Quality control for firms that perform audits and reviews of historical financial information, and other assurance and related services engagements* and ISA (UK and Ireland) 220 (Revised June 2016) *Quality control for an audit of financial statements* will take effect for periods commencing on or after 17 June 2016.

ISQC (UK and Ireland) 1 (Revised June 2016) sets out requirements and provides guidance for professional accountants on systems of quality control for audits and review work on historical financial information and ISA (UK and Ireland) 220 (Revised June 2016) provides guidance on quality control procedures specifically applicable to audits.

The revisions incorporate amendments relating to the EU Audit Directive and Audit Regulation which are required to be implemented by all EU countries. The revisions mainly affect audits of public interest entities, in particular, surrounding independence requirements and engagement quality control reviews.

For earlier periods, the versions of ISQC (UK and Ireland) 1 and ISA (UK and Ireland) 220 issued in October 2009 and applicable to periods ending on or after 15 December 2010 should be used.

In September 2010, the ICAEW issued a practical guide for firms on the implementation of the ISQC (UK and Ireland) 1 entitled *Quality Control in the Audit Environment*. It is detailed in **3.2.2**.

Audit quality continues to be an important theme for the FRC and for standard setters and regulators internationally as well as for companies themselves.

In November 2006, a discussion paper was issued by the Financial Reporting Council (FRC) entitled *Promoting Audit Quality*. This led to the publication in February 2008 of *The Audit Quality Framework* which was designed to support effective communication between auditors, audit committees, preparers, investors and other stakeholders on audit quality. Details of these papers are given in **3.4**.

In February 2014, the IAASB issued a Paper entitled *A Framework for Audit Quality: Key Elements that create an Environment for Audit Quality*. The IAASB expects that the Framework will generate discussion, and positive actions to achieve a continuous improvement to audit quality (see **3.5**).

In March 2015, the FRC issued an Audit Quality Practice Aid for audit committees to assist them in evaluating audit quality in their assessment of the effectiveness of the external audit process. The FRC was responding to requests for guidance in this area, in light of the UK Corporate Governance Code provision that the audit committee report should include an explanation as to how it has assessed the effectiveness of the external audit process.

Promoting audit quality is a key theme of the extensive proposals issued by the FRC in September 2015 to update ethical standards, audit quality control standards and auditing standards, together with revisions to the UK Corporate Governance Code and associated guidance for directors and audit committees.

In addition, it is a key theme of the IAASB's consultation issued in December 2015. The Invitation to Comment, *Enhancing Audit Quality in the Public Interest: A Focus on Professional Scepticism, Quality Control and Group Audits* (the ITC) highlights the board's discussions on the topics of professional scepticism, quality control and group audits – and flags potential standard-setting activities the IAASB may undertake to enhance audit quality (see **3.5**).

3.2   ISQC (UK and Ireland) 1 (Revised June 2016)

3.2.1   Basic requirement

ISQC (UK and Ireland) 1 (Revised June 2016) requires firms to establish and maintain a system of quality control which is designed to provide reasonable assurance that the firm and its personnel comply with professional standards and regulatory and legal requirements, including relevant ethical requirements, and that reports issued by the firm or engagement partners are appropriate in the circumstances.

Firms need to take into consideration the scale and complexity of the firm's activities and be able to demonstrate to the competent authority that the policies and procedures designed to achieve compliance with the requirements of ISQC (UK and Ireland) 1 (Revised June 2016) are appropriate given the scale and complexity of activities of the firm.

ISQC (UK and Ireland) 1 (Revised June 2016) has been written to apply to statutory audits of financial statements and other public interest assurance engagements (which means any other assurance engagement carried out in accordance with performance standards issued by the FRC). Not all requirements apply equally to all types of engagement. To avoid confusion, this chapter considers the requirements that apply to statutory audits.

3.2.2   ICAEW implementation guidance

To assist the auditor with implementing the requirements of ISQC (UK and Ireland) 1, the Audit and Assurance Faculty of the ICAEW issued a practical implementation guide *Quality Control in the Audit Environment*, in September 2010. The guide has since been archived by the ICAEW as it is no longer current, and has not been updated to the most recent version of the ISQC. However, it may still be useful reading for sole practitioners or firms with only one or two responsible individuals.

3.2.3   Elements of a system of quality control

ISQC (UK and Ireland) 1 (Revised June 2016) sets out six areas which should be addressed by a firm's quality control policies and procedures, documented and communicated to the firm's personnel:

- leadership responsibilities for quality within the firm (**3.2.4**);
- ethical requirements (**3.2.5**);
- acceptance and continuance of client relationships and specific engagements (**3.2.6**);
- human resources (**3.2.7**);
- engagement performance (**3.2.8**); and
- monitoring (**3.2.10**).

These are discussed in greater detail below.

The policies and procedures are not restricted to professional staff, but the firm is required to ensure that its owners or shareholders, as well as the members of the administrative, management and supervisory bodies of the firm, do not intervene in the carrying out of an audit in any way which jeopardises the independence and objectivity of the engagement team. The firm is required to have:

- sound administrative and accounting procedures;
- internal quality control mechanisms that are designed to secure compliance with decisions and procedures at all levels of the firm;
- effective procedures for risk assessment; and
- effective control and safeguard arrangements for the firm's information processing systems.

3.2.4   Leadership

From the very top of the organisation, the firm should establish policies which promote a culture of quality. ISQC (UK and Ireland) 1 (Revised June 2016) states that this should be demonstrated practically, with actions and messages from all levels of the firm's management emphasising their commitment to quality. This should also be demonstrated in the firm's overall business strategy, which should promote the need for quality.

The firm's managing board of partners, or equivalent, will maintain ultimate responsibility for the firm's system of quality control, but operational responsibility may be delegated to someone with sufficient and appropriate experience, ability and authority.

In order to promote an appropriate culture, firms should recognise that the overall business strategy is subject to an overriding requirement to achieve quality in its work and take care to ensure that:

- commercial considerations never override the quality of performance;
- audit partners and staff are always sufficiently independent and approach audits with a mindset of professional scepticism;
- performance evaluation, compensation and promotion demonstrate the firm's commitment to quality; and
- sufficient appropriate resources are devoted to the development, documentation and support of the firm's quality control policies and procedures.

3.2.5 Ethical requirements

The firm should have procedures in place to provide it with assurance that its personnel comply with relevant ethical requirements. The Audit Directive also requires the firm to establish appropriate and effective organisational and administrative arrangements for dealing with and recording incidents which have, or may have, serious consequences for the integrity of the firm's activities.

The application material in ISQC (UK and Ireland) 1 (Revised June 2016) explains that 'relevant ethical requirements' ordinarily comprises Parts A and B of the International Ethics Standards Board for Accountants' *Code of Ethics for Professional Accountants* (the IESBA Code) and national requirements that are more restrictive. It also makes clear that in the UK and Ireland, the firm and its personnel are subject to the FRC's *Ethical Standards*[1] and ethical requirements imposed by the auditor's, or assurance practitioner's, own professional body (see **Chapters 1** and **2**).

All audit partners and staff should have appropriate training on ethical matters including on the contents of the Ethical Standard (see **Chapter 2**), and specific guidance available within the firm. They should also be made aware of who or what to consult if they are uncertain on an ethical matter.

In relation to independence, the firm should ensure that it:

- is able to communicate its independence requirements to personnel and any others bound by them; and
- has established appropriate and effective organisational and administrative arrangements to prevent, identify, eliminate or manage and disclose any threats to the firm's independence.

---

[1] The FRC proposes to replace the Ethical Standards with a single revised Ethical Standard for periods commencing 17 June 2016. Full details are in **Chapter 2**.

To adhere to these requirements, sufficient information must be held about the engagements undertaken by the firm, including the scope of the services provided to each client. Changes to the information should be notified to the person responsible for maintaining it on a timely basis.

Firms should also ensure that they have policies and procedures for informing the relevant individual when breaches of independence take place. The engagement partner and others who need to take action should be informed of the breach promptly.

In addition, the firm should obtain annual declarations of independence from all personnel who are required to be independent by the *Ethical Standard*. This requirement can be most easily met by using a standard form.

Firms should set policies and procedures to be applied to mitigate the familiarity threat that may arise where the same senior personnel are used on an audit for a long period of time. These may include rotation of partners or other audit personnel. In the case of listed companies, rotation periods should be set in accordance with the requirements of the *Ethical Standard*.

3.2.6   Client acceptance and continuance

The firm's policies and procedures should ensure that it:

- considers the integrity of each client;
- is competent and has the resources to provide the service; and
- can comply with ethical requirements.

The information should be gathered or reviewed at the commencement of the relationship with the client, when accepting recurring work in second or subsequent years or when accepting a new engagement from an existing client. Example matters to be considered are set out in **Table 1**.

Where issues are discovered that cause concern, but the engagement continues, the issues, and their resolution should be fully documented.

If the firm later discovers something that would have led it to declining the engagement, it should take legal advice and consider resigning.

The firm also needs to have policies and procedures addressing the circumstances where the firm obtains information that would have caused it to decline the engagement had that information been available earlier. This will include considering:

(a) the professional and legal responsibilities that apply to the circumstances; and

(b) the possibility of withdrawing from the engagement or from both the engagement and the client relationship.

Where the auditor ceases to hold office as auditor, he provides the successor auditor with access to all relevant information concerning the entity, including information concerning the most recent audit (see **Chapter 38**).

Before accepting or continuing an audit engagement, the firm assesses:

(a) whether the firm complies with relevant independence and objectivity requirements in the Ethical Standards;

(b) whether there are threats to the firm's independence, and the safeguards applied to mitigate those threats;

(c) whether the firm has the competent personnel, time and resources needed in order to carry out the audit in an appropriate manner; and

(d) whether the key audit partner is eligible for appointment as a statutory auditor.

Public interest entities

In addition to points (a) to (d) above, for a public interest entity, the firm assesses:

(a) whether the firm complies with the audit fees and the prohibition of the provision of non-audit services requirements in the FRC's Ethical Standard;

(b) whether the conditions for the duration of the audit engagement in accordance with the Audit Regulation are complied with; and

(c) without prejudice to UK or Irish anti-money laundering requirements, the integrity of the members of the supervisory, administrative and management bodies of the public interest entity.

TABLE 1: Examples of matters to consider when accepting or reaccepting a client

Client integrity

Consider:

- the identity and business reputation of the client's principal owners, key management, related parties and those charged with governance;
- the nature of the client's operations, including its business practices;
- information concerning the attitude of the client's principal owners, key management and those charged with governance towards such matters as aggressive interpretation of accounting standards and the internal control environment;
- whether the client is aggressively concerned with keeping the firm's fees as low as possible;
- indication of an inappropriate limitation in the scope of work;
- indications that the client might be involved in money laundering or other criminal activities;
- the identity and business reputation of related parties; and
- the reasons for the proposed appointment of the firm and non-reappointment of the previous firm (if relevant).

Firm resources and capabilities

Consider:

- whether firm personnel have knowledge of relevant industries or subject matters;
- if firm personnel have experience with relevant regulatory or reporting requirements or the ability to gain the necessary skills and knowledge effectively;
- whether the firm has sufficient personnel with the necessary capabilities and competence;
- the availability of experts, if needed;
- whether individuals meeting the criteria and eligibility requirements to perform engagement quality control reviews are available, where applicable; and
- whether the firm can complete the engagement within the reporting deadline.

3.2.7   Human resources

Firms should have policies and procedures to ensure that they have sufficient capable, competent and committed staff. These should, for example, cover:

- recruitment;
- performance evaluation;
- capabilities;
- competence;
- career development;
- promotion;
- compensation; and
- the number of staff needed.

Firms should allocate appropriately experienced and qualified staff to each engagement, together with an engagement partner who has the competence, capabilities and authority to perform the role and whose responsibilities are clearly defined and understood. The identity and role of the engagement partner should be communicated to key members of the client's management team and those charged with governance.

For audits, the firm must designate at least one key audit partner (including the engagement partner), who must be selected using the criteria of securing audit quality, independence and competence. The firm must assign to that key audit partner sufficient resources and personnel that have the necessary competence and capabilities to carry out the firm's duties appropriately.

Firms should also:

(a) establish appropriate policies and procedures to ensure that the firm's personnel and any other people under the firm's control who are directly involved in the audit activities, have appropriate knowledge and experience for the duties assigned; and
(b) have in place adequate remuneration policies, including profit sharing policies, providing sufficient performance incentives to secure audit quality. In particular, the revenue from providing non-audit services to the audited

entity must not form part of the performance evaluation and remuneration of any person involved in, or able to influence, the audit.

The firm is also required to establish appropriate policies and procedures to ensure that outsourcing of important audit functions is not undertaken in such a way as to impair the quality of the firm's internal quality control and the ability of the competent authorities to supervise the firm's compliance with professional standards and applicable legal and regulatory requirements.

3.2.8   Engagement performance

ISQC (UK and Ireland) 1 (Revised June 2016) requires firms to implement policies and procedures to provide it with assurance that its engagements are performed in accordance with professional and legal standards. The aim is to ensure consistently high quality engagements, and this can be accomplished through the use of manuals, software tools and standardised documentation as applicable.

The engagement team should be sufficiently briefed prior to commencing their work, adequately supervised throughout the engagement and their work reviewed by a more experienced team member.

Policies and procedures regarding the review of work are determined on the basis that work of less experienced team members is reviewed by more experienced engagement team members.

Firms also need to:

- establish an internal quality control system to ensure the quality of the audit which at least covers the policies and procedures for carrying out audits, coaching, supervising and reviewing employees' activities and organising the structure of the audit file;
- ensure that responsibility for the internal quality control system lies with a person who is eligible for appointment as a statutory auditor;
- establish appropriate policies and procedures for carrying out audits, coaching, supervising and reviewing the activities of the firm's personnel and organising the structure of the audit file; and
- use appropriate systems, resources and procedures to ensure continuity and regularity in the carrying out of the firm's audit activities.

Consultation

Firms need to establish policies and procedures for consultation and ensure that sufficient resources are available so that:

- appropriate consultation takes place on difficult or contentious issues;
- sufficient resources are available to enable the consultation to occur;
- the details of the consultation are documented and agreed with the consultee; and
- conclusions are implemented.

Small firms may need to make arrangements with others outside their firm in order to implement such policies. Arrangements for consultations with fellow professionals should be made as soon as it becomes clear that an issue exists and the person being consulted should be provided with full information on which to base his opinion. This includes the situation where the engagement team needs to consult with an individual, or organisation, with expertise in a specialised area of accounting or auditing, for example, a member of a financial reporting technical team, whether internal or external.

Engagement quality control review

For certain engagements, the firm should implement engagement quality control reviews to ensure that significant judgments made by the engagement team undergo an objective evaluation. The policies for such reviews should:

- require reviews for audits of listed companies; and
- set out criteria against which all other work should be assessed to see if it requires a review.

When setting these criteria, firms would consider the nature of the engagement, including the extent to which it involves a matter of public interest, any unusual circumstances or risks surrounding the work and whether a review is required by law.

The review should be completed before any report is issued.

Policies should also be developed to set out:

- the nature, extent and timing of the engagement quality control review;
- eligibility criteria for reviewers; and
- documentation requirements.

Nature, timing and extent of review

An engagement quality control review will usually involve discussions with the engagement partner, a review of the financial statements, consideration of the audit report and review of selected working papers. The engagement quality control review must be completed before the auditor's report is signed, however, documentation of that review may occur after the signing of the auditor's report providing that any matters raised by the reviewer were resolved before the audit report was signed.

In all engagement quality control reviews carried out in accordance with the firm's policy, the reviewer should consider the firm's compliance with the FRC's Ethical Standard in relation to the engagement, form an independent opinion as to the adequacy of any safeguards applied and consider the adequacy of the documentation of the engagement partner's consideration of the objectivity and independence of the firm and its personnel.

Engagement quality control reviews of audits of listed clients include considering:

- the engagement team's evaluation of the firm's independence in relation to the specific engagement;
- significant risks identified during the engagement and the responses to those risks;
- judgments made, particularly with respect to materiality and significant risks;
- whether appropriate consultation has taken place on matters involving differences of opinion or other difficult or contentious matters, and the conclusions arising from those consultations;
- the significance of corrected and uncorrected misstatements identified during the engagement and the actions taken in relation to them;
- the matters to be communicated to those charged with governance and other parties such as regulatory bodies;
- whether working papers selected for review reflect the work performed in relation to the significant judgments and support the conclusions reached; and
- the appropriateness of the report to be issued.

Where the review is for an engagement other than the audit of a listed company, some or all of the above considerations will be relevant.

Public interest entities

For audits of public interest entities, the firm requires that:

(a) before the audit report and the additional report to the audit committee are issued, an engagement quality control review is done to assess whether the key audit partner could reasonably have come to the opinion and conclusions expressed in the draft of these reports; and

(b) the review is to be performed by an engagement quality control reviewer who is eligible for appointment as a statutory auditor and not involved in the performance of the audit to which the EQCR relates.

Where the audit is carried out by a firm and all the statutory auditors of that firm were involved in the carrying-out of the audit, the firm needs to arrange for another firm to perform an engagement quality control review. Documents or information disclosed to the engagement quality control reviewer for this purpose shall be subject to professional secrecy.

Eligibility of reviewers

The firm's policies should set out the technical qualifications, experience and authority required of quality control reviewers together with the extent to which the quality control reviewer can be consulted by the engagement partner during the audit without compromising the reviewer's objectivity. Procedures should be in place to allow replacement of the quality control reviewer where his ability to perform an objective review is impaired.

What constitutes an appropriate degree of qualifications, experience and authority will depend on the circumstances of the engagement but for the audit of the financial statements of listed companies, for example, the application material to the standard suggests that the reviewer is likely to be someone who is sufficiently experienced to act as an engagement partner on listed company audits.

Care should be taken to ensure that the objectivity of the engagement quality control reviewer is not impaired and:

- where practicable, he is not appointed by the engagement partner;
- he takes no part in the audit (other than in connection with his review) and does not make decisions for the team;
- he is not used routinely for consultation by the engagement partner or team on significant matters of judgment; and
- he is not subject to other considerations that would threaten his objectivity.

For sole practitioners or small firms, suitably qualified external persons may be contracted to perform quality control reviews.

Review documentation

There should be documentation on file that the review occurred, that it was completed before the report was issued and that the reviewer is not aware of any unresolved matters that suggest that the conclusions of the engagement team were not appropriate.

Differences of opinion

There should be firm policies about resolution and documentation of differences of opinion within the engagement team. The firm's report should never be issued until any such differences have been resolved.

For public interest entities, the firm establishes procedures for determining the manner in which any disagreement between the key audit partner and the engagement quality control reviewer are to be resolved.

3.2.9 Engagement documentation

There should be policies and procedures for engagement teams to complete the assembly of final engagement files on a timely basis after the engagement reports have been finalised. For audits, this is 'ordinarily not more than 60 days after the date of the auditor's report'.

Policies and procedures should also be established that are designed to maintain the confidentiality, safe custody, integrity, accessibility and retrievability of engagement documentation.

ISQC (UK and Ireland) 1 (Revised June 2016) states that firms may implement controls to avoid alteration or loss of engagement documentation, whether on paper, electronic or using other media, including those that:

- ensure that details of who created, changed or reviewed the working papers, and when that occurred, can be clearly seen;
- protect the integrity of the information, particularly if it is transmitted or shared with other members of the engagement team via the internet;
- prevent unauthorised changes to documentation; and
- allow access to the working papers to those that are authorised to have it.

Confidentiality, safe custody, integrity, accessibility and retrievability of engagement documentation may be improved by implementing further controls such as:

- the use of passwords to restrict access to electronic documentation to authorised users;
- appropriate back-up routines throughout the engagement;
- procedures for distributing documentation to audit team members, retrieving it and collating it at the end of the engagement; and
- procedures for restricting access to, and ensuring proper distribution and storage of, hardcopy engagement documentation.

Where hardcopy documentation is scanned for storage and retention purposes, the following controls may be relevant:

- ensuring scanned copies reflect the entire content of the original paper documentation, including manual signature, cross references and annotation;
- integrating scanned copies into the engagement file, including indexing them and signing them off as necessary; and
- enabling the scanned copies to be retrieved and printed as necessary.

ISQC (UK and Ireland) 1 (Revised June 2016) also states that policies and procedures should be implemented to ensure that firms retain engagement documentation for the period required by law or regulation. Requirements for audit working papers are set out in **12.6**.

3.2.10 Monitoring

Monitoring the firm's quality control policies and procedures

Each firm should have procedures to monitor their quality control policies and to ensure that they are complied with in practice. Evaluation of the system of quality control will include:

- analysis of:
  - changes in professional standards and regulatory and legal requirements;
  - written confirmation by staff of compliance with policies and procedures on independence;
  - continuing professional development and training; and
  - decisions related to acceptance and continuance of engagements;
- suggestions for corrective actions and improvements to the system;
- communication of weaknesses in the system to those in authority; and
- follow-up procedures to ensure that modifications are made as suggested.

Monitoring should also include a periodic review of completed engagements on a cyclical basis, typically with at least one engagement for each engagement partner in an inspection cycle (which should be no longer than three years). The monitoring inspector will be separate from the engagement partner or the quality control reviewer and may select engagements without prior notification. For small firms or sole practitioners, an external person may be engaged, or arrangements established with another small firm to provide personnel on a reciprocal basis.

ISQC (UK and Ireland) 1 (Revised June 2016) also requires firms to:

(a) monitor and evaluate the adequacy and effectiveness of the firm's systems, internal quality control mechanisms and arrangements established in accordance with ISQC (UK and Ireland) 1 (Revised June 2016) and take appropriate measures to address any deficiencies;

(b) carry out an annual evaluation of the internal quality control system, referred to in paragraph **3.2.8**; and

(c) keep records of the findings of the evaluation required by paragraph (a) above and any proposed measure to modify the internal quality control system.

The reviewer should consider whether any deficiencies found are:

- systemic, repetitive or significant which require prompt corrective action; or
- not indicative of failings in the firm's quality control system,

and an appropriate report should be given at the end of the work.

Where deficiencies are found, they should be communicated to the engagement partner and recommendations made for remedial action. Recommendations may include one or more of the following:

- taking action in relation to an individual engagement or member of personnel;
- informing those in charge of training and professional development;
- changing quality control policies and procedures; and
- disciplinary action against offenders.

Where an incorrect report is found to have been issued, firms should seek legal advice.

At least annually, a summary of the findings of the quality control review process should be provided to the managing board of partners, or equivalent. This should include details of the process undertaken, its conclusions and information about any systemic failures. Where the firm is part of a network of firms, this summary should also be sent to appropriate individuals in the network.

External monitoring of group audits

Where the firm is subject to a quality assurance review or an investigation concerning a group audit, the firm is responsible for complying with, and ensuring the group engagement team also comply with, any request by the authority:

(a)   for relevant audit documentation retained by the group engagement team;

(b)   to deliver any additional documentation of the work performed by any component auditor from a non-EEA member state, including that component auditor's working papers relevant to the group audit, where the authority is unable to obtain audit documentation of the work carried out by that component auditor.

As such the firm needs to establish policies and procedures, which require that, in order to comply with any request under point (b) above, the group engagement team either:

(a)   retain copies of the documentation of the work carried out by the relevant component auditor for the purpose of the group audit (including the component auditor's working papers relevant to the group audit);

(b)   obtain the agreement of the relevant component auditor that the group engagement team shall have unrestricted access to such documentation on request;

(c)   retain documentation to show that the group engagement team has undertaken the appropriate procedures in order to gain access to the audit documentation, together with evidence supporting the existence of any impediments to such access; or

(d)   take any other appropriate action.

3.2.11   Complaints

ISQC (UK and Ireland) 1 (Revised June 2016) also requires firms to have procedures for handling complaints or allegations that work performed does not comply with professional standards, or with the firm's own system of quality control, whether these arise from inside or outside the firm.

The firm is also required to keep records of any complaints made in writing about the performance of the audits carried out.

3.2.12   Documentation of quality control system

Firms are required to have sufficient documentation to provide evidence that their quality control system is operating effectively. ISQC (UK and Ireland) 1 does not set a standard form for this documentation, but points out that the content of documentation will vary depending on the size of the firm, the number of offices, and the nature and complexity of the firm's practice and organisation.

A frequently used method is to create an ISQC (UK and Ireland) 1 (Revised June 2016) file documenting both the firm's policies and procedures. The level and length of the documentation required will depend on the size of the firm and need not be onerous. It is likely that documentation of a number of the areas is already covered by the firm's standard audit documentation, and cross references to other documentation may suffice in a number of areas. Alternatively, procedures may already be in place, but not formally documented. The documentation should be easily accessible by staff and partners involved in audit work and they should be required to read and understand it and be made aware of any updates or changes as they are made.

Firms also need to keep any engagement documentation that is of importance for monitoring compliance with this ISQC (UK and Ireland) and other applicable legal requirements. This includes documenting whether:

(a)   the firm complies with the independence and objectivity requirements in the Ethical Standards;

(b)   there are threats to the firm's independence, and the safeguards applied to mitigate those threats;

(c)   the firm has the competent personnel, time and resources needed in order to carry out the audit in an appropriate manner; and

(d)   the key audit partner is eligible to be appointed as a statutory auditor.

Firms are required to keep the documents and information required by ISQC (UK and Ireland) 1 and the documentation requirements of other applicable ISAs (UK and Ireland) for at least six years from the date of the auditor's report. This period may be longer if necessary to satisfy the requirements of any applicable laws or regulation relating to data protection and to meet the requirements for any applicable administrative and judicial proceedings.

The firm also needs to:

(a)   keep records of any breaches (other than breaches which the firm reasonably considers to be minor breaches) of professional standards and applicable legal and regulatory requirements;

(b)   keep records of any consequences of any breach recorded in (a), the measures taken to address such a breach and to modify the firm's internal quality control system; and

(c)   prepare an annual report containing an overview of any measures taken under (b) and communicate that report internally.

ISQC (UK and Ireland) 1 also requires the firm to maintain a client account record detailing the following for each audit client:

(a)   client's name, address and place of business;

(b)   name of the key audit partner; and

(c)   fees charged for the audit and fees charged for other services in any financial year.

3.3 ISA (UK and Ireland) 220 (Revised June 2016) Quality Control for an Audit of Financial Statements

3.3.1 General requirement

ISA (UK and Ireland) 220 (Revised June 2016) requires the auditor to implement quality control procedures for the individual audit engagement. ISQC (UK and Ireland) 1 (Revised June 2016) (see **3.2** above) sets out the detailed requirements for quality control systems for audits and reviews of historical financial information and ISA (UK and Ireland) 220 (Revised June 2016) sets out the details of how those systems should be applied to audit engagements. The ISA deals largely with engagement partner responsibilities as set out in the following paragraphs.

3.3.2 Leadership responsibilities for quality

The engagement partner is responsible for the overall quality on each of his audit engagements. His actions and appropriate messages to the other members of the engagement team should emphasise:

- the importance to audit quality of:
  - performing work that complies with professional standards and applicable legal and regulatory requirements;
  - complying with the firm's quality control policies and procedures;
  - issuing audit reports that are appropriate to the circumstances; and
  - the team's ability to raise concerns without fear of reprisal; and

- the fact that quality is essential in performing audits.

3.3.3 Ethical requirements

Throughout the audit, the engagement partner is required to remain alert for any evidence of non-compliance by his team with relevant ethical requirements. If any such matters come to his attention, it is his responsibility, in consultation with others to determine the appropriate action. He also forms a conclusion on compliance with independence requirements applicable to the audit engagement.

3.3.4 Acceptance and continuance

The engagement partner needs to be satisfied that appropriate procedures regarding the acceptance and continuance of client relationships and audit engagements have been followed and ensures conclusions reached are appropriate. If he obtains information that would have caused the firm to decline the engagement, had the information been available sooner, then he communicates that to the firm promptly so that the firm and engagement partner can take the necessary action.

3.3.5   Assignment of the team

The engagement partner is responsible for ensuring that the team, and any auditor's experts who are not part of the team, collectively have the appropriate competence and capabilities to perform the engagement in accordance with the relevant standards and enable an appropriate audit report to be issued.

3.3.6   Engagement performance

The engagement partner takes responsibility for:

- the direction, supervision and performance of the engagement in accordance with professional standards;
- his audit report being appropriate to the circumstances;
- reviews being performed in accordance with the firm's review policies and procedures;
- being satisfied that sufficient appropriate audit evidence has been obtained to support the conclusions reached and for the audit report to be issued;
- ensuring that members of the engagement team undertake appropriate consultation on difficult or contentious matters, that the resulting conclusions are agreed with the party consulted and that they are implemented;
- ensuring that an engagement quality control review is appropriately carried out, where required by the firm's policies; and
- ensuring that any differences of opinion, whether between the engagement team, those consulted, the engagement partner or the engagement quality control reviewer are dealt with and resolved in accordance with the firm's policies.

The key audit partner is also required to be actively involved in carrying-out the audit.

Public interest entities

For public interest entities, the engagement quality control reviewer, also considers the following:

(a) the independence of the firm from the entity;

(b) the significant risks relevant to the audit and which the key audit partner has identified during the audit and the measures that he has taken to adequately manage those risks;

(c)   the reasoning of the key audit partner, in particular with regard to the level of materiality and the significant risks referred to in (b);

(d)   any request for advice to external experts and the implementation of such advice;

(e)   the nature and scope of the corrected and uncorrected misstatements that were identified during the audit;

(f)   the subjects discussed with the audit committee and the management and/or supervisory bodies of the entity;

(g)   the subjects discussed with competent authorities and, where applicable, with other third parties; and

(h)   whether the documents and information selected from the file by the engagement quality control reviewer support the opinion of the key audit partner as expressed in the draft audit report and the additional report to the audit committee.

The engagement quality control reviewer discusses his assessment of the above and results of his review with the key audit partner.

3.3.7   Monitoring

ISQC 1 (Revised June 2016) requires the firm to have a monitoring process in place (see **3.2.10**), designed to provide the firm with reasonable assurance that its policies and procedures relating to quality control are relevant, adequate and operating effectively. The engagement partner is responsible for considering the results of the firm's monitoring process and considering whether any deficiencies noted may affect the audit engagement.

3.3.8   Documentation

The engagement partner is responsible for ensuring that the audit is appropriately documented, including documentation of the following:

- issues identified regarding compliance with ethical requirements and how they were resolved;
- conclusions on compliance with applicable independence requirements;
- conclusions regarding the acceptance and continuance of client relationships and audit engagements;
- the nature and scope of, and conclusions from, consultations undertaken during the audit;
- all significant threats to the firm's independence as well as the safeguards applied to mitigate those threats; and
- those matters it is required to assess before accepting or continuing a statutory audit engagement in accordance with ISQC (UK and Ireland) 1 (Revised June 2016).

The engagement quality control reviewer is responsible for documenting that:

- the procedures required by the firm's policies on EQCR have been performed;
- the EQCR has been completed on or before the date of the audit report; and
- he is not aware of any unresolved matters that would cause him to believe that the significant judgments the team made and the conclusions it reached were not appropriate.

Public interest entities

For public interest entities, the engagement quality control reviewer is required to:

(a) keep a record of the results of the review, together with the considerations underlying those results; and
(b) record at least the following:

    (i) the oral and written information provided by the key audit partner to support the significant judgments as well as the main findings of the audit procedures carried out and the conclusions drawn from those findings, whether or not at the request of the engagement quality control reviewer; and

    (ii) the opinions of the key audit partner, as expressed in the draft of his audit report and his report to the audit committee.

For public interest entities, the auditor is required to keep a record of the results of the EQCR, together with the considerations underlying those results in the audit documentation.

3.4   FRC Audit Quality Framework

3.4.1   Background

In the early part of the 21st century, as a result of a number of high profile corporate collapses including Enron and WorldCom, and the subsequent break up of Arthur Andersen, a major international accounting firm, the quality of financial reporting and the effectiveness of the external audit process came under increasing scrutiny and criticism. Various reforms were introduced and legislators, including the UK government and the EU implemented measures aimed at improving corporate governance and financial reporting and increasing regulation of the auditing profession.

Against this background, in November 2006, the FRC issued a discussion paper, *Promoting Audit Quality*, addressing the FRC's objective of 'promoting and maintaining confidence in the audit process and the resulting audit report as a key component of the corporate reporting and governance regime and the effective operation of capital markets'. In order for this objective to be met, users of the financial statements must be able to rely on the audit report.

The paper notes that there is no single agreed definition of audit quality and that an auditor's opinion as to whether financial statements give a 'true and fair' view is subjective. Different views may be held as to the nature and extent of evidence needed to support such an opinion.

The approach taken in the paper is therefore to identify the 'drivers' that are central to achieving a high quality audit and consider the threats to them.

Following responses to the discussion paper in February 2008, the FRC issued its *Audit Quality Framework*. The Framework was intended to complement existing guidance and regulations and promote the previously identified key drivers of audit quality.

3.4.2 Promoting audit quality

Despite changes aimed at improving audit quality, the discussion paper identified the following concerns about audit quality which were still felt by commentators:

- changing business environment and increasing complexity of financial reporting, particularly in relation to the increasing requirement for estimates and valuations;
- audits possibly not detecting management fraud;
- relationships between executive management and the auditor;
- lack of transparency in auditor's work and judgments; and
- an increasingly prescriptive approach to audit.

The FRC identified four main drivers of audit quality. These were the:

- culture within the audit firm;
- skills and personal qualities of the audit partners and staff;
- quality of the audit process; and
- reliability and usefulness of audit reporting.

Audit firm culture

The discussion paper states that audit quality 'can be driven by audit firms creating an environment where achieving high quality is valued, invested in and rewarded'. It identifies a number of indicators that enhance audit quality, including respect for underlying auditing and ethical standards, partner and staff development systems and the promotion of consultation on difficult issues. Threats to quality oriented cultures include over-emphasis on winning and retaining audits or on non-audit services and excessive cost cutting in times of economic downturn.

Skills of partners and staff

The key drivers of audit quality in this area are subdivided into the skills required of partners and staff, the training provided to them and the appraisal process they undergo. Threats that may undermine quality in this area include failure to retain experienced staff, insufficient or ineffective training and lack of effective mentoring to develop the necessary personal characteristics.

Audit process

The discussion paper sets out the following characteristics of an effective audit process:

- an audit team appropriately structured for the engagement with relevant experience and knowledge;
- availability of high quality technical support;
- a well-structured audit methodology which provides a good framework to obtain sufficient appropriate audit evidence, ensures compliance with auditing standards, requires appropriate documentation and ensures effective review;
- objectives under ethical standards being achieved; and
- effective quality control procedures.

The paper identifies possible threats, including the increased use of computerised audit methodologies which may be over-prescriptive and reduce the importance of auditor judgment and a focus on producing documentation to the detriment of performing procedures properly.

Reliability of audit reporting

The discussion paper recognises that the structure of the audit report is specified by law and auditing standards and as such acts as 'a signal rather than a source of new information'. This means that confidence in the report is inextricably linked to the presumed quality of the audit process. This quality is best clarified through clear communication between the auditor and audit committee, as it is in this forum that the auditor can provide further information about the process followed, key risks identified and issues found.

The FRC are aware that confidence in the audit report may be undermined by the concerns of some users and commentators. These concerns include whether auditors are fulfilling their responsibilities in relation to the adequacy of a company's accounting records and whether audit reports should contain more information about key issues.

3.4.3   Factors outside the auditor's control

In addition, the discussion paper warns that some factors which affect audit quality will remain outside the control of the auditor. It lists these as:

- the approach taken by management;
- contributions made by audit committees;
- the role of shareholders and commentators;

- litigation as a driver of audit quality;
- the approach of regulators; and
- pressures caused by tight reporting deadlines.

3.4.4   The Audit Quality Framework

For each key driver identified above, including factors outside the auditor's control, the Framework outlines a number of indicators, which are features that are likely to provide a positive contribution to audit quality. Some examples are listed in **Table 2**.

TABLE 2: Example indicators of key drivers of audit quality

Driver	Indicators
Firm culture	• leadership ensures robust system for client acceptance and continuation
	• leadership creates an environment where achieving high quality is valued, invested in and rewarded
	• leadership ensures that financial decisions do not drive actions and decisions having a negative effect on audit quality
	• leadership promotes the merits of consultation
Skills of audit partners and staff	• junior staff provided with appropriate mentoring and training
	• partners and staff exhibit professional scepticism in their work
Effectiveness of the audit process	• well-structured audit methodology and tools, including active involvement of partners and managers in the planning process, efficient and effective methods for collection of audit evidence and appropriate documentation
	• high quality technical support is available
	• collection of audit evidence is not inappropriately constrained by financial pressures
Reliability and usefulness of reporting	• audit reports are written to be clear and unambiguous
	• auditors properly conclude as to the truth and fairness of the financial statements
	• good communications with audit committees

Factors outside control of the auditor	• audit committees that are active, professional and robust in dealing with issues identified during the audit
	• supportive shareholders
	• realistic reporting deadlines
	• regulatory environment

3.5   International developments

In February 2014, the IAASB issued a Paper entitled *A Framework for Audit Quality: Key Elements that create an Environment for Audit Quality* based on a Consultation Paper issued in January 2013. The objectives of the Framework include:

• raising awareness of the key elements of audit quality;
• encouraging key stakeholders to explore ways to improve audit quality; and
• facilitating greater dialogue between key stakeholders on the topic.

The IAASB issued the Framework in order to generate discussion, and positive actions to achieve a continuous improvement to audit quality. It is not however, a substitute for auditing standards, standards of quality control or other regulatory requirements with which the auditor must comply, and does not itself create new standards or impose requirements on the auditor.

The framework identifies the following key elements that create an environment in which quality audits can be performed:

• inputs;
• processes;
• outputs;
• interactions with other in the supply chain; and
• contextual factors.

The framework explains that quality audits involve the auditor exhibiting appropriate values, ethics and attitudes as well as being sufficiently knowledgeable, skilled and experienced, and having sufficient time to devote to the work. The auditor must also apply a rigorous audit process and quality control procedures.

Quality audits result in outputs that are useful and timely and involve the auditor interacting appropriately with other stakeholders including management, those charged with governance, users of financial statements and regulators.

Quality audits also require the auditor to respond appropriately to external factors including business practices and law, financial reporting and corporate governance frameworks and broader cultural factors.

In July 2015, the Public Company Accounting Oversight Board (PCAOB) in the US issued paper 2015-05 seeking public comment on the content and possible uses of a group of potential 'audit quality indicators'.

The indicators are a series of quantitative measures that may provide new insights about how to evaluate the quality of audits and how high quality audits are achieved. Taken together with qualitative context, the indicators may inform discussions among those concerned with the financial reporting and auditing process, for example, among audit committees and audit firms. Enhanced discussions, in turn, may strengthen audit planning, execution, and communication. Use of the indicators may also stimulate competition among audit firms focused on the quality of the firms' work and, thereby, increase audit quality overall.

Building on its 2014 framework for Audit Quality, in December 2015, the IAASB released an Invitation to Comment, *Enhancing Audit Quality in the Public Interest: A Focus on Professional Scepticism, Quality Control and Group Audits* (the ITC). The IAASB asks how it can improve its standards on quality control and proposes a new quality management approach (QMA) to the issue of quality control. Specific issues it has identified that need to be addressed in revising its existing standards ISQC1 and ISA 220 include:

- at the firm level:
    - monitoring (internal and external) and remediation activities;
    - quality control policies and procedures when operating as part of a network; and
    - transparency reports;

- and at an engagement level:
    - engagement partner responsibilities; and
    - engagement quality control reviews and reviewers.

4 THE AUDIT REPORT

4.1 Introduction

The form and content of the auditor's report are dictated by the nature of the engagement, the type of entity concerned and ISAs (UK and Ireland). Where an entity is required by law to have an audit, the applicable law generally sets out the matters on which the auditor is required to report. In other cases, these may be determined by the auditor's engagement letter with the client. In all cases where the audit is carried out in accordance with ISAs (UK and Ireland), the overall form of the report must comply with the ISAs, which also specify additional information to be included and how and when the auditor's opinion on the financial statements should be modified. The manner in which the audit report should be signed is set out in the *Companies Act* 2006 and Audit Regulations. This chapter examines the auditor's report on the annual financial statements of a company reporting in accordance with the *Companies Act* 2006. Modifications to the auditor's report are discussed in **Chapter 5**.

Other reports by auditors on financial information are considered in **Chapter 6**, while other reports under the *Companies Act* are considered in **Chapter 7**. Reports by the auditor to the regulator on investment businesses and insurance intermediaries are considered in **Chapter 9**. Compilation reports on accounts prepared by accountants are considered in **Chapter 8**.

Recent developments in the area of audit reporting derive from changes to ISA (UK and Ireland) 700 for periods commencing on or after 1 October 2014 as well as the *Companies, Partnerships and Groups (Accounts and Reports) Regulations* 2015 which affect the auditor's responsibilities in relation to the directors' report, strategic report and, where applicable, separate report on corporate governance. These are considered further below.

4.2 Standards and guidance

The current version of ISA (UK and Ireland) 700 *The independent auditor's report on financial statements* was issued in September 2014 and provides standards and guidance on the form and content of the auditor's report.

This update to ISA (UK and Ireland) 700 is effective for the audits of financial statements for periods commencing on or after 1 October 2014.

The 2014 revisions to the ISA supported changes to the UK Corporate Governance Code (the Code) and Guidance for Audit Committees that were also updated by the FRC in September 2014.

The main changes in the recent revisions to ISA (UK and Ireland) 700 are set out in **4.3.1**.

Further major changes to auditor reporting standards will take effect for audits of all entities for periods commencing on or after 17 June 2016. These are set out in a number of final draft new and revised ISAs (UK and Ireland) issued by the FRC in April 2016 in conjunction with implementation of the EU Audit Regulation and Directive and adoption of revised standards issued by the IAASB. Further details are given in **4.3.2**.

4.2.1   Other guidance

In ISA (UK and Ireland) 700 (revised September 2014), the FRC refers readers to 'the most recent version of the Bulletin, *Compendium of Illustrative Auditor's Reports on United Kingdom Private Sector Financial Statements*' for example, company reports. The most recent version is Bulletin 2010/2 (Revised) *Compendium of Illustrative Auditor's Reports on United Kingdom Private Sector Financial Statements for periods ended on or after 15 December 2010*. This Bulletin provides guidance on the application in the UK of ISA (UK and Ireland) 700 and contains a number of illustrative examples of auditor's reports covering different situations and different types of entity. It was revised in February 2011 to reflect the requirements of an updated version of ISA (UK and Ireland) 700, which was effective for periods ending on or after 23 March 2011. It was further updated in March 2012 to update example reports for charities and friendly societies following changes in legislation and guidance applicable to those entities.

However, the examples in the revised Bulletin do not reflect changes to ISAs (UK and Ireland), legislative changes and changes to the Listing Rules and the Code since March 2012. To provide an update on these matters in April 2014, the FRC issued Bulletin 4: *Recent developments in company law, the Listing Rules and Auditing Standards that affect United Kingdom Auditor's Reports*. This Bulletin was revised in June 2015 and provides guidance in respect of:

- the *Companies Act* requirement for large and medium sized companies to produce a strategic report;
- the option for companies to provide members with a strategic report and supplementary material in place of the company's full annual report – replacing the previous option to provide summary financial statements;
- amendment of the regulations specifying the content of the directors' remuneration report for quoted companies;
- changes to the Listing Rules regarding disclosure of directors' remuneration; and
- changes to ISA (UK and Ireland) 700 in October 2012 and June 2013.

The Bulletin includes several example reports, one for a FRSSE company and several more taken from the 2010/2 Bulletin and updated. The FRC does not currently have any plans to update Bulletin 2010/2. Further example reports can be found in *CCH Preparing Audit Reports* and on CCH Online.

At the time of writing, Bulletin 2010/2 and Bulletin 4 have not been updated to reflect:

- reports on the financial statements of micro-entities;
- changes arising from the Code (for periods commencing on or after 1 October 2014);
- changes to the Listing Rules with respect to the Code provisions in respect of which the auditor is expected to review the company's compliance statement; and
- changes arising from the *Companies Partnerships and Groups (Accounts and Reports) Regulations* 2015 in respect of the auditor's report on the strategic report and the directors' report and, where applicable, the auditor's report on a separate governance statement. These changes affect all companies and take effect for periods commencing on or after 1 January 2016 but may take effect for earlier periods (commencing on or after 1 January 2015) at the company's option or where the company takes advantage of other provisions of the Regulations such as the change in small company thresholds.

In January 2003, the Audit and Assurance Faculty of the ICAEW issued Technical Release Audit 1/03, *The audit report and auditors' duty of care to third parties* following an earlier judgment in the Scottish courts, *Royal Bank of Scotland v Bannerman Johnstone Maclay and others* ('Bannerman'). The aim of Audit 1/03 is to assist the auditor in managing the risk of inadvertently assuming a duty of care to third parties in relation to his audit reports. Further details are discussed in **4.22**.

In April 2006, the Audit and Assurance faculty of the ICAEW issued AAF 02/06, *Identifying and managing certain risks arising from the inclusion of reports from auditors and accountants in prospectuses (and certain other investment circulars)*. This publication develops the principles in Audit 01/03 for reporting accountants.

APB Bulletin 2008/6 *The senior statutory auditor under the United Kingdom Companies Act 2006* provides guidance on interpretation of the requirements of the *Companies Act* in respect of the role of the senior statutory auditor and the signature of the auditor's report.

4.3 Changes to auditor reporting standards

4.3.1 Recent changes

In June 2013, the FRC issued a revision to ISA (UK and Ireland) 700, effective for audits of financial statements for periods commencing on or after 1 October 2012. This change required auditors reporting on companies which apply the Code to explain more about their work by:

(a) providing an overview of the scope of the audit, showing how this addressed the risk and materiality considerations;

(b) describing the risks of material misstatement that had the greatest effect on the overall audit strategy, the allocation of resources in the audit and directing the efforts of the engagement team; and

(c) providing an explanation of how the auditor applied the concept of materiality in planning and performing the audit.

The revised standard also included an amended 'scope' paragraph to reflect the auditor's new responsibility imposed by a revision to ISA (UK and Ireland) 720 to read other information with a view to identifying any information that is materially incorrect based on, or materially inconsistent with the knowledge he has acquired in the course of performing the audit.

The revision in September 2014 applies to periods commencing on or after 1 October 2014 and only affects those auditors reporting on companies that apply the Code. The revision requires the auditor to provide a statement regarding the directors' assessment of the principal risks that would threaten the solvency or liquidity of the entity – see **4.12.4**.

4.3.2 Forthcoming changes

In April 2016, as part of a suite of revised ISAs (UK and Ireland) incorporating changes arising from the EU Audit Regulation and Directive and from recent changes to ISAs issued by the IAASB, the FRC issued final draft versions of:

- ISA (UK and Ireland) 700 (Revised June 2016) *Forming an opinion and reporting on financial statements*;
- ISA (UK and Ireland) 701 *Communicating key audit matters in the independent auditor's report*;
- ISA (UK and Ireland) 705 (Revised June 2016) *Modifications to the opinion in the independent auditor's report*; and
- ISA (UK and Ireland) 706 (Revised June 2016) *Emphasis of Matter paragraphs and Other Matter paragraphs in the independent auditor's report*.

Subject to legislation, it is intended that the changes proposed in these new and revised standards will come into effect for accounting periods commencing on or after 17 June 2016 and so will affect June 2017 year ends and entities with short accounting periods.

Significant changes are also proposed to ISA (UK and Ireland) 570 (Revised June 2016) *Going concern* (see **Chapter 11**) and ISA (UK and Ireland) 720 (Revised June 2016) *The auditor's responsibilities relating to other information* (see **Chapter 34**) which will in future set out considerations for the auditor's report in respect of these matters.

ISAs (UK and Ireland) 705 and 706 deal with modifications to the auditor's reports and the revised versions are not significantly different from the current versions. Further details are given in **Chapter 5**.

The revisions to ISA 700 and related standards will have a significant impact on the content, wording and format of the auditor's report which will, in future, start with the opinion on the financial statements, a practice already common in reports for listed companies. Other wording changes will include much more detailed explanation of auditor's and directors' responsibilities including responsibilities in relation to going concern although much of this may be relegated to a website such as the one currently maintained by the FRC. There will also be specific requirements for audit reports on public interest entities.

In view of the uncertainties surrounding the exact format and wording of reports and the lack of officially approved examples, no examples of the new style reports have been included in this edition of *Implementing GAAS* but these will be available in due course on CCH Online.

4.3.3 Key Audit Matters

ISA (UK and Ireland) 701 *Communicating key audit matters in the independent auditor's report* is a new standard based on the recently issued international version, with certain specific UK additions and requirements derived from the EU Audit Regulation. It will require the communication of certain matters in the audit report, referred to as 'key audit matters' – similar to the requirements applicable previously under ISA 700 to entities stating compliance with the Code. The new standard will apply to listed companies, public interest entities, entities choosing voluntarily to explain their compliance with the Code and other entities where the auditor decides to communicate key matters in the audit report.

Key audit matters are those matters that in the auditor's professional judgment were of most significance in the audit of the financial statements of the current period. Key audit matters are selected from matters communicated with those charged with governance. In determining what are key audit matters, the auditor considers:

- areas of higher assessed risk of material misstatement or significant risk identified in accordance with ISA (UK and Ireland) 315 (Revised June 2016);
- significant auditor judgments relating to areas of significant management judgment including accounting estimates; and
- the effect on the audit of significant transactions or events in the period.

4.4 Aim of the audit report

When reporting on a set of financial statements, the auditor's objective is to form an opinion on the financial statements and to express that opinion clearly in a written report.

ISA (UK and Ireland) 700 requires that auditor's reports should contain a clear expression of opinion based on review and assessment of the conclusions drawn from evidence obtained in the course of the audit.

In forming his opinion, the auditor should evaluate whether:

- there is sufficient appropriate audit evidence as to whether the financial statements as a whole are free from material misstatement, whether due to fraud or error;
- uncorrected misstatements are material, individually or in aggregate (including consideration of the qualitative aspects of the entity's accounting practices and indicators of possible bias in management's judgments);
- in respect of a true and fair framework, the financial statements, including the disclosures, give a true and fair view; and
- in respect of all frameworks the financial statements have been prepared in all material respects in accordance with the framework, including the requirements of applicable law;

and, in particular, whether:

- the financial statements adequately refer to or describe the relevant financial reporting framework;
- the financial statements adequately disclose the significant accounting policies selected and applied;
- the accounting policies selected and applied are consistent with the applicable financial reporting framework, and are appropriate in the circumstances;
- accounting estimates are reasonable;
- the information presented in the financial statements is relevant, reliable, comparable and understandable;
- the financial statements provide adequate disclosures to enable the intended users to understand the effect of material transactions and events on the information conveyed in the financial statements; and
- the terminology used in the financial statements, including the title of each financial statement, is appropriate.

4.5 Contents of an audit report

The ISA (UK and Ireland) requires that an audit report is in writing and should contain:

- a title (see **4.6**);
- details of the addressee(s) of the report (see **4.7**);
- identification of the financial statements which have been audited (see **4.8**);
- the responsibilities of those charged with governance (see **4.9**);
- the responsibilities of the auditor (see **4.9**);
- the scope of the audit of the financial statements (see **4.10**);
- the auditor's opinion(s) on the financial statements (see **4.11**);
- the auditor's opinion(s) on other matters (see **4.11**);

- details of the auditor's responsibilities to report by exception on certain matters (see **4.11**);
- the date of the auditor's report (see **4.13**);
- the location of the office where the auditor is based (see **4.14**); and
- the auditor's signature (see **4.15**).

The standard recommends that using a standard format with appropriate headings will help the user to understand the report. However, it also points out that the report should reflect the particular engagement.

In practice, most reports on unlisted companies follow a standard format based on that used by the FRC in its illustrative examples of audit reports. However, following the issue in June 2013 of a revised version of ISA (UK and Ireland) 700, auditors of listed companies and other entities that comply with the Code have been experimenting with the order of topics and sub-headings used in their reports in order to make them more informative and easier to understand. In particular, most auditors are now choosing to place the opinion at the beginning of the report for such entities in order that shareholders will hopefully then find it easier to focus on the opinion and the key risks addressed in arriving at that opinion.

4.5.1   Entities that report on application of the Code

ISA 700 also contains specific requirements for audit reports relating to entities that are required, or choose voluntarily, to report on how they have applied the Code. These include:

- a description of significant risks, description of how the auditor has applied the concept of materiality and an overview of the scope of the audit including how the auditor has responded to the significant risks;
- a report, by exception, where the auditor has identified 'other information' in the annual report that is materially incorrect or inconsistent with the knowledge he has gained in the course of the audit; and
- a statement regarding whether the auditor has anything to add to the directors' statements required by the Code in relation to risk assessment, going concern and liquidity.

Further details of these requirements are given in **4.12**.

4.6   Title

The term 'Independent Auditor' is usually used in the title in order to distinguish the report from reports that might be issued by others who have not complied with the FRC's *Ethical Standards for Auditors* (see **Chapter 2**).

4.7 Addressee

From a risk management point of view, it is important that the auditor correctly identifies the addressee(s) of his report. Where the auditor is reporting on the financial statements of a UK company, the *Companies Act* 2006 requires that he reports to the members of the company, as the audit is undertaken on their behalf. Audit reports for such companies are therefore usually addressed to 'the members' or 'the shareholders'.

For other types of reporting entity, the addressee of the report will depend on the terms of the engagement and/or applicable legislation. For example, where the auditor is reporting on the financial statements of a pension scheme, he will usually address his report to the trustees, although in some cases, the trust deed of the scheme or applicable legislation may require that the report also be addressed to the members.

An introductory paragraph may be followed by a 'Bannerman' paragraph clarifying the purpose of the report, as discussed in ICAEW Technical Release Audit 1/03 which was issued to assist auditors in managing the risk of inadvertently assuming a duty of care to third parties in relation to their audit reports. The Technical Release is discussed in detail in section **4.22** below.

4.8 Identification of financial statements

The auditor's report should identify the financial statements that have been audited; this is normally achieved via an introductory paragraph. This identification section should refer to the pages of the report that contain the financial statements and the date of, and period covered by, the financial statements, and is intended to ensure that there is no confusion over the subject matter of the auditor's report. As noted in paragraph **4.20**, problems may arise where the Annual Report is to be published electronically and the statements covered by the audit report may not be determined from page numbers alone. Here, the auditor is required to refer explicitly to the primary statements and notes covered by the audit report.

In practice, many auditors now identify the financial statements that are the subject of the report by identifying the primary financial statements by name and referring also to the related notes. It is, however, still acceptable for the auditor to identify the audited financial statements by reference to page numbers.

4.9 Respective responsibilities of those charged with governance and the auditor

Those charged with governance are responsible for the preparation of the financial statements and auditors are responsible for auditing and expressing an opinion on those financial statements in accordance with applicable legal requirements and ISAs (UK and Ireland). The auditor's report should state these responsibilities clearly. The report should also state that ISAs (UK and Ireland) require the auditor to comply with the *Ethical Standards for Auditors*.

4.10　Description of the generic scope of an audit

The report should include a description of the generic scope of an audit by either:

- cross referring to a 'Statement of the Scope of an Audit' that is maintained on the FRC's website (www.frc.org.uk/auditscopeukprivate) for any private sector entity;
- including the description of the scope of an audit from **Table 1** below (NB when this option is used the wording used should be exactly as set out below); or
- cross referring to a 'Statement of the Scope of an Audit' that is included elsewhere within the Annual Report.

When the Statement of the Scope of an Audit is included elsewhere in the Annual Report, the format in **Table 1** should also be used, although this option is rarely used in practice.

TABLE 1: Statement of the Scope of an Audit to be included in the auditor's report

An audit involves obtaining evidence about the amounts and disclosures in the financial statements sufficient to give reasonable assurance that the financial statements are free from material misstatement, whether caused by fraud or error. This includes an assessment of:

- whether the accounting policies are appropriate to the [*describe nature of entity*] circumstances and have been consistently applied and adequately disclosed;
- the reasonableness of significant accounting estimates made by [*describe those charged with governance*]; and
- the overall presentation of the financial statements.

In addition, we read all the financial and non-financial information in the [*describe the annual report*] to identify material inconsistencies with the audited financial statements and to identify any information that is apparently materially incorrect based on, or materially inconsistent with, the knowledge acquired by us in the course of performing the audit. If we become aware of any apparent material misstatements or inconsistencies, we consider the implications for our report.

4.11   Auditor's opinions

ISA (UK and Ireland) 700 (revised September 2014) requires that the auditor's report should contain a clear expression of the auditor's opinion on the financial statements and on any further requirements of statute or the particular engagement.

The opinions may be unqualified or qualified. Qualified opinions are considered in detail in **Chapter 5**.

4.11.1   Opinion on financial statements

The opinion required from the auditor will be dictated by the applicable reporting framework, including applicable legislation, and will be intended to provide the addressee of the report with reasonable assurance that the financial statements are free from material misstatement.

For UK companies, *Companies Act* 2006, s. 495 requires the auditor to express an opinion as to whether the financial statements:

- give a true and fair view of the entity's financial position at the end of the reporting period and of its profit/loss for that period;
- have been properly prepared in accordance with the applicable reporting framework; and
- have been prepared in accordance with the provisions of the *Companies Act* 2006.

The auditor's opinion should indicate the financial reporting framework upon which the financial statements are based. For UK companies, this will normally be stated as:

- UK Generally Accepted Accounting Practice;
- (where the FRSSE is applied) UK Generally Accepted Accounting Practice applicable to Smaller Entities;
- International Financial Reporting Standards (IFRSs) as adopted by the European Union; or
- (for consolidated financial statements of fully listed companies) International Financial Reporting Standards (IFRSs) as adopted by the European Union and Article 4 of the IAS Regulation.[1]

Auditors may also be asked to report on compliance with a second financial reporting framework, such as International Financial Reporting Standards (IFRSs) as issued by the IAASB. In this situation, the second opinion must be clearly separated in the opinion section by the use of a subheading.

---

[1] Article 4 of the IAS Regulation (1606/2002/EC) applies to companies with securities that are admitted to trading on a regulated market in an EU member state and requires such companies to apply EU adopted IFRS in their consolidated accounts. This requirement therefore applies to fully listed companies in the UK, but not to those traded on AIM, which is not a regulated market for this purpose.

4.11.2   Opinion on other matters

When the auditor gives an opinion arising from other responsibilities, that opinion should be set out in a separate section of the auditor's report, following the opinion on the financial statements.

Other reporting requirements may be set out in legislation or by the terms of engagement agreed with the entity. Where this is the case, these opinions should be clearly distinguished from the opinion on the financial statements.

For UK companies, the *Companies Act* 2006 requires that the auditor expresses opinion(s) on:

Strategic report and directors' report:

- whether the information given in the strategic report (if any) and the directors' report is consistent with the financial statements; and
- (for companies applying the *Companies, Partnerships and Groups (Accounts and Reports) Regulations* 2015) whether any such strategic report and directors' report have been prepared in accordance with applicable legal requirements. The auditor shall also state whether, in the light of the knowledge and understanding of the company and its environment obtained in the course of the audit, he has identified any material misstatements in the strategic report (if any) and the directors' reports and, if applicable, give an indication of the nature of each of the misstatements.

Directors' Remuneration Report:

- (for quoted companies only) whether the information given in the part of the directors' remuneration report to be audited is consistent with the financial statements.

Separate corporate governance statement:

Rule 7.2 in the Financial Conduct Authority's *Disclosure Rules and Transparency Rules* sourcebook requires listed companies to disclose certain information. Normally this is done in a Corporate Governance section within the directors' report but as an alternative, some of this information may be disclosed in a separate corporate governance statement. Where a company produces such a separate corporate governance statement, the auditor states:

- whether, in his opinion, based on the work undertaken in the course of the audit, the information given in the statement in compliance with rules 7.2.5 and 7.2.6 in the *Disclosure Rules and Transparency Rules* sourcebook made by the Financial Conduct Authority (information about internal control and risk management systems in relation to financial reporting processes and about capital structures) is consistent with the financial statements;
- (for companies applying the *Companies, Partnerships and Groups (Accounts and Reports) Regulations* 2015) whether the separate corporate governance statement has been prepared in accordance with applicable legal requirements. The auditor shall also state whether, in the light of the

knowledge and understanding of the company and its environment obtained in the course of the audit, he has identified any material misstatements in the statement and, if applicable, give an indication of the nature of each of the misstatements; and

- (for companies applying the *Companies, Partnerships and Groups (Accounts and Reports) Regulations* 2015) the auditor must also state whether in his opinion, based on the work undertaken in the course of the audit, rules 7.2.2, 7.2.3 and 7.2.7 in the Disclosure Rules and Transparency Rules sourcebook made by the Financial Conduct Authority (information about the company's corporate governance code and practices and about its administrative, management and supervisory bodies and committees) have been complied with, if applicable.

An example extract form an auditor's report where a listed company has produced a separate corporate governance statement is given in **42.7**.

Other reporting frameworks may require other additional opinions.

4.11.3   Reporting by exception

If the auditor is required to report by exception, he should describe his responsibilities under the heading 'Matters on which we are required to report by exception' and include a suitable conclusion(s) in respect of such matters.

All UK companies

For UK companies, the auditor is required to consider, and report by exception if:

- adequate accounting records have not been kept by the company or returns adequate for the purposes of the audit have not been received from branches not visited by the auditor;
- the financial statements are not in agreement with the accounting records and returns;
- certain disclosures of directors' remuneration have not been made (that is the information required under the *Small Companies and Groups (Accounts and Directors' Report) Regulations* 2008 or the *Large and Medium-sized Companies and Groups (Accounts and Reports) Regulations* 2008, as applicable); or
- the auditor has not received all the information and explanations he requires for his audit.

Small companies

Where a small company has prepared its accounts in accordance with the small companies regime or has taken advantage of either of the small companies' exemptions relating to the directors' report or the preparation of a strategic report, the auditor is required to report by exception if, in his opinion, the directors were not entitled to do so.

Other entities

Legislation and reporting frameworks applicable to other entities may require similar or additional exception reporting.

4.12 Entities that report on application of the Code

4.12.1 Listing Rules

Listing Rule LR 9.8.10R requires that a premium listed company must ensure that the auditors review each of the following before the annual report is published:

- the statements made by the directors, in accordance with the *UK Corporate Governance Code* and related FRC guidance, regarding going concern and longer-term viability; and
- the parts of the statement required by LR 9.8.6R(6) (corporate governance) that relate to the company's compliance with provisions C1.1, C2.1, C2.3 and C3.1 to C3.8 of the *UK Corporate Governance Code*.

These matters are usually referred to by the auditor under the heading of matters on which the auditor is required to report by exception (see **Table 3**).

4.12.2 Significant risks and scope of audit

For those entities required, and those that choose voluntarily, to report on how they have applied the Code, or to explain why they have not, ISA 700 requires the auditor's report to:

(a) describe those assessed risks of material misstatement that were identified by the auditor and which had the greatest effect on: the overall audit strategy; the allocation of resources in the audit; and directing the efforts of the engagement team;

(b) provide an explanation of how the auditor has applied the concept of materiality in planning and performing the audit. This explanation needs to specify the threshold used by the auditor as being materiality for the financial statements as a whole; and

(c) provide an overview of the scope of the audit, including an explanation of how the scope addressed the assessed risks of material misstatement disclosed in (a) and was influenced by the application of materiality as disclosed in (b).

When describing these matters, it is important that they are set out in a way which is useful to the users of the financial statements. This means the matters need to be described:

(a) so that a user is able to understand their significance in the context of the audit of the financial statements as a whole and not as discrete opinions on separate elements of the financial statements;

(b) in a way that the user is able to relate them directly to the specific circumstances of the audited entity, that is, they should not be generic or abstract matters written in standardised language; and

(c) in a manner that complements the description of significant issues relating to the financial statements, which are required to be set out in the separate section of the annual report describing the work of the audit committee in discharging its responsibilities. See **42.5**.

4.12.3 Reporting by exception

For those entities required, and those that choose voluntarily, to report on how they have applied the Code, or to explain why they have not, ISA 700 requires the auditor to report by exception when he identifies information in the annual report that is:

- materially inconsistent with either the information in the audited financial statements or the knowledge acquired by the auditor in the course of performing the audit;
- apparently materially incorrect based on the knowledge acquired by the auditor in the course of performing the audit; or
- otherwise misleading.

For such entities, matters that the auditor shall report on by exception include circumstances where the annual report includes:

- a statement given by the directors that they consider the annual report and accounts taken as a whole is fair, balanced and understandable and provides the information necessary for shareholders to assess the entity's performance, business model and strategy, that is inconsistent with the knowledge acquired by the auditor in the course of performing the audit;
- a section describing the work of the audit committee that does not appropriately address matters communicated by the auditor to the audit committee;
- an explanation, as to why the annual report does not include such a statement or section, that is materially inconsistent with the knowledge acquired by the auditor in the course of performing the audit; or
- other information that, in the auditor's judgment, contains a material inconsistency or a material misstatement of fact.

4.12.4 *Statement on the directors' assessment of solvency and liquidity*

With effect for audits of periods commencing on or after 1 October 2014, for those entities required, or who voluntarily choose to report on how they have applied the Code, or to explain why they have not, the auditor is required to provide a further statement on the directors' assessment of the principal risks that would threaten the solvency or liquidity of the entity, having regard to the work he performed in relation to going concern, see **Chapter 11**.

The statement will set out whether the auditor has anything material to add or draw attention to in relation to:

- the directors' confirmation in the annual report that they have carried out a robust assessment of the principal risks facing the entity, including those that would threaten its business model, future performance, solvency or liquidity;
- the disclosures in the annual report that describe those risks and explain how they are being managed or mitigated;
- the directors' statement in the financial statements about whether they considered it appropriate to adopt the going concern basis of accounting, and their identification of any material uncertainties to the entity's ability to continue to do so over a period of at least 12 months from the date of approval of the financial statements; and
- the directors' explanation in the annual report as to how they have assessed the prospects of the entity, over what period they have done so and why they consider that period to be appropriate, and their statement as to whether they have a reasonable expectation that the entity will be able to continue in operation and meet its liabilities as they fall due over the period of their assessment, including any related disclosures drawing attention to any necessary qualifications or assumptions.

4.13 Date

ISA (UK and Ireland) 700 requires that:

- before the auditor can give an opinion on the financial statements, they must have been approved by the directors and the auditor must have considered all of the available evidence; and
- the auditor's report has to be dated as at the date the opinion is expressed.

The significance of the date of the auditor's report is that he is informing the reader that he is aware of events up to that date and has considered the effect of these on the financial statements.

Before the auditor signs the audit report, the following must have occurred:

- receipt of the approved financial statements, together with any accompanying information, from the directors;
- review of all the documents which the auditor is required to consider in addition to the financial statements, for example, the strategic report (if any) and the directors' report; and
- completion of all the procedures thought necessary by the auditor to be able to form an opinion, including a post balance sheet events review.

The senior statutory auditor must sign and date the report expressing an opinion on the financial statements for distribution with the financial statements. Firms must therefore have procedures to ensure reports are not signed before the above events have occurred.

Although the date of the auditor's report has to be after the directors have approved the financial statements, it does not mean that the auditor cannot commence his work until the directors have approved the financial statements. Rather, he cannot conclude it until this has happened. In many cases, the preparation of the financial statements will take place at the same time as the auditor is gathering evidence.

Although he will normally be in a position to give his opinion at the same date as the financial statements are approved, it does not have to be on the same day. Unless the auditor has gathered all his evidence and completed his work at that time (including a post balance sheet event review), he is unable to sign his report despite the directors approving the financial statements.

Where the date the opinion is expressed is before the final printing of the financial statements, the auditor will have to ensure the drafts on which he forms his opinion are sufficiently clear for him to assess the overall presentation. One area to be especially aware of is where the directors have approved the profit and loss account and the balance sheet, but the notes have yet to be finally completed. In such cases, the auditor will have to delay giving his opinion until they are finished.

Where the date the auditor signs his report is later than the date of approval, he may need to obtain additional assurances from the directors that there have been no events in the intervening period that would affect the financial statements. He will also need to have his own procedures for reviewing subsequent events and assessing their impact on the financial statements.

4.14 Auditor's location

The report should also state the location of the auditor's office, typically, the city or town in which the auditor (or senior statutory auditor) responsible for the opinion is based.

4.15   Signature

4.15.1   Audit regulations

Audit regulations require that an audit report in respect of the audit of UK entities must:

- state the name of the firm as it appears in the Register;
- include the words 'Statutory Auditor' or 'Statutory Auditors' after the name of the firm;
- and if required by law, state the name of the responsible individual who was in charge of the audit, be signed by this person in his own name and include the words 'Senior Statutory Auditor' after the name of the responsible individual.

An audit report has to include the description 'Statutory Auditor' but there is nothing to prevent a firm adding any other appropriate description, such as 'chartered accountants'.

4.15.2   Senior statutory auditor

Where the auditor is a firm, the *Companies Act* 2006 sets out the requirement for the senior statutory auditor to sign the auditor's report in his own name for and on behalf of the audit firm. Guidance with respect to the term 'senior statutory auditor' was published by the APB in April 2008 as Bulletin 2008/6, *The 'senior statutory auditor' under the United Kingdom Companies Act 2006*.

The senior statutory auditor is required to sign in his own name for reports:

- prepared in accordance with the *Companies Act* 2006, s. 495, 496 and 497, that is audit reports which provide a true and fair opinion;
- on voluntary revisions of annual accounts and reports (see **6.3**); and
- on the special auditor's reports on abbreviated accounts (see **6.2**).

This requirement has been effective for accounting periods since those commencing on or after 6 April 2008.

In signing an auditor's report in his own name as the senior statutory auditor, the individual does not take on any additional legal responsibility for the audit or the report than he would previously have had prior to the *Companies Act* 2006.

If more than one partner is involved in an audit, it is important to determine which individual is acting as the engagement partner (as defined in ISAs (UK and Ireland)) and therefore, assumes the role of senior statutory auditor.

The Bulletin suggests that it would be pragmatic for the audit firm to have a contingency plan as to who would succeed as senior statutory auditor in the event that the audit is at an advanced stage but the senior auditor is unable to sign the auditor's report.

If another audit partner is actively involved in the audit engagement, a suitable contingency plan may be for that other partner to work in parallel with the senior statutory auditor and be able to take over as senior statutory auditor if the need arises.

If no other partner has worked in parallel with the senior statutory auditor, then the Bulletin is of the view that in such exceptional circumstances it is permissible for the engagement quality control reviewer to be appointed as the replacement senior statutory auditor where:

- the engagement quality control reviewer has completed his or her review; and
- the audit is at an 'advanced stage' as defined by Bulletin 2008/2[2], which deals with the auditor's association with preliminary announcements.

This is subject to the condition that the engagement quality control reviewer is eligible to be appointed as the senior statutory auditor.

Once an engagement quality control reviewer has been appointed as a replacement senior statutory auditor, he can no longer act as the engagement quality control reviewer because his objectivity may have been impaired through assuming the role of senior statutory auditor.

4.15.3   Signing

The requirements of the *Companies Act* 2006 for the senior statutory auditor to physically sign the auditor's report in his own name, extends only to the copy of the auditor's report to be provided to the client upon completion of the audit. In all but this 'signing copy', the name of the senior statutory auditor needs to be stated, but the signature does not need to be reproduced. The copy of the auditor's report sent to the Registrar of Companies requires the name of the senior statutory auditor to be stated, together with the name of the statutory auditor, but does not require an actual signature.

Under s. 503(3) of the 2006 Act, only the senior statutory auditor can sign the 'signing copy' of the auditor's report. If he is absent at the time of signing, the signature can be obtained by electronic means, such as e-mail or fax. If, for example, due to illness or other absence, another partner needs to sign the audit report, he cannot do so on behalf of the senior statutory auditor but would need to take full responsibility for that role himself. This would involve familiarising himself with the audit and audit judgments made to the extent necessary for him to assume the role of senior statutory auditor.

---

[2] Bulletin 2008/2 considers an audit to be at an advanced stage when it is complete subject only to the following:
  (a) clearing outstanding matters which are unlikely to have a material effect on the financial statements;
  (b) completing audit procedures on the detail of note disclosures on the financial statements that will not have a material impact on the primary financial statements and completing the auditor's reading of 'other information' in the annual report in accordance with ISA (UK and Ireland) 720;
  (c) updating the subsequent events review covering the period to the date of the auditor's reports on the financial statements; and
  (d) obtaining final written representations from management and establishing that the financial statements have been reviewed and approved by the directors.

4.15.4   Joint auditors

Where a company has appointed joint auditors, each audit firm will designate its own senior statutory auditor. When the auditor's report is signed, each firm's senior statutory auditor must sign the report in his own name for and on behalf of his firm.

4.16   Unmodified auditor's reports examples

ISA (UK and Ireland) 700 refers to example auditor's reports in the most recent version of the Bulletin *Compendium of Illustrative Auditor's Reports on United Kingdom Private Sector Financial Statements*. The current version is Bulletin 2010/2 (Revised) published in February 2011 as supplemented and updated by FRC Bulletin 4: *Recent developments in company law, the Listing Rules and Auditing Standards that affect United Kingdom Auditor's Reports* revised in June 2015.

A simple auditor's report for a non-listed company not preparing group accounts is provided in **Table 2**. The example in **Table 3** is for a premium listed company. Further variations are set out in Bulletin 2010/2 but may need to be adapted in accordance with Bulletin 4 and other recent developments.

Further example reports can be found in the book *CCH Preparing Audit Reports*, published by Wolters Kluwer and available on CCH Online.

TABLE 2: Example simple auditor's report

- *Company does not prepare group accounts.*
- *UK GAAP used for individual company financial statements.*
- *Company does not meet the Companies Act definition of a quoted company.*
- *Financial statements contain no surrounding information other than the Directors' Report.*

Independent auditor's report to the members of XYZ Limited

We have audited the financial statements of [entity name] for the year ended [date] which comprise [state the primary financial statements such as the Profit and Loss Account, the Balance Sheet, the Cash Flow Statement, the Statement of Total Recognised Gains and Losses] and the related notes. The financial reporting framework that has been applied in their preparation is applicable law and United Kingdom Accounting Standards (United Kingdom Generally Accepted Accounting Practice).[1]

Respective responsibilities of directors and auditor

As explained more fully in the Directors' Responsibilities Statement [set out [on pages …]], the directors are responsible for the preparation of the financial statements and for being satisfied that they give a true and fair view. Our responsibility is to audit and express an opinion on the financial statements in accordance with applicable law and International Standards on Auditing (UK and Ireland). Those standards required us to comply with the Auditing Practices Board's (APB's) Ethical Standards for Auditors.

Scope of the audit of the financial statements

A description of the scope of an audit of financial statements is [provided on the FRC's website at www.frc.org.uk/auditscopeukprivate]/[set out [on page x] of the Annual Report].

Opinion on financial statements

In our opinion, the financial statements:

- give a true and fair view of the state of the company's affairs as at … and of its profit [loss] for the year then ended;
- have been properly prepared in accordance with United Kingdom Generally Accepted Accounting Practice; and
- have been prepared in accordance with the requirements of the *Companies Act* 2006.

Opinion on other matters prescribed by the Companies Act 2006

In our opinion, the information given in the [Strategic Report and the] Directors' Report for the financial year for which the financial statements are prepared is consistent with the financial statements [and [the Strategic Report and] the Directors' Report [have/ has] been prepared in accordance with applicable legal requirements.

In the light of the knowledge and understanding of the company and its environment obtained in the course of the audit, we have identified no material misstatements in [the Strategic Report and] the Directors' Report][2].

Matters on which we are required to report by exception

We have nothing to report in respect of the following matters where the *Companies Act* 2006 requires us to report to you if, in our opinion:

- adequate accounting records have not been kept or returns adequate for our audit have not been received from branches not visited by us; or
- the company's financial statements are not in agreement with the accounting records and returns; or
- certain disclosures of directors' remuneration specified by law are not made; or
- we have not received all the information and explanations we required for our audit.

[Signature]
John Smith (Senior statutory auditor)
For and on behalf of ABC LLP, Statutory Auditor
Address
Date

---

[1] The auditor may include a 'Bannerman Statement' as part of the opening section of his report (see **4.22**).
[2] Applies only for periods commencing on or after 1 January 2016 and for earlier periods where the company has applied the *Companies, Partnerships and Groups (Accounts and Reports) Regulations* 2015.

TABLE 3: Example auditor's report for a premium listed company using IFRSs

- *Group and parent company financial statements not presented separately.*
- *IFRSs as adopted by the European Union used for both group and parent company financial statements.*
- *Company meets the Companies Act definition of a quoted company and has a premium listing in the UK.*
- *Company's Corporate Governance statement required by DTR is included in the Directors' Report.*
- *Section 408 exemption relating to parent company's own income statement not taken.*
- *Auditor chooses to refer to FRC website for description of scope of an audit.*

Independent auditor's report to the members of XYZ Limited

We have audited the financial statements of [entity name] for the year ended [date] which comprise [specify the financial statements such as the Group and Parent Company Statements of Comprehensive Income, Statements of Changes in Equity, Balance Sheets and Statements of Cash Flow] and the related notes. The financial reporting framework that has been applied in their preparation is applicable law and International Financial Reporting Standards (IFRSs) as adopted by the European Union.[3]

Respective responsibilities of directors and auditors

As explained more fully in the Directors' Responsibilities Statement [set out [on page ...]], the directors are responsible for the preparation of the financial statements and for being satisfied that they give a true and fair view. Our responsibility is to audit and express an opinion on the financial statements in accordance with applicable law and International Standards on Auditing (UK and Ireland). Those standards required us to comply with the Auditing Practices Board's (APB's) Ethical Standards for Auditors.

Scope of the audit of the financial statements

A description of the scope of an audit of financial statements is provided on the FRC's website at www.frc.org.uk/auditscopeukprivate.

Opinion on financial statements

In our opinion, the financial statements:

- give a true and fair view of the state of the group's and of the parent company's affairs as at ... and of the group's and the parent company's profit [loss] for the year then ended;
- have been properly prepared in accordance with IFRSs as adopted by the European Union; and
- have been prepared in accordance with the requirements of the *Companies Act* 2006 and, as regards the group financial statements, Art. 4 of the IAS Regulation.

Our assessment of risks of material misstatement

[Insert a description of those specific assessed risks of material misstatement that were identified by the auditor and which had the greatest effect on the audit strategy; the allocation of resources in the audit; and directing the efforts of the engagement team.]

Our application of materiality

[Insert an explanation of how the auditor applied the concept of materiality in planning and performing the audit. Such explanation shall specify the threshold used by the auditor as being materiality for the financial statements as a whole.]

An overview of the scope of our audit

[Insert an overview of the scope of the audit, including an explanation of how the scope addressed the assessed risks of material misstatement and was influenced by the auditor's application of materiality.]

[The disclosures about the above three matters are made in a manner that complements the description of significant issues relating to the financial statements required to be set out in the separate section of the annual report describing the work of the audit committee in discharging its responsibilities].

Opinion on other matters prescribed by the Companies Act 2006

In our opinion:

- the part of the Directors' Remuneration Report to be audited has been properly prepared in accordance with the *Companies Act* 2006; and
- the information given in the Strategic Report and the Directors' Report for the financial year for which the financial statements are prepared is consistent with the financial statements [and the reports have been prepared in accordance with applicable legal requirements.

In the light of the knowledge and understanding of the company and its environment obtained in the course of the audit, we have identified no material misstatements in the Strategic Report and the Directors' Report][4].

Statement regarding the directors' assessment of principal risks, going concern and longer term viability of the company

We have nothing material to add or to draw attention to in relation to:

- the directors' confirmation in the annual report that they have carried out a robust assessment of the principal risks facing the entity, including those that would threaten its business model, future performance, solvency or liquidity;
- the disclosures in the annual report that describe those risks and explain how they are being managed or mitigated;
- the directors' statement in the financial statements about whether they considered it appropriate to adopt the going concern basis of accounting in preparing them and their identification of any material uncertainties over the entity's ability to continue over a period of at least 12 months from the date of approval of the financial statements; and

- the directors' explanation in the annual report as to how they have assessed the prospects of the entity, over what period they have done so and why they consider that period to be appropriate, and their statement as to whether they have a reasonable expectation that the entity will be able to continue in operation and meet its liabilities as they fall due over the period of their assessment, including any material disclosures drawing attention to any necessary qualifications or assumptions.

Matters on which we are required to report by exception

We have nothing to report in respect of the following:

Under the ISAs (UK and Ireland), we are required to report to you if, in our opinion, information in the annual report is:

- materially inconsistent with the information in the audited financial statements; or
- apparently materially incorrect based on, or materially inconsistent with, our knowledge of the Group acquired in the course of performing our audit; or
- is otherwise misleading.

In particular, we are required to consider whether we have identified any inconsistencies between our knowledge acquired during the audit and the directors' statement that they consider the annual report is fair, balanced and understandable and whether the annual report appropriately discloses those matters that we communicated to the audit committee which we consider should have been disclosed.

Under the *Companies Act* 2006, we are required to report to you if, in our opinion:

- adequate accounting records have not been kept by the parent company, or returns adequate for our audit have not been received from branches not visited by us;
- the parent company financial statements and the part of the Directors' Remuneration Report to be audited are not in agreement with the accounting records and returns;
- certain disclosures of directors' remuneration specified by law are not made; or
- we have not received all the information and explanations we required for our audit.

Under the Listing Rules, we are required to review:

- the directors' statements, [set out on pages ...], in relation to going concern and longer term viability; and
- the part of the Corporate Governance Statement relating to the company's compliance with the provisions of the UK Corporate Governance Code specified for our review.

[Signature]
John Smith (Senior statutory auditor)
For and on behalf of ABC LLP, Statutory Auditor
Address
Date

[3] The auditor may include a 'Bannerman Statement' as part of the opening section of his report (see **4.22**).
[4] Applies only for periods commencing on or after 1 January 2016 and for earlier periods where the company has chosen to apply the *Companies, Partnerships and Groups (Accounts and Reports) Regulations* 2015.

4.17 Directors' Responsibility Statements

ISA (UK and Ireland) 700 requires that the auditor should distinguish between his responsibilities and those of the directors. This is achieved by making reference in the auditor's report to a statement contained elsewhere in the financial statements or accompanying information.

Legal advice on the exact wording of the Statement of Directors' Responsibilities may be sought in complex situations and the wording applicable to publicly traded companies will vary depending on the rules of the market on which its securities are traded.

Example wording for a description of the directors' responsibilities in various scenarios are given in **Tables 4–6**.

Example wording of a paragraph for inclusion at the foot of the directors' responsibilities statement in situations where financial statements are to be published on a website is given in **Table 7**. See also further considerations in section **4.20**.

TABLE 4: Example wording of a description of the directors' responsibilities for inclusion in a non-publicly traded company's financial statements, reporting under UK GAAP

The directors are responsible for preparing the Directors' Report and the financial statements in accordance with applicable law and regulations.

Company law requires the directors to prepare financial statements for each financial year. Under that law, the directors have elected to prepare the financial statements in accordance with United Kingdom Generally Accepted Accounting Practice (United Kingdom Accounting Standards and applicable law). Under company law, the directors must not approve the financial statements unless they are satisfied that they give a true and fair view of the state of affairs of the company and of the profit or loss of the company for that period.

In preparing these financial statements, the directors are required to:

- select suitable accounting policies and then apply them consistently;
- make judgments and accounting estimates that are reasonable and prudent;
- [except for small or medium-sized companies] state whether applicable UK Accounting Standards have been followed, subject to any material departures disclosed and explained in the financial statements;
- prepare the financial statements on the going concern basis unless it is inappropriate to presume that the company will continue in business.

The directors are responsible for keeping adequate accounting records that are sufficient to show and explain the company's transactions and disclose with reasonable accuracy at any time the financial position of the company and enable them to ensure that the financial statements comply with the *Companies Act* 2006. They are also responsible for safeguarding the assets of the company and hence for taking reasonable steps for the prevention and detection of fraud and other irregularities.

TABLE 5: Example wording of a description of the directors' responsibilities for inclusion in a non-publicly traded company's financial statements, reporting under IFRS

The directors are responsible for preparing the Directors' Report and the financial statements in accordance with applicable law and regulations.

Company law requires the directors to prepare financial statements for each financial year. Under that law, the directors have elected to prepare the financial statements in accordance with International Financial Reporting Standards as adopted by the European Union. Under company law, the directors must not approve the financial statements unless they are satisfied that they give a true and fair view of the state of affairs of the company and of the profit or loss of the company for that period. In preparing these financial statements, the directors are required to:

- select suitable accounting policies and then apply them consistently;
- make judgments and accounting estimates that are reasonable and prudent;
- state whether the financial statements have been prepared in accordance with IFRSs as adopted by the European Union;
- prepare the financial statements on the going concern basis unless it is inappropriate to presume that the company will continue in business.

The directors are responsible for keeping adequate accounting records that are sufficient to show and explain the company's transactions and disclose with reasonable accuracy at any time the financial position of the company and to enable them to ensure that the financial statements comply with the *Companies Act* 2006. They are also responsible for safeguarding the assets of the company and hence for taking reasonable steps for the prevention and detection of fraud and other irregularities.

[*Where financial statements are published on a website, see **4.20.2***]

Financial statements are published on the group's website in accordance with legislation in the United Kingdom governing the preparation and dissemination of financial statements, which may vary from legislation in other jurisdictions. The maintenance and integrity of the group's website is the responsibility of the directors. The directors' responsibility also extends to the ongoing integrity of the financial statements contained therein.

TABLE 6: Example wording of a description of the directors' responsibilities for inclusion in consolidated financial statements of an AIM traded company

- *Group accounts prepared under IFRS.*
- *Parent company accounts prepared under IFRS.*

The directors are responsible for preparing the Directors' Report and the financial statements in accordance with applicable law and regulations.

Company law requires the directors to prepare financial statements for each financial year. Under that law, the directors have, as required by the AIM Rules of the London Stock Exchange, elected to prepare the group financial statements in accordance with International Financial Reporting Standards as adopted by the European Union and have elected to prepare the parent company financial statements in accordance with United Kingdom Generally Accepted Accounting Practice (United Kingdom accounting standards and applicable law). Under company law, the directors must not approve the financial statements unless they are satisfied that they give a true and fair view of the state of affairs of the company and the group and of the profit or loss of the company and the group for that period.

In preparing these financial statements, the directors are required to:

- select suitable accounting policies and then apply them consistently;
- make judgments and accounting estimates that are reasonable and prudent;
- state whether the group financial statements have been prepared in accordance with IFRS as adopted by the European Union;
- state, with regard to the parent company financial statements, whether applicable UK Accounting Standards have been followed, subject to any material departures disclosed and explained in the financial statements;
- prepare the financial statements on the going concern basis unless it is inappropriate to presume that the company and the group will continue in business.

The directors are responsible for keeping adequate accounting records that are sufficient to show and explain the company's transactions and disclose with reasonable accuracy at any time the financial position of the company and to enable them to ensure that the financial statements comply with the *Companies Act* 2006. They are also responsible for safeguarding the assets of the company and hence for taking reasonable steps for the prevention and detection of fraud and other irregularities.

TABLE 7: Example paragraph for inclusion at the foot of the statement of directors' responsibilities where financial statements are to be published on a website

The directors are responsible for the maintenance and integrity of the corporate and financial information included on the company's website. Legislation in the United Kingdom governing the preparation and dissemination of the financial statements and other information included in annual reports may differ from legislation in other jurisdictions.

4.18   Small companies

4.18.1   *The Financial Reporting Standard for Smaller Entities and FRS 105*

The Financial Statement for Smaller Entities ('FRSSE') was introduced in 1997 as a one-stop alternative financial reporting standard for smaller entities.

It incorporated into one standard the applicable accounting and disclosure requirements of the *Companies Act* and simplified accounting and disclosure requirements derived from other accounting standards. Entities applying the FRSSE do not need to concern themselves with the requirements of other accounting standards but may refer to such standards for guidance in situations not covered by the FRSSE.

Companies applying the FRSSE must state in the financial statements that they have done so.

For accounting periods commencing before 1 January 2016, the FRSSE may be applied by small companies entitled to take advantage of the small companies regime under the *Companies Act* 2006, and other entities that would be so entitled if they were companies. The small company limits are set out in **Chapter 36**.

The FRSSE was revised to take account of developments in UK GAAP and the issue of FRS 102 *The Financial Reporting Standard applicable in the UK and Ireland.* The revised FRSSE takes effect for periods beginning on or after 1 January 2015 but earlier application is permitted. For earlier periods, the FRSSE (effective April 2008) applies.

The FRSSE has, however, been withdrawn for periods commencing from 1 January 2016 and in future those who have applied the FRSSE will instead need to apply either FRS 102 *The Financial Reporting Standard applicable in the UK and Republic of Ireland* or FRS 105 *The Financial Reporting Standard applicable to the Micro-entities Regime.*

Example wording for an unmodified audit report for a company preparing financial statements under the FRSSE is given in **Table 8**.

TABLE 8: Example unmodified auditor's report for a company preparing financial statements under the FRSSE

- *Company qualifies as a small company.*
- *Company does not prepare group financial statements.*
- *Company does not prepare a strategic report.*

Independent auditor's report to the members of XYZ Limited

We have audited the financial statements of [entity name] for the year ended [date] which comprise [state the primary financial statements such as the Profit and Loss Account, the Balance Sheet, the Cash Flow Statement, the Statement of Total Recognised Gains and Losses, the Reconciliation of Movements in Shareholders' Funds] and the related notes. The financial reporting framework that has been applied in their preparation is applicable law and the Financial Reporting Standard for Smaller Entities [Effective January 2015] (United Kingdom Generally Accepted Accounting Practice applicable to Smaller Entities).[5]

Respective responsibilities of directors and auditor

As explained more fully in the Directors' Responsibilities Statement [set out [on pages …]], the directors are responsible for the preparation of the financial statements and for being satisfied that they give a true and fair view. Our responsibility is to audit and express an opinion on the financial statements in accordance with applicable law and International Standards on Auditing (UK and Ireland). Those standards required us to comply with the Auditing Practices Board's (APB's) Ethical Standards for Auditors [, including 'APB Ethical Standard – Provisions Available for Small Entities (Revised)', in the circumstances set out in note [x] to the financial statements].

Scope of the audit of the financial statements

A description of the scope of an audit of financial statements is [provided on the FRC's website at www.frc.org.uk/auditscopeukprivate]/[set out [on page x] of the Annual Report].

Opinion on financial statements

In our opinion, the financial statements:

- give a true and fair view of the state of the company's affairs as at … and of its profit [loss] for the year then ended;
- have been properly prepared in accordance with United Kingdom Generally Accepted Accounting Practice applicable to Smaller Entities; and
- have been prepared in accordance with the requirements of the *Companies Act* 2006.

Opinion on other matters prescribed by the Companies Act 2006

In our opinion, the information given in the Directors' Report for the financial year for which the financial statements are prepared is consistent with the financial statements [and the Directors' Report has been prepared in accordance with applicable legal requirements.

In the light of the knowledge and understanding of the company and its environment obtained in the course of the audit we have identified no material misstatements in the Directors' Report][6].

Matters on which we are required to report by exception

We have nothing to report in respect of the following matters where the *Companies Act* 2006 requires us to report to you if, in our opinion:

- adequate accounting records have not been kept or returns adequate for our audit have not been received from branches not visited by us; or
- the financial statements are not in agreement with the accounting records and returns; or
- certain disclosures of directors' remuneration specified by law are not made; or
- we have not received all the information and explanations we required for our audit; or

- the directors were not entitled to [prepare the financial statements in accordance with the small companies regime] [and] [take advantage of the small companies' exemption in preparing the directors' report] [and] [take advantage of the small companies exemption from the requirement to prepare a strategic report].

[Signature]
John Smith (Senior statutory auditor)
For and on behalf of ABC LLP, Statutory Auditor
Address
Date

[5] The auditor may include a 'Bannerman Statement' as part of the opening section of his report (see **4.22**).
[6] Applies only for periods commencing on or after 1 January 2016 and for earlier periods where the company has chosen to apply the *Companies, Partnerships and Groups (Accounts and Reports) Regulations* 2015.

4.18.2   The small companies regime

Small companies and groups, to which the small companies regime set out in the *Companies Act* 2006 applies, are subject to reduced accounting and reporting requirements in comparison with large and medium sized companies, and other companies not eligible to apply the small companies regime. These requirements and the conditions attached to their applicability are set out in the Act itself and in the *Small Companies and Groups (Accounts and Directors' Report Regulations)* 2008 (SI 2008/409). Where a company prepares its accounts in accordance with the provisions applicable to small companies subject to the small companies regime, the balance sheet must contain a statement to that effect in a prominent position above the signature.

Companies subject to the small companies regime are entitled to take advantage of certain exemptions ('the small companies exemption') relating to the information required to be shown in the directors' report. Where they take advantage of this, the directors' report must include a statement to this effect.

Companies subject to the small companies regime are exempt from the requirement to prepare a strategic report but do not need to make a statement to that effect.

Where the directors of a company:

- have prepared accounts in accordance with the small companies regime; or
- take advantage of the small companies' exemption from the requirement to prepare a strategic report; or
- take advantage of the small companies' exemption in preparing the directors' report

and, in the opinion of the auditor, were not entitled to do so, then the auditor must state that fact in his report.

The principal implications for the auditor's report are:

- where no strategic report is prepared, the 'opinion on other matter prescribed by the *Companies Act*' needs to refer only to the consistency of the directors' report with the financial statements; and
- matters on which the auditor is required to report by exception should include a reference to the directors' entitlement to apply the small companies regime and take advantage of exemptions.

See **Table 8** for example wording.

Changes to the small companies' regime were made by the *Companies, Partnerships and Groups (Accounts and Reports) Regulations* 2015 (SI 2015/980) including the introduction of 'abridged' accounts and changes to filing requirements including the abolition of abbreviated accounts. These changes apply for periods commencing on or after 1 January 2016 but may be applied early by some small companies for periods commencing on or after 1 January 2015. Further details including implications for the auditor's report are given in **Chapter 6**.

4.18.3   Micro-entities

A new category of small company, the 'micro-entity', was created by amendments to the *Companies Act* 2006 introduced by the *Small Companies (Micro-Entities Accounts) Regulations* 2013 (SI 2013/3008).

Subject to certain exceptions and conditions, a micro-entity is an entity falling within the small companies regime which meets two out of three of the following conditions in each of two consecutive years:

- turnover not more than £632,000;
- total assets not more than £316,000;
- number of employees not more than ten.

Micro-entities are subject to considerably simplified requirements relating to the preparation and filing of accounts. These are set out in the *Small Companies and Groups (Accounts and Directors' Report) Regulations* 2008 as amended by the *Small Companies (Micro-Entities' Accounts) Regulations* 2013. Where a company takes advantage of these provisions, the balance sheet must contain, in a prominent position above the signature, a statement to that effect.

Where a company qualifies as a micro-entity and takes advantage of any of the micro-entity provisions, it may not submit abbreviated accounts (see **Chapter 6**).

The accounts of a micro-entity are still required to give a true and fair view but the *Companies Act* 2006 has been amended to clarify that, in their consideration of whether the accounts give a true and fair view, the directors must disregard:

- where the accounts contain only micro-entity minimum accounting items, any provisions of accounting standards that would require disclosure of information additional to those items; and
- in relation to a micro-entity minimum accounting item contained in the accounts, any provisions of accounting standards that would require the accounts to contain further information in relation to that item;

but where the accounts contain an item of information additional to the micro-entity minimum accounting items, they must have regard to any provision of an accounting standard which relates to that item.

Audit implications

Most companies entitled to the micro-entity provisions will also claim exemption from audit. However, in situations where an audit is required, in his consideration of whether the accounts give a true and fair view, the auditor must also disregard or have regard to the provisions of accounting standards as set out above.

In his report, the auditor should refer to the micro-entity provisions when describing the applicable reporting framework and in his opinion on the financial statements. See **Table 9** for example wording for an auditor's report.

TABLE 9: Example unmodified auditor's report for a micro-entity

- *Company applying micro-entity provisions.*
- *Company does not prepare a strategic report.*
- *Company has not prepared a directors' report (periods commencing on or after 1 January 2015).*

Independent auditor's report to the members of XYZ Limited

We have audited the financial statements of [entity name] for the year ended [date] which comprise [state the primary financial statements such as the Profit and Loss Account, the Balance Sheet and the related notes]. The financial reporting framework that has been applied in their preparation is applicable law including the micro-entity provisions of the *Companies Act* 2006 (United Kingdom Generally Accepted Accounting Practice applicable to Micro-Entities).[7]

Respective responsibilities of directors and auditor

As explained more fully in the Directors' Responsibilities Statement [set out [on pages …]], the directors are responsible for the preparation of the financial statements and for being satisfied that they give a true and fair view. Our responsibility is to audit and express an opinion on the financial statements in accordance with applicable law and International Standards on Auditing (UK and Ireland). Those standards required us to comply with the Auditing Practices Board's (APB's) Ethical Standards for Auditors [including 'APB Ethical Standard – Provisions Available for Small Entities (Revised)', in the circumstances set out in note [x] to the financial statements].

Scope of the audit of the financial statements

A description of the scope of an audit of financial statements is [provided on the FRC's website at www.frc.org.uk/auditscopeukprivate]/[set out [on page x] of the Annual Report].

Opinion on financial statements

In our opinion, the financial statements:

- give a true and fair view of the state of the company's affairs as at … and of its profit [loss] for the year then ended;
- have been properly prepared in accordance with United Kingdom Generally Accepted Accounting Practice applicable to Micro-Entities; and
- have been prepared in accordance with the requirements of the *Companies Act* 2006.

Matters on which we are required to report by exception

We have nothing to report in respect of the following matters where the *Companies Act* 2006 requires us to report to you if, in our opinion:

- adequate accounting records have not been kept or returns adequate for our audit have not been received from branches not visited by us; or
- the financial statements are not in agreement with the accounting records and returns; or
- certain disclosures of directors' remuneration specified by law are not made; or
- we have not received all the information and explanations we required for our audit; or
- the directors were not entitled to [prepare the financial statements in accordance with the small companies regime].

[Signature]
John Smith (Senior statutory auditor)
For and on behalf of ABC LLP, Statutory Auditor
Address
Date

7 The auditor may include a 'Bannerman Statement' as part of the opening section of his report (see **4.22**).

4.19 Reporting on the Directors' Remuneration Report

4.19.1 Introduction

With effect from 1 August 2002, the UK Government brought into force Regulations that require quoted companies to prepare a Directors' Remuneration Report for each financial year. This report contains specified information, some of which is subject to audit. On implementation of the *Companies Act* 2006, the regulations were replaced by requirements set out in the *Large and Medium-sized Companies and Groups (Accounts and Reports) Regulations* 2008 (SI 2008/410), Sch. 8.

In 2013, the Government introduced the most comprehensive reforms of the framework for directors' remuneration in over a decade. The reforms aimed to address failures in corporate governance by empowering shareholders to engage effectively with companies on pay. As part of this process, the *Large and Medium-sized Companies and Groups (Accounts and Reports) (Amendment) Regulations* 2013 (SI 2013/1981) resulted in major revisions to the Sch. 8 requirements which apply for financial years ending on or after 1 October 2013.

Under the new regulations, the Directors' Remuneration Report (DRR) is divided into three parts:

- an annual statement from the chairman of the remuneration committee (this will summarise the major decisions on directors' remuneration, details of any substantial changes relating to directors' remuneration made during the year and the context in which the changes occurred);
- the company's policy on directors' remuneration (the 'remuneration policy'). This will be subject to a binding shareholder vote at least every three years; and
- information on how the remuneration policy was implemented in the financial year being reported on (the 'implementation report'). This will be put to an annual advisory shareholder vote.

The *Companies Act* 2006, s. 497 requires the auditor of quoted companies to include within his report on the annual accounts his opinion as to whether the 'auditable part' of the Directors' Remuneration Report has been properly prepared in accordance with the *Companies Act*.

4.19.2 Companies affected by the rules

The regulations apply to 'quoted' companies. A quoted company is defined as a company incorporated under the *Companies Act* 2006:

- whose equity share capital has been included in the official list; or
- is officially listed in an European Economic Area (EEA) state; or
- is admitted to dealing on either the New York Stock Exchange of the exchange known as Nasdaq.

The definition does not include companies traded on the Alternative Investment Market (AIM) or entities with listed debt or non-equity shares only.

4.19.3 The 'auditable part' of the Directors' Remuneration Report

The auditor is required to report on the disclosures in the 'auditable part' of the Directors' Remuneration Report. The 'auditable part' is the part which contains the information required by the *Large and Medium-sized Companies and Groups (Accounts and Reports) Regulations* 2008 (SI 2008/410), Sch. 8, para. 4–17 as amended by the *Large and Medium-sized Companies and Groups (Accounts and Reports) (Amendment) Regulations* 2013 (SI 2013/1981).

4.19.4 Reporting on the Directors' Remuneration Report

The auditor reports on the Directors' Remuneration Report as part of his report on the financial statements. As he is not required to audit all of the information in the Directors' Remuneration Report, he must clearly identify the elements that have been audited. If this cannot be done by cross-reference, the auditor should set out the particulars that have been audited within the auditor's report. It is not satisfactory for the auditor to describe what he has audited as 'the disclosures required by Pt. 3 of Sch. 8 to the *Large and Medium-sized Companies and Groups (Accounts and Reports) Regulations* 2008 (SI 2008/410)'.

An example of the auditor's report in relation to the Directors' Remuneration Report is included in **Table 3**, although it should be noted that the requirement is not restricted to reports on premium listed companies.

4.20   Electronic publication of audit reports

4.20.1   Background

APB Bulletin 2001/1 *The Electronic Publication of Auditors' Reports* was published in response to changes in company law enabling companies to meet their statutory reporting obligations to shareholders by distributing financial statements and certain other reports electronically, or by posting them on a website. This Bulletin was withdrawn in March 2012 as references contained in it were outdated and an updated version of much of the principal guidance is included in the Appendix to ISA (UK and Ireland) 720.

The *Companies Act* 2006 set out additional requirements to facilitate electronic communication with shareholders. It is discussed in **4.20.2** below.

4.20.2   Electronic publication of audit reports

Companies may either send their members copies of the annual financial statements by electronic means or post the annual financial statements on their website and advise their members of this, rather than post hard copies to them.

It is important to note that the auditor's duty of care is not extended solely as a result of his report being published in electronic rather than hard-copy form. In addition, as information published on websites is available in many countries with different legal requirements, it must be clear which legislation governs the preparation and dissemination of financial statements.

Additional work to provide assurance on the integrity of an entity's website is considered a separate engagement and is not covered here.

Directors' responsibilities

The fact that financial statements are reproduced or published electronically does not change the responsibilities of the directors concerning preparation, dissemination and signing of financial statements.

At the request of the Department of Trade and Industry, the Institute of Chartered Secretaries and Administrators (ICSA) has issued guidance (in 2007 and updated periodically since) on information published on corporate websites. If a company wishes to publish its financial statements on its website, the auditor should enquire whether the directors have obtained a copy of this guidance and are following its recommendations relating to the presentation of the annual report and accounts.

The main ICSA recommendations are set out in **Table 10**. The auditor should be aware of these, as non-compliance of any of these by an entity may mean the auditor is unable to agree to the electronic publication of his audit report.

TABLE 10: Summary of ICSA recommendations for electronic publication of the annual report and accounts

- inclusion of a 'watermark' or 'banner' on each page containing statutory or audited information to ensure that the status of that information is clear;
- add a warning message each time a user moves from or to a statutory or audited part of a website;
- not mixing statutory and non-statutory or audited and unaudited information on any one page;
- including a link to the statutory part of the website on the homepage;
- at an early stage ask the auditor for clearance for the publication of audited information on the website;
- ask the auditor to confirm that he agrees with the way information is being presented, including the exact format of his audit report;
- listed companies should have procedures in place to ensure that no price sensitive information is published prior to notification of the relevant authorities; and
- ensure they comply with the *Companies Act* 2006, s. 434, which states that statutory accounts must be published with the relevant auditor's report and that non-statutory accounts must be accompanied by a statement that they are not statutory accounts.

The directors' responsibility statement should include reference to the fact that legislation in the United Kingdom governing the preparation and dissemination of financial statements may differ from legislation in other jurisdictions.

Hard-copy reports cannot be amended unless a revised printed version is issued to shareholders. However, it is easy for all or part of an electronic report to be amended without it being apparent that a revision has occurred. Inaccurate information may be placed on a website by a company employee (either accidentally or maliciously) or by a person outside the organisation who is able to gain access to the website.

Directors should therefore establish a regular procedure for checking that statutory or audited information has not been tampered with. The auditor will have no further responsibility for either the controls in place or the integrity of the information on a website once it is issued in electronic form. The FRC recommends that directors state clearly in their statement of responsibilities that the maintenance and integrity of the website is their responsibility alone. If the directors' statement does not make this clear such as in **Table 5** above, or if the auditor otherwise considers it appropriate, he should add a note to the bottom of his audit report. Example wording is given in **Table 11** below.

Where the auditor is aware that the financial statements no longer agree to the set the directors have approved, he should inform the directors and request that they be amended immediately. If the necessary amendments are not made, the auditor should obtain legal advice and consider resignation.

Auditor's considerations

When a company publishes its annual report on a website or distributes it electronically, the auditor should:

- review the process used to derive the electronically published financial statements from the manually signed version;
- check the electronic version is identical in content to the manual accounts; and
- check that conversion to the electronic version has not distorted the overall presentation (e.g. by use of different fonts or colour to highlight certain information).

In addition, for future reference, it is recommended the auditor should retain a printed copy or disk of the electronic version that he has reviewed.

The auditor is not expected to perform the above procedures on any prior period information. Prior period information should be clearly identified as such, or the auditor should request management to delete it.

Auditor's report

In considering whether the wording of the auditor's report is suitable for electronic publication, issues to be considered include:

- identifying the financial statements that have been audited and the information that has only been reviewed or read by the auditor; and
- limiting the auditor's association with any other information distributed with the annual report.

In addition, it is important that the auditor's report indicates clearly the nationality of the accounting standards used in the preparation of the financial statements and the nationality of the auditing standards applied.

In addition, the auditor should ensure that his report gives sufficient details of his address to enable readers to understand in which country the auditor is located.

Where the directors' responsibility statement does not include the statement relating to different legislation requirements in different jurisdictions referred to above, the auditor should include a statement at the foot of his report. Example wording is given in **Table 11** below.

TABLE 11: Example wording for the Directors Responsibility Statement

1. The maintenance and integrity of the [name of entity] website is the responsibility of the directors; the work carried out by the auditor does not involve consideration of these matters and, accordingly, the auditor accepts no responsibility for the changes that may have occurred to the financial statements since they were initially presented on the website.
2. Legislation in the United Kingdom governing the preparation and dissemination of financial statements may differ from legislation in other jurisdictions.

Hard-copy annual reports will have page numbers by which the auditor can identify the financial statements that have been audited in his report. Where Hypertext Mark-up Language (HTML) has been used to publish annual reports on a website, page numbers are often no longer included and thus identification of audited information is difficult. Where a Portable Document Format (PDF) file is used, page numbers generally continue to be effective.

Therefore, where page numbers are no longer an effective way of identifying audited information, the FRC recommends that the auditor's report describes, by name, the primary statements that comprise the financial statements. The same technique can be used to identify information that has been reviewed, or read, by the auditor.

The problem of identifying other information in the annual report, which the auditor has neither audited, reviewed nor read, is exacerbated by the use of hyperlinks that allow the user to move easily from one area of the website to another. To reduce misunderstandings, the auditor should request that readers are warned when they move from an audited to an unaudited part of the website. An additional safeguard is for the auditor to request that all audited information, such as disclosures relating to directors' emoluments, are included within the financial statements. If the scope of the audit report is not clear because of the use of hyperlinks, the report itself should list in detail all the areas within its scope.

Where the auditor is not satisfied with the proposed presentation of the audited financial statements and his report, he should request that the presentation is amended. If the presentation is not amended, the auditor should refuse to give his consent for the electronic release of his audit report. If the report is used without his consent, the auditor should seek legal advice and consider resigning from the engagement.

The electronic report should have the same date as the manually signed version. Amending the manual report for electronic publication (such as the substitution of the names of primary statements for page numbers) does not constitute a new audit opinion. The auditor is not required to perform any further subsequent events work, as the date of the opinion has not changed.

Engagement letters

The responsibilities of directors and the auditor in relation to the electronic publication of financial statements should be clarified in the engagement letter. The engagement letter should also state that directors must seek the consent of their auditor for the electronic publication of the audit report. This will ensure that the auditor has a right to request amendments to the wording or presentation of an electronic audit report.

The engagement letter should note that:

- the auditor recognises that the company may wish to publish its financial statements and the auditor's report on its website or distribute them electronically;
- the presentation of the financial information and auditor's report is the responsibility of the directors;
- the directors should advise the auditor in advance of the intended electronic publication;
- the auditor reserves the right to withhold consent to the electronic publication of his report if the audited financial statements or the audit report itself are presented in an inappropriate way;
- the directors are responsible for controls over the maintenance and security of the website;
- examination of the controls over maintenance and integrity are outside the scope of the audit; and
- where applicable, directors are responsible for establishing and controlling the process for electronically distributing the Annual Report to shareholders and the Registrar of Companies.

4.21 [section left blank]

4.22 The Bannerman Case

4.22.1 Introduction

As a result of the legal judgment in the Scottish Court of Session in the *Bannerman* case, auditors have considered whether they should include additional wording in their audit reports to protect against exposure to third party claims. The ICAEW issued Technical Release Audit 1/03 in January 2003, and this guidance contains a suitable wording for inclusion in audit reports. They have discussed the format and inclusion of such wording with Leading Counsel.

In the *Bannerman* case, the judge held that, although there was no direct contact between Bannerman (the auditor) and the third party, knowledge gained by Bannerman through the course of his normal audit work was sufficient, in the absence of any disclaimer, to create a duty of care towards the third party. The absence of a disclaimer was an important circumstance supporting the finding of a duty of care by the judge.

4.22.2   Auditor's responsibilities

The Technical Release is clear that the responsibilities of the auditor are not changed as a result either of the *Bannerman* case or the release of 1/03. It states that 'the best risk management policy is for firms to take the steps that are necessary to carry out quality audits'.

4.22.3   Recommended wording

It is clear that the auditor automatically assumes responsibility for the audit report to the shareholders as a body. The *Bannerman* case indicates that the absence of a disclaimer may, depending on the facts of the case, make the auditor liable to third parties.

The ICAEW therefore suggests the following wording is included in the first or second paragraph of all audit reports for UK companies.

> 'This report is made solely to the company's members, as a body, in accordance with Chapter 3 of Part 16 of the *Companies Act* 2006. Our audit work has been undertaken so that we might state to the company's members those matters we are required to state to them in an auditor's report and for no other purpose. To the fullest extent permitted by law, we do not accept or assume responsibility to anyone other than the company and the company's members as a body, for our audit work, for this report, or for the opinions we have formed.'

The wording, or a variation of it, may also be suitable for inclusion in other reports issued by auditors.

It is important to note that the inclusion of this paragraph in audit reports does not mean that the auditor can never agree to take on responsibilities to third parties, or that they may inadvertently assume a duty of care through subsequent comments or actions inconsistent with the wording of this paragraph. Where the auditor is aware of circumstances which may give rise to a duty of care, he should disclaim this responsibility by writing a letter to the third party in line with guidance in Technical Release Audit 4/00 (see **Chapter 40**).

4.22.4   Engagement letters

The Technical Release also contains suggested wording for inclusion in an engagement letter, to inform clients about the clarification paragraph in the audit report. This is not mandatory, and is set out in **Chapter 14**.

4.22.5   Further developments

In February 2015, the High Court found in favour of Grant Thornton (GT) in relation to a negligence claim brought against it by Barclays Bank. The dispute arose after Barclays relied on two non-statutory audits carried out for the Von Essen Hotels Group (VEH) in 2006 and 2007 in continuing to fund VEH under a loan facility. The bank alleged GT had been negligent in producing the reports because it failed to uncover fraudulent overstatements of VEH's financial position, causing Barclays financial loss when VEH became insolvent and could not repay the loan.

Each of the reports produced by GT included a *Bannerman* style disclaimer which stated that the report was made solely to VEH's director and that the auditor did not accept responsibility to anyone other than VEH and its director for its audit work. Barclays argued that this disclaimer was 'unreasonable'. The judge, however, considered the disclaimer was 'clear on its face', 'could not have been misunderstood' and 'would have been read and understood by anyone at Barclays who had read the two page reports'. He noted that 'Grant Thornton made it clear that it was not prepared to assume responsibility to Barclays in respect of these reports. There was nothing unreasonable in that stance, as between two sophisticated commercial parties, where the approach of auditors limiting their responsibilities is well known.'.

This is the first case in which the lawfulness of a *Bannerman* clause in an auditor's report had been considered. Although it related to non-statutory rather than statutory financial statements, it illustrates the potential value of a *Bannerman* clause, clearly identifying the addressee of the report and limiting or excluding liability to others by way of a prominent and clearly expressed disclaimer.

5 MODIFIED AUDITOR'S REPORTS

5.1 Introduction

In **Chapter 4**, the content and format of unmodified auditor's reports was considered. Where the auditor is unable to issue an unmodified report, his report may follow a number of formats, which are discussed below.

Standards relating to modified auditor's reports are provided by ISAs (UK and Ireland) 705 *Modifications to the opinion in the independent auditor's report* and 706 *Emphasis of matter paragraphs and other matter paragraphs in the independent auditor's report*. Example wording is also contained in Bulletin 2010/2 (Revised) *Compendium of illustrative auditor's reports on United Kingdom private sector financial statements for periods ended on or after 15 December 2010.* Although the example reports in this Bulletin have not been updated for legislative and other changes to reporting requirements, the illustrative wording of the basis of opinion and opinion paragraphs remains relevant and is included in this book. Some of these changes are considered in Bulletin 4: *Recent developments in Company Law, The Listing Rules and Auditing Standards that affect United Kingdom Auditor's Reports* issued by the FRC and last updated in June 2015 although this has not been updated for the April 2016 ISAs.

The current versions of ISAs (UK and Ireland) 705 and 706 are effective for the audit of financial statements for periods commencing on or after 1 October 2012. The most recent version of ISA (UK and Ireland) 700 (Revised) is effective for periods commencing on or after 1 October 2014.

In April 2016, the FRC issued a final draft of a number of revised ISAs which, subject to legislation, will apply to audits of financial statements for periods commencing on or after 17 June 2016. The revised standards incorporate amendments relating to the EU Audit Directive and Audit Regulation which are required to be implemented by all EU countries and align the auditor reporting standards in the UK and Ireland more closely with recently revised standards issued by the IAASB.

The revisions will lead to:

- a number of wording and format changes in the audit report;
- setting the 'opinion' paragraph as the first paragraph in the report, followed directly by the 'basis for opinion' paragraph;
- additional requirements for public interest entities; and
- further details and guidance for other sections.

The revisions will not lead to any significant change in the basic form of modified audit opinions (as set out in **5.4**) but will result in significant changes to the standards themselves and to the presentation of information in the auditor's report.

The revised ISAs will be applicable for periods commencing on or after 17 June 2016. This chapter does not fully reflect the changes which will be introduced by ISA (UK and Ireland) 705 and 706 (Revised June 2016) as the precise impact on UK audit reports has not yet been interpreted. Although early adoption is permitted, the revised ISAs are not applicable until periods beginning 17 June 2016, i.e. those ending in mid-2017. As such, the previous versions of ISAs will still be applicable for years ending prior to mid-2017 and the next version of this book will incorporate the revisions in more detail.

5.2 Modifications

An auditor's report may be considered to be modified in the following situations:

- matters that affect the auditor's opinion on the financial statements (see **5.4**):

  - disclaimer of opinion;
  - adverse opinion;
  - qualified opinion;

- matters that affect the auditor's opinion on other matters (such as consistency of the strategic report and directors' report);
- matters that do not affect the auditor's opinions:

  - emphasis of matter;
  - other matter; and

- matters that the auditor is required to report by exception.

Table 1 contains a navigation aid to help the auditor select the correct type of report. Note, however, that this focuses on the auditor's opinion on the financial statements and does not include consideration of modifications arising for other reasons as set out above. In addition, it does not deal with modifications to the auditor's opinion on the financial statements arising from going concern issues (see **Chapter 11**).

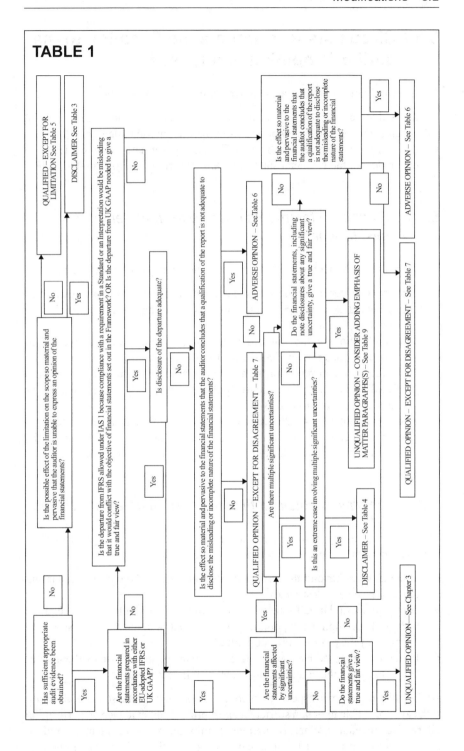

TABLE 1

5.3 Circumstances when a modification to the auditor's opinion is required

Modified opinions on financial statements are issued where either:

- the auditor concludes that, based on the evidence obtained, the financial statements as a whole are not free from material misstatement; or
- the auditor is unable to obtain sufficient appropriate audit evidence to conclude that the financial statements are free from material misstatement.

5.3.1 Financial statements not free from material misstatement

A material misstatement of the financial statements may arise in relation to:

(a) the appropriateness of the selected accounting policies (for example, when the selected accounting policies are not consistent with the applicable financial reporting framework);

(b) the application of the selected accounting policies (for example, when management has not applied the selected accounting policies consistently with the financial reporting framework, including when management has not applied the selected accounting policies consistently between periods or to similar transactions and events); or

(c) the appropriateness or adequacy of disclosures in the financial statements (for example, when the financial statements do not include all of the disclosures required by the applicable financial reporting framework).

5.3.2 Inability to obtain sufficient appropriate audit evidence

The auditor's inability to obtain sufficient appropriate audit evidence (also called a limitation on the scope of the audit) may arise due to:

- circumstances beyond the control of the entity (e.g. the entity's accounting records have been destroyed);
- circumstances relating to the nature or timing of the auditor's work (e.g. the timing of the auditor's appointment is such that he is unable to observe the counting of the physical inventories); or
- limitations imposed by management (e.g. management prevents the auditor from observing the counting of the physical inventories).

An inability to perform a specific procedure does not limit the scope of the audit if the auditor is able to obtain sufficient appropriate audit evidence by performing alternative procedures. Where limitations are imposed by management, the auditor also needs to consider further implications, such as the auditor's assessment of fraud risks and consideration of engagement continuance.

5.3.3   Imposed limitation of scope

ISA (UK and Ireland) 705 refers to cases where directors or management restrict access to information such that an effective audit cannot be carried out. This may occur where there is a statutory requirement for an audit but the owners are indifferent to the requirement, for example:

- an owner-managed business; or
- an overseas controlled entity which requires an on-shore report.

In these cases, the owners or directors may be prepared to accept a disclaimed opinion for a nominal fee so long as they have a set of accounts that may be filed at Companies House.

If the auditor is aware, before accepting an audit engagement that the directors of the entity, or those who appoint its auditor, will impose a limitation on the scope of his work, which he considers is likely to result in the need to issue a disclaimer of opinion on the financial statements, ISA (UK and Ireland) 210 (Revised June 2016) *Agreeing the terms of audit engagements* requires that he should not accept that engagement.

Where the auditor becomes aware after accepting an engagement of such a restriction, ISA (UK and Ireland) 705 requires that he should consider whether to resign if the limitation is not removed. Alternatively, he may decide to continue the engagement but disclaim an opinion and then not seek reappointment. Factors he would take into account in deciding on the most appropriate course of action are the extent to which any work is complete and what is in the best public interest.

Where the auditor does withdraw from the engagement as a result of the imposition of such a limitation, this may be a matter for the auditor to consider including in any statement of circumstances made in connection with his ceasing to hold office as auditor, or in response to professional enquiries made by the possible successor auditor.

In addition, before withdrawing, the auditor needs to communicate to those charged with governance any matters regarding misstatements identified during the audit that would have given rise to a modification of the opinion (see para **5.10**). **Chapter 38** gives guidance on statements to be made on cessation as auditor.

5.4   Types of modified opinion

There are three possible outcomes, as illustrated in **Table 2**:

- *'disclaimer' of opinion*, where the auditor is unable to obtain sufficient audit evidence on which to base an opinion on the financial statements and the possible effects of undetected misstatements could be both material and pervasive; or (rarely) where it is not possible to form an opinion on the financial statements due to the potential interaction of multiple uncertainties and their possible cumulative effect on the financial statements;

- *'adverse' opinion*, where the auditor concludes that the effects of misstatements, either individually or in aggregate, are both material and pervasive to the financial statements; and
- *qualified opinion*, where the auditor concludes that the effects of the misstatements, individually or in aggregate, are material but not pervasive to the financial statements; or where the auditor is unable to obtain sufficient appropriate audit evidence on which to base his opinion, but he concludes that the possible effects of undetected misstatements, if any, could be material but not pervasive.

The effects of misstatements are considered to be pervasive when they are not limited to specific elements or items in the financial statements or, if they are so limited, the affected items represent a substantial proportion of the financial statements. In addition, misstatements in respect of disclosures will be pervasive if they are considered to be fundamental to a user's understanding of the financial statements.

TABLE 2: Types of modified opinion

Effect	*Inability to obtain sufficient appropriate audit evidence*	*Financial statements are materially misstated*
Material but not pervasive	Qualified opinion	
Material and pervasive	Disclaimer	Adverse

5.4.1 Adverse opinions or disclaimers of opinion

Where the auditor has expressed an adverse opinion or disclaimed an opinion on the financial statements as a whole, the auditor cannot issue an unmodified opinion on a part of the financial statements under the same financial reporting framework. To include an unmodified opinion in the same report in these circumstances would contradict the auditor's adverse opinion or disclaimer of opinion on the financial statements as a whole.

This does not, however, prevent the auditor from issuing a disclaimer of an opinion regarding the results of operations and cash flows, and an unmodified opinion on the balance sheet position. This is not a contradiction since the auditor has not expressed a disclaimer of opinion on the financial statements as a whole.

5.5 Form and content of the audit report when opinion is modified

5.5.1 Basis for modification paragraph

Where the auditor modifies his opinion, the auditor's report should include a paragraph, immediately before the opinion paragraph, describing the matter giving rise to the modification. This paragraph should be headed *Basis for Qualified Opinion/Adverse Opinion/Disclaimer of Opinion on Financial Statements*, as appropriate. On implementation of ISA (UK and Ireland) 706 (Revised June 2016), the *Basis for Opinion* paragraph will follow immediately after the opinion paragraph rather than precede it.

If there is a material misstatement of the financial statements that relates to specific amounts in the financial statements (including quantitative disclosures), the auditor includes in the basis for modification paragraph a description and quantification of the financial effects of the misstatement, unless impracticable. For example, the auditor may be able to quantify the effects on income tax, income before taxes, net income and equity if inventory is overstated.

If it is not practicable to quantify the financial effects, he says so in this paragraph.

If there is a material misstatement that relates to narrative disclosures, he includes in the basis for modification paragraph an explanation of how the disclosures are misstated.

If there is a material misstatement of the financial statements that relates to the non-disclosure of information required to be disclosed, the auditor shall:

(a)   discuss the non-disclosure with those charged with governance (see para **5.10**);
(b)   describe in the basis for modification paragraph the nature of the omitted information; and
(c)   unless prohibited by law or regulation, include the omitted disclosures, provided it is practicable to do so and the auditor has obtained sufficient appropriate audit evidence about the omitted information.

If the modification results from an inability to obtain sufficient appropriate audit evidence, the auditor includes in the basis for modification paragraph the reasons for that inability.

Even if the auditor has expressed an adverse opinion or disclaimed an opinion on the financial statements, he still describes in the basis for modification paragraph the reasons for any other matters of which the auditor is aware that would have required a modification to the opinion, and the effects thereof.

5.5.2   Opinion paragraph

When the auditor modifies the audit opinion, the auditor shall use the heading *Qualified Opinion on Financial Statements, Adverse Opinion on Financial Statements,* or *Disclaimer of Opinion on Financial Statements*, as appropriate, for the opinion paragraph.

5.5.3   Qualified opinion

When the auditor expresses a qualified opinion due to a material misstatement in the financial statements, he states that, in his opinion, except for the effects of the matter(s) described in the Basis for Qualified Opinion on Financial Statements paragraph:

(a)   the financial statements present fairly, in all material respects (or give a true and fair view of) when reporting in accordance with a fair presentation framework; or

(b)   the financial statements have been prepared, in all material respects, in accordance with the applicable financial reporting framework when reporting in accordance with a compliance framework.

When the modification arises from an inability to obtain sufficient appropriate audit evidence, the auditor uses the corresponding phrase 'except for the possible effects of the matter(s) ...' for the modified opinion.

5.5.4   Adverse opinion

When the auditor expresses an adverse opinion, he states that, in the auditor's opinion, because of the significance of the matter(s) described in the Basis for Adverse Opinion on Financial Statements paragraph:

(a)   the financial statements do not present fairly (or give a true and fair view of) when reporting in accordance with a fair presentation framework; or

(b)   the financial statements have not been prepared, in all material respects, in accordance with the applicable financial reporting framework when reporting in accordance with a compliance framework.

5.5.5   Disclaimer of opinion

When the auditor disclaims an opinion due to an inability to obtain sufficient appropriate audit evidence, he is required to state that:

(a)   because of the significance of the matter(s) described in the Basis for Disclaimer of Opinion on Financial Statements paragraph, the auditor has not been able to obtain sufficient appropriate audit evidence to provide a basis for an audit opinion on the financial statements; and accordingly

(b)   he does not express an opinion on the accompanying financial statements.

5.5.6   Description of auditor's responsibilities when the auditor disclaims an opinion

When the auditor disclaims an opinion due to an inability to obtain sufficient appropriate audit evidence, he amends the introductory paragraph of his report to state that he was engaged to audit the financial statements, rather than that he has audited the financial statements.

5.6   Examples

In the example in **Table 3**, the evidence available to the auditor was limited because he was not able to observe all physical stock and confirm trade debtors due to limitations placed on the scope of his work by the directors of the company. The limitation on the scope of the audit is considered by the auditor to be both material and pervasive such that he is unable to form an opinion on the financial statements and issues a report disclaiming an opinion on the financial statements.

Table 4 gives an example of a disclaimer where the auditor has concluded it is not possible to form an opinion on the financial statements due to the potential interaction of multiple uncertainties and their possible cumulative effect on the financial statements.

The example in **Table 5** is qualified 'except for' any adjustments that might have been found to be necessary, had it been possible to obtain sufficient evidence concerning stock. The limitation on scope was determined by the auditor to be material but not pervasive to the financial statements.

In assessing whether there is a limitation on the scope of the audit, the auditor must have regard to the evidence that he would reasonably expect to be available to support a particular figure or disclosure. In all cases where there is a lack of evidence that may lead to a limitation of scope, the auditor should take all possible steps to obtain alternative evidence to support an unqualified opinion.

TABLE 3[1]: Extract from report with disclaimer of opinion: Auditor unable to attend stocktaking and confirm trade debtors

Basis for disclaimer of opinion on financial statements

The audit evidence available to us was limited because we were unable to observe the counting of physical stock having a carrying amount of £X and send confirmation letters to trade debtors having a carrying amount of £Y due to limitations placed on the scope of our work by the directors of the company. As a result of this, we have been unable to obtain sufficient appropriate audit evidence concerning both stock and trade debtors.

Disclaimer of opinion on financial statements

Because of the significance of the matter described in the Basis for Disclaimer of Opinion on Financial Statements paragraph, we have not been able to obtain sufficient appropriate audit evidence to provide a basis for an audit opinion. Accordingly, we do not express an opinion on the financial statements.

Opinion on other matter prescribed by the Companies Act 2006

Notwithstanding our disclaimer of an opinion on the financial statements, in our opinion, the information given in the [Strategic Report and the] Directors' Report for the financial year for which the financial statements are prepared is consistent with the financial statements.

Matters on which we are required to report by exception

Arising from the limitation of our work referred to above:

- we have not obtained all the information and explanations that we considered necessary for the purpose of our audit; and
- we were unable to determine whether adequate accounting records had been kept.

We have nothing to report in respect of the following matters where the *Companies Act* 2006 requires us to report to you if, in our opinion:

- returns adequate for our audit have not been received from branches not visited by us; or
- the financial statements are not in agreement with the accounting records and returns; or
- certain disclosures of directors' remuneration specified by law are not made.

[1] This example is based on existing ISAs and has not been updated to reflect changes to audit reporting ISAs which will take effect for periods commencing 17 June 2016.

TABLE 4[2]: Extract from report with disclaimer of opinion: Multiple uncertainties

Basis for disclaimer of opinion on financial statements

In seeking to form an opinion on the financial statements, we considered the implications of the significant uncertainties disclosed in the financial statements concerning the following matters:

- [significant uncertainty 1];
- [significant uncertainty 2];
- [significant uncertainty 3].

There is potential for the uncertainties to interact with one another such that we have been unable to obtain sufficient appropriate audit evidence regarding the possible effect of the uncertainties taken together.

Disclaimer of opinion on financial statements

Because of the significance of the possible impact of the uncertainties, described in the Basis for Disclaimer of Opinion on Financial Statements paragraph, to the financial statements, we have not been able to obtain sufficient appropriate audit evidence to provide a basis for an audit opinion. Accordingly, we do not express an opinion on the financial statements.

Opinion on other matter prescribed by the Companies Act 2006

Notwithstanding our disclaimer of an opinion on the financial statements, in our opinion, the information given in the [Strategic Report and the] Directors' Report for the financial year for which the financial statements are prepared is consistent with the financial statements.

Matters on which we are required to report by exception

We have nothing to report in respect of the following matters where the *Companies Act 2006* requires us to report to you if, in our opinion:

- adequate accounting records have not been kept or returns adequate for our audit have not been received from branches not visited by us; or
- the financial statements are not in agreement with the accounting records and returns; or
- certain disclosures of directors' remuneration specified by law are not made; or
- we have not received all the information and explanations we required for our audit.

[2] This example is based on existing ISAs and has not been updated to reflect changes to audit reporting ISAs which will take effect for periods commencing 17 June 2016.

TABLE 5[3]: Extract from report with qualified opinion: Limitation on scope – Auditor not appointed at the time of the stocktaking

Basis for qualified opinion on financial statements

With respect to stock having a carrying amount of £X the audit evidence available to us was limited because we did not observe the counting of the physical stock as at 31 December 20X1, since that date was prior to our appointment as auditor of the company. Owing to the nature of the company's records, we were unable to obtain sufficient appropriate audit evidence regarding the stock quantities by using other audit procedures.

Qualified opinion on financial statements

In our opinion, except for the possible effects of the matters described in the Basis for Qualified Opinion paragraph, the financial statements:

● give a true and fair view of the state of the company's affairs as at [date] and of its profit [loss] for the year then ended;
● have been properly prepared in accordance with United Kingdom Generally Accepted Accounting Practice; and
● have been prepared in accordance with the requirements of the *Companies Act* 2006.

Opinion on other matter prescribed by the Companies Act 2006

In our opinion, the information given in the [Strategic Report and the] Directors' Report for the financial year for which the financial statements are prepared is consistent with the financial statements.

Matters on which we are required to report by exception

In respect solely of the limitation on our work relating to stock, described above:

● we have not obtained all the information and explanations that we considered necessary for the purpose of our audit; and
● we were unable to determine whether adequate accounting records had been kept.

We have nothing to report in respect of the following matters where the *Companies* Act 2006 requires us to report to you if, in our opinion:

● returns adequate for our audit have not been received from branches not visited by us; or
● the financial statements are not in agreement with the accounting records and returns; or
● certain disclosures of directors' remuneration specified by law are not made.

[3] This example is based on existing ISAs and has not been updated to reflect changes to audit reporting ISAs which will take effect for periods commencing 17 June 2016.

5.6.1 Material misstatement

ISA (UK and Ireland) 705 requires that where the auditor concludes that there is a material misstatement either with the accounting treatment or the disclosure of a matter in the financial statements and the effect is material to the financial statements, he should:

- describe the substantive factors giving rise to the material misstatement, the implications for, and, where practicable, a quantification of the effect on, the financial statements; and either
- issue an adverse opinion where the possible effect is so material and pervasive that the financial statements are seriously misleading; or
- issue a qualified opinion indicating that it is expressed except for the effects of the matter giving rise to the material misstatement.

The examples given in Bulletin 2010/2 include an adverse (**Table 6**) and a qualified 'except for' opinion (**Table 7**).

As illustrated in **Table 6**, reference may be made to further information and explanations in the financial statements where this would assist the user's understanding of the issue.

TABLE 6[4]: Extract from report with adverse opinion: No provision made for losses expected to arise on long-term contracts

Basis for adverse opinion on financial statements

As more fully explained in note X to the financial statements, no provision has been made for losses expected to arise on certain long-term contracts currently in progress, as the directors consider that such losses should be off-set against amounts recoverable on other long-term contracts. In our opinion, provision should be made for foreseeable losses on individual contracts as required by [*specify accounting standard*]. If losses had been so recognised the effect would have been to reduce the carrying amount of contract work in progress by £X, the deferred tax liability by £Y and the profit for the year and retained earnings at 31 December 20X1 by £Z.

Adverse opinion on financial statements

In our opinion, because of the significance of the matter described in the Basis for Adverse Opinion paragraph, the financial statements:

- do not give a true and fair view of the state of the company's affairs as at 31 December 20 ... and of its profit for the year then ended; and
- have not been properly prepared in accordance with United Kingdom Generally Accepted Accounting Practice.

In all other respects, in our opinion the financial statements have been prepared in accordance with the requirements of the *Companies Act* 2006.

Opinion on other matter prescribed by the Companies Act 2006

Notwithstanding our adverse opinion on the financial statements, in our opinion, the information given in the [Strategic Report and the] Directors' Report for the financial year for which the financial statements are prepared is consistent with the financial statements.

Matters on which we are required to report by exception

We have nothing to report in respect of the following matters where the *Companies Act* 2006 requires us to report to you if, in our opinion:

- adequate accounting records have not been kept or returns adequate for our audit have not been received from branches not visited by us; or
- the financial statements are not in agreement with the accounting records and returns; or
- certain disclosures of directors' remuneration specified by law are not made; or
- we have not received all the information and explanations we required for our audit.

[4] This example is based on existing ISAs and has not been updated to reflect changes to audit reporting ISAs which will take effect for periods commencing 17 June 2016.

TABLE 7[5]: Extract from report with qualified opinion: Disagreement

Basis for qualified opinion on financial statements

Included in the debtors shown on the balance sheet is an amount of £ … due from a company which has ceased trading. XYZ plc has no security for this debt. In our opinion, the company is unlikely to receive any payment and full provision of £ … should have been made. Accordingly, debtors should be reduced by £Y, the deferred tax liability should be reduced by £X and profit for the year and retained earnings should be reduced by £Z.

Qualified opinion on financial statements

In our opinion, except for the effects of the matter described in the Basis for Qualified Opinion paragraph, the financial statements:

- give a true and fair view of the state of the company's affairs as at 31 December 20 … and of its profit for the year then ended;
- have been properly prepared in accordance with United Kingdom Generally Accepted Accounting Practice; and
- have been prepared in accordance with the requirements of the *Companies Act* 2006.

- *Opinion on other matter prescribed by the Companies Act 2006*

In our opinion, the information given in the [Strategic Report and the] Directors' Report for the financial year for which the financial statements are prepared is consistent with the financial statements.

Matters on which we are required to report by exception

We have nothing to report in respect of the following matters where the *Companies Act* 2006 requires us to report to you if, in our opinion:

- adequate accounting records have not been kept or returns adequate for our audit have not been received from branches not visited by us; or
- the financial statements are not in agreement with the accounting records and returns; or
- certain disclosures of directors' remuneration specified by law are not made; or
- we have not received all the information and explanations we required for our audit.

[5] This example is based on existing ISAs and has not been updated to reflect changes to audit reporting ISAs which will take effect for periods commencing 17 June 2016.

5.6.2   Multiple uncertainties

The auditor should issue a disclaimer of opinion in the case of multiple uncertainties where the cumulative nature and possible effects of the uncertainties are such that it is not possible to form an opinion on the financial statements as a whole despite having obtained sufficient audit evidence about each individual uncertainty. Such situations are expected to be extremely rare.

5.6.3   Modifications to opinions on other matters

Where the auditor is unable to give an unqualified opinion regarding the consistency of the information given in the Strategic Report (where applicable) or the Directors' Report, he should explain the reason for this and modify his opinion in the auditor's report accordingly. An example where the information contained in the strategic report is inconsistent with the financial statements is given in **Table 8**.

In the case of a quoted company, where the auditor is unable to provide an opinion as to whether the part of the Directors' Remuneration Report to be audited has been properly prepared in accordance with the *Companies Act* 2006, he should explain the reason for this and modify his opinion in the auditor's report accordingly. The auditor must also include in his report, so far as he is reasonably able to do so, a statement giving the required particulars.

TABLE 8[6]: Extract from report with qualified opinion on consistency of strategic report with financial statements

Qualified opinion on other matter prescribed by the Companies Act 2006

In our opinion, the information given in the seventh paragraph of the Strategic Report is not consistent with the financial statements. That paragraph states without amplification that 'the company's trading for the period resulted in a 10% increase in profit over the previous period's profit'. The profit and loss account, however, shows that the company's profit for the period includes a profit of £Z which did not arise from trading but arose from the disposal of assets of a discontinued operation. Without this profit on the disposal of assets, the company would have reported a profit for the year of £Y, representing a reduction in profit of 25% over the previous period's profit on a like for like basis. Except for this matter, in our opinion, the information given in the Strategic Report and the Directors' Report is consistent with the financial statements.

[6] This example is based on existing ISAs and has not been updated to reflect changes to audit reporting ISAs which will take effect for periods commencing 17 June 2016.

5.7 Emphasis of Matter

In some circumstances, the auditor may consider it necessary to draw the user's attention to a matter that is already presented or disclosed in the financial statements but which is, in the auditor's judgment, of such importance that it is fundamental to the user's understanding of the financial statements. The auditor does this by adding an Emphasis of Matter paragraph to his audit report to highlight the matter. Typical examples are:

- an uncertainty relating to the future outcome of major litigation;
- a subsequent event occurring between the date of the financial statements and the date of the auditor's report;
- early (permitted) application of a new accounting standard that has a pervasive effect on the financial statements in advance of its effective date; and
- a major catastrophe that has had a significant effect on the entity's financial position.

An Emphasis of Matter paragraph can only be used to refer to information already presented or disclosed in the financial statements.

In addition, an Emphasis of Matter paragraph should not be used where the matter has not been determined as a key audit matter for communication in the audit report (see **Chapter 4**). (In other words, where a matter is a key matter and key matters are reported separately in the audit report then the auditor cannot use Emphasis of Matter as an alternative presentation.) However, the application material notes that in the UK and Ireland, law or regulation may require an

Emphasis of Matter paragraph relating to something that is also disclosed as a key matter – in which case, the auditor is not precluded from doing so.

Where the auditor decides to include an Emphasis of Matter paragraph in his report, he:

- uses an appropriate heading, such as *Emphasis of Matter*;
- includes a clear reference to the matter being emphasised and to where the relevant disclosures can be found in the financial statements; and
- indicates that the auditor's opinion is not modified in respect of the matter.

Table 9 gives an example of an Emphasis of Matter paragraph which describes the matter, the effect on the financial statements and, where practicable, quantifies it. Where quantification is not possible, this should be stated. A reference to the notes to the financial statements alone is not sufficient. The explanation in the audit report must be such that a reader can appreciate the principal points at issue and their implications.

When applied in conjunction with the new ISA (UK and Ireland) 700, ISA (UK and Ireland) 706 (Revised June 2016) no longer requires an Emphasis of Matter paragraph where there is a material uncertainty related to going concern that is adequately described in the financial statements. Instead this will be dealt with in the auditor's report by inclusion of a separate section in the report headed 'Material Uncertainty in Relation to Going Concern' (see paragraph **11.12.4**).

Where an entity is required, or elects, to prepare its financial statements on a basis other than that of going concern, the auditor may consider it appropriate or necessary to include an Emphasis of Matter paragraph in his report to draw the user's attention to the basis in which the financial statements have been prepared and the reasons for its use.

An Emphasis of Matter paragraph is not a substitute for expressing a qualified or adverse opinion, or for disclaiming an opinion, where the circumstances of the engagement require it.

TABLE 9: Example Emphasis of Matter paragraph: Uncertain outcome of a lawsuit

Emphasis of Matter – uncertain outcome of a lawsuit

In forming our opinion on the financial statements, which is not modified, we have considered the adequacy of the disclosures made in the financial statements concerning the possible outcome of litigation against B Limited, a subsidiary of the company, for an alleged breach of environmental regulations. The future settlement of this litigation could result in additional liabilities and the closure of B Limited's business, whose net assets included in the consolidated balance sheet total £ ... and whose profit before tax for the year was £ ... Details of the circumstances relating to this significant uncertainty are described in note ...

5.8 Other Matter paragraphs

Where the auditor considers that a matter other than those presented or disclosed in the financial statements is relevant to the user's understanding of the audit, and that it is necessary to communicate it then ISA (UK and Ireland) 706 requires that this be done by the inclusion of a paragraph in the auditor's report setting out details of the matter. The information should be included in a separate section under the heading *Other Matter* or another appropriate heading.

An Other Matter paragraph may not be used where ISA (UK and Ireland) 701 applies and the auditor has determined that the matter is a key matter to be communicated in the audit report.

Other Matter paragraphs may be used:

- when the matter has not been determined to be a key audit matter to be communicated in the auditor's report;
- where the entity has prepared another set of financial statements (e.g. consolidated financial statements prepared under IFRS and entity financial statements prepared in accordance with UK GAAP). In this case, the auditor may use an Other Matter paragraph referring to the fact that the entity has prepared another set of financial statements on which the auditor has reported separately; and
- where general purpose financial statements have been prepared for a specific purpose. In this situation, the auditor may include an Other Matter paragraph stating that the report is prepared solely for the intended users and may not be distributed to or used by third parties.

Where comparative information in the financial statements is derived from prior period financial statements that were not audited, ISA (UK and Ireland) 710 *Comparative information – corresponding figures and comparative financial statements* requires that the auditor's report includes an Other Matter paragraph stating that comparative figures are unaudited.

ISA (UK and Ireland) 560 *Subsequent events* requires the use of an Emphasis of Matter paragraph or an Other Matter paragraph in circumstances where:

(a) a new or amended audit report is issued following amendment to the financial statements to reflect facts that became known after the date of the original audit report but before issue of the financial statements and where the auditor's procedures on subsequent events are restricted to the amendment of the financial statements as described in the relevant note therein; or

(b) management prepare new or amended financial statements to reflect facts that became known after the financial statements were originally issued and the auditor issues a new or amended audit report on those financial statements.

ISA (UK and Ireland) 720 (Revised June 2016) *The auditor's responsibilities relating to other information* requires an Other Matter paragraph to be included in the auditor's report where, on reading the other information, the auditor identifies a material inconsistency with the financial statements requiring revision of the other information and management refuses to make the revision.

5.9 Placement

The placement of an Emphasis of Matter paragraph or Other Matter paragraph in the auditor's report depends on the nature of the information to be communicated, and the auditor's judgment as to the relative significance of the information to intended users compared to other elements of the report.

5.10 Communication with those charged with governance

When the auditor expects to modify the opinion in his report, he should communicate with those charged with governance the circumstances that led to the expected modification and the proposed wording of the modification.

Similarly, if the auditor expects to include an Emphasis of Matter or an Other Matter paragraph in his report, he should communicate with those charged with governance regarding the proposed wording of this paragraph.

Doing this not only allows the auditor to give notice to those charged with governance of the intended modification and the reasons for the modification, but gives him the opportunity to seek the concurrence of those charged with governance regarding the facts of the matter; and gives those charged with governance an opportunity, where appropriate, to provide the auditor with further information and explanations in respect of the matter giving rise to the expected modification.

6 OTHER REPORTS ON FINANCIAL INFORMATION

6.1 Introduction

This chapter considers other reports that auditors may be required to make on a company's financial information. It covers reports on:

- abbreviated accounts (**6.2**);
- revised financial statements and reports (**6.3**);
- preliminary announcements (**6.4**);
- reporting implications when a small company takes advantage of filing exemptions under the small companies regime (**6.5**); and
- summary financial statements.

This chapter does not cover engagements to review historical financial statements. Such engagements are covered in **Chapter 41**.

Engagements to report on special purpose financial statements are covered in **41.4**.

Rules regarding the preparation of abbreviated accounts for filing purposes and auditors' reports thereon are contained in the *Companies Act* 2006 and, for small companies, the *Small Companies and Groups (Accounts and Directors' Report) Regulations* 2008 (SI 2008/409). Abbreviated accounts are not permitted for filing purposes for accounting periods commencing on or after 1 January 2016 or where companies early adopt changes to the small company regime (for example by applying new small company size limits or Section 1A of FRS 102). APB Bulletin 2008/4 *The special auditor's report on abbreviated accounts in the United Kingdom* has now been withdrawn by the FRC.

Rules regarding revision of financial statements or reports are contained in the *Companies (Revision of Defective Accounts and Reports) Regulations* 2008 (SI 2008/373). Guidance for auditors is found in Bulletin 2008/5 *Auditor's reports on revised accounts and reports, in the United Kingdom* for periods after 6 April 2008.

For preliminary announcements, guidance comes from Bulletin 2008/2 *The auditors' association with preliminary announcements made in accordance with the requirements of the UK and Irish listing rules*. The Listing Rules of the Financial Conduct Authority also contain rules regarding the issue of preliminary statements of results by listed companies.

Abridged accounts may be prepared by small companies following the small companies regime for periods commencing on or after 1 January 2015.

6.2 Abbreviated accounts

6.2.1 Legal background

Companies which meet the criteria set out in the *Companies Act* 2006 for small and medium-sized companies, and which prepare their accounts under UK GAAP, are entitled to file abbreviated accounts with the Registrar of Companies for periods commencing prior to 1 January 2016, provided that they are not early adopting changes to the small companies regime (see **6.5**). For periods commencing on or after 1 January 2016, abbreviated accounts will not be permitted in any case. Abbreviated accounts must be prepared in accordance with the 2006 Act, s. 444 (small companies) or s. 445 (medium-sized companies) as applicable. There is no provision for group accounts to be prepared on an abbreviated basis.

Where abbreviated accounts are submitted to the Registrar they must be accompanied by a special auditor's report under the 2006 Act, s. 449 unless the company has claimed exemption from audit.

Those companies who have elected to prepare their individual accounts using IFRSs cannot file abbreviated accounts but may still be entitled to exemptions applicable to companies subject to the small companies regime.

6.2.2 Guidance

Guidance for the auditor in respect of abbreviated accounts is provided in the ICAEW's Helpsheet *Abbreviated Accounts*. The FRC's Bulletin 2008/4 *The Special Auditor's Report on Abbreviated Accounts in the United Kingdom* has now been withdrawn although reference is still made to this Bulletin below, since it remains relevant to those auditing abbreviated accounts for periods commencing prior to 1 January 2016.

6.2.3 Auditor's report

Where abbreviated accounts are prepared to be delivered to the Registrar, they must be accompanied by a copy of a special report of the auditor, unless the company has claimed exemption from audit. The *Companies Act* does not state to whom the report should be addressed, but the Bulletin stated that the report should be addressed to the company. Despite the fact that abbreviated accounts must be properly prepared in accordance with the relevant provisions they are not intended to be 'true and fair' and the auditor's opinion is limited to whether:

- the company is entitled to deliver abbreviated accounts in accordance with the section in question; and
- the abbreviated accounts are properly prepared in accordance with regulations under that section.

The report should be dated as close as possible to the date of the report on the full financial statements, and preferably on the same day. If there is a significant delay in reporting on the abbreviated accounts, it may give the impression that the report on the full accounts is being 'updated'. In practical terms, this means that the auditor may be required by the directors to confirm informally in advance of the preparation of abbreviated accounts that the exemptions are available. Where the report on the abbreviated accounts is dated later than that on the full financial statements, the abbreviated report should state that the auditor has not considered the effect of any events between the two dates.

If the auditor cannot confirm that the directors are entitled to the exemptions, he should report this to the directors and full accounts will have to be filed with the Registrar.

If the report on the full financial statements is qualified, abbreviated accounts may be prepared so long as they are an accurate extract. However, if the qualification relates to one of the criteria by virtue of which the company is entitled to deliver abbreviated accounts, the auditor should consider the maximum possible misstatement that this could give rise to. Where this means that the company would exceed the limits, full accounts will have to be filed with the Registrar. If the auditor has disclaimed on the financial statements then this will normally prevent him from assessing the criteria at all.

A reproduction of the report given on the full financial statements is not required unless the report on the full financial statements has been qualified. Where this is the case, the Act requires that the report given on the full financial statements is reproduced in full together with sufficient material either in the accounts or following the auditor's report, to ensure that the reader is able to understand the qualification.

This does not apply where the auditor's report on the full accounts contained an emphasis of matter but an unqualified opinion on the financial statements. However, the Bulletin noted that in this situation the APB considered it necessary that the auditor's report on the abbreviated accounts should include such a paragraph together with any further material necessary for an understanding of the report.

In addition, if the report on the full financial statements contains a statement under the *Companies Act* 2006, s. 498(2)(a) or (b) (accounts, records or returns inadequate or accounts not agreeing with records and returns) or the *Companies Act* 2006, s. 498(3) (failure to obtain necessary information and explanations), the special report should set out that statement in full under the heading 'other information'.

Under the *Companies Act* 2006, where the auditor is a firm, the report must be signed by the senior statutory auditor in his own name for and on behalf of the auditor in the same way as for the audit report on the full financial statements.

An example of a report on abbreviated accounts is shown in **Table 1** below.

TABLE 1: Report on abbreviated accounts

Independent auditor's report to XYZ Limited under the Companies Act 2006, s. 449

We have examined the abbreviated accounts of XYZ Limited set out on pages … to …, together with the financial statements of the company for the year ended … prepared under the *Companies Act* 2006, s. 449[1].

Respective responsibilities of directors and auditors

The directors are responsible for preparing the abbreviated accounts in accordance with the *Companies Act* 2006, s. 444 [s. 445 if medium-sized]. It is our responsibility to form an independent opinion as to whether the company is entitled to deliver abbreviated accounts to the Registrar of Companies and whether the abbreviated accounts have been properly prepared in accordance with those provisions and to report our opinion to you.

Basis of opinion

We conducted our work in accordance with Bulletin 2008/4 issued by the Auditing Practices Board. In accordance with that Bulletin we have carried out the procedures we consider necessary to confirm, by reference to the financial statements, that the company is entitled to deliver abbreviated accounts and that the abbreviated accounts are properly prepared.

Opinion

In our opinion, the company is entitled to deliver abbreviated accounts prepared in accordance with the *Companies Act* 2006, s. 444(3) [s. 445(3) if medium-sized], and the abbreviated accounts have been properly prepared in accordance with those provisions.

Other information

[*This section is only to be included where there is such information*]

[signature] John Smith (senior statutory auditor)

for and on behalf of ABC LLP, Statutory Auditor

Address

Date

[1] The auditor may include a 'Bannerman Statement' as part of the opening section of his report (see **4.22**).

It is preferable for the same auditor to report on both full and abbreviated sets of accounts. If there is to be a change of auditor and the new auditor is to report on the abbreviated accounts, he only needs to perform additional work if he has grounds to doubt the accuracy of his predecessor. Where such a change occurs, it should be indicated in the report.

It would not be appropriate to prepare an assurance review report (under ISRE 2400) on abbreviated accounts, as these are not intended to give a true and fair view. If a company obtains an assurance review report over its full accounts, and files abbreviated accounts at Companies House, the assurance review report does not cover the abbreviated accounts and should not be filed with them. However, the company may use a note in the abbreviated accounts to publicise the fact that it has obtained an assurance review report over its full accounts. Example wording is given in TECH 09/13 AAF.

6.3   Revised financial statements and reports

6.3.1   Legal background

The *Companies Act* 2006 allows directors to withdraw financial statements, strategic reports or directors' reports which have been found to be defective after they have been filed with the Registrar of Companies. In addition, the court, on application from the Secretary of State, has powers to make directors revise defective accounts or reports.

Detailed rules regarding revision of financial statements or reports are set out in the *Companies (Revision of Defective Accounts and Reports) Regulations* 2008 (SI 2008/373).

6.3.2   Guidance

Guidance for the auditor in these situations is contained in *Bulletin 2008/5 Auditor's reports on revised accounts and reports in the United Kingdom*. It should be noted that the Bulletin does not reflect revisions to the regulations arising from the *Companies (Revision of Defective Accounts and Reports) (Amendment) Regulations* 2013 (SI 2013/1971) relating to strategic reports, or revisions to ISA (UK and Ireland) 700 (Revised June 2016) *Forming an opinion and reporting on financial statements*.

6.3.3   Types of revision

Revision may be by:

- issue of replacement financial statements and/or strategic or directors' reports, as applicable;
- supplementary note, to be appended to the existing financial statements, strategic report or directors' report.

In each case, the auditor has to report on the revision and the directors' statement of the reason why the original financial statements, or report(s), are now considered incorrect. They must consider if the statement by the directors of the reason for the revision is sufficient for the reader to obtain a clear picture of the relevant facts. It is also necessary to consider if the method of revision is appropriate and whether any further adjustments are necessary.

Where the only revision is to the strategic report or directors' report, the auditor has to make a positive statement that it is consistent with the information in the financial statements.

Bulletin 2008/5 sets out individual example reports under the *Companies Act 2006* for:

- revision by replacement; and
- revision by supplementary note

and both are reproduced in **Tables 2** and **3** below.

It is possible to revise abbreviated financial statements where these alone prove to be defective. In these instances, the auditor is only required to report on the preparation of the abbreviated financial statements, rather than the revision.

Where either the full revision or supplementary note option is chosen, there should be a statement of directors' responsibilities under the Regulations. As with the annual financial statements, this may be either in the auditor's report or elsewhere in the financial statements or accompanying information. In addition to the normal responsibility statement that would accompany annual financial statements, the responsibilities that should be noted are shown in **Table 4.**

Where it is necessary to qualify such a report, the considerations are the same as for reports on other financial statements. For example, if the auditor considers that the reasons for the revision given by the directors are inadequate he should qualify and give further details in his report.

Where the auditor is a firm, the auditor's report must be signed by the senior statutory auditor in his own name for and on behalf of the auditor in the same way as for the audit report on the full financial statements.

TABLE 2[2]: Annual financial statements revised by replacement under CA 2006

Independent auditor's report to the members of XYZ Limited

We have audited the revised financial statements of XYZ Limited for the year ended … which comprise [state the primary financial statements such as the Profit and Loss Account, the Balance Sheet, the Cash Flow Statement, the Statement of Total Recognised Gains and Losses] and the related notes. These revised financial statements have been prepared under the accounting policies set out therein and replace the original financial statements approved by the directors on …

The revised financial statements have been prepared under the *Companies (Revision of Defective Accounts and Report) Regulations* 2008 and accordingly do not take account of events which have taken place after the date on which the original financial statements were approved.[3]

Respective responsibilities of directors and auditor

As explained more fully in the Directors' Responsibilities Statement [set out [on pages …]], the directors are responsible for the preparation of the revised financial statements and for being satisfied that they give a true and fair view. Our responsibility is to audit and express an opinion on the revised financial statements in accordance with applicable law and International Standards on Auditing (UK and Ireland). Those standards require us to comply with the Auditing Practices Board's (APB's) Ethical Standards[4] for Auditors.

Scope of the audit of the financial statements

A description of the scope of an audit of financial statements is [provided on the FRC's website at www.frc.org.uk/auditscopeukprivate]/[set out [on page x][5] of the Annual Report].

The audit of revised financial statements includes the performance of additional procedures to assess whether the revisions made by the directors are appropriate and have been properly made.

Opinion on revised financial statements

In our opinion:

- the revised financial statements give a true and fair view, seen as at the date the original financial statements were approved, of the state of the company's affairs as at … and of its profit for the year then ended;
- the revised financial statements have been properly prepared in accordance with United Kingdom Generally Accepted Accounting Practice seen as at the date the original financial statements were approved;
- the revised financial statements have been properly prepared in accordance with the provisions of the *Companies Act* 2006 as they have effect under the *Companies (Revision of Defective Accounts and Reports) Regulations* 2008; and
- the original financial statements for the year ended … failed to comply with the requirements of the *Companies Act* 2006 in the respects identified by the directors in the statement contained in note … to these revised financial statements.

Emphasis of matter – revision of …

In forming our opinion on the revised financial statements, which is not modified, we have considered the adequacy of the disclosures made in note x to these revised financial statements concerning the need to revise the … The original financial statements were approved on … and our previous report was signed on that date. We have not performed a subsequent events review of the period from the date of our previous report to the date of this report.

Opinion on other matters prescribed by the Companies Act 2006

In our opinion, the information given in the [[revised] Strategic Report and the] [revised] Directors' Report for the financial year for which the revised financial statements are prepared is consistent with the revised financial statements.

Matters on which we are required to report by exception

We have nothing to report in respect of the following matters where the *Companies Act* 2006 requires us to report to you if, in our opinion:

- adequate accounting records have not been kept or returns adequate for our audit have not been received from branches not visited by us; or
- the company's revised financial statements are not in agreement with the accounting records and returns; or
- certain disclosures of directors' remuneration specified by law are not made; or
- we have not received all the information and explanations we required for our audit.

[Signature] John Smith (senior statutory auditor)
For and on behalf of ABC LLP, Statutory auditor
Address
Date

---

[2] This example is based on existing ISAs and has not been updated to reflect changes to audit reporting ISAs which will take effect for periods commencing 17 June 2016.
[3] The auditor may include a 'Bannerman Statement' as part of the opening section of his report (see **4.22**).
[4] The FRC proposes to replace the Ethical Standards with a single revised Ethical Standard for periods commencing 17 June 2016. Full details are in **Chapter 2**.
[5] Please refer to **Table 1** in **4.10** for wording to be included.

TABLE 3[6]: Annual financial statements revised by supplementary note under CA 2006

Independent auditor's report to the members of XYZ Limited

We have audited the revised financial statements of XYZ Limited for the year ended … which comprise [state the primary financial statements such as the Profit and Loss Account, the Balance Sheet, the Cash Flow Statement, the Statement of Total Recognised Gains and Losses] and the related notes. These revised financial statements replace the original financial statements approved by the directors on … and consist of the attached supplementary note together with the original financial statements which were circulated to members on …

The revised financial statements have been prepared under the *Companies (Revision of Defective Accounts and Report) Regulations* 2008 and accordingly do not take account of events which have taken place after the date on which the original financial statements were approved.[7]

Respective responsibilities of directors and auditor

As explained more fully in the Directors' Responsibilities Statement [set out [on pages …]], the directors are responsible for the preparation of the revised financial statements and for being satisfied that they give a true and fair view. Our responsibility is to audit and express an opinion on the revised financial statements in accordance with applicable law and International Standards on Auditing (UK and Ireland). Those standards required us to comply with the Auditing Practices Board's (APB's) Ethical Standards for Auditors.

Scope of the audit of the financial statements

A description of the scope of an audit of financial statements is [provided on the FRC's website at www.frc.org.uk/auditscopeukprivate]/[set out [on page x][8] of the Annual Report].

The audit of revised financial statements includes the performance of additional procedures to assess whether the revisions made by the directors are appropriate and have been properly made.

Opinion on revised financial statements

In our opinion:

- the revised financial statements give a true and fair view, seen as at the date the original financial statements were approved, of the state of the company's affairs as at ... and of its profit for the year then ended;
- the revised financial statements have been properly prepared in accordance with United Kingdom Generally Accepted Accounting Practice seen as at the date the original financial statements were approved;
- the revised financial statements have been properly prepared in accordance with the provisions of the *Companies Act* 2006 as they have effect under the *Companies (Revision of Defective Accounts and Reports) Regulations* 2008; and
- the original financial statements for the year ended ... failed to comply with the requirements of the *Companies Act* 2006 in the respects identified by the directors in the statement contained in the supplementary note.

Emphasis of matter – revision of ...

In forming our opinion on the revised financial statements, which is not modified, we have considered the adequacy of the disclosures made in the supplementary note concerning the need to revise the ... The original financial statements were approved on ... and our previous report was signed on that date. We have not performed a subsequent events review of the period from the date of our previous report to the date of this report.

Opinion on other matters prescribed by the Companies Act 2006

In our opinion, the information given in the [[revised] Strategic Report and the] [revised] Directors' Report for the financial year for which the revised financial statements are prepared is consistent with the revised financial statements. *Matters on which we are required to report by exception*

We have nothing to report in respect of the following matters where the *Companies Act* 2006 requires us to report to you if, in our opinion:

- adequate accounting records have not been kept or returns adequate for our audit have not been received from branches not visited by us; or
- the company's revised financial statements are not in agreement with the accounting records and returns; or
- certain disclosures of directors' remuneration specified by law are not made; or
- we have not received all the information and explanations we required for our audit.

[Signature] John Smith (senior statutory auditor)
For and on behalf of ABC LLP, Statutory auditor
Address
Date

[6] This example is based on existing ISAs and has not been updated to reflect changes to audit reporting ISAs which will take effect for periods commencing 17 June 2016.
[7] The auditor may include a 'Bannerman Statement' as part of the opening section of his report (see **4.22**).
[8] Please refer to **Table 1** in **4.10** for wording to be included.

TABLE 4: Directors' responsibilities with regard to revised financial statements under CA 2006

Under the *Companies Act* 2006, s. 454, the directors have the authority to revise financial statements or a directors' report if they do not comply with the Act. The revised financial statements must be amended in accordance with the *Companies (Revision of Defective Account and Report) Regulations* 2008 and in accordance therewith do not take account of events which have taken place after the date on which the original financial statements were approved. The Regulations require that revised financial statements show a true and fair view as if they were prepared and approved by the directors, as at the date of the original financial statements.

There is no specific guidance on what the auditor should do if he does not agree that there are grounds for revision but the directors decide to go ahead with the revision. However, as the auditor must give an opinion on whether the revision is in accordance with the Regulations and these only permit revision in certain circumstances, where he disagrees with it, he will have to give an adverse opinion. This is because the revised financial statements have not been prepared in accordance with the Regulations and may also be on the grounds that in his opinion the original financial statements did comply with the requirements of the *Companies Act*.

The auditor will need to assess whether the discovery that leads to the revision indicates that adequate accounting records have not been kept and the effect this has on his report.

There is no duty on the auditor to search for further evidence after he has signed his report, but if he does become aware of anything that he should have known at the original date of signing he should inform the directors immediately and consider whether revision is necessary.

When deciding on the best course of action once an error is discovered, various factors should be taken into consideration, including the proximity to the next set of financial statements. It may be better to make a prior year adjustment rather than carry out a revision, if the error is discovered during the course of the next year's audit due to the costs and value of the information that will result from a revision. This is not precluded by the Regulations and will often be the best course of action if a significant amount of time has elapsed since the incorrect financial statements were produced.

6.3.4 Procedures

In determining the extent of audit procedures necessary, the auditor should analyse the matter giving rise to the revision and consider:

- whether the nature of the matter suggests that errors in the financial statements may be pervasive, for example the discovery of fraud;
- whether the facts discovered since the approval of the financial statements affect past assumptions in areas of judgment, for example provisions;
- the extent of any consequential changes to the form of financial statements which arise from the matter. For example, group financial statements may be required for the first time; and
- any steps taken by the directors to investigate and correct the defect.

Where the auditor has changed since the date of the original financial statements which have subsequently been found to be defective, the new auditor should make the required reports, unless the previous auditor has been specifically engaged by management and he is still eligible to report as 'registered auditor'.

Where the auditor reporting on the original and revised financial statements is the same, it is unlikely that a re-performance of the original audit will be required. However, in determining the extent of his examination, the auditor should assess the risk of other misstatements in the original accounts. Where different auditors are reviewing the revised accounts, the amount of work that is necessary will depend on the reason for the revision and their assessment of risk.

Based on their assessment of this, they should determine appropriate review procedures to identify any significant events in the period since the approval of the original financial statements. Such a review must be sufficient to:

- ensure that the factors which have led the directors to determine that the original financial statements were defective have been properly reflected in the proposed adjustments; and
- identify any further adjustments which should be made to the revised accounts.

The auditor would therefore normally undertake the following specific procedures:

- review of the original audit plans (and programmes) in the light of the analysis of the matter leading to revision and the extent to which additional audit evidence is required should be considered;
- reassessment of the various matters of judgment involved in the preparation of the original financial statements;
- obtaining evidence specific to the adjustments made to the original financial statements;
- review of the period after the date on which the original financial statements were approved;

- review of the revised financial statements to the extent that, in conjunction with the conclusions drawn from the other audit evidence obtained, there is a reasonable basis for the opinion on the financial statements; and
- consideration of any legal and regulatory consequences of the revision.

Each of these steps may in turn indicate a need for further procedures.

Engagements to report on revised directors' reports should be conducted following the principles outlined above.

6.4 Preliminary announcements

6.4.1 Background

Under the Listing Rules of the United Kingdom Listing Authority, a listed company may choose to publish a preliminary announcement, but is not required to do so. However, when a company does issue a preliminary announcement it is required by the Listing Rules to have agreed the announcement with the company's auditor prior to publication, although the Listing Rules do not set out what form the agreement with the auditor should take. Neither do they set out the extent of work expected of the auditor.

6.4.2 Guidance

The main guidance for auditors on this issue is in APB Bulletin 2008/2 *The Auditors' Association with Preliminary Announcements Made in Accordance with Requirements of the UK and Irish Listing Rules*. The Bulletin:

- reflects the change in the Listing Rules to move from a mandatory to a permissive regime for the publication of preliminary announcements;
- reflects the change in the Listing Rules to require preliminary announcements to give details of any likely modification (rather than qualification) of the auditor's report required to be included with the annual financial report;
- reflects the introduction of ISAs (UK and Ireland) but has not been updated for the latest revisions; and
- continues to emphasise the need for the auditor to consider the way in which alternative performance measures and management commentary are presented in preliminary announcements before agreeing to their release.

6.4.3 Terms of engagement

From the auditor's point of view, the objective of the engagement is to report that the preliminary figures are consistent with the financial statements which are being or have been audited.

The scope of any engagement to review a preliminary announcement should be clearly established with the client and any public statements must also make this clear. The terms of the engagement should be set out either in a separate engagement letter or by incorporating them within the standard engagement letter.

In particular, the auditor is required to agree the contents of the preliminary statement.

The Bulletin contains example paragraphs for inclusion in an engagement letter where a preliminary announcement is being made. These are shown in **Table 5** (audit complete) and **Table 6** (audit not yet complete).

TABLE 5: Example paragraphs for an engagement letter where audit will be complete

Review of preliminary announcement

The Listing Rules state that 'a preliminary statement of annual results … must be agreed with the company's auditor prior to publication'. As directors of the company, you are responsible for preparing and issuing any preliminary announcement and ensuring that we agree to its release.

We undertake to review the preliminary announcement having regard to Bulletin 2008/2 *The Auditors' Association with Preliminary Announcements Made in Accordance with the Requirements of the UK and Irish Listing Rules*, issued by the Auditing Practices Board. Accordingly, our review will be limited to checking the accuracy of extraction of the financial information in the preliminary announcement from the audited financial statements of the company for that year, considering whether any 'alternative performance measures' and associated narrative explanations may be misleading and reading the management commentary, including any comments on, or separate presentation of, the final interim period figures, and considering whether it is in conflict with the information that we obtained in the course of our audit.

You will provide us with such information and explanations as we consider necessary for the purposes of our work. We shall request sight of the preliminary announcement in sufficient time to enable us to complete our work. The Board/Committee of the Board will formally approve the preliminary announcement before we agree to it.

TABLE 6: Example paragraphs for an engagement letter where audit will not be complete

Review of preliminary announcement

The Listing Rules state that 'a preliminary statement of annual results … must be agreed with the company's auditor prior to publication'. As directors of the company, you are responsible for preparing and issuing the preliminary announcement and ensuring that we agree to its release.

We undertake to review the preliminary announcement having regard to Bulletin 2008/2 *The Auditors' Association with Preliminary Announcements Made in Accordance with the Requirements of the UK and Irish Listing Rules* issued by the Auditing Practices Board. Accordingly, our review will be limited to checking the accuracy of extraction of the financial information in the preliminary announcement from the audited financial statements of the company for that year, considering whether any 'alternative performance measures' and associated narrative explanations may be misleading and reading the management commentary, including any comments on, or separate presentation of, the final interim period figures, and considering whether it is in conflict with the information that we have obtained in the course of our audit.

You will provide us with such information and explanations as we consider necessary for the purposes of our work. We shall request sight of the preliminary announcement in sufficient time to enable us to complete our work. The Board/Committee of the Board will formally approve the preliminary announcement before we agree to it. You will also make available to us the proposed text of the company's annual report.

We will not agree to the release of the preliminary announcement until the audit is complete subject only to the following:

- clearing outstanding audit matters which we are satisfied are unlikely to have a material impact on the financial statements or disclosures insofar as they affect the preliminary announcement;
- completing audit procedures on the detail of note disclosures to the financial statements that will not have a material impact on the primary financial statements and completing our reading of the other information in the annual report in accordance with ISA (UK and Ireland) 720 (Revised June 2016) *The auditor's responsibilities relating to other information*;
- updating the subsequent events review to cover the period between the date of the preliminary announcement and the date of our auditor's report on the financial statements; and
- obtaining final signed written representations from management and establishing that the financial statements have been reviewed and approved by the directors.

The scope of our work will be necessarily limited in that we will only be able to check the consistency of the preliminary announcement with draft financial statements on which our audit is incomplete. Accordingly, we shall not, at that stage, know whether further adjustments may be required to those draft financial statements. Consequently, there is an unavoidable risk that the company may wish to revise its preliminary announcement in the light of audit findings or other developments occurring between the preliminary announcement being notified to a regulatory information service and the completion of the audit.

In the event that we disagree with the release of the preliminary announcement, we will send you a letter setting out the reasons why.

6.4.4 Procedures

A preliminary announcement may be based on financial statements where the audit report has been finalised, or on financial statements whose audit is at an advanced stage. Whilst there is the expectation that the figures in the preliminary announcement will be consistent with those in the final audited financial statements, this cannot be guaranteed where the full financial statements are yet to be approved.

The Bulletin defines an 'advanced stage' as being where the audit has been completed, including appropriate reviews by personnel not otherwise involved in the audit, subject only to the following:

- clearing outstanding audit matters which the auditor is satisfied are unlikely to have a material impact on the financial statements or disclosures in the preliminary announcement;
- completing audit procedures on the detail of note disclosures to the financial statements that will not have a material impact on the primary financial statements and completing their reading of the other information in the annual report in accordance with ISA (UK and Ireland) 720 (Revised June 2016) *The auditor's responsibilities relating to other information*;
- updating the subsequent events review to cover the period between the issue of the preliminary announcement and the date of the auditor's report on the financial statements; and
- obtaining final signed written representations, where relevant, from management and establishing that the financial statements have been reviewed and approved by the directors.

The Bulletin provides a list of audit procedures which will normally be carried out by the auditor in relation to the preliminary announcement, regardless of whether that announcement is based on a draft statement or extracted from audited financial statements:

- checking that the figures in the preliminary announcement covering the full year have been accurately extracted from the audited or draft financial statements and reflect the presentation to be adopted in the audited financial statements. For example, any summarisation should not change the order in which items are presented where this is specified by law or accounting standards;
- considering whether the information (including the management commentary) is consistent with other expected contents of the annual report of which the auditor is aware; and
- considering whether the financial information in the preliminary announcement is misstated. A misstatement exists when the information is stated incorrectly or presented in a misleading manner. A misstatement may arise, for example, as a result of an omission of a significant change of accounting policy disclosed or due to be disclosed in the audited financial statements.

The auditor should also consider whether the preliminary announcement includes the directors' statements in connection with the publication of non-statutory accounts required by the *Companies Act* 2006, s. 435.

6.4.5 Alternative performance measures

Bulletin 2008/2 recognises that preliminary announcements may disclose non-GAAP performance measures (such as EBITDA) or pro forma information intended to give a different view of performance by including or excluding items or transactions that would otherwise be reflected in statutory financial statements or by presenting such information in a different way. Whilst such 'alternative performance measures' (APMs) are often of use to shareholders, they have the greatest potential to be misleading when:

- given greater prominence than the statutory numbers;
- there is no description of the APM;
- the APMs resemble defined performance measures but do not actually have the characteristics of the defined measures; or
- adjusted numbers are not reconciled to the statutory numbers.

Therefore Bulletin 2008/2 recommends that prior to the auditor agreeing the release of a preliminary announcement, he should consider whether:

- appropriate prominence has been given to the statutory numbers;
- any APMs are clearly and accurately described, stating the purpose for which it has been prepared;
- any APMs are reconciled to the statutory numbers; and
- any APMs are not misleading in the form or context in which they are given.

6.4.6 Management commentary

The auditor should read any management commentary in the preliminary statement, together with any other narrative disclosures and any final interim period figures, and consider whether they are in conflict with the information that he has obtained in the course of his work. If it is available, the auditor should also read the text of any Chairman's Statement, operating and financial review or similar document to be included in the annual report to ensure no discrepancies with the preliminary statement.

6.4.7 Directors' approval

The preliminary statement should state the date on which it was approved by the directors. The auditor does not agree the preliminary announcement until the Board has formally approved its entire content.

6.4.8 Modification of the auditor's report

The Listing Rules require that where an auditor is likely to issue a modified report (that is a qualified or adverse opinion, disclaimer of opinion or emphasis of matter), any preliminary announcement should make reference to this. The directors should give adequate prominence to this information in the announcement and the auditor should consider whether this is the case.

When giving details of the likely modification, care should be taken to comply with the *Companies Act* 2006, s. 435 which states that an auditor's report on the statutory accounts cannot be published with non-statutory accounts.

6.4.9 Reporting

The auditor is not required to prepare an audit report on the preliminary announcement. However, the Bulletin recommends that, to avoid possible misunderstanding and to make explicit his agreement to the preliminary announcement, he should issue a letter to the company to signify his agreement. An example of this letter is shown in **Table 7**. This report should not be published with the announcement.

TABLE 7: Example report on preliminary announcement

Dear Sirs

In accordance with the terms of our engagement letter dated [ ], we have reviewed the attached proposed preliminary announcement of XYZ plc for the year ended [ ]. Our work was conducted having regard to Bulletin 2008/2 *The Auditor's Association with Preliminary Announcements Made in Accordance with the Requirements of the UK and Irish Listing Rules* issued by the Auditing Practices Board. As directors, you are responsible for preparing and issuing the preliminary announcement.

Our responsibility is solely to give our agreement to the preliminary announcement having carried out the procedures specified in the Bulletin as providing a basis for such agreement. In this regard, we agree to the preliminary announcement being notified to a Regulatory Information Service.

[*Insert paragraph* below only where the preliminary announcement is made before the audit is complete.]

Yours faithfully

* As you are aware we are not in a position to sign our auditor's report on the annual financial statements as they have not yet been approved by the directors and we have not yet *insert significant procedures that are yet to be completed, for example completing the subsequent events review and obtaining final representations from directors.* Consequently, there can be no absolute certainty that we will be in a position to issue an unmodified audit opinion on financial statements consistent with the results and financial position reported in the preliminary announcement. However, at the present time, we are not aware of any matters that may give rise to a modification to our report. In the event that such matters do come to our attention, we will inform you immediately.

6.4.10 Announcements not agreed

Where the auditor is not in agreement with the content of the preliminary announcement, he should communicate this to the directors in a letter setting out the reasons for this disagreement and advising the directors not to release the announcement to a Regulatory Information Service.

Where he becomes aware that the company has released the announcement, without first obtaining his consent, he should first ascertain the reasons for this. If the announcement was released inadvertently, the Bulletin advises the auditor to remind the directors of their obligations under the Listing Rules to obtain the auditor's agreement. However, where an announcement with which the auditor disagrees has been released, the Bulletin advises taking legal advice with a view to notifying the Listing Authority of the fact that the announcement had not been agreed.

6.5   New small companies regime

6.5.1   Legal background

The *Companies, Partnerships and Groups (Accounts and Reports) Regulations* 2015 (SI 2015/980) made various amendments to the *Companies Act* 2006 and the *Small Companies and Groups (Accounts and Directors' Report) Regulations* 2008 (SI 2008/409) and introduced significant changes to the small companies regime. Companies are entitled to adopt the new provisions of the Act and Regulations for periods commencing on or after 1 January 2015 and are required to apply them for periods commencing on or after 1 January 2016.

Under the new regime, small companies may prepare their accounts for members using the full small company formats set out in the regulations or may alternatively prepare simplified accounts (referred to as 'abridged accounts') in which certain of the prescribed format items are combined. For example, an abridged format 1 profit and loss account will start at the gross profit/loss line rather than turnover and in an abridged format 2 profit and loss account, the first five lines in the format are combined into one heading of 'gross profit or loss'. In an abridged balance sheet, items need only be analysed to the levels indicated by letters and roman numerals in the formats. For example, within fixed assets, tangible assets would need to be disclosed, but would not need to be further analysed into land and buildings and plant and machinery. Companies preparing abridged accounts should note, however, that such accounts must still give a true and fair view and FRS 102 notes that in order to achieve this, small entities may need to provide additional disclosure that is necessary in the notes to the financial statements, for example in relation to disaggregating the information in the income statement or balance sheet.

If a company wishes to prepare abridged accounts, it must obtain unanimous agreement of all shareholders. This means that if one shareholder does not agree to the abridgement, then the company must instead prepare a full set of financial statements for the period in question. It is worth noting that shareholders' agreement to prepare abridged accounts for the preceding financial year does not cover all subsequent accounting periods and such a decision must be taken on an annual basis.

Abbreviated accounts are not permitted under the new regime and instead the accounts filed with the registrar must be the same accounts as those prepared for members. There are, however, a number of filing exemptions and a small company need not file its directors' report or its profit and loss account (or notes thereto). This applies whether the accounts prepared for members were full accounts or abridged accounts. Where advantage is taken of either of these exemptions, there must be a statement on the balance sheet to the effect that the annual accounts and reports have been delivered to the registrar in accordance with the provisions of the small companies regime.

Where a company has prepared abridged accounts, the revised Companies Act also requires a statement from the directors to the registrar that all shareholders have consented to the abridgement.

6.5.2 Auditor's report

Where the accounts are audited, the auditor's report is essentially the same regardless of whether the accounts are full accounts or abridged accounts although, where applicable, the auditor may choose to make reference to the fact that the accounts have been prepared as abridged accounts. Unlike abbreviated accounts, there is no requirement for a 'special' auditor's report.

As noted above, the accounts prepared for members, whether abridged or not, need to be filed at Companies House, although the profit and loss account may be removed before filing. Where the accounts have been audited but no profit and loss account is filed the auditor's report should also not be filed. Instead the notes to the filed accounts should include a note summarising the auditor's report on the full financial statements. An example is given in **Table 8**. The note must:

(a)　state whether the auditor's report was qualified or unqualified;

(b)　where that report was qualified, disclose the basis of the qualification (reproducing any statement under s. 498(2)(a) or (b) (accounting records) or s. 498(3) (information and explanations not obtained), if applicable);

(c)　where that report was unqualified, include a reference to any matters to which the auditor drew attention by way of emphasis; and

(d)　state:

(i)　the name of the auditor and (where the auditor is a firm) the name of the person who signed the auditor's report as senior statutory auditor; or

(ii)　if the conditions in s. 506 (circumstances in which names may be omitted) are met, that a resolution has been passed and notified to the Secretary of State in accordance with that section.

TABLE 8: Example Auditor's Report

Note X – Auditor's report on the financial statements

The financial statements of the company for the financial year ended 31 December 20XX prepared for members, from which these financial statements have been extracted, were audited by the company's auditors, ABC LLP.

The auditor's report on those financial statements was [unqualified/qualified (explain basis of qualification/unqualified but contain an emphasis of matter paragraph as follows (…)]. The report was signed by [name] as senior statutory auditor for and on behalf of ABC LLP, statutory auditor on [date].

6.5.3   Guidance

The ICAEW issued a helpsheet, *Abridged accounts for small companies* in December 2015. The helpsheet provides example formats for financial statements under the new rules.

6.6   Summary financial statements

Under the *Companies Act* 2006, s. 426(1) and the *Companies (Summary Financial Statement) Regulations* 2008, companies in the United Kingdom used to be able to send summary financial statements (SFSs) to their shareholders instead of the full report and accounts.

These summary financial statements used to be accompanied by a statement from the company's auditor that the summary statement was consistent with the full accounts and that it complied with s. 426(1) and the Regulations.

This concept of summary financial statements, however, was removed from the *Companies Act* 2006, s. 426 by the *Strategic Report and Directors' Report Regulations* 2013. With effect from 1 October 2013, companies are now able to send to shareholders, with their agreement, a copy of the strategic report instead of the full annual financial statements. There is no requirement to include the auditor's report.

Other entities, for example, non-corporate registered charities may still choose to produce summary financial statements and companies may produce summary financial statements for other purposes. Whilst the FRC has withdrawn APB Bulletin 2008/3 *The Auditor's Statement on the Summary Financial Statement in the United Kingdom* which related to the statutory requirement, many auditors still refer to this for guidance on procedures to be applied and the form of their report. Alternatively, reference may be made to the IAASB's ISA 810 (Revised) *Engagements to Report on Summary Financial Statements*, the latest version of which was issued in March 2016.

Further guidance on charities is given in **Chapter 43**.

7 OTHER STATUTORY REPORTS BY AUDITORS

7.1 Introduction

This chapter considers the other types of reports that auditors may be required to make under the *Companies Act* 2006. It covers the reports on:

- distributions;
- purchase and redemption of own shares;
- re-registration of companies;
- allotment of shares otherwise than for cash; and
- transfer of non-cash assets.

The guidance on the form of these is contained in Bulletin 2008/9 *Miscellaneous reports by auditors required by the United Kingdom Companies Act 2006*. For some reports, there is additional guidance on the procedures necessary to support such reports and the source of this has been noted below.

Under the *Companies Act* 2006, there is no longer a requirement for the auditor of a private company to make a report on the directors' statutory declaration to provide financial assistance for the purchase of its own shares or those of a holding company. This is effective in relation to financial assistance given on or after 1 October 2008.

7.2 Distributions

7.2.1 Legal background

A company may only make a distribution out of distributable reserves and must justify any distribution by reference to profits, losses, assets, liabilities, provisions, share capital and reserves shown in the 'relevant accounts'. Generally, the relevant accounts will be the company's last annual accounts except where:

- a distribution would be found to contravene the requirements of the *Companies Act* by reference to the last annual accounts – in which case special 'interim' accounts may be used instead (see **7.2.3**); or
- a distribution is proposed to be declared in the company's first accounting reference period, before any annual accounts have been prepared – in which case special 'initial' accounts may be prepared for the purpose of justifying the distribution. (This is covered in section **7.2.4**.)

Where interim or initial accounts are prepared, these accounts should be sufficient to enable a reasonable judgment to be made as to the items mentioned above and hence, as to the availability of distributable profits. However, in the case of a public company, the accounts must be 'properly prepared' or have been so prepared except for matters not material for the purposes of determining distributable profits. 'Properly prepared' in this context means prepared under the accounting provisions of the *Companies Act* for individual company accounts, applying such modifications as are necessary to reflect the fact that the accounts are not the annual accounts of the company.

In the case of a parent company, group accounts are not required.

7.2.2   *Distributions made by reference to annual accounts*

The *Companies Act* 2006, s. 837(4) requires that where the auditor's report on a company's annual financial statements contains a qualification, before those statements may be used to justify a distribution, it is necessary for the company's auditor to make a further statement as to whether the qualification is material for the purposes of determining the company's distributable profits. This statement must, in the case of a private company, be circulated to members of the company or, in the case of a public company, be laid before the members in general meeting.

The auditor's statement may be issued as a separate report to the members and sent to the company for distribution to members, or as an additional paragraph in the normal auditor's report on the financial statements. This will depend upon the individual circumstances.

The required statement is restricted to the consideration of the effect of the last qualification on the company's distributable profits. The auditor is required to state whether the subject matter of the qualification is material for determining whether the proposed distributions, and any which have not yet been proposed, are permitted. Some qualifications will not be material because of their nature, for example, if the qualification related to the misclassification of creditors due within one year, there would be no effect on distributable profits.

Other qualifications will by their nature be potentially material. For example, a qualification for failure to make a provision in respect of the carrying value of properties could have an adverse effect on the distributable reserves of the company. Here the auditor would have to assess the maximum potential write down, if known, before he could say whether the proposed distribution was permitted.

It should be noted that an emphasis of matter paragraph which states that the auditor's opinion on the financial statements is not qualified does not count as a qualification of the auditor's report for this purpose and as a consequence will not result in the need for a report under s. 837(4).

If the auditor is unable to quantify the effect of the qualification, its effect would have to be assessed as material for the purposes of determining the distributable reserves, unless he can conclude that the qualification either does not impact distributable profits or that its possible impact could only be favourable. In this case, the auditor would have to state either that the qualification is material or that he is unable to form an opinion whether it is material.

A disclaimer of opinion on the financial statements as a whole would be material as the auditor would be unable to form an opinion on the amount at which the company's distributable profits are stated.

Whatever opinion is given, legally the company could pay a dividend so long as a statement, irrespective of its conclusion, is laid before the members. It is only when the auditor does not provide such a statement that the distribution is illegal. However, where the auditor has concluded that the effect of a qualification is or could be material the directors would be unwise to make a distribution without first establishing that the company did in fact have sufficient distributable reserves.

The following tables provide suitable wordings for these reports. **Table 1** is where a separate report is given and the amount of the proposed distribution is known. If the proposed dividend is as yet unquantified, the wording in **Table 2** should be used or if a statement is to be made about 'any distribution' **Table 3** should be used. If a separate report is not required, the additional paragraph should be based on **Table 4**.

If a separate statement is made, the date used should be that on which the statement is completed and will need to be by the date of the distribution.

TABLE 1: Report required on company's ability to make a distribution

Statement of the Independent Auditor to the [members/shareholders] of XYZ Limited pursuant to the Companies Act 2006, s. 837(4)

We have audited the financial statements of XYZ Limited for the year ended ... in accordance with International Standards on Auditing (United Kingdom and Ireland) and have expressed a qualified opinion thereon in our report dated ...[1]

Respective responsibilities of directors and auditor

[*Summarisation of directors' responsibilities with respect to the financial statements referred to in the introductory paragraph.*] They are also responsible for considering whether the company, subsequent to the balance sheet date, has sufficient distributable profits to make a distribution at the time the distribution is made.

Our responsibility is to report whether, in our opinion the subject matter of our qualification of our auditors' report on the financial statements for the year ended ... is material for determining, by reference to those financial statements, whether the distribution proposed by the company is permitted under the *Companies Act* 2006, s. 830 [s. 831/832[2]]. We are not required to form an opinion on whether the company has sufficient distributable reserves to make the distribution proposed at the time it is made.

Opinion

In our opinion, the subject matter of that qualification is not material for determining, by reference to those financial statements, whether [the distribution of £ ... /the interim/final dividend for the year ended ... of £ ...] proposed by the company is permitted under the *Companies Act* 2006, s. 830 (*s. 831/832*).

Statutory Auditor

Address

Date

[1] The auditor may include a 'Bannerman Statement' as part of the opening section of his report (see **4.22**).
[2] Section 831 should be used for public companies and s. 831 and 832 if the company is also an investment company.

TABLE 2: Alternative opinion paragraph where amount of distribution not known

In our opinion, the subject matter of that qualification is not material for determining, by reference to those financial statements, whether a distribution of not more than £ ... by the company is permitted under the *Companies Act* 2006, s. 830 (*s. 831/832*).

TABLE 3: Alternative opinion paragraph concerning ability to make 'any distribution'

In our opinion, the subject matter of that qualification is not material for determining, by reference to those financial statements, whether any distribution proposed by the company is permitted under the *Companies Act* 2006, s. 830 (*s. 831/832*).

TABLE 4: Additional paragraphs concerning ability to make a distribution for audit report on annual accounts

Statement pursuant to Companies Act 2006, [s. 837(4)/839(6[3])].

Respective responsibilities of directors and auditor

In addition to their responsibilities described above, the directors are also responsible for considering whether the company, subsequent to the balance sheet date, has sufficient distributable profits to make a distribution at the time the distribution is made.

Our responsibility is to report whether, in our opinion the subject matter of our qualification of our auditors' report on the financial statements for the year ended ... is material for determining, by reference to those financial statements, whether the distribution proposed by the company is permitted under the *Companies Act* 2006, s. 830 [s. 831/832[4]]. We are not required to form an opinion on whether the company has sufficient distributable reserves to make the distribution proposed at the time it is made.

> ### Opinion on other matter required by the Companies Act
>
> In our opinion, the subject matter of the above qualification is not material for determining whether [the distribution of £ ... /the interim/final dividend for the year ended ... of £ ...] proposed by the company is permitted under the *Companies Act* 2006, s. 830 (*s. 831/832*).
>
> [3] Section 837(4) applies where the last annual accounts are used. Section 839(6) applies where initial accounts are used and are qualified.
> [4] Section 831 should be used for public companies and s. 831 and 832 if the company is also an investment company.

7.2.3   Distributions made by reference to 'interim' accounts

Where interim accounts are prepared to justify a distribution, no auditor's report is required, although, in the case of a public company, the interim accounts must be filed with the Registrar of Companies.

7.2.4   Distributions made by reference to 'initial' accounts

Where a company wishes to make a distribution during its first accounting period, or after its end but before the accounts for that period have been circulated to members or laid before the members in general meeting, initial accounts have to be prepared in accordance with the *Companies Act* 2006, s. 839, as set out in **7.2.1** above. In the case of a private company, there is no requirement for a report by the auditor, but in the case of a public company, the auditor must report in accordance with the *Companies Act* 2006, s. 839(5) whether, in his opinion, the initial accounts have been properly prepared.

The auditor's report may be addressed to the directors and should identify the period covered by the initial accounts.

The auditor is required to express an opinion on whether the accounts have been properly prepared in accordance with the *Companies Act* 2006, s. 395–397 with any modifications necessary to reflect the fact that the accounts are not prepared in respect of a financial year of the company. This means, in effect, that the accounts give a true and fair view and are prepared in accordance with the accounting provisions of the Act.

Although the opinion provided by the auditor is not an audit opinion, the work done by the auditor in order to determine whether the accounts are properly prepared will not be dissimilar to that required to support an audit opinion on annual financial statements.

An example unqualified report is shown in **Table 5**.

If the auditor's opinion on the initial accounts is qualified, then the auditor must make a statement as to whether, in his opinion, the subject matter of the qualification is material for the purposes of determining whether the company has sufficient distributable reserves. See **Table 4** above for example paragraphs for inclusion in the report.

In the case of a distribution by a public company based on initial accounts, the initial accounts, the auditor's report thereon, and any statement made by the auditor in respect of a qualified opinion on the initial accounts, must be filed with the Registrar of Companies.

TABLE 5: Report on initial accounts of a public company wishing to make a distribution

Report of the Independent Auditor to the directors of XYZ Plc under the Companies Act 2006, s. 839(5)

We have examined the initial accounts of XYZ plc for the period from ... to ... which comprise [state the primary financial statements such as the Profit and Loss Account, the Balance Sheet, the Cash Flow Statement, the Statement of Total Recognised Gains and Losses] and the related notes. The initial accounts have been prepared under the accounting policies set out therein.[5]

Respective responsibilities of directors and auditor

As described ... the directors are responsible for the preparation of the initial accounts in accordance with applicable law and United Kingdom Accounting Standards (United Kingdom Generally Accepted Accounting Practice).

Our responsibility is to report to you our opinion as to whether the initial accounts have been properly prepared within the meaning of the *Companies Act* 2006, s. 839(4).

Opinion

In our opinion, the initial accounts for the period from ... to ... have been properly prepared within the meaning of the *Companies Act* 2006, s. 839(4).

[Signature]
John Smith (senior statutory auditor)
for and on behalf of ABC LLP, Statutory Auditor
Address
Date

[5] The auditor may include a 'Bannerman Statement' as part of the opening section of his report (see **4.22**).

7.3   Purchase and redemption of own shares

7.3.1   Legal background

Where a private company decides to redeem or purchase its own shares wholly or partly out of capital, this has to be approved by a special resolution of the company. A directors' declaration is required concerning the amount by which the purchase price exceeds any available profits (the permissible capital payment) and the solvency of the company. This statement has to be accompanied by an auditor's report.

The auditor's report should be addressed to the directors and states that the amount specified as the permissible capital payment has been properly determined and that the solvency statement is reasonable. The report should be made and dated in the week prior to the meeting which passes the special resolution.

7.3.2   Guidance

The auditor's report:

- should not be dated earlier than the declaration;
- cannot be qualified and should not be issued unless unqualified.

An example of the report is shown in **Table 6**.

There is no published guidance on the procedures that are necessary to support such a report. In general, before giving the report the auditor must:

- be satisfied that the directors' assumptions are realistic and consistently applied;
- review the cash flow forecasts;
- review asset and liability values, including provisions and future commitments;
- confirm that any support being received from lenders or group companies will be continued; and
- ensure that the permissible capital payment calculation is correct, taking into account any movements since the relevant accounts were prepared. These relevant accounts need not be audited but must be sufficient to enable a reasonable judgment to be made as to the financial position of the company.

TABLE 6: Report for private company redeeming or purchasing shares out of capital

Report of the Independent Auditor to the Directors of XYZ Limited pursuant to the Companies Act 2006, s. 714(6)

We report on the attached statement of the directors dated ..., prepared pursuant to the *Companies Act* 2006, in connection with the company's proposed [purchase]/ [redemption] of ... (*number*) [ordinary]/[preferred] shares by a payment out of capital.[6]

Basis of opinion

We have inquired into the state of the company's state of affairs in order to review the bases for the directors' statement.

Opinion

In our opinion, the amount of £ ... specified in the directors' statement as the permissible capital payment for the shares to be [purchased]/[redeemed] is properly determined in accordance with the *Companies Act* 2006, s. 710–712.

We are not aware of anything to indicate that the opinion expressed by the directors in their statement as to any of the matters mentioned in the *Companies Act* 2006, s. 714(3) is unreasonable in all the circumstances.

Statutory Auditor
Address
Date

[6] The auditor may include a 'Bannerman Statement' as part of the opening section of his report (see **4.22**).

7.4   Re-registration of companies

7.4.1   Legal background

When a private company wishes to re-register as a public company, it has to deliver certain documents to the Registrar of Companies before it will be issued with a new certificate of incorporation. These include a copy of the company's balance sheet, at a date not more than seven months before the application, together with an auditor's report on that balance sheet which is either:

- unqualified; or
- qualified and the auditor expresses an opinion that the qualification is not material for determining the net assets of the company,

and a further written statement from the auditor. If the last financial statements are at a date more than seven months before, an up-to-date balance sheet will need to be prepared and audited.

The auditor's statement should confirm that the company's net assets are not less than the total of its share capital and non-distributable reserves.

7.4.2   Guidance

The procedures to support such a report may be restricted to a simple examination of the amounts in the relevant financial statements. The report should indicate that the work is limited to such an examination.

If the balance sheet is qualified, the auditor will have to state that this is not material for the purposes of determining whether at the balance sheet date the net assets of the company were not less than the aggregate of its called-up share capital and non-distributable reserves. The considerations required for this are similar to those for the effect of qualifications on distributions. Where this is the case, an extra paragraph will need to be inserted in the auditor's statement as illustrated in **Table 7**.

The auditor's report should not be dated earlier than the date of the audit report on the relevant balance sheet.

If there has been a change of auditor, the new auditor can accept the balance sheet audited by his predecessor unless the audit report contains a material qualification. The new auditor should refer in his report to the firm that has carried out the audit of the relevant balance sheet.

The following examples should be used:

- a balance sheet from the previous annual financial statements is reported on without qualification (**Table 7**);
- a balance sheet from the previous annual financial statements is reported on with a qualification in respect of proper preparation in accordance with the *Companies Act* 2006, but the qualification is not material (**Table 8**);
- a specially prepared balance sheet is reported on without qualification (**Table 9**); and
- a specially prepared balance sheet is reported on with a qualification in respect of proper preparation in accordance with the *Companies Act* 2006, but the qualification is not material (**Table 10**).

TABLE 7: Statement required when a private company wishes to re-register as a public company – previous balance sheet with no qualification

Statement of the Independent Auditor to the directors of XYZ Limited for the purpose of he Companies Act 2006, s. 92(1)(b) and (c)

We have examined the balance sheet and related notes of XYZ Limited as at ... which formed part of the financial statements for the year then ended which were audited by [us]/[name of firm].[7]

Respective responsibilities of directors and auditor

The company's directors are responsible for the preparation of the balance sheet and related notes.

It is our responsibility to:

- report on whether the balance sheet has been properly prepared in accordance with the requirements of the *Companies Act* 2006; and
- form an independent opinion, based on our examination, concerning the relationship between the company's net assets and its called up share capital and undistributable reserves at the balance sheet date.

Opinion concerning proper preparation of balance sheet

In our opinion, the audited balance sheet as at … has been properly prepared in accordance with the requirements of the *Companies Act* 2006.

Statement on net assets

In our opinion, at … the amount of the company's net assets (within the meaning given to that expression by the *Companies Act* 2006, s. 831(2)) was not less than the aggregate of its called-up share capital and undistributable reserves.

Statutory Auditor

Address

Date

[7] The auditor may include a 'Bannerman Statement' as part of the opening section of his report (see **4.22**).

TABLE 8: Statement required when a private company wishes to re-register as a public company – previous balance sheet with non material qualification

Statement of the Independent Auditor to the directors of XYZ Limited for the purpose of the Companies Act 2006, s. 92(1)(b) and (c)

We have examined the balance sheet and related notes of XYZ Limited as at … which formed part of the financial statements for the year then ended which were audited by [us]/[name of firm].[8]

Respective responsibilities of directors and auditor

The company's directors are responsible for the preparation of the balance sheet and related notes.

It is our responsibility to:

- report on whether the balance sheet has been properly prepared in accordance with the requirements of the *Companies Act* 2006; and
- form an independent opinion, based on our examination, concerning the relationship between the company's net assets and its called up share capital and undistributable reserves at the balance sheet date.

Qualified opinion concerning proper preparation of balance sheet

[We]/[Name of firm] audited the financial statements for the year ended … and expressed a qualified opinion regarding the proper preparation of the balance sheet in accordance with the requirements of the *Companies Act* 2006.

The matter giving rise to [our]/[the] qualification is not material for determining by reference to the balance sheet at … whether, at that date, the amount of the company's net assets (within the meaning given to that expression by the *Companies Act* 2006, s. 831(2)) was not less than the aggregate of its called-up share capital and undistributable reserves.

Statement on net assets

In our opinion, at ... the amount of the company's net assets (within the meaning given to that expression by the *Companies Act* 2006, s. 831(2)) was not less than the aggregate of its called-up share capital and undistributable reserves.

Statutory Auditor
Address
Date

[8] The auditor may include a 'Bannerman Statement' as part of the opening section of his report (see **4.22**).

TABLE 9: Report for re-registration where new balance sheet prepared and is unqualified

Report of the Independent Auditor to the directors of XYZ Limited for the purpose of the Companies Act 2006, s. 92(1)(b) and (c)

We have audited the balance sheet and related notes of XYZ Limited as at ... set out on pages ... to ... which have been prepared under the accounting policies set out therein.[9]

Respective responsibilities of directors and auditor

The company's directors are responsible for the preparation of the balance sheet and related notes.

It is our responsibility to:

- report on whether the balance sheet has been properly prepared in accordance with the requirements of the *Companies Act* 2006 that would have applied if it had been prepared for a financial year of the company with such modifications as are necessary by reason of that fact; and
- form an independent opinion concerning the relationship between the company's net assets and its called up share capital and undistributable reserves at the balance sheet date.

Opinion concerning proper preparation of balance sheet

In our opinion, the audited balance sheet as at ... has been properly prepared in accordance with the requirements of the *Companies Act* 2006, which would have applied had the balance sheet been prepared for a financial year of the company.

Statement on net assets

In our opinion, at ... the amount of the company's net assets (within the meaning given to that expression by the *Companies Act* 2006, s. 831(2)) was not less than the aggregate of its called-up share capital and undistributable reserves.

Statutory Auditor
Address
Date

[9] The auditor may include a 'Bannerman Statement' as part of the opening section of his report (see **4.22**).

TABLE 10: Report for re-registration where new balance sheet prepared and has a non material qualification

Report of the Independent Auditor to the directors of XYZ Limited for the purpose of the Companies Act 2006, s. 92(1)(b) and (c)

We have audited the balance sheet and related notes of XYZ Limited as at ... set out on pages ... to ... which have been prepared under the accounting policies set out therein.[10]

Respective responsibilities of directors and auditor

The company's directors are responsible for the preparation of the balance sheet and related notes.

It is our responsibility to:

- report on whether the balance sheet has been properly prepared in accordance with the requirements of the *Companies Act* 2006 that would have applied if it had been prepared for a financial year of the company with such modifications as are necessary by reason of that fact; and
- form an independent opinion concerning the relationship between the company's net assets and its called up share capital and undistributable reserves at the balance sheet date.

Qualified opinion concerning proper preparation of balance sheet

[Except for [*describe area of non-compliance with CA 2006*] in our opinion the balance sheet and related notes as at ... have been properly prepared in accordance with the provisions of the *Companies Act* 2006, which would have applied had the balance sheet been prepared for a financial year of the company.][11]

[Because [*describe area of non-compliance with CA 2006*] in our opinion the balance sheet and related notes as at ... have not been properly prepared in accordance with the provisions of the *Companies Act* 2006, which would have applied had the balance sheet been prepared for a financial year of the company.][12]

However, in our opinion, this matter is not material for determining by reference to the balance sheet at ... whether, at that date, the amount of the company's net assets (within the meaning given to that expression by the *Companies Act* 2006, s. 831(2)) was not less than the aggregate of its called-up share capital and undistributable reserves.

Statement on net assets

In our opinion, at ... the amount of the company's net assets (within the meaning given to that expression by the *Companies Act* 2006, s. 831(2)) was not less than the aggregate of its called-up share capital and undistributable reserves.

Statutory Auditor
Address
Date

[10] The auditor may include a 'Bannerman Statement' as part of the opening section of his report (see **4.22**).
[11] Use this wording if the auditor has expressed a qualified opinion concerning the proper preparation of the balance sheet.
[12] Use this wording if the auditor has expressed an adverse opinion concerning the proper preparation of the balance sheet.

7.5 Allotment of shares otherwise than for cash

7.5.1 Legal background

All companies may allot shares and receive payment for them in something other than cash. However, where the company concerned is a public company, during the six months prior to the allotment, it is necessary to obtain a report on the value of the asset to be received instead of cash.

This report should be prepared by independent accountants. This is either the company's auditor, or a firm suitably qualified to be the company's auditor, i.e. a registered auditor. The accountants are entitled to rely on an expert, who is not connected with the company, to make a valuation of part or all of the asset.

If the company's own statutory auditor is requested to undertake a valuation in accordance with the *Companies Act* 2006, s. 599, the standards and guidance in *Ethical Standard 5[1] (Revised)* are applied (see **Chapter 2**).

The report should be addressed to the company and sent to the company secretary for distribution to the allottees. It should include the following information:

- the nominal value of the shares in question;
- any premium payable on them;
- a description of the consideration;
- a description of the part of the consideration valued by the independent accountants, the method used and the date of the valuation; and
- the extent to which the nominal value of the shares and any premium are to be treated as paid up by the consideration and in cash.

If the valuation was carried out by someone else, the independent accountants should give their opinion on whether that valuation is reasonable and provide details on the expert's qualifications, the method used, and the amount and the date of the valuation. The expert must be independent of the company.

Where the allotment of shares represents only part of the consideration for the asset, the report should apply to as much of the value as is attributable to the shares. It must state what valuations have been made to determine the proportion of the consideration and the reasons for and methods of that valuation.

[1] The FRC proposes to replace the Ethical Standards with a single revised Ethical Standard for periods commencing 17 June 2016. Full details are in **Chapter 2.**

7.5.2   Guidance

The accountants' work will consist of:

- either valuing the consideration themselves or assessing whether it is reasonable to accept an external valuation;
- confirming that the value of the consideration is not less than the total amount to be treated as being paid up on the shares, together with any premium; and
- considering whether there has been any change in the value of the asset since the valuation and confirming that it has not diminished. Where they have used an expert to provide the valuation it may be necessary to obtain written confirmation that there has been no diminution since the original valuation exercise.

The report, which must not be qualified, is shown in **Table 11**. If it were qualified the company registrars would be unable to issue the share certificates.

TABLE 11: Report where shares allotted other than for cash

Report of the Independent [Valuer] [Auditor] to XYZ Plc for the purposes of the Companies Act 2006, s. 593(1)

We report on the value of the consideration for the allotment to … [*name of allottee*] of … shares, having a nominal value of […] each, to be issued at a premium of … pence per share. The shares and share premium are to be treated as fully paid up.

The consideration for the allotment to … [*name of allottee*] is [the freehold building situated at … [*address*]] and … [*number*] shares, having a nominal value of […] each in Blue Chip plc.[13]

Basis of valuation

The freehold building was valued on the basis of open market value by [*name of expert*], a Fellow of the Royal Institution of Chartered Surveyors.

The shares in Blue Chip plc were valued by us on … on the basis of the price shown in The Stock Exchange Daily Official List at …

Opinion

In our opinion:

- it is reasonable to accept the valuation made by [name of expert];
- the methods of valuation of the freehold building and of the shares in Blue Chip plc were reasonable in all the circumstances; and
- there appears to have been no material change in the value of either part of the consideration since the date(s) at which the valuations were made.

On the basis of the valuations, in our opinion, the value of the total consideration is not less than the aggregate of the nominal value and share premium to be treated as paid up by the consideration.

Qualified independent person
Address
Date

[13] The auditor may include a 'Bannerman Statement' as part of the opening section of his report (see **4.22**).

7.6 Transfer of non-cash assets to a public company by one of its members

7.6.1 *Legal background*

A similar report to that described in **7.5** above is required when a public company, in the first two years following its registration, purchases a non-cash asset from one of its members for a consideration of at least one-tenth of the nominal value of its issued share capital. The Act does not allow such a purchase without approval by an ordinary resolution of the company and the submission of a report by independent accountants.

7.6.2 *Guidance*

This report must be prepared by independent accountants and must be made to the company in the six months preceding the allotment of shares.

As with the report made in **7.5** above, if the company's own statutory auditor is requested to undertake a valuation in accordance with the *Companies Act* 2006, s. 599, the standards and guidance in *Ethical Standard 5 (Revised)* are applied (see **Chapter 2**).

Instead of being sent to the allottees, it will be addressed to the company and sent to the members and will detail the asset to be purchased by the company, together with details of the valuation. Again, this report must not be qualified.

An example report is set out in **Table 12**.

TABLE 12: Report where non-cash assets are transferred to a public company by certain of its members

Report of the Independent [Valuer] [Auditor] to XYZ Plc for the purposes of the Companies Act 2006, s. 599

We report on the transfer of non-cash assets to XYZ plc ('the Company') by subscribers to the Company's memorandum of association.

The consideration to be received by the Company is [a freehold building situated at … [*address*]] ('the consideration to be received').

The consideration to be given by the Company is [number] shares, having a nominal value of […] each in LMN plc ('the consideration to be given').[14]

Basis of valuation

The freehold building was valued on the basis of open market value by [name of expert], a Fellow of the Royal Institution of Chartered Surveyors.

The shares in LMN Plc were valued by us on … on the basis of the price shown in The Stock Exchange Daily Official List at …

Opinion

In our opinion:

- it is reasonable to accept the valuation made by [name of expert];
- the methods of valuation of the freehold building and of the shares in LMN Plc were reasonable in all the circumstances; and
- there appears to have been no material change in the value of either part of the consideration since the date(s) at which the valuations were made.

On the basis of the valuations, in our opinion, the value of the total consideration to be received by the Company is not less than the value of the consideration to be given by the Company.

Qualified independent person

Address

Date

[14] The auditor may include a 'Bannerman Statement' as part of the opening section of his report (see **4.22**).

8 COMPILATION REPORTS ON ACCOUNTS PREPARED BY ACCOUNTANTS

8.1 Introduction

As audit exemption thresholds have crept steadily upwards over recent years, accountants have found themselves increasingly preparing financial statements for companies and charities where no audit is required. Statutory financial statements will, however, still be required to give a true and fair view and will be used by clients for the same purposes as audited financial statements. Although not required to do so, accountants will often wish to attach a report to financial statements they have prepared or compiled to indicate their involvement in the process and to make clear the extent of their responsibilities.

Some of the considerations arising when companies become exempt from the audit requirement are detailed in section **8.5**.

8.2 Guidance

The Audit and Assurance Faculty of the ICAEW has issued a number of iterations of guidance on the form and content of reports issued by accountants who prepare accounts on behalf of clients. The most recent versions are:

- TECH 07/16 AAF *Chartered accountants' reports on the compilation of financial statements of incorporated entities* (revised March 2016), which replaced AAF 02/10; and
- TECH 08/16 AAF *Chartered accountants' reports on the compilation of historical financial information of unincorporated entities* (revised March 2016), which replaced AAF 03/10.

In March 2016, TECH 07/16 AAF and TECH 08/16 AAF were issued as revisions to AAF 02/10 and AAF 03/10 respectively. The changes in the revised technical releases have been reflected in this chapter. The update has been carried out to reflect changes such as new UK GAAP and it is recommended that the guidance be applied as soon as possible. The revisions are not, however, intended to change existing best practice.

The guidance in TECH 07/16 AAF for incorporated entities is also applicable to the compilation of financial statements of Limited Liability Partnerships (LLPs).

TECH 07/16 AAF and TECH 08/16 AAF remind accountants that the five fundamental ethical principles of integrity, objectivity, competence, performance and courtesy apply to compilation engagements as they do to audits. It also reminds them that no tests are required on the assertions underlying the information they are presented with and therefore reporting accountants can express no assurance on the financial statements.

8.3 Incorporated entities

8.3.1 Terms of engagement

TECH 07/16 AAF states that there must be clear understanding between the client and the accountants regarding the terms of the engagement. An example engagement letter extract is given in **Table 1**.

In addition, accountants should consider whether it is appropriate to include a section on the limitation of the accountants' liability.

TABLE 1: Engagement letter extracts for the compilation of unaudited financial statements

Your responsibilities as directors

As directors of the company, you are responsible for maintaining adequate accounting records and for preparing financial statements which give a true and fair view and which have been prepared in accordance with the *Companies Act* 2006 ('the Act'). As directors, you must not approve the financial statements unless you are satisfied that they give a true and fair view of the assets, liabilities, financial position and profit or loss of the company.

In preparing financial statements, you are required to:

(1) select suitable accounting policies and then apply them consistently;
(2) make judgments and estimates that are reasonable and prudent; and
(3) prepare financial statements on a going concern basis unless it is inappropriate to presume that the company will continue in business.

You are also responsible for such internal control as you determine is necessary to enable the preparation of financial statements that are free from material misstatement whether due to fraud or error.

You are also responsible for safeguarding the assets of the company and hence for taking reasonable steps to prevent and detect fraud and other irregularities.

You have undertaken to make available to us, as and when required, all the company's accounting records and related financial information, including minutes of management and shareholders' meetings, necessary to carry out our work. You will make full disclosure to us of all relevant information.

Scope of the accountants' work

You have asked us to assist you in the preparation of the financial statements. We will compile the annual financial statements for your approval based on the accounting records maintained by you and the information and explanations given to us by you. We shall plan our work on the basis that no report is required by statute or regulation for the year, unless you inform us in writing to the contrary. In carrying out our engagement, we will make enquiries of management and undertake any procedures that we judge appropriate but are under no obligation to perform procedures that may be required for assurance engagements such as audits or reviews.

You have advised us that the company is exempt from an audit of the financial statements. We will not carry out any work to determine whether or not the company is entitled to audit exemption. However, should our work indicate that the company is not entitled to the exemption, we will inform you of this.

Our work will not be an audit of the financial statements in accordance with International Standards on Auditing (UK and Ireland). Consequently, our work will not provide any assurance that the accounting records or the financial statements are free from material misstatement, whether caused by fraud, other irregularities or error and cannot be relied on to identify weaknesses in internal controls.

Since we have not carried out an audit, nor confirmed in any way the accuracy or reasonableness of the accounting records maintained by the company, we are unable to provide any assurance as to whether the financial statements that we prepare from those records present a true and fair view.

We have a professional duty to compile financial statements that conform with generally accepted accounting principles from the accounting records and information and explanations given to us. Furthermore, as directors, you have a duty to prepare financial statements that comply with the Act and applicable accounting standards. Where we identify that the financial statements do not conform to accepted accounting principles or if the accounting policies adopted are not immediately apparent this will need to be disclosed in the financial statements.

We have a professional responsibility not to allow our name to be associated with financial statements which may be misleading. Therefore, although we are not required to search for such matters, should we become aware, for any reason, that the financial statements may be misleading, we will discuss the matter with you with a view to agreeing appropriate adjustments and/or disclosures in the financial statements. In such circumstances where adjustments and/or disclosures that we consider appropriate are not made or where we are not provided with appropriate information, and as a result, we consider that the financial statements are misleading, we will withdraw from the engagement.

As part of our normal procedures, we may request you to provide written confirmation of any information or explanations given by you orally during the course of our work.

Form of the accountants' report

We shall report to the Board of Directors, with any modifications that we consider may be necessary, that in accordance with this engagement letter and in order to assist you to fulfil your responsibilities, we have compiled, without carrying out an audit, the financial statements from the accounting records of the company and from the information and explanation supplied to us.

Liability provisions

We will perform the engagement with reasonable skill and care. The total aggregate liability to the Company and the Board of Directors, as a body, of whatever nature, whether in contract, tort or otherwise, of [name of accountants] for any losses whatsoever and howsoever caused arising from or in any way connected with this engagement shall not exceed [amount].

8.3.2   Directors' responsibilities

Although they have asked their accountants to compile the financial statements, directors are ultimately responsible for ensuring that the company maintains adequate accounting records and for preparing financial statements which give a true and fair view. The accounts of micro-entities, where the exemptions available are taken advantage of and the legal disclosure requirements are met, are presumed to give a true and fair view. Other company accounts must have been prepared in accordance with the *Companies Act* 2006 and the applicable financial reporting framework.

In addition, directors are required to:

- select suitable accounting policies and then apply them consistently;
- make judgments and estimates that are reasonable and prudent;
- state whether applicable UK accounting standards have been followed, subject to any material departures disclosed and explained in the financial statements; and
- prepare financial statements on a going concern basis unless it is inappropriate to presume that the company will continue in business.

They are also responsible for safeguarding the assets of the company and for taking steps for the prevention and detection of fraud and other irregularities.

8.3.3   Accountants' procedures

Accountants will plan their work, and this includes obtaining a general understanding of the business and operations of the company and the accounting principles and practices of the industry in which the company operates.

Accountants also consider whether the financial statements are consistent with their understanding of the company, but are under no obligation to perform procedures that may be required for an audit or other type of assurance engagement.

There is no mandatory requirement to document the work that has been carried out; however, adequate documentation will demonstrate that the work performed is of the requisite quality and has been performed in accordance with the terms of engagement. Accountants may use a disclosure checklist or software package to check that all relevant disclosures have been made.

Accountants will also consider obtaining written confirmation of oral representations made by management.

8.3.4 Misleading financial statements

Although accountants are not reviewing or auditing the financial statements, they may become aware that the financial statements are misleading. For example, they may be aware that there are significant misclassifications or disclosure omissions within the financial statements, or instances of non-compliance with applicable requirements of the *Companies Act* or accounting standards. If this is the case, the matter should be discussed with management with a view to making adjustments or giving additional disclosures. If such amendments are not made, accountants should withdraw from the engagement.

It should be noted that where accounts have been prepared using the micro-entity option, there is no requirement for the disclosure of a going concern note or a note of accounting policies. If the accounts have been properly prepared to include the minimum requirements under this regime, they will be presumed to give a true and fair view. However, should the micro-entity choose to include items in addition to the minimum requirements, the accountant must consider the relevant accounting standard in relation to that item and whether proper disclosure has been made.

Accountants also need to remember that they are bound by the Code of Ethics not to be knowingly associated with misleading information, including instances where the information may be misleading because of omissions. This may be relevant where the accounts of micro-entities are presumed to be true and fair but, on rare occasions, may be considered misleading perhaps due to the absence of key information.

If the accountant considers the financial statements to be misleading, he should discuss the matter with the client and hope to make relevant adjustments or disclosures. If management refuse to take any action, the accountant will consider withdrawing from the engagement.

In rare circumstances, accountants may conclude that they do not need to withdraw from the engagement despite apparent departures from accounting standards or incomplete information, for example due to inadequacies in the accounting records. In these situations, where appropriate disclosure has been made in the financial statements, the accountants may wish to highlight the matter by inclusion of an explanatory paragraph in their compilation report.

There may be rare occasions when professional accountants form an opinion that the information disclosed in accordance with the micro-entity regime is misleading.

8.3.5 Approving financial statements

The financial statements should be approved and signed by the directors before the accountants' report is signed.

The directors are statutorily responsible for their company's accounts. They are required to approve the accounts and the balance sheet should state the name of the directors signing the accounts on behalf of the board.

Under the *Companies Act* 2006, s. 475, a company is not entitled to audit exemption unless its balance sheet contains a statement by the directors to that effect. In addition, the directors must, on the face of the balance sheet, state that the members of the company have not required the company to obtain an audit of its accounts and acknowledge their responsibilities for complying with the requirements of the *Companies Act* with respect to keeping accounting records and the preparation of accounts.

8.3.6 Accountants' reports

The aim of the accountants' report is for readers to draw comfort from the fact that the accounts have been compiled by a chartered accountant who is subject to the ethical and other guidance issued by the Institute. The report will normally be addressed to the directors of the company.

The report should not be signed as 'registered auditor' or 'statutory auditor'.

An example report is given in **Table 2**.

The financial statements should contain a reference to the fact that they are unaudited, either on the front cover or on each page of the financial statements.

TABLE 2: Example accountants' report

Chartered Accountants'/Accountant's Report to the Board of Directors on the preparation of the Unaudited Statutory Accounts of XYZ Ltd for the year ended xxx

In order to assist you to fulfil your duties under the *Companies Act* 2006, we have prepared for your approval the accounts of XYZ Limited for the year ended xxx [as set out on pages x-x which comprise [*insert name of statements*] and the related notes from the company's accounting records and from information and explanations you have given us.

As a practising member/member firm of the Institute of the Chartered Accountants in England and Wales (ICAEW), we are subject to its ethical and other professional requirements which are detailed at www.icaew.com/en/members/regulations-standards-and-guidance/.

[This report is made to the Board of Directors of XYZ Limited, as a body, in accordance with the terms of our engagement letter dated xxx. Our work has been undertaken [solely to prepare for your approval the accounts of XYZ Limited and state those matters that we have agreed to state to the Board of Directors of XYZ Limited, as a body, in this report] in accordance with ICAEW Technical Release 07/16 AAF. To the fullest extent permitted by law, we do not accept or assume responsibility to anyone other than XYZ Limited and its Board of Directors, as a body, for our work or for this report.]

[It is your duty to ensure that XYZ Limited has kept adequate accounting records and to prepare statutory accounts that give a true and fair view of the assets, liabilities, financial position and profit [/loss] of XYZ Limited. You consider that XYZ Limited is exempt from the statutory audit requirement for the year.]

[We have not been instructed to carry out an audit or a review of the accounts of XYZ Limited. For this reason, we have not verified the accuracy or completeness of the accounting records or information and explanations you have given to us and we do not, therefore, express any opinion on the statutory accounts.]

[We draw your attention to note x in the financial statements which discloses and explains ...]

Signature

Typed name of professional accountant

Chartered Accountants

Address

Date

8.4 Unincorporated entities

8.4.1 Scope of guidance

TECH 08/16 AAF is intended to give general guidance to accountants when they compile historical financial information for their clients, and covers situations where the request is by unincorporated entities for a specific purpose, such as for tax purposes, partnership accounts or for grant claims. TECH 08/16 AAF replaced AAF 03/10.

However, where a set of financial statements which comply fully with the provisions of UK GAAP are requested for an unincorporated entity, the guidance in TECH 07/16 AAF should be followed (see **8.3**).

TECH 08/16 AAF may also be of use when accountants compile historical financial information, other than financial statements, for incorporated entities.

8.4.2 Professional ethics

When compiling historical financial information for unincorporated entities, accountants are bound by all ethical and other guidance laid down by the ICAEW. They should not, therefore compile, or allow their names to be associated with, financial information which they consider to:

- contain a materially false or be misleading statement;
- contain statements or information furnished recklessly; or
- omit or obscure information required to be included where such omission or obscurity would be misleading.

If the accountant has been associated with such information, he should take steps to disassociate himself.

8.4.3 Accounting basis

Accountants are not required to test assertions underlying the information which they are compiling and therefore are not able to express any assurance on the financial information being compiled.

There is no statutory requirement for the financial information of most unincorporated entities to give a true and fair view and it is acceptable to compile the information on an accounting basis other than full UK GAAP. The appropriate accounting basis should be discussed with the clients and clearly defined so that the accountants can compile the information.

The accounting basis, purpose and limitations of the information presented should be fully disclosed in a note to the financial information and referred to in the accountants' report.

8.4.4 Terms of engagement

As with compilations performed under TECH 07/16 AAF, there must be clear understanding between the client and the accountants regarding the terms of the engagement. An example engagement letter extract for the compilation of historical financial information under TECH 08/16 AAF is provided in **Table 3**.

In addition, accountants should consider whether it is appropriate to include a section on the limitation of the accountants' liability.

TABLE 3: Engagement letter extracts for the compilation of historical financial information for unincorporated entities

Client's responsibilities

You will be responsible for the reliability, accuracy and completeness of the accounting records.

You have undertaken to make available to us, as and when required, all your accounting records and related financial information, including minutes of management meetings, necessary to carry out our work. You will provide us with all the information and explanations relevant to the purpose and compilation of the financial information.

Scope of the accountants' work

You have asked us to assist you in the preparation of [insert type of information required] for [insert purpose]. We will compile the financial information for your approval based on the accounting records maintained by you and the information and explanations given to us by you.

We shall plan our work on the basis that no report is required by statute or regulation, unless you inform us in writing to the contrary. In carrying out our engagement, we will make enquiries of [management] and undertake any procedures that we judge appropriate but are under no obligation to perform procedures that may be required for assurance engagements such as audits or reviews.

Our work will not be an audit of the financial information in accordance with Auditing Standards. Consequently, our work will not provide any assurance that the accounting records or the financial information are free from material misstatement, whether caused by fraud, other irregularities or error and cannot be relied on to identify weaknesses in internal controls.

Since we have not carried out an audit, nor confirmed in any way the accuracy or reasonableness of the accounting records maintained by the company, we are unable to provide any assurance as to whether the financial information that we prepare from those records presents a true and fair view.

We have a professional duty to compile financial information that conforms with generally accepted accounting principles selected by management as being appropriate for the purpose for which the information is prepared. The accounting basis on which the information has been compiled, its purpose and limitations will be disclosed in an accounting policy note to the financial information and will be referred to in our accountants' report.

We also have a professional responsibility not to allow our name to be associated with financial information which we believe may be misleading. Therefore, although we are not required to search for such matters, should we become aware, for any reason, that the financial information may be misleading, we will discuss the matter with you with a view to agreeing appropriate adjustments and/or disclosures in the financial information. In circumstances where adjustments and/or disclosures that we consider appropriate are not made or where we are not provided with appropriate information, and as a result we consider that the financial information is misleading, we will withdraw from the engagement.

As part of our normal procedures, we may request you to provide written confirmation of any information or explanations given by you orally during the course of our work.

You will approve and sign the financial information thereby acknowledging responsibility for it, including the appropriateness of the accounting basis on which it has been compiled, and for providing us with all information and explanations necessary for its compilation.

Form of the accountants' report

We shall report to you that in accordance with this engagement letter we have compiled, without carrying out an audit, the financial information from the accounting records of the entity and from the information and explanation supplied to us. The report should not be used for any purpose other than as set out in this engagement letter.

Liability provisions

We will perform the engagement with reasonable skill and care. The total aggregate liability to you, of whatever nature, whether in contract, tort or otherwise, of [name of accountants] for any losses whatsoever and howsoever caused arising from or in any way connected with this engagement shall not exceed [amount].

8.4.5   Client's responsibilities

The client is responsible for the reliability, accuracy and completeness of the accounting records of the entity and for disclosing all relevant information to the accountant.

8.4.6 Planning

Having agreed a basis and format for the financial information, the accountant will plan the engagement. The level of planning will vary depending on the complexity and completeness of the client's accounting records and the reporting accountant's experience of the business.

8.4.7 Procedures

As in **8.3.3** above, reporting accountants will obtain a general understanding of the operations of the entity, consider whether the financial information is consistent with their understanding of the business and check whether relevant disclosures have been made. In addition, they will obtain written representations from management, particularly in relation to estimates and the reliability, accuracy and completeness of information provided to them.

The accountants are under no obligation to perform procedures that would be necessary to enable them to give assurance on the financial information.

There is no mandatory requirement to document the work carried out, although full documentation will assist with performing a good quality engagement.

8.4.8 Misleading financial information

Accountants compiling financial information for unincorporated entities have the same responsibilities towards misleading financial information as accountants working for incorporated entities (see **8.3.4**).

8.4.9 Approval of financial information

Although there is no statutory duty for the financial information of unincorporated entities to be signed or approved by the client, it is recommended that the client does sign the information to acknowledge their responsibility for it. An example wording is given in **Table 4**.

TABLE 4: Example wording for approval of financial information

In accordance with the engagement letter dated […], I/we approve the financial information which comprises [state the financial information compiled]. I/we acknowledge my/our responsibility for the financial information, including the appropriateness of the applicable financial reporting framework as set out in note [x], and for providing [the accountants] with all information and explanations necessary for its compilation.

8.4.10 Accountants' reports

As stated in **8.3.6** above, the aim of the accountants' report is to help users derive comfort from the fact that the financial information has been compiled by an accountant who is subject to the ethical and other guidance issued by the ICAEW. It also clarifies that an audit has not taken place. An example report wording for the compilation of financial information for unincorporated entities is given in **Table 5**.

TABLE 5: Example accountants' report for the compilation of financial information for unincorporated entities

Chartered Accountants'/Accountant's Report to [Entity] on Unaudited Financial Information of XYZ

In accordance with the engagement letter dated [date], we have prepared for your approval the financial information of [the entity] for the year [/period] which comprises [*insert names of statements*] and the related notes from the entity's accounting records and from information and explanations you have given to us.

As a practising member [/member firm] of the Institute of Chartered Accountants in England and Wales (ICAEW), we are subject to its ethical and other professional requirements which are detailed at www.icaew.com/en/members/regulations-standards-and-guidance/.

[This report is made solely to you in accordance with the terms of our engagement letter dated [date].] Our work has been undertaken [solely to prepare for your approval the financial information of [entity] and state those matters that we have agreed to state to you in this report] in accordance with ICAEW Technical release TECH 08/16 AAF. [To the fullest extent permitted by law, we do not accept or assume responsibility to anyone other than [addressee of this report] for our work or for this report.]

[You have approved the [financial information] [for the year/period] and have acknowledged your responsibility for it, for the appropriateness of the financial reporting framework adopted and for providing all information and explanations necessary for its compilation.

We have not verified the accuracy or completeness of the accounting records or information and explanations you have given to us and we do not, therefore, express any opinion on the financial information.]

Signature

Typed name of professional accountant

Chartered Accountants

Address

Date

8.5   Companies claiming audit exemption

8.5.1   Ineligible companies

Many companies that fulfil the size criteria for audit exemption (profit and loss, balance sheet or number of employees) are still required to have an audit. This may be because they are 'ineligible' under the legislation, such as public, banking and insurance companies, trade unions, employers' associations, certain companies that are members of groups and companies regulated under the *Financial Services Act*. An audit may also be required where the company's constitution requires it or where it is requested by the provider of finance.

8.5.2   Requirements when a company becomes exempt

Where a client company becomes audit exempt, either as a result of changing exemption limits, or due to changes in its size, the auditor should not continue to perform an audit without telling the client about the options available. Discussing these options will allow the auditor to point out the advantages of continuing with the annual audit process.

8.5.3   Engagement letters

Where there is a significant change in the nature of the services provided, a new engagement letter will be required. Therefore, when a client becomes audit exempt and takes advantage of that exemption a new engagement letter will be required, assuming the practitioner continues to act in some other capacity for that client. Where the client becomes entitled to take advantage of audit exemption but chooses not to do so it may nevertheless be desirable to issue a new engagement letter setting out the situation clearly.

8.5.4   Resignation procedures

Where a client becomes audit exempt and an audit is no longer requested for other reasons, the auditor does not, in theory, have to resign from office.

However, in order to avoid unnecessary risk relating to his position as auditor and risk arising should the exemption status of the company change in future, the auditor may wish to resign from office when an audit is no longer required. Normal procedures should be followed regarding statements to be made by the auditor on cessation of office (see **Chapter 38**).

The former Department of Trade and Industry (now Department for Business Industry and Skills) has advised that audit exemption is not, in itself, an issue that should be brought to the attention of members or creditors on the resignation of an auditor.

9 REPORTS TO FINANCIAL REGULATORS

9.1 Legal background

The auditor of certain regulated entities has special reporting responsibilities in addition to his responsibility to report on the financial statements of the entity. These may include:

- requirements to report to regulators on certain specific matters, such as the entity's procedures with regard to client assets;
- a more general statutory duty to report to regulators where matters come to the attention of the auditor in the course of his audit that may be of significance to the regulator in the performance of its functions; and
- a right to report to the regulator matters that fall outside the statutory duty to report, where the auditor considers it appropriate to do so in the public interest.

Regulators for this purpose are primarily the Financial Conduct Authority (FCA) and the Prudential Regulation Authority (PRA) but may include other bodies if empowered to act in this capacity by future legislation.

Details regarding the auditor's responsibilities are set out in applicable legislation, for example, the *Financial Services and Markets Act* 2000, the *Financial Services Act* 2012 and the EU Audit Regulation (Regulation EU 537/2014 of the European Parliament and of the Council) and the rules of the relevant regulator. Auditors of regulated entities should ensure that they are aware of their responsibilities in this respect.

Whilst this is a familiar area to auditors in the financial services sector, the widening scope of businesses now authorised and regulated by the FCA has broadened the auditor's responsibilities in this area which now covers insurance intermediaries, consumer credit and debt management activities as well as businesses more usually thought of as falling under a financial services umbrella.

In addition, as a result of the EU Audit Regulation which applies from 17 June 2016, public interest entities are now also included in the definition of regulated entities and auditors of public interest entities have a statutory duty to report to a regulator should certain matters come to their attention (see **9.7**).

9.2 Types of report

Two types of report made by the auditor to the regulator are covered in this chapter:

- opinions on client money and custody assets (**9.4** and **9.5**);
- special ad hoc reports on regulatory matters of material significance (**9.6**); and
- reports to the regulator in respect of public interest entities (**9.7**).

Opinions on interim profits are covered in **Chapter 46**.

9.3 Auditing standards and guidance

The following standards and guidance are relevant:

- Section B of ISA (UK and Ireland) 250 (Revised June 2016) *The auditor's statutory right and duty to report to regulators of public interest entities and regulators of other entities in the financial sector*;
- Practice Note 21 (Revised) *The audit of investment businesses in the United Kingdom*;
- FRC Assurance Standard *Providing assurance on client assets to the Financial Conduct Authority*, issued November 2015 (the Client Asset Assurance Standard).

This chapter has been updated to reflect the proposed changes in final draft ISAs issued by the FRC in April 2016. Subject to legislative changes in progress at the time of writing, it is expected that Section B of ISA (UK and Ireland) 250 (Revised June 2016) *The auditor's statutory right and duty to report to regulators of public interest entities and regulators of other entities in the financial sector* will take effect for periods commencing on or after 17 June 2016.

For earlier periods, ending on or after 15 December 2010, Section B of ISA 250 (UK and Ireland) *The auditor's right and duty to report to regulators in the financial sector* as issued in October 2009 is effective.

Practice Note 21 (Revised) was issued in December 2007 and updated earlier guidance to reflect the changes in regulatory arrangements and changes to Auditing Standards to that date. The sections of the Practice Note relating to providing assurance on client assets were superseded in October 2011 by Bulletin 2011/2, which also brought insurance intermediaries within its scope. When published, that Bulletin:

(a) contained all of the FRC's extant guidance relating to the provision of assurance to the FSA on client assets; and
(b) was the material referred to in SUP 3.10.5B G to which the FSA expected CASS auditors to have regard for reports issued on or after 30 September 2011.

Bulletin 3 was issued by the FRC in March 2013 to supplement the guidance contained in Bulletin 2011/2 for CASS auditors providing assurance to the FSA on client assets where the firm has outsourced certain services or functions to a third party administrator ('TPA').

Bulletin 2011/2 and Bulletin 3 were superseded in November 2015 by the FRC's Client Asset Assurance Standard which is effective for periods commencing 1 January 2016. This chapter has been updated to reflect the requirements of this Assurance Standard.

This chapter considers only the reports of auditors to regulators. Other aspects of the audits of investment businesses are covered in **Chapter 46**.

9.4 Respective responsibilities

A regulated business's management are required to:

- prepare financial statements which give a true and fair view of the state of affairs and the profit or loss for the period;
- establish and maintain adequate accounting and other records and systems of control;
- ensure clients' assets are protected and the rules on clients' assets are followed; and
- ensure that the entity complies with laws and regulations that apply to its activities, and for preventing non-compliance and detecting any that occurs.

The entity's auditor is required to prepare a report to the regulator on an annual basis stating whether the business complied with the FCA Rules concerning client assets (including client money) at the relevant dates.

The auditor should always be aware of any changes to the regulator's Rules during the period and the impact this will have on his report.

Details of the Rules applicable to auditors are contained within the FCA and PRA Handbooks.

The auditor must also notify the FCA or PRA, as applicable, if he is removed from office, resigns before the end of his term of office or is not reappointed. Any matters relevant to the removal, resignation or non-reappointment should be included in this communication. If there are no such matters, this must also be stated.

9.5 Client assets

The main purpose of the CASS (Client Asset) Rules, which are contained in the Business Standards section of the FCA's Handbook, is to ensure that the regulated business safeguards client assets, both in its day-to-day business and in the event of its insolvency. Chapter 6 of the CASS Rules contains the rules which a regulated business must comply with when it holds and/or safeguards and administers custody assets, whilst Chapter 7 sets out rules relating to when such a firm holds client money. Chapter 5 deals with client money arising in relation to insurance mediation (for example, broking) activities. Auditors have to report on this compliance under section 3.10 of the Supervision (SUP) section of the Handbook. Chapter 11 deals with client money arising in connection with debt management activities.

9.5.1 Background

Most firms that carry on investment business fall within the ambit of FCA rule SUP 3.10 regarding client assets. Such firms must appoint an auditor to prepare and submit a Client Assets Report to the FCA (a 'CASS auditor'). This may be the statutory auditor or another auditor engaged for this purpose. Similar rules apply to insurance intermediaries although not all insurance intermediaries are required to appoint a CASS auditor (see **9.5.12**). The CASS auditor's report must be made annually (or for a period of not more than 53 weeks) and provide an opinion on whether the firm:

- has maintained systems adequate to comply with the FCA's client money and custody rules (and if relevant, collateral and mandate rules) throughout the year; and
- was in compliance with those rules at the period end date.

The CASS auditor is also required to provide a schedule of breaches of CASS rules.

Where no CASS auditor has been appointed, the statutory auditor should be alert for circumstances that indicate that a CASS auditor is required. If the statutory auditor becomes aware of such circumstances, a report should be made to the firm and the FCA.

9.5.2 Determining whether a client assets report is required

The decision tree in **Table 1** assists with determining whether a client assets report is required by the FCA, and if so, which sort is required.

TABLE 1: Decision tree to determine whether a client assets report is required by the FCA

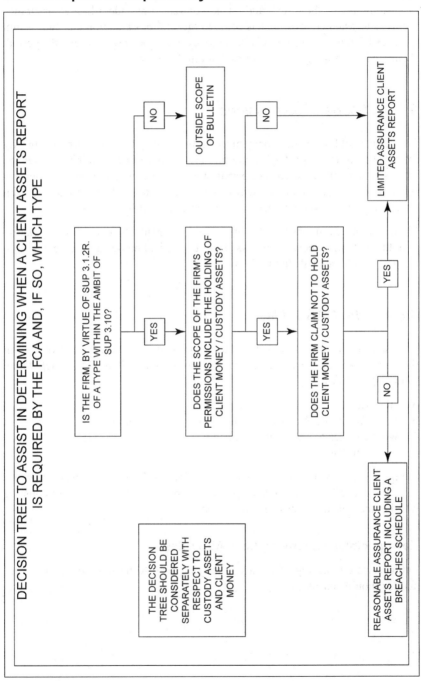

DECISION TREE TO ASSIST IN DETERMINING WHEN A CLIENT ASSETS REPORT IS REQUIRED BY THE FCA AND, IF SO, WHICH TYPE

THE DECISION TREE SHOULD BE CONSIDERED SEPARATELY WITH RESPECT TO CUSTODY ASSETS AND CLIENT MONEY

IS THE FIRM, BY VIRTUE OF SUP 3.1.2R, OF A TYPE WITHIN THE AMBIT OF SUP 3.10?

NO → OUTSIDE SCOPE OF BULLETIN

YES

DOES THE SCOPE OF THE FIRM'S PERMISSIONS INCLUDE THE HOLDING OF CLIENT MONEY / CUSTODY ASSETS?

NO → LIMITED ASSURANCE CLIENT ASSETS REPORT

YES

DOES THE FIRM CLAIM NOT TO HOLD CLIENT MONEY / CUSTODY ASSETS?

YES → LIMITED ASSURANCE CLIENT ASSETS REPORT

NO → REASONABLE ASSURANCE CLIENT ASSETS REPORT INCLUDING A BREACHES SCHEDULE

Limited assurance reports

Where a firm involved in investment business claims not to hold client money or custody assets, the CASS auditor is required to provide a limited assurance report as to whether anything has come to the auditor's attention that causes him to believe that the firm did hold client money or custody assets during the period. Example reports are given in **Tables 7, 8 and 9** below.

9.5.3 Scope of permissions

Firms must not hold client money or assets unless they have the correct authority from the FCA to do so. CASS auditors are required to determine whether the firm is acting within its scope of permissions. In order to determine whether this is the case, the CASS auditor will discuss the matter with those charged with governance and view the firm's Scope of Part IV Permissions notice.

If the auditor determines that the firm is acting outside its permission in relation to holding client money, custody assets or both client money and custody assets, a report should be made to the FCA.

9.5.4 The CASS rules

The main role of the CASS rules is to ensure that client assets are protected in the event of an insolvency of the firm. The provisions within CASS include the following suffixes:

- 'R' – Rule;
- 'E' – Evidential Provision, a rule which is not binding in its own right, but will be linked to a binding rule; and
- 'G' – Guidance.

A reportable breach will occur when a bindable rule is contravened. Where a firm has not followed a guidance provision, the CASS auditor should consider whether the linked rule has been breached.

Key principles underlying the CASS rules

Table 2 sets out the key principles underlying the CASS rules, which the CASS auditor should consider:

TABLE 2: Principles underlying the CASS rules

Principle	CASS 3 Collateral	CASS 5 Insurance Intermediaries	CASS 6 Custody Assets	CASS 7 Client Money	CASS 8 Mandates	CASS 11 Debt Management Firms
Identification: The firm should identify all sources of client assets and mandates in its business	X	X	X	X	X	X
Protecting client assets: The firm should make adequate arrangements to safeguard client ownership rights on the insolvency of the firm	X	X	X	X		X
Organisational arrangements: The firm's organisational arrangements should be adequate such that they comply with the CASS Rules	X	X	X	X	X	X
• Arrangements in respect of registration and recording of legal titles			X			
• Segregation of client money		X		X		X
• Safe custody assets used only as permitted by the CASS Rules	X		X			

Accurate records and accounts: The firm should have records and accounts that are maintained with sufficient accuracy (and on a timely basis) to enable the firm to comply with the CASS Rules	X	X	X	X	X	X
Reconciliations: The firm should perform internal and external reconciliations in accordance with the CASS Rules at the requisite frequency in order to rectify discrepancies		X	X	X		X
Rectify discrepancies in reconciliations: The firm should ensure that discrepancies arising from reconciliations are rectified appropriately		X	X	X		X
Trust: The firm should notify and obtain acknowledgement of trust status over client money		X		X		X
Non-statutory trust: The firm should ensure that the conditions for establishing a non-statutory trust are met		X				

Custody agreements: The firm should have appropriate custody agreements setting out the status of client custody accounts and prohibiting inappropriate liens		X			
Client money distributions: The firm should ensure that client money distributions are carried out in accordance with the CASS Rules	X		X		X

9.5.5 Scope of the Assurance Standard

The Client Asset Assurance Standard covers the following CASS Rules:

- *Collateral* (CASS 3) – these rules address arrangements whereby a firm is given the right to use a client's asset, and is allowed to treat the asset as if the firm has legal title and associated rights to it, subject to the requirement to return equivalent assets to the client upon satisfaction of the client's obligation to the firm;
- *Client Money* (CASS 5 and CASS 7 and CASS 11) – money of any currency that a firm holds for or on behalf of a client in connection with investment business or insurance mediation activity or debt management activities;
- *Client Money Distributions* (CASS 5.6 and 7A) – these rules aim to facilitate the timely return of client money to a client if the firm or a third party holding the client money fails;
- *Custody Assets* (CASS 6) – in relation to a non-MiFID ('Markets in Financial Instruments Directive' which allows firms incorporated and authorised in an EEA member state to provide those authorised services in another EEA member state) business, custody assets include:
  - a designated investment held for or on behalf of a client (otherwise known as a safe custody investment); and
  - any other asset, which is or may be held with a designated investment, held for, or on behalf of, a client.

For MiFID businesses, custody assets are financial instruments that the firm holds which belong to a client; and

- **Mandates** (CASS 8) – these rules apply to engagements where the firm controls rather than holds client assets or can enter arrangements that create liabilities on behalf of a client.

9.5.6 Accepting the engagement

In accordance with ISQC (UK and Ireland) 1 *Quality control for firms that perform audits and reviews of historical financial information and other assurance and related services engagements*, see **Chapter 3**, an engagement partner and the audit staff must have appropriate experience and competence to act for a client. Therefore, members of the CASS engagement team must have a knowledge and understanding of the CASS and other FCA Rules sufficient to perform the engagement. This may mean that the statutory audit team are not best placed to perform the CASS audit for complex firms and a specialist team may be used instead.

Where the statutory audit team and the CASS audit team are from the same firm, the terms of engagement for the CASS audit may be included in a separate section of the main engagement letter. Typically, the CASS auditor will refer in the engagement letter to the:

- responsibility of the directors or senior management to comply with applicable legislation and the FCA Handbook rules and guidance including the need to keep the FCA informed about the affairs of the firm;
- statutory right and duty of the CASS auditor to report directly to the FCA in certain circumstances; and
- requirement to cooperate with the CASS auditor, including allowing access to records information and explanations.

The FCA do not approve the appointment of the CASS auditor and so is not usually an addressee of the engagement letter. However, CASS auditors are required to cooperate with the FCA and notify them when they cease to hold office.

9.5.7 Assurance procedures

The FRC's Client Asset Assurance Standard sets out, in diagram form, the process required to form an opinion on compliance with the CASS Rules. This is set out in **Table 3**. The procedures involved include those required to form an opinion on:

- the adequacy of systems and controls; and
- compliance with the CASS Rules at the period end date (shown in the diagram as shaded boxes).

Actual or potential breaches of the rules may be identified at any stage of the process.

The Standard also sets out examples of specific procedures for both reasonable assurance and limited assurance engagements in the main body of the guidance and in the Appendix.

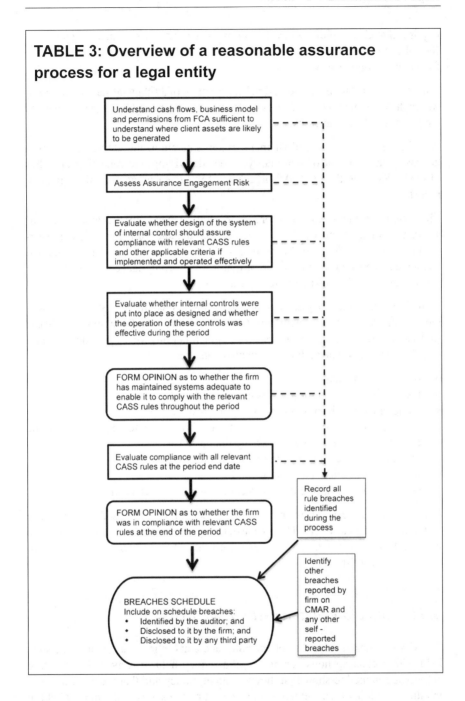

TABLE 3: Overview of a reasonable assurance process for a legal entity

Understand cash flows, business model and permissions from FCA sufficient to understand where client assets are likely to be generated

Assess Assurance Engagement Risk

Evaluate whether design of the system of internal control should assure compliance with relevant CASS rules and other applicable criteria if implemented and operated effectively

Evaluate whether internal controls were put into place as designed and whether the operation of these controls was effective during the period

FORM OPINION as to whether the firm has maintained systems adequate to enable it to comply with the relevant CASS rules throughout the period

Evaluate compliance with all relevant CASS rules at the period end date

Record all rule breaches identified during the process

FORM OPINION as to whether the firm was in compliance with relevant CASS rules at the end of the period

Identify other breaches reported by firm on CMAR and any other self-reported breaches

BREACHES SCHEDULE
Include on schedule breaches:
• Identified by the auditor; and
• Disclosed to it by the firm; and
• Disclosed to it by any third party

9.5.8   *Planning the engagement*

The objective of the CASS Rules is to ensure that client assets are safeguarded if the firm becomes insolvent. For this reason, the FRC's Assurance Standard requires that CASS auditors develop an 'insolvency mind-set', meaning that they should conduct their procedures against a level of stress which presumes that the firm may become insolvent.

This is in contrast to the traditional risk assessment of a financial statements audit, where the level of audit procedures performed is determined by the assessment of the various risks to the entity.

Also in contrast to a typical financial statements audit, the CASS auditor will not apply the concept of materiality when identifying and reporting breaches of CASS Rules to the FCA. All breaches, of whatever monetary value, must be reported.

The extent of the CASS auditor's work will depend on the assessment of assurance engagement risk. This is the risk that the auditor incorrectly expresses an unmodified opinion when reporting to the FCA that the firm has maintained adequate systems during the period or that it was in compliance with the relevant rules at the period end when in fact it was not.

In making the initial assessment of engagement risk, the CASS auditor will meet with senior management, the CASS compliance officer and the CF10a (individual approved for the CASS oversight function) for CASS medium and CASS large firms. The auditor would also consider:

- operations manuals;
- the firm's documentation of systems and controls;
- compliance monitoring programmes and results;
- records maintained by the firm of any rule breaches and notifications to the FCA that may have occurred during the period;
- the results of recent inspection visits made by the FCA;
- the register of client complaints; and
- any section 166 Skilled Persons Reports that may have been performed.

CASS auditors must ensure that they consider all systems used by the entity in relation to client assets. This is particularly relevant where client assets are held on deposit overnight, and are, therefore subject to different arrangements at different times of the day.

9.5.9   Statutory and non-statutory trusts

The CASS rules require that client bank accounts, client transaction accounts held with a clearing house or broker and money held in respect of mediation activity are named to show that they are client money and that the bank or other institution holding them acknowledges in writing the status of the money held in the account and the limitation of right of set off or counterclaim with other entity accounts.

The CASS auditor should consider whether the:

- client bank accounts and client transaction accounts include in their titles an appropriate description to distinguish them as client money;
- relevant acknowledgement letters relating to the trust status have been sent to and received from the bank/institution at which accounts have been opened;
- acknowledgement from the bank/institution has been received in the prescribed period set out by the CASS rules;
- body of the notification letters complies with the specific requirements set out in CASS 7;
- acknowledgment letters sufficiently distinguish the account to which they refer; and
- letters can be dated and attributed to the responsible party (i.e. the letterhead and signatory identifies their position within the firm).

9.5.10   Reconciliations

The CASS auditor is required to review client asset reconciliations as part of his work. These can often be complex in nature and a suitably senior member of the CASS audit team should be involved in performing this review to evaluate whether the justifications given for reconciling items are reasonable.

The CASS auditor should be particularly cautious in relation to:

- infrequent or sporadic reconciliations;
- poorly implemented system changes which lead to reconciling items;
- an excessive number of manual corrections or corrections caused by poor systems;
- the inclusion of non-client bank accounts in the reconciliation;
- client staff appearing to lack understanding of the CASS rules;
- a failure to escalate reconciling items to the appropriate level of management by client staff;
- poor documentation; and
- the reconciliation being performed by a person involved in the recording or movement of assets, resulting in a lack of segregation of duties.

9.5.11   Custody arrangements

The CASS auditor is required to ensure that the firm has complied with the rules in CASS 6.3 where custody assets held on behalf of a client are placed in an account with a third party.

The auditor should:

- obtain and document an understanding of the contractual terms between the firm and the third party;
- understand how the firm monitors the systems and controls in place at the third party;

- consider relevant reports from the third party's statutory auditor, internal auditor or other regulatory agencies; and
- consider whether they have access to all the information they require from the third party.

Failure to obtain sufficient information from the third party will result in a limitation in scope, which will affect the opinion in the client assets report.

9.5.12 Insurance intermediaries

CASS 5 governs firms undertaking insurance mediation activity and holding client money. Many of the requirements are similar to those governing client money held by investment businesses, however there are some significant differences of which CASS auditors must be aware and these are set out in the rules themselves.

In addition:

- insurance intermediaries holding no more than £30,000 client money in a statutory trust are not required to appoint a CASS auditor; and
- insurance intermediaries are not required to appoint a CASS auditor to give a limited assurance report when they claim not to hold client money.

Insurance intermediaries may use non-statutory trusts in accordance with rule CASS 5.4. This allows them to make advances of credit from the client money account to the firm's clients. The conditions and requirements surrounding use of non-statutory trusts are many and varied, including ensuring that the firm obtains, and keeps current, written confirmation from its CASS auditor that the firm has in place systems and controls which are adequate to ensure that the firm is able to monitor and manage its client money transactions and any credit risk arising from the operation of non-statutory trusts.

9.5.13 Debt management firms

Debt management firms now fall within the scope of FCA regulation. CASS Rule 11 extends CASS Rules and reporting requirements to such firms which are defined as firms which:

(a) carry on the activities of debt counselling or debt adjusting with a view to an individual entering into a particular debt solution;

(b) carry on the activity of debt counselling where an associate carries on debt adjusting with that aim (or vice versa); or

(c) is a not for profit debt advice body.

During a transitional period, some debt management firms are operating under interim permissions from the FCA and may not be required to comply in full with CASS rules. Auditors of such firms should check the firm's authorisation status and the rules that apply in the particular circumstances.

9.5.14   Mandates

Where a firm holds a mandate in respect of investment business or insurance mediation activity (except where it relates to a reinsurance contract) which allows the firm to control a client's assets or liabilities, that firm must establish and maintain adequate systems and internal controls which include:

- an up to date list of the authorities and any conditions placed by the client or the firm's management on their use;
- a record of all transactions entered into using the authority and internal controls to ensure that they are within the scope of the authority of the person and the firm entering into the transaction;
- the details of the procedures and authorities for giving and receiving of instructions under the authority;
- where the firm holds a passbook or similar document belonging to the client, internal controls for the safeguarding (including against loss, unauthorised destruction, theft, fraud or misuse) of any passbook or similar document belonging to the client and held by the firm.

The CASS auditor is required to perform procedures in relation to mandates to provide reasonable assurance that the firm maintained adequate systems to enable it to comply with the mandate rules and that the firm was in compliance with the mandate rules at the period end date. Bulletin 2011/2 gives example procedures in the appendix.

9.5.15   Using the work of the internal audit function

Where the client entity has an internal audit function, the scope of which covers control over client assets, the CASS auditor should consider the extent to which the work of the internal audit function is relevant for his purposes. The CASS auditor will, at least, wish to familiarise himself with the findings of the internal audit function and consider the implications thereof for his own work and reporting responsibilities.

Further guidance on matters to be considered when using the work of the internal audit function are set out in the FRC's Client Asset Assurance Standard and in **Chapter 31**.

The findings of internal audit in relation to breaches of CASS rules are of particular importance to the CASS auditor because the CASS auditor must report all CASS breaches in his CASS report and this includes any CASS breaches identified by the internal audit function. Whatever extent the CASS auditor relies on the work of internal audit, the responsibility for the client asset report will remain entirely with the CASS auditor.

9.5.16 Using the work of an expert

Although CASS auditors are expected to have a good knowledge of the CASS rules, there can sometimes be complex arrangements in place which may mean that CASS Rules are not applicable to an individual client money or asset balance or to the overall holdings of a particular client.

In these situations, it is important that the CASS auditor understands the underlying terms of client agreements to ascertain whether exemption provisions are correctly applied. The involvement of a legal specialist is likely to be required in such situations, and the guidance in section **31.3** will apply.

9.5.17 Reporting

A report on a client asset engagement is quite different to a report on financial statements as the engagement is specifically undertaken to address the needs of the FCA who are the users of the report.

If there has been any breach of a CASS rule during the year, a qualified or adverse opinion must be given as the concept of materiality does not apply as in the audit of financial statements. However, if all breaches identified in the period have been rectified by the period end, the CASS auditor may give a modified opinion on the period and a clean opinion on the period end compliance with CASS rules (see **Table 4**).

An adverse opinion is likely to be given where the breaches identified are indicative of a 'systemic or pervasive failure to comply with the principle of protecting client assets'. Considerations include:

- the extent to which clients might lose their assets if the firm had gone into administration while the breach persisted;
- whether there has been a breach of the requirement to keep proper records of client assets; and
- whether the firm has failed to carry out, or incorrectly carried out to a significant extent, the reconciliations or client money calculations required by the CASS Rules.

The client asset report contains two parts:

- the CASS auditor's opinion; and
- the breaches schedule.

Every breach within the period identified by the CASS auditor, the firm or notified by another party including the FCA itself, must be listed in the breaches schedule and if no breaches were found, a nil return must be made. Information about the severity, duration and frequency of each breach must also be given, together with details of the circumstances that gave rise to each breach and any remedial action undertaken.

The CASS auditor must deliver a draft of its client asset report to the firm prior to submitting it to the FCA so that the firm has an adequate period of time to consider the findings and provide the CASS auditor with comments explaining the circumstance that gave rise to the breaches included in the breaches schedule and to provide details of remedial action.

CASS auditors are required to submit their report to the FCA within four months of the end of the period covered with a copy of the final report also provided to the firm. For insurance intermediaries, the report must be delivered to the firm, rather than the FCA, within the same time period.

Examples of qualified, adverse, clean and limited assurance reports are set out in **Tables 4 to 9**.

TABLE 4: Example qualified reasonable assurance report

Reasonable assurance report on client assets by the independent auditor to the Financial Conduct Authority in respect of [name of firm], FCA reference number [number]

Part 1: Auditor's Opinion on Client Assets

We report in respect of [Firm name] ('the firm') on the matters set out below for the period started [dd/mm/yyyy] and ended [dd/mm/yyyy] ('the period').

Our report has been prepared as required by SUP 3.10.4R and is addressed to the Financial Conduct Authority (FCA) in its capacity as regulator of financial services firms under the *Financial Services and Markets Act* 2000.

Basis of opinions

We have carried out such procedures as we considered necessary for the purposes of this report in accordance with the Client Asset Assurance Standard issued by the Financial Reporting Council.

The opinions relate only to the period, or as at the date, specified. The opinions do not provide assurance in relation to any future period or date as changes to systems or controls subsequent to the date of this report may alter the validity of our opinions.

Qualified opinion on adequacy of systems during the period

In our opinion, except for the failure of the firm to perform a reconciliation of ... in March 20xx, as described in item 1 of the attached breaches schedule, the firm has maintained systems adequate to enable it to comply with the custody rules, collateral rules, mandate rules and client money rules throughout the period since the last date at which a report was made.

Unmodified opinion on compliance at period end date

In our opinion, the firm was in compliance with the custody rules, collateral rules, the mandate rules and the client money rules as at the period end date.

Other matters

This report should be read in conjunction with the Breaches Schedule that we have prepared and which is appended.

[Signature]

Address

John Smith for and on behalf of [Name of audit firm]

Date

Breaches Schedule

Part 2: Identified CASS Breaches that have occurred during the period

[Firm name], FCA reference number [number], for the period started [dd/mm/yyyy] and ended [dd/mm/yyyy]

In accordance with SUP 3.10.9AR, Columns A to D have been completed by and are the responsibility of the auditor. In accordance with SUP 3.11.1G, Column E has been completed by the firm. The auditor has no responsibility for the content of Column E.

Column A	Column B	Column C	Column D	Column E
Item No	Rule Reference(s)	Identifying Party	Breach Identified	Firm's Comment
1. (Illustrative details to be inserted)				

TABLE 5: Example adverse reasonable assurance report

Assurance report on client assets by the independent auditor to the Financial Conduct Authority in respect of [name of firm], FCA reference number [number]

Part 1: Auditor's Opinion on Client Assets

We report in respect of [Firm name] ('the firm') on the matters set out below for the period started [dd/mm/yyyy] and ended [dd/mm/yyyy] ('the period').

Our report has been prepared as required by SUP 3.10.4R and is addressed to the Financial Conduct Authority (FCA) in its capacity as regulator of financial services firms under the *Financial Services and Markets Act* 2000.

Basis of opinions

We have carried out such procedures as we considered necessary for the purposes of this report in accordance with the Client Asset Assurance Standard issued by the Financial Reporting Council.

The opinions relate only to the period, or as at the date, specified. The opinions do not provide assurance in relation to any future period or date as changes to systems or controls subsequent to the date of this report may alter the validity of our opinions.

Adverse opinion on adequacy of systems during the period

In our opinion, because of the systemic failure of the firm to carry out reconciliations of ... as described in lines 1 to 5 of the attached breaches schedule the firm did not maintain systems adequate to enable it to comply with the client money rules throughout the period since the last date at which a report was made.

Adverse opinion on compliance at period end date

In our opinion, because of the failure to perform the reconciliations described in lines 1 to 5 of the attached breaches schedule the firm was not in compliance with the client money rules as at the period end date.

Claim not to hold custody assets

The scope of the firm's permissions did not allow it to hold custody assets.

The directors of the firm have stated that the firm did not hold custody assets during the period. Based on review procedures performed, nothing has come to our attention that causes us to believe that the firm held custody assets during the period.

Other matters

This report should be read in conjunction with the Breaches Schedule that we have prepared and which is appended.

[Signature]

Address

John Smith for and on behalf of [Name of audit firm]

Date

Breaches schedule

Part 2: Identified CASS Breaches that have occurred during the period

[Firm name], FCA reference number [number], for the period started [dd/mm/yyyy] and ended [dd/mm/yyyy].

In accordance with SUP 3.10.9AR, Columns A to D have been completed by and are the responsibility of the auditor. In accordance with SUP 3.11.1G, Column E has been completed by the firm. The auditor has no responsibility for the content of Column E.

Column A	Column B	Column C	Column D	Column E
Item No	Rule Reference(s)	Identifying Party	Breach Identified	Firm's Comment
1. (Illustrative details to be inserted)				

TABLE 6: Example unmodified reasonable assurance report

Reasonable assurance report on client assets by the independent auditor to the Financial Conduct Authority in respect of [name of firm], FCA reference number [number]

Part 1: Auditor's Opinion on Client Assets

We report in respect of [Firm name] ('the firm') on the matters set out below for the period started [dd/mm/yyyy] and ended [dd/mm/yyyy] ('the period').

Our report has been prepared as required by SUP 3.10.4R and is addressed to the Financial Conduct Authority (FCA) in its capacity as regulator of financial services firms under the *Financial Services and Markets Act* 2000.

Basis of opinions

We have carried out such procedures as we considered necessary for the purposes of this report in accordance with the Client Asset Assurance Standard issued by the Financial Reporting Council.

The opinions relate only to the period, or as at the date, specified. The opinions do not provide assurance in relation to any future period or date as changes to systems or controls subsequent to the date of this report may alter the validity of our opinions.

Unmodified opinions on adequacy of systems during the period

In our opinion, the firm has maintained systems adequate to enable it to comply with the custody rules, collateral rules, mandate rules and client money rules throughout the period since the last date at which a report was made.

In our opinion [name of nominee companies], subsidiaries of the firm which are nominee companies during the period in whose name custody assets are registered, those nominee companies have maintained throughout the period systems for the custody, identification and control of custody assets which:

(a)   were adequate; and
(b)   included reconciliations at appropriate intervals between the records maintained (whether by the firm or the nominee company) and statements or confirmations from custodians or from the person who maintained the record of legal entitlement.

Unmodified opinion on compliance at period end date

In our opinion, the firm was in compliance with the [custody rules,] [collateral rules,] [the mandate rules] [and] [the client money rules] as at the period end date.

Unmodified opinion on secondary pooling event

In our opinion, in relation to the secondary pooling event during the period, the firm has complied with the rules in [CASS 5.6] [and] [CASS 7A] in relation to that pooling event.

Other matters

Our opinion expressed above does not extend to the appended Breaches Schedule.

[Signature]

Address

John Smith for and on behalf of [Name of audit firm]

Date

Breaches schedule

Part 2: Identified CASS Breaches that have occurred during the period

[Firm name], FCA reference number [number], for the period started [dd/mm/yyyy] and ended [dd/mm/yyyy].

In accordance with SUP 3.10.9AR, Columns A to D have been completed by and are the responsibility of the auditor. In accordance with SUP 3.11.1G, Column E has been completed by the firm. The auditor has no responsibility for the content of Column E.

Column A	Column B	Column C	Column D	Column E
Item No	Rule Reference(s)	Identifying Party	Breach Identified	Firm's Comment
			No breaches were identified	

TABLE 7: Example unmodified opinion limited assurance report where firm has permission to hold both client money and client assets and claims to hold neither

Limited assurance report on client assets by the independent auditor to the Financial Conduct Authority in respect of [name of firm], FCA reference number [number]

We report in respect of [Firm name] ('the firm') on the matters set out below for the period started [dd/mm/yyyy] and ended [dd/mm/yyyy] ('the period').

Our report has been prepared as required by SUP 3.10.4R and is addressed to the Financial Conduct Authority (FCA) in its capacity as regulator of financial services firms under the *Financial Services and Markets Act* 2000.

Basis of opinion

We have carried out such procedures as we considered necessary for the purposes of this report in accordance with the Client Asset Assurance Standard issued by the Financial Reporting Council.

The opinions relate only to the period, or as at the date, specified. The opinions do not provide assurance in relation to any future period or date.

Unmodified opinion

The directors of the firm have stated that the firm did not hold client money or custody assets during the period. Based on review procedures performed, nothing has come to our attention that causes us to believe that the firm held client money or custody assets during the period.

[Signature]

Address

John Smith for and on behalf of [Name of audit firm]

Date

TABLE 8: Example unmodified opinion limited assurance report where firm does not have permissions to hold client money and client assets and claims to hold neither

Limited assurance report on client assets by the independent auditor to the Financial Conduct Authority in respect of [name of firm], FCA reference number [number]

We report in respect of [Firm name] ('the firm') on the matters set out below for the period started [dd/mm/yyyy] and ended [dd/mm/yyyy] ('the period').

Our report has been prepared as required by SUP 3.10.4R and is addressed to the Financial Conduct Authority (FCA) in its capacity as regulator of financial services firms under the *Financial Services and Markets Act* 2000.

Basis of opinion

We have carried out such procedures as we considered necessary for the purposes of this report in accordance with the Client Asset Assurance Standard issued by the Financial Reporting Council.

The opinions relate only to the period, or as at the date, specified. The opinions do not provide assurance in relation to any future period or date.

Unmodified opinion

The scope of the firm's permissions did not allow it to hold custody assets.

The directors of the firm have stated that the firm did not hold client money or custody assets during the period. Based on review procedures performed, nothing has come to our attention that causes us to believe that the firm held client money or custody assets during the period.

[Signature]

Address

John Smith for and on behalf of [Name of audit firm]

Date

TABLE 9: Example modified limited assurance report on client assets where a firm holds client money but does not have permission to do so

Limited assurance report on client assets by the independent auditor to the Financial Conduct Authority in respect of [name of firm], FCA reference number [number]

We report in respect of [Firm name] ('the firm') on the matters set out below for the period started [dd/mm/yyyy] and ended [dd/mm/yyyy] ('the period').

Our report has been prepared as required by SUP 3.10.4R and is addressed to the Financial Conduct Authority (FCA) in its capacity as regulator of financial services firms under the *Financial Services and Markets Act* 2000.

Basis of opinion

We have carried out such procedures as we considered necessary for the purposes of this report in accordance with the Client Asset Assurance Standard issued by the Financial Reporting Council.

The opinions relate only to the period, or as at the date, specified. The opinions do not provide assurance in relation to any future period or date.

Modified opinion on client money

The scope of the firm's permissions allowed it to hold custody assets but not to hold client money.

The directors (or equivalent corporate officers) of the firm have stated that the firm did not hold client money or custody assets during the period. Arising from the findings of our review procedures, it came to our attention that, contrary to its permissions, the firm held client money [include information about how much client money is involved and the circumstances leading to the firm holding such client money] during [specify period during which client money was held].

Unmodified opinion on custody assets

Based on review procedures performed, nothing has come to our attention that causes us to believe that the firm held custody assets during the period.

[Signature]

Address

John Smith for and on behalf of [Name of audit firm]

Date

9.6   Special ad hoc reports

The *Financial Services and Markets Act* 2000, the *Financial Services Act* 2012 and regulations made under them (including the *FSMA 2000 (Communications by Auditors) Regulations* 2001 (SI 2001/2587)) impose a statutory duty on the auditors of an authorised firm, or the auditor of an entity closely linked to an authorised firm, to communicate certain matters to the regulator relevant to the regulator's functions, which has come to his attention 'in the capacity of auditor' during his audit work. The FRC's Assurance Standard on Client Assets notes that the FCA has confirmed that this duty applies also to a CASS auditor who is not appointed as statutory auditor of the entity.

Other regulations clarify the matters to be reported and extend the application of the statutory duty to information to which auditors of a financial institution become aware in their capacity as auditors of other entities with close links to the financial institution.

The EU Audit Regulation which applies for audits of accounting periods commencing on or after 17 June 2016 imposes a new duty to report to regulators on auditors of public interest entities. This is reflected in the requirements of ISA (UK and Ireland) 250 (Revised June 2016) and is considered in **9.7**.

9.6.1   Auditing standards and guidance

Standards and guidance on the implications of and the procedures necessary under these regulations are contained in Section B of ISA (UK and Ireland) 250 (Revised June 2016) *The auditor's right and duty to report to financial regulators*. This includes:

- the right and duty to report to regulators;
- material significance;
- procedures;
- reporting;
- communication with the regulator; and
- relationship with other reporting responsibilities.

Practice Notes have also been developed for different types of entity – for example, Practice Note 19 covers Banks and Building Societies and Practice Note 20 covers Insurers. Where entities are governed by more than one regulator, the auditor should ensure that they follow the guidance in each relevant Practice Note.

9.6.2   Right and duty to report

The auditor of a regulated entity is required to bring to the attention of the regulator information of which he becomes aware in the course of the work required to fulfil his audit responsibilities, which in his opinion is:

- relevant to the regulator's functions (such as breaches of regulator's Rules or concerns about the fit and proper status of management); and
- of material significance to the regulator.

For this purpose, Section B of ISA (UK and Ireland) 250 (Revised June 2016) defines a regulated entity as being an individual, company or other type of entity which is:

(i) authorised to carry on business in the financial sector which is subject to statutory regulation; or

(ii) a public interest entity (defined in **1.6.4**).

The auditor has a statutory duty to report certain other information, typically breaches of regulations which may come to his attention during his work. The auditor is not required to perform any additional procedures to search out these matters. This statutory duty applies only to information which comes to the auditor in his capacity as auditor. Guidance on what constitutes information gained in his capacity as auditor is given in the ISA (UK and Ireland).

If the information is discovered by someone not involved in the audit, but it is of relevance to the audit, and the work that it related to, it should be taken into account as if it were audit evidence. If the work is not relevant to the audit then it is unlikely that it will give rise to a duty to report.

Where information is discovered in the course of work performed for another client the auditor has no right to breach his duty of confidentiality in respect of it. However, he may choose to make enquiries during the audit of the regulated entity to establish whether the information can be substantiated from that source.

The guidance stresses that firms should ensure that they have suitable lines of communication so that any information which may give rise to a duty to report is brought to the attention of the partner responsible for the audit, usually by enquiries of other members of the firm as part of the audit planning and completion.

The statutory right to report to the regulator is not affected if the auditor ceases to hold office. Hence, if he is aware of information, this may be reported either before or after ceasing to hold office.

The auditor may have a right to report certain matters direct to the regulator in addition to those which he has a duty to report. This right will usually be exercised where the auditor considers that doing so is necessary to protect the interests of those for whose benefit the regulator is required to act.

9.6.3 'Material significance'

'Material significance' is defined in ISA (UK and Ireland) 250 (Revised June 2016) as being where the regulator is likely to investigate a matter because of its nature or potential financial impact. Material significance does not mean the same as materiality in the context of the audit of financial statements. Whilst an event may be trivial in its financial impact, it may be of a nature or type likely to change the perception of the regulator. Further guidance concerning particular types of regulated entity is contained in the Practice Notes.

Under the *Financial Services and Markets Act*, statutory definitions are provided for matters giving rise to a duty to report. They are generally matters which the auditor has a reasonable cause to believe will, or may be, of material significance in determining whether:

- a person is a fit and proper person to carry on investment or other regulated business; or
- disciplinary action or powers of intervention should be used to stop investors suffering loss.

Although the particular nature of the various sectors are considered in the legislation, in general the definitions incorporate the following terms:

- circumstances indicating that the regulated entity's authorisation could be revoked;
- there is, has been, or may have been, either:
  - a failure to fulfil specified requirements; or
  - a contravention of other provisions of the Rules which is likely to be of material significance to the regulator concerned for the exercise of its functions;
- there is a doubt as to the entity's status as a going concern; and
- the auditor concludes that his report on the entity's financial statements should include a qualified opinion.

Practice Note 21 gives additional guidance on the meaning of material significance in relation to investment businesses. It states that any breach of the regulator's Rules may be reportable, whether an isolated or recurring breach, depending on size or significance, and the auditor must use his judgment in determining whether a breach will be of material significance to the regulator. In doing so, the auditor must consider both the facts of the matter and their implication.

Status of regulated entities, directors and senior management as fit and proper persons

When planning the audit, the auditor must familiarise himself with any guidance issued by the regulator on the information that it takes into consideration when deciding whether the fit and proper requirement has been met.

Generally, the regulator assesses entities against three broad measures:

- honesty;
- competence; and
- solvency.

Although the auditor cannot be expected to make judgments on competence, soundness of judgment and diligence, there may be persuasive evidence which calls the appropriateness of some of the entity's actions into question. Therefore, the auditor should be alert for any indication of shortfalls in any of the following areas:

- probity, honesty, skill, care and integrity;
- attention to establishing satisfactory compliance arrangements;
- attention to compliance with notification requirements;
- observing appropriate standards of market practice; and
- openness with the regulator.

Any report on the fitness and propriety of the entity, or any of its directors or management, should be made to the regulator without prior reference to the directors of the entity.

Risk of loss – client assets

The auditor should report any identified deficiency in client assets which cannot be explained or accounted for, as well as any suspicions that misappropriation of assets may occur. Immediate action is required to ensure that the regulator can take appropriate action to protect client assets from future loss.

Risk of loss – financial position

Areas of material significance to the regulator will be those that indicate:

- the occurrence or possibility of a material loss to the regulated entity; or
- the breach, or likelihood of breach, by the entity of the requirements concerning the adequacy of its financial resource or solvency requirements.

A material loss to the business will include an event leading to a loss which is material in meeting the entity's solvency or capital adequacy requirements, or the requirement of a subsidiary, related or nominee company. This may include litigation against the entity, which may give rise to contingent liabilities and costs in defending the action.

An entity may be required to notify the regulator if its financial resources fall below a multiple of the financial requirement (e.g. 110%). Failure to make this notification will also be regarded by the regulator as having material significance.

Compliance with requirements for the management of its affairs

Areas that the auditor is likely to be aware of as a result of his work include:

- significant concerns over the internal control environment;
- disagreements or lack of evidence about amounts in the financial statements which cannot be resolved;
- material breaches of client asset rules and the rules requiring suitable systems in relation to client assets;

- evidence of business being conducted outside the entity's authorised scope; and
- significant matters affecting the regulated businesses' appointed representatives.

Doubt as to the entity's status as a going concern

Any doubt as to the entity's ability to continue to undertake investment business should be reported to the regulator.

9.6.4   Procedures

Section B of ISA (UK and Ireland) 250 (Revised June 2016) stresses that neither the legislation nor the ISA require the auditor to perform any extra work to discover information that may give rise to a duty to report. The duty relates only to work performed to fulfil other reporting responsibilities where the auditor must be alert to instances which would give rise to a duty to report.

Although there is no obligation to perform additional procedures, time must still be spent complying with the regulator's Rules. When planning, time must be allocated to understanding the Rules. Additionally, if matters which may give rise to the duty have been found, further procedures are necessary to assess whether the matter should be reported, and if so, how.

The duty does not only cover matters which are in the financial statements or are covered by the requirements of the auditor's standard report to the regulator, as there may be implications for the regulator's functions in any information discovered during the audit. For example, where information comes to light which could cast doubt on the fit and proper status of the management, this should be investigated and reported if appropriate, even though it is not a matter that the annual report to the regulator covers.

Closely linked entities

During planning, the auditor should establish whether any closely linked entities exist, of which he is also auditor. A closely linked entity is a:

- parent undertaking;
- subsidiary undertaking;
- parent undertaking of a subsidiary undertaking; or
- subsidiary undertaking of a parent undertaking.

Where such entities exist and are commonly audited, the auditor considers the significance of the entities and the nature of the issues that might arise which may be of material significance to the regulator. The audit engagement partner should contact the audit engagement partner of the closely linked entity to inform them of the audit firm's responsibility to report to the regulator and notify them of circumstances which might be of material significance to the regulator. These would include:

- activities or uncertainties within the closely linked entity which might significantly impair the financial position of the regulated entity;
- money laundering; and
- if the closely linked entity is itself regulated, matters that the auditor of the closely linked entity are intending to report to its regulator.

Prior to completion of the audit, the auditor of the regulated entity should obtain written confirmation that such circumstances do not exist from the other audit team. If circumstances do exist, further information may need to be obtained from the other auditors and the closely linked entity itself.

There is no duty for the auditors of the closely linked entity to make a report to the regulator, unless they are themselves regulated.

Planning

As part of his assessment of the accounting systems and internal controls, the auditor should consider the control environment, including the attitude of management to compliance with the relevant regulator's Rules. The auditor should also assess whether the business is being conducted outside its authorisation as this could result in a need to report.

Application material in the ISA notes that in the context of a regulated entity, the auditor's understanding of the entity and its environment needs to extend to applicable statutory provisions, the rules of the regulator and guidance on application of those rules issued by the regulator or other relevant authority, including the FRC.

Supervision and control

ISA (UK and Ireland) 250 also requires staff involved in regulated business audits to obtain a sufficient knowledge of what constitutes reportable matters to be able to identify them. Practice Note 21 states that as a basic minimum, the knowledge of all staff involved in the audit of a regulated business will extend to:

- the provisions of the Regulations concerning the auditor's duty to report to the regulators (*FSMA 2000 (Communication by Auditors) Regulations* 2001);
- Section B of ISA (UK and Ireland) 250 (Revised June 2016);
- Practice Note 21;
- the *Principles for Businesses and Thresholds Conditions* set out in the FCA's Handbook; and
- the types of business which require authorisation by other regulatory authorities.

In addition, and depending on the individual's role in the engagement, understanding will be required of the regulator's Rules and guidance relating to matters on which auditors are routinely required to report, in particular section 3 of the regulator's *Supervision Manual*.

Other staff who are only involved in non-audit work for a regulated entity are not required to have a detailed knowledge of the regulator's Rules nor to bring any information to the attention of the audit partner. However, there should be procedures in firms to ensure that any relevant relationship is notified to the partner responsible for the audit by other departments of the firm.

Identifying matters requiring a report

When the auditor becomes aware of matters that he suspects may give rise to a report to the regulator, he should:

- obtain evidence to assess the implications for reporting;
- determine whether the matter is of material significance to the regulator; and
- consider whether the breach is criminal conduct that gives rise to criminal property, and therefore should be reported to the relevant authority.

It is necessary to perform these procedures in this order because not all matters may be of material significance and this may only be apparent once the matter has been investigated further. Minor breaches may be reportable if they indicate a general lack of compliance which calls into question the fit and proper status. Breaches which have been rectified and reported by the entity itself do not normally need to be reported by the auditor, but if they have not been rectified or reported then a report may be required.

It is not necessary to collect sufficient evidence to determine the full implications of the matter before deciding to report. It is only necessary that there are reasonable grounds. What constitutes reasonable grounds is a matter for professional judgment. Such a judgment will be based on:

- discussions with management and staff; and
- a review of correspondence and documents relating to the matter.

Certain matters, such as a loss of client money, may be so serious as to necessitate an immediate report to the regulator to prevent further losses being sustained.

The evidence obtained by the auditor should be documented so that his decision whether to proceed with a report can be clearly demonstrated should the need arise in the future.

Items reportable on an ad hoc basis

Appendix 6 to Practice Note 21 sets out a number of 'themes' within which 'relevant requirements' or matters of concern which may give rise to a statutory duty to report are likely to fall. These are reproduced in **Table 10**.

> ## TABLE 10: Examples of items reportable on an ad hoc basis
>
> - controllers, directors and senior management who may not be 'fit and proper';
> - serious breaches of law/regulations;
> - potential disciplinary action against the firm or directors;
> - undertaking activities outside the scope of their permission;
> - failure to comply with limitations or restriction on permission or individual requirements;
> - false or misleading information given to the regulator or matters concealed;
> - problems with another 'regulator', or overseas regulators;
> - breaches of prudential limits and/or any financial limits;
> - significant actual or potential loss by investors, e.g. loss of customer assets or breach of client money rules; where there appear to be conflicts of interest; where there appears to be systemic abuse of advice or discretionary decisions; or as identified by complaints or by cases where a customer sues under FSMA, s. 150;
> - failure to clearly allocate responsibilities between senior managers or to implement clear reporting lines;
> - major systems and control weaknesses (including major reconciliation failures and backlogs);
> - possible going concern issues; and
> - adverse skilled person's report or qualified auditor's report.

Cumulative minor breaches

Minor breaches would not normally be of material significance to the regulator and give rise to an ad hoc report. However, the auditor of a regulated entity is required to review whether the cumulative effect of a number of minor breaches is such as to give rise to a duty to report to the regulator. The auditor may wish to seek legal advice on whether such a report would be necessary.

The facts and circumstances of his decision to report or not should be clearly documented in the audit working papers.

Use of other auditors

In group audit situations, the group auditor is not necessarily expected to have all the knowledge of components of the group that component auditors may have acquired in the course of their audits. However, the auditor of a regulated entity (including a public interest entity) should establish arrangements such that other auditors bring to their attention any matters that may give rise to a duty to report to a regulator.

9.6.5   Reporting

ISA (UK and Ireland) 250 (Revised June 2016) does not suggest a format for the report, only that it should be 'in a form and manner which will facilitate appropriate action'. The report should be made without delay and may be made orally, so long as it is followed up in writing. Normally, the auditor should agree the report to the regulator with the directors before it is made and a copy of the report should be sent to the directors.

Where a statutory duty to report arises, the auditor must report the matter, even if it has already been reported by another party, including the directors.

Where the matter in question casts doubt on the integrity of those charged with governance or their competence to conduct the business of the regulated entity, then the auditor should report as soon as practicable to the regulator without informing those charged with governance. Application material in the ISA notes that in such extreme cases speed is of the essence and that the auditor may wish to take legal advice.

Where the matter involves evidence or suspicion of fraud or criminal activity that would fall within the scope of money laundering regulations, auditors need also to consider their responsibilities under these regulations (see **Chapter 18**) and be careful to avoid any activity that would amount to 'tipping off'.

Auditor's right to report directly to regulators

Under FSMA 2000, auditors are not held to breach any duty by communicating in good faith to the regulator, information or an opinion on a matter that they reasonably believe is relevant to any functions of the regulator. This only applies to information obtained as auditors. Auditors should ensure compliance with legislation relating to 'tipping off' (see **Chapter 18**).

In addition to the statutory duty to report directly, the auditor has a right to do so where he believes the matter to be relevant to the regulator's function and the directors have not informed the regulator themselves. On discovery of such a matter, the auditor should inform the directors in writing that, in his opinion, it should be reported, and if he does not obtain evidence within a reasonable period that the directors have reported it, he should do so himself.

The auditor may wish to take legal advice before deciding on what, and in what form, to report. However, it is important to balance this against the need for prompt reporting to protect the interests of investors.

9.6.6   Form of report

Section B of ISA (UK and Ireland) 250 (Revised June 2016) states that the report should include the following:

- the name of the regulated entity;
- the statutory power under which the report was made;
- a statement that it has been prepared in accordance with ISA (UK and Ireland) 250 (Revised June 2016), Section B;
- a description of the context in which the report is given;

- a description of matters giving rise to the report;
- a request that the regulator confirms receipt of the report; and
- the name of the auditor making the report, the date of the written report and, if appropriate, the date of the oral report and the name of the person to whom it was made.

The description of the matter should give an indication of the extent of any discussions with the directors on the matter.

The context of the report will depend on several matters such as:

- the nature of the appointment from which the report derives;
- the interpretation of the relevant legislation;
- the extent to which the auditor has investigated the matter;
- whether the matter has been discussed with the directors; and
- whether steps have been taken to rectify the matter.

9.6.7 Communication by the regulator

The regulator may pass on to the auditor any information which it considers relevant to his function. Auditors are bound by the confidentiality provisions set out in the *Financial Services and Markets Act* 2000, Pt. XXIII (Public record, disclosures of information and cooperation). Communications of this nature must be treated as confidential by the auditor and must not be disclosed to his client or any other party without the express permission of the regulator or the other party. The regulator will indicate if anyone at the client has been informed of the matter.

The regulator has confirmed that it will take the initiative in communicating with auditors. The most likely matters are those which may affect the opinion that the auditor gives on the financial statements. However, the auditor should not assume that no communication from the regulator means that there is nothing that may be materially significant.

Where information has been brought to his attention, the auditor may need to amend his approach, but there is no requirement to change the scope of his work or actively investigate the matter further, unless specifically requested to do so by the regulator.

9.6.8 Relationship with other reporting responsibilities

Where matters have been reported directly to regulators, the auditor should consider the implications for his report on the financial statements. These are most likely to give rise to contingencies or other uncertainties which should be disclosed in the financial statements.

Table 11 provides a flowchart showing actions to be taken when a breach is suspected.

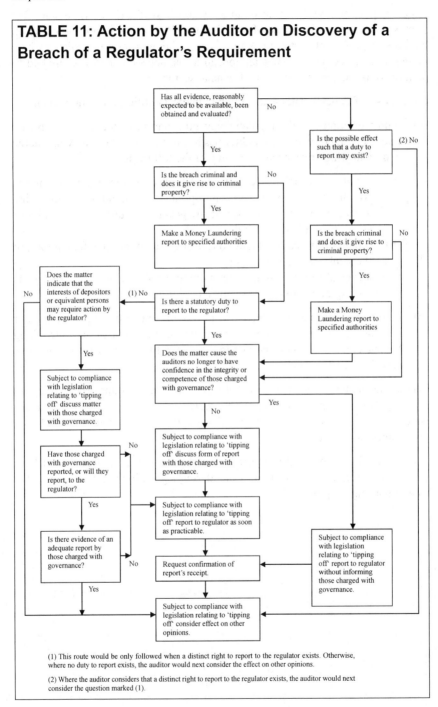

TABLE 11: Action by the Auditor on Discovery of a Breach of a Regulator's Requirement

(1) This route would be only followed when a distinct right to report to the regulator exists. Otherwise, where no duty to report exists, the auditor would next consider the effect on other opinions.

(2) Where the auditor considers that a distinct right to report to the regulator exists, the auditor would next consider the question marked (1).

9.7 Public interest entities

A new requirement was introduced into Section B of ISA (UK and Ireland) 250 (Revised June 2016) by virtue of the EU Audit Regulation imposing a duty on auditors of public interest entities to report to the appropriate regulator where certain matters come to their attention, in a manner similar to that applied to auditors of regulated entities in the financial sector.

For audits of financial statements of public interest entities, the auditor shall:

(a) report promptly to the regulator any information concerning that public interest entity of which the auditor has become aware while carrying out the audit and which may bring about any of the following:

   (i)   a material breach of the laws, regulations or administrative provisions which lay down, where appropriate, the conditions governing authorisation or which specifically govern pursuit of the activities of such public interest entity;

   (ii) a material threat or doubt concerning the continuous functioning of the public interest entity; or

   (iii) a refusal to issue an audit opinion on the financial statements or the issuing of an adverse or qualified opinion;

(b) report any information referred to in (i)–(iii) above of which the auditor becomes aware in the course of carrying out the audit of an undertaking having close links with the public interest entity for which they are also carrying out the audit.

Where the matter giving rise to a duty to report casts doubt on the integrity or competence of those charged with governance, the report to the regulator should be made as soon as possible and without informing those charged with governance in advance.

When considering making a report to the regulator, the auditor should have regard to the requirements of money laundering legislation and in particular the rules regarding 'tipping off'.

10 COMMUNICATING WITH MANAGEMENT AND THOSE CHARGED WITH GOVERNANCE

10.1 Introduction

Auditors are required by ISAs (UK and Ireland) to communicate with management and/or those charged with governance on a number of matters relating to the audit.

In addition, auditors may be requested to provide other reports to management and those charged with governance in connection with their audit work – for example, on the adequacy of the company's system of internal control, on significant findings and on possible improvements to the financial and accounting efficiency of the business. The timing, form and content of such reports should be covered in the engagement letter between the auditor and his client.

This chapter considers the principal requirements of the ISAs, particularly in the context of ISA (UK and Ireland) 260 (Revised June 2016) *Communication with those charged with governance* and ISA (UK and Ireland) 265 *Communicating deficiencies in internal control to those charged with governance and management*.

This chapter has been updated to reflect the proposed changes contained in final draft ISAs issued by the FRC in April 2016. Subject to legislative changes in progress at the time of writing it is expected that ISA (UK and Ireland) 260 (Revised June 2016) will take effect for periods commencing on or after 17 June 2016. Although ISA 265 (UK and Ireland) was not revised, it does contain some amended application material in respect of public interest entities.

The revision to ISA (UK and Ireland) 260 (Revised June 2016) includes changes affecting public interest entities due to the Audit Regulation and Directive, these are detailed in the chapter and include the requirement to communicate certain matters in an additional report to the audit committee (see **10.7.2**). In addition, the communication surrounding planned scope and timing of audit work has been clarified and this is covered in **10.6.3**.

For earlier periods, commencing on or after 1 October 2014, the version of ISA (UK and Ireland) 260 issued in September 2014 applies.

The current version of ISA (UK and Ireland) 265 was issued in October 2009 and is effective for the audit of financial statements for periods ending on or after 15 December 2010. ISA (UK and Ireland) 265 is discussed in **10.10** below.

ISA (UK and Ireland) 260 (Revised June 2016) sets standards and provides guidance on:

- determining the appropriate person(s) within the governance structure for communications;
- matters to be communicated;
- the communication process; and
- documentation of that communication.

ISA (UK and Ireland) 265 considers the specific case of reporting significant deficiencies in internal control.

10.2 Determining those charged with governance

ISA (UK and Ireland) 260 (Revised June 2016) defines those charged with governance as including 'the directors (executive and non-executive) of a company or other body, the members of an audit committee where one exists, the partners, proprietors, committee of management or trustees of other forms of entity, or equivalent persons responsible for directing the entity's affairs and preparing its financial statements'.

Depending on the nature and circumstances of the entity, management, i.e. those persons who perform senior management functions, may include some or all of those charged with governance, for example the executive directors of a company. Non-executive directors are not usually part of management.

The auditor needs to determine the appropriate person or people within the governance structure with whom to communicate. Where the auditor communicates with a sub-group of those charged with governance, for example, an audit committee, he should consider whether it is appropriate also to communicate with the governing body as a whole.

For audits of public interest entities, ISAs require certain matters to be communicated to an audit committee, and ISA (UK and Ireland) 260 requires the auditor to include these matters in an additional report to the audit committee (see **10.7.2**). If the entity does not have an audit committee, the additional report to the audit committee is to be submitted to the body performing equivalent functions within the entity.

10.3 Aims of reports to those charged with governance

The auditor should aim to develop a constructive working relationship with those charged with governance, whilst retaining his independence and objectivity, and under ISA (UK and Ireland) 260 (Revised June 2016), one of his objectives is to promote effective two-way communication with those charged with governance.

The main purposes of such communication are:

- to assist the auditor and those charged with governance in understanding matters related to the audit. This includes communicating clearly the responsibilities of the auditor in relation to the audit and an overview of the planned timing and scope of the work;
- to assist the auditor in obtaining information from those charged with governance that is relevant to the audit. This includes the auditor making enquiries of those charged with governance regarding their knowledge of actual or suspected fraud, non-compliance with laws and regulations and their reasons for not adjusting misstatements in the financial statements detected by the auditor; and
- to assist those charged with governance in fulfilling their responsibilities in relation to the financial reporting process, thereby reducing the risks of material misstatement in the financial statements. This includes communication by the auditor of audit findings and other matters of governance interest.

All reports to the client should be relevant to the particular client, and the auditor should consider the extent, form and frequency of reports in relation to the size and nature of the client. The attitude of those charged with governance and the importance of the issues to be raised may also affect the format and timing of reports. For example, reports of relatively minor matters to a small client may be best handled orally via a meeting or telephone conversation rather than by a formal written report. These considerations are discussed further in **10.4** below.

All reports should be made on a timely basis to allow those charged with governance to take appropriate action. Timely communication throughout the audit contributes to the achievement of robust two-way dialogue between those charged with governance and the auditor. The speed with which the auditor reports will depend on the nature of the issue arising, but matters relating to the qualitative aspects of the entity's accounting and financial reporting will usually be communicated prior to the approval of the financial statements. When ISA (UK and Ireland) 701 applies (see **Chapter 4**), the auditor may communicate preliminary views about key audit matters when discussing the planned scope and timing of the audit, and he also may have more frequent communications to further discuss such matters when communicating about significant audit findings.

10.4   The communication process

10.4.1   Establishing expectations

At an early stage in their relationship, the auditor should agree the level of detail and timing of communication between himself and those charged with governance.

This will vary depending on the circumstances of the client. The auditor should also clarify that he will only report matters which he considers relevant to those charged with governance as a result of his normal audit procedures, and will not perform additional procedures specifically to determine other matters to report.

Such communication is often made in the engagement letter (see **Chapter 14**). The auditor is required to set out that he is responsible for forming and expressing an opinion on the financial statements which have been prepared by those charged with governance and that the audit does not relieve those charged with governance of their responsibility for the financial statements.

10.4.2   Form of communication and documentation

Certain communications need to be made in writing. These are:

- agreement to the terms of the engagement (engagement letter);
- in the case of a listed[1] entity:
  - the communications regarding auditor independence specified in **10.6.5**; and
  - any contingent fee arrangements for non-audit services provided by the auditor or members of the same network;
- in the case of a public interest entity[2]:
  - the communications regarding independence set out in **10.6.5**;
  - the additional report to the audit committee must be in writing. This report is to be signed and dated by the engagement partner; and
  - upon request by either the auditor or the audit committee, the auditor shall discuss key matters arising from the audit, referred to in the additional report to the audit committee (see **10.7.2**), and in particular any deficiencies communicated;
- significant deficiencies in internal control (see **10.10**); and
- matters on which the auditor is required to obtain written representations (representation letter – see **32.4**).

In addition, the auditor should communicate in writing with those charged with governance regarding significant findings from the audit if, in his professional judgment, oral communication would not be adequate.

Due to the nature and sensitivity of fraud involving senior management, or fraud that results in a material misstatement in the financial statements, the auditor may also consider it necessary to report such matters in writing.

---

[1] A listed entity is one whose shares, stock or debt are quoted or listed on a recognised stock exchange, or are marketed under the regulations of a recognised stock exchange or other equivalent body.
In the UK and Ireland, this includes those listed on the London Stock Exchange (including those admitted to trading on the Alternative Investments Market), ISDX Markets and the Irish Stock Exchange (including those admitted to trade on the Irish Enterprise Securities Market). It does not include entities whose quoted or listed shares, stock or debt are in substance not freely transferable or cannot be traded freely by the public or the entity.
[2] See **1.6.4** for definition.

Other communications may be made orally. However, the auditor may judge that for effective communication a written communication is issued even if its content is limited to explaining that there is nothing he wishes to draw to the attention of those charged with governance. To avoid doubt, where there are no matters the auditor wishes to communicate in writing, he may issue a written communication to that effect.

Where communication has been made in writing, the auditor should retain a copy as part of the audit documentation.

ISA (UK and Ireland) 260 (Revised June 2016) requires that where matters are communicated orally, a record should be retained in the audit documentation showing what was communicated, to whom and when. In many cases, this will be a copy of the minutes of a meeting at which the issue was discussed.

Additionally, for audits of public interest entities, the auditor is required to retain any other data and documents that are important in supporting the additional report to the audit committee (see **10.7.2**) as part of the audit documentation.

Typically, the auditor will discuss his findings with management or those with direct responsibility for an area, where appropriate to do so, before reporting them to those charged with governance. This should ensure that all facts are clarified as well as providing management with an opportunity to provide further explanations. Where it will aid the understanding of those charged with governance, the auditor may include details of comments made by management in his final communication.

10.4.3 Addressees

The auditor should use judgment to determine to whom he communicates certain matters. This may be contrary to the arrangement agreed at the start of the audit if the matter is sufficiently important to require reporting directly to the board or governing body.

For listed companies and other entities where they have been constituted, reports will often be made to the audit committee. However, auditors and boards should understand that a report to the audit committee will only form part of the auditor's overall obligation to report to those charged with governance and additional reports to other parts of the client's organisation may also be required, such as reports direct to the remuneration committee or to individual departments. In any case, it is important that the report is seen by those who have the authority to implement the recommendations included therein. If the report is presented in sections of varying importance, it may be appropriate for the more detailed matters to be referred directly to the division or branch to which they relate.

10.4.4 Form of reports

Where a written report is made, the form of report will depend on the type of organisation concerned and the matters to be communicated. A report covering findings from the audit may typically be formed of a covering letter (see **Table 1**) and a schedule of points raised.

TABLE 1: Reports to those charged with governance covering letter

Private & Confidential

The Directors

XYZ Plc

1 High Street

London W1

24 June 20XX

Dear Sirs

XYZ Plc

Following our recent audit of your company, we are writing to advise you of various matters which came to our attention.

We set out on the attached schedule the major areas of weakness which we noted, together with our recommendations. These recommendations have already been discussed with … and their comments have been included.

As the purpose of the audit is to form an opinion on the company's financial statements, you will appreciate that our examination cannot necessarily be expected to disclose all shortcomings of the system and for this reason, the matters raised may not be the only ones which exist.

We should appreciate your comments as to how you propose to deal with the matters raised in this letter. If you require any further information or advice, please contact us.

We have prepared this letter for your use only. It should not be disclosed to a third party and we can assume no responsibility to any person to whom it is disclosed without our written consent.

We would like to take this opportunity to thank you and your staff for your help and co-operation during the course of our audit.

Yours faithfully

ABC & Co

10.5 Adequacy of communications

The responsiveness of those charged with governance to communications from the auditor may be considered when assessing the effectiveness of the entity's control environment. This may also affect the auditor's assessment of the risks of material misstatements. The auditor may consider:

- the appropriateness and timeliness of actions taken by those charged with governance following the auditor's recommendations;
- how open those charged with governance appear to be when communicating with the auditor;
- the willingness of those charged with governance to meet with the auditor; and
- the ability of those charged with governance to comprehend the recommendations made by the auditor.

ISA (UK and Ireland) 260 (Revised June 2016) also requires the auditor to evaluate, as part of the audit process, whether the two-way communication between him and those charged with governance has been adequate for the purposes of his audit. In other words, have those charged with governance provided all the information expected of them in response to the auditor's enquiries and have they understood and responded appropriately to matters communicated to them by the auditor. If not, the auditor should consider the effects on his risk assessment and his ability to obtain sufficient appropriate audit evidence and take further action as necessary.

10.6 Matters to be communicated

10.6.1 Overview

There are a number of matters that the auditor is required to communicate to those charged with governance which are covered in this chapter:

- his responsibilities in relation to the audit of the financial statements (see **10.6.2**);
- the form, timing and expected general content of communications (see **10.4** above);
- an overview of the planned scope and timing of the audit (see **10.6.3**);
- significant findings from the audit (see **10.6.4**);
- significant deficiencies in internal control (see **10.10**); and
- certain matters regarding independence and objectivity (see **10.6.5**); and
- (for audits of public interest entities) matters to be contained in an additional report to the audit committee (see **10.7.2**).

In addition to ISAs (UK and Ireland) 260 and 265, a number of other ISAs (UK and Ireland) also contain specific requirements relating to matters to be communicated to those charged with governance in specific circumstances.

Where appropriate, these requirements are referred to in other chapters and a summary of these is below:

- ISQC (UK and Ireland) 1 (Revised June 2016), identity and role of the engagement partner (see **3.2.7**);
- ISA (UK and Ireland) 240 (Revised June 2016), requires the auditor to make inquiries of those charged with governance to determine whether they have knowledge of any actual, suspected or alleged fraud affecting the entity (**16.4.3**); where applicable to discuss reasons for withdrawal from the engagement (**16.6**); and when applicable to inform the entity of any suspected irregularities, including fraud and ask them to take action (**16.8.1**);
- ISA (UK and Ireland) 250 (Revised June 2016), requires enquiries as to whether the entity is in compliance with laws and regulations (**17.5.1**); and inform them of any suspected non-compliance (**17.8.1** and **17.8.4**);
- ISA (UK and Ireland) 450 (Revised June 2016), requires uncorrected misstatements and their effects to be communicated (**15.9**);
- ISA (UK and Ireland) 505, requires communication if management refuse to allow the auditor to send a confirmation request and it is considered unreasonable (**23.8.1**);
- ISA (UK and Ireland) 510 (Revised June 2016), requires communication if any errors in prior period financial statements are considered to affect the current year (**19.3**);
- ISA (UK and Ireland) 550, requires communication of any significant matters arising during the audit in connection with the entity's related parties (**20.8**);
- ISA (UK and Ireland) 560, requires communication about any subsequent events that may have happened, discussion about any facts which become known to the auditor after the date of his report but before the date the financial statements are issued (**33.3**); in certain situations to ask those charged with governance not to issue the financial statements (**33.4**); facts that become known after the financial statements have been issued (**33.5**); circumstances in which the auditor believes the financial statements need to be amended (**33.5**);
- ISA (UK and Ireland) 570 (Revised June 2016), requires communication of events or conditions identified that may cast significant doubt on the entity's ability to continue as a going concern (**11.14**);
- ISA (UK and Ireland) 600 (Revised June 2016), requires communication of certain matters in a group situation (**30.15**);
- ISA (UK and Ireland) 610 (Revised June 2013), requires communication about the use of the work of the internal audit function (**31.2.3**);
- ISA (UK and Ireland) 700 (Revised June 2016), communication where the auditor does not intend to disclose the name of the engagement partner in the audit report;
- ISA (UK and Ireland) 701, requires communication of key audit matters (**4.3.3**);
- ISA (UK and Ireland) 705 (Revised June 2016), requires certain communications where there is an imposed limitation of scope or an inability to obtain sufficient appropriate audit evidence (**5.3.3**), material misstatements due to the non-disclosure of information (**5.5.1**) and expected modifications to the opinion (**5.7**);

- ISA (UK and Ireland) 706 (Revised June 2016), communication of an expected Emphasis of Matter or Other Matter paragraph (**5.9**);
- ISA (UK and Ireland) 710, certain communications about misstatements in prior period financial statements (**19.3**); and
- ISA (UK and Ireland) 720 (Revised June 2016), requires certain communications where misstatements are identified in other information (**34.5.1**).

The auditor communicates 'audit matters of governance interest' to those charged with governance. These are matters arising from the audit of financial statements and which, in the opinion of the auditor, are both important and relevant to those charged with governance in their role of overseeing the financial statements and disclosure process. Only matters which have come to the auditor's attention as a result of the audit will be reportable, and the auditor is not required to perform additional procedures to identify matters of governance interest.

10.6.2   Auditor's responsibilities

The auditor needs to communicate his responsibilities to those charged with governance, including that:

- he is responsible for forming and expressing an opinion on the financial statements that have been prepared by management with oversight from those charged with governance; and
- the audit does not relieve management or those charged with governance of their responsibilities.

This is usually covered by the engagement letter (see **Chapter 14**). In all cases, the auditor should ensure that those charged with governance are provided with a copy of the engagement letter.

10.6.3   Planned scope and timing

The ISA states that auditors of all entities should inform those charged with governance of the planned scope and timing of the work they plan to perform, including any limitations thereon. This includes communicating about the significant risks identified by the auditor. Also where the auditor is required or decides to communicate key audit matters (see **Chapter 4**), the overview of the planned scope and timing of the audit should include communication about the most significant assessed risks of material misstatement (whether or not due to fraud) the auditor identified, including those that had the greatest effect on the overall audit strategy; the allocation of resources; and directing the efforts of the engagement team. Matters that might be communicated in outline include:

- how the auditor plans to address the significant risks of material misstatement, whether due to fraud or error;
- how the auditor plans to address areas of higher assessed risks of material misstatement;

- the concept of materiality and its application to the audit;
- the approach the auditor will use in relation to assessing and relying on internal controls;
- the nature and extent of specialised skill or knowledge needed to perform the planned audit procedures or evaluate the audit results, including the use of an auditor's expert;
- the extent, if any, that reliance can be placed on the internal audit function;
- where relevant, the work to be performed by other auditors and how the auditor intends to ensure the adequacy of the work of those other auditors;
- when ISA (UK and Ireland) 701 applies (see **Chapter 4**), the auditor's preliminary views about matters that may be areas of significant auditor attention in the audit and therefore may be key audit matters; and
- the auditor's planned approach to addressing the implications on the individual statements and the disclosures of any significant changes within the applicable financial reporting framework or in the entity's environment, financial condition or activities.

The nature and detail of the planning information communicated will depend on the size and nature of the entity and precisely how those charged with governance operate. The auditor needs to take care when communicating with those charged with governance about the planned scope and timing of the audit to ensure that he does not compromise the effectiveness of the audit, particularly where some or all of those charged with governance are involved in managing the entity. For example, communicating the nature and timing of detailed audit procedures may reduce the effectiveness of those procedures by making them too predictable.

Where the audit team considers that there has been no change in this information from one year to the next, there is no requirement to reproduce it. Instead, the auditor need only make those charged with governance aware that no change has taken place.

10.6.4   Significant findings from the audit

The following areas are those that the auditor should communicate to those charged with governance:

- the auditor's views on the qualitative aspects of the entity's accounting practices and financial report – this will include the auditor's opinions on the accounting policies used, the appropriateness of accounting estimates, the potential impact of uncertainties and apparent misstatements in other material issued with the financial statements;
- any significant difficulties encountered during the audit, such as:
  - significant delays by management, the unavailability of entity personnel or an unwillingness by management to provide information necessary for the auditor to perform his procedures;
  - an unreasonably brief time within which to complete the audit;

- extensive unexpected effort required to obtain sufficient appropriate audit evidence;
- the unavailability of expected information;
- restriction imposed on the auditor by management; and
- management's unwillingness to make or extend its assessment of the entity's ability to continue as a going concern when required;

● significant matters discussed with management, unless all of those charged with governance are involved in managing the entity, such as:

- significant events or transactions that occurred during the year;
- business conditions affecting the entity, and business plans and strategies that may affect the risks of material misstatement;
- concerns about management's consultations with other accountants on accounting or auditing matters;
- discussions or correspondence in connection with the initial or recurring appointment of the auditor regarding accounting practices, the application of auditing standards, or fees for audit or other services; and
- significant matters on which there was disagreement with management, except for initial differences of opinion because of incomplete facts or preliminary information that are later resolved by the auditor obtaining additional relevant facts or information.

● written representations the auditor is requesting, unless all of those charged with governance are involved in managing the entity;
● any other significant matters which the auditor considers relevant to the oversight of the financial reporting process, this may include modifications to the overall audit strategy and audit plan, material misstatements of the other information that have been corrected, and other matters considered by the engagement quality control reviewer;
● uncorrected misstatements (see below);
● the final draft of the management letter for signature;
● expected modifications to the auditor's report – to ensure that those charged with governance are aware of the proposed modification, that there are no disputed facts and that those charged with governance have an opportunity to provide further information so that a modification is no longer required;
● significant deficiencies in internal control identified during the audit;
● matters specifically required by other ISAs (UK and Ireland) to be communicated to those charged with governance; and
● any other matters of governance interest.

ISA (UK and Ireland) 260 (Revised June 2016) also requires the auditor to explain, where relevant, why significant accounting policies, which are acceptable under the applicable financial reporting framework are not considered appropriate in the particular circumstances of the entity. Examples may include the effect of accounting policies in controversial or emerging areas where there may be a lack of guidance, areas where estimates are significant, or the effect of the timing of a transaction in relation to the period in which they are recorded.

Unadjusted misstatements

Where the auditor finds uncorrected misstatements, he should report them to the entity's management and request that they be corrected. These misstatements should be clearly distinguished as either errors of fact or matters of judgment. There is no requirement to report those misstatements which are 'clearly trivial' or inconsequential whether taken individually or in aggregate.

Where any of these misstatements are not corrected by management they are reported to those charged with governance. If those charged with governance refuse to make any of the adjustments, the auditor should discuss the matter with them and consider the implications for his report. The auditor should also obtain written representations from those charged with governance that explain why they have not been corrected.

Even where management has corrected the misstatements, the auditor may consider that including the details of the misstatement in his communications may assist those charged with governance with their role, including considering the effectiveness of the system of internal control.

Where matters previously reported have not been rectified by those charged with governance, the auditor considers repeating the point. Failing to do so may lead to the auditor giving the impression that he is satisfied that the matter has been addressed.

Guidance on unadjusted misstatements is detailed in ISA (UK and Ireland) 450 (Revised June 2016) *Evaluation of misstatements identified during the audit* (see **Chapter 15**).

10.6.5   Integrity, independence and objectivity

For all companies, listed and unlisted, *Ethical Standard 1*[3] requires that those charged with governance should be told of any significant facts and matters which may impact the auditor's objectivity and independence.

The communication should include the key issues considered by the engagement partner such as:

- the principal threats, if any, to objectivity and independence identified by the auditor;
- any safeguards implemented with an explanation of why they were thought to be effective;
- any independent partner review;
- the overall assessment of threats and safeguards; and
- information about the general policies and processes employed by the audit firm to maintain independence and objectivity.

---

[3] The FRC has replaced the Ethical Standards with a single revised Ethical Standard for periods commencing 17 June 2016. Full details are in **Chapter 2**.

Listed entities

ISA (UK and Ireland) 260 (Revised June 2016) states that for listed companies, the auditor should, at least annually:

- disclose in writing and discuss as appropriate:

  - all relationships between the audit firm and its related entities and the client entity and its related entities that may reasonably be thought to bear on the firm's independence and the objectivity of the audit engagement partner and audit staff; and
  - the related safeguards that are in place to eliminate identified threats to independence or reduce them to an acceptable level; and

- where it is the case, confirm in writing to the audit committee that, in his professional judgment, the firm is independent within the meaning of regulatory and professional requirements and the objectivity of the audit engagement partner and audit staff is not impaired.

In addition, for listed entities, the engagement partner should provide the audit committee with details of all non-audit services provided to the entity and the fees charged in relation thereto as well as details of any inconsistencies between the *Ethical Standards* and the company policy for the supply of non-audit services and any apparent breach of that policy.

Public interest entities

ISA (UK and Ireland) 260 (Revised June 2016) requires that for all public interest entities, the auditor shall:

- confirm annually in writing to the audit committee that the statutory auditor, the audit firm and partners, senior managers and managers, conducting the statutory audit are independent from the audited entity; and
- discuss with the audit committee the threats to the auditor's independence and the safeguards applied to mitigate those threats.

This includes identifying the ethical requirements relevant to the group audit that are applicable to component auditors.

10.7   Communication with audit committees

10.7.1   Companies applying the UK Corporate Governance Code

In the case of entities that are required, and those that choose voluntarily, to report on how they have applied the UK Corporate Governance Code, or to explain why they have not, the auditor shall communicate to the audit committee the information that the auditor believes will be relevant to:

- the board (in the context of fulfilling its responsibilities under Code provisions C.1.1, C.1.3, C.2.1, C.2.2 and C.2.3) and, where applicable, the audit committee (in the context of fulfilling its responsibilities under Code provision C.3.4) – see **42.5**; and
- the audit committee (in the context of fulfilling its responsibilities under Code provision C.3.2) to enable them to understand the rationale and the supporting evidence the auditor has relied on when making significant professional judgments in the course of the audit and in reaching an opinion on the financial statements.

This will include information about the auditor's views on business risks, significant accounting policies, valuations of assets and liabilities and disclosure thereof, the effectiveness of internal control, the robustness of the directors' risk assessment process and the directors' explanation in the annual report as to how they have assessed the prospects of the entity. ISA (UK and Ireland) 260 (Revised June 2016) gives further details of these matters.

10.7.2   Public interest entities

In addition to this, for public interest entities, the auditor is required to submit an additional written report to the audit committee of the entity not later than the date of the auditor's report explaining the results of the audit. This report should cover a number of matters set out in ISA (UK and Ireland) 260 (Revised June 2016), including at least, where applicable:

(a)   the declaration of independence referred to in **10.6.5**;

(b)   the identity of key audit partner(s)[4];

(c)   where any of the auditor's activities are carried out by another firm that is not a member of the same network or by an external expert, that fact together with confirmation of the independence of external experts or other firms used;

(d)   a description of the nature, frequency and extent of communication with the audit committee;

(e)   a description of the scope and timing of the audit;

(f)   where more than one auditor has been appointed, a description of the distribution of tasks;

(g)   a description of the methodology used, including an explanation of any substantial differences to the previous year, even if the previous year's audit was carried out by another firm. This includes being able to describe the methodology used, including which categories of the balance sheet have been directly verified and which categories have been verified based on system and compliance testing, including an explanation of any substantial

---

[4] The key audit partner is defined in UK legislation as:

(i)   the statutory auditor designated by an audit firm for a particular audit engagement as being primarily responsible for carrying out the statutory audit on behalf of the audit firm;

(ii)   in the case of a group audit, the statutory auditor designated as being primarily responsible for carrying out the statutory audit at the level of the group and the statutory auditor designated as being primarily responsible at the level of material subsidiaries; or

(iii) the statutory auditor who signs the audit report.

variation in the weighting of system and compliance testing when compared to the previous year;

(h) the quantitative level(s) of materiality applied and the qualitative factors considered when setting the levels;

(i) a report and explanation of judgments about events or conditions identified that may cast significant doubt on the entity's ability to continue as a going concern and provide a summary of all support measures that have been taken into account when making a going concern assessment;

(j) a report on any significant deficiencies in the internal financial control system and/or in the accounting system and whether or not they have been resolved by management;

(k) any significant matters involving actual or suspected non-compliance with laws and regulations identified in the course of the audit;

(l) valuation methods applied including any impact of changes of such methods;

(m) the scope of consolidation and the exclusion criteria applied by the entity to the non-consolidated entities, if any;

(n) identify any audit work performed in relation to consolidated financial statements other than by members of the same network to which the group auditor belongs;

(o) whether all requested explanations and documents were provided by the entity;

(p) a report of any significant difficulties encountered in the course of the audit, any significant matters arising from the audit, and any other matters arising from the audit that in the auditor's professional judgment, are significant to the oversight of the financial reporting process.

10.8   Groups

Where a parent undertaking is preparing group financial statements, the auditor brings to the attention of those charged with governance any matters arising through the audit of components which he judges to be of significance in the context of the group.

There is a statutory requirement for the auditor of corporate subsidiaries in the UK to supply information, on request, to the parent company auditor. Where no statutory obligation exists (for example, for non-corporate or overseas components), the group auditor may need to seek permission to communicate with the component auditor.

Further detail on communicating with those charged with governance in group situations is given in **30.15**.

10.9   Third parties

Reports issued by the auditor to those charged with governance on the matters referred to in this chapter will usually be solely for the use of the addressees.

If the auditor wishes to disclose its contents to a third party, he should obtain permission from the client before releasing it. In practical terms, once the report has been sent, the auditor has little control over it and it may be given to third parties without the knowledge of the auditor. The auditor should therefore ensure that his report contains an appropriate disclaimer, as shown in **Table 1**, so that any third parties who see the report understand it was not prepared for their benefit.

In the public or regulated sectors, the auditor may have a duty to submit a copy of his report to the relevant regulatory or funding bodies and therefore the disclaimer will not be appropriate. However, any communication with those charged with governance is confidential and the auditor will require prior consent from those charged with governance before sending a copy to the regulator or funding body.

Where reports are required by such third parties, the auditor should show due consideration for the requirements of those bodies when compiling his reports.

10.10 Communicating deficiencies in internal control

10.10.1 Identifying and reporting deficiencies

The auditor is required to obtain an understanding of internal control sufficient to allow him to identify and assess risks of material misstatement and to plan audit procedures which address those risks. The auditor is not required to identify deficiencies with the sole purpose of reporting them to those charged with governance or management.

Where the auditor has identified deficiencies in internal control ISA (UK and Ireland) 265 *Communicating deficiencies in internal control to those charged with governance and management* sets out the requirements that apply in determining the manner in which they are communicated to management or those charged with governance, as appropriate. This does not preclude the auditor from reporting any other deficiencies in internal control identified during the course of his work.

10.10.2 Significant deficiency

A deficiency in internal control exists when:

- a control is designed, implemented or operated in such a way that it is unable to prevent, or detect and correct, misstatements in the financial statements on a timely basis; or
- a control necessary to prevent, or detect and correct, misstatements in the financial statements on a timely basis is missing.

A deficiency is a 'significant deficiency' when, either in isolation or in combination with other deficiencies, it is of sufficient importance to merit the attention of those charged with governance. This will depend not only on whether a material misstatement has actually occurred, but also on the likelihood that a misstatement could occur, and the potential magnitude of the misstatement. Therefore significant deficiencies can exist without a misstatement having been identified.

When determining whether a deficiency or combination of deficiencies in internal control constitutes a significant deficiency, the auditor may consider:

- likelihood of the deficiencies leading to material misstatements in the financial statements in the future;
- susceptibility to loss or fraud of the related asset or liability;
- subjectivity and complexity of determining estimated amounts, such as fair value accounting estimates;
- financial statements amounts exposed to the deficiencies;
- volume of activity that has occurred or could occur in the account balance or class of transactions exposed to the deficiency or deficiencies;
- importance of the controls to the financial reporting process; for example:
  - general monitoring controls (such as oversight of management);
  - controls over the prevention and detection of fraud;
  - controls over the selection and application of significant accounting policies;
  - controls over significant transactions with related parties;
  - controls over significant transactions outside the entity's normal course of business;
  - controls over the period-end financial reporting process (such as controls over non-recurring journal entries);
- cause and frequency of the exceptions detected as a result of the deficiencies in the controls; and
- interaction of the deficiency with other deficiencies in internal control.

10.10.3   Reporting of significant deficiencies

All significant deficiencies should be reported on a timely basis and in writing to those charged with governance. In addition, management should also be notified in writing of any significant deficiencies reported to those charged with governance.

When reporting significant deficiencies to those charged with governance, the auditor should include in his written communication:

- a description of the deficiencies and an explanation of their potential effects; and
- sufficient information to allow those charged with governance and management to understand the context of the communication. In particular, the auditor should explain that the:

  - purpose of the audit was for the auditor to express an opinion on the financial statements;
  - audit included consideration of internal control relevant to the preparation of the financial statements in order to design audit procedures that are appropriate in the circumstances but not for the purpose of expressing an opinion on the effectiveness of internal control; and
  - matters being reported are limited to those deficiencies that the auditor has identified during the audit and that the auditor has concluded are of sufficient importance to merit being reported to those charged with governance.

The auditor may include suggestions for remedial actions and management's own responses as well as details of any steps taken to verify whether management's responses have been implemented.

The auditor may also include in his reports:

- an indication that if he had performed more extensive procedures on internal control more reportable deficiencies may have been discovered, or it may have been concluded that some of the reported deficiencies may not have needed to be reported; and
- an indication that the report has been provided for the purposes of those charged with governance only, and that it may not be suitable for other purposes.

Public interest entities

For audits of public interest entities, ISA (UK and Ireland) 260 (Revised June 2016) requires the auditor to communicate in the additional report (see **10.7.2**) to the audit committee any significant deficiencies in the entity's internal financial control system or in the accounting system, and whether or not the deficiencies reported have been resolved by management.

10.10.4   Reporting of other deficiencies

Other deficiencies not considered to be significant deficiencies need not be reported in writing but should be communicated to management at an appropriate level of responsibility on a timely basis. Obviously, such deficiencies may be included in the written report to those charged with governance if the auditor and client consider it appropriate to do so.

11   GOING CONCERN

11.1   Introduction

The auditor's consideration of the appropriateness of the use of the going concern basis of accounting and of disclosures relating to the solvency or liquidity of the company is an area that has attracted much attention from standard setters and regulators. Recent changes to the UK Corporate Governance Code ('the Code') and accompanying guidance for directors, Listing Rules and ISAs on going concern and auditor reporting have made changes in this area for companies that explain their compliance with the Code. Further changes affecting all entities are introduced by changes to ISAs (UK and Ireland) deriving from the EU Audit Directive and taking effect from 17 June 2016.

Directors have a responsibility to prepare financial statements on the going concern basis of accounting unless it is inappropriate to do so. This involves an assessment of, and judgments about, the future. If they decide the basis is inappropriate, assets may need to be written down to recoverable amounts or reclassified, and liabilities restated to reflect changes in amount or date of maturity. Directors must also consider whether there are material uncertainties regarding the entity's ability to continue as a going concern (or to continue to adopt the going concern basis of accounting) and ensure that these are disclosed in the financial statements where appropriate. The auditor must assess whether directors have carried out this assessment on a realistic basis and whether the consequences, where relevant, and any disclosures regarding uncertainties are adequately reflected in the financial statements.

Recent changes to auditing standards and related guidance make a distinction between the use of the going concern basis of accounting, which is prescribed except in specific limited circumstances, and adequacy of disclosures regarding the directors' consideration of the company's viability, including risks and uncertainties relating to the company's future solvency or liquidity that may impact on its ability to continue in business as a going concern.

11.2   Auditing standards and other guidance

This chapter has been updated to reflect the changes contained in final draft versions of revised ISAs (UK and Ireland) issued by the FRC in April 2016. Subject to legislative changes in progress at the time of writing it is expected that ISA (UK and Ireland) 570 (Revised June 2016) *Going Concern* will take effect for periods commencing on or after 17 June 2016. For earlier periods, commencing on or after 1 October 2014, the version of ISA (UK and Ireland) 570 issued in September 2014 applies.

Changes in the 2016 version of the ISA are numerous and result from the EU Directive, IAASB updates and UK specific amendments. The chapter has been updated throughout to include these requirements.

Key changes include:

- use of the term 'going concern basis of accounting' rather than 'going concern assumption';
- an EU Directive requirement for the auditor to maintain professional scepticism when reviewing future cash flow relevant to the entity's ability to continue as a going concern;
- requirement for a specific auditor conclusion regarding management's use of the going concern basis of accounting;
- greater emphasis on consideration of adequacy of disclosures including a requirement for the auditor to consider adequacy of disclosures where there are matters that may cast significant doubt on the entity's ability to continue as a going concern but no material uncertainty exists; and
- consideration of whether going concern is a key audit matter for the purposes of ISA 701 even where no material uncertainty has been identified.

Guidance for directors of companies applying the UK Corporate Governance Code was issued by the FRC in September 2014 in conjunction with changes to the Code, ISA (UK and Ireland) 570 and ISA (UK and Ireland) 700 taking effect from 1 October 2014. *Guidance on Risk Management, Internal Control and Related Financial and Business Reporting* revises and replaces the previous document *Going Concern and Liquidity Risk: Guidance for Directors of UK Companies 2009*.

Guidance for those entities which do not apply the Code was issued in April 2016, titled *Guidance on the Going Concern Basis of Accounting and Reporting on Solvency and Liquidity Risks*.

In early 2011, the Financial Reporting Council requested Lord Sharman to lead an inquiry into going concern and liquidity risks. The Panel's final report was published in June 2012 and has since resulted in a number of revisions to ISAs (UK and Ireland) and to the Code. The Sharman Inquiry is considered in **11.21**.

Older, but still potentially relevant, guidance is also contained in the APB's Bulletin 2008/10 *Going concern issues during the current economic conditions* published in December 2008 to supplement Bulletin 2008/1 *Audit issues when financial market conditions are difficult and credit facilities may be restricted*, which provided more general guidance and is covered in **Chapter 37**. Bulletin 2008/10 is discussed in **11.20**.

11.3   General requirement

In preparing financial statements, it is the responsibility of those charged with governance to determine whether it is appropriate to apply the going concern basis of accounting and whether any assumptions and uncertainties are adequately disclosed.

The auditor's objectives are to:

- obtain sufficient appropriate audit evidence regarding, and conclude on, the appropriateness of those charged with governance's use of the going concern basis of accounting in the preparation of the financial statements;
- conclude, based on the audit evidence obtained, whether a material uncertainty exists related to events or conditions that may cast significant doubt on the entity's ability to continue as a going concern; and
- report in accordance with ISA (UK and Ireland) 570 (Revised June 2016).

The ISA focuses on the auditor's responsibility to assess how the directors have satisfied themselves that the financial statements have been prepared on an appropriate basis and whether the financial statements contain adequate disclosures relating to going concern, including the existence of any material uncertainties in relation to the entity's ability to continue as a going concern.

11.4 The entity's responsibilities

Under the going concern basis of accounting, an entity will be assumed to continue in business for the foreseeable future without the intention or need to liquidate, cease trading or seek protection from its creditors. Assets and liabilities will, therefore, be recorded assuming that they will be traded or settled in the normal course of business.

Those charged with governance may prepare financial statements under either IFRS or UK accounting standards. The requirements relating to going concern are similar under the two frameworks and entities should prepare their accounts on a going concern basis unless the entity has ceased trading or is being liquidated, or the directors either intend or have no realistic alternative but to cease trading or liquidate the entity. Most financial statements will therefore be prepared on a going concern basis even where there is uncertainty regarding the entity's ability to remain a going concern. Under UK accounting standards, in assessing whether the going concern basis of accounting is appropriate, those charged with governance take into account all available information about the future, which is at least, but is not limited to, 12 months from the date when the financial statements are authorised for issue.

When those charged with governance are aware, in making their assessment, of material uncertainties related to events or conditions that cast significant doubt upon the entity's ability to continue as a going concern, the entity must disclose those uncertainties. When an entity does not prepare financial statements on a going concern basis, it shall disclose that fact, together with the basis on which it prepared the financial statements and the reason why the entity is not regarded as a going concern.

IAS 1 contains almost identical requirements to UK accounting standards but requires that the directors' assessment covers a period of at least 12 months from the balance sheet date. In practice, however, for UK entities, those charged with governance are usually expected to consider a period of 12 months from the date of approval.

Non-compliance with an accounting standard will usually lead to a qualification of the auditor's opinion. Where the assessment period is less than 12 months from the date of approval of the financial statements, under either framework, the auditor may need to refer to this in the audit report.

When making their assessment, those charged with governance should be aware that:

- the outcome of an event is less certain the further it is likely to occur from the date the assessment is made;
- judgments can only be made on the basis of information available at the time. Subsequent events can contradict a decision which was reasonable at the time it was made; and
- any judgment will be affected by the size and complexity of the entity, its type of business and how susceptible its activities are to outside influences.

The auditor should also consider these factors when forming an opinion on the assessment made by those charged with governance.

11.5   The auditor's responsibilities

The auditor's responsibilities are to evaluate the assessment made by those charged with governance of the use of the going concern basis of accounting, conclude on the existence of material uncertainties, consider the disclosures made in the financial statements and in other information (see **Chapter 34**) and to report appropriately.

11.6   Risk assessment procedures and related activities

When carrying out his risk assessment procedures (see **Chapter 21**), the auditor should consider whether events or conditions exist that may cast significant doubt over the entity's ability to continue as a going concern. He should determine whether those charged with governance have already performed a preliminary assessment of their ability to continue as a going concern, and:

- if such an assessment has been performed, he should discuss it with those charged with governance to determine whether they have identified events or conditions that, individually or collectively, may cast significant doubt on the entity's ability to continue as a going concern, and, if so, their plans to address them; or

- if such an assessment has not yet been performed, the auditor discusses with those charged with governance the basis for the intended use of the going concern basis of accounting, and inquires of them whether events or conditions exist that, individually or collectively, may cast significant doubt on the entity's ability to continue as a going concern.

The auditor should also remain alert throughout the audit for evidence of events or conditions that may cast significant doubt on the entity's ability to continue as a going concern.

If such events or risks are identified, the auditor may need to revise his risk assessment and may need to reconsider the nature and timing of his procedures in response to the assessed risks of material misstatement (see **Chapter 21**).

11.6.1 Significant doubt about the entity's ability to continue as a going concern

Examples of events or circumstances which may cause doubt about the entity's ability to continue as a going concern are given in **Table 1**.

TABLE 1: Events or circumstances which may cause doubt about the entity's ability to continue as a going concern

Financial

- net liability or net current liability position;
- necessary borrowing facilities have not been agreed;
- fixed-term borrowing approaching maturity without realistic prospects of renewal or repayments; or excessive reliance on short-term borrowings to finance long-term assets;
- major debt repayment falling due where refinancing is necessary to the entity's continued existence;
- major restructuring of debt;
- indications of withdrawal of financial support by debtors and other creditors;
- negative operating cash flows indicated by historical or prospective financial statements;
- adverse key financial ratios;
- substantial operating losses or significant deterioration in the value of assets used to generate cash flows;
- major losses or cash flow problems which have arisen since the balance sheet date;
- arrears or discontinuance of dividends;
- inability to pay creditors on due dates;
- inability to comply with the terms of loan agreements;

- reduction in normal terms of trade credit;
- change from credit to cash-on-delivery transactions with suppliers;
- inability to obtain financing for essential new product development or other essential investments;
- substantial sales of fixed assets not intended to be replaced.

Operating

- loss of key management without replacement;
- loss of key staff without replacement;
- loss of a major market, franchise, licence or principal supplier;
- labour difficulties or shortages of important suppliers;
- fundamental changes in the market or technology to which the entity is unable to adapt adequately;
- excessive dependence on a few product lines where the market is depressed;
- technical developments which render a key product obsolete.

Other

- non-compliance with capital or other statutory requirements;
- pending legal or regulatory proceedings against the entity that may, if successful, result in claims that are unlikely to be satisfied;
- changes in legislation or government policy expected to adversely affect the entity;
- issues which involve a range of possible outcomes so wide that an unfavourable result could affect the appropriateness of the going concern basis.

11.7   Evaluating the entity's assessment of going concern

ISA (UK and Ireland) 570 (Revised June 2016) requires that the auditor evaluates the assessment made by those charged with governance of the entity's ability to continue as a going concern. It also requires that the auditor maintains professional scepticism throughout the audit and in particular when reviewing future cash flow relevant to the entity's ability to continue as a going concern.

In his evaluation, the auditor should consider the same period as used by those charged with governance. If this covers a period of less than 12 months from the date of approval of the financial statements, the auditor should request those charged with governance to extend the period of their assessment. If they fail to do so, this may have implications for the auditor's report.

In making his evaluation, the auditor considers whether those charged with governance's assessment have included all relevant information of which the auditor is aware as a result of the audit.

The auditor's procedures may involve:

- holding discussions with those charged with governance;
- examining appropriate supporting documentation; and
- planning and performing procedures designed to identify any material matters which could impact on the entity's ability to continue as a going concern, including considering the process followed to make the assessment, the assumptions on which the assessment is based and plans for the future.

The issues the auditor should consider may include the:

- period assessed by those charged with governance;
- system for identifying future risks;
- existence/quality of budgets or forecasts;
- appropriateness of assumptions;
- sensitivity of budgets;
- adequacy of borrowing facilities; and
- the entity's plans for resolving going concern problems.

The extent of the procedures carried out will depend on the headroom between financial requirements and the facilities available. The more demonstrably healthy the company, the less extensive the procedures may need to be.

11.7.1   Possible audit procedures

Some possible procedures that the auditor may consider are shown in **Table 2**.

TABLE 2: Possible audit procedures

Forecasts and budgets

Review cash flow forecasts and budgets, where available, from the expected date of approval of the financial statements. Perform sensitivity analysis on the key components of forecasts and budgets.

Consider the assumptions used in preparing the forecasts, for example:

- anticipated levels of sales;
- projected winning of new customers;
- expected cash collection performance;
- capital expenditure programme;
- timing of anticipated payments to HMRC;
- basis of payment terms to existing suppliers;
- ensure forecasts represent the timing of cash flows, not profits;
- where forecasts assume an increase in sales, ensure that associated costs (advertising, sales/admin staff, distribution, increased stock levels etc), are also factored in; and
- ensure the entity has the capacity to deliver at the increased sales level forecast.

Assess reliability of directors' previous forecasting.

Borrowing facilities

Confirm the existence and terms of facilities.

> Establish the date for renewal of facilities.
> Assess the future intentions of lenders via discussion or correspondence.
> Assess possible breaches of any borrowing covenants imposed by lenders.
> Check for any arrears of interest on current borrowings.
> Review the value of any assets granted as security for borrowings.
> Review correspondence between directors and lenders.

Contingent liabilities

Consider possible exposure to contingent liabilities arising, for example, from:

- legal proceedings;
- guarantees or warranties; and
- retentions.

Assess potential intra-group guarantees (e.g. unlimited multilateral guarantees).

Review possible breaches of grant conditions leading to repayment of grants.

Financial risk

Review directors' assumptions about projected foreign currency exchange rates.

Consider exposure to major fixed-price contracts.

Financial adaptability

Assess entity's ability to adapt to unexpected events, for example:

- disposal of fixed assets;
- leasing;
- debt restructuring;
- share capital issue;
- financial support from group companies; and
- new sources of finance.

11.7.2 Borrowing facilities

When considering adequacy of borrowing facilities, the auditor may need to make an assessment of the intentions of the company's bankers or other providers of finance, where:

- there is a low margin of financial resources available;
- the company's facilities are shortly due for renewal;
- he is aware of previous difficulties in agreeing facilities and the bankers have imposed further conditions for continued lending;

- the directors have projected a significant deterioration in the cash position; or
- the company has recently breached or is likely to breach its borrowing covenants.

Such an assessment may include:

- reviewing correspondence between directors and their bankers; and
- meeting with the directors and bankers to clarify the latter's intentions.

The auditor may, despite the above, decide it is necessary to obtain confirmation from bankers of the existence and terms of facilities.

If he is neither able to satisfy himself about the existence and terms of facilities or about the bankers' future intentions, the auditor needs to consider whether this represents a material uncertainty that should be disclosed in the financial statements and may have implications for his report (see paragraph **11.11**).

11.8   Events after the period considered by those charged with governance

The 12-month period is not intended to be a hard cut-off point and the auditor should also make enquiries regarding management's knowledge of events or conditions beyond the period of their assessment that may cast significant doubt on the entity's ability to continue as a going concern.

Events this far in the future are unlikely to be certain, but the auditor should consider the possible significance of any such event which is made known to him up until the date of his audit report. For example, it may be that the company's cash flow forecasts show a significant dependence on the availability of a loan facility. Where those charged with governance know, or suspect, that company's situation will make renewal of the facility difficult they should take this into account in their assessment even where the renewal date is later than 12 months after the date of approval of the financial statements.

However, the auditor has no responsibility to design audit procedures, other than enquiry, to discover such events or conditions.

11.9   Additional procedures when events or conditions are identified

If events or conditions have been identified that may cast significant doubt on the entity's ability to continue as a going concern, the auditor shall obtain sufficient appropriate audit evidence to determine whether or not a material uncertainty exits related to events or conditions that may cast significant doubt on the entity's ability to continue as a going concern. This is done through performing additional audit procedures, including consideration of mitigating factors. These procedures shall include:

- where those charged with governance have not yet performed an assessment of the entity's ability to continue as a going concern, requesting them to make their assessment;
- evaluating those charged with governance's plans for future actions in relation to their going concern assessment, whether the outcome of these plans is likely to improve the situation and whether their plans are feasible in the circumstances;
- where the entity has prepared a cash flow forecast, and analysis of the forecast is a significant factor in considering the future outcome of events or conditions in the evaluation of those charged with governance's plans for future action:
    - evaluating the reliability of the underlying data generated to prepare the forecast; and
    - determining whether there is adequate support for the assumptions underlying the forecast.
- considering whether any additional facts or information have become available since the date on which those charged with governance made their assessment; and
- requesting written representations from those charged with governance regarding their plans for future action and the feasibility of these plans.

11.10 Auditor conclusions

The auditor evaluates whether sufficient appropriate audit evidence has been obtained and concludes on the appropriateness of management's use of the going concern basis of accounting.

Based on the audit evidence obtained, the auditor concludes whether, in his judgment, a material uncertainty exists related to events or conditions that, individually or collectively, may cast significant doubt on the entity's ability to continue as a going concern. A material uncertainty exists when the magnitude of its potential impact and the likelihood of occurrence is such that, in the auditor's judgment, appropriate disclosure of the nature and implications of the uncertainty is necessary for the fair presentation of the financial statements.

11.10.1 Entities applying the UK Corporate Governance Code

For those entities required, or who voluntarily choose to report on how they have applied the UK Corporate Governance Code, the auditor shall read the following and consider them in the light of the auditor's knowledge obtained in the audit:

- the directors' confirmation in the annual report that they have carried out a robust assessment of the principal risks facing the entity, including those that would threaten its business model, future performance, solvency or liquidity (Code Provision C2.1);
- the disclosures in the annual report that describe those risks and explain how they are being managed or mitigated (Code Provision C2.1);
- the directors' statement in the financial statements about whether they considered it appropriate to adopt the going concern basis of accounting in preparing them, and their identification of any material uncertainties to the entity's ability to continue to do so over a period of at least 12 months from the date of approval of the financial statements (Code Provision C1.3); and
- the directors' explanation in the annual report as to how they have assessed the prospects of the entity, over what period they have done so and why they consider that period to be appropriate, and their statement as to whether they have a reasonable expectation that the entity will be able to continue in operation and meet its liabilities as they fall due over the period of their assessment, including any related disclosures drawing attention to any necessary qualifications or assumptions (Code Provision C2.2).

The auditor determines whether he has anything material to add or to draw attention to in his audit report in relation to these disclosures and reports.

Matters the auditor considers when determining whether there is anything to add or to emphasise in his audit report, include:

- whether he is aware of information that would indicate that the annual report and accounts taken as a whole are not fair, balanced and understandable in relation to the principal risks facing the entity including those that would threaten its business model, future performance, solvency or liquidity; and
- matters relating to the robustness of the directors' assessment of the principal risks facing the entity and its outcome, including the related disclosures in the annual report and accounts, that the auditor communicated to the audit committee and that are not appropriately addressed in the section of the annual report that describes the work of the audit committee.

11.11   Adequacy of disclosures

The auditor has a responsibility to consider the requirements of the applicable financial reporting framework and the adequacy of disclosures, whether or not he considers a material uncertainty to exist.

A material uncertainty exists when the potential impact of the events or conditions and the likelihood of them occurring is such that appropriate disclosure is necessary to achieve fair presentation. The auditor needs to conclude on whether such a material uncertainty exists regardless of whether or how the applicable financial reporting framework defines a material uncertainty.

Even when no material uncertainty exists, the auditor is required to evaluate whether the financial statements provide adequate disclosure about events or conditions that may cast significant doubt on the entity's ability to continue as a going concern.

Paragraph **11.11.1** considers the situation where events or conditions have been identified and a material uncertainty does exist and paragraph **11.11.2** where no material uncertainty exists.

11.11.1   Adequacy of disclosures when events or conditions have been identified and a material uncertainty exists

If the auditor concludes that the use of the going concern basis of accounting is appropriate but that there remains a material uncertainty, he should determine whether the financial statements:

- disclose adequately the principal events or conditions that may cast significant doubt on the entity's ability to continue as a going concern and those charged with governance's plans to deal with these events or conditions; and
- disclose clearly that the material uncertainty exists and that it may cast significant doubt on the entity's ability to continue as a going concern and, therefore, that it may be unable to realise its assets and discharge its liabilities in the normal course of business.

11.11.2   Adequacy of disclosures when events or conditions have been identified but no material uncertainty exists

If events or conditions have been identified that may cast significant doubt on the entity's ability to continue as a going concern but, based on the audit evidence obtained the auditor concludes that no material uncertainty exists, the auditor evaluates whether, in view of the requirements of the applicable financial reporting framework, the financial statements provide adequate disclosures about these events or conditions.

11.12   Implications for the auditor's report

11.12.1   Auditor's conclusions

The auditor may conclude that:

- use of the going concern basis of accounting is not appropriate in the circumstances;

- use of the going concern basis is appropriate and no material uncertainty exists; or
- use of the going concern basis is appropriate but one or more material uncertainties exist.

11.12.2 Going concern basis of accounting inappropriate

Where the financial statements have been prepared using the going concern basis of accounting, but in the auditor's judgment, the use of the going concern assumption is inappropriate, the auditor would give an adverse opinion in his report, as shown in **Table 3**. This applies regardless of whether the financial statements include disclosure of the inappropriateness of those charged with governance's use of the going concern basis of accounting.

Where the use of the going concern basis of accounting is inappropriate and those charged with governance have elected to prepare the financial statements on an alternative basis (such as a liquidation basis), which the auditor considers to be acceptable, and have made appropriate disclosures in the financial statements regarding the basis of preparation and the reasons for it then the auditor may be able to give an unqualified opinion on the financial statements. In these circumstances he may consider it appropriate or necessary to include an Emphasis of Matter paragraph (see **Chapter 5**) drawing attention to the basis of preparation and the relevant disclosures in the financial statements.

11.12.3 Going concern basis of accounting is appropriate and no material uncertainty has been identified

If the auditor is required or has decided to communicate key audit matters (see **Chapter 4**), where he concludes that the use of the going concern basis of accounting is appropriate and no material uncertainty has been identified, he nevertheless needs to consider whether a key audit matter relating to going concern exists. If so, he communicates it in his report in accordance with ISA (UK and Ireland) 701, see **4.3.3**.

Where the auditor is required to report by exception on going concern issues, for example for entities that are required, and those that choose voluntarily, to report on how they have applied the UK Corporate Governance Code, or to explain why they have not, he includes a separate section in the audit report with the heading of 'Conclusions in relation to going concern' (or other appropriate heading).

11.12.4 Use of going concern basis of accounting is appropriate but a material uncertainty exists

Adequate disclosure of a material uncertainty is made in the financial statements

If adequate disclosure is made, the audit opinion would be unmodified, but the auditor's report would contain a separate section under the heading 'Material Uncertainty Related to Going Concern' to bring readers' attention to the note(s) disclosing the matter(s) in the financial statements. The section should also state that these events or conditions indicate that a material uncertainty exists that may cast significant doubt on the entity's ability to continue as a going concern and that the auditor's opinion is not modified in respect of the matter.

Table 7 sets out an example paragraph. (Note that under the previous version of the ISA this would have been regarded as an emphasis of matter paragraph.)

Adequate disclosure of a material uncertainty is not made in the financial statements

Where the relevant disclosures about the material uncertainty are not made or are inadequate, the auditor expresses a qualified or adverse opinion, as appropriate. In the 'Basis for Qualified (Adverse) Opinion' section of the auditor's report, he states that a material uncertainty exists that may cast significant doubt on the entity's ability to continue as a going concern and that the financial statements do not adequately disclose this matter. See example in **Table 4**.

11.12.5 Other considerations

Where those charged with governance have not extended their assessment when required to do so, the auditor needs to consider whether they have complied with the relevant accounting framework and needs to consider the implications for his report.

Where financial statements have been prepared on a basis other than that of going concern and the auditor considers that adequate disclosure of this has not been made then he may need to qualify his opinion or express an adverse opinion.

In extreme circumstances, where there are multiple significant uncertainties, a disclaimer of opinion may be suitable.

11.12.6 Small and micro-entities

In the case of small and micro-entities in the UK, the applicable accounting framework may not contain the same requirements in relation to disclosure of material uncertainties as are imposed on other entities. The auditor is nevertheless required to consider management's assessment of the applicability of the going concern basis and the adequacy of disclosures in relation to any material uncertainties that exist and should consider the implications for his report where he considers that disclosure of such uncertainties is not adequate for the purposes of a true and fair view (see **8.3.4**).

11.12.7   Entities applying the UK Corporate Governance Code

Having considered the various disclosures and reports referred to in **11.10.1** above the auditor determines whether he has anything material to add or to draw attention to in his audit report in relation to these disclosures and reports, and reports in accordance with ISA (UK and Ireland) 720 (Revised June 2016). Where he has nothing to add or to draw attention to, he reports that fact. See **4.12.4**.

11.13   Entity unwilling to make or extend its assessment

If the auditor believes it is necessary to request those charged with governance to make or extend their assessment, and they are unwilling to do so, the auditor considers the implications for his audit report. In such circumstances, a qualified opinion or a disclaimer of opinion may be appropriate, because it may not be possible for the auditor to obtain sufficient appropriate audit evidence regarding the use of the going concern basis of accounting, for example, such as evidence regarding the existence of plans that those charged with governance have put in place or the existence of other mitigating factors.

11.13.1   Those charged with governance not taking adequate steps

Where the auditor is of the opinion that those charged with governance have not taken adequate steps to assess the reasonableness of the going concern basis of accounting, he would give a qualified opinion or disclaim an opinion on the financial statements. Such a qualification would be a limitation on the scope of the auditor's work as he is unable to obtain all the information and explanations which he considers necessary for the purpose of his audit. Depending on the severity of the limitation, the extract examples in **Tables 5** and **6** could be used.

11.14 Communication with those charged with governance

Unless all those charged with governance are involved in managing the entity, the auditor communicates with those charged with governance, those events or conditions identified that may cast significant doubt on the entity's ability to continue as a going concern. This includes whether the events or conditions constitute a material uncertainty, whether the use of the going concern basis of accounting for the preparation of the financial statements is appropriate, the adequacy of related disclosures in the financial statements, and, where applicable, the implications for the audit report.

11.14.1 Public interest entities

For audits of public interest entities, ISA (UK and Ireland) 260 (Revised June 2016) requires the auditor in the additional report to the audit committee to:

- explain the judgments about events or conditions identified in the course of the audit that may cast significant doubt on the entity's ability to continue as a going concern and whether they constitute a material uncertainty; and
- provide a summary of all guarantees, comfort letters, undertakings of public intervention and other support measures that have been taken into account when making a going concern assessment.

11.15 Significant delay in the approval of financial statements

If there is a significant delay in the approval of the financial statements by those charged with governance, the auditor inquires as to the reasons. If the auditor believes the delay may be related to events or conditions relating to the going concern assessment, he performs additional audit procedures as necessary as well as considering the effect on his conclusion regarding the existence of a material uncertainty.

11.16 Example report extracts

The extracts of example audit reports in **Tables 3** to **7** illustrate the following situations:

> **Table 3** – an example adverse opinion, where the financial statements have been prepared using the going concern basis of accounting, but in the auditor's judgment, the use of the going concern basis of accounting is inappropriate.

Table 4 – an example of a disagreement over inadequate disclosure of going concern problems.

Table 5 – an example of a limitation of scope where the auditor is of the opinion that those charged with governance have not taken adequate steps to assess the reasonableness of the going concern basis of accounting.

Table 6 - an example of a disclaimer of opinion where the auditor is of the opinion that those charged with governance have not taken adequate steps to assess the reasonableness of the going concern basis of accounting.

Table 7 – an example paragraph where a material uncertainty exists and is adequately disclosed.

TABLE 3: Example adverse opinion

Basis for adverse opinion on financial statements

As explained in note x to the financial statements, the company's financing arrangements expired and the amount outstanding was payable on 31 December 20XX [a past date]. The company has been unable to re-negotiate or obtain replacement financing and the directors of the company are considering whether the company should be entering insolvency proceedings [but are continuing to investigate alternative sources of finance]. These events indicate a material uncertainty which may cast significant doubt on the company's ability to continue as a going concern and, therefore, it may be unable to realise its assets and discharge its liabilities in the normal course of business. The financial statements (and notes thereto) do not disclose this fact and have been prepared on the going concern basis.

Adverse opinion on financial statements

In our opinion, because of the significance of the matter described in the Basis for Adverse Opinion paragraph:

- the financial statements do not give a true and fair view of the state of the company's affairs as at 31 December 20 ... and of its profit [loss] for the year then ended; and
- have not been properly prepared in accordance with United Kingdom Generally Accepted Accounting Practice.

In all other respects, in our opinion the financial statements have been prepared in accordance with the requirements of the *Companies Act* 2006.

Opinion on other matter prescribed by the Companies Act 2006

Notwithstanding our adverse opinion on the view given by the financial statements, in our opinion, the information given in the [Strategic Report and the] Directors' Report for the financial year for which the financial statements are prepared is consistent with the financial statements.

TABLE 4[4]: Example of disagreement over inadequate disclosure of going concern problems

Basis for qualified opinion on financial statements

The company's financing arrangements expire and amounts outstanding are payable on 19 July 20XX. The company has been unable to re-negotiate or obtain replacement financing. This situation indicates the existence of a material uncertainty which may cast significant doubt on the company's ability to continue as a going concern and therefore it may be unable to realise its assets and discharge its liabilities in the normal course of business. The financial statements (and notes thereto) do not fully disclose this fact.

Qualified opinion on financial statements

In our opinion, except for the incomplete disclosure of the information referred to in the Basis for Qualified Opinion paragraph, the financial statements:

- give a true and fair view of the state of the company's affairs as at 31 December 20 ... and of its profit for the year then ended;
- have been properly prepared in accordance with United Kingdom Generally Accepted Accounting Practice; and
- have been prepared in accordance with the requirements of the *Companies Act* 2006.

[4] This example is based on existing ISAs and has not been updated to reflect changes to audit reporting ISAs which will take effect for periods commencing 17 June 2016.

TABLE 5[5]: Example of limitation of scope

Basis for qualified opinion on financial statements

The audit evidence available to us was limited because the directors of the company have prepared cash flow forecasts and other information needed for the assessment of the appropriateness of the going concern basis of preparation of the financial statements for a period of only nine months from the date of approval of these financial statements. We consider that the directors have not taken adequate steps to satisfy themselves that it is appropriate for them to adopt the going concern basis because the circumstances of the company and the nature of the business require that such information be prepared, and reviewed by the directors and ourselves, for a period of at least 12 months from the date of approval of the financial statements. Had this information been available to us, we might have formed a different opinion on the financial statements.

Qualified opinion on financial statements

In our opinion, except for the possible effects of the matter described in the Basis for Qualified Opinion paragraph, the financial statements:

- give a true and fair view of the state of the company's affairs as at 31 December 20 ... and of its profit for the year then ended;
- have been properly prepared in accordance with United Kingdom Generally Accepted Accounting Practice; and
- have been prepared in accordance with the requirements of the *Companies Act* 2006.

Opinion on other matter prescribed by the Companies Act

In our opinion, the information given in the [Strategic Report and the] Directors' Report for the financial year for which the financial statements are prepared is consistent with the financial statements.

Matters on which we are required to report by exception

In respect solely of the limitation on our work relating to the assessment of the appropriateness of the going concern basis of preparation of the financial statements, described above, we have not obtained all the information and explanations that we considered necessary for the purpose of our audit.

We have nothing to report in respect of the following matters where the *Companies Act* 2006 requires us to report to you if, in our opinion:

- adequate accounting records have not been kept or returns adequate for our audit have not been received from branches not visited by us; or
- the financial statements are not in agreement with the accounting records and returns; or
- certain disclosures of directors' remuneration specified by law are not made.

[5] This example is based on existing ISAs and has not been updated to reflect changes to audit reporting ISAs which will take effect for periods commencing 17 June 2016

TABLE 6[6]: Disclaimer of opinion

Basis for disclaimer of opinion on financial statements

The evidence available to us to confirm the appropriateness of preparing the financial statements on the going concern basis was limited because the company has not prepared any profit or cash flow projections for an appropriate period subsequent to the balance sheet date. As a result, and in the absence of any alternative evidence available to us, we have been unable to form a view as to the applicability of the going concern basis, the circumstances of which, together with the effect on the financial statements should this basis be inappropriate, are set out in note x to the financial statements.

Disclaimer of opinion on financial statements

Because of the significance of the matter described in the Basis for Disclaimer of Opinion on Financial Statements paragraph, we are unable to form an opinion as to whether the financial statements:

- give a true and fair view of the state of the company's affairs as at 31 December 20.. and of its profit [loss] for the year then ended;
- have been properly prepared in accordance with United Kingdom Generally Accepted Accounting Practice; and
- have been prepared in accordance with the requirements of the *Companies Act* 2006.

Opinion on other matter prescribed by the Companies Act 2006

Notwithstanding our disclaimer of an opinion on the financial statements, in our opinion, the information given in the [Strategic Report and the] Directors' Report for the financial year for which the financial statements are prepared is consistent with the financial statements.

Matters on which we are required to report by exception

In respect solely of the limitation of our work referred to above, we have not obtained all the information and explanations that we considered necessary for the purpose of our audit.

We have nothing to report in respect of the following matters where the *Companies Act* 2006 requires us to report to you if, in our opinion:

- adequate accounting records have not been kept or returns adequate for our audit have not been received from branches not visited by us; or
- the financial statements are not in agreement with the accounting records and returns; or
- certain disclosures of directors' remuneration specified by law are not made.

[6] This example is based on existing ISAs and has not been updated to reflect changes to audit reporting ISAs which will take effect for periods commencing 17 June 2016.

TABLE 7: Example paragraph where a material uncertainty exists and is adequately disclosed

Material uncertainty related to going concern

In forming our opinion, which is not modified, we have considered the adequacy of the disclosures made in Note 1 of the financial statements concerning the company's ability to continue as a going concern. The company incurred a net loss of £x during the year ended … and, at that date, the company's current liabilities exceeded its total assets by £y. These conditions, along with the other matters explained in note 2 to the financial statements, indicate the existence of a material uncertainty which may cast significant doubt about the company's ability to continue as a going concern. The financial statements do not include the adjustments that would result if the company was unable to continue as a going concern.

11.17　Regulated entities

Where the entity is regulated, it may be necessary to inform the regulator at an early stage of the intention to use an explanatory paragraph or qualify the audit report. This may lead to corrective action being requested by the regulator, which may serve to reduce the concerns that led to the proposal to include the explanatory paragraph or qualify the audit report.

11.18　Groups

The provisions of ISA (UK and Ireland) 570 (Revised June 2016) apply to group financial statements as well as individual company ones. However, the going concern basis may be appropriate for the preparation of group financial statements, even though it may not be for one or more of the individual entities within the group. Where this is the case, the auditor should ensure that he documents his considerations, and those of the directors, fully.

11.19　Preliminary announcements

Where a company prepares a preliminary announcement, the Listing Rules of the UK Listing Authority require that the preliminary announcement of full year results include a reference to any likely modification or emphasis of matter paragraph that may be contained in the auditor's report to be issued with the annual financial report. The announcement should also be agreed with the auditor. Although there is no reference in these requirements to going concern, best practice suggests that the auditor would not agree a preliminary statement that made no reference to significant concerns where these existed.

11.20　Bulletin 2008/10

11.20.1　The need for guidance

As referred to in **11.2**, Bulletin 2008/10 *Going Concern issues during the current economic conditions* was issued in response to the severe economic conditions described as the 'credit crunch' affecting the UK and Irish economies in the latter half of 2007 and subsequently. Economic conditions had deteriorated and the APB considered it appropriate to issue further guidance regarding the auditor's evaluation of the directors' assessment of going concern, and the implications for the auditor's report.

11.20.2   General principles

An important principle underlying the Bulletin is that economic recession in itself would not give rise to a material uncertainty that causes significant doubt and causes the auditor to issue a report containing an emphasis of matter paragraph. It is only where there are matters which are specific to the entity that such an uncertainty would arise.

It is still therefore necessary for the process set out in ISA (UK and Ireland) 570 (Revised June 2016) to be followed whereby those charged with governance assess the applicability of the going concern basis of accounting and make disclosures regarding any material uncertainty around it, whilst the auditor assesses and evaluates what those charged with governance have done and reports accordingly where there is a material uncertainty that may cast significant doubt on the entity's ability to continue as a going concern.

11.20.3   Detailed considerations

The Bulletin goes into more detail about how economic recession may affect the various stages of this process and amongst other things makes the following points:

- the process directors go through to make the disclosures around risk referred to above will provide useful audit evidence;
- the need for the assessment by both the directors and the auditor to start early. As this process will often result in board papers or possibly in remediation plans so the earlier the issues are addressed the better;
- because the risks in relation to the entity not being a going concern are so pervasive, they must be borne in mind throughout the audit;
- because the future outcome of implementing plans may be an important part of the assessment of going concern, then specific representations relating to these matters may be needed;
- the understandability of disclosures is an important feature given that the disclosures may be made in numerous places in the financial statements;
- the extent of disclosure is not an indicator that there is a material uncertainty that causes significant doubt. A lengthy disclosure may be as a result of explaining why this is not the case; and
- the issue of facility renewal is likely to be problematic but need not result in significant doubt (see **11.20.4**).

11.20.4   Availability of finance

One impact of difficult economic conditions may be the limited availability of finance from both suppliers and customers as well as banks and other lenders. Companies often find themselves needing to renew facilities before the end of the period over which going concern is being assessed. In these cases, bankers may be reluctant to confirm that facilities will continue to be available. This in itself is not a reason to doubt the ability of the entity to continue as a going concern.

The Bulletin refers to a number of reasons why a bank may be reluctant to confirm that a facility will be available in the future, including:

- the bank responding that in the current economic environment, as a matter of policy, it is not providing such confirmations to its customers and their auditors;
- the entity and its bankers are engaged in negotiations about the terms of a facility (e.g. the interest rate), so there is no evidence that the bank is reluctant to lend to the company; or
- the bank renewed a rolling facility immediately prior to the date of the issuance of the annual report and accounts and is reluctant to go through the administrative burden to confirm that the facility will be renewed on expiry.

The absence of a confirmation on its own does not constitute a significant doubt. The Bulletin makes the point that there needs to be other reasons specific to the entity which lead to the belief that the bankers are refusing to confirm ongoing facilities.

Even in this event, directors and auditors should consider whether alternative strategies or sources of finance are available. The auditor should assess the directors' plans for future action, including plans to liquidate assets, borrow money or restructure debt, reduce or delay expenditure or increase capital. Where alternative strategies are in place, the auditor should consider whether these:

- are realistic;
- have a reasonable expectation of resolving the problem; and
- are likely to be put into place effectively by the directors.

If this is the case, the auditor may decide it is unnecessary to include an emphasis of matter paragraph in his report.

11.21   The Sharman Inquiry into going concern and liquidity risks

Lord Sharman was asked by the Financial Reporting Council in early 2011 to lead an enquiry to:

- identify lessons for companies and auditors addressing going concern and liquidity risks; and
- recommend measures, if any, which are necessary to improve the existing reporting regime and related guidance for companies and auditors in relation to these matters.

The initial findings of the inquiry were published in November 2011 and the final findings in June 2012.

Evidence gathered by Lord Sharman strongly indicated an expectation gap between the needs of investors and management assessment in relation to going concern. The report was clear that the requirement to make adequate and useful going concern disclosures should not discourage management from sensible risk taking which would cause their business not to grow.

The inquiry report recommended that going concern reporting move towards a disclosure model whereby the directors always report how they arrived at the going concern statement, as part of their discussion of strategy and principal risks in the company's narrative report. The audit committee report would also illustrate the effectiveness of the directors' process by:

- confirming that a robust risk assessment had been made;
- providing an explanation of the material risks to going concern considered and addressed; and
- identifying any material risks which have not been resolved.

Since 2012, the FRC has worked to implement the recommendations of the Sharman Panel and has made various amendments to ISAs (UK and Ireland) 260, 570 and 700 as well as a revision to the UK Corporate Governance Code ('the Code'), applicable for financial years beginning on or after 1 October 2014.

Accompanying the revised Code, the FRC has issued *Guidance on Risk Management, Internal Control and Related Financial and Business Reporting*. This guidance revises, integrates and replaces the previous editions of the FRC's *Internal Control: Revised Guidance for Directors on the Combined Code and Going Concern and Liquidity Risk: Guidance for Directors of UK Companies*, and reflects changes made in the 2014 version of the Code. It aims to bring together elements of best practice for risk management; prompt boards to consider how to discharge their responsibilities in relation to the existing and emerging principal risks faced by the company; reflect sound business practice; and highlight related reporting responsibilities. This guidance includes guidance for directors on determining whether to adopt the going concern basis and determining whether there are material uncertainties.

Following on from this, the FRC also decided to issue separate, simplified guidance for those companies which do not apply the Code. This was published in April 2016 as *Guidance on the Going Concern Basis of Accounting and Reporting on Solvency and Liquidity Risks*. The guidance is intended to provide a practical guide for directors of non-Code companies, bringing together the requirements of company law, accounting standards, auditing standards, other regulation and existing FRC guidance relating to reporting on the going concern basis of accounting, solvency risk and liquidity risk and reflects developments in the FRC's thinking as a consequence of the Sharman Inquiry. It incorporates recent developments in the corporate reporting framework and the strategic report.

12 DOCUMENTATION

12.1 Introduction

This chapter has been updated to reflect the changes contained in final draft ISAs issued by the FRC in April 2016. Subject to legislative changes in progress at the time of writing, it is expected that ISA (UK and Ireland) 230 (Revised June 2016) *Audit documentation* will take effect for the audit of financial statements for periods commencing on or after 17 June 2016. For earlier periods, ending on or after 15 December 2010, the version of ISA (UK and Ireland) 230 issued in October 2009 applies. The ISA provides standards on documentation covering:

- form of working papers;
- content of working papers;
- changes to audit documentation after the date of the auditor's report;
- assembly of the final audit file; and
- confidentiality, safe custody and retention of audit documentation.

Changes in the 2016 version include Audit Directive requirements for statutory audits regarding retention of documents and closure of the audit file (see paragraphs **12.3**, **12.4** and **12.6**).

Other ISAs contain documentation requirements and application material relating to specific aspects of the audit. These are covered in the chapters of this book dealing with the relevant topics.

ISQC (UK and Ireland) 1 and Audit Regulations also contain requirements regarding ownership, custody and confidentiality of working papers (see paragraph **12.6**).

Whilst audit documentation remains the property of the auditor, the Companies Act requires certain information to be made available to successor auditors (see **Chapter 38**).

Auditors may also be asked in other situations to grant access to their files to third parties, usually acting on behalf of a prospective purchaser of, or provider of finance to, the entity. Guidance on steps that may be taken by the auditor to mitigate risk in these situations is provided in ICAEW Technical Release Audit 04/03 *Access to Working Papers by Investigating Accountants* (see paragraph **12.7**).

12.2 Purpose of documentation

ISA (UK and Ireland) 230 (Revised June 2016) requires that the auditor should document matters which are important in providing audit evidence to support his opinion and evidence that the audit was carried out in accordance with ISAs (UK and Ireland).

Working papers are any material the auditor obtains, prepares or retains in the course of his audit. This may be in paper form but may also include, for example, film, scanned documents, computer discs or electronic files, including e-mail.

Working papers provide a record of supervision and review, the planning and performance of the audit by the staff and the evidence to support the audit opinion. They provide the individuals responsible for approving the audit report with the means to satisfy themselves that the work delegated has been properly performed. Other advantages of working papers are that they are seen as providing a source of reference that may be used in subsequent years and that they encourage a methodical approach.

12.3   Form and content

Working papers should be sufficiently complete and detailed so as to provide an overall understanding of the audit. They should contain information on planning the audit, the nature, timing and extent of the audit procedures performed and the results and conclusions from the procedures.

Working papers should be sufficient to allow an 'experienced auditor, having no previous connection with the audit' to be able to understand:

- the nature, timing and extent of the audit procedures performed to comply with the ISAs (UK and Ireland) and applicable legal and regulatory requirements;
- the results of the audit procedures performed, and the audit evidence obtained; and
- significant matters arising during the audit, the conclusions reached thereon, and significant professional judgments made in reaching those conclusions.

For statutory audits of financial statements, the ISA requires the auditor to retain any other data and documents in the audit documentation that are of importance in support of his report.

An experienced auditor is an individual (whether internal or external to the firm) who has practical audit experience, and a reasonable understanding of:

- audit processes;
- ISAs and applicable legal and regulatory requirements;
- the business environment in which the entity operates; and
- auditing and financial reporting issues relevant to the entity's industry.

The ISA states that it may be necessary for that experienced auditor to hold discussions with the auditor to obtain a detailed understanding.

Because of a wide variety of circumstances in which working papers have to be prepared and the many types of business transactions to which they relate, it is not practicable to lay down a standard form for their preparation suitable for each and every situation. How the relevant information can best be shown, what audit procedures need to be applied and how their results can best be summarised is a matter for the particular circumstances. They should, however, be set out in such a fashion that the salient facts are readily apparent.

12.3.1   Factors affecting form and content of working papers

Working papers should be designed for each assignment and the factors set out in **Table 1** will determine their extent.

TABLE 1: Factors affecting form and content and extent of working papers

- the nature of the engagement;
- the identified risks of material misstatement;
- the extent of judgment required in performing the work and evaluating the results;
- the significance of the audit evidence obtained;
- the nature and extent of exceptions identified;
- the need to document a conclusion or the basis for a conclusion not readily determinable from the documentation of the work performed or audit evidence obtained; and
- the specific methodology and technology the auditor uses.

The use of standardised working papers, such as checklists, specimen letters and a standard index may aid efficiency and control, but the auditor should be aware of the dangers of following a standard approach mechanically. Professional judgment should be exercised when such aids are used.

If schedules have been drawn up by the client, the auditor requires evidence that they have been properly prepared before relying on them.

As indicated above, the term 'working papers' refers to the record of all of the evidence that the auditor considers necessary to collect in order to support an opinion. This may relate to the current year or be of a permanent nature, i.e. of continuing importance and as a result, be filed separately. The specific nature will depend on the assignment. Examples of the content of working papers are shown in **Table 2**.

TABLE 2: Contents of working papers

- information on the legal nature of the client, including copies of important documents;
- information concerning the industry and the economic and legislative environments within which the entity operates;
- evidence of the planning process, including any changes;
- notes on the accounting and internal control systems including extracts from the entity's internal control manual;
- assessment of inherent and control risks at the financial statements and assertion level;
- consideration of and conclusions on the work of internal audit;
- analyses of transactions and balances, including significant ratios and trends;
- audit programmes showing the nature, timing and extent of the audit procedures performed in response to risks at the assertion level, and the conclusions thereon;
- evidence that the work performed by assistants was supervised and reviewed;
- an indication as to who performed the audit procedures and when they were performed;
- correspondence with other auditors, experts and third parties;
- details of audit procedures applied where components of the financial statements are audited by another auditor;
- correspondence with the entity, including reports to management and notes of discussions with management concerning audit matters;
- letters of representation from management;
- a summary of the significant aspects of the audit, the conclusions reached and how matters have been resolved and the views of those charged with governance; and
- copies of the approved financial statements and auditor's reports.

12.3.2   Documenting characteristics of items tested

The ISA requires the auditor to include in his documentation details of the identifying characteristics of the items or matters tested. The characteristics recorded will vary depending on the items being tested, but may specifically identify the actual items testing, e.g. for a detailed test of entity-generated purchase orders, the auditor may identify the actual documents tested by providing their purchase order number, or alternatively, indicate the population as a whole, e.g. for a review of credit notes over a certain amount, the auditor may document the scope of the procedure and the threshold value above which items were reviewed.

Recording the items tested at this level of detail allows the subsequent investigation of exceptions or inconsistencies as well as enabling the audit team to be accountable for its work.

Typically, however, copies of the entity's records will only be required when they are necessary for an experienced auditor to understand the work performed and the conclusions reached.

12.3.3   Judgment areas

ISA 230 requires that working papers should include the auditor's reasoning on all significant matters which require the exercise of judgment, together with the auditor's conclusions thereon.

The ISA provides examples of items which would be deemed to be 'significant matters':

* matters that give rise to significant risks;
* results of audit procedures which indicate either that financial information could be materially misstated or that there is a need to revise the auditor's previous assessment of the risks of material misstatement;
* circumstances where the auditor has significant difficulty in performing his procedures;
* the entity's ability to continue as a going concern; and
* findings that could result in a modification to the auditor's report.

The working papers should note the relevant facts at the time the judgment was reached. This is particularly important where it concerns a difficult area which may be questioned later with the benefit of hindsight. The ISA suggests that use of a summary of significant matters cross-referenced to detailed working papers may aid consideration of these matters together with assisting with review of the work performed and conclusions reached. This may form part of a 'completion memorandum'.

The ISA also requires the auditor to document any discussion held with management and others, including those charged with governance, about significant matters.

Where the auditor has found information that contradicts his final conclusion on a significant matter the inconsistency should be documented on file, together with an explanation of how the final conclusion was reached. This does not mean, however, that incorrect or superseded documentation should be retained on file.

12.3.4   Documentation of departures from ISAs (UK and Ireland)

Where it is necessary to depart from the requirements of the basic or essential procedures in an ISA, the auditor is required to document the alternative procedures followed and the reasons for the departure. This does not apply to procedures that are not relevant to the engagement, e.g. the auditor need not apply the standards in ISA (UK and Ireland) 510 (Revised June 2016) regarding initial engagements for ongoing audits.

12.3.5 Identification of the preparer and reviewer of documentation

The performer of audit work should be clearly identified on each piece of documentation, including the date on which his work was performed. There is no requirement to provide on each piece of documentation evidence of who reviewed the audit work. The documentation should indicate, however, who reviewed each element of the audit work and when. This may be on a control sheet rather than by, for example, initialling and dating each sheet of documentation itself.

12.3.6 Specific documentation requirements

In addition to documentation requirements specified elsewhere in ISAs, ISQC (UK and Ireland) 1 (Revised June 2016) requires that for statutory audits, the engagement documentation must include any other data and documents that are of importance for monitoring compliance with the ISQC and other applicable legal requirements.

This includes documenting whether:

(a) the firm complies with the independence and objectivity requirements in the Ethical Standards;

(b) there are threats to the firm's independence, and the safeguards applied to mitigate those threats;

(c) the firm has the competent employees, time and resources needed in order to carry out the audit in an appropriate manner; and

(d) the key audit partner is eligible to be appointed as a statutory auditor.

Firms are required to keep the documents and information required by ISQC (UK and Ireland) 1 and the documentation requirements of other applicable ISAs (UK and Ireland) for at least six years from the date of the auditor's report. This period may be longer if necessary to satisfy the requirements of any applicable laws or regulation relating to data protection and to meet the requirements for any applicable administrative and judicial proceedings.

ISA (UK and Ireland) 220 (Revised June 2016) specifies certain documentation requirements where engagement quality control reviews are carried out.

ISQC (UK and Ireland) 1 (Revised June 2016) also specifies certain matters that need to be documented at the firm level regarding the firm's systems, procedures and controls.

12.4   Assembly of the final audit file

ISA (UK and Ireland) 230 (Revised June 2016) requires the final audit file to be assembled on a timely basis. The requirements of ISQC (UK and Ireland) 1 (Revised June 2016) suggest this should be within 60 days of the date of the auditor's report (see **3.2.9**) and for statutory audits, ISA (UK and Ireland) 230 (Revised June 2016) requires the file to be closed within this 60-day period.

For statutory audits of financial statements, the auditor is required to keep any other data and documents that are of importance for monitoring compliance with ISAs (UK and Ireland) and other applicable legal requirements.

The final assembly of the audit file is an administrative process and should not involve any further audit work or the drawing of new conclusions. Only administrative changes can be made to the audit documentation, such as:

- deleting or discarding superseded documentation;
- sorting, collating or cross-referencing working papers;
- signing off completion checklists relating to the file assembly process; or
- documenting audit evidence that the auditor has obtained, discussed and agreed with the relevant members of the audit team before the date of his report.

Other audit documentation must not be deleted or discarded before the end of the retention period.

12.5   Changes to audit documentation

ISA (UK and Ireland) 230 (Revised June 2016) states that exceptional circumstances may arise which require the auditor to perform new procedures after the date of the audit report or modify existing documentation, such as in response to comments received during monitoring inspections performed by internal or external parties. The ISA requires the auditor to record who made the changes and when, the consequential changes to documentation, the reasons for the changes and the effect on his previous conclusions.

12.6   Confidentiality, custody, ownership and retention of working papers

ISQC (UK and Ireland) 1 (Revised June 2016) (see **3.2.9**) contains specific requirements that the auditor should adopt appropriate procedures for maintaining the confidentiality and safe custody of his working papers. It is the auditor's responsibility to ensure that the audit working papers are kept safely. He should bear in mind that his work is strictly confidential.

The audit working papers are the property of the auditor. Papers relating to accountancy work will normally be the property of the client although this will depend on the particular circumstances. Certain papers may be made available to clients but care should be taken not to undermine the independence or validity of the audit process. Because of their confidential nature, they should not be divulged to third parties without the client's permission, although some third parties, for example HMRC, may have a right of access in certain circumstances. However, whatever the circumstances, they should not be seen as a substitute for the client's accounting records.

Audit Regulation 3.11 states that 'A Registered Auditor must keep all audit working papers which auditing standards require for an audit for a period of at least six years. The period starts with the end of the accounting period to which the papers relate'. The actual length of time they are kept for will be a matter of judgment based on the auditor's own needs, those of the client and any regulatory requirements. However, it suggests that prior to their destruction, a review is carried out to ensure that there is no need to refer to them again.

This conflicts slightly with the application material in ISA (UK and Ireland) 230 (Revised June 2016), which states that audit documentation should normally be retained for a period of at least five years from the audit report date (or date of the group auditor's report, if later). It also conflicts with a new requirement in ISQC (UK and Ireland) 1 (Revised June 2016) which originates from the EU Audit Directive and requires that for statutory audits, engagement documentation must be retained for at least six years from the date of the audit report.

Where evidence is held electronically, audit firms should ensure that they retain at least one version of any, otherwise superseded, information technology applications required to access old audit documentation. This may include both proprietary word-processing or spreadsheet tools which may have been upgraded, or any internally developed audit tools which have become obsolete or have been replaced or revised. The ability to retrieve working papers and other documentation is also an issue if it was originally prepared on paper and has later been scanned or microfiched for storage.

It is important that the auditor has procedures in place to ensure that the integrity of data is maintained when it is stored electronically such as introducing appropriate back-up routines and use of restricted passwords.

Where working papers are produced by sub-contractor auditors, Audit Regulation 3.12 requires that 'A Registered Auditor must make arrangements so that if any of its audit work is carried out by another firm, then:

(a) all the audit working papers created by that firm are returned to the Registered Auditor; or
(b) the other firm agrees to keep those papers as required by regulation 3.11 and allows the Registered Auditor unrestricted access to the papers for whatever reason.'

Working papers of component auditors in group situations are considered in **Chapter 30**.

12.7   Access to working papers

When a company becomes a target for potential purchasers, the purchaser's investigating accountants will frequently want access to the audit working papers to assist in their investigations. The granting of access to working papers in these circumstances involves issues of confidentiality and also the possibility that the auditor may be alleged to have accepted an additional duty of care.

The Audit Faculty of the ICAEW issued Audit 4/03: *Access to Working Papers by Investigating Accountants*, to attempt to facilitate the agreement of access to working papers in these situations and update previous guidance. It recommends that access to papers is granted on the basis of client authorisation and 'release' letters. These seek to deal with confidentiality issues and limit as far as possible additional risks.

12.7.1   Working paper ownership and access

The working papers of the auditor are his legal property and he has the right to restrict or decline access to them, except where there is a change of auditor, as described in **Chapter 38**. The auditor would not provide access to his working papers or provide explanations on those papers until he has received:

- an authorisation letter signed by the vendor and the target company permitting the auditor to give access (**Table 3**); and
- a release letter signed by the prospective purchaser and its investigating accountant in which they agree that the auditor does not assume any duties or liabilities as a result of granting access (**Table 4**).

The release letter also requires the purchaser to indemnify the auditor for any loss suffered in the event of the purchaser or investigating accountant failing to comply with his obligations in the release letter.

In addition, to assist in excluding any other duty of care which may arise, and to reinforce the importance and purpose of audit working papers, the guidance suggests:

- attaching a 'notice' to the working papers when access is provided which summarises the characteristics, and records the exclusion of liability (see Attachment 1 in the example letter in **Table 4**); and
- obtaining an undertaking from the purchaser and investigating accountants to include such a standard notice in the text of their due diligence report.

This assumes that the purchaser and investigating accountant will not allow the working papers to be viewed by another third party without written consent from the auditor. Whether this will be granted depends on the circumstances, and will usually be dependent on the signing of a formal release letter. In many cases, the auditor controls access to the files by requiring the investigating accountants to view them on the auditor's premises.

The auditor would normally give access to all working papers. If some are withdrawn, he should inform the investigating accountants and purchaser that this is the case.

The example letters in **Tables 3** and **4** should be tailored to the circumstances. In particular, references to tax papers should be omitted where access to such papers is not provided.

TABLE 3: Client authorisation letter

Private and Confidential

The Directors
[Vendor]
[Address]

The Directors
[The Company]
[Address]
[Date]

Dear Sirs

Proposed sale of [Company Limited ('the Company') by [XYZ plc] ('the Vendor') to [ABC plc] ('the Purchaser')

In relation to the proposed sale by the Vendor [of the ordinary shares of the Company] to the Purchaser ('the Proposed Transaction') in which you requested this firm to allow [the Purchaser and/or] the Purchaser's accountants [PQR & Co] ('the Investigating Accountants') access to this firm's working papers relating to the statutory audit[s] of the Company's [and its subsidiaries'] financial statements for the year ended 31 December 20XX ('the Audit Working Papers').]

[As you are aware, this firm has not yet completed this year's statutory audit[s] of the Company's [and its subsidiaries'] financial statements, and therefore, the Audit Working Papers for this year are incomplete. Further this firm is not able to give any opinion on those financial statements and has not done so. Nevertheless, I understand that the Purchaser and the Investigating Accountants still wish the Investigating Accountants to review such Audit Working Papers as are available to date.]

[In addition, you requested this firm to allow the Investigating Accountants to review the taxation returns and computations of the Company [and its subsidiaries], so far as in the possession of this firm, as submitted to and/or agreed with the UK HM Revenue & Customs for each of the last [insert number] years[, working papers relating to those returns and computations] and copies of the correspondence and related documents passing between this firm and the UK HM Revenue & Customs in respect of those returns and computations (together, 'the Tax Papers').]

This firm's general policy is not to allow third parties to have access to the working papers in the possession of this firm. However, this firm is content to allow such access to the Audit Working Papers [and the Tax Papers] ([together] 'the Papers'), but only on the basis of the guidance contained in Technical Release 04/03 issued by the Institute of Chartered Accountants in England and Wales. In accordance with that guidance I am now writing to confirm your agreement to the terms set out in this letter and to secure the authorisation of the Company [and its subsidiaries] for that access.

As a condition of providing access to the Investigating Accountants and responding to any requests for information and explanations in relation to the Papers in the course of or in connection with their review of the Papers, this firm requires that the Purchaser and the Investigating Accountants agree to the terms of the letter enclosed.

As you will appreciate, the Audit Working Papers were created for the sole purpose of the statutory audit[s] of the Company's [and its subsidiaries'] financial statements [and the Tax Papers were prepared and/or obtained for the purpose of calculating and agreeing the Company's [and its subsidiaries'] UK tax liabilities]. The Papers were not created for the purpose of the Proposed Transaction. Consequently, the information in the Papers should not be treated as suitable for the purposes of the Proposed Transaction. Furthermore, it is not this firm's function or responsibility to provide to the Purchaser or the Investigating Accountants any Papers that may come into existence, or information that may come to this firm's attention, after [date].

Accordingly, this firm requires the Vendor and its directors and the Company [(and its subsidiaries)] and [its] [their] directors to agree to the following conditions:

(a)   They each accept the risk, and do not and will not hold this firm responsible, if the Investigating Accountant's review of the Papers or any information or explanations that this firm gives to them in relation to the Papers or in connection with their review of the Papers:

    (i)   results in or contributes to the termination or reduction of the interest of the Purchaser in, or to the alternation to the proposed terms of, the Proposed Transaction, or otherwise affects the Proposed Transaction or the prospects of its maturing into a binding transaction; or

    (ii)   causes an action or proceeding to be brought at any time against the Vendor or its directors or the company [(or any of its subsidiaries)] or [its] [their] directors [respectively]; or

    (iii)   results in the Purchaser, the Investigating Accountants or any other person or entity using or misusing any confidential information obtained from a review of the Papers or from any information or explanations given by this firm.

(b)   They each accept that, to the fullest extent permitted by law, this firm owes them no duty of care or other obligation and has no liability to them, in relation to or in connection with the Proposed Transaction as a result of granting the Investigating Accountants access to the Papers or any information or explanations that this firm gives in relation to the Papers or in connection with the review by the Investigating Accountants of the Papers.

The audit of the financial statements of the [Company/Companies] was undertaken by and is the sole responsibility of this firm, that is [insert full, exact name of UK firm carrying out the audit]. In paragraph (a) and (b) above references to 'this firm', where appropriate in the context, shall have an extended meaning so that they include, in addition to [insert full, exact name of the UK firm carrying out the audit], [partners/ directors/members], employees and agents of this firm [and any person or organisation associated with this firm through membership of the international association of professional service firms to which this firm belongs and their [partners/directors/ members], employees and agents]. This letter is for the benefit of all those included within the reference to this firm and each of them may enforce in their own right all of the terms of this letter.

Please confirm that the Company [and its subsidiaries] authorise[s] this firm to allow access to the Papers and to give information or explanations on the terms described above by signing the enclosed copy of this letter on behalf of the Vendor and its directors and the Company and its directors [and its subsidiaries and their directors] and returning it to this firm marked for the attention of ....

Yours faithfully

....

ACKNOWLEDGEMENT

Acknowledged and agreed, for and on behalf of [Vendor] and the directors of [Vendor].

....
Director   Date

Acknowledged and agreed, for and on behalf of [the Company] and the directors of [the Company].

....
Director   Date

[Acknowledged and agreed, for and on behalf of [subsidiaries] and the directors of [subsidiaries].

....
Director   Date]

TABLE 4: Release letter to prospective purchaser and investigating accountants

(The Release Letter assumes a proposed purchase of a company and that both Audit Working Papers and Tax Papers are to be made available. It must be amended as appropriate for the circumstances of each transaction.)

Private and Confidential

[Purchaser]
[Address]

[Investigating Accountants]
[Address]
[Date]

Dear Sirs

Proposed Acquisition of [Company] Limited

(1)   In connection with the proposed acquisition by [ABC plc] ('the Purchaser') of [Company] Limited ('the Company') ('the Proposed Transaction') the Company [(and the subsidiary undertakings identified in Attachment 2)] [(together 'the Companies')] [has/have] requested this firm to allow [the Purchaser and/or] [name of Firm of Accountants] (the 'Investigating Accountants') access to this firm's working papers relating to the statutory audit[s] [(including the audits currently in progress)] of the financial statements of the [Company/Companies] for the year[s] ended [date] ('the Audit Working Papers') [and the taxation returns and computation of the [Company/Companies], so far as in this firm's possession, as submitted to and/or agreed with the UK HM Revenue & Customs for each of the last [number] years[, working papers relating to those returns and computations] and copies of the correspondence and related documents passing between this firm and the UK HM Revenue & Customs in respect of those returns and computations (together 'the Tax Papers')]. [[The Company/ Companies] [has/have] authorised this firm at this firm's discretion to give information or explanations in relation to the Audit Working Papers [and the Tax Papers]]. The Audit Working Papers [and the Tax Papers together] are also referred to below as 'the Papers'.

(2)   The Purchaser and the Investigating Accountants should note that this firm has not reported on the [Company's/Companies'] financial statements for any period subsequent to [date] [nor have any tax liabilities of the [Company/ Companies] been agreed for any subsequent period to [date]] and significant events may well have occurred since [that date/those dates]. It is not this firm's function or responsibility to provide to the Purchaser or the Investigating Accountants any Audit Working Papers [or Tax Papers] that may come into existence, or information that may come to this firm's attention, at any point after [date].

(3)   This firm does not accept or assume responsibility to anyone other than the [Company/Companies] and the [Company's/Companies' respective] members as a body, for its audit work, for its audit report(s) or for the opinions it has formed. The statutory audit is undertaken in order that this firm might report to the [Company's/Companies' respective] members, as a body, in accordance with Chapter 3 of Part 16 of the *Companies Act* 2006. The audit procedures and the Audit Working Papers were designed and created solely for the purpose of enabling this firm to form and state an opinion to the [Company's/ Companies' respective] members as a body, in accordance with the statutory requirements for audit, on whether the financial statements of [the Company/the Companies], which are the responsibility of the directors of the [the Company/ the Companies], give a true and fair view of the state of affairs of [the Company/ the Companies] as at the end of the relevant financial year and of the profit and loss for the period then ended. This firm's auditing procedures were designed to enable this firm to express an opinion on [the Company's/the Companies' respective] financial statements as a whole or not, for example and save where otherwise expressly stated, on individual account balances, financial amounts, financial information or the adequacy of financial, accounting or management systems. [The Tax Papers were prepared and/or obtained solely for the purpose of calculating and/or agreeing [the Company's/the Companies'] tax liabilities.]

(4) This firm's audit(s) of the [Company's/Companies'] financial statements, and the Audit Working Papers prepared or obtained in connection therewith, [was/ were] not planned or conducted in contemplation, or for the purpose, of the Proposed Transaction. [Nor were the Tax Papers.] Further, the scope of an audit is normally substantially narrower than an investigation on behalf of a potential purchaser. Moreover, there are a number of inherent limitations in audited financial statements [and the calculation or agreement of tax liabilities] as the Investigating Accountants will be able to advise.

(5) Therefore, items of possible interest to the Purchaser may not have been specifically addressed for the purposes of the audit [or of calculating and agreeing [the Company's/the Companies'] tax liabilities]. The user of professional judgment and assessment of materiality for the purpose of this firm's audit [or of calculating and agreeing [the Company's/the Companies'] tax liabilities] means that matters may have existed that would have been assessed differently by the Purchaser or the Investigating Accountants for the purposes of the Proposed Transaction. This firm does not warrant or represent that the information in the Papers, or that information or explanations given by this firm in relation to the Papers or in connection with the review by the Investigating Accountants of the Papers, is appropriate for the purposes of the Purchaser or the Investigating Accountants. The Audit Working Papers were not created for, and should not be treated as suitable for, any purpose other than the Statutory Audit. [The Tax Papers were not created for, and should not be treated as suitable for, any purpose other than [calculating and agreeing [the Company's/the Companies'] tax liabilities.]

(6) For the foregoing reasons, neither the Papers nor the information or explanations given by this firm in relation to the Papers or in connection with the review by the Investigating Accountants of the Papers can in any way serve as a substitute for other enquiries and procedures that the Purchaser and Investigating Accountants would (or should) otherwise undertake and judgments they must make for the purpose of satisfying themselves regarding [the Company's/the Companies' respective] financial condition or for any other purpose in connection with the Proposed Transaction. No one should rely for any purpose whatsoever upon the Papers or any information or explanations that this firm may give in relation to them or in connection with the review by the Investigating Accountants of them.

(7) This firm is prepared to grant the [Purchaser and/or the] Investigating Accountants access to the papers and at this firm's discretion to give information and explanations in relation to the Papers or in connection with the review by the Investigating Accountants of the Papers, on condition that the Purchaser and the Investigating Accountants acknowledge and accept the foregoing paragraphs (including that the position in respect of this firm's audit reports on the [Company's/Companies'] financial statements will remain as stated in paragraph 3 above following the grant of access to the Papers and giving of information and explanations in relation to the Papers) and agree to the following conditions upon which access to the Papers is granted and the explanations and information referred to are given:

(1) The Purchaser and the Investigating Accountants accept, agree and acknowledge:

(a) for the purposes of this letter, the expression 'the information' shall mean the Papers and any information and explanations given by this firm in relation to the Papers or in connection with the review by the Investigating Accountants of the papers;

(b)   where any information or explanation is given by this firm, the onus shall be upon the Purchaser and the Investigating Accountants to verify any such information or explanation direct with [the Company/ the Companies] rather than seek to rely on this firm;

(c)   to the fullest extent permitted by law, this firm owes no duty to them, whether in contract or in tort or under statute or otherwise (including in negligence) with respect to or in connection with the information or its provision or in relation to the audit reports on the [Company's/ Companies'] financial statements;

(d)   if, notwithstanding the terms of this letter, they do rely upon any of the information or the audit reports on the [Company's/Companies] financial statements for any purpose, they will do so entirely at their own risk;

(e)   they will not bring any actions, proceedings, or claims against this firm where the action, proceeding or claim in any way relates to or concerns or is connected with the use of or reliance on the information or the audit reports on the [Company's/Companies'] financial statements;

(f)   to the fullest extent permitted by law, this firm has no liability to them for any loss or damage suffered or costs incurred by them, arising out of or in connection with the information or its use or the audit reports on the [Company's/Companies'] financial statements, however such loss or damage is caused;

(g)   they will not refer to the information nor allow access to it or any report derived therefrom to any person or entity without this firm's prior written consent. (However the Investigating Accountants will not need to obtain such consent in order to disclose and discuss the same (i) with [the Company/the Companies] for the purpose of obtaining information or verification from [the Company/the Companies] in respect of any report to be prepared by the Investigating Accountants in connection with the Proposed Transaction; (ii) with the Purchaser's legal advisers but then only on the basis that the firm will have no duty or liability to them; or (iii) otherwise as required by a Court or by statute.) Where this firm is willing to give written consent, this firm will require as a condition of such consent that the other person or entity agrees in writing to be bound by and to observe the terms set out in this letter, as if references to the Purchaser were a reference to the other person or entity.

(2)   To the fullest extent permitted by law, the Purchaser agrees to indemnify and hold harmless this firm against all actions, proceedings and claims brought or threatened against this firm, and all loss, damage and expense (including legal expenses) relating thereto where such action, proceeding or claim has arisen out of or results from or is connected with the failure of the Purchaser, or any of its professional advisers or the Investigating Accountants to comply with the terms of this letter.

(3)   Without limiting the obligation in paragraph 7(1)(g) above, the Purchaser and the Investigating Accountants agree to ensure that the notice attached as Attachment 1 to this letter is attached to any document obtained as a result of the Investigating Accountants' access to the Papers and is included in any note or report or other document in which they make reference to the information.

(8) The audit of the financial statements of the [Company/Companies] was undertaken by and is the sole responsibility of this firm, that is [insert full, exact name of UK firm carrying out the audit]. In paragraph 7(1)(c) to (g) and 7(2) of this letter all references to 'this firm' (except for the first and the last two references in the paragraph 7(1)(g) shall have an extended meaning so that they include, in addition to [insert full, exact name of the UK firm carrying out the audit], [partners/directors/members], employees and agents of this firm [and any person or organisation associated with this firm through membership of the international association of professional service firms to which this firm belongs and their [partners/directors/members], employees and agents. This letter is for the benefit of all of those referred to in the previous sentence and each of them may enforce in their own right all of the terms of this letter.

(9) This letter sets out the entire agreement as between the Purchaser and the Investigating Accountants and this firm in relation to the conditions upon which access to the Papers is given by this firm and upon which information and explanations in relation to the Papers or in connection with the review by the Investigating Accountants are given by this firm to the Purchaser and the Investigating Accountants. It replaces all prior agreements or understandings (if any) between or amongst the Purchaser, the Investigating Accountants and this firm in that regard.

(10) The terms of the agreement shall be governed solely by English law, and the Courts of England and Wales shall have exclusive jurisdiction in respect of any dispute arising out of it or in connection with it. [The Purchaser, the Investigating Accountants, and this firm irrevocably waive any right to object to proceedings being brought in those Courts, to claim that the proceedings have been brought in an inappropriate forum, or to claim that those Courts do not have jurisdiction.]

(11) Please confirm the agreement of the Purchaser and the Investigating Accountants to, and acceptance of, the provisions of this letter by signing, dating and returning to us a copy of this letter.

Yours faithfully

[Firm]

The Purchaser hereby acknowledges that it agrees to and accepts the provisions of this letter.

_____   [Date]

Director

The Investigating Accountants hereby acknowledge that they agree to and accept the provisions of this letter.

_____   [Date]

Director

Attachment 1 to Release Letter

Notice of the Auditor

(1)   [Firm name] ('the Auditor'), the auditor of [Company name] ('the Company') [and the subsidiary undertakings identified in the attached List of Subsidiary Undertakings (together 'the Companies')], has, on certain conditions, allowed [name of Investigating Accountants] ('the Investigating Accountants') to have access to the Auditor's working papers relating to the statutory audit of the [Company's/Companies'] financial statements for the [year/period] ended [date] ('the Audit Working Papers') and certain matters in the Auditor's files relating to the Auditor's engagement as the [Company's/Companies'] tax agent and adviser ('the Tax Papers').

(2)   The Auditor does not accept or assume responsibility to anyone other than [the Company/the Companies] and the [Company's/Companies' respective] members as a body, for its audit work, for its audit report[s] or for the opinions it has formed. To the fullest extent permitted by law, the Auditor does not accept or assume responsibility to anyone as a result of the access given to the Audit Working Papers and Tax Papers or for any information or explanation given to the Investigating Accountants in relation to the Audit Working Papers and Tax Papers or in connection with the review by the Investigating Accountants of the Audit Working Papers and Tax Papers.

(3)   The Audit Working Papers were not created for, and should not be treated as suitable for, any purpose other than the statutory audit. The statutory audit is undertaken in order that the Auditor might report to the [Company's/Companies' respective] members, as a body, in accordance with Chapter 3 of Part 16 of the *Companies Act* 2006. The audit work of the Auditor is undertaken so that the Auditor might state to the [Company's/Companies' respective] members those matters it is required to state to them in an auditor's report and for no other purpose. The Tax Papers were not created for, and should not be treated as suitable for, any purpose other than calculating and agreeing the [Company's/Companies'] tax liabilities.

Attachment 2 to Release Letter

List of companies referred to in paragraph 1 for which access to the Audit Working Papers [and the Tax Papers] is to be provided.

12.7.2   *Further explanations*

If an auditor provides further explanation which extends to matters beyond the content of his working papers, he increases the risk of assuming a duty of care. In particular, the auditor should take care not to give oral representations about matters arising after the date of the audit report.

If further explanations are sought, the auditor is advised to re-emphasise the matters in the Notice in Attachment 1 to the release letter, in **Table 4**, at the time, perhaps by reading this out, or circulating a copy of the Notice at the beginning of the meeting any meeting at which such matters are to be discussed.

If matters outside the auditor's working papers are to be discussed, the auditor considers whether this is appropriate. If the risks can be managed, he may wish to structure this as a separate engagement with appropriate liability protection in a separate engagement letter.

Auditors are recommended not to agree to any request by the investigating accountants to review or approve their due diligence report. Such requests do not give the auditor any added protection and may serve to confuse auditors' roles in transactions.

12.7.3   Access for other parties

The example release letter in **Table 4** assumes a simple investment transaction where an existing corporate entity purchases a subsidiary of the vendor. There are other situations where the release letter may require amendment.

Syndicated financings

In syndicated financings, the investigating accountants may be requested to provide copies of their investigation report, incorporating information derived from the audit working papers, to other parties who were not identified at the time the release letter was signed, and therefore could not be party to it. Providing this information without the auditor's consent would be in breach of paragraph 7(1)(g) of the release letter.

It might be appropriate for the lead bank or equity provider to sign a modified release letter containing the following paragraph:

> *This letter is addressed to [Lead Bank/Lead Equity Provider] for itself and on behalf of all [Banks/Equity Providers] listed in the [Loan/Equity Agreement] (together 'the [Banks/Equity Providers']). By signing and accepting the terms of this letter, [Lead Bank/Equity Provider] warrants and represents that it has authority to accept the same on its own behalf and as agent for the [Banks/Equity Providers].*

The lead bank or equity provider may seek to amend paragraph 7(2) of the letter to seek to provide an indemnity for its own breaches only. If this is agreed, the auditor should be aware of the risks of another bank or equity provider passing information on to another party.

Alternatively, each bank or equity provider should sign a release letter in its own right. This may be difficult where the draft investigating accountants' report is circulated to potential finance parties as a basis for their decision whether or not to go ahead with the finance. Technical Release Audit 4/03 contains detailed guidance on this situation.

Flotations

Where access is provided in connection with a flotation, the auditor is advised to obtain a release letter signed by the:

- firm acting as reporting accountants;
- new company incorporated for the purpose of the float; and
- sponsor.

The auditor should obtain legal advice about limiting liability where no new company has been incorporated.

Where the reporting accountants are preparing an accountants' report (a short form report), there is no need to attach or refer to the Notice. Paragraph 7(3) of the release letter should be amended accordingly.

Vendor due diligence

Where a vendor has instructed a firm of accountants to prepare a due diligence report that will eventually be addressed to a purchaser, the auditor will require the vendor and the target company to sign an authorisation letter. The wording of that letter will be extended to include an indemnity from the vendor, as it is the vendor, rather than the purchaser, who will control the distribution of the due diligence report.

The auditor will also require a release letter signed by the investigating accountants, based on **Table 4**, but without the indemnity paragraph 7(2). Risks to unknown potential purchasers will be managed in much the same way as for financing syndicates above.

Alternatively, the auditor may be prepared to acknowledge that the investigating accountants will require permission to circulate his report to prospective purchasers, and replace paragraphs 7(1)(g) and 7(2) with **Table 5**.

TABLE 5: Alternative paragraph 7(1)(g) and 7(2) for use in vendor due diligence situations

(g) they will not refer to the Information nor allow access to it or any report derived therefrom to any person or entity without this firm's prior written consent. The Investigating Accountants may allow access to the Information or any part thereof, in the form of a report of Investigating Accountants incorporating or referring to any part of the Information, to any prospective purchaser of the Company ('Prospective Purchaser') provided that the Investigating Accountants obtain the express prior agreement and acknowledgement of each Prospective Purchaser, addressed to this firm, that (a) this firm has, to the fullest extent permitted by law, no duty or liability and assumes no responsibility to the Prospective Purchaser or its professional advisers, whether in contract or tort or under statue or otherwise (including in negligence), with respect to or in connection with the Information or any part thereof the report and that (b) Prospective Purchaser will not disclose (including by reference or by copy, in whole or in part) any Information, including without limitation the report, to any other person or entity. Prior to the Investigating Accountants addressing to any party

---

acquiring interest in the Company ('Purchaser') any report incorporating or referring to any part of the Information, the Investigating Accountants shall procure that Purchaser binds itself to this firm and accepts all the provisions of a letter in the terms of this letter (but adjusted to refer to Purchaser), together with an obligation in the following terms:

(2) To the fullest extent permitted by law, Purchaser agrees to indemnify and hold harmless this firm against all actions, proceedings and claims brought or threatened against this firm and all loss, damage and expense (including legal expenses) relating thereto, where such action, proceedings or claim has arisen out of or results from or is connected with the failure of Purchaser, or any of its professional advisers or Investigating Accountants to comply with the terms of this letter.

Where the vendor due diligence report is prepared by the same firm as the auditor, the firm may manage its risk relating to the purchaser or prospective purchaser by:

- requiring the purchaser to agree the terms of the release letter before agreeing to address the vendor due diligence report to them; or
- placing an obligation on the vendor to ensure that the purchaser signs the release letter.

Business refinancing where there is no acquisition

Where a firm of accountants are instructed to report to funders in respect of a proposed refinancing of the entity, it is recommended that the auditor obtains a signed release letter from the funders and investigating accountants prior to releasing the audit working papers.

12.7.4   Investigating accountants from the same firm as the auditor

Where the auditor and investigating accountants are from the same firm, there still remains a risk from releasing audit working papers to a purchaser.

In this situation, some firms will wish to amend the release letter so that it is addressed only to the purchaser. The indemnity may also be restricted to breaches by the purchaser only.

12.7.5   Change of auditor

Where there is a change of auditor, guidance on access to working papers by the successor auditor is covered in **Chapter 38**.

13 PLANNING

13.1 Introduction

This chapter has been updated to reflect the changes contained in final draft ISAs issued by the FRC in April 2016. Subject to legislative changes in progress at the time of writing, it is expected that ISA (UK and Ireland) 300 (Revised June 2016) *Planning an audit of financial statements* will take effect for the audit of financial statements for periods commencing on or after 17 June 2016. For earlier periods ending on or after 15 December 2010, the version of ISA (UK and Ireland) 300 issued in October 2009 applies. The ISA provides guidance on the planning process covering:

- the role and timing of planning;
- involvement of key engagement team members;
- preliminary engagement activities;
- planning activities;
- documentation; and
- considerations for initial audit engagements.

Changes in the 2016 version of the ISA include additional application material, originating from the IAASB's own amendments, specifically relating to the audit of disclosures in the financial statements (see **13.5.1**). These derive from the IAASB's disclosures project (see **Chapter 1**) which identified a need to focus the auditor's attention on disclosures at an early stage in the audit process.

13.2 Planning the work

Planning is discussed in the context of recurring audits and is described as 'not a discrete phase of an audit, but rather a continual and iterative process that often begins shortly after (or in connection with) the completion of the previous audit and continues until the completion of the current audit engagement'. However, some planning activities will, by necessity, have to be completed at the beginning of the audit, such as understanding the legal and regulatory framework within which the entity operates and briefing the audit team.

The objectives of planning include:

- ensuring that appropriate attention is directed to important areas of the audit;
- ensuring that potential problems are identified;
- organising and managing the engagement properly;
- assisting with proper allocation of work to engagement team members;
- where appropriate, assisting with the coordination of work performed by other auditors or specialists;
- facilitating review; and
- enabling the audit to be performed in an effective and timely manner.

The guidance stresses that planning varies according to the size of the entity and complexity of the audit. In the case of a smaller audit where accountancy assistance is provided by the auditor, the audit plan should take account of any areas of audit risk identified, and evidence obtained, during that exercise.

13.3   Preliminary engagement activities

In order to ensure that the auditor has considered any events or circumstances which may affect his ability to plan to reduce the risk of material misstatement to an acceptable level, he should:

- perform client and audit engagement acceptance procedures in accordance with ISA (UK and Ireland) 220 (Revised June 2016) *Quality control for an audit of financial statements* (see **Chapter 3**);
- evaluate compliance with ethical and independence requirements (see **Chapters 2** and **3**); and
- establish the terms of the engagement, in accordance with ISA (UK and Ireland) 210 (Revised June 2016) *Agreeing the terms of audit engagements* (see **Chapter 14**).

The factors affecting client acceptance and ethical and independence issues should be continually re-evaluated during the audit as circumstances may change. However, the main element of this work should be performed before any other audit procedures are started and, for continuing engagements, this may be at the end of the prior year's audit.

13.4   The overall audit strategy

The auditor should set an overall strategy for the audit which sets the scope, timing and direction of the audit and assists with the development of the more detailed audit plan. This will involve:

- identifying the characteristics of the engagement that define its scope, i.e. what reporting requirements are there, what financial reporting framework is the client using, what group companies are covered;
- ascertaining the reporting objectives of the engagement to plan the timing of the audit and the nature of the communications required;
- considering the factors that, in the auditor's professional judgment, are significant in directing the engagement team's efforts;
- considering the results of preliminary engagement activities and, where applicable, whether knowledge gained on other engagements performed by the engagement partner for the entity is relevant; and
- ascertaining the nature, timing and extent of resources necessary to perform the engagement.

Developing this overall audit strategy helps the auditor to determine matters such as which members of the audit team should be used for specific audit areas and whether experts are needed for complex areas. For example, using appropriately experienced team members for high risk areas, how many team members to attend the inventory count, the extent of review of other auditor's work, the timing of such work and how these team members and resources are to be managed, directed and supervised.

Table 1 sets out a list of matters the auditor may consider when determining his overall audit strategy.

TABLE 1: Matters to consider when determining the overall audit strategy

Scope of the audit engagement

- the financial reporting framework on which the financial information to be audited has been prepared, including any need for reconciliations to another financial reporting framework;
- industry specific reporting requirements such as reports mandated by industry regulators;
- the expected audit coverage, including the number of locations of components to be included;
- the nature of the control relationships between a parent and its components that determine how the group is to be consolidated;
- the extent to which components are audited by other auditors;
- the nature of the business segments to be audited, including the need for specialised knowledge;
- the reporting currency to be used including any need for currency translation for the financial information audited;
- the need for a statutory audit of standalone financial statements in addition to an audit for consolidation purposes;
- whether the entity has an internal audit function and if so, whether, in which areas and to what extent, the work of the function can be used for the purposes of the audit;
- the entity's use of service organisations and how the auditor may obtain evidence concerning the design or operation of controls performed by them;
- the expected use of audit evidence obtained in prior audits, for example, audit evidence related to risk assessment procedures and tests of controls;
- the effect of information technology on the audit procedures, including the availability of data and the expected use of computer-assisted audit techniques;
- the coordination of the expected coverage and timing of the audit work with any reviews of interim financial information and the effect on the audit of the information obtained during such reviews;

- the discussion of matters that may affect the audit with firm personnel responsible for performing other services to the entity; and
- the availability of client personnel and data.

Reporting objectives, timing of the audit and communications required

- the entity's timetable for reporting, such as at interim and final stages;
- the organisation of meetings with management and those charged with governance to discuss the nature, extent and timing of the audit work;
- the discussion with management and those charged with governance regarding the expected type and timing of reports to be issued and other communications, both written and oral, including the auditor's report, management letters and communications to those charged with governance;
- the discussion with management regarding the expected communications on the status of audit work throughout the engagement and the expected deliverables resulting from the audit procedures;
- communication with auditors of components regarding the expected types and timing of reports to be issued and other communications in connection with the audit of components;
- the expected nature and timing of communications among engagement team members, including the nature and timing of team meetings and timing of the review of work performed; and
- whether there are any other expected communications with third parties, including any statutory or contractual reporting responsibilities arising from the audit.

Direction of the audit

- with respect to materiality:
  - setting materiality for planning purposes;
  - setting and communicating materiality for auditors of components;
  - reconsidering materiality as audit procedures are performed during the course of the audit;
  - identifying the material components and account balances;
- audit areas where there is a higher risk of material misstatement;
- the impact of the assessed risk of material misstatement at the overall financial statement level on direction, supervision and review;
- the selection of the engagement team (including, where necessary, the engagement quality control reviewer) and the assignment of audit work to the team members including the assignment of appropriately experienced team members to areas where there may be higher risks of material misstatement;
- engagement budgeting, including considering the appropriate amount of time to set aside for areas where there may be higher risks of material misstatement;
- the manner in which the auditor emphasises to engagement team members the need to maintain a questioning mind and to exercise professional scepticism in gathering and evaluating audit evidence;

- results of previous audits that involved evaluating the operating effectiveness of internal control including the nature of identified weaknesses and action taken to address them;
- evidence of the commitment of those charged with governance to the design and operation of sound internal control including evidence of appropriate documentation of such internal control;
- changes within the applicable financial reporting framework, such as changes in accounting standards, which may involve significant new or revised disclosures, particularly relevant with the introduction of new UK GAAP;
- volume of transactions which may determine whether it is more efficient for the auditor to rely on internal control;
- importance attached to internal control throughout the entity to the successful operation of the business;
- processes management uses to identify and prepare the disclosures required by the applicable financial reporting framework, including disclosures containing information that is obtained from outside the general and subsidiary ledgers;
- significant business developments affecting the entity, including changes to information technology and business process, changes in key management and acquisitions, mergers and divestments;
- significant industry developments such as changes in industry regulations and new reporting requirements; and
- other significant relevant developments such as changes in the legal environment affecting the entity.

13.5   Audit plan

As well as setting an overall audit strategy, ISA (UK and Ireland) 300 (Revised June 2016) requires the auditor to develop a detailed audit plan to address the various matters identified in the overall audit strategy in detail. The plan needs to include:

- a description of the nature, timing and extent of planned risk assessment procedures sufficient to assess the risks of material misstatement in accordance with ISA (UK and Ireland) 315 (Revised June 2016) (see **Chapter 21**);
- a description of the nature, timing and extent of planned further audit procedures at the assertion level for each material class of transactions, account balance and disclosure in accordance with ISA (UK and Ireland) 330 (Revised June 2016) (see **Chapter 21**); and
- details of other planned procedures that are required to be carried out so that the engagement complies with ISAs (UK and Ireland).

The audit plan is more detailed than the overall audit strategy in that it includes the specific nature, timing and extent of audit procedures to be performed by engagement team members. Planning for these audit procedures takes place over the course of the audit as the audit plan for the engagement develops. For example, planning of the auditor's risk assessment procedures occurs early in the audit process. However, planning the nature, timing and extent of specific further audit procedures depends on the outcome of those risk assessment procedures. In addition, the auditor may begin the execution of further audit procedures for some classes of transactions, account balances and disclosures before planning all remaining further audit procedures.

Although audit firms may have a bank of standard tests which are used to form the basis of an audit plan, these must be tailored to the individual circumstances of each audit.

13.5.1 Disclosures

Determining the nature, timing and extent of planned risk assessment procedures, and further audit procedures, as they relate to disclosures is important in light of both the wide range of information and the level of detail that may be encompassed in those disclosures. Further, certain disclosures may contain information that is obtained from outside of the general and subsidiary ledgers, which may also affect the assessed risks and the nature, timing and extent of audit procedures to address them.

Rather than leaving disclosures until the end of the audit, consideration of disclosures early in the audit assists the auditor in giving appropriate attention to, and planning adequate time for, addressing disclosures in the same way as classes of transactions, events and account balances. Early consideration may also help the auditor to determine the effects on the audit of:

- significant new or revised disclosures required as a result of changes in the entity's environment, financial condition or activities (for example, a change in the required identification of segments and reporting of segment information arising from a significant business combination);
- significant new or revised disclosures arising from changes in the applicable financial reporting framework (for example, the introduction of new UK GAAP, changes to disclosures where a small company ceases to be eligible for the small companies regime or a change in framework from UK GAAP to IFRS);
- the need for the involvement of an auditor's expert to assist with audit procedures related to particular disclosures (for example, disclosures related to pension or other retirement benefit obligations); and
- matters relating to disclosures that the auditor may wish to discuss with those charged with governance.

13.6 Documentation

ISA (UK and Ireland) 300 (Revised June 2016) requires that the auditor should document the overall audit strategy, the audit plan and any significant changes made during the audit engagement to the overall audit strategy or the audit plan, and the reasons for such changes.

This will act as a record of the key decisions considered necessary to properly plan the audit and communicate significant matters to the engagement team.

Documentation of the audit plan also acts as a record that the planning has been properly completed, which can be reviewed and approved before further work is undertaken.

13.7   Initial audit engagements

Much of the planning for ongoing or initial engagements will be identical, however, the first time auditor will not be able to draw on his knowledge of the client from earlier work. In addition to the procedures detailed above, the first time an auditor acts for a client, as part of planning he should also:

- perform the client acceptance procedures set out by ISA (UK and Ireland) 220 (Revised June 2016);
- follow up any matters discussed with management or those charged with governance as part of the process followed to select him as auditor;
- communicate with the predecessor auditor to arrange review of his working papers (see **Chapter 38**);
- consider the audit procedures necessary to obtain sufficient appropriate audit evidence regarding opening balances (see **Chapter 19**);
- assign appropriately experienced audit firm personnel; and
- perform the procedures required by the firm's quality control systems, such as appointment of a technical or concurring partner.

13.8   Changes to planning decisions during the course of the audit

The ISA explains that the planning decisions should be reviewed and revised as necessary during the course of the audit. The results of the audit tests or new information may lead to changes in the approach adopted or the assessment of risks and materiality and these should be formally documented.

13.9   Direction, supervision and review

As part of the audit planning, the auditor needs to plan time for the direction, supervision and review of others' work. The nature, timing and extent of the direction and supervision of audit team members and review of their work will depend on a number of factors including their experience and the complexity of the areas in which they are working. For areas of higher risk of material misstatement, the extent of direction and supervision may be increased.

Direction, supervision and review is not relevant where the audit work is carried out by the audit engagement partner who is a sole practitioner. However, that individual must be content that the audit has been performed in accordance with ISAs, and a sole practitioner may plan to consult with an outside source on particularly difficult or complex areas.

13.10   Communications with those charged with governance

The auditor may discuss elements of the planning with those charged with governance to improve the efficiency and effectiveness of the audit. However, the overall audit strategy and the audit plan remain the auditor's responsibility.

14 ENGAGEMENT LETTERS

14.1 Introduction

This chapter has been updated to reflect the changes contained in final draft ISAs issued by the FRC in April 2016. Subject to legislative changes in progress at the time of writing, it is expected that ISA (UK and Ireland) 210 (Revised June 2016) *Agreeing the terms of audit engagements* will take effect for the audit of financial statements for periods commencing on or after 17 June 2016. For earlier periods, ending on or after 15 December 2010, the version of ISA (UK and Ireland) 210 issued in October 2009 applies. The ISA provides guidance on engagement letters issued by the auditor covering:

- agreeing terms of engagement in writing;
- respective responsibilities of the auditor and those charged with governance;
- imposed limitations on audit scope;
- changes to the terms of the audit engagement;
- recurring audits; and
- changes in engagements.

In addition, ISA (UK and Ireland) 210 (Revised June 2016) includes guidance on the preconditions for an audit (see **14.3** below).

Changes in the 2016 version of ISA (UK and Ireland) 210 (Revised June 2016) are confined to the application material and relate largely to additional information that the auditor may request from management for the audit and example paragraphs for inclusion in an engagement letter. In addition, the application material considers the implications of the special accounting frameworks applicable to small companies and micro-entities (see **14.6** below).

In June 2008, the Financial Reporting Council issued guidance on auditor liability limitation agreements. It is outlined in **14.5** below.

Further guidance and general principles on risk management, including engagement letters, can be found in TECH 09/15BL *Managing the professional liability of accountants*.

The ICAEW has issued a helpsheet *Engagement Letters*, which provides example wording for engagement letters in a variety of scenarios. This helpsheet was last updated in February 2015 but was in the process of being updated at the time of writing.

14.2 Purpose

ISA (UK and Ireland) 210 (Revised June 2016) requires that the auditor and the client should agree on the terms of the engagement and these terms should be recorded in writing.

The purpose of an engagement letter is to:

- define clearly the extent of the auditor's responsibilities;
- minimise the possibility of any misunderstanding between the client and the auditor; and
- provide written confirmation of the auditor's acceptance of appointment, the scope of the audit and the form of the report.

There may be occasions when an engagement letter is not appropriate, but the terms should still be agreed in some other form of contract.

It is important that the letter takes account of the relevant legislative requirements and should be tailored for each assignment.

The ISA is primarily concerned with the audit of annual financial statements but the guidance to it notes that its principles can be applied to other audit related assignments, such as reporting on interim financial information or review of UK Corporate Governance Code compliance statements (see **Chapter 42** and **Chapter 39** for examples of appropriate engagement letters).

The guidance in the ISA does not encompass other services such as tax and accounting and separate letters may be required for each such service. Such services may be included in the audit engagement letter, but if so, the paragraphs must be clearly distinguished from those relating to the audit.

14.3   Preconditions for an audit

An auditor should only accept or continue with an audit when the basis upon which it is to be performed has been agreed. This will involve:

- establishing whether the preconditions for an audit are present; and
- confirming the understandings of the auditor and those charged with governance.

The preconditions for an audit are only present when the auditor can determine that the financial reporting framework to be applied by those charged with governance is acceptable and that those charged with governance understand and acknowledge their responsibility for:

- the preparation of the financial statements in accordance with that financial reporting framework;
- internal control systems that are adequate to ensure that financial statements can be prepared that are free from material misstatement; and
- providing the auditor with access to information relevant to the preparation of the financial statements, additional information requested by the auditor and individuals from whom the auditor may wish to gather audit evidence.

Additional information that the auditor may request from management for the purpose of the audit may include when applicable, matters related to other information in accordance with ISA (UK and Ireland) 720 (Revised June 2016) – see **Chapter 34**.

14.4 Contents

An engagement letter should be sent to each new client as soon after the acceptance of the appointment as possible and certainly before the commencement of any audit work.

The principal contents of an audit engagement letter may vary for each client, but reference would generally be made to:

- the objective of the audit of the financial statements;
- those charged with governance's responsibility for the financial statements;
- the scope of the audit, including reference to applicable legislation, regulations or pronouncements of professional bodies to which the auditor adheres;
- the form of any reports or other communication of results of the engagement;
- where applicable, the requirement for the auditor to communicate key audit matters in the auditor's report in accordance with ISA (UK and Ireland) 701 (see **Chapter 4**);
- the fact that because of the test nature and other inherent limitations of an audit, together with the inherent limitations of internal control, there is an unavoidable risk that even some material misstatement may remain undiscovered; and
- the need for unrestricted access to whatever records, documentation and other information is requested in connection with the audit.

The auditor may also include:

- arrangements regarding the planning and performance of the audit;
- expectation of receiving written confirmation of oral representations made by management;
- expectation that management will provide access to all information of which management is aware that is relevant to the preparation of the financial statements, including information relevant to disclosures;
- agreement of management to make draft financial statements available to the auditor on a timely basis including all information relevant to their preparation, whether obtained from within or outside of the general and subsidiary ledgers (including all information relevant to the preparation of disclosures), and any 'other information', as defined in ISA (UK and Ireland) 720 (Revised June 2016) – see **Chapter 34**;
- expectation that management will inform the auditor of any facts that may affect the financial statements of which management may become aware during the period from the date of the auditor's report to the date the financial statements are issued;

- descriptions of any other letters or reports the auditor expects to issue to the client;
- any confidentiality of other letters and reports to be issued and, where appropriate, the conditions, if any, on which permission might be given to make those reports available to others;
- basis on which fees are computed and any billing arrangements;
- complaint procedures;
- arrangements concerning the involvement of other auditors, experts or internal audit;
- for an initial audit, arrangements to be made with the predecessor auditor;
- a restriction of audit liability, where this is possible;
- a reference to any further agreements between auditor and client; and
- a request for the client to confirm acceptance of the terms of engagement.

When the auditor is not required to communicate key audit matters, it may be helpful for him to make reference in the terms of the audit engagement to the possibility of communicating key audit matters in the auditor's report.

Extracts from an example engagement letter for a company preparing financial statements under the *Companies Act* 2006 is shown in **Table 1**.

TABLE 1: Example terms for inclusion in an engagement letter for the audit of a non-listed company

Your responsibilities as directors

1.1 As directors of the company, you are responsible for ensuring that the company maintains adequate accounting records and for preparing financial statements which give a true and fair view and have been prepared in accordance with the *Companies Act* 2006. As directors, you must not approve the financial statements unless you are satisfied that they give a true and fair view of the assets, liabilities, financial position and profit or loss of the company.

1.2 In preparing the financial statements, you are required to:

- select suitable accounting policies and then apply them consistently;
- make judgments and estimates that are reasonable and prudent; and
- prepare the financial statements on the going concern basis unless it is inappropriate to presume that the company will continue in business.

1.3 You are also responsible for such internal control as you determine is necessary to enable the preparation of financial statements that are free from material misstatement whether due to fraud or error.

1.4 You are also responsible for safeguarding the assets of the company and hence for taking reasonable steps to prevent and detect fraud and other irregularities.

1.5 You are also responsible for making available to us, as and when required, all the company's accounting records and all other relevant records and related information, including minutes of all management and shareholders' meetings.

We are entitled to require from the company's officers such other information and explanations as we think necessary for the performance of our duties as auditors. Each director is required to take all steps that he ought to take as a director in order to make himself aware of any relevant audit information and to establish that we are aware of that information.

1.6 If financial information, which includes a report by us or is otherwise connected to us, is to be published on the company's website or by other electronic means, you agree to inform us in advance of the electronic publication. You agree that any such information will only be published in an appropriate context and be presented in a manner that is not misleading. The maintenance and integrity of the company's website is the responsibility of the directors. The directors' responsibility also extends to the ongoing integrity of the financial statements contained therein.

Our responsibilities as auditor

2.1 We have a statutory responsibility to report to the members whether in our opinion the financial statements give a true and fair view and have been properly prepared in accordance with the relevant accounting framework and whether they have been prepared in accordance with the *Companies Act* 2006.

2.2 We are also required to report whether the information given in the strategic report (if any) and the directors' report is consistent with those financial statements, and whether any such strategic report and the directors' report have been prepared in accordance with applicable legal requirements. We are required to state whether we have identified any material misstatements and, if so, give an indication of their nature.[1]

2.3 In arriving at our opinions, we are required to consider the following matters, and to report on any in respect of which we are not satisfied:

   (a) whether adequate accounting records have been kept by the company and proper returns adequate for our audit have been received from branches not visited by us;

   (b) whether the company's financial statements are in agreement with the accounting records and returns; and

   (c) whether we have obtained all the information and explanations which we consider necessary for the purposes of our audit.

   In addition, there are certain other matters which, according to the circumstances, may need to be dealt with in our report. For example, where the financial statements do not give details of directors' remuneration or of their transactions with the company, the *Companies Act* 2006 requires us to disclose such matters in our report.

2.4 We have a professional responsibility to report if the financial statements do not comply in any material respect with applicable accounting standards, unless in our opinion the non-compliance is justified in the circumstances. In determining whether or not the departure is justified, we consider:

   (a) whether the departure is required in order for the financial statements to give a true and fair view; and

   (b) whether adequate disclosure has been made concerning the departure.

2.5 Our professional responsibilities also include:

   • a description in our report of the directors' responsibilities for the financial statements and for assessing the company's ability to continue as a going concern[2]; and

- considering whether other information in documents containing audited financial statements is consistent with those financial statements and does not contain any information that is apparently materially incorrect based on, or materially inconsistent with the knowledge acquired by us in the course of performing the audit.

2.6 Our audit report will be made solely to the company's members, as a body, in accordance with Part 3 of Chapter 16 of the *Companies Act* 2006. Our audit work will be undertaken so that we might state to the company's members those matters we are required to state to them in an auditor's report and for no other purpose. To the fullest extent permitted by law, we do not accept or assume responsibility to anyone other than the company and the company's members as a body, for our audit work, the audit report, or for the opinions we will form.

2.7 [Where appropriate] As the company is a subsidiary undertaking we may be requested to co-operate with auditors of the parent undertaking and to provide them with information and explanations as necessary for the purposes of their audit of the parent undertaking. You agree that we may communicate with group auditors and respond to any reasonable requests for information for this purpose.

2.8 In the event that we cease to act as statutory auditors for the company, we are required to make available, if requested, all relevant information concerning the audit to our successors (if any) as statutory auditors. You agree to cover any reasonable costs of making such information available that we may incur in fulfilling our statutory duty.

Scope of Audit

3.1 Our audit will be conducted in accordance with International Auditing Standards (UK and Ireland). Those standards require us to comply with ethical requirements. In carrying out the audit, we will exercise professional judgment and maintain professional scepticism throughout the audit.

3.2 We shall:

- obtain an understanding of the accounting and internal control systems in order to assess their adequacy as a basis for the preparation of the financial statements and to establish whether adequate accounting records have been maintained by the company;
- identify and assess the risks of material misstatement of the financial statements, whether due to fraud or error and design and perform audit procedures responsive to those risks; and
- expect to obtain such appropriate evidence as we consider sufficient to enable us to form a reasonable basis for our conclusions.

3.3 Our procedures will include an assessment of:

- whether the accounting policies are appropriate to the company's circumstances and have been consistently applied and adequately disclosed;
- the reasonableness of significant accounting estimates made by the directors;
- the appropriateness of management's use of the going concern basis of accounting and, based on the audit evidence obtained, whether a material uncertainty exists related to events or conditions that may cast significant doubt on the Company's ability to continue as a going concern; and
- the overall presentation of the financial statements.

If we conclude that a material uncertainty exists in relation to the Company's ability to continue as a going concern, we are required to draw attention in our auditor's report to the related disclosures in the financial statements or, if such disclosures are inadequate, to modify our opinion.

In addition, we will read all the financial and non-financial information to be published with the financial statements to identify material inconsistencies with the audited financial statements and to identify any information that is apparently materially incorrect based on, or materially inconsistent with, the knowledge acquired by us in the course of performing the audit. If we become aware of any apparent material misstatements or inconsistencies, we will discuss them with you and consider the implications for our report.

3.4 The nature and extent of our procedures will vary according to our assessment of the company's accounting system and, where we wish to place reliance on it, the internal control system, and may cover any aspect of the business's operations that we consider appropriate. Our audit is not designed to identify all significant weaknesses in the company's systems but, if such weaknesses come to our notice during the course of our audit which we think should be brought to your attention, we shall report them to you. Any such report may not be provided to third parties without our prior written consent. Such consent will be granted only on the basis that such reports are not prepared with the interests of anyone other than the company in mind and that we accept no duty or responsibility to any other party as concerns the reports.

3.5 As part of our normal audit procedures, we may request you to provide written confirmation of certain oral representations which we have received from you during the course of the audit on matters having a material effect on the financial statements. In connection with representations and the supply of information to us generally, we draw your attention to the *Companies Act* 2006, s. 501, under which it is an offence for an officer of the company to mislead the auditors.

3.6 In order to assist us with the examination of your financial statements, we shall request sight of all documents or statements, including any chairman's statement, strategic review and the directors' report, which are due to be issued with the financial statements. We are also entitled to attend all general meetings of the company and to receive notice of all such meetings.

3.7 The responsibility for safeguarding the assets of the company and for the prevention and detection of fraud, error and non-compliance with law or regulations rests with yourselves. However, we shall endeavour to plan our audit so that we have a reasonable expectation of detecting material misstatements in the financial statements or accounting records (including those resulting from fraud, error and non-compliance with law or regulations), but our examination should not be relied upon to disclose all such material misstatements or frauds, errors or instances of non-compliance as may exist.

3.8 **(Where appropriate)** We shall not be treated as having notice, for the purposes of our audit responsibilities, of information provided to members of our firm other than those engaged on the audit (e.g. information provided in connection with accounting, taxation and other services).

3.9 Once we have issued our report, we have no further direct responsibility in relation to the financial statements for that financial year. However, we expect that you will inform us of any material event occurring between the date of our report and that of the Annual General Meeting which may affect the financial statements.

3.10 To ensure that there is effective two-way communication between us and to comply with the requirements of International Standards on Auditing (UK and Ireland) we will:

- contact you prior to the audit to discuss any relevant matters, the planned scope and timing of the audit and to agree any required action; and
- contact you after the audit to discuss any matters arising from the audit and to confirm any agreed action.

We will of course contact you more frequently and regularly about audit and other matters during the course of the audit.

3.11 **(Where appropriate)** The scope of the audit does not extend to providing assurance on the accuracy of iXBRL tagging in the financial statements. We therefore accept no responsibility for tagging inaccuracies detected by HMRC or others.

[1] Applies for periods commencing on or after 1 January 2016 or where small company accounting regulations have been applied early.

[2] For periods commencing on or after 17 June 2016.

14.4.1   Recurring audits

Once agreed, the letter will remain in force until it is replaced, but should be reviewed annually to ensure that it is appropriate to the client's circumstances. If a change has taken place, then a new letter may need to be sent.

A new engagement letter may be appropriate when there is:

- any indication that the client misunderstands the objective and scope of the audit;
- any revised or special terms of the audit engagement;
- a recent change of management;
- a significant change in ownership;
- a significant change in the client's business;
- a change in the financial reporting framework adopted for the preparation of the financial statements; or
- a change in legal or professional requirements.

Where a new letter is not considered necessary, it may nevertheless be appropriate to remind the client of the original letter.

14.4.2   Groups of companies

The ISA does not deal with group or joint audits. However, accepted practice suggests that where the same firm of auditors is appointed for several companies within a group, they should consider whether separate letters should be sent to each board. The decision will be influenced by:

- who appoints the auditor of the component;
- whether a separate audit report is to be issued on the component;

- whether the terms are the same for each component;
- legal requirements;
- the extent of any work performed by other auditors; and
- the degree of ownership by the parent.

Where a group letter is sent, it should clearly identify the companies concerned and confirmation should be obtained from each board.

Where joint auditors are appointed the audit engagement should be described in similar terms by each firm and that a joint letter be sent if there are no additional services provided by either party.

Further guidance on group audits is in **Chapter 30**.

14.4.3   Changes in terms

The ISA states that the auditor 'shall not agree to a change in the terms of the audit engagement where there is no reasonable justification for doing so'. If he considers the changes appropriate, the auditor obtains written agreement to them.

Such situations arise from:

- changes in circumstances affecting the need for the service;
- misunderstandings as to the nature of the audit originally requested; or
- restrictions of the scope of the engagement.

Where the auditor considers the changes inappropriate, normally because it may lead to the recipients of his report being misled in some way, he should consider his position and, if necessary, take legal advice. If he decides to withdraw from the engagement, he should consider whether the reasons for this have to be notified to any party. For example, under the *Companies Act* 2006, the outgoing auditor must send a notice of any circumstances which he considers should be brought to the attention of the members or creditors of the company. He may also need to provide a statement of reasons for his ceasing to hold office to the appropriate audit authority (see **Chapter 38**).

14.4.4   Disengagement

Where the auditor ceases to hold office in circumstances where no other auditor is appointed, it may be appropriate to write to the client to formally terminate the appointment. This situation may arise where an audit client becomes eligible for and claims exemption from audit or where an insolvency practitioner is appointed as administrator or liquidator. Further guidance is in **Chapter 38**.

14.5 Liability limitation

14.5.1 Background

The *Companies Act* 2006, s. 532 provides that any provision that exempts an auditor from any liability in connection with the audit shall be void, except in the case of liability limitation agreements as set out below.

From 6 April 2008, when the *Companies Act* 2006, s. 532–538 came into force, auditors were permitted to limit their liability to their statutory audit clients as long as they obtain the agreement (under a liability limitation agreement) of the company and its shareholders.

Other legislation may permit or prohibit liability limitation arrangements in respect of statutory audit for other types of entities. Where legislation is silent on the subject, contractual limitation of liability may well be possible, provided that the contract terms do not fall foul of the *Unfair Contract Terms Act* 1977.

Provisions of the *Companies Act* 2006, s. 532–538 do not apply to statutory audit of limited liability partnerships (LLPs).

14.5.2 FRC guidance

Guidance on the use of auditor liability agreements was published by the Financial Reporting Council in June 2008. The guidance outlines the measures to improve auditor liability that are allowed under the *Companies Act* 2006, gives specimen clauses for use in agreements, and explains the process to be followed for obtaining shareholder approval.

However, there were issues with introducing this into practice, mainly caused by the US authorities' non-acceptance of these agreements and the unwillingness of major companies and auditors to implement them without acceptance by the US authorities. As a result, these agreements are rarely used in practice.

14.5.3 Liability limitation agreements

A liability limitation agreement will limit the liability owed by the auditor in relation to negligence, breach of duty or breach of trust occurring during the course of the audit. In order for the liability agreement to be valid, it must:

- cover only one financial year;
- be approved by a resolution of the company's shareholders, as follows:

    - for public companies, at a general meeting;
    - for private companies, by written resolution, if preferred;

- for group companies, by each company in the group, not just the holding company; and

- be 'fair and reasonable'.

The courts can ultimately decide whether a liability limitation agreement is 'fair and reasonable'.

The actual limit on liability can be set out a number of different ways:

- based on the auditor's proportionate share of the responsibility for any loss;
- purely by reference to the 'fair and reasonable' test;
- a cap of liability (either in monetary terms or the basis of an agreed formula); or
- a combination of some or all of the above.

The FRC guidance sets out specimen 'principal terms' for each method of limiting liability above, together with example clauses which can be added to the relevant principal terms to form a liability limitation agreement.

The liability limitation agreement can be entered into at any time before the accounts for the year are approved. The existence of any such agreement and its principal terms must be disclosed in a note to the company's annual accounts.

14.5.4   Liability limitation – other services

Where an engagement letter covers both an audit in respect of which limitation of liability is prohibited and non-audit services in respect of which the auditor wishes to limit his liability, the letter should make clear that any limitation of liability applying to the non-audit services does not apply to the audit.

14.6   Small companies and micro-entities

The application material in ISA (UK and Ireland) 210 (Revised June 2016) notes that EU law imposes restrictions on the number of disclosures that can be prescribed by law or accounting standards for small companies and micro-entities even though the financial statements of those entities are required to give a true and fair view. This means that such companies, when preparing financial statements in compliance with prescribed requirements may not include all the disclosures considered necessary for the purposes of a true and fair view, particularly in relation to matters relating to the use of the going concern assumption.

In the case of a small company, it is not sufficient for the auditor to conclude that the financial statements give a true and fair view simply because they contain all the prescribed disclosures and the auditor in this case may wish to draw attention in the engagement letter to the fact that additional disclosures may be required if he is to give an unqualified opinion.

In the case of micro-entities, the situation is slightly more complicated, although it is expected that the vast majority of such companies will take advantage of audit exemption. For these companies, the law presumes that compliance with the prescribed requirements is sufficient to give a true and fair view. The auditor is thus precluded from insisting on additional disclosures. As this financial reporting framework does not acknowledge that to achieve fair presentation of the financial statements it may be necessary for management to either provide additional disclosures or to depart from a requirement of the framework, it is not considered to be a fair presentation framework as defined in ISA (UK and Ireland) 200. Accordingly, this financial reporting framework is considered to be a compliance framework. Under ISA 700 (UK and Ireland) (Revised June 2016), an auditor can only provide an unmodified opinion in respect of a fair presentation framework and would therefore be unable to do so for micro-entities as to do so may result in the auditor's report being misunderstood by users.

The guidance notes that it may be possible for the auditor to mitigate the potential misunderstanding through the prominent inclusion of an Other Matter paragraph addressing this in the auditor's report in accordance with ISA (UK and Ireland) 706 (Revised June 2016). In this situation, the engagement letter should also refer to the proposed form of report.

15   MATERIALITY AND THE AUDIT

15.1   Introduction

This chapter has been updated to reflect the changes contained in final draft ISAs issued by the FRC in April 2016. Subject to legislative changes in progress at the time of writing, it is expected that ISA (UK and Ireland) 320 (Revised June 2016) *Materiality in planning and performing an audit* will take effect for the audit of financial statements for periods commencing on or after 17 June 2016. For earlier periods, the previous version of ISA (UK and Ireland) 320, issued in October 2009, applies.

Similarly, it is expected that the changes in ISA (UK and Ireland) 450 (Revised June 2016) *Evaluation of misstatements identified during the audit* will take effect for the audit of financial statements for periods commencing on or after 17 June 2016. Materiality considerations in the context of a group audit engagement are also considered in ISA (UK and Ireland) 600 (Revised June 2016) *Special considerations – audits of group financial statements* (see **Chapter 30**).

Changes in the 2016 versions of ISAs (UK and Ireland) 320 and 450 derive from the IAASB's disclosure project (see **Chapter 1**) and emphasise that consideration of the nature of potential misstatements in disclosures is relevant to the design of audit procedures relating to those disclosures and that in evaluating the overall effect of all misstatements, the auditor should consider the nature of uncorrected misstatements as well as their size.

15.2   Materiality

The term 'materiality' is used in financial reporting frameworks in relation to the preparation and presentation of financial statements. Misstatements are considered to be material if they, individually or in aggregate, can be reasonably expected to influence the economic decisions of users of the financial statements. Materiality is determined both by the size and nature of an item, judged in relation to the surrounding circumstances.

The auditor's determination of materiality is a matter of professional judgment and will be affected by the auditor's perception of the financial information needs of users of the financial statements. There is no mathematical definition of materiality, as it has both qualitative and quantitative aspects.

The concept of materiality is applied by the auditor in both planning and performing the audit and when evaluating the effect of identified misstatements on the audit. Materiality judgments are also used when considering the effect of any uncorrected misstatements on the financial statements.

15.3 The need to consider materiality

The auditor plans and performs his audits so as to obtain reasonable assurance that the financial statements are free from material misstatement. However, whether an item is to be considered as material is a matter of professional judgment. The relationship of materiality to audit risk should also be considered.

The consideration of materiality should not simply be a matter of amount, the nature of the error should also be assessed. For example, if the auditor finds an illegal payment of an otherwise immaterial amount, this may lead to a material contingent liability, a material loss of assets or a material loss of revenue, and the effects on the audit report should be considered. Similarly, a failure to disclose a breach of regulatory requirements may result in the imposition of restrictions, which could impair a company's ability to operate.

The auditor also needs to be aware of qualitative misstatements. For example, an inadequate description of an accounting policy which would mislead users of financial statements is material to those users. The auditor should remain alert for possible bias in management judgments, particularly in relation to the entity's accounting practices. A misstatement may also arise due to the omission of a disclosure needed for the financial statements to achieve a fair presentation beyond those disclosures specifically required by the accounting framework; for an example in relation to disclosures for micro-entities, see **8.3.4**.

The level of materiality may be influenced by:

- legal and regulatory requirements;
- the level of exposure of the financial statements;
- whether the company is using the financial statements to negotiate additional finance or a listing on the Stock Exchange; and
- the auditor's previous experience of the company.

The auditor may use a benchmark such as a percentage of turnover, net assets or profit before tax as a starting point for determining materiality, but such calculated benchmarks should be adjusted as necessary for the factors listed above and other qualitative factors to determine the value of materiality to be used when planning and performing the audit.

For some classes of transactions, account balances or disclosures, a misstatement of less than the materiality set for the financial statements as a whole could be expected to influence the decision making of users, and for these areas, a lower materiality figure may be set.

The expected degree of accuracy of certain statutory disclosures, such as directors' emoluments, may make normal materiality considerations irrelevant.

15.4 Materiality and audit risk

When planning the audit, the auditor will assess the risk of material misstatement of the financial statements and plan how to respond to those risks throughout the audit. This risk assessment also helps the auditor to continually assess whether the materiality assessment remains valid throughout the course of the audit.

Materiality is also considered when determining whether any significant risks exist (see **Chapter 21**).

The assessment of materiality helps the auditor to determine the type and extent of testing required to reduce audit risk to an acceptably low level.

Materiality is used specifically in:

- *Planning the audit.* At this stage, materiality assists the auditor in deciding what areas need to be addressed, where material misstatement is likely to occur and whether any significant risks exist, so that his approach is efficient and effective.
- *Planning individual audit procedures.* Materiality is used to determine what items to examine and whether to use sampling and the extent of testing to be carried out on the particular transaction class or account balance. This enables specific audit procedures to be selected to support the opinion whilst reducing to a low level the risk of giving an inappropriate opinion.

When designing the detailed audit procedures, the auditor should consider the nature of potential disclosure errors (for example, appropriate disclosure of valuations for a company with significant investment property). However, it is not expected that in practice procedures can be designed to detect all possible misstatements that could be material by nature.

15.4.1 Performance materiality

'Performance materiality' is the amount or amounts set by the auditor at less than the general materiality level, so that the probability of the aggregate of uncorrected and undetected misstatements exceeding materiality is reduced to an appropriately low level. Performance materiality may be set as a single figure for the financial statements as a whole or, separately for some or all individual classes of transactions, account balances or disclosures. The level of performance materiality is a matter of judgment. It will depend on the auditor's understanding of the entity and the nature and extent of misstatements identified in previous audits, which determine expectations relating to misstatements in the current period.

15.5 Revision to materiality assessments

ISA (UK and Ireland) 320 (Revised June 2016) sets out additional guidance in relation to revisions to materiality assessments. If information comes to light during the course of the audit which would have influenced the auditor's assessment of materiality had it been known when materiality was determined, the materiality level (or levels for particular classes of transactions, account balances or disclosures) should be adjusted. The amendment and the reason for it should be clearly documented on the audit file.

If materiality levels are lowered, the auditor should consider whether performance materiality should also be decreased. In addition, where misstatements are found during the audit which exceed the auditor's initial expectations, consideration should be given to the need to reduce performance materiality.

Where revisions are made to materiality, the auditor should consider the implications for his audit approach and, if necessary, modify the nature, timing and extent of planned audit procedures. If his revised assessment results in a lower level of materiality, the auditor may find it necessary to carry out more audit work.

15.6 Uncorrected misstatements

15.6.1 During the audit

Guidance on evaluating misstatements is set out in ISA (UK and Ireland) 450 (Revised June 2016) *Evaluation of misstatements identified during the audit*.

In evaluating whether the financial statements give a true and fair view, the auditor is required to assess the materiality of the aggregate of uncorrected misstatements. Uncorrected misstatements arise from:

- specific misstatements identified by the auditor, including those from a previous financial period to the extent that they impact on the current financial statements; and
- the auditor's best estimate of other misstatements which cannot be quantified specifically, i.e. projected errors.

The various errors found during the audit should be assessed in aggregate as the audit progresses to ensure that there is no material misstatement in the financial statements. If the auditor is of the opinion that these may be material, he will need to consider reducing audit risk by extending audit procedures or requesting management to adjust the financial statements. If no adjustment is made after such a request, he will need to consider the effect on his report.

Misstatements that are individually and in aggregate 'clearly trivial' can be omitted from this aggregation. If there is debate over whether an item is 'clearly trivial', the ISA states that by generating such a debate the item cannot be considered trivial.

Misstatements in disclosures that are not 'clearly trivial' also need to be accumulated to enable the auditor to evaluate their effect on the disclosures and financial statements as a whole. Where these are misstatements due to their nature or circumstances rather than size, they cannot simply be added together as monetary amounts can be, however, the auditor still needs to evaluate those misstatements individually and in aggregate to determine whether they are material.

If the aggregate of uncorrected errors approaches materiality, the auditor should consider whether undetected errors could make this total material. In such a situation, he may perform additional procedures or request that the identified errors are adjusted.

15.6.2   At the completion phase

Once all audit tests have been completed and prior to evaluating the effect of uncorrected misstatements, ISA (UK and Ireland) 320 (Revised June 2016) states that the auditor should reassess his materiality judgments in light of the entity's actual financial results.

The auditor should then consider whether any uncorrected misstatements are material either individually or in aggregate.

Each individual misstatement should be evaluated, considering the size of the misstatement and the particular circumstances, to determine its effect on relevant account balances, transactions or disclosures. The auditor should also consider whether any materiality levels for each account balance, transaction or disclosure has been breached.

Where a number of immaterial misstatements have been identified within the same account balance or class of transactions, this may lead the auditor to reconsider his assessment of the risk of material misstatement for that account balance or class of transactions.

The auditor should also be aware of areas where errors are likely to be material by their nature and without aggregation, for example the disclosure of directors' emoluments.

In addition to simply aggregating the monetary value of misstatements, the auditor also needs to consider the circumstances surrounding the misstatement as some may be considered to be material, even if they are lower than materiality levels. For example, where the misstatement has an effect on compliance with regulatory requirements or compliance with covenants, or where it affects a value on which management bonuses are calculated, such circumstances would be likely to affect the auditor's consideration of materiality.

15.6.3 Disclosures

When considering misstatements in disclosures at the completion stage, any misstatements that are not clearly trivial are also accumulated, to help the auditor to evaluate the effect of the misstatements on the relevant disclosures and the financial statements as a whole.

Determining whether a misstatement in a qualitative disclosure is material, and aggregating such misstatements, is a matter that involves the exercise of professional judgment. Some examples of where such misstatements may be material include:

- inaccurate or incomplete descriptions of information about the objectives, policies and processes for managing capital for entities with insurance and banking activities;
- the omission of information about the events or circumstances that have led to an impairment loss (e.g. a significant long-term decline in the demand for a metal or commodity) in an entity with mining operations;
- the incorrect description of an accounting policy relating to a significant item in the financial statements; and
- the inadequate description of the sensitivity of an exchange rate in an entity that undertakes international trading activities.

15.7 Documentation

ISA (UK and Ireland) 450 (Revised June 2016) sets out a number of documentation requirements in relation to misstatements identified during the audit. The requirements are to clearly document on file:

- the amount below which a misstatement would be regarded as clearly trivial;
- all misstatements accumulated during the audit and whether they have been corrected; and
- the auditor's conclusions as to whether uncorrected misstatements are material individually or in aggregate, and the basis for that conclusion.

15.8 Communication of misstatements

The auditor should provide details of all misstatements, other than those which are clearly trivial, to the appropriate level of management, with a request that they be corrected. Uncorrected misstatements will need to be brought to the attention of those charged with governance, and the auditor may consider it appropriate to bring corrected misstatements to their attention as well, in accordance with ISA (UK and Ireland) 260 (Revised June 2016) (see **Chapter 10**).

15.9   Written representations

The auditor should obtain written representations from those charged with governance to confirm their opinion that uncorrected misstatements are immaterial both individually and in aggregate. The ISA requires that this representation, which would normally be contained in a management representation letter (see **Chapter 32**), be accompanied by a list of uncorrected misstatements.

Where misstatements that have been reported to those charged with governance remain uncorrected, the auditor should obtain a written representation from those charged with governance as to their reasons for not making the necessary corrections.

15.10   FRC Thematic Review

In December 2013, the FRC published the results of an Audit Quality Thematic Review on the subject of materiality. The review looked at the consideration and application of materiality by the six largest audit firms and identified a number of key messages for firms including:

- promoting the use of judgment in setting materiality levels, including performance materiality;
- auditors should demonstrate consideration of risk in setting performance materiality and not automatically default to the highest level allowed under the firm's guidance; and
- auditors should ensure that materiality is appropriately addressed when planning analytical procedures. For example, analytical procedures where expected or permitted variances exceed performance materiality are unlikely to provide much in the way of useful audit evidence.

16 FRAUD AND ERROR

16.1 Introduction

This chapter covers the responsibilities of the auditor in relation to fraud. It does not cover non-compliance with law and regulations, which is covered in **Chapter 17**.

This chapter has been updated to reflect the changes contained in final draft ISAs issued by the FRC in April 2016. Subject to legislative changes in progress at the time of writing, it is expected that ISA (UK and Ireland) 240 (Revised June 2016) *The auditor's responsibilities relating to fraud in an audit of financial statements* will take effect for the audit of financial statements for periods commencing on or after 17 June 2016. For earlier periods, the previous version of ISA (UK and Ireland) 240, issued in October 2009, applies. It provides guidance on auditing fraud covering:

- the definition of fraud and error;
- the responsibilities of those charged with governance;
- auditor's responsibilities;
- assessment of the risks of material misstatement due to fraud;
- evaluating audit evidence;
- written representations;
- reports to management;
- communication with those charged with governance;
- communication with the authorities; and
- documentation.

Changes in the 2016 version relate largely to Audit Directive requirements for statutory audits of public interest entities regarding communication with management and those charged with governance where the auditor suspects that irregularities have occurred, or may do so (see paragraphs **16.8** and **16.9**).

16.2 Definitions

The auditor plans and performs audit procedures to reduce audit risk to an acceptably low level. As part of this process, the ISA requires him to consider the risk of material misstatement in the financial statements due to fraud.

Misstatements can arise from either fraud or error. The main difference between fraud and error is whether the action that resulted in the misstatement was intentional or unintentional.

16.2.1 Fraud

Fraud is an intentional act by one or more individuals among management, those charged with governance, employees, or third parties, involving the use of deception to obtain an unjust or illegal advantage.

Although fraud has a wide legal definition, for the purpose of the ISA, the auditor is only concerned with fraud that causes a material misstatement in the financial statements.

Fraudulent financial reporting involves intentional misstatements in financial statements to deceive the users of those financial statements. It may be a result of:

- falsification or alteration of records and documents;
- misappropriation of assets or theft;
- suppression or omission of the effects of transactions from records or documents;
- recording fictitious transactions;
- wilful misrepresentation of transactions or of an entity's state of affairs; or
- intentional misapplication of accounting policies.

Fraud often involves management override of controls using such techniques as intentionally:

- recording fictitious journal entries, particularly close to the end of the accounting period;
- adjusting assumptions and changing judgments used when performing accounting estimates;
- omitting, advancing or delaying recognition of items in the financial statements;
- omitting, obscuring or misstating disclosures required by the applicable financial reporting framework, or disclosures that are necessary to achieve fair presentation;
- concealing facts that could affect the amounts recorded in the financial statements;
- engaging in complex transactions which aim to misrepresent the financial position or performance of the entity; or
- altering records and terms related to significant and unusual transactions.

16.2.2 Error

Error is distinguished from fraud and is defined as unintentional mistakes in the financial statements. It may arise from:

- mathematical or clerical mistakes in the underlying records and accounting data;
- oversight or misinterpretation of facts; or
- unintentional misapplication of accounting policies.

As part of his assessment of an error, the auditor should decide its cause and whether it was intentional or unintentional.

16.3   Responsibilities of those charged with governance

As stewards of the company, both those charged with governance and management have a fiduciary duty towards the owners of the company. Those charged with governance also have a statutory duty to maintain adequate accounting records and prepare financial statements that give a 'true and fair view'. Those charged with governance are responsible for the prevention and detection of fraud and error. It is not possible to achieve absolute assurance against fraud and error, but the implementation and continued operation of adequate accounting and internal control systems may reduce the likelihood of such occurrences.

An additional responsibility is that, under the *Companies Act* 2006, s. 501, it is a criminal offence to give auditors information or explanations which are misleading, false or deceptive.

Those charged with governance should take steps to prevent and detect fraud, and these may include:

* creating a culture of honesty and ethical behaviour, including setting a proper tone;
* developing an appropriate control environment;
* hiring, training and promoting appropriate employees; and
* requiring periodic confirmation by employees of their responsibilities and taking appropriate action in response to actual, suspected or alleged fraud.

16.4   Responsibilities of the auditor

The position has not altered since the pronouncement of Lord Justice Lopes in *Re Kingston Cotton Mill Company* (1896) that an auditor 'is a watchdog ... not a bloodhound'. The auditor's responsibilities are thus very much tied in with the duty to report on financial statements and are restricted by the concept of 'reasonable assurance'.

ISA (UK and Ireland) 240 (Revised June 2016) expects the auditor to recognise that fraud or error may materially affect the financial statements when planning his work and when evaluating and reporting his findings.

Compliance with Auditing Standards will not guarantee that the financial statements are free from material misstatement. The risk of undetected misstatement will be higher with regard to those resulting from fraud or error due to:

- the inherent limitations of the accounting and internal control systems and the use of audit sampling to test them;
- the persuasive, rather than conclusive, nature of the evidence generally obtained by the auditor;
- frauds sometimes taking place over a number of years but only being discovered when they become material;
- audit procedures which are planned to detect error may not be appropriate to detect fraud which does not immediately affect the financial statements; and
- frauds often involving collusion or intentional misrepresentations to the auditor.

Often auditors are less likely to detect fraud perpetrated by management than fraud perpetrated by employees. This is because management are frequently in a position to directly or indirectly manipulate accounting records or override control procedures.

Because fraud or errors are subsequently discovered which were not detected by the audit, it does not mean that the audit was defective. The guidance stresses that although the auditor cannot prevent fraud and error, the very fact that an annual audit is carried out may act as a deterrent.

16.4.1 Professional scepticism

Auditors should maintain an attitude of professional scepticism throughout the audit. Professional scepticism requires an enquiring mind and a critical questioning of the audit evidence, and is particularly important when considering the risks of material misstatement due to fraud. Even when management and those charged with governance have been found previously to be honest and trustworthy, a sceptical view should be maintained. However, as auditors are not trained to be experts in the authentication of documents, they will accept records and documents as genuine as long as there is no evidence to the contrary.

16.4.2 Engagement team discussion

ISA (UK and Ireland) 315 (Revised June 2016) requires the auditor to discuss any susceptibilities of the financial statements to material misstatement (see **21.3.3**), and ISA (UK and Ireland) 240 (Revised June 2016) requires this discussion to include particular emphasis on those risks arising from fraud.

The discussion should include the engagement partner and key staff, and the engagement partner has a responsibility to ensure that those engagement team members not present at the discussion are informed of matters relevant to their work. Areas that the discussion would normally consider are set out in **Table 1**.

TABLE 1: Considerations for the engagement team discussion

- how and where they believe the financial statements (including disclosures) may be susceptible to material misstatement due to fraud, how management could perpetrate and conceal fraudulent financial reporting and how assets of the entity could be misappropriated;
- circumstances that might be indicative of earnings management and how earnings may be managed fraudulently;
- the risk that management may attempt to present disclosures in a manner that may obscure a proper understanding of the matters disclosed (for example, by including too much immaterial information or by using unclear or ambiguous language);
- the known external and internal factors affecting the entity that may create an incentive for management or others to commit fraud;
- management's involvement in overseeing employees with access to cash or other assets susceptible to misappropriation;
- any unusual or unexplained changes in behaviour or lifestyle of management or employees which have come to the attention of the engagement team;
- the important of maintaining an air of professional scepticism;
- types of circumstances that might be indicative of fraud;
- how an element of unpredictability will be incorporated into the nature, timing and extent of the audit procedures to be performed;
- the audit procedures selected to respond to the risk of fraud and whether some types of procedures are more effective than others;
- any allegations of fraud that have come to the auditor's attention; and
- the risk of management override of controls.

After the initial discussion, it is important that the engagement team members continue to communicate and discuss their findings.

Where a small audit is being carried out entirely by the engagement partner, that partner must consider the susceptibility of the entity to fraud during the planning and execution of the work.

16.4.3   Risk assessment

ISA (UK and Ireland) 240 (Revised June 2016) requires an assessment of the risk that fraud or error may lead to misstatement. It sets out the following areas for consideration.

Management and others within the entity

The auditor should enquire about the entity's:

- assessment of the risk that the financial statements may be materially misstated by fraud;
- process for identifying and responding to the risks of fraud in the entity including any specific risks of fraud that have been identified or account

balances, classes of transactions or disclosures for which a risk of fraud is likely to exist;

- communication, if any, with those charged with governance regarding its fraud risk identification procedures; and
- communication, if any, to employees regarding its views on business practices and ethical behaviour.

The auditor should also ask those charged with governance, management and the internal audit function about any actual, suspected or alleged fraud affecting the entity. Where there is an internal audit function, the auditor should ask appropriate individuals within the function about the risk of fraud, whether the internal audit function has performed any procedures to detect fraud in the period and whether management and those charged with governance have responded satisfactorily to any findings resulting from those procedures.

Others to whom the auditor may direct enquiries about fraud include:

- operating personnel not directly involved in the financial reporting process;
- employees with different levels of authority;
- employees involved in initiating, processing or recording complex or unusual transactions and those who supervise or monitor such employees;
- in-house legal counsel;
- chief ethics officer or equivalent; and
- the person or persons who deal with allegations of fraud.

Those charged with governance

Those charged with governance have a duty to oversee the systems for monitoring risk, financial control and compliance with the law and this will include the entity's assessment of the risks of fraud and controls put in place to mitigate specific risks of fraud that have been identified. The auditor should understand how those charged with governance fulfil this responsibility, and this may give insight into the susceptibility of the entity to fraud, the adequacy of internal control and the competence and integrity of management.

Unusual or unexpected relationships

Any unusual results from analytical review work should make the auditor consider the possibility of fraudulent financial reporting.

Other information

Any other information that comes to the auditor's attention should be considered as a possible indicator of fraudulent financial reporting. The engagement team discussion (see **16.4.2**) may be particularly useful in this respect. In addition, work performed as part of acceptance or reacceptance procedures, and work done for the entity in other capacities may be of use.

Fraud risk factors

After his work on understanding the entity and its environment is complete, the auditor should consider whether it indicates that one or more fraud risk factor is present. Examples include the:

- need to meet expectations of third parties to obtain additional financing; or
- granting of significant bonuses if unrealistic profit targets are met.

Fraud risk factors may not necessarily indicate that a fraud has occurred or is likely to occur and the auditor uses his judgment to assess whether the existence of a fraud risk factor does actually affect the risk of material misstatement of the financial statements.

Fraud risk factors are generally classified as:

- an incentive or pressure to commit fraud, e.g. profitability being threatened by changes in the market;
- a perceived opportunity to commit fraud, e.g. the handling of large amounts of cash; and
- an ability to rationalise the fraudulent action, e.g. a known history of violations against laws and regulations.

Auditors are encouraged to increase their focus on identifying fraud risk factors when assessing the risks of the financial statements being materially misstated due to fraud and in particular, they should ensure their approach is tailored to the entity they are auditing.

16.4.4   Identification and assessment of fraud risk

As part of his work of identifying and assessing the risk of material misstatement at the financial statements and assertion level, the auditor should assess the risks of material misstatement due to fraud. Fraud risks will automatically be significant risks (see **21.3.7**) and therefore, the auditor should evaluate the design of the related controls and determine whether they have been implemented.

The assessment of fraud risk is a three-stage process. The auditor uses his professional judgment to:

- identify risks of fraud through risk assessment procedures;
- relate the risks of fraud to the assertions; and
- consider the likely size of the potential misstatement and the likelihood of the risk occurring.

Not all fraud risks will have related controls, as the entity's management and those charged with governance may believe that some risks are so remote that the implementation of controls to mitigate them is not necessary.

Revenue recognition

As material misstatement due to fraud often results in an understatement or overstatement of revenue, ISA (UK and Ireland) 240 (Revised June 2016) states that the auditor ordinarily assumes that there are risks of fraud in revenue recognition. This means that these risks will be significant risks and the three-stage assessment noted above should be followed, together with consideration of associated controls.

The assumption that there are risks of fraud in revenue recognition may be rebutted, for example, where there is a single type of simple revenue transaction, such as leasehold revenue from a single unit rental property.

16.4.5   Responses to fraud risk

Responses to fraud risk

Where the risk of material misstatement in the financial statements due to fraud has been identified, the auditor will respond in ways that have an overall effect on how the audit is conducted. This means that professional scepticism will be increased in all areas which may lead to an increased need to corroborate explanations and representations, and take greater care when examining documentation in relation to material matters.

In his overall response to the risk of material misstatement due to fraud, the auditor is required by ISA (UK and Ireland) 240 (Revised June 2016) to pay particular attention to:

- the assignment and supervision of suitably experienced personnel and experts;
- the accounting policies used by the entity, particularly those related to subjective and complex areas; and
- the selection, nature and timing of audit procedures, including incorporating an element of unpredictability in his audit plan.

Responses at the assertion level

The auditor's responses to the risk of material misstatement from fraud at the assertion level may include changing the nature, extent and timing of tests planned. He will aim to obtain more relevant and reliable audit evidence and additional corroborative evidence. This may include a greater reliance on observation and inspection procedures or, where relevant, CAATs. The auditor may conclude that better quality evidence will be obtained by performing more, or all, of his procedures at the period end, rather than during an interim visit, unless the fraud risk has arisen from improper revenue recognition during an interim period, which may be best investigated earlier in the audit process. More extensive testing may also be suitable in response to the increased risk assessment.

Table 2 sets out possible audit procedures to address the assessed risks of material misstatement due to fraud.

TABLE 2: Example audit procedures to address the assessed risks of material misstatement due to fraud

- visiting locations or performing certain tests on a surprise or unannounced basis. For example, observing stock at locations where auditor attendance has not been previously announced or counting cash at a particular date on a surprise basis;
- requesting that stocks be counted at the end of the reporting period or on a date closer to period end to minimise the risk of manipulation of balances in the period between the date of completion of the count and the end of the reporting period;
- altering the audit approach in the current year. For example, contacting major customers and suppliers orally in addition to sending written confirmations, sending confirmation requests to a specific party within an organisation, or seeking more or different information;
- performing a detailed review of the entity's year end adjusting entries and investigating any that appear unusual as to nature or amount;
- for significant and unusual transactions, particularly those occurring at or near year end, investigating the possibility of related parties and the sources of financial resources supporting the transactions;
- performing substantive analytical procedures using disaggregated data. For example, comparing sales and costs of sales by location, line of business or month to expectations developed by the auditor;
- conducting interviews of personnel involved in areas where a risk of material misstatement due to fraud has been identified, to obtain their insights about the risk and whether, or how, controls address the risk;
- when other independent auditors are auditing the financial statements of one or more subsidiaries, division or branches, discussing with them the extent of work necessary to be performed to address the risk of material misstatement due to fraud resulting from transactions and activities among these components;
- if the work of an expert becomes particularly significant with respect to a financial statement item for which the risk of misstatement due to fraud is high, performing additional procedures relating to some or all of the expert's assumptions, methods or findings to determine that the findings are not unreasonable, or engaging another expert for that purpose;
- performing audit procedures to analyse selected opening balance sheet accounts of previously audited financial statements to assess how certain issues involving accounting estimates and judgments, for example, a provision for sales returns, were resolved with the benefit of hindsight;
- performing procedures on account or other reconciliations prepared by the entity, including considering reconciliations performed at interim periods;
- performing computer-assisted techniques to test for anomalies in a population;
- testing the integrity of computer-produced records and transactions;
- seeking additional audit evidence from sources outside of the entity being audited.

Responses to management override of controls

The extent of the risk that management may use their position to override controls to manipulate accounting records and prepare fraudulent financial statements will vary from entity to entity. However, there will be some risk in all entities, and the ISA deems this to be a significant risk (see **21.3.7**). Therefore, in accordance with ISA (UK and Ireland) 315 (Revised June 2016) specific procedures should be planned and performed to address this risk. ISA (UK and Ireland) 240 (Revised June 2016) requires the auditor to:

- test the appropriateness of journal entries recorded in the general ledger and other adjustments made in the preparation of financial statements;
- review accounting estimates for biases that could result in material misstatement due to fraud; and
- obtain an understanding of the business rationale of significant transactions that the auditor becomes aware of that are outside the normal course of business for the entity, or that otherwise appear to be unusual given the auditor's understanding of the entity and its environment.

The auditor's assessment of the risk of material misstatement due to fraud may lead him to perform additional procedures to those set out above.

Journal entries

The financial reporting process is often manipulated by the recording of inappropriate or unauthorised journal entries or other adjustments. When considering which journals or adjustments to test, the auditor considers:

- his assessment of the risks of material misstatement, which may indicate a type of class or adjustments for testing;
- whether there are effective controls over journal entries and adjustments;
- the nature of evidence that can be obtained, particularly when journal entries are made electronically;
- the typical characteristics of fraudulent journal entries, including entries:
  - made to unrelated, unusual or seldom-used accounts;
  - made by individuals who do not usually make journal entries;
  - recorded at the end of the period or as post-closing entries that have little or no explanation or description;
  - made either before or during the preparation of the financial statements; or
  - containing round numbers or consistent ending numbers;
- the nature and complexity of the accounts involved, as fraudulent entries may be made to accounts that:
  - contain transactions that are complex or unusual in nature;
  - contain significant estimates and period end adjustments;
  - have been prone to misstatements in the past;

- have not been reconciled on a timely basis or contain unreconciled differences;
- contain intercompany transactions; or
- are otherwise associated with an identified risk of material misstatement due to fraud; and

- those journals processed outside the normal course of business.

Accounting estimates

Fraudulent financial reporting is often performed through intentional misstatement of accounting estimates. Therefore, the ISA suggests that, when the auditor is reviewing accounting estimates, he should consider whether the estimates indicate a bias on the part of the entity's management. The auditor may also perform a retrospective review of management judgments and assumptions in the prior year to see if any bias is indicated in the current period.

If a bias is indicated, the auditor should consider whether the circumstances represent a risk of material misstatement due to fraud.

Business rationale of transactions

The auditor aims to understand the rationale of unusual business transactions in order to consider whether the transactions have been entered into to conceal fraudulent financial reporting or misappropriation of assets. The auditor should consider whether:

- the transaction appears overly complex;
- management has discussed the nature of, and accounting for, the transaction with those charged with governance;
- management is placing emphasis on the need for a particular accounting treatment;
- transactions involving related parties have been properly reviewed and approved by those charged with governance; and
- the transaction involves previously unidentified related parties or parties that do not have the substance to support the transaction without the assistance of the entity being audited.

16.5 Evaluating audit evidence

In accordance with ISA (UK and Ireland) 330 (Revised June 2016), once audit evidence has been obtained, the auditor should revisit his assessment of the risk of material misstatement and consider whether it remains valid or needs amendment. This includes the risk of material misstatement due to fraud. If the risk assessment requires amendment, further audit procedures may be required.

The auditor's overall analytical review procedures at the end of the audit should include consideration of whether there is an indication of material misstatement due to fraud. For example, uncharacteristically large amounts of income being reported in the last few weeks of the accounting period may indicate fraudulent activity.

Any misstatements discovered during the audit process should be considered as possible indicators of fraud. If fraud is indicated, the auditor should reconsider the reliability of management representations.

The auditor must consider the severity of the fraud and its impact on his report. Where a suspected fraud has caused a misstatement that is not material to the financial statements, the auditor considers its implications to the rest of his evidence. For example, a petty cash fraud perpetrated by a clerk is not likely to impact the auditor's opinions. However, if the same fraud was perpetrated by management, the auditor may consider that it is indicative of a more pervasive problem with the integrity of management.

16.6 Auditor unable to continue the engagement

ISA (UK and Ireland) 240 (Revised June 2016) states that there may be situations where the auditor is required to question his ability to continue performing an audit. These may include:

- the entity does not take the appropriate action regarding fraud that the auditor considers necessary in the circumstances, even where the fraud is not material to the financial statements;
- auditor's consideration of the risk of material misstatement due to fraud and the results of audit tests indicate a significant risk of material and pervasive fraud; or
- the auditor has significant concerns about the competence or integrity of management or those charged with governance.

In such situations, the auditor should:

- consider whether it is appropriate to withdraw from the engagement;
- determine his professional and legal responsibilities, including responsibilities to report his inability to continue the engagement with the person or person who made the audit appointment or any relevant regulatory authority.

16.7 Management representations

ISA (UK and Ireland) 240 (Revised June 2016) requires the auditor to obtain written representations from management and those charged with governance that:

- it acknowledges its responsibility for the design, implementation and maintenance of internal controls to prevent and detect fraud;

- it has disclosed to the auditor the results of its assessment of the risk that the financial statements may be material misstated as a result of fraud;
- it has disclosed to the auditor its knowledge of fraud or suspected fraud affecting the entity involving:

  - management;
  - employees who have significant roles in internal control; or
  - others where the fraud could have a material effect on the financial statements; and

- it has disclosed to the auditor its knowledge of any allegations of fraud, or suspected fraud, affecting the entity's financial statements, communicated by employees, former employees, analysts, regulators or others.

16.8   Communication with management and those charged with governance

Where the auditor has identified a fraud, or has indications that a fraud may exist, this should be communicated to an appropriate level of management as soon as possible.

If fraud is identified involving:

- management;
- employees who have significant roles in internal control; or
- others where the fraud could have a material effect on the financial statements,

the auditor should communicate with those charged with governance as soon as practicable. Communication may be oral or in writing, but where fraud involves senior management or results in material misstatement of the financial statements, the nature and sensitivity of such matters may be such that the auditor considers it appropriate to report in writing.

If the integrity or honesty of management or those charged with governance is doubted, the auditor considers seeking legal advice before continuing with his work.

In addition, the auditor should inform those charged with governance about any significant deficiencies in the design and implementation of internal controls to prevent and detect fraud, or other matters related to fraud which may have come to his attention.

16.8.1   Public interest entities

For public interest entities, when the auditor suspects that irregularities, including fraud with regard to the financial statements, may occur or have occurred, he informs the entity and asks it to investigate the matter and take appropriate measures to deal with the issue and to prevent any recurrence. Where the entity does not investigate these matters, the auditor informs the relevant authorities (see **16.9**).

If the entity investigates the matter but does not, in the auditor's judgment, take appropriate measures to deal with any fraud and prevent future occurrences, the auditor considers whether he needs to take further action.

16.9 Communication with the authorities

The auditor's duty of confidentiality will be overridden by the requirements of the anti-money laundering regulations and the *Proceeds of Crime Act* 2002, which impose a duty on the auditor to report all suspicions that a criminal offence giving rise to any direct or indirect benefit from criminal conduct has been committed. Further details are given in **Chapter 18**.

16.9.1 Public interest entities

The disclosure in good faith to the relevant authorities, by the auditor, of any irregularities referred to in **16.8** above does not constitute a breach of any contractual or legal restriction on disclosure of information in accordance with the Audit Regulation.

16.10 Documentation

As part of his understanding of the entity as required by ISA (UK and Ireland) 315 (Revised June 2016), the auditor should document:

- the significant decisions reached during the engagement team discussion about the susceptibility of the entity's financial statements to material misstatement due to fraud (see **16.4.2** above); and
- the identified and assessed risks of material misstatement due to fraud at the financial statements level and at the assertion level.

The auditor should also document:

- his planned responses to the assessed risk of material misstatement due to fraud at the financial statements level and the nature, timing and extent of audit procedures planned, with those procedures linked back to the assessed risks of material misstatement due to fraud at the assertion level;
- the results from the procedures planned;
- communications about fraud made to management and those charged with governance; and
- if he has assessed that there is no risk of material misstatement due to fraud related to revenue recognition, his reasons for this conclusion.

17 CONSIDERATION OF LAWS AND REGULATIONS

17.1 Introduction

This chapter covers the responsibility of the auditor to consider laws and regulations in the context of an audit.

It does not cover fraud and error, which are covered in **Chapter 16** or money laundering which is covered in **Chapter 18**.

This chapter has been updated to reflect the changes contained in final draft ISAs issued by the FRC in April 2016. Subject to legislative changes in progress at the time of writing, it is expected that ISA (UK and Ireland) 250 (Revised June 2016) will be issued in its final draft form. The ISA (UK and Ireland) has two parts: Section A covers *Consideration of laws and regulations in an audit of financial statements* and Section B covers *The auditor's statutory right and duty to report to regulators of public interest entities and regulators of other entities in the financial sector*.

Section A is based on international ISA 250, but Section B is entirely UK and Ireland specific. Both will take effect for the audits of financial statements for periods commencing on or after 17 June 2016. For earlier periods ending on or after 15 December 2010, the version of ISA (UK and Ireland) 250 issued in October 2009 applies.

Section A of the ISA covers:

- types of law and regulation;
- auditor's consideration of compliance; and
- reporting non-compliance.

Section B of the ISA is detailed in **Chapter 9**.

Changes in the 2016 version relate largely to Audit Directive requirements for statutory audits of public interest entities regarding communication with the entity where the auditor suspects that irregularities have occurred or may occur (see paragraph **17.8.4**).

17.2 Legal and regulatory framework

An entity's legal and regulatory framework is the laws and regulations to which it is subjected. The legal and regulatory framework will vary from entity to entity. Some laws and regulations will have a direct effect on the financial statements as they determine the amounts to be reported and disclosures in the financial statements. Examples of such laws and regulations include those governing taxation and pension rights.

Other laws and regulations do not have a direct effect on the amounts in the financial statements, but compliance with them is fundamental to the ability of the business to operate. These include compliance with the terms of an operating licence, compliance with regulatory solvency requirements or compliance with environmental regulations. Non-compliance with these laws and regulations will have an effect on the financial statements by calling the going concern assumption into doubt or requiring additional disclosure of matters in the accounts.

The amount of law and regulation that an entity is governed by will depend on the industry it operates in and its constitution. For example, some sectors are heavily regulated, such as banks or pharmaceutical companies, whilst others are only subject to 'general' laws such as health and safety regulations. The further removed the non-compliance is from what is reflected in the financial statements, the less likely the auditor is to recognise it.

17.3 Management responsibility

It is management's responsibility to ensure that the entity complies with laws and regulations and that they establish procedures to prevent and detect non-compliance. To do this, they would normally set up procedures whereby they:

- maintain a register of significant laws and regulations as they affect the entity;
- monitor relevant legal requirements and ensure operating procedures and conditions meet them;
- institute and operate an appropriate system of internal control;
- develop and publish within the entity relevant codes of conduct;
- ensure employees are properly trained and understand the relevant codes of conduct;
- monitor compliance with the code;
- engage legal advisers to assist in monitoring; and
- maintain a record of complaints.

In larger entities, these methods may be supplemented by the establishment of:

- a wide-ranging internal audit function;
- a legal department;
- a compliance department; and/or
- an audit committee.

In certain industries, these compliance procedures may be imposed by regulations, such as the financial services sector.

Non-compliance with laws and regulations may lead to financial penalties being imposed on an entity or a loss of its business. Therefore, the implications of any non-compliance, either suspected or actual, should be assessed using appropriate accounting standards, such as FRS 102 or IAS 37 *Provisions, Contingent*

Liabilities and Contingent Assets, with regard to the inclusion and/or disclosure in the financial statements of such liabilities. In serious cases, this may also affect the directors' consideration of going concern.

17.4   Responsibility of the auditor

The auditor has no responsibility for the prevention of illegal acts or duty to report them except in certain restricted circumstances. However, the annual audit and the auditor's right to report in the public interest may act as a deterrent. The auditor may also highlight areas where illegal acts could occur, and suggest practical solutions in his reports to management (see **Chapter 10**).

Under ISA (UK and Ireland) 200 (Revised June 2016) the auditor 'should plan and perform the audit with an attitude of professional scepticism recognising that the audit may reveal conditions or events that would lead to questioning whether an entity is complying with laws and regulations'.

The guidance goes on to stress that an audit cannot be expected to detect all possible non-compliance. There is always a risk that material misstatement arising from non-compliance will not be detected, but the level of risk will be affected by:

- whether the non-compliance can be captured by the system of internal controls and accounting system;
- the inherent limitations of the internal control system and the use of audit testing;
- the fact that the auditor obtains evidence which is persuasive rather than conclusive; and
- non-compliance may involve concealment.

The risk will also be affected by management's ethos as regards compliance as well as consideration of any relevant codes of conduct. A review of management's procedures and controls together with relevant correspondence with those authorities responsible for regulation in industries where specific laws and regulations may be expected to have such a fundamental effect may be useful.

As part of the planning process, the auditor should obtain a general understanding of the legal and regulatory framework applicable to the client and its industry. The auditor should also consider the procedures the entity follows to ensure that it complies with this framework. Procedures would include:

- using and updating existing knowledge of the entity's industry, regulatory and other external factors;
- enquiring of those charged with governance about the entity's policies and procedures for complying with laws and regulations;
- enquiring of those charged with governance as to the regulations that may be expected to have a fundamental effect on the operations of the entity;

- discussing the policies for identifying, evaluating and accounting for litigation claims with those charged with governance; and
- discussing the legal and regulatory framework with auditors of subsidiaries in other countries.

During the audit, the auditor may also become aware of circumstances or issues which do not affect the financial statements and thus, are not obviously within the auditor's remit except insofar as they may give rise to possible liabilities or going concern issues.

These might include, for example:

- fraud or theft not materially affecting the financial statements;
- insider dealing, market abuse, bribery and other acts of dishonesty;
- money laundering (see **Chapter 18**);
- tax offences;
- offences relating to health and safety or employment legislation;
- environmental offences;
- bankruptcy or insolvency offences.

Whilst accountants (including auditors) have an over-arching ethical obligation to preserve the confidentiality of information of their clients, this does not apply where disclosure to an appropriate authority is justified:

- by legal authority;
- in the public interest; or
- to protect a member's own interests.

The auditor may therefore find that he has knowledge of actions which, as a professional, he needs to report to an appropriate person, despite the information not affecting the financial statements. Guidance on this is given in 'Professional Conduct in relation to defaults or unlawful acts guidance' attached to the ICAEW Code of Ethics.

17.5   Consideration of compliance

17.5.1   Laws with a direct effect on the financial statements

Evidence should be obtained by the auditor of compliance with laws and regulations which have a direct effect on the financial statements under ISA (UK and Ireland) 250 (Revised June 2016). Examples of such laws are:

- those which determine the form and content of an entity's financial statements – for example, the *Large and Medium-sized Companies and Groups (Accounts and Reports) Regulations* 2008 (SI 2008/410) or the *Small Companies and Groups (Accounts and Directors' Report) Regulations* 2008 (SI 2008/409);

- those which determine when a company is prohibited from making a distribution – for example, the *Companies Act* 2006, s. 830;
- those which oblige the auditor to report in accordance with specific statutory requirements – for example, failure of a company to maintain adequate accounting records, or disclosure of directors' remuneration; and
- financial reporting requirements for specific industries – for example, the *Friendly and Industrial and Provident Societies Act* 1968.

The Taxes Acts are a special case and the extent to which they need to be considered by the auditor depends on whether that firm also acts as tax advisors. If they do not, their only consideration will be the material misstatement of the tax liability. Where the auditor is also the tax advisor, even though different people may be involved in each service, those responsible for the audit should inform the partner responsible for tax advice of any non-compliance they come across during the course of their work, in addition to assessing the effect of the matter on the financial statements.

Where laws determine the form and content of an entity's financial statements or, alternatively, are reportable on by the auditor, the auditor has a responsibility to properly plan, perform and evaluate his audit with these in mind. In doing this, the auditor must aim to give himself a reasonable expectation of identifying non-compliance and any resulting misstatements in the financial statements which would be important to the user, although not necessarily material in quantitative terms. The auditor, therefore, must have regard to these laws when planning his audit, by understanding them and then testing compliance with them.

To identify instances of non-compliance with laws which have a direct effect on the financial statements, the ISA requires the auditor to:

- review correspondence with relevant authorities;
- make enquiries of those charged with governance to ascertain whether they are aware of any non-compliance; and
- obtain written confirmation from the directors that they have disclosed to the auditor all possible non-compliance, together with the consequences that may arise.

17.5.2   Laws affecting the operations of the entity

In addition, in the UK and Ireland, the auditor should plan and perform procedures which are designed to identify possible or actual instances of non-compliance with the laws and regulations within which the entity conducts its business and which are central to the entity's ability to continue operating. These may include environmental restrictions or non-compliance with terms of an operating licence.

17.6 Money laundering

The auditor should be aware that instances of possible or actual non-compliance with laws and regulations discovered during the audit may incur obligations for partners and staff to report money laundering offences to the authorities. Further guidance is given in **Chapter 18**.

17.7 Non-compliance

The auditor may receive specific information from testing which may alert him to the possibility that illegal acts have occurred. For example:

- investigation by government departments;
- payment of fines or penalties;
- large payments for unspecified services or loans to consultants;
- excessive sales commissions;
- purchasing at prices significantly above or below market price;
- unusual payments in cash, cheques payable to bearer or transfers to numbered bank accounts;
- unusual transactions with companies registered in tax havens;
- payments for goods or services made to a country other than that where goods originated;
- existence of an accounting system or part of one which fails, whether by design or accident, to give an adequate audit trail;
- unauthorised or improperly recorded transactions; or
- media comment.

When the auditor becomes aware of possible non-compliance, he should obtain an understanding of the nature of the act and the circumstances in which it has occurred, and sufficient other information to evaluate the possible effect in the financial statements.

Evaluating the effect on the financial statements involves considering:

- any contingent liabilities, such as fines;
- whether the going concern assumption is still appropriate; and
- the extent of required disclosure.

The consideration may involve matters outside the knowledge of the auditor and in these cases, expert advice should be sought on the effect on the financial statements. ISA (UK and Ireland) 620 (Revised June 2016) *Using the work of an auditor's expert* sets out the procedures that the auditor should follow in such circumstances (see **31.3**).

Once the auditor believes there is non-compliance, ISA (UK and Ireland) 250 (Revised June 2016) requires him to:

- document his findings, including taking copies of original records which give rise to suspicions and make full notes or minutes of conversations with management on the subject if appropriate;
- report them direct to a third party if necessary; and
- discuss them with the directors, subject to consideration of the risk of 'tipping off' (see **Chapter 18**).

Where management does not provide sufficient information about the suspected non-compliance to demonstrate that the entity is in fact complying, the auditor should consider taking legal advice. In normal circumstances, he would consult the entity's lawyers, but if he believes that it is not appropriate or he is unable to consult them, the auditor may obtain his own legal advice. If there is still insufficient information concerning the non-compliance, then the auditor should consider the implications for his report, and whether there is any obligation to report to third parties.

However, it is not just the effect on the audit report that should be considered. The auditor needs to assess the reliability of management representations he has received in the light of the suspected non-compliance. This may be particularly important where the non-compliance includes:

- an apparent failure of specific control procedures;
- involvement of management; and
- any concealment of the act.

The guidance cites the example of a series of instances which, although financially immaterial, are 'symptomatic of management's probity' and cast doubt on the integrity of the financial statements.

17.8   Reporting

17.8.1   *Reporting to those charged with governance*

The discovery of non-compliance should normally be reported to those charged with governance and where the non-compliance is believed to be intentional and material this report should be made as soon as is practicable.

The non-compliance should be reported to the next level of management who are not suspected of being involved. Where it is suspected senior management are involved it may be necessary to report the matter to the audit committee, or in the case of money laundering directly to the appropriate authority. Legal advice may be required if the auditor believes that no higher authority exists or that his report may not be acted on. If money laundering or some other reportable event is suspected, it may be appropriate to report suspicions directly to the relevant authority.

17.8.2   Reporting to owners/members

Where a non-compliance has a material effect on the financial statements, and it has not been adequately reflected in those financial statements, the auditor should issue a qualified audit report.

If management have not given sufficient evidence for the auditor to conclude that the entity is free from non-compliance, a limitation of scope opinion should be given. This will be either a disclaimer of opinion or a qualified opinion depending on the severity of the limitation.

If the auditor is unable to determine whether a non-compliance has occurred as a result of circumstances rather than management intervention, a limitation of scope opinion will also be suitable.

In all the above situations, and where there is the suspicion of money laundering, the auditor must consider whether issuing his audit report would be considered to be 'tipping off' (see **Chapter 18**). In such a situation, the auditor should obtain specialist legal advice.

The auditor should not refrain from qualifying his report or omitting an explanatory paragraph because the matter has since been corrected. He should base his assessment on the adequacy of the view given by the financial statements.

The consideration of the disclosure of the non-compliance will focus on going concern issues and contingencies. In particular:

- whether shareholders require the information to assess the performance of the directors;
- any potential consequences for the operational future of the company; and
- any contingencies such as fines or litigation costs.

The disclosure should be sufficient to provide a true and fair view enabling users to 'appreciate the significance of the information disclosed'. Normally, full disclosure of the potential consequences will be necessary to give a true and fair view.

Where there is no specific disclosure requirement, the auditor must assess the potential financial consequences and, in particular, have regard to whether non-compliance or its consequences are material to the financial statements and the probability of the act or its consequences recurring.

17.8.3   Reporting to third parties

Where the auditor becomes aware of an actual or suspected non-compliance which gives rise to a statutory duty to report, he should do so to the appropriate authority without delay. The guidance in Section B of ISA (UK and Ireland) 250

(Revised June 2016), which covers reporting to regulators in such circumstances (see **Chapter 9**), should be adapted for non-regulated entities whose auditor is under a statutory duty to report, for example where he suspects money laundering.

ISA (UK and Ireland) 250 (Revised June 2016) requires the auditor who becomes aware of suspected or actual non-compliance to:

- consider if the matter should be reported to 'a proper authority in the public interest'; and where this is the case
- discuss the matter with the board and the audit committee, except in cases where he no longer has confidence in the integrity of the directors (see below).

Once he has reached a decision, the auditor should then notify the directors in writing that he is of the opinion that the matter is reportable. If the directors do not report the matter themselves, or do not provide evidence that they have already reported the matter, the auditor should report directly. The auditor may take legal advice before making a decision on whether the matter needs to be reported.

Where the auditor has lost confidence in the integrity of the directors as a result of the suspected or actual non-compliance, he may report extreme cases directly to the proper authority in the public interest, without discussing the matter with the board.

Reporting to third parties may lead to some concerns regarding the apparent breach of confidentiality and what is meant by the public interest. The guidance in the ISA considers both in detail.

17.8.4   Public interest entities

For public interest entities, when the auditor suspects that irregularities, including fraud with regard to the financial statements, may occur or have occurred, he informs the entity and asks it to investigate the matter and take appropriate measures to deal with the issue and to prevent any recurrence. Where the entity does not investigate these matters, the auditor informs the relevant authorities.

The disclosure in good faith to the relevant authorities, by the auditor, of any irregularities referred to above does not constitute a breach of any contractual or legal restriction on disclosure of information in accordance with the Audit Regulation.

The auditor considers whether to take further action when the entity investigates the matter referred to above but where the measures taken by management or those charged with governance, in the auditor's judgment, were not appropriate to deal with the actual or potential risks of fraud identified or would fail to prevent future occurrences of fraud or other irregularities.

17.9 Resignation

The guidance suggests that as a last resort, where the auditor cannot obtain the necessary information, or where management or those charged with governance do not take the remedial action that the auditor considers appropriate in the circumstances, or the auditor wishes to inform the shareholders and creditors of his concerns but has no immediate opportunity to do so, or where management refuse to issue financial statements, he should consider withdrawing from the engagement.

18 MONEY LAUNDERING

18.1 Introduction

Chapter 17 deals with laws and regulations and the need for the auditor to take them into account in the course of his audits. One area which is of great concern to auditors in relation to this is money laundering. Until 1 March 2004, the specific duties of an auditor in the UK to report money laundering suspicions extended only to the suspected proceeds of drug trafficking or terrorist funds. From that date, the *Money Laundering Regulations* 2003 were introduced which extended the *Proceeds of Crime Act* 2002 to accountants. This legislation extended money laundering reporting to include possessing or in any way dealing with, or concealing, the proceeds of any criminal conduct, where criminal conduct is defined as conduct which constitutes an offence in any part of the United Kingdom, or is an indictable offence in the Republic of Ireland.

The *Serious Organised Crime and Police Act* 2005 made some changes to the Anti-Money Laundering reporting requirements.

Further changes were made by the *Money Laundering Regulations* 2007, which came into effect from 15 December 2007.

The *Money Laundering Regulations* 2007 apply not just to auditors but to all accountants, and to others including legal professionals, estate agents, financial institutions and credit institutions. This chapter is concerned with how these regulations impact on the responsibilities of auditors specifically and outlines various sources of guidance which have been published.

The principal guidance for auditors is set out in Practice Note 12 (Revised) (see **18.3**). ISA (UK and Ireland) 250 (Revised June 2016) requires the auditor to obtain an understanding of law and regulations applicable to the entity being audited. Section B of the ISA sets out requirements in respect of the auditor's right and duty to report to financial regulators.

18.2 Consequences for accountants in practice

In February 2004, the Consultative Committee of Accounting Bodies (CCAB) issued guidance for all accountants which was replaced in August 2008 by *Anti-Money Laundering Guidance for the Accountancy Sector*, also published by the CCAB. Relevant guidance from the document is included throughout this chapter.

Under this guidance, accountants in practice must report any suspicions or grounds for suspicion to the National Crime Agency (NCA) into which the previous responsible body, the National Crime Intelligence Squad (NCIS) has been subsumed. Firms must:

- appoint a nominated officer (a money laundering reporting officer (MLRO)) to receive reports of suspicions from colleagues and pass them on to the NCA;
- train partners and staff on the requirements of the legislation, and how to recognise and report money laundering suspicions;
- verify the identity of new clients and keep records of the evidence obtained; and
- establish appropriate internal procedures to prevent or halt money laundering.

Sole practitioners are not required to appoint a MLRO, but in other respects are recommended to follow the CCAB guidance.

In assessing whether an individual had knowledge or suspicion of money laundering which he should have reported, the courts are likely to take into account the level of skill and experience held by that individual, including any professional qualification. Willful blindness will also be seen as having knowledge.

18.3   Practice Note 12 (Revised)

18.3.1   Introduction

Practice Note 12, *Money Laundering – Guidance for Auditors on UK legislation* was originally issued in May 1997. It has undergone a continued programme of updates to ensure that it addresses new legislation as it is published. The most recent update, issued in September 2010, reflects the legislation effective at 31 August 2010. The Practice Note concentrates on the impact of the legislation on the auditor's responsibilities when auditing and reporting on financial statements; it does not provide general guidance on the legislation.

18.3.2   What is money laundering?

The 2007 Regulations include the concealing, disguising, converting, transferring, removing, using, acquiring or possessing of property which constitutes or represents a benefit from any criminal conduct within the scope of reportable offences. Criminal conduct is defined as 'conduct which constitutes an offence in any part of the UK or would constitute such an offence if it occurred in any part of the UK'. As a result, the auditor is more likely to come into contact with matters that should be reported.

The definition of money laundering is illustrated by examples of offences set out in Appendix 1 to Practice Note 12.

As the number of reportable incidences increase, so does the likelihood of auditors falling foul of the offence of 'tipping off'. Many of the procedures set out in ISA (UK and Ireland) 250 (Revised June 2016) may constitute 'tipping off' if actioned where an incidence of money laundering is discovered or suspected. Examples include:

- discussing non-compliances with management or those charged with governance;
- issuing a qualified audit report;
- issuing a report to a regulatory authority; or
- resigning his position as auditor.

In such situations, the auditor should discuss his actions with experts in the NCA.

The appendix to the Practice Note contains a number of situations where suspicions of money laundering may be reportable. With the changing legislation surrounding money laundering, the Practice Note suggests that each case is assessed individually in relation to the current rules and independent advice obtained as necessary.

The *Serious Organised Crime and Police Act* 2005 states that it is not necessary for auditors to report money laundering suspicions where the suspect cannot be identified and the whereabouts of the proceeds are unknown. Commentators are assuming that this change also includes situations where an auditor knows that his client keeps records of suspected shoplifters or other minor criminals, but does not need to access those records for the purposes of the audit. The CCAB guidance states that if the whereabouts of the criminal property is known or information is held that might assist in locating the property, a report is still required.

Whilst the definition of money laundering has been widened the scope of the audit has not been extended. The auditor is required to make a report when information comes to his attention in the normal course of his work. All incidences should be reported, not just those which are material to the financial statements. Failure to make a report is a criminal offence and auditors, both partners and staff, face criminal penalties if they breach the requirements. The auditor is not required to undertake any further work to determine whether an offence has been committed; the suspicion alone is reportable.

The final CCAB guidance amended requirements for auditors who discover conduct overseas which would have been an offence if committed in the UK. Previously, all such incidents were reportable, but now auditors are not required to report conduct giving rise to criminal property if it was:

- reasonably believed to have taken place outside of the UK;
- was lawful under the criminal law of the place where it occurred; and
- the maximum sentence if the conduct had occurred in the UK would have been less than 12 months.

Therefore when considering non-UK parts of a group audit, the UK parent company auditor will need to consider whether information obtained as part of the group audit procedures, such as discussions with subsidiary auditors or discussions with UK or non-UK directors, gives rise to a reportable offence.

18.3.3 Procedures

Training

Firms are required to implement training programmes to ensure that their partners and staff are aware of the *Proceeds of Crime Act* 2002, the *Money Laundering Regulations* 2007, the *Terrorism Act* 2000 and the *Serious Organised Crime and Police Act* 2005.

Risk assessment

Professional firms are likely to have systems in place to minimise professional, client and legal risk. Money laundering risk assessment procedures will probably be integrated within these other systems.

Firms should assess each client in relation to their money laundering risk. Money laundering risk is the risk that:

- the client is involved in money laundering; or
- the firm may be used to launder money or provide the means to launder money, for example by handling client money.

From their considerations, firms can put together a simple matrix of money laundering risk and combine this with their client acceptance procedures to ensure that sufficient client due diligence work is performed.

Even where clients are only subject to simple due diligence and are considered low risk, firms should always gain an understanding of:

- who the client is;
- who owns the client (including its ultimate beneficial owners – see below);
- who controls it;
- the purpose and intended nature of their business relationship with the client;
- the nature of the client;
- the client's source of funds; and
- the client's business and economic purpose.

Client identification

Client identification procedures under the 2007 Regulations fall into a number of different areas:

- general client identification;
- simplified client due diligence;
- enhanced client due diligence;
- politically exposed person;
- identification of beneficial owner;
- third party reliance;
- ongoing monitoring; and
- electronic identification.

General client identification

Under the 2007 Regulations, firms are required to perform client identification procedures for all new and existing clients.

The auditor must ensure that he has on file sufficient evidence to prove that the identity of the client has been verified and suitable evidence has been retained. The method of verification is not set out in the Regulations, but the CCAB guidance provides suggested evidence for companies and individuals, and this is reproduced in **Tables 1** and **2**.

TABLE 1: Example client identification procedures suggested by the CCAB guidance

For private companies and LLPs

If a representative of the company has been met face to face and the client has been assessed as normal money laundering risk:

- obtain full company search from Companies House (or equivalent information obtained through a commercial provider of registry information); or
- obtain certified copies taken from original documents evidencing details of incorporation or registration, registered office and list of directors and shareholders/members; and
- identify any shareholder/member in the entity holding more than 25% of the equity (rights to either income, capital or voting), or if there is no holding over 25%, the largest holding. This step should be repeated until the ultimate beneficial owners have been identified.

If no representative of the company has been met face to face and/or the client has been assessed as high money laundering risk:

- select individual(s) and entities that is/are capable of exercising significant influence over this entity either as an appointed director, or as a shadow director or equivalent, identify it/them according to whether a legal or natural person;
- select any shareholder/member in the entity holding more than 25% of the equity (rights to either income, capital or voting), or where no holding over 25%, the largest holding and identify it/them according to whether a legal or natural person. This step should be repeated until appropriate ultimate beneficial owners have been verified.

For all entities that are a money service business, verify HMRC registered number by obtaining a certified copy of their certificate.

For listed or regulated entities

Obtain either a printout from the relevant regulator's or exchange's website (and annotate), or obtain direct written confirmation from the regulator or exchange, to confirm the regulated or listed status of the entity (ensure that basic details of name, address, any membership or registration details, and any disciplinary details where applicable are provided).

TABLE 2: Example client identification procedures suggested by the CCAB guidance for individuals

If the individual has been met face to face and has been assessed as normal money laundering risk, obtain either:

- photo identity; or
- non-photo identity and proof of address (cannot be a PO Box) or date of birth.

If the individual has not been met face to face and/or has been assessed as higher money laundering risk, obtain either:

- photo identity and another piece of evidence; or
- non-photo identity, proof of address (no PO Boxes) or date of birth, plus an additional piece of evidence.

Suitable sources of evidence of identity are:

- photo identity:
  - valid passport;
  - valid photocard driving licence (full or provisional);
  - national identity card (issued by EEA member states and Switzerland);
  - firearms certificate or shotgun licence;
  - identity card issued by the Electoral Office for Northern Ireland;

- non-photo identity:
  - documents issued by a government department, incorporating the person's name and residential address or their date of birth, such as:
    - a current UK full driving licence old version (not provisional licence);
    - evidence of entitlement to a state or local authority funded benefit, tax credit, pension, educational or other grant;
    - documents issued by HMRC, such as PAYE coding notices and statements of account;
    - end of year tax certificates.

Suitable sources of evidence of address or date of birth are:

- instrument of a court appointment (such as a grant of probate, bankruptcy);
- current council tax demand letter or statement;
- current (within the last three months) bank statements, or credit/debit card statements issued by a regulated financial sector firm in the UK, EU or Joint Money Laundering Steering Group equivalent jurisdiction (but not statements printed off the internet);
- a file note of a visit by a member of the firm to the address concerned;
- an electoral register search showing residence in the current or most recent electoral year;
- a recent (last available) utility bill;
- valid photocard driving licence (full or provisional);
- a current UK full driving licence old version (not provisional licence);
- evidence of entitlement to a state or local authority funded benefit, tax credit, pension, educational or other grant;

- documents issued by HMRC, such as PAYE coding notices and statements of account;
- a firearms/shotgun licence;
- a solicitor's letter confirming a recent house purchase or land registry confirmation (the auditor must also verify the previous address).

Client identification procedures should be applied when:

- a business relationship is established;
- an occasional transaction is carried out;
- there is a suspicion of money laundering or terrorist financing; or
- there are doubts about the veracity or adequacy of the documents or data previously obtained.

Simplified client due diligence

Simplified due diligence means that the customer due diligence measures required on establishing a business relationship, carrying out an occasional transaction or doubting the veracity of documents previously obtained is not obligatory.

Clients who may be subject to simplified due diligence are:

- credit or financial institutions subject to the provisions of the money laundering directive or equivalent overseas requirements;
- companies listed on a regulated EEA market or equivalent overseas requirements; or
- UK public authorities and certain public authorities in the EU and EEA.

The right to simplified due diligence is revoked if a suspicion of money laundering or terrorist financing arises in relation to that client.

Enhanced client due diligence

Enhanced due diligence must be performed where the auditor has assessed his client as having a higher money laundering risk or where the client has not been physically present for identification purposes. The additional information to be gathered in these circumstances is set out in **Tables 1** and **2** above.

In addition, if a business relationship or occasional transaction is to be undertaken with a politically exposed person (see below), the firm must:

- provide approval from senior management before the relationship is established;
- take adequate measures to establish the source of wealth and funds which are involved; and
- conduct enhanced monitoring of any relationship entered into.

Politically Exposed Person

A Politically Exposed Person (PEP) is defined as a person 'who is or has, at any time in the preceding year been entrusted with a prominent public function by a state other than the United Kingdom, a community institution or an international body' or a family member or known close associate of such as person. PEPs must always be subject to enhanced due diligence.

Identification of beneficial owner

Under previous guidance it was prudent, but not obligatory to identify the beneficial owners of a client, that is any individual who owns more than 25% of the shares or voting rights. Under the 2007 Regulations, it is now a requirement for the auditor to perform this investigation and document the results in his files.

Third party reliance

Under the 2007 Regulations, the auditor may now rely on third parties such as regulated credit or financial institutions, lawyers, other audit firms, external accountants, insolvency practitioners and tax advisors when completing his customer due diligence work. Any reliance is subject to the consent of the third party, and the auditor will remain liable for any failures to comply with the requirements.

Ongoing monitoring

The 2007 Regulations contain a requirement for customer due diligence to be kept under review, although no prescribed periodic review is given. Where updates to a client's risk profile indicates that customer due diligence may require updating, additional work should be performed. In addition, the following should trigger a review of customer due diligence:

- at the start of new engagements and when planning for recurring engagements;
- when a previously stalled engagement restarts;
- whenever there is a change of control and/or ownership of the client;
- when there is material change in the level, type or conduct of business; and
- where any cause for concern, or suspicion, has arisen (in such cases, care must be taken to avoid making any disclosure which could constitute 'tipping off' (see **18.3.4** below)).

Electronic identification

Electronic resources are an acceptable part of client due diligence and can be used as stand alone evidence of verification of identity.

Engagement letters

For new clients, a form of pre-engagement communication may be of use in explaining the procedures being undertaken. The requirement for obtaining additional evidence of clients' identities may also be explained in the engagement letter for ongoing clients. The example in **Table 3** could be used for both purposes.

TABLE 3: Example client identification wording

Client identification

As with other professional services firms, we are required to identify our clients for the purposes of the UK anti-money laundering legislation. We are likely to request from you, and retain, some information and documentation for these purposes and/or to make searches of appropriate databases. If we are not able to obtain satisfactory evidence of your identity within a reasonable time, there may be circumstances in which we are not able to proceed with the audit appointment.

It may also be useful to include a paragraph similar to the example in **Table 4** to inform clients of the auditor's responsibility to report suspicions or knowledge that a money laundering offence has taken place.

TABLE 4: Example money laundering reporting wording for engagement letter

Money laundering reporting

The provision of audit services is a business in the regulated sector under the *Proceeds of Crime Act* 2002 and, as such, partners and staff in audit firms have to comply with this legislation which includes provisions which may require us to make a money laundering disclosure in relation to information we obtain as part of our normal audit work. It is not our practice to inform you when such a disclosure is made or the reasons for it because of the restrictions imposed by the 'tipping off' provisions of the legislation.

Where a decision is taken to include paragraphs such as those in **Tables 3** and **4** in engagement letters, this should be done for all clients. Where the paragraphs are included in only some of the auditor's engagement letters, the inclusion of these paragraphs may be seen as 'tipping off'.

18.3.4   Tipping off

Previously, anyone who had knowledge or suspicion that a money laundering offence has occurred should be aware that various actions may mean that they breached the 'tipping off' requirements, that is disclosing information to any person or individual where doing so was likely to prejudice an investigation. Changes in legislation mean that this offence is now limited to people in the regulated sector. This includes auditors, external accountants, insolvency practitioners and tax advisers. Therefore auditors should:

- ensure that any further investigation consists only of steps that the auditor would have performed as part of his normal audit work;

- obtain clearance from their MLRO before any further investigation is performed;
- consider whether the wording of a qualified audit report will fall foul of the tipping off regulations, consulting with the law enforcement agency for agreement as necessary;
- issue their report on a timely basis, as an unnecessary delay may be construed as tipping off; and
- take advice on the precise dating of the s. 394 statement if they decide to resign from the engagement in order to avoid tipping off.

18.3.5   Reporting to the MLRO and NCA

Subject to the Privilege Reporting Exemption, introduced by the CCAB guidance (see **18.3.6** below), all suspicions or knowledge of money laundering offences must be reported to the firm's MLRO or, for sole practitioners, direct to the National Crime Agency (NCA). The MLRO must then report the matter 'as soon as is practicable' to the NCA, and at the latest up to one month after the audit report is signed. There is no de minimis limit for reporting, or provision for a report not to be made where the auditor considers that the NCA is already aware of the matter, so all incidences, however small, will warrant a report. The *Serious Organised Crime and Police Act* paved the way for the introduction of mandatory reporting forms, and the NCA is currently reviewing its system for reporting including the use of 'standard' and 'limited intelligence value' reports. For sole practitioners making reports directly to the NCA, the NCA disclosure forms are available on its website www.nationalcrimeagency.gov.uk and these can be submitted electronically.

Reporting to the NCA does not relieve the auditor from other statutory duties such as reporting to the FCA for entities in the financial sector or other regulators for entities such as pension schemes and charities. The need to report to the NCA is likely to be a matter of 'material significance' to a regulator, and therefore will require to be reported to them. Again, the auditor should ensure that he does not breach tipping off regulations in making reports to regulators.

18.3.6   Privilege reporting exemption

As is the case with lawyers, a 'relevant professional adviser' can also be exempted from reporting in privileged circumstances. The exemption is only in relation to money laundering reports and no other legal professional privilege is extended.

A relevant professional adviser is an accountant, auditor or tax adviser who is a member of a professional body which:

- tests the competence of those seeking admission; and
- imposes and maintains professional and ethical standards, as well as imposing sanctions for non-compliance with those standards.

The exemption also extends to those in partnership with such an adviser, or employed by them.

If a relevant professional adviser obtains knowledge or suspicion of money laundering in privileged circumstances, he should still make a report to his MLRO, who in turn assesses whether the adviser is exempted from reporting under POCA, s. 330(6). There is no exemption if the information is passed to the adviser with the intention of furthering the criminal act. The details of the information and the consideration of whether to make a report should be fully documented by the MLRO.

Privileged circumstances

There are two types of privileged circumstances; those relating to legal advice and those to litigation.

In relation to legal advice, for a privileged circumstance to exist:

- there needs to be a confidential communication (written or oral) between the relevant professional adviser and his client, or a representative of the client, in which the client seeks or the relevant professional adviser gives legal advice;
- that communication must take place within the confines of a professional relationship between them, including an initial meeting which does not progress to a business relationship; and
- the communication must relate to legal advice (i.e. advice concerning the rights, liabilities and obligations or remedies of the client under the law).

Examples where relevant professional advisers may fall within privileged circumstances in relation to legal advice include:

- advice on taxation matters, where the tax adviser is giving advice on the interpretation or application of any element of tax law and in the process is assisting a client to understand his tax position;
- advice on the legal aspects of a takeover bid, for example on points under the Companies Act legislation;
- advice on duties of directors under the Companies Act;
- advice to directors on legal issues relating to the *Insolvency Act* 1986; and
- advice on employment law.

In relation to litigation, for a privileged circumstance to exist:

- there must be a confidential communication (written or oral) between the relevant professional adviser and the client or third party;
- the confidential communication must be made for the dominant purpose (i.e. the overriding purpose) of being used in connection with actual, pending or contemplated litigation.

Examples where relevant professional advisers may fall within privileged circumstances in relation to litigation include:

- assisting a client by taking a witness statement from him or from third parties in respect of litigation;
- representing a client, as permitted, at a tax tribunal; and
- when instructed as an expert witness by a solicitor on behalf of a client in respect of litigation.

Conducting audit work, routine book-keeping, accounts preparation or tax compliance assignments do not in themselves give rise to privileged circumstances.

18.3.7   The auditor's report on the financial statements

Where it is suspected that money laundering has occurred, the auditor should be wary about breaching the regulations relating to 'tipping off' when issuing his audit report. When considering the nature of his audit report, the auditor should apply the concept of materiality, considering whether the disclosure of the:

- crime itself;
- consequences of the crime; or
- outcome of any subsequent investigation by police or other investigatory body

may have a material effect on the financial statements.

19 OPENING BALANCES AND COMPARATIVES

19.1 Introduction

This chapter has been updated to reflect the changes contained in the final draft ISAs issued by the FRC in April 2016. Subject to legislative changes in progress at the time of writing, it is expected that ISA (UK and Ireland) 510 (Revised June 2016) *Initial audit engagements – opening balances* will take effect for periods commencing on or after 17 June 2016. ISA (UK and Ireland) 710 *Comparative information – corresponding figures and comparative financial statements* was not revised as part of the FRC's project and the version issued in April 2016 is the same as that issued in October 2009, though with an additional paragraph in application material relating to public interest entities.

For earlier periods, ending on or after 15 December 2010, the version of ISA (UK and Ireland) 510 *Initial audit engagements – opening balances* and ISA (UK and Ireland) 710 *Comparative information – corresponding figures and comparative financial statements* issued in October 2009 are effective.

The revision incorporates amendments relating to the EU Audit Directive and Audit Regulation which are required to be implemented by all EU countries.

Changes in the 2016 version of ISA 510 relate to the audit of public interest entities (see **19.3.3**) and changes in ISA 710 are restricted to the application material.

19.2 The auditor's responsibilities

ISAs (UK and Ireland) 510 and 710 require the auditor to obtain sufficient evidence to ensure that accounts derived from the previous financial statements are:

- free from material misstatement; and
- incorporated appropriately in the current financial statements.

In the UK, the auditor has no statutory responsibility to report specifically on corresponding or comparative amounts. Comparatives are, however, an essential component of financial statements produced under UK GAAP or IFRS financial reporting frameworks and the auditor, therefore has a responsibility to ensure that these amounts have been correctly extracted and, where appropriate, properly restated to achieve consistency and comparability.

Particular care needs to be taken in years where accounting policies are changed as a result of new accounting standards or as a result of making a change from one accounting framework to another, for example, where the entity is changing from

UK GAAP to the new FRS 102. For further details on the change to FRS 102, see **Chapter 37**. Further guidance is available on CCH Online and Navigate GAAP.

19.3 Opening balances

As part of his audit evidence, the auditor should confirm under ISA (UK and Ireland) 510 (Revised June 2016) that:

- opening balances have been appropriately brought forward;
- opening balances are free from material error or misstatement; and
- appropriate accounting policies are consistently applied, or where there are changes, these are adequately accounted for and disclosed.

Evidence may be obtained by:

- for an incoming auditor, reviewing the predecessor auditor's working papers to obtain evidence regarding the opening balances;
- evaluating whether audit procedures performed in the current period provide evidence relevant to the opening balances; or
- performing specific audit procedures to obtain evidence regarding the opening balances.

Where such evidence cannot be obtained, the auditor should consider the implications for his report. An example of the report is shown in **Table 1**.

If the auditor obtains audit evidence that the opening balances contain misstatements that could materially affect the current period's financial statements, he needs to perform such additional audit procedures as are appropriate in the circumstances to determine the effect on the current period's financial statements. If he then concludes that such misstatements exist in the current period's financial statements, he communicates the misstatements with the appropriate level of management and with those charged with governance (see **Chapter 10**).

TABLE 1[1]: Unable to obtain evidence regarding opening balances

Extract from the independent auditor's report to the shareholders of XYZ Ltd

Basis for qualified opinion on financial statements

The evidence available to us was limited because we were not appointed as auditor of the company until [*date*] and in consequence it was not possible for us to perform the auditing procedures necessary to obtain sufficient appropriate audit evidence as regards [*specify and evaluate the balances involved*] included in the preceding years' financial statements at £ ... Any adjustment to [*these figures*] would have a consequential effect on the profit for the year ended 31 December 20 ...

Qualified opinion on financial statements

In our opinion, except for the possible effect of the matter described in the Basis for Qualified Opinion paragraph, the financial statements:

- give a true and fair view of the state of the company's affairs as at [date] and of its profit [loss] for the year then ended;
- have been properly prepared in accordance with United Kingdom Generally Accepted Accounting Practice; and
- have been prepared in accordance with the requirements of the *Companies Act* 2006.

Matters on which we are required to report by exception

In respect solely of the limitation on our work relating to [*specify balances involved*]:

- we have not obtained all the information and explanations that we considered necessary for the purpose of our audit; and
- we were unable to determine whether adequate accounting records had been maintained.

We have nothing to report in respect of the following matters where the *Companies Act* 2006 requires us to report to you if, in our opinion:

- returns adequate for our audit have not been received from branches not visited by us; or
- the financial statements are not in agreement with the accounting records and returns; or
- certain disclosures of directors' remuneration specified by law are not made.

¹ This example is based on existing ISAs and has not been updated to reflect changes to audit reporting ISAs which will take effect for periods commencing 17 June 2016.

19.3.1   Continuing auditors

Where the previous report was unqualified and the current audit has not cast any doubt on the opening balances, the auditor may limit his procedures to ensuring that:

- the opening balances have been brought forward correctly; and
- the accounting policies have been consistently applied, or if there has been a change in policy that this is accounted for and disclosed properly.

In cases where the previous report was qualified, the auditor should, in addition to those procedures noted above, consider whether the matter giving rise to the qualification has been resolved and properly dealt with in the current financial statements. Even if it is resolved, it may still give rise to a qualification (see **19.4.1** below).

19.3.2   Incoming auditors

The guidance to the ISA (UK and Ireland) suggests that the sufficiency and appropriateness of the evidence the incoming auditor requires depends on:

- the entity's accounting policies;
- whether the previous financial statements were audited, and if so, whether the report was qualified;
- the nature of the opening balances and the risk of misstatement in the current financial statements; and
- the materiality of the opening balances relative to the current financial statements.

This means that in general, more evidence is expected to support balances from previous years which affect the current year's results, for example, stock or debtors, where these are material. Where the level of activity has increased significantly and the relative importance of these figures is diminished, less evidence would be necessary.

The incoming auditor must carry out more extensive procedures than the continuing auditor and these will include:

- consultations with management and review of the previous period's accounting records and control procedures; and
- substantive procedures on the opening balances, if other procedures on the current period to confirm the opening position do not provide sufficient evidence.

In situations where the previous financial statements were not audited and where the auditor is unable to obtain sufficient appropriate evidence from alternative procedures, he should consider the implications for his report. This will usually lead to a qualification, or in rare cases a disclaimer, on the basis of a limitation of scope depending on the effect of the unaudited figures on the financial statements. An example of such a qualified report where the company took advantage of audit exemption in the previous year is shown in **Table 2**. In such situations, the auditor may also need to qualify his opinion in respect of comparability of the comparatives and include an Other Matter paragraph (see **19.5**).

19.3.3   Public interest entities

For public interest entities, an incoming auditor is also required to obtain an understanding of the predecessor auditor's methodology used to carry out the audit, sufficient to enable him to communicate with those charged with governance those matters required by ISA (UK and Ireland) 260 (Revised June 2016), see **10.7.2**. This includes being able to describe the methodology used, including which categories of the balance sheet have been directly verified and which categories have been verified based on system and compliance testing, including an explanation of any substantial variation in the weighting of system and compliance testing when compared to the previous year. This applies even where the previous year's audit was carried out by a predecessor auditor and may lead to the incoming auditor becoming aware of a possible misstatement in corresponding figures.

For public interest entities, the Audit Regulation also specifically requires the predecessor auditor to grant the successor auditor access to the additional report to the audit committee in respect of previous years.

TABLE 2: Previous year's figures are unaudited

Extract from the independent auditor's report to the shareholders of XYZ Limited[2]

Basis for qualified opinion on financial statements

The evidence available to us was limited because we were appointed as auditors during the year and we have been unable to carry out auditing procedures necessary to obtain adequate assurance regarding the opening balances and comparative figures because the financial statements for the year ended 31 December 20 ... were unaudited. Any adjustments to the opening balances would have a consequential effect on the profit for the year. In addition, the amounts shown as corresponding amounts for the year ended 31 December 20 ... may not be comparable with the figures for the current period.

Qualified opinion on financial statements

In our opinion, except for the possible effects of the matter described in the Basis for Qualified Opinion paragraph, the financial statements:

- give a true and fair view of the state of the company's affairs as at [date] and of its profit [loss] for the year then ended;
- have been properly prepared in accordance with United Kingdom Generally Accepted Accounting Practice; and
- have been prepared in accordance with the requirements of the *Companies Act* 2006.

Other matter

Comparative information in the financial statements is derived from the company's prior period financial statements which were not audited.

Matters on which we are required to report by exception

In respect solely of the limitation on our work relating to opening balances:

- we have not obtained all the information and explanations that we considered necessary for the purpose of our audit; and
- we were unable to determine whether adequate accounting records had been maintained.

We have nothing to report in respect of the following matters where the *Companies Act* 2006 requires us to report to you if, in our opinion:

- returns adequate for our audit have not been received from branches not visited by us;
- the financial statements are not in agreement with the accounting records and returns; or
- certain disclosures of directors' remuneration specified by law are not made.

[2] This example is based on existing ISAs and has not been updated to reflect changes to audit reporting ISAs which will take effect for periods commencing 17 June 2016.

19.4 Comparatives

As with opening balances, the auditor should obtain evidence that comparatives are not materially misstated. ISA (UK and Ireland) 710 requires that evidence is obtained to confirm that:

- accounting policies are consistent, or if there has been a change that this is properly accounted for and disclosed;
- the comparative figures agree with those in the previous financial statements and are free from material error in the context of the current financial statements; and
- where comparatives have been adjusted because of material errors and misstatements that this is properly disclosed.

Where the auditor is unable to obtain such evidence, he should consider the implications for his report.

For the continuing auditor, as long as he has no concerns about prior year items, procedures are normally restricted to ensuring that the comparatives have been correctly brought forward and disclosed.

The ISA requires the auditor to obtain a specific written representation regarding any restatement made to correct a material misstatement in prior period financial statements that affects the comparative information.

19.4.1 Qualified reports

The reasons for a qualified report in one period may have knock-on effects into the next. The effect of a qualification on a subsequent period depends on whether or not the matter has been resolved:

(a) when the matter is unresolved, and is material in the context of the current period's opening balances as well as comparatives, the auditor should qualify the current period audit report in respect of opening balances and comparatives;

(b) where the matter is unresolved and does not effect the opening balances, but is material to the comparatives shown in the current financial statements, the auditor should qualify his report in respect of the comparatives; and

(c) where the matter has been resolved, but is material to the current period, the auditor should include an emphasis of matter paragraph in his report on the current period explaining how it has been dealt with.

In (a), the qualified opinion would describe the matter and its effect on the current and preceding years' figures. An example of this would be where in a previous year the company had made a provision for the permanent diminution in value of a fixed asset which the auditor did not believe was necessary. In subsequent years, he would qualify his report in respect of the consequential understatement of the depreciation charge and corresponding understatement of the asset and give an 'except for' opinion.

A further example would be a disagreement over the necessity for a provision against a debtor. **Table 3** shows the opinion paragraph that would be appropriate.

Where an auditor's report on the previous year contained a limitation of scope disclaimer covering all aspects of the report, it would be unlikely that he could satisfy himself on the profit and loss account or the cash flow statement in the next year, even if he obtained sufficient evidence that the balance sheet for that year showed a true and fair view.

TABLE 3: Preceding period was qualified and the matter has not been resolved

Extract from independent auditor's report to the shareholders of XYZ Ltd[3]

Basis for qualified opinion on financial statements

Included in the debtors shown on the balance sheet of 31 December 20 ... and 31 December 20 ... is an amount of £Y which is the subject of litigation and against which no provision has been made. In our opinion, full provision of £Y should have been made in the year ended 31 December 20 ... reducing profit before tax for the year ended 31 December 20 ... and net assets at 31 December 20 ... and 31 December 20 ... by that amount.

Qualified opinion on financial statements

In our opinion, except for the possible effects of the matter described in the Basis for Qualified Opinion paragraph, the financial statements:

- give a true and fair view of the state of the company's affairs as at [date] and of its profit [loss] for the year then ended;
- have been properly prepared in accordance with United Kingdom Generally Accepted Accounting Practice; and
- have been prepared in accordance with the requirements of the *Companies Act* 2006.

Where this occurs, it normally affects areas such as stock and work in progress or debtors and creditors at the beginning of the period, uncertainty about which directly affects the profit and loss account and the cash flow statements. Where the effect is material, either a qualification or disclaimer on the grounds of limitation of scope is needed, depending on the effect of the limitation on the audit procedures and the significance of the amounts involved to the financial statements. An example of such a disclaimer is shown in **Table 3** of **Chapter 5**.

An example of (b) might be a limitation of scope in respect of the accounting records kept in the first six months of the year which had been destroyed by a fire but which had not led to a qualification in respect of the balance sheet. In the subsequent year, there would be an 'except for' opinion in respect of the corresponding profit and loss figures as the auditor would still not have sufficient evidence on them.

Similarly, if there was a change in auditor in the previous period and that previous report contained the limitation of scope shown in **Table 5** of **Chapter 5**, the subsequent report will refer to this, as shown in **Table 4** below.

Situation (c) would result from a fundamental uncertainty which was not properly disclosed in the previous financial statements resulting in a disagreement which has now been resolved.

TABLE 4: Previous qualification not affecting opening balances

Extract from independent auditor's report to the shareholders of XYZ Ltd[4]

Basis for qualified opinion on financial statements

The evidence available to us was limited in relation to the comparatives in the current year's financial statements which are derived from the financial statements for the year ended 31 December 20 … In our report on those financial statements we stated that, because we were appointed as auditor on 30 June 20 … it was not possible for us to perform the auditing procedures necessary to obtain sufficient appropriate audit evidence concerning the quantities and condition of certain stock and work in progress included in the balance sheet at 31 December 20 ... at £ ... Any adjustment to this figure would have a consequential effect on the profit for the year ended 31 December 20 ... and, consequently, our opinion on the financial statements for the year ended 31 December 20 ... was qualified because of this limitation in audit scope. Accordingly the amounts shown as cost of sales and profit for the year ended 31 December 20 ... may not be comparable with the figures for the current period.

Qualified opinion on financial statements

In our opinion, except for the possible effects of the matter described in the Basis for Qualified Opinion paragraph, the financial statements:

- give a true and fair view of the state of the company's affairs as at [date] and of its profit [loss] for the year then ended;
- have been properly prepared in accordance with United Kingdom Generally Accepted Accounting Practice; and
- have been prepared in accordance with the requirements of the *Companies Act* 2006.

Matters on which we are required to report by exception

In respect solely of the limitation on our work relating to stock and work in progress:

- we have not obtained all the information and explanations that we considered necessary for the purpose of our audit; and
- we were unable to determine whether adequate accounting records had been maintained.

We have nothing to report in respect of the following matters where the *Companies Act* 2006 requires us to report to you if, in our opinion:

- returns adequate for our audit have not been received from branches not visited by us; or
- the financial statements are not in agreement with the accounting records and returns; or
- certain disclosures of directors' remuneration specified by law are not made.

[4] This example is based on existing ISAs and has not been updated to reflect changes to audit reporting ISAs which will take effect for periods commencing 17 June 2016.

In contrast, where the auditor issues a qualified report because of disagreement over an accounting policy, but this no longer exists following a change in accounting policy, which has been properly disclosed and adjustments made to the prior year, no qualification is necessary as the matter has been resolved and dealt with correctly.

Where an issue over which there was a disagreement has been resolved but not satisfactorily, for example, where the disagreement over the accounting policy was resolved by adjusting the current year's figures when the auditor considered a prior year adjustment was required, then both current period and comparatives would be qualified on the basis of disagreement.

For audits under the *Companies Act* 2006, there is no direct requirement to report on comparatives, apart from the fact that they are a 'disclosure requirement' under relevant UK law. Any qualification should therefore be in terms of this requirement. If corresponding amounts are presented solely as good practice, the audit report reference should be made as an explanatory paragraph.

The guidance to the ISA considers what the auditor should do when he becomes aware of a material misstatement which affects the previous financial statements, which had an unqualified audit opinion. If the previous financial statements have been revised (see **Chapter 6**) the auditor needs to ensure that the comparatives agree with the revised financial statements. Where the previous year's financial statements have not been reissued but the comparatives adjusted, no qualification is necessary as long as the matter is properly disclosed. Where no adjustment or disclosure has been made, the auditor needs to consider whether the misstatements in the opening balances will give rise to misstatements in this period's financial statements or whether the comparatives are materially misstated. Both of which, in the absence of adjustments, will lead to qualifications as discussed above.

19.5   Incoming auditors – comparatives

Where the comparative figures have been audited by another auditor, the new auditor assumes responsibility for them as part of the financial statements as a whole. He should assess them in the light of his knowledge of the client and the previous financial statements.

If the comparative figures have not been audited, for example, where advantage had been taken of audit exemption, the auditor should ensure that the financial statements clearly disclose the fact that the comparatives are unaudited, but also needs to ensure that he is not aware of any possible material misstatement in those figures. In situations where the auditor is unable to satisfy himself that no material misstatement exists in the comparative figures, he will qualify his opinion on the financial statements on the basis that the comparative information may not be comparable.

If the auditor encountered significant difficulty in obtaining sufficient appropriate audit evidence that the opening balances do not contain misstatements that materially affect the current period's financial statements, he may determine this to be a key audit matter in accordance with ISA (UK and Ireland) 701 – see **4.3.3**.

Regardless of any potential qualification of the auditor's opinion, in all situations where the previous financial statements were not audited, the auditor should include an 'Other Matter paragraph' (see **5.9**) in his report stating that comparative figures are unaudited. An example is shown in **Table 2**.

20 RELATED PARTIES

20.1 Introduction

Accounting standards require certain disclosures of related party transactions, and the auditor's task is to obtain reasonable assurance that the disclosures made are complete and accurate. The nature of related party transactions makes them difficult to identify, and the auditor may thus be faced with a high level of risk that he will not detect related party transactions which should be, but are not, disclosed in the financial statements.

In addition, the definitions of related parties in accounting standards are not always easy to apply in practice. In deciding whether parties are related, it is necessary to consider the substance of the relationships either between individuals and the reporting entity or between different individuals and entities. In preparing financial statements, directors must address the question of whether related party relationships exist in such circumstances and the auditor must judge the reasonableness of this assessment. This may involve the auditor in areas that are outside his normal areas of expertise.

Standards and guidance for the auditor is found in ISA (UK and Ireland) 550 *Related parties* which was issued in October 2009 and is effective for the audit of financial statements for periods ending on or after 15 December 2010. This ISA was not revised as part of the FRC's project to revise ISAs in April 2016, and as such, the 2009 version remains applicable.

Further guidance on the audit of related parties was issued by the Audit and Assurance Faculty of the ICAEW in 2010. Further details are provided in **20.12** below.

20.2 Auditing standards

ISA (UK and Ireland) 550 covers:

- the existence and disclosure of related parties;
- evidence relating to transactions with related parties;
- disclosures relating to control of the entity;
- management representations;
- communication with those charged with governance; and
- documentation.

The ISA was updated following a number of corporate scandals where fraudulent financial reporting arose through the involvement of related parties. The 2009 revision focused guidance on the identification and assessment of risk of material misstatement associated with related party relationships and transactions and on performing appropriate procedures to respond to such risks. The guidance takes a risk-based approach to the difficult issue of identifying related party relationships and transactions not disclosed to the auditor by management or those charged with governance.

20.3 General requirement

The auditor has a responsibility to perform audit procedures to identify, assess and respond to the risks of material misstatement arising from the entity's failure to appropriately account for or disclose related party relationships, transactions or balances in accordance with the requirements of the financial reporting framework. In order to do this, the auditor firstly needs to understand, as part of his knowledge of the business, the relevant disclosure requirements in legislation and accounting standards.

The auditor's understanding of related parties should be sufficient to:

- recognise fraud risk factors; and
- conclude whether the financial statements are fairly presented and are not misleading.

Many related party transactions are in the normal course of business and may carry no higher risk of material misstatement of the financial statements than similar transactions with unrelated parties. However, related party transactions may be difficult to detect due to:

- reticence on the part of the directors to disclose sensitive transactions;
- accounting systems not being designed to identify these transactions;
- a lack of controls over such transactions; and
- the complexity of the definition of a related party in applicable accounting standards.

In certain instances, related party transactions may be concealed in whole, or in part, from the auditor for fraudulent purposes. ISA (UK and Ireland) 240 *The auditor's responsibilities relating to fraud in an audit of financial statements* (see **Chapter 16**) provides guidance on the auditor's responsibility to consider fraud and error in financial statements and this includes fraudulent related party transactions.

The auditor's risk of not detecting related party transactions is compounded when transactions are:

- without charge;
- not self-evident to the auditor;
- with a party that the auditor could not reasonably know was a related party; or
- actively concealed by the directors.

Directors are responsible for the identification and disclosure of related party transactions. However, in addition to their responsibility to ensure that the disclosures are complete and accurate, the auditor should consider the effect they may have on other items within the financial statements, such as the tax liability. He must also be aware that the reliability of evidence may be reduced if it is obtained from related parties and also that transactions with them may be motivated by considerations other than ordinary business, such as window dressing.

ISA (UK and Ireland) 550 requires that the audit team discussion required by ISA (UK and Ireland) 315 (see **Chapter 21**), also includes consideration of fraud or error that may arise as a result of related party relationships and transactions.

20.4 Materiality

Where related parties are concerned, it is particularly important for the auditor to consider not just the monetary amount of any misstatements, but also their nature. A misstatement of a related party transaction may be significant to users of the financial statements (and hence material) even if its monetary value is low, depending on the nature of the relationship with the related party.

20.5 Existence and disclosure of related parties

ISA (UK and Ireland) 550 requires the auditor to assess the risk of undisclosed material related party transactions when planning his audit.

As part of his initial risk assessment procedures in accordance with ISA (UK and Ireland) 315, the auditor will make enquiries of management regarding:

- the identity of related parties, including changes from prior periods;
- the nature of relationships with those related parties; and
- whether any transactions were entered into with those related parties during the period, and if so, the type and purpose of those transactions.

The ISA requires that the auditor also gains an understanding of controls in place over related party transactions by understanding controls over the:

- identification, accounting and disclosure of related party relationships and transactions;
- authorisation and approval of significant transactions and arrangements with related parties; and
- authorisation and approval of significant transactions and arrangements outside the normal course of business.

As transactions between related parties may not be at arm's length, there may be an actual or perceived conflict of interest. For this reason, many entities will require that such transactions are authorised by those charged with governance.

This means that such transactions are often recorded in the minutes of meetings, for example, meetings of directors. This is less likely for owner-managed entities where procedures are often less formalised.

Relevant information about related parties should be shared with the whole audit team, for example as part of the engagement team discussion (see **21.3.4**).

20.5.1 Responses to assessed risks

Undisclosed related parties

The auditor should remain alert to indicators of the existence of related parties and related party transactions when inspecting records and documents throughout the audit. ISA (UK and Ireland) 550 requires the auditor to inspect the following documents for indications of unidentified related parties:

- bank and legal confirmations obtained as part of the auditor's procedures;
- minutes of meetings of shareholders and of those charged with governance; and
- such other records or documents considered necessary by the auditor.

The auditor will also review prior year working papers to determine names of known related parties.

In addition, **Table 1** sets out other documents that the auditor is likely to view as part of his audit procedures which may uncover previously undisclosed related parties.

TABLE 1: Records or documents that the auditor may inspect to uncover related parties

- third party confirmations obtained by the auditor (in additional to bank and legal confirmations);
- entity income tax returns;
- information supplied by the entity to regulatory authorities;
- shareholder registers to identify the entity's principal shareholders;
- statements of conflicts of interest from management and those charged with governance;
- records of the entity's investments and those of its pension plans;
- contracts and agreements with key management or those charged with governance;
- significant contracts and agreements not in the entity's ordinary course of business;
- specific invoices and correspondence from the entity's professional advisors;
- life insurance policies acquired by the entity;
- significant contracts re-negotiated by the entity during the period;
- reports of the internal audit function; and
- documents associated with the entity's filings with a securities regulator (such as prospectuses).

Where there is an indication of an increased risk of material misstatement in relation to related parties, the auditor should perform additional tests to those listed as appropriate. Many of these procedures, such as review of prior year working papers, will often need to be carried out in any case as part of the auditor's planning to gain sufficient knowledge of the business.

If previously unidentified related parties are discovered, they should be reported to all members of the audit team immediately, as this information could affect the results of work they are performing or have already performed, including the assessment of the risk of material misstatement, which may need revision. The auditor should also make enquiries of management to determine all transactions with the newly identified related party so that they can be evaluated.

If non-disclosure of the related party by management appears intentional it may be indicative of a risk of material misstatement due to fraud, and the auditor should evaluate the implications for the audit and his report. It may also cast doubt over other representations made by management.

The extent of substantive testing required to obtain sufficient audit evidence following the procedures in **Table 1** will vary depending on the auditor's assessment of the entity's internal control over related party transactions. When assessing the control activities the auditor should concentrate on controls over the authorisation and recording of related party transactions.

The auditor should also be aware of related party transactions which may not be included in the information provided by the entity. **Table 2** sets out a number of circumstances where the auditor may wish to investigate further if he becomes aware of them during other audit testing.

TABLE 2: Examples of unusual circumstances

- transactions which have unusual terms such as very low interest rates;
- transactions which appear to lack a logical business rationale, such as the sale of an asset for what appears to be less than market value;
- transactions in which substance differs from form;
- transactions processed or approved in a non-routine manner or by personnel who do not ordinarily deal with such transactions, for example, a sale authorised by the chief executive rather than the sales manager;
- high volume or significant transactions with certain customers or suppliers compared to others;
- unrecorded transactions such as the receipt or provision of management services at no charge; and
- unusual transactions which are entered into shortly before or after the end of the reporting period, such as a large sale just before the year end which is later cancelled.

If the auditor discovers significant related party transactions which had not previously been identified by management or disclosed to the auditor,

ISA (UK and Ireland) 550 requires that the auditor considers whether other such related party relationships or transactions exist. If the non-disclosure appears intentional, and is therefore indicative of a risk of material misstatement due to fraud, the auditor should evaluate the implications for the audit as a whole.

Related party transactions outside the entity's normal course of business

If the auditor discovers related party transactions which appear outside the entity's normal course of business, ISA (UK and Ireland) 550 requires that he:

- inspects the underlying contracts to determine whether the:

    - business rationale, or lack thereof, is indicative of fraudulent activity;
    - terms are consistent with management's explanations;
    - transactions have been appropriately accounted for; and

- obtains evidence that the transactions have been appropriately authorised and approved.

The ISA also requires that any such significant related party transactions outside the entity's normal course of business are treated as giving rise to a significant risk (see **21.3.7**).

Arm's length transactions

If management assert that a related party transaction has been conducted on terms equivalent to an arm's length transaction, ISA (UK and Ireland) 550 requires that the auditor should obtain evidence to support that assertion.

In order to verify their assertion, management may:

- compare the terms of the related party transaction with those of an identical or similar transaction with an unrelated party;
- engage an external expert to determine a market value and confirm market terms and conditions for the transaction; or
- compare the terms of the transaction with broadly similar transactions in the open market.

Evaluating the information provided by management may include:

- considering the appropriateness of the processes undertaken by management to support their assertion;
- verifying internal or external data used as evidence by management;
- evaluating whether assumptions used by management are reasonable.

20.6   Evidence

The reliability of the audit evidence regarding related parties may be of concern when it is either:

- limited, such as an instruction from one group company to another to pay a management charge; or
- created by the related party, such as the confirmation of a loan.

In order to assess reliability where evidence is limited, the guidance suggests that the auditor should consider:

- discussing the matter with management;
- confirming the terms and amount of the transaction with the related party; and
- corroborating the explanation with the related party.

Where the evidence is created by the related party, the auditor should consider:

- inspecting any additional evidence held by the related party; or
- confirming explanations with persons associated with the transaction such as lawyers and bankers.

20.7   Control disclosures

Accounting frameworks usually require disclosures relating to the control of the entity. Where this is the case, ISA (UK and Ireland) 550 expects the auditor to obtain appropriate evidence in this respect, usually via enquiry of management. It is suggested that these management representations may be confirmed with the controlling party if considered appropriate.

20.8   Representations from those charged with governance

ISA (UK and Ireland) 550 requires the auditor to obtain written confirmation from those charged with governance that information concerning related parties and control provided to them is complete and that the disclosures in the financial statements regarding related party transactions are adequate (see **Chapter 32**).

Where an entity requires its management and those charged with governance to confirm their interests in writing, the auditor should inspect these documents. In such cases, the guidance suggests that the confirmations may be jointly addressed to the company and the auditor.

20.9 Communication with those charged with governance

Examples of items which the auditor may report in his communications with those charged with governance in respect of related party transactions include:

- intentional or unintentional non-disclosure of related parties or significant related party transactions, which may alert those charged with governance to relationships and transactions of which they had not previously been aware;
- significant related party transactions which have not been appropriately authorised and approved, which may give rise to suspected fraud;
- disagreements with management regarding the accounting for and disclosure of significant related party transactions;
- non-compliance with laws and regulations which prohibit or restrict certain types of related party transactions; and
- difficulties in identifying the party that ultimately controls the entity.

20.10 Documentation

ISA (UK and Ireland) 550 includes a formal requirement for the names and nature of the relationship with all related parties be documented on the audit file.

20.11 Reporting

If the auditor is unable to obtain sufficient appropriate evidence on related party matters or the disclosures are not adequate, he should consider the implications for his report.

Where the auditor believes that there is more information which could have been obtained but he has been unable to do so, this is a limitation of scope which could lead to a qualified or disclaimed opinion as set out in **5.4**. For example, such a report would be appropriate where he suspects a related party transaction but has not been able to obtain all the evidence to which he is reasonably entitled to determine the matter.

In instances where the auditor has sufficient evidence to know that the disclosure is incorrect or he considers the disclosures inadequate because the directors are unwilling to disclose information, he should consider giving a qualified or adverse opinion on the basis of misstatement of the financial statements (see **5.4**). ISA (UK and Ireland) 705 requires that, where practicable and unless prohibited by law or regulation, the auditor should include in his report a description and quantification of any misstatement and details of any omitted disclosures. The *Companies Act* 2006 also requires the auditor to include details in his report of omitted or misstated disclosures where these relate to details of directors' remuneration, pensions, or compensation for loss of office required under the Act.

20.12   The audit of related parties in practice

20.12.1   Introduction

In February 2010, the Audit and Assurance Faculty of the ICAEW issued a paper entitled *The Audit of Related Parties in Practice* as it believed that the publication of the revised version of ISA (UK and Ireland) 550 in October 2009 required a significant shift in the focus of work carried out by the auditor in this area. The paper was based on an earlier Exposure Draft published in 2008.

The aim of the paper is to provide practical advice to auditors on auditing related party transactions via a five-point action plan.

The paper voices concerns that the auditor has previously seen his work in relation to related parties and related party transactions as a mere check on disclosures made under accounting standards, rather than focusing on this as an area where material misstatement may occur as a result of fraud or error. ISA (UK and Ireland) 550 aims to redress this balance by requiring procedures to identify, assess and respond to risks of material misstatement associated with related parties. It focuses on fraud risk factors linked to related party transactions, and creates a stronger parallel to the requirements of ISA (UK and Ireland) 240. It recommends that there is focus on and an understanding of the controls in place in respect of related parties, and that the auditor inspects documents for evidence of undisclosed related parties.

The Audit and Assurance Faculty guidance highlights common pitfalls when auditing related parties and related party transactions, and provides suggestions to improve audit quality in this area. It emphasises the importance of proper planning in this area, involving the whole audit team.

20.12.2   The five-point action plan

The Audit and Assurance Faculty guidance contains a five-point plan highlighting specific areas where existing audit work on related parties and related party transactions could be enhanced to improve the quality of the audit. It is reproduced in **Table 3**.

TABLE 3: The five-point action plan

(1)   Plan your work on the audit of related parties and related party transactions thoroughly.

- Plan the audit of related parties and related party transactions by updating existing information, and where possible, obtain a list of related parties from clients or compile a list based on discussions with clients.
- Ask management about changes from the prior period, the nature of the relationships, whether any transactions have been entered into and the type and purpose of the transactions.

- Plan for concerns raised by audit team members and others to be considered and reviewed by suitably experienced staff.
- Brief all audit team members on related party relationships and transactions and the risks of material misstatement due to fraud or error that could arise from such transactions.
- Ensure that the client understands what related parties are and why the relevant disclosure requirements are necessary.
- Speak to the right person 'in authority' at the client who can answer questions.
- Plan for concerns raised by audit team members and others to be considered and reviewed by suitably experienced staff.
- Brief all audit team members on related party relationships and transactions and the risks of material misstatement due to fraud or error that could arise from such transactions.
- Ensure that all staff are informed about any changes to related party relationships throughout the engagement and are aware of the need to bring such changes to the attention of the rest of the team.

(2) Focus on the risk of material misstatement that might arise from related party transactions.

- Understand the nature, size and complexity of the businesses and use family trees or document group structures to help identify related parties and relationships between the client and related parties.
- Follow up indicators of the existence of undisclosed related parties or related party transactions.
- Consider the impact of undisclosed related party relationships and transactions as a potential fraud risk.
- Consider the qualitative aspects of materiality.
- Emphasise the importance of the audit team remaining alert for related party relationships and transactions as the audit proceeds.
- Discuss related party relationships with others within the firm who provide services to the client, such as tax, accounting or corporate finance departments.

(3) Understand the internal controls at the company to identify related parties and to record related party transactions.

- Understand the controls, if any, that management has put in place to identify, account for and disclose related party transactions and to approve significant transactions with related parties, and significant transactions outside the normal course of business.
- If few or no processes are in place for dealing with related party relationships and transactions, seek to obtain an understanding of those relationships and transactions by asking management.

(4) Design procedures to respond to risks identified.

- Perform procedures to confirm identified related party relationships and transactions and identify others including:
  - inspecting bank and legal confirmations obtained as part of other audit procedures;
  - inspecting minutes of shareholder and management meetings and any other records or documents considered necessary, such as regulatory returns, tax returns and records of investments.

- Where the existence of related party relationships or transactions that management has not previously identified or disclosed is indicated, communicate the information to team members promptly, and:
  - request management to identify all such transactions;
  - ask why controls failed to identify or disclose the related parties or transactions;
  - perform appropriate substantive procedures;
  - reconsider the risk that further unidentified or undisclosed relationships or transactions may exist and evaluate the implications for the audit.
- Consider any fraud risk factors in the context of the requirements of ISA (UK and Ireland) 240.
- Establish the nature of significant transactions outside the company's normal course of business and whether related parties could be involved, by inquiring of management.
- Consider any arm's-length transactions and obtain supporting evidence from third parties.
- Treat significant related party transactions outside the normal course of business as significant risks and inspect relevant documentation to evaluate the business rationale of the transactions, whether they have been appropriately authorised and approved, whether the terms are consistent with management's explanations and whether they have been appropriately accounted for.
- Document the identity of related parties and the nature of related party relationships.

(5) Perform completion procedures.

- Obtain a representation that management has disclosed the identity of related parties, relationships and transactions of which they are aware and that related parties and transactions have been appropriately accounted for and disclosed.
- Communicate significant related party matters arising during the audit to those charged with governance unless all of those charged with governance are involved in its management.
- Ensure that the accounting for and disclosures of related parties and related party transactions are appropriate.
- Consider the implications of the findings from work performed on related parties and related party transactions for the audit opinion.

21 AUDIT RISK ASSESSMENT AND THE AUDITOR'S RESPONSE

21.1 Introduction

Three ISAs set out the process involved in assessing and responding to the risk of material misstatement in an entity. These are:

- ISA (UK and Ireland) 315 (Revised June 2016) *Identifying and assessing the risks of material misstatement through understanding the entity and its environment*;
- ISA (UK and Ireland) 330 (Revised June 2016) *The auditor's responses to assessed risks*; and
- ISA (UK and Ireland) 240 (Revised June 2016) *The auditor's responsibilities relating to fraud in an audit of financial statements*, which is covered in **Chapter 16**.

This chapter has been updated to reflect the changes contained in final draft ISAs issued by the FRC in April 2016. Subject to legislative changes in progress at the time of writing, it is expected that the final draft versions of these three ISAs (UK and Ireland) will take effect for the audit of financial statements for periods commencing on or after 17 June 2016. For earlier periods, ending on or after 15 December 2010, the versions of these ISAs issued in October 2009 apply.

Changes in ISA (UK and Ireland) 315 relate to the audit of disclosures as a result of the IAASB's disclosure project (see **Chapter 1**). These changes are covered at various points throughout the chapter and include:

- a requirement that the auditor's understanding of relevant information systems should extend to systems relating to information that is disclosed in the financial statements but comes from outside the general and subsidiary ledgers;
- a requirement for the auditor to consider both quantitative and qualitative aspects of disclosures when identifying and assessing risks of misstatement; and
- application material suggesting that consideration should be given to disclosure requirements as part of the engagement team discussion to assist in early identification of risks relating to disclosures.

Changes in ISA (UK and Ireland) 330 include Audit Regulation requirements for public interest entities (see **21.4.2**) and audit of disclosures (covered in **21.4.2**, **21.4.3** and **21.4.5**).

21.2 General overview

The auditor is required to assess risks of material misstatement in order to determine the nature, timing and extent of further audit procedures necessary to obtain sufficient appropriate audit evidence which enables the auditor to express an opinion on the financial statements at an acceptably low level of audit risk. Audit risk is a function of the risk of material misstatement of the financial statements (i.e. the risk that the financial statements are materially misstated prior to audit) and the risk that the auditor will not detect such misstatements ('detection risk').

The auditor determines what the risk of material misstatement is and seeks to reduce his detection risk by performing audit tests based on that assessment. This involves focusing on what could lead to a misstatement at the assertion level and planning tests to address these areas.

The auditor considers the risk of material misstatement at the overall financial statements level which may affect many assertions. This type of risk often relates to a failing in the control environment, such as management override of certain internal controls, and may be particularly indicative of a risk of fraud.

In addition, the risk of material misstatement at class of transaction, account balance and disclosure level should also be considered as this often determines the extent, nature and timing of audit tests at assertion level.

21.2.1 The components of audit risk

As stated above, audit risk is a function of the risk of material misstatement and detection risk. The risk of material misstatement is the entity's risk, and can be further broken down into:

- inherent risk; and
- control risk.

Inherent risk is the susceptibility of an assertion to material misstatement assuming that there are no related controls. The misstatement could be material either individually or when aggregated with other misstatements. This will vary depending on the nature of the assertion, transaction or account balance being considered. For example, items subject to complex calculations or accounting estimates are likely to have a higher inherent risk than others. External circumstances may create business risks which increase the inherent risk of some assertions, e.g. technological developments may render some stock obsolete, increasing the inherent risk of stock valuation.

Control risk is the risk that a material misstatement will not be prevented, or detected and corrected by the entity's internal control. The misstatement may be material either individually or when aggregated with other misstatements. There will always be some control risk as no internal control system is infallible.

Inherent and control risks may be assessed individually or using a combined assessment depending on the auditor's preferred methods and practical considerations.

Detection risk is the risk that the auditor will not detect a misstatement that exists in an assertion that could be material, either individually or when aggregated with other misstatements. Detection risk cannot be eliminated completely as the auditor does not usually examine all of a class of transactions, account balance or disclosure. In addition, the auditor may select the wrong audit procedure or misinterpret the results of a procedure.

For a given level of audit risk the level of detection risk bears an inverse relationship to the assessment of the risk of material misstatement. That is, the higher the risk of material misstatement, the less detection risk can be accepted and therefore more assurance is required from audit procedures, which are inevitably increased both in number and quality as a result.

21.3   Identifying and assessing risks

21.3.1   *Requirements*

ISA (UK and Ireland) 315 (Revised June 2016) *Identifying and assessing risks of material misstatement through understanding the entity and its environment* sets out requirements on understanding the entity, including its internal control and using this understanding to assess the risks of material misstatement in the financial statements. The ISA covers:

- risk assessment procedures and related activities;
- the required understanding of the entity and its environment, including the entity's internal control;
- identifying and assessing the risks of material misstatement; and
- documentation.

21.3.2   *Background*

ISA (UK and Ireland) 315 (Revised June 2016) requires the auditor to identify and assess the risks of material misstatement, whether due to fraud or error, at the financial statements and assertion levels, through understanding the entity and its environment, including the entity's internal control, thereby providing a basis for designing and implementing responses to the assessed risks of material misstatement.

The risk assessment should be made at the financial statement and assertion levels, and ISA (UK and Ireland) 330 (Revised June 2016) *The auditor's responses to assessed risks* (see below) sets out the auditor's responsibility to plan and perform audit procedures relating to these identified risks.

Further guidance in relation to the risk of material misstatement arising from fraud and error is set out in ISA (UK and Ireland) 240 (Revised June 2016) *The auditor's responsibilities relating to fraud in an audit of financial statements* (see **Chapter 16**).

21.3.3   Risk assessment procedures and related activities

Procedures

Although concentrated at the early stages of the audit, procedures to obtain an understanding of the entity, its environment and internal control, will be performed throughout the audit. Audit procedures designed and performed to obtain such an understanding are defined by the ISA as 'risk assessment procedures'. Such procedures may also provide evidence about transactions, balances, disclosures or the operation of controls, although they were not specifically designed to.

The ISA requires the auditor to perform the following risk assessment procedures to obtain an understanding of different aspects of the entity and its environment:

- enquiries of management, of appropriate individuals within the internal audit function (if the function exists) and others within the entity;
- analytical procedures; and
- observation and inspection.

Much information may come from management, but other directors or staff may be able to provide different perspectives which highlight the risk of material misstatement. Information may also be obtained through enquiries with the internal audit function, if the entity has such a function. For example, talking to sales personnel may uncover a change in sales trends or contractual arrangements with customers, or meeting with the internal audit function may highlight potential problems with the design or effectiveness of the internal control system.

Analytical procedures may identify unusual transactions or trends which may indicate material misstatements. At the risk assessment stage such analytical procedures tend to be at a high level and are therefore likely only to provide a broad initial indication of a misstatement which will require further investigation.

Observation and inspection may support management representations or may provide information directly. Procedures will normally include:

- observation of entity activities and operations;
- inspection of documents (such as business plans and strategies), records and internal control manuals;
- reading reports (such as quarterly management reports and minutes of directors' meetings);
- visits to the entity's premises; and
- tracing transactions through the information systems relating to financial reporting, i.e. walkthroughs.

Prior year information

For ongoing audits, information gained at the prior year's audit will be of use when performing risk assessment procedures in the current year. However, the ISA requires the auditor to determine whether changes have occurred since the previous audit that may affect the relevance of such information in the current audit. The continuing relevance of such information can be determined by performing system walkthroughs.

Information gathered during any interim review may also be relevant to the year end risk assessment procedures, but its ongoing accuracy should also be verified.

In addition, information gathered in previous audits may highlight particular types of transactions and other events or account balances (and related disclosures) where the auditor experienced difficulty in performing the necessary audit procedures, for example, due to their complexity.

21.3.4   Engagement team discussion

ISA (UK and Ireland) 315 (Revised June 2016) introduced a requirement for the engagement partner and other key members of the engagement team to discuss the susceptibility of the entity's financial statements to material misstatement. This meeting is often combined with the fraud discussion outlined in **16.4.2**. The meeting should include all key members of the engagement team, but the exact participants, timing and extent of the meeting are matters of professional judgment. Typically, such a discussion would include the engagement partner, audit manager and senior and tax manager, where such services are provided. More junior members of the engagement team may be included to enable them to gain a better understanding of how the results of the work assigned to them affect other aspects of the audit. The presence of the engagement partner is not to be underestimated as he is key in setting the overall tone and direction of the audit and his knowledge and experience both of the client, its industry and auditing in general will provide essential inputs to the risk assessment process.

The engagement team must also consider whether experts assigned to the team, such as IT or valuation specialists, should participate in the meeting.

The discussion provides an opportunity for more experienced engagement team members to share their knowledge of the entity. It allows the engagement team members to exchange information about the business risks to which the entity is subject and about how and where the financial statements might be susceptible to material misstatement due to fraud or error. It is an opportunity for the engagement team members to gain a better understanding of the potential for material misstatement of the financial statements in the specific areas assigned to them, and to understand how the results of the audit procedures that they perform may affect other aspects of the audit including the decisions about the nature, timing, and extent of further audit procedures.

The discussion should emphasise the need for professional scepticism and, in accordance with the requirements of ISA (UK and Ireland) 240 (Revised June 2016) *The auditor's responsibilities relating to fraud in an audit of financial statements* particular importance should be given to the susceptibility of the entity's financial statements to material misstatement due to fraud.

As part of the discussion, there should be consideration of the disclosure requirements of the applicable financial reporting framework to assist in identifying early in the audit where there may be risks of material misstatement in relation to disclosures.

Further meetings may be held during the course of the engagement to allow team members to communicate and share information gained during the audit which may affect the assessment of risk or the audit procedures performed.

21.3.5 Understanding the entity and its environment, including the entity's internal control

Detailed areas

The following areas should be included in the auditor's understanding of the entity and its environment:

- industry, regulatory and other external factors, including the applicable financial reporting framework;
- nature of the entity, including:

  - its operations;
  - its ownership and governance structures;
  - the types of investment that the entity is making and plans to make, including investments in special-purpose entities; and
  - the way that the entity is structured and how it is financed to enable the auditor to understand the classes of transactions, account balances, and disclosures to be expected in the financial statements;

- the selection and application of accounting policies;
- objectives and strategies and the related business risks that may result in a material misstatement of the financial statements; and
- measurement and review of the entity's financial performance.

Table 1 sets out examples of items that the auditor may consider in relation to the items above. Internal control is considered in **21.3.6** below.

Nature of the entity

A full understanding of the nature of the entity, its operations, governance and the way it is structured will help to ensure that any risks relating to group structures or the need for consolidation are identified. Such knowledge will also assist with identifying related party transactions.

The ISA also requires the auditor to consider whether the accounting policies selected and applied by the entity are suitable given the business and its industry. The auditor should consider new financial reporting standards that may be relevant to the entity and situations where the entity has changed its accounting policies, as well as ensuring adequate disclosure has been made of all relevant issues in the financial statements.

Objectives, strategies and related business risks

A business will define overall plans, or 'objectives' to respond to a variety of internal and external factors. To implement these objectives, practical 'strategies' are used. The risk that events or circumstances will mean that strategies cannot be implemented and objectives are not achieved is 'business risk'.

Business risk is a wider concept than the risk of material misstatement of the financial statements, but understanding business risk will increase the likelihood of identifying such risk. Whether a business risk will result in a risk of material misstatement will depend on the entity's circumstances. Examples of conditions that may indicate a risk of material misstatement are given in **Table 2**.

Smaller entities may not have formal, documented objectives and strategies. Therefore, to understand the business risk for such entities, the auditor must make enquiries and observations of management.

TABLE 1: Example items to consider when gaining an understanding of the entity and its environment

Industry, regulatory and other external factors

- Industry conditions:
  - the market and competition, including demand, capacity and price competition;
  - cyclical or seasonal activity;
  - product technology relating to the entity's products; and
  - energy supply and cost.
- Regulatory environment:
  - accounting principles and industry-specific practices;
  - regulatory framework for a regulated industry, including requirements for disclosures;
  - legislation and regulation that significantly affect the entity's operations, including direct supervisory activities;
  - taxation (corporation tax and other);

- government policies currently affecting the conduct of the entity's business such as:
  - monetary, including foreign exchange controls:
  - fiscal;
  - financial incentives (e.g. grant programmes);
  - tariffs and trade restrictions; and
- environmental requirements affecting the industry and the entity's business.

- Other external factors:

  - general level of economic activity (e.g. recession or growth);
  - interest rates and availability of financing; and
  - inflation, currency revaluation.

Nature of the entity

- Business operations:

  - nature of revenue sources (e.g. manufacture, wholesale, banking, insurance or other financial services, import/export trading, utilities, transportation and technology products and services);
  - products or services and markets (e.g. major customers and contracts, terms of payment, profit margins, market share, competitors, experts, pricing policies, reputation of products, warranties, order book, trends, marketing strategy and objectives, manufacturing processes);
  - conduct of operations (e.g. stages and methods of production, business segments, delivery or products and services, details of declining or expanding operations);
  - alliances, joint ventures and outsourcing activities;
  - involvement in electronic commerce including internet sales and marketing activities;
  - geographic dispersion and industry segmentation;
  - location of production facilities, warehouses and offices;
  - key customers;
  - important suppliers of goods and services (e.g. long-term contracts, stability of supply, terms of payment, imports. methods of delivery such as 'just in time');
  - employment (e.g. by location, supply, wage levels, union contracts, pension benefits, share option or incentive bonus arrangements and government regulation related to employment matters);
  - research and development activities and expenditure; and
  - transactions with related parties.

- Investments:

  - acquisitions, mergers or disposals of business activities (planned or recently executed);
  - investment and dispositions of securities and loans;
  - capital investment activities, including investments in plant and equipment and technology and any recent or planned changes; and

- investments in non-consolidated entities, including partnerships, joint ventures and special-purpose entities.
- Financing:

  - group structure – major subsidiaries and associated entities, including consolidated and non-consolidated structures;
  - debt structure, including covenants, restrictions, guarantees and off-balance sheet financing arrangements;
  - leasing of property, plant or equipment for use in the business;
  - parent companies (local, foreign, business reputation and experience);
  - related parties; and
  - use of derivate financial instruments.

- Financial reporting practices:

  - accounting principles and industry specific practices;
  - revenue recognition;
  - accounting for fair values;
  - stock (e.g. locations and quantities);
  - foreign currency assets, liabilities and transactions;
  - industry specific significant classes of transactions, account balances and related disclosures in the financial statements (e.g. loans and investments for banks, trade debtors and stock for manufacturers, research and development for pharmaceuticals);
  - accounting for unusual or complex transactions including those in controversial or emerging areas; and
  - financial statements presentation and disclosure.

Objectives and strategies and related business risks

- Existence of objectives relating to:

  - industry developments (a potential business risk might be that the entity does not have the personnel or expertise to deal with the changes in the industry);
  - new products and services (a potential related business risk might be that there is increased product liability);
  - expansion of the business (a potential business risk might be that the demand has not been accurately estimated);
  - new accounting requirements (a potential business risk might be incomplete or improper implementation or increased costs);
  - regulatory requirements (a potential business risk might be increased legal exposure);
  - current and prospective financing requirements (a potential business risk might be the loss of financing due to the entity's inability to meet requirements); and
  - use of IT (a potential business risk might be that systems and processes are incompatible).

- Effects of implementing a strategy, particularly any effects that will lead to new accounting requirements (a potential business risk might be incomplete or improper implementation).

Measurement and review of the entity's financial performance

- key ratios and operating statistics;
- key performance indicators;
- employee performance measures and incentive compensation policies;
- trends;
- use of forecasts, budgets and variance analyses;
- analyst reports and credit rating reports;
- competitor analyses;
- period-on-period financial performance (revenue growth, profitability, leverage).

TABLE 2: Examples of conditions that may indicate a risk of material misstatement, including risks relating to disclosures

- operations in regions that are economically unstable, e.g. countries with significant currency devaluation or highly inflationary economies;
- operations exposed to volatile markets, e.g. futures trading;
- high degree of complex regulation;
- going concern and liquidity issues including loss of significant customers;
- constraints on the availability of capital and credit;
- changes in the industry in which the entity operates;
- changes in the supply chain:
- developing or offering new products or services, or moving into new lines of business;
- expanding into new locations;
- changes in the entity such as large acquisitions or reorganisations or other unusual events;
- entities or business segments likely to be sold;
- complex alliances and joint ventures;
- use of off-balance sheet finance, special purpose entities and other complex financing arrangements;
- significant transactions with related parties;
- lack of personnel with appropriate accounting and financial reporting skills;
- changes in key personnel including departure of key executives;
- weaknesses in internal control, especially those not addressed by management;
- incentives for management and employees to engage in fraudulent financial reporting;
- inconsistencies between the entity's IT strategy and its business strategies;
- changes in the IT environment;
- installation of significant new IT systems related to financial statements;
- enquiries into the entities' operations or financial results by regulatory or government bodies;
- past misstatements, history of errors or a significant amount of adjustments at period end;
- significant amount of non-routine or non-systematic transactions including intercompany transactions and large revenue transactions at period end;

- transactions that are recorded based on management's intent, e.g. debt refinancing, assets to be sold and classification of marketable securities;
- application of new accounting pronouncements;
- accounting measurements that involve complex processes;
- events or transactions that involve significant measurement uncertainty, including accounting estimates, and related disclosures;
- omission, or obscuring, of significant information in disclosures;
- pending litigation and contingent liabilities, e.g. sales warranties, financial guarantees and environmental remediation.

Measurement and review of financial performance

By understanding which areas management are keen to monitor and review, the auditor can make assumptions about the areas which management perceive to be of relatively high risk. In turn, the existence of such performance measures may create a pressure on management, which may lead to motivation to misstate the financial statements.

Information used by management to monitor performance may include key performance indicators (both financial and non-financial), budgets, variance analysis, segment information and divisional, departmental or other level performance reports, and comparison of an entity's performance with that of competitors. Much of this information is likely to be internally generated and the auditor must consider whether it is likely to be accurate and precise enough to detect material misstatement.

Although smaller entities may not have formal performance review procedures, management are still likely to focus on a number of performance indicators. The auditor can observe these in the same way as for larger entities.

21.3.6   Internal control

Components of internal control

ISA (UK and Ireland) 315 (Revised June 2016) requires the auditor to obtain an understanding of internal control relevant to the audit in order to identify types of misstatement and design audit procedures. Internal control is the process designed, implemented and maintained to provide reasonable assurance about the achievement of the entity's objectives with regard to reliability of financial reporting, effectiveness and efficiency of operations and compliance with applicable laws and regulations.

Internal control consists of five components:

- the control environment;
- the entity's risk assessment process;

- the information system, including the related business processes, relevant to financial reporting and communication;
- control activities; and
- monitoring of controls.

Each of these is considered in detail below.

The design and implementation of internal control will vary from entity to entity and will differ depending on the entity's size and complexity. For smaller entities, the five components above may be blurred with an owner-manager taking sole responsibility for elements of each of them. Although the components of internal control may not be clearly distinguished in a smaller entity, their purpose will still stand.

Ordinarily, the auditor will be concerned with those controls relevant to the preparation of financial statements. Controls over information not directly relevant to the financial statements may also be of concern to the auditor if that information is used in the design or performance of an audit procedure, for example production statistics or controls, or pertains to the detection of non-compliance with laws and regulations. Therefore in assessing whether a control is relevant to the audit, the auditor considers:

- materiality;
- the significance of the related risk;
- the size of the entity;
- the nature of the entity's business;
- the diversity and complexity of the entity's operations;
- applicable legal and regulatory requirements;
- the circumstances and the applicable component of internal control;
- the nature and complexity of the systems that are part of the entity's internal control; and
- whether, and how, a specific control, individually or in combination with others, prevents, or detects and corrects, material misstatement.

Once the auditor has determined which controls are relevant to the audit he should evaluate the design of each control and determine whether it has been properly implemented. When evaluating the design of the control, the auditor considers whether it is capable of preventing, detecting or correcting material misstatements. If a control is poorly designed it may lead to a weakness which should be reported to those charged with governance.

Obtaining an understanding of a control is not the same as testing its operating effectiveness. In order to obtain assurance that a control is mitigating the risk of material misstatement, the control must be found to be operating effectively throughout the period.

Control environment

ISA (UK and Ireland) 315 (Revised June 2016) states that the auditor should obtain an understanding of the control environment and includes within the control environment the governance and management functions and the attitudes, awareness, and actions of those charged with governance and management concerning the entity's internal control and its importance in the entity. The control environment sets the tone of an organisation, influencing the control consciousness of its people.

When evaluating the design of the entity's control environment, the auditor considers how the following elements have been incorporated:

- communication and enforcement of integrity and ethical values;
- commitment to competence;
- participation of those charged with governance, including their independence from management;
- management's philosophy and operating style, their approach to taking risks and attitude to financial reporting and financial reporting staff;
- organisational structure and how activities are planned, executed, controlled and reviewed;
- assignment of authority and responsibility; and
- human resources policies and practices, such as recruitment, training and evaluating.

In understanding the control environment, the auditor must also consider whether the policies have actually been implemented. This will involve enquiries and corroboration using observation techniques or review of documents. For some controls, documentary evidence may be limited. For example, a commitment to ethical values is often demonstrated rather than documented. In smaller entities, communication between management and other personnel may be particularly informal. In such situations, the auditor's observations will be important.

An entity's control environment has a pervasive effect on assessing the risk of material misstatement. Even the best documented and implemented internal control system will be rendered useless by a poor management attitude which allows control environment weaknesses and thinks little of overriding controls. However, the existence of a satisfactory control environment can be a positive factor when assessing the risk of material misstatement, and may allow the auditor to have more confidence in the reliability of internally generated audit evidence.

The risk assessment process

The entity's risk assessment process is the way in which they identify the business risks that are relevant to financial reporting and determine actions to address those risks. The auditor is required to obtain an understanding of this process. This will involve considering how management identifies business risks, estimates their significance, assesses the likelihood of them occurring and determines actions to manage them.

The entity's process can assist the auditor in identifying risks of material misstatement, however, if the auditor discovers material risks which were not identified by the entity's process he considers whether there is a weakness which should be reported to those charged with governance.

The information system

The auditor is required to obtain an understanding of the information system insofar as it relates to financial reporting objectives. This will include gaining an understanding of the accounting system. The ISA sets out the following areas that the auditor should consider:

- the classes of transactions which are significant to the financial statements;
- the procedures by which transactions are initiated, recorded, processed and reported in the financial statements (these may be IT based or manual);
- the records supporting the above processes, held either electronically or manually;
- how other events are captured, i.e. those that are not normal transactions for the entity;
- the process used to prepare the financial statements from the accounting records; and
- controls surrounding journal entries, including non-standard journal entries used to record non-recurring, unusual transactions or adjustments.

This understanding of the information system relevant to financial reporting needs to include relevant aspects of that system relating to information disclosed in the financial statements that is obtained from within or outside of the general and subsidiary ledgers.

Financial statements may contain information that is obtained from outside of the general and subsidiary ledgers, such as information:

- from lease agreements, such as renewal options or future lease payments;
- produced by an entity's risk management system;
- on fair values;
- from models, or from other calculations used to develop estimates, including information relating to the underlying data and assumptions used in those models;
- about sensitivity analyses derived from financial models that demonstrates that management has considered alternative assumptions;
- obtained from an entity's tax returns and records; and
- obtained from analyses prepared to support management's assessment of the entity's ability to continue as a going concern.

The auditor should also be aware of whether and how controls are overridden and how incorrect processing of transactions is dealt with once it has been discovered. In addition, the auditor should consider how information is transferred from the processing system to the general ledger or the financial reporting systems.

The auditor should also consider whether the entity's information system is suitable for its circumstances. This will involve gaining an understanding of the entity's business processes and how transactions originate during these processes.

As part of understanding the information system, the auditor should also consider how the roles and responsibilities within the system are communicated to the individuals involved in the day-to-day running of that system. A risk of material misstatement may be reduced by the entity ensuring that all roles are set out in suitably detailed policy or financial reporting manuals.

Control activities

The auditor's risk assessment procedures performed to date will have provided a good indication of the areas where a risk of material misstatement exists. When assessing an entity's control activities, the auditor will concentrate on those areas where material misstatements are more likely to occur.

Control activities are the policies and procedures that help ensure that management directives are carried out. In order to understand an entity's control activities, the auditor considers how a particular activity, individually or in conjunction with others, prevents, detects or corrects a material misstatement. Specific control activities may include:

- authorisation (e.g. of payments);
- performance reviews;
- information processing;
- physical controls (e.g. over assets); or
- segregation of duties.

Specifically, the ISA requires the auditor to consider how the entity has responded to risks arising from IT. The auditor should consider how control activities have responded to different risks posed by the advent of IT systems, and consider whether the integrity of the information and security of the data has been maintained. **Table 3** provides examples of areas where risks may differ when the system is automated rather than manual.

TABLE 3: Traits of an automated system

Examples of areas where risk may differ from that associated with a manual system include:

- lack of transaction trails;
- uniform processing of transactions – clerical error is less of a risk in an information systems (IS) environment but there is a risk of a programming error resulting in large numbers of similar transactions being incorrectly processed;
- lack of segregation of duties;
- potential to alter data without visible signs of this being done;
- lack of human involvement may mean that errors are not detected as quickly;
- automatic transactions carried out by the IS;
- potential for increased management supervision using analytical tools available via the IS; and
- potential for using computer assisted audit techniques.

IT controls can be categorised as 'general IT controls' or 'application controls'. General IT controls are policies and procedures that relate to many applications and assist with ensuring that the information system operates properly. Examples are controls over access to IT systems or development of new systems. Application controls typically operate at a more detailed level, can be preventative or detective in nature and aim to ensure the integrity of the accounting records. Examples include numerical sequence checks or checks to ensure that items are suitably authorised.

Monitoring of controls

ISA (UK and Ireland) 315 (Revised June 2016) requires the auditor to gain an understanding of what the entity does to monitor its own controls. This monitoring should encompass both the day-to-day operation of the controls and the overall design of the control system. Where the information used to monitor the controls is taken from the information system itself, the auditor considers how the entity ensures it is reliable.

Where the entity has an internal audit function, the auditor should obtain an understanding of the nature of the internal audit function's responsibilities, its organisational status and the activities performed, or to be performed. Further guidance can be found in **Chapter 31**.

Manual and automated elements of internal control

An entity's system of internal control is likely to include both manual and automated elements. For smaller companies, there is likely to be a greater emphasis on manual procedures, but even for some large entities, elements of their internal control system may still rely heavily on manual intervention. The benefits and risks of using automated controls are set out in **Table 4**.

TABLE 4: Benefits and risks of using automated controls

Benefits – an entity is able to:

- consistently apply predefined business rules and perform complex calculations in processing large volumes of transactions or data;
- enhance the timeliness, availability and accuracy of information;
- facilitate the additional analysis of information;
- enhance the ability to monitor the performance of the entity's activities and its policies and procedures;
- reduce the risk that controls will be circumvented; and
- enhance the ability to achieve effective segregation of duties by implementing security controls in applications, databases and operating systems.

Risks

- reliance on systems or programmes that are inaccurately processing data, processing inaccurate data, or both;

- unauthorised access to data that may result in destruction of data or changes to data, including the recording of unauthorised or non-existent transactions or inaccurate recording of transactions. Particular risks occur where multiple users access a common database;
- the possibility of IT personnel gaining access privileges beyond those necessary to perform their assigned duties thereby breaking down segregation of duties;
- unauthorised changes to data in master files;
- unauthorised changes to systems or programmes;
- failure to make necessary changes to systems or programmes;
- inappropriate manual interventions; and
- potential loss of data or inability to access data as required.

Manual systems or elements of systems may be more suitable when judgment and discretion are required, such as for:

- large, unusual or non-recurring transactions;
- circumstances where errors are difficult to define, anticipate or predict;
- changing circumstances that require a control response outside the scope of an existing automated control; or
- monitoring the effectiveness of automated controls.

However, manual controls are generally less reliable than automated controls as they rely on people to perform them. Therefore, it cannot be assumed that a manual control has been applied consistently.

Limitations of internal control

Internal control, however well designed and implemented, can at best only provide reasonable assurance about achieving an entity's financial reporting objectives. Even automated controls are subject to some human involvement and, therefore, human error. There may have been errors at the programming stage, operatives may input data incorrectly and individuals receiving reports from the system may not understand the purpose of such reports.

In addition, all controls are subject to override by collusion of one or more individuals. In smaller entities formal segregation of duties may be impossible, and the potential for override of controls by an owner-manager may be great.

21.3.7 Identifying and assessing the risks of material misstatement

Relating risks to assertions

The auditor identifies risks in the financial statements by obtaining an understanding of the entity and its environment, including relevant controls that relate to risks and by considering the classes of transactions, account balances and disclosures (including both the qualitative and quantitative aspects of disclosures).

He then relates the risks identified to the financial statements assertions. The assertions considered by the auditor are set out in **Table 5**, although the audit approaches of different firms may use different terminologies. This means that each risk is considered in terms of the financial statements balance or balances it may affect and what that effect might be. For example, a risk that goods may have been incorrectly invoiced to customers without being despatched may impact the existence and valuation of turnover and trade debtors.

The auditor then considers whether the risk is such that the effect on the financial statements would be material and then how likely it is that this will occur. Potential misstatements in individual statements and disclosures may be judged to be material due to size, nature or circumstances.

The auditor will next consider whether controls have been identified which are likely to prevent or detect and correct material misstatement arising from each risk. Often individual controls do not completely address a risk, but the controls within a particular process or system may together address an assertion. However, the less directly a control relates to an assertion, the less effective that control may be in preventing or detecting and correcting risks related to the assertion.

Once risks have been allocated to assertions and matched with controls, the auditor can plan tests of controls and substantive tests to gain his audit evidence.

TABLE 5: Audit assertions

Assertions about classes of transactions and events, and related disclosures, for the period under audit

- occurrence – transactions and events that have been recorded or disclosed have occurred, and such transactions and events pertain to the entity;
- completeness – all transactions and events that should have been recorded have been recorded, and all related disclosures that should have been included in the financial statements have been included;
- accuracy – amounts and other data relating to recorded transactions and events have been recorded appropriately, and related disclosures have been appropriately measured and described;
- cut-off – transactions and events have been recorded in the correct accounting period;
- classification – transactions and events have been recorded in the proper accounts;
- presentation – transactions and events are appropriately aggregated or disaggregated and clearly described, and related disclosures are relevant and understandable in the context of the requirements of the applicable financial reporting framework.

Assertions about account balances, and related disclosures, at the period end

- existence – assets, liabilities and equity interests exist;
- rights and obligations – the entity holds or controls the right to assets, and liabilities are the obligations of the entity;

- completeness – all assets, liabilities and equity interests that should have been recorded have been recorded, and all related disclosures that should have been included in the financial statements have been included;
- accuracy, valuation and allocation – assets, liabilities and equity interests have been included in the financial statements at appropriate amounts and any resulting valuation or allocation adjustments have been appropriately recorded, and related disclosures have been appropriately measured and described;
- classification – assets, liabilities, and equity interests have been recorded in the proper accounts;
- presentation – assets, liabilities, and equity interests are appropriately aggregated or disaggregated and clearly described, and related disclosures are relevant and understandable in the context of the requirements of the applicable financial reporting framework.

Assertions about other disclosures

The assertions described above, adapted as appropriate, may also be used by the auditor in considering the different types of potential misstatements that may occur in disclosures not directly related to recorded classes of transactions, events, or account balances. As an example of such a disclosure, the entity may be required to describe its exposure to risks arising from financial instruments, including how the risks arise; the objectives, policies and processes for managing the risks; and the methods used to measure the risks.

Pervasive risks

Although many risks can be related to specific assertions, some risks may affect the financial statements as a whole, typically as a result of a weak control environment. Examples would be concerns about the integrity of the entity's management or untrained or inexperienced staff in a key accounting role.

In severe situations, the weakness of internal control may raise doubts about the auditability of the financial statements, for example unscrupulous management may lead to a very high risk of management misrepresentation in the financial statements or very poor accounting records may mean that insufficient audit evidence is available to support an unqualified audit opinion. In such cases, the auditor may issue a qualification or disclaimer of opinion, but if the situation is severe, the only action available to the auditor is to resign.

Significant risks

As part of his risk assessment, the auditor may decide that certain risks are 'significant risks'. Significant risks require special audit consideration as a result of the nature of the risk or the magnitude or likelihood of the error which may result. Significant risks often arise from non-routine transactions or judgmental matters as a result of:

- greater management intervention to specify the accounting treatment;
- greater manual intervention during data collection and processing;

- complex calculations or accounting principles, which may also be unfamiliar; and
- the difficulty of planning and implementing effective controls over non-routine transactions.

In determining whether a risk is a significant risk, the ISA requires the auditor to consider:

- whether the risk is a risk of fraud;
- whether the risk is related to recent significant economic, accounting or other developments and, therefore, requires specific attention;
- the complexity of transactions;
- whether the risk involves significant transactions with related parties;
- the degree of subjectivity in the measurement of financial information related to the risk, especially those measurements involving a wide range of measurement uncertainty; and
- whether the risk involves significant transactions that are outside the normal course of business for the entity, or that otherwise appear to be unusual.

Having identified significant risks, the auditor considers the controls, if any, in place to mitigate those risks. As such risks are often as a result of non-routine transactions, there may not be controls specific to each risk, but rather general procedures for responding to such risks such as approval processes for any transaction falling outside of the standard accounting process.

If the auditor wishes to rely on the operating effectiveness of controls to mitigate a significant risk, he will plan and perform tests of controls. In addition, substantive procedures should be planned to address the significant risk. This is covered further in ISA (UK and Ireland) 330 (Revised June 2016), which is discussed below.

Other ISAs identify certain matters that are presumed to give rise to significant risks and will therefore warrant special audit consideration:

- ISA (UK and Ireland) 240 (Revised June 2016) states that:
  - where assessed risks of material misstatement are due to fraud, they must be treated as significant risks;
  - there is a presumed risk of fraud in relation to revenue recognition. This presumption may be rebutted, otherwise, revenue recognition will be a significant risk; and
  - when making his assessment of risks due to fraud, in all entities the auditor should presume that there is a risk of fraud arising from management override of controls. This presumption may not be rebutted, and as a fraud risk, this will always give rise to a significant risk;
- ISA (UK and Ireland) 550 requires that the auditor should treat identified significant related party transactions that are outside the entity's normal course of business as giving rise to significant risks.

Risks that cannot be mitigated by substantive procedures alone

At the risk assessment stage, the auditor should be aware of any risks which may not be mitigated by planning and performing substantive tests alone. Such risks are likely to arise in an environment where much of the entity's information is initiated, recorded, processed or reported electronically with little or no manual intervention. In such an integrated system, audit evidence may only be available electronically and its sufficiency and appropriateness will depend on the effectiveness of the controls over its accuracy and completeness. If such controls are not operating properly, the potential for fictitious transactions to be created or existing transactions to be amended without detection may be large.

In such a situation, the auditor should plan and perform tests of controls to satisfy themselves that controls are working to eliminate any risk of material misstatement. Due to the nature of such systems, the use of CAATs will be required (see **Chapter 37**).

Revision of risk assessment

The auditor's assessment of the risks of material misstatement at the assertion level may change during the course of the audit as additional audit evidence is obtained. Where audit evidence is obtained from performing further audit procedures, or new information is obtained, either of which is inconsistent with the audit evidence on which the auditor originally based the assessment, the auditor should revise the assessment and modify the further planned audit procedures accordingly.

21.3.8   Communicating with those charged with governance

Where the auditor finds significant deficiencies in the design or implementation of internal control, or a risk of material misstatement which has not been addressed by one or more controls, he should inform those charged with governance as soon as practical.

21.3.9   Documentation

ISA (UK and Ireland) 315 (Revised June 2016) requires the auditor to document:

- the engagement team's discussion about the likelihood of material misstatement arising from fraud or error and the significant decisions reached;
- his understanding of the entity and its environment, assessment of the component parts of internal control, risk assessment procedures and sources of his information;

- risks of material misstatement by financial statement area and assertion;
- significant risks; and
- risks that cannot be mitigated by substantive tests alone.

There are many techniques that may be used to document these areas:

- narrative descriptions;
- questionnaires;
- checklists; and
- flow charts.

These may be used in isolation or in combination. The extent and form of the documentation to support the assessment will depend on the complexity of the systems and the extent of the auditor's procedures required to assess them.

21.4 Responses to assessed risks

ISA (UK and Ireland) 330 (Revised June 2016) *The auditor's responses to assessed risks* covers:

- overall responses;
- audit procedures responsive to the assessed risks of material misstatement at the assertion level;
- adequacy of presentation and disclosure;
- evaluating the sufficiency and appropriateness of audit evidence; and
- documentation.

21.4.1 Overall responses

The first stage is for the auditor to respond to any risks of material misstatement at the overall financial statements level. Responses may include:

- emphasising the need for professional scepticism;
- assigning more experienced audit staff;
- using specialists or experts;
- providing additional supervision; and
- incorporating further elements of unpredictability in the selection of audit tests.

The auditor may also decide to perform all audit procedures at the period end date rather than during any interim visit. Only if the auditor has confidence in the effectiveness of the control environment may some audit procedures be performed at an interim date.

Where there are concerns about the control environment, the auditor is likely to use a substantive approach, rather than a combined approach which also relies on tests of controls.

21.4.2   Responses at the assertion level

Procedures planned by the auditor should link directly to his risk assessment. The auditor should consider:

- the significance of the risk;
- the likelihood that a material misstatement will occur;
- the characteristics of the class of transactions, account balance or disclosure involved;
- the nature of the specific controls used by the entity and in particular whether they are manual or automated; and
- whether the auditor expects to obtain audit evidence about related controls.

The auditor may plan to perform tests of controls alone, tests of controls combined with substantive procedures or follow a purely substantive testing route. The latter approach may be used where the risk assessment procedures have not identified any effective controls relevant to the assertion or because testing the operating effectiveness of controls would be inefficient. For smaller entities a fully substantive approach would probably be used as the number of control activities are likely to be limited.

Nature of procedures

The higher the auditor's assessment of risk, the more reliable and relevant the audit evidence must be. This will affect both the types of audit procedures performed and their mix. Where the auditor has considered related controls in his assessment of material misstatement, he should test the effective operation of those controls. Where the auditor uses information produced by the entity's information system in his testing, the accuracy and completeness of that information should be verified. For example, if analytical procedures include comparisons to budget data, the accuracy and completeness of the budget data should be considered.

Timing of procedures

The higher the assessed risk of material misstatement, the more likely the auditor is to consider that performing substantive procedures at period end rather than at an interim date would be most effective. A disadvantage of performing all procedures at the period end is that the auditor may lose the ability to identify and address significant matters at an early stage. Another strategy might be to perform procedures unannounced or at unpredictable times.

In considering when to perform his procedures, the auditor considers:

- the control environment;
- when information is available;
- the nature of the risk, for example risks relating to the state of work in progress would be performed at the period end;
- the period or date to which the audit evidence relates; and

- the timing of the preparation of the financial statements, particularly for those disclosures that provide further explanation about amounts recorded in the statement of financial position, the statement of comprehensive income, the statement of changes in equity or the statement of cash flows.

Extent of procedures

The extent of any audit procedure is a matter of judgment based on the materiality, the assessed risk and the degree of assurance the auditor plans to obtain. The use of CAATs may allow more extensive testing of electronic transactions and account files (see **Chapter 37**).

Tests of controls

The auditor should perform tests of controls when:

- substantive procedures alone do not provide sufficient evidence; or
- the auditor's risk assessment includes the expectation that controls are operating effectively.

Typically, an enquiry will form part of the auditor's testing of controls, but an enquiry will not be sufficient in itself and should be combined with other procedures such as observation, inspection or reperformance. The type of testing will be determined by the details of the control itself. For example, some controls are documented and review of this documentation may provide evidence about the effective operation of the control. Others may not be documented, such as control activities performed by a computer, where the use of CAATs may be required.

Controls are generally tested throughout the period. Testing at one point in time only may be effective for some areas such as for controls over the entity's physical stock count at the period end. When testing has only covered part of the period, alternative audit procedures should normally be used for the remainder.

Relying on prior periods' assessments

If the auditor plans to rely on evidence about the operating effectiveness of controls obtained in prior periods he should ensure, through observation or inspection, that the controls have not changed. If controls have changed, he must test the operating effectiveness of those controls in the current audit. Even if they have not changed, the ISA requires that the operating effectiveness should be retested at least once every third audit. When there are a number of controls which are not being retested each year, a proportion of them should be tested at each audit.

In considering whether it is acceptable to rely on the testing carried out in prior periods, the auditor considers:

- the effectiveness of other elements of internal control, including the control environment, the entity's monitoring of controls and risk assessment process;

- the characteristics of the control, including whether it is manual or automated;
- the effectiveness of general IT controls;
- the effectiveness of the control and its application by the entity, including the nature and extent of failures of the control in prior audits;
- whether the lack of change in a control is itself a risk, given changing circumstances elsewhere; and
- the risk of material misstatement and the extent of reliance placed on the control.

Where the operation of one or more controls is intended to mitigate a significant risk (see **21.3.7** above) evidence about the operating effectiveness of the control must be made in the current period.

Extent of tests of controls

Matters that the auditor considers when deciding on the extent of tests of controls include:

- how frequently the control is performed during the period;
- the length of time during the audit period that the auditor is relying on the operating effectiveness of the control;
- the quality of the audit evidence likely to be obtained;
- the extent to which other controls related to the assertion will provide audit evidence;
- the extent to which the control is relevant to the assessment of risk; and
- expected deviations in the control (although if this is too high, no reliance may be placed on the control).

The more the auditor relies on the operating effectiveness of controls, the greater the extent of testing required.

Where controls are automated, the auditor will not gain additional assurance from increasing the extent of testing of the control. The control should function consistently throughout the period unless the application is changed. Once the auditor is content that the control is operating as intended, usually by testing it once only, testing should concentrate on ensuring that the application is not changed without appropriate change controls and testing.

Substantive procedures

The auditor should plan and perform substantive procedures for each material class of transactions, account balance and disclosure, regardless of their risk. In addition, the auditor is required by the ISA to:

- agree or reconcile information in the financial statements to the underlying accounting records, including agreeing or reconciling information in disclosures, whether such information is obtained from within or outside of the general and subsidiary ledgers; and
- examine material journal entries and other adjustments made during the course of preparing the financial statements.

Where the risk assessment process has identified a significant risk (see **21.3.7**), substantive procedures should be planned and performed in response to that risk. Substantive procedures may be analytical procedures or tests of detail. Substantive analytical procedures are generally more applicable to large volumes of transactions that tend to be predictable over time and suit gathering evidence about existence and valuation assertions. When designing substantive analytical procedures, the auditor should consider:

- the suitability of using substantive analytical procedures given the assertions;
- the reliability of the data, whether internal or external, used to generate ratios and comparisons;
- whether the expected results are sufficiently precise to identify a material misstatement and the desired level of assurance; and
- the amount of any difference in recorded amounts from expected values that is acceptable.

If substantive procedures are performed at an interim date, the auditor should perform further tests (either tests of controls, substantive tests or a combination of both) to cover the remaining time to the period end. The decision whether it is worthwhile performing substantive procedures at an interim date will depend on the:

- control environment and other relevant controls;
- availability of information at the date of the interim procedure;
- the objective of the test;
- the assessed risk of material misstatement;
- the nature of the class of transactions or account balance and related assertions being tested; and
- the ability of the auditor to perform additional tests to cover the period between the interim testing and the period end.

If testing has occurred at an interim date and has detected misstatements, the auditor would usually modify the assessment of risk and the nature, timing or extent of further audit procedures to be performed at the period end.

Relying on prior periods' work

Unlike for tests of controls, it is not sufficient to rely on substantive procedures performed in prior periods to obtain evidence to address a risk of material misstatement in the current period. If any assurance is to be taken from work performed in prior periods, the audit evidence and related subject matter must not change fundamentally. An example would be where legal opinion was obtained about the structure of a securitisation in the prior period, and that securitisation has not changed.

Extent of substantive procedures

The greater the risk of material misstatement, the greater the extent of substantive procedures. Substantive procedures may also be extended if there are unsatisfactory results from the work performed on tests of controls.

For tests of detail, the extent of testing is often thought of in terms of the sample size. ISA (UK and Ireland) 530 contains details on the use of sampling and other methods to select items for testing (see **Chapter 26**).

External confirmation procedures may be relevant in some situations and further details can be found in **Chapter 23**. Although external confirmations may provide relevant audit evidence relating to certain assertions, there are some assertions for which external confirmations provide less relevant audit evidence. For example, an external confirmation provides more evidence about the existence of a debtor balance than it does about its recoverability.

Public interest entities

For public interest entities, the ISA includes an explicit requirement (derived from the Audit Regulation) that the auditor needs to assess the valuation methods applied to the various items in the financial statements including the impact of any changes. He is also required to communicate in his additional report to the audit committee, his assessment of the valuation methods used including the impact of any changes in such methods (see **10.7.2**). Such procedures may also be appropriate for other entities.

21.4.3   Presentation of the financial statements

The ISA requires the auditor to plan and perform procedures to determine that the overall presentation of the financial statements is in line the requirements of the applicable accounting framework. In making this evaluation, the auditor considers whether the financial statements are presented in a manner that reflects the appropriate:

- classification and description of financial information and the underlying transactions, events and conditions; and
- presentation, structure and content of the financial statements.

21.4.4   Evaluating audit evidence

Throughout the audit, the auditor is required to evaluate whether his original assessment of the risk of material misstatement requires amending. For example, the auditor may be required to amend his assessment as a result of:

- a higher level of misstatements being discovered than planned during the performance of substantive procedures;
- failures of the entity's controls during the period; or
- discrepancies coming to light as a result of the overall analytical review of the financial statements at the completion stage of the audit.

Changes to the assessment may require changes to the nature, timing and extent of the audit procedures.

At the completion of the audit procedures, the auditor is required to conclude whether sufficient appropriate audit evidence has been obtained to reduce the risk of material misstatement in the financial statements to an acceptably low level. The factors influencing what constitutes sufficient appropriate audit evidence are set out at **23.2.2**. Where he concludes that the evidence obtained is not sufficient, the auditor should attempt to gather further information. Where this is not possible, he should issue a qualified or disclaimer of opinion audit report.

21.4.5   Documentation

The auditor should ensure that the following are fully documented:

- overall responses to address the assessed risks of material misstatement at the financial statements level;
- nature, timing and extent of further audit procedures;
- linkage of those procedures with assessed risks at the assertion level;
- results of audit procedures; and
- where using evidence about the operating effectiveness of controls obtained in prior audits, the justification for relying on that work.

The auditor's documentation should demonstrate that information in the financial statements agrees or reconciles with the underlying accounting records, including agreeing or reconciling disclosures.

22 SERVICE ORGANISATIONS

22.1 Introduction

ISA (UK and Ireland) 402 *Audit considerations relating to an entity using a service organisation* was issued in October 2009 and is effective for the audit of financial statements for periods ending on or after 15 December 2010. This ISA was not revised as part of the FRC's project to revise ISAs in April 2016 and as such, the 2009 version remains applicable.

ISA (UK and Ireland) 402 sets out requirements on the procedures necessary to assess the impact of a reporting entity's use of a service organisation, specifically:

- understanding the services provided by a service organisation, including internal control;
- responding to the assessed risks of material misstatement;
- subservice organisations;
- responding to the risks of material misstatement;
- fraud, non-compliance with laws and regulations and uncorrected misstatements; and
- reporting by the auditor of the user entity ('the user auditor').

A 'service organisation' is defined for this purpose as a third-party organisation (or segment of a third-party organisation) that provides services to user entities that are part of those entities' information systems relevant to financial reporting. Use of service organisations is often referred to as 'outsourcing'.

Guidance on issuing reports on service organisations is given in AAF 01/06 *Assurance reports on internal controls of service organisations made available to third parties* and ISAE 3402, *Assurance Reports on Controls at a Third Party Service Organisation*. These are covered in **Chapter 40**.

22.2 Understanding the services provided by a service organisation, including internal control

The auditor is required to identify whether the reporting entity uses service organisations and then to consider the impact of this on the client's internal control, the auditor's assessment of the risk of material misstatement and his procedures. The guidance notes that the outsourcing of an activity by an entity to a service organisation does not relieve its directors of their responsibilities nor does it alter those of the auditor. As not all outsourced activities have a significant effect on the reporting entity's financial statements, the auditor needs to assess initially whether those activities are relevant to financial reporting and hence whether the service provider is a service organisation as defined above.

Service organisation services that are relevant to the audit include:

- information processing;
- maintenance of the user entity's accounting records;
- management or custody of assets; and
- initiation or execution of transactions on behalf of the entity.

Examples of ways in which different activities undertaken by service organisations can affect the risk of misstatement are given in **Table 1**.

TABLE 1: Characteristics of service organisation activities which may increase risk
Outsourced Accounting Functions

Degree of risk	Characteristics	Examples
High	• Complex transactions	• Maintenance of both accounting records and preparation of budgets and reports control
	• Those undertaking accounting work need extensive business or specialist knowledge	• Accounting records of retail business
	• Delegated authority to initiate and execute transactions	
	• Effective controls only possible on 'real time' basis	
	• Reversal of outsourcing costly/ difficult	
	• High cost of performance failure (e.g. misleading management reports leading to poor decision making)	
	• High proportion of finance functions outsourced	
Medium	• Some business knowledge needed but parameters for necessary judgments can be identified and agreed in advance	• Outsourcing of accounting records by a supplier of raw materials
	• Transactions can be initiated but execution requires approval from entity	• Credit control
	• Execution of transactions on instruction from entity	• Leasing arrangements

---

	• Analytical techniques insufficient for adequate degree of control	
	• Discrete functions outsourced	
Low	• Little requirement for judgment in processing transactions	• Processing salary payments
	• Non-complex transactions	• Preparation of invoices
	• Little business knowledge required	• Data entry
	• Analytical control techniques effective	
	• Effects of failure can be contained	
	• Easy to rearrange/find alternative service organisations	
	• Low proportion of discrete functions outsourced	

Services provided by a service organisation will be relevant when those services, and the controls over them, effectively form part of the entity's information system relevant to financial reporting. Controls at the service organisation may be relevant to the audit, such as controls over the safeguarding of assets. A service organisation's services will be part of the entity's information system if those services affect any of the following:

- the classes of transactions that are significant to the user entity's financial statements;
- the procedures by which the user entity's transactions are initiated, recorded, processed, corrected as necessary, transferred to the general ledger and reported in the financial statements;
- the related accounting records, supporting information and specific accounts in the user entity's financial statements;
- how the user entity's information system captures events and conditions, other than transactions, that are significant to the financial statements;
- the financial reporting process used to prepare the financial statements; and
- controls surrounding recurring and non-recurring journal entries.

The auditor should obtain and document an understanding of the contract terms, whether agreed orally or in writing, and the way in which the reporting entity monitors the service organisation's activities so that it can meet its fiduciary and other legal responsibilities. This will assist the auditor in his consideration of the impact of the arrangement on his assessment of risk (see **22.3**).

When obtaining an understanding of internal control relevant to the audit, the user auditor evaluates the design and implementation of relevant controls at the user entity that relate to the services provided by the service organisation, including those that are applied to the transactions processed by the service organisation.

For example, if a user entity uses a service organisation to process payroll, the user entity may establish controls over the submission and receipt of payroll information that could prevent, or detect, material misstatements. These controls may include comparing the data submitted to the service organisation with reports received from the service organisation after the data has been processed and recomputing a sample of the payroll amounts for accuracy and reviewing the total payroll amount for reasonableness. In such a situation, the user auditor may perform tests of the user entity's controls over payroll processing that would provide a basis for him to conclude that the user entity's controls are operating effectively for the assertions related to payroll transactions.

The user auditor determines whether a sufficient understanding of the nature and significance of the services provided by the service organisation and their effect on the user entity's internal control relevant to the audit has been obtained to provide a basis for the identification and assessment of risks of material misstatement.

If the auditor is unable to ascertain sufficient information about the operation of controls at the service organisation from the user entity, ISA (UK and Ireland) 402 requires that he performs one or more of the following procedures:

- obtain a type 1 report on the description and design of controls, or a type 2 report (see below) on the description and design of controls and their operating effectiveness, if available;
- contact the service entity, through the user entity, to obtain specific information;
- visit the service organisation and perform procedures that will provide the necessary information about controls; or
- use another auditor to perform those procedures for him.

22.2.1   Using a type 1 or type 2 report

Type 1 and type 2 reports are prepared under International Standards on Assurance Engagements (ISAE) 3402 *Assurance Reports on Controls at a Third Party Service Organisation* with guidance from AAF 01/06 (see **Chapter 40.7**) and are used to support the auditor's understanding of the service organisation. Type 1 and type 2 reports provide differing levels of assurance to the user auditor and, as a result, have different impacts on the remaining work to be carried out.

A type 1 report is a report on the description and design of the controls at a service organisation and contains:

(i) the service organisation's description of its system;
(ii) a written assertion by the service organisation that, in all material respects, and based on suitable criteria, the description fairly presents the service organisation's system as designed and implemented as at the specified date and the controls related to the control objectives stated in the service

organisation's description of its system were suitably designed as at the specified date; and

(iii) a service auditor's assurance report that gives reasonable assurance on (ii) above.

A type 2 report is a report on the description and design and also operating effectiveness of the controls at a service organisation and contains:

(i)   the service organisation's description of its system;

(ii) a written assertion by the service organisation that, in all material respects, and based on suitable criteria, the description fairly presents the service organisation's system as designed and implemented throughout the specified period, the controls related to the control objectives stated in the service organisation's description of its system were suitably designed throughout the specified period, and the controls operated effectively throughout the specified period; and

(iii) a service auditor's assurance report that gives reasonable assurance on (ii) above and also includes a description of the tests of controls and the results thereof.

In order to determine the sufficiency and appropriateness of the audit evidence provided by the type 1 or type 2 report, the auditor needs to be satisfied as to:

- the service auditor's professional competence and independence from the service organisation; and
- the adequacy of the standards under which the report was issued, particularly where the service auditor practices outside of the United Kingdom.

Where the auditor plans to use a type 1 or type 2 report as audit evidence to support his understanding about the design and implementation of controls at the service organisation, the ISA requires him to:

- evaluate whether the description and design of controls at the service organisation is at a date or for a period that is appropriate for the auditor's purposes;
- evaluate the sufficiency and appropriateness of the evidence provided by the report for the understanding of the user entity's internal control relevant to the audit; and
- determine whether complementary user entity controls identified by the service organisation are relevant to the user entity and, if so, obtain an understanding of whether the user entity has designed and implemented such controls.

22.2.2   *Accounting records*

Outsourcing all or part of their accounting records does not diminish the responsibilities of those charged with governance in relation to those records. Therefore, for each material element of the accounting records maintained by a service organisation, the auditor should obtain and document an understanding of the way the accounting records are maintained and how those charged with governance ensure the accounting records meet any relevant legal obligations. Under UK company law, those charged with governance must retain ownership of the accounting records and allow the auditor to access them at any time.

The ISA requires that the auditor should assess whether the arrangements for maintaining all or part of the entity's accounting records by a service organisation have any effect on his reporting responsibilities in relation to accounting records.

The guidance notes that the wording of UK company law is such that it requires companies to keep records rather than cause them to be kept, and thus the wording of the contract with the service organisation will need to be reviewed to determine whether the entity retains ownership of those records. It is suggested that the auditor may wish to seek legal advice where there is any doubt on this matter.

22.3 Responding to the assessed risks of material misstatement

The ISA requires the auditor to use his understanding of the arrangement to:

- assess whether he can obtain sufficient appropriate audit evidence on the relevant financial statement assertions from the records held at the reporting entity; and if not
- determine effective procedures to obtain audit evidence either by direct access to the records kept by the service organisation or through information obtained from the service organisation or its auditor.

Where the auditor requires evidence concerning balances representing assets held by or transactions undertaken by the service organisation, he may consider the efficiency and effectiveness of the following procedures:

- inspecting records and documents held by the reporting entity;
- establishing the effectiveness of controls;
- obtaining representations to confirm balances and transactions from the service organisation;
- performing analytical review procedures on the records maintained by the reporting entity or the returns from the service organisation;
- inspecting records and documents held by the service organisation;
- requesting the service organisation auditor or the reporting entity's internal audit function to perform specified procedures; and
- reviewing information from the service organisation and its auditor concerning the design and operation of its controls systems.

As noted in **22.2** above, when the user auditor's risk assessment includes an expectation that controls at the service organisation are operating effectively, he obtains evidence about this from one or more of the following:

- obtaining a type 2 report;
- performing appropriate tests of control at the service organisation; or
- using another auditor to perform tests of control at the service organisation on his behalf.

22.4   Subservice organisations

If the service organisation itself outsources some of its activities to another service organisation, the auditor should consider whether those activities are relevant to the audit of the user entity's financial statements. If they are, the requirements of ISA (UK and Ireland) 402 should be applied also to the operations of the other service organisations.

22.5   Fraud, non-compliance with laws and regulations and uncorrected misstatements

ISA (UK and Ireland) 402 requires the auditor to enquire of management of the user entity whether the service organisation has reported to them any incidences of fraud, non-compliance with applicable laws and regulations and uncorrected misstatements affecting the financial statements of the user entity. Terms of the contract between the user entity and the service organisation may require that such disclosure is made.

If such incidents have been reported, the auditor should consider any impact they may have on the nature, timing and extent of his audit procedures.

22.6   Reporting

If the auditor is unable to obtain sufficient appropriate audit evidence regarding the services provided by the service organisation which are relevant to the audit of the financial statements, then the auditor should modify his opinion in accordance with ISA (UK and Ireland) 705 (Revised June 2016). Such a limitation on scope may arise where:

- the auditor is unable to obtain a sufficient understanding of the services provided by the service organisation and does not have a basis for the identification and assessment of the risks of material misstatement;

- the auditor's risk assessment includes an expectation that controls at the service organisation are operating effectively but he is unable to obtain sufficient appropriate audit evidence about the operating effectiveness of these controls; or
- sufficient appropriate audit evidence is only available from records held at the service organisation and the auditor is unable to obtain direct access to those records.

Whether the auditor expresses a qualified opinion or disclaims an opinion depends on the individual situation and circumstances.

Where the auditor's report is not modified it should not refer to the work of a service auditor.

If reference to the work of the service auditor is relevant to an understanding of a modification in the auditor's report, the report should make clear that the reference does not diminish the auditor's responsibility for the audit opinion. The auditor may also need to seek the consent of the service auditor before making such a reference.

Examples of modifications in audit reports arising from limitations in scope are shown in **Table 3** and **Table 5** in **Chapter 5**.

23 AUDIT EVIDENCE

23.1 Introduction

There are three ISAs covering various elements of the subject of audit evidence. These are:

- ISA (UK and Ireland) 500 *Audit evidence*;
- ISA (UK and Ireland) 501 *Audit evidence – specific considerations for selected items*; and
- ISA (UK and Ireland) 505 *External confirmations.*

The current versions of these ISAs (UK and Ireland) were issued in October 2009 and are effective for the audit of financial statements for periods ending on or after 15 December 2010. These three ISAs were not revised as part of the suite of revised ISAs issued by the FRC in April 2016. See **1.6.4** for further details.

ISA (UK and Ireland) 500, including the use of management's experts, is considered in paragraphs **23.2** and **23.3**.

ISA (UK and Ireland) 501 covers:

- attendance at stocktaking – see paragraph **23.5**. Further guidance on this subject is provided by Practice Note 25 *Attendance at stocktaking*;
- enquiries about litigation and claims – see paragraph **23.6**; and
- segment information – see paragraph **23.7**.

ISA (UK and Ireland) 505 is considered in paragraph **23.8**.

In addition to the guidance on external confirmations given in this chapter, guidance on bank confirmations is contained in **Chapter 24**.

In August 2010, the Auditing Practices Board published a Discussion Paper entitled *Auditor Scepticism: Raising the Bar*. Its publication followed criticism of the auditing profession by external commentators and Regulators following the banking crisis and also responded to comments by the Audit Inspection Unit (AIU) on the need for firms to exercise greater professional scepticism in its 2009/10 Annual Report. This is considered in **23.9** below along with other related publications.

23.2 The nature of audit evidence

23.2.1 Concept of audit evidence

ISA (UK and Ireland) 500 *Audit evidence* requires the auditor to obtain sufficient appropriate audit evidence to be able to draw reasonable conclusions on which to base his opinion. The *Auditor's Code* (see **1.5**) also requires the auditor to act with professional skill which demands an expertise in accumulating and assessing the evidence necessary to form an audit opinion.

Audit evidence is obtained from a combination of inquiry, inspection, observation, tests of controls and substantive procedures (including confirmation, recalculation, reperformance and analytical procedures).

It is defined as information used by the auditor in arriving at the conclusions on which his opinion is based and includes:

- information from source documents and accounting records underlying the financial statement assertions; and
- information from other sources such as previous audits and a firm's client acceptance procedures.

23.2.2 Sufficient appropriate evidence

The ISA contains a discussion on what 'sufficient appropriate evidence' means. Sufficiency is seen as a measure of the quantity of audit evidence, and appropriateness is a measure of its quality, including its relevance and its reliability.

The auditor is rarely able to rely on conclusive evidence, but uses persuasive evidence which is supported by information from different sources. He seeks reasonable, but not absolute, assurance that there are no material misstatements and may choose to rely on sample data, extracted either statistically or judgmentally, in order to form his opinion on a particular balance or class of transaction. Reasonable assurance will be obtained when the auditor has obtained sufficient appropriate audit evidence to reduce audit risk (i.e. the risk that the auditor expresses an inappropriate opinion when the financial statements are materially misstated) to an acceptably low level.

Audit evidence is cumulative in nature and the decision on whether there is sufficient appropriate evidence is a matter for the auditor's judgment and is influenced by:

- the assessment of the nature and degree of risk of material misstatement at both the financial statement level and at the account balance or transaction level;
- the nature of the accounting and internal control systems and the assessment of the control environment;
- the materiality of the item being examined;
- previous experience of the client and the auditor's knowledge of the business;
- the results of auditing procedures and work on preparing the financial statements; and
- the source and reliability of information available.

The reliability of audit evidence can be judged using the following general criteria:

- external evidence, for example, confirmation obtained from third parties, is generally more reliable than internal evidence;
- evidence from the entity's records and systems is generally more reliable when the related accounting and internal control system is satisfactory;
- evidence obtained directly by the auditor is generally more reliable than that obtained from the entity;
- evidence in the form of documents and written representations is generally more reliable than oral representations; and
- original documents are generally more reliable than photocopies or facsimiles.

Where the auditor performs procedures on information produced by the entity, he should first satisfy himself as to the accuracy and completeness of the information. For example, if the auditor is verifying provisions against debtors outstanding at the year end, using an aged debts list prepared by the entity, he should first satisfy himself that the listing is complete and correctly aged by checking invoices raised in the period for inclusion on the listing where appropriate and amounts on the listing back to dated invoices. He also needs to ensure that the information is sufficiently precise and detailed for his purposes, for example, performance measures used by management may not be precise enough to detect material misstatements where the same information is used by the auditor.

Consistency is obviously important in deciding the sufficiency and appropriateness of the evidence obtained – see paragraph **23.2.7**. The auditor also needs to consider the relationship between the cost of obtaining evidence and its usefulness bearing in mind that the difficulty and expense of obtaining evidence is not a valid reason for not obtaining it.

23.2.3   Sources of evidence

Some audit evidence is obtained by performing procedures to test the accounting records. For example, analysis and review, reperforming procedures followed in the financial reporting process, and reconciling information may help the auditor to determine that the accounting records are internally consistent and agree to the financial statements.

Where the auditor is able to corroborate evidence from different sources or items of a different nature, he will usually obtain more assurance than from those items considered individually. For example, corroborating information obtained from a source independent of the entity, may increase the assurance the auditor obtains from internally generated information, such as accounting records, minutes of meetings, etc.

23.2.4   Using assertions to gather audit evidence

ISA (UK and Ireland) 315 (Revised June 2016) requires that the auditor's consideration of the risk of material misstatement is made at assertion level (see **Chapter 21**). When seeking to obtain audit evidence from audit procedures the auditor should consider the extent to which the evidence supports the relevant financial statement assertions.

The term 'assertions' refers to the individual representations made by management and which make up the financial statements. The assertions considered by the auditor are set out in paragraph **21.3.6**, although the audit approaches of different firms may use different terminologies.

23.2.5   Audit procedures

The auditor uses audit procedures to:

- obtain an understanding of the entity and its environment and determine audit risk;
- test the operating effectiveness of controls; and
- detect material misstatements at the assertion level.

The objective of testing the operating effectiveness of controls is to test the design of control systems by aiming to establish whether the system is capable of preventing and detecting material misstatement. When testing the operation of controls, the auditor seeks to establish whether the controls have operated for the whole of the period under review. Where controls are not effective, such testing may indicate the existence of audit risk.

Substantive procedures are planned and performed in order to determine audit risk and then in response to the risk of material misstatement assessed at the planning stage. The auditor uses one or more of the types of audit procedure listed below.

The nature and timing of audit procedures will depend on the information available to the auditor. Where information is held in electronic form, the auditor may carry out Computer Assisted Audit Techniques (CAATs) (see **Chapter 37**).

Inspection of records or documents

This consists of examining records or documents whether internal or external, in paper form, electronic form or other media. It provides evidence of different degrees of persuasiveness depending on the nature and source of the documentation. The criteria used in assessing the reliability of evidence in general are noted at **23.2.2** above, and they should be applied to the type of evidence that can be obtained by inspection. For example, depending on the case, different degrees of reliability will apply to documentary evidence:

- created and provided by third parties;
- created by third parties and held by the entity; and
- created and held by the entity.

Some documentation will give direct evidence about existence, but may not provide evidence of ownership or value, for example share or bond certificates.

Inspection of tangible assets

This consists of physical examination of the assets. Again, the inspection of tangible assets provides evidence of their existence but alone is not sufficient to provide evidence of their ownership or value.

Observation

This consists of inspecting a particular process or procedure being performed by others. It is particularly useful where an internal control procedure does not leave an audit trail or for 'one off' procedures such as stocktakes. It is normally used in combination with other procedures.

Enquiry

This consists of seeking information from knowledgeable persons both inside and/or outside the entity. This may either be written or oral. Its reliability will vary depending on its source in a similar way to the evidence resulting from inspection.

An important part of the enquiry process is evaluation of the responses received, which may lead to amending the audit plan or performing additional audit procedures.

Enquiry alone is not sufficient to provide evidence of material misstatement or to confirm the effectiveness of controls. For example, in relation to management intentions, in addition to making enquiries, the auditor should consider management's past history of carrying out its stated intentions and obtain written representation of oral responses.

Confirmation

Confirmation is a type of enquiry and involves obtaining information directly from a third party. For example, a debtors' circularisation obtains confirmation of outstanding balances directly from the entity's debtors. Further information is provided in ISA (UK and Ireland) 505 *External confirmations* (see **23.8**).

Recalculation

Recalculation involves checking the mathematical accuracy of documents or records, and may be done through the use of CAATs (see **Chapter 37**).

Reperformance

This describes the independent reperformance of calculations, for example, the calculations on a sales invoice or on a debtors' listing. Again, CAATs may be used to perform this task.

Analytical procedures

These involve the analysis of relationships between items of financial data both within the financial statements and between the financial statements and other internally and externally produced data. These are discussed in greater detail in **Chapter 25**.

23.2.6 *Selection and sampling of items for testing*

Where the auditor designs tests of controls or substantive procedures, he determines the best method of selecting the items for testing so as to be effective in meeting the purpose of the audit procedure. The methods available for selecting the items to test are:

- selecting all items (100% examination);
- selecting specific items; and
- audit sampling.

The auditor chooses which method, or combination of methods, is appropriate depending on the particular circumstances, including the risks related to the assertion being tested and the practicality and efficiency of the different means. Further details on these selection methods are given in **26.4**.

23.2.7 *Dealing with inconsistent or potentially unreliable evidence*

Where evidence is inconsistent, for example, one piece of evidence leads the auditor to believe a company owns an asset whilst another piece of evidence throws doubt on this, or where the auditor has doubts about the reliability of information to be used as evidence, he will need to consider what modifications or additional procedures are necessary to resolve the matter. He will also need to consider the effect of the matter on other areas of the audit and ultimately on his opinion.

23.3   Management's experts

23.3.1   Using the work of a management's expert

Where information to be used as audit evidence has been prepared using the work of a management's expert, such as actuarial calculations, valuations or engineering data, the auditor should ensure that, to the extent necessary, he:

(a)   evaluates the competence, capabilities and objectivity of that expert;

(b)   obtains an understanding of the work of that expert; and

(c)   evaluates the appropriateness of that expert's work as audit evidence for the relevant assertion.

Where the auditor uses his own expert (as opposed to work of the management's expert), reference should be made to ISA (UK and Ireland) 620 (Revised June 2016) (see **Chapter 31**).

The nature, timing and extent of audit procedures in relation to work performed by management's experts will be affected by many factors such as:

- the nature and complexity of the matter;
- the risks of material misstatement;
- the availability of alternative sources of evidence;
- the nature, scope and objectives of the management's expert's work;
- whether the management's expert is employed by the entity, or is a party engaged by it to provide relevant services;
- the extent to which management can exercise control or influence over the work of the management's expert;
- whether the management's expert is subject to technical performance standards or other professional or industry requirements;
- the nature and extent of any controls over the management's expert's work;
- the auditor's knowledge and experience of the management's expert's field of expertise; and
- the auditor's previous experience of the work of that expert.

23.3.2   Evaluating the expert's competence, capabilities and objectivity

In order to evaluate the competence, capabilities and objectivity of management's expert, the auditor will need to evaluate evidence from a variety of sources, such as:

- personal experience with previous work of that particular expert;
- discussions with the expert and with others familiar with his work;
- knowledge of the expert's qualifications, membership of a professional body or industry association, licence to practice, etc.;

- published books or papers written by the expert;
- an auditor's expert, where used, who assists the auditor in obtaining sufficient appropriate audit evidence with respect to the information produced by the management's expert.

The auditor may also need to consider the relevance of the management's expert's competence for the matter in question. For example, a particular actuary used by management may specialise in property insurance but have limited expertise regarding pension calculations.

The auditor will also need to consider the objectivity of the management's expert, which may be threatened by a range of circumstances, such as self-interest, advocacy, familiarity, self-review and intimidation threats. Although safeguards may reduce such threats, they are unlikely to eliminate all threats to a management's expert's objectivity.

23.3.3   Obtaining an understanding of the expert's work

The auditor needs to obtain an understanding of the work of the management's expert including:

- whether the expert's work has any areas of speciality within it that are relevant to the audit;
- whether any professional standards or regulatory requirements apply;
- what assumptions and methods are used by management's expert and whether they are generally accepted within that expert's field and appropriate for financial reporting purposes; and
- the nature of the internal and external data the expert uses.

23.3.4   Evaluating the appropriateness of the expert's work

In order to evaluate the appropriateness of the management's expert's work as audit evidence, the auditor needs to consider:

- the relevance and reasonableness of the expert's findings or conclusions, their consistency with other audit evidence, and whether they are appropriately reflected in the financial statements;
- the relevance and reasonableness of any significant assumptions and methods used by the expert; and
- the relevance, completeness and accuracy of any source data used by the expert.

23.4   Specific considerations

ISA (UK and Ireland) 501 *Audit evidence – specific considerations for selected items* provides guidance on:

- attendance at stocktaking;
- enquiries about litigation and claims; and
- segment information.

These are discussed in sections **23.5**, **23.6** and **23.7** below.

23.5   Attendance at stocktaking

23.5.1   Introduction

In addition to the requirements and guidance in ISA (UK and Ireland) 501 *Audit evidence – specific considerations for selected items*, further guidance is given in Practice Note 25 *Attendance at stocktaking*. The current version of Practice Note 25 was issued in February 2011 and covers:

- assessment of risks and internal controls;
- audit evidence;
- audit procedures before, during and after the stocktake;
- work in progress;
- the use of experts; and
- stock held by third parties.

23.5.2   Assessment of risks and internal controls

ISA (UK and Ireland) 315 (Revised June 2016) states that the auditor should use professional judgment to ascertain levels of audit risk. Example factors to consider when assessing risks relating to existence of stock are set out in **Table 1**.

TABLE 1: Example risk factors relating to existence of stock

- reliability of accounting and stock recording systems including, in relation to work in progress, the systems that track location, quantities and stages of completion;
- timing of stocktakes relative to the year end date, and the reliability of records used in any roll forward of balances;
- location of stock, including stock on consignment and items held at third-party locations;

- physical controls over stock, and its susceptibility to theft or deterioration;
- objectivity, experience and reliability of the stock counters and of those monitoring their work;
- degree of fluctuation in stock levels;
- nature of stock, for example, whether specialist knowledge is needed to identify the quantity, quality and/or identity of stock items; and
- difficulty in carrying out the assessment of quantity, for example, whether a significant degree of estimation is involved.

The assessment of risk should also include consideration of frauds that influence stock levels. These may include the risk of false sales involving the movement of stock to another location, movement of stock to sites with different stocktaking dates, using inappropriate estimation techniques, or amendment or falsification of stock count sheets.

23.5.3   Audit evidence

Where stock is material or there is a risk of material misstatement, ISA (UK and Ireland) 501 requires the auditor to attend a stocktake, unless it is 'impracticable' to do so. As well as giving evidence about the existence assertion, attending a stocktake may also provide evidence in respect of completeness and valuation of stock.

The main sources of evidence for the existence of stock are:

- evidence from audit procedures which confirm the reliability of the accounting records upon which the amount in the financial statements is based;
- evidence from tests of controls over stock, including the reliability of stock counting procedures; and
- substantive evidence from the physical inspection tests undertaken by the auditor.

The amount and type of evidence required depends on the auditor's risk assessment.

Entities may or may not maintain detailed stock records. Where these are kept, the auditor should check that these records are up to date, that adequate stocktaking procedures are used, and that all material differences between physical and book stock are investigated and corrected.

Where no continuous stock records are maintained, the year-end stock figure will be derived from a full year-end stock count. In this situation, it would be preferable for stocktaking to be completed at the year-end date but, where necessary, the count may be on a different date and updated for stock movements between that date and year-end.

In both situations, attendance at the stocktake would be beneficial, either to confirm that accurate stock records are maintained or, where no stock records exist, to ensure that the count to determine year-end stock is accurate.

If the auditor is unable to attend on the count date, he should take or observe physical counts on another date and perform audit procedures on the transactions between the two counts. If the auditor cannot attend, for example, due to the nature and location of the stock he should consider whether alternative audit evidence is available to support the existence and condition of stock at the period end date. If there is no suitable and adequate alternative, the auditor would be required to give a limitation of scope opinion in his audit report.

23.5.4   Audit procedures before, during and after the stocktake

Table 2 outlines example procedures that may be used before, during and after the stocktake. It does not provide an exhaustive list.

TABLE 2: Example audit procedures

Before the stocktake:

- perform analytical procedures and discuss findings with management;
- discuss client stocktaking arrangements and instructions with management;
- gain familiarity with the nature and volume of the stock, the identification of high value items, the method of accounting for stock and the conditions giving rise to obsolescence;
- consider the location of the stock and assess the implications of this for stock control and recording;
- consider the quantity and nature of work in progress, the quantity of stock held by third parties and whether expert valuers or stocktakers will be required;
- review the system of internal control and accounting relating to stock;
- consider any involvement of internal audit; and
- consider the results of previous stocktakes and review prior year working papers.

During the stocktake:

- ascertain whether client staff are following instructions;
- perform test counts to ensure that procedures and internal controls relating to the stocktake are operating effectively. Counting should be checked in both directions, i.e. from physical stock to stock sheet and vice versa;
- request recounts where results are not satisfactory;
- copy extracts of stocktaking records for subsequent testing;
- check the sequence of stock count records;
- consider whether the procedures for identifying damaged, obsolete and slow moving stock operate properly;

- ensure that stock held for third parties is separately identified and accounted for;
- consider the adequacy of cut-off procedures to ensure stock movements are included or excluded from the year-end stock figure as necessary.

After the stocktake:

- follow up details of last serial numbers of goods inwards and outwards records to check cut-off;
- check copies of stock sheets are correctly reflected in final stock figures;
- review whether continuous stock records have been adjusted to the amounts physically counted and that differences have been investigated; and
- follow up queries and notify senior management of serious problems encountered during the stocktake.

Some entities use computer-assisted techniques to perform stocktakes, for example, using hand held scanners. This may lead to there being no stock sheets, no physical count records and no paper records available at the time of the count. In such circumstances, the auditor should consider the IT environment surrounding the stocktake and consider the need for specialist assistance to evaluate the techniques used and the controls in place.

23.5.5 Work in progress

Management may use accounting systems and internal controls to determine the completeness and accuracy of records of work in progress, and there may not be a stocktake. However, the auditor may still find it beneficial to observe the work in progress as it may help with understanding the entity's control systems and processes and with determining the stage of completion of construction or engineering work in progress.

23.5.6 The use of experts

The auditor should determine whether expert help is required prior to attending the stocktake. Assistance may be required to substantiate quantities (e.g. a quantity surveyor) or to determine the nature and condition of specialist stock.

Where management involve a specialist third party stocktaker, common practice for farms, petrol stations and public houses, this does not eliminate the need for the auditor to obtain audit evidence as to the existence of stock.

23.5.7   Stock held by third parties

If stock is held at a third party location, e.g. in public warehouses, the ISA requires the auditor to perform one or both of the following:

- request confirmation from the third party as to the quantities and condition of stock held on behalf of the entity; and
- perform inspection or other audit procedures appropriate in the circumstances.

If such stock is material the auditor should consult ISA (UK and Ireland) 402 *Audit considerations relating to an entity using a service organisation* to ascertain how to obtain sufficient audit evidence (see **Chapter 22**).

23.6   Enquiries about litigation and claims

Requirements and guidance for the auditor when dealing with pending litigation against the company on which he is reporting is given in ISA (UK and Ireland) 501 *Audit evidence – specific considerations for selected items.*

In addition, useful guidance can be found in the old, but still relevant, ICAEW statement AUDIT 2/95 – *The Ascertainment and Confirmation of Contingent Liabilities Arising from pending Legal Matters* which covers the auditor's problems concerning contingencies arising from pending litigation against the entity upon which he is reporting.

23.6.1   Audit procedures

The auditor should design and perform audit procedures to determine whether a risk of material misstatement may arise from any litigation or claims involving the entity. These must include:

- enquiries of management and, where applicable, others within the entity;
- reviewing minutes of meetings with those charged with governance and correspondence between the entity and its legal advisers; and
- reviewing legal expense accounts.

Procedures the auditor may use to verify the existence of claims, although they will not necessarily provide sufficient evidence of the likely amount that the company may be responsible for, include:

- reviewing the system of recording claims and the procedure for bringing these to the attention of management;
- discussing with management arrangements for instructing solicitors;
- examining board minutes and correspondence for potential claims;
- examining legal expense accounts, bills from solicitors or estimates of unbilled charges;

- obtaining a list of matters referred to solicitors with estimates of the possible ultimate liabilities;
- making enquiries of those charged with governance; and
- obtaining written representations that there are no further matters of which the directors are aware.

If the auditor assesses a risk of material misstatement regarding litigation or claims that have been identified, or where audit procedures indicate that other material litigation or claims might exist, the auditor must seek direct communication with the entity's external legal advisers. This should be done through a letter of enquiry prepared by management and sent by the auditor requesting that the legal advisers communicate directly with the auditor. If management refuses to give permission for this communication or the legal advisers refuse, or are prohibited from responding appropriately, and the auditor is unable to obtain sufficient appropriate evidence from alternative procedures, then he will modify his opinion (see **Chapter 5**).

The auditor may make a general inquiry to the legal advisor, asking the advisor to inform the auditor of any litigation and claims of which they are aware, together with an assessment of the outcomes and the financial implications. However, the Council of the Law Society has advised solicitors in the UK that they are not recommended to comply with such general requests for information. As such, the auditor may seek communication through a letter of specific inquiry which includes:

- a list of litigation and claims;
- where available, management's assessment of the outcome of each identified litigation and claim, along with management's estimate of the financial implications; and
- a request that the legal advisor confirms the reasonableness of management's assessments and provides further information if management's list is considered to be incomplete or incorrect.

Example extracts from a letter of enquiry to be sent to the client's legal advisor are included below. They are to be typed on the client's headed notepaper and sent out by the auditor.

The example in **Table 3** is to be used in situations where management are not aware of litigation or claims that the auditor considers to be relevant to his audit and where:

- a risk of material misstatement regarding litigation or claims that has been identified; or
- audit procedures performed have indicated that other material litigation or claims may exist.

Table 4 is to be used in situations where management are aware of litigation or claims that the auditor considers to be relevant to his audit and where:

- a risk of material misstatement regarding litigation or claims that has been identified; or
- audit procedures performed have indicated that other material litigation or claims may exist.

TABLE 3: Example of a 'negative' enquiry

Dear Sirs

[*Client name/List of companies*]

In connection with the preparation and audit of our accounts for the year ended [*date*], we as the directors of the company/ies stated above, have confirmed to our auditors that there are no litigation or claims on which you have been consulted greater than £[*amount*].

We should be grateful if you would write directly to our auditors on the following:

(1) Confirming that you are not aware of any litigation or claims on which you have been consulted greater than £[*amount*]. If this is not the case, providing detail of the litigation or claims including:

    (a) an assessment of the outcome of the litigation or claim;

    (b) an estimate of the financial implications; and

    (c) an estimate of the legal costs to complete.

(2) Details of monies held by you on behalf of the company/ies; and

(3) Giving an estimate of the amount of any unbilled fees and expenses due to you at [*date*].

Please send your response to:
For the attn of: [*Name*]
[*Name of Audit Firm*]
[*Audit Firm address*]

Your letter should include matters that existed at [*date*] and during the period from that date to the date of your letter.

Yours faithfully

_____

[*Client Signatory*]

TABLE 4: Example of a 'positive' enquiry

Dear Sirs

[*Client name/List of companies*]

In connection with the preparation and audit of our accounts for the year ended [*date*], we as the directors of the company/ies stated above, have given our auditors details of litigation and claims on which you have been consulted. These are as follows:

[*List of litigation and claims. Where available this to include management's assessment of the outcome of each identified litigation or claim and their estimate of the financial implications, including costs involved.*]

Claims where the outcome is likely to be less than £[*amount*] have been excluded.

We should be grateful if you would write directly to our auditors on the following:

(1) Confirming whether in your opinion our assessments are reasonable;
(2) Providing any additional information that you consider necessary including an explanation of those matters on which your view may differ from those stated;
(3) Confirming that you are not aware of any items which should be included but which have been omitted;
(4) Details of monies held by you on behalf of the company/ies; and
(5) Giving an estimate of the amount of any unbilled fees and expenses due to you at [*date*].

Please send your response to:
For the attn of: [*Name*]
[*Name of Audit Firm*]
[*Audit Firm address*]

Your letter should include matters that existed at [*date*] and during the period from that date to the date of your letter.

Yours faithfully

[*Client Signatory*]

There may also be situations where the auditor considers it necessary to meet with the entity's legal advisers to discuss the likely outcome of claims. This may be the case where the auditor determines the matter is a significant risk or is complex, or if there is disagreement between management and the entity's legal advisers. Where such meetings take place, they usually include a representative of management and they take place with management's permission.

Where there are matters which are being dealt with by solicitors but the auditor is unable to take photocopies of documents because of legal privilege, he should prepare file notes of the evidence he has reviewed.

There are occasions when solicitors do not reply directly to requests on the grounds that letters written concerning the merits of litigation involving a client would be discoverable by the other party to the litigation. In such situations, the auditor needs to consider the adequacy of the evidence available to him to support the treatment and disclosure of the issue in the financial statements.

23.6.2   Written representations

The auditor also needs to obtain written representations from management and those charged with governance that all known actual or possible litigation and claims that should be considered in relation to the financial statements have been disclosed to the auditor and accounted for and disclosed in accordance with the applicable financial reporting framework.

23.7   Segment information

When segmental information is material to the financial statements, the auditor should plan and perform procedures to obtain sufficient appropriate audit evidence about the presentation and disclosure of the segment information. This will usually be by:

- obtaining an understanding of the methods used by management to determine the segmental information and:
  - evaluating whether such methods are likely to result in disclosure in accordance with the financial reporting framework; and
  - where necessary, testing the application of those methods; and

- performing analytical or other procedures considered appropriate in the circumstances.

This is likely to involve discussion with those charged with governance about the techniques used to determine the segmental information and analytical techniques. Guidance is given in ISA (UK and Ireland) 501 *Audit evidence – specific considerations for selected items.*

23.8   External confirmations

23.8.1   Use of external confirmations

As stated above, audit evidence is more reliable when it is obtained from independent sources outside the entity. ISA (UK and Ireland) 505 *External confirmations* provides guidance on using external confirmations to provide sufficient appropriate audit evidence at assertion level.

External confirmations are frequently used in connection with account balances and their components, such as debtors' circularisations, which are discussed in detail in section **23.8.2**. However, they need not be limited to this and may be used to confirm the terms of agreements or transactions an entity has with third parties. Examples of where external confirmations may be used are:

- bank balances and other information with bankers (see **Chapter 24**);
- stocks held by third parties at bonded warehouses for processing or on consignment;
- property title deeds held by lawyers or financiers for safe custody or as security;
- investments purchased from stockbrokers but not delivered at the balance sheet date;
- loans from lenders; and
- accounts payable and receivable balances.

The assertions covered by external confirmations will vary. For example, in the case of goods held on consignment, evidence will be obtained about existence and rights and obligations assertions, but not about the value. Confirmation about the completeness assertion can be obtained by contacting certain parties. For example, evidence about completeness of accounts payable balances can be obtained by circularising suppliers with a nil balance at the year end to determine whether all liabilities to them have been recorded. This means that external confirmation requests must be tailored to the specific audit objective.

All confirmation requests are usually sent on the entity's headed paper and contain the management's authorisation to disclose the information requested. ISA (UK and Ireland) 505 states that in order to have control over the process, the auditor must design the confirmation request, determine the parties to contact and the information to be requested, send the requests himself and make all follow up requests, where applicable. All responses should be sent directly to the auditor, not to the entity.

The auditor may use positive or negative confirmations, or a combination of both. Positive confirmations ask respondents to reply and either confirm information or provide data themselves. Negative confirmations ask for responses only in the event of a disagreement with the information provided in the request. There is an additional risk with negative confirmations that the auditor will assume that information was correct when the respondent simply chooses not to respond. The auditor should not use negative confirmation requests as the sole substantive audit procedure to address an assessed risk of material misstatement unless:

- the risk of material misstatement has been assessed as low and the related controls have been assessed as operating effectively;
- the population subject to negative confirmation comprises a large number of small, homogeneous account balances, transactions or conditions;
- a very low exception rate is expected; and
- the auditor is not aware of circumstances or conditions that would cause recipients of negative confirmation requests to disregard such requests.

With positive confirmations the response rate tends to be lower the more information the auditor requests. However, by requesting information from respondents, the value of audit evidence is greater than where they are asked only to confirm a balance included in the request. In order to obtain good quality responses the auditor should consider to whom the confirmation request is addressed.

If those charged with governance refuse to allow the auditor to obtain direct confirmations the auditor should consider whether this is reasonable, whether alternative suitable audit evidence is available and whether a limitation of audit scope has arisen. Similarly where no response is obtained from a positive confirmation or where the response has not provided sufficient reliable evidence, the auditor should perform alternative procedures. Where no response has been obtained he would normally first attempt to contact the recipient of the confirmation to elicit a response.

ISA (UK and Ireland) 505 requires that where the auditor has doubts about the reliability of a response he should consider whether additional procedures are required. Doubts about the reliability of a response may arise because it was not received by the auditor directly or appeared not to come from the original intended confirming party. If a confirming party uses a third party to coordinate its response, the auditor should perform procedures to confirm that the respondent was indeed authorised to respond on behalf of the original contact.

Once any alternative procedures have been performed, the auditor evaluates whether the results in total have provided sufficient appropriate audit evidence, and where this is not the case, he considers the implications for his report.

23.8.2   Debtors' confirmations

As noted above, the auditor may decide to carry out a circularisation of the company's trade debtors as part of his audit procedures.

The auditor cannot approach the debtors directly as only the client can authorise third parties to divulge information to the auditor but generally, if asked, the management will authorise the circularisation. Where the client refuses, the auditor needs to consider whether he is able to obtain sufficient alternative evidence and the implications for his report.

Where a circularisation is performed on a sample basis it may not provide sufficient evidence on its own, but may influence the extent of any other tests carried out.

There are two methods that can be used when requesting information from the debtor. These are:

- *positive*: where the debtor is requested to confirm the accuracy of the balance shown or state in what respect he disagrees; or
- *negative*: where the debtor only replies if the amount stated is disputed.

In either case, the reply should be sent directly to the auditor. The choice of method will be a matter for the auditor's judgment, but there are certain factors which may influence this decision, including:

- the strength of the system of internal controls;
- whether there are any suspicions of irregularities;
- the number and size of accounts;
- whether there are amounts which are likely to be in dispute; and
- the number of bookkeeping errors.

Where there are doubts about the accuracy of the sales ledger or where there is a small number of large balances, more confidence will be gained from a positive circularisation. However, if errors are not expected or there is a large number of small balances then a negative one may be more appropriate.

In most cases, a sample of debtors' balances based on the complete population will be tested. However, the following should be considered when selecting the sample:

- old, unpaid accounts;
- accounts written off during the period;
- accounts with credit balances;
- accounts with nil balances; and
- accounts which have been paid by the date of the examination.

The request is usually accompanied by a statement of the account, either the normal monthly statement if the circularisation is carried out at the same time as these are sent out, or a specially printed one if the circularisation is at any other time. Where a positive response is required, a pre-paid reply envelope is normally included.

The request may be as a specially prepared letter or as an attachment to the statement. An example of a positive circularisation is shown in **Table 5**.

Where requests are returned as undelivered they should be sent to the auditor, who will need to consider what action to take.

When the positive method is used and replies are not received, the auditor should make every effort to ensure that some response is obtained. It may be that a member of the client's staff can be used to do this, but the auditor will need to ensure that the clearance procedure is properly performed. It may be necessary to use other audit tests to provide evidence of the validity of the debtor where no reply is received in a positive circularisation, as every item selected must be concluded upon.

The responses may indicate inaccuracies in the part of the population that is not tested and further work may be necessary.

TABLE 5: Example of positive debtors' circularisation letter

[Client entity letter head]

[Trade Debtor Name and Address]

Dear Sir

As part of their normal audit procedures, we have been requested by our auditors, ABC & Co, to ask you to confirm direct to them the balance on your account at 31 December 20 ... This request is made for audit purposes only and remittances should be sent to us in the normal way.

According to our records, the balance at that date in our favour was as shown by the enclosed statement of your account. If the balance is in agreement with that shown by your records, please sign the confirmation below and return it in the enclosed reply-paid envelope to ABC & Co. Please do this even if the account has been settled.

If the balance is not in agreement with that shown by your records, will you please send the confirmation to our auditors showing, if possible, details of the items making up the difference.

Your co-operation in this matter is greatly appreciated.
Yours faithfully
[Client]

....

ABC & Co Auditors
1 High Street
London

Dear Sirs

We confirm that according to our records a balance of £ ... was owing by us to XYZ plc at 31 December 20 ...

Name of company or individual: _____

Signed: _____

Position held: _____

Items making up difference if any: _____

23.9   Auditor scepticism

23.9.1   Background

Professional scepticism is an essential feature of an audit, particularly in relation to the auditor's evaluation of the sufficiency and appropriateness of audit evidence. ISAs (UK and Ireland) define professional scepticism as 'an attitude that includes a questioning mind, being alert to conditions which may indicate possible misstatement due to error or fraud, and a critical assessment of audit evidence'.

In recent years, a number of papers have been issued on the subject, including:

- in August 2010, the Auditing Practices Board's Discussion Paper *Auditor Scepticism: Raising the Bar* following challenges from regulators on whether sufficient auditor scepticism was shown by audit firms in relation to the banking crisis;
- in March 2012, a feedback paper based on the responses received, together with a further APB Paper *Professional Scepticism: Establishing a Common Understanding and Reaffirming its Central Role in Delivering Audit Quality*;
- in February 2012, the IAASB issued a question and answer paper on the issue; and
- in December 2015, the IAASB issued an *Invitation to Comment, Enhancing Audit Quality in the Public Interest: A Focus on Professional Skepticism, Quality Control and Group Audits*.

23.9.2   A sceptical mind

The papers all accept that a sceptical mind is a requirement of a rigorous audit performed with due professional care. The degree of scepticism required is less clear cut. Too little scepticism influences both the effectiveness and efficiency of the audit, too much risks an unnecessary increase in costs.

Prior to commencement of an audit, an auditor may have a neutral mindset (that is he does not assume either that the financial statements are misstated or correct or that management are honest or dishonest) or a more questioning approach, sometimes known as 'presumptive doubt'. Both ISA (UK and Ireland) 200 (Revised June 2016) and ISA (UK and Ireland) 240 (Revised June 2016) suggest that the auditor should lean towards holding a position of presumptive doubt at the start of the audit 'recognising the possibility that a material misstatement due to fraud could exist'. This initial mindset is largely a personal attribute, and the audit firms need to consider a number of character traits which underlie auditor scepticism when recruiting auditors:

- curiosity and a questioning mind;
- deferral of judgment and not making premature conclusions;
- understanding management behaviour and motivations;
- self-confidence; and
- freedom of action.

Such a sceptical mindset can be acquired or learned through effective training and procedures and auditors are also likely to become more sceptical when they have been personally involved in an investigation of an audit failure.

Audit firm procedures are also of particular importance when responding to negative findings from audit testing. The nature and extent of additional work to be performed is likely to be a decision taken by the hierarchy of the audit team and will be strongly influenced by the firm's policies, procedures and methodologies.

23.9.3   Throughout the audit

An attitude of professional scepticism is necessary throughout all stages of the audit, it is not simply something to attempt to document at the end of the engagement.

At the acceptance stage, the engagement partner should be challenging the integrity of the client. This top down approach is essential and the partner should drive the audit approach from planning through to sign off and he should encourage staff to adopt a more questioning mentality. Its importance must be stressed at the audit team discussion in relation to fraud (see **16.4.2**) and the engagement partner should set expectations regarding the importance of professional scepticism through his direction and supervision of the engagement, particularly in his review of the work involved. Due to the characteristics of fraud, which may include sophisticated schemes, concealment and collusion, professional scepticism is particularly relevant when considering fraudulent activity. The engagement partner should also encourage members of the audit team to seek guidance on difficult or contentious matters.

Professional scepticism also includes being alert to audit evidence that contradicts other evidence obtained or causes the auditor to question the reliability of documents or responses by management. This requires the auditor to assess audit evidence critically, and exercise judgment in reaching conclusions. Professional scepticism is closely interrelated with professional judgment and both are key elements of audit quality.

Whilst scepticism is important at all stages of the audit, it is particularly relevant where there are areas which are more complex, significant or highly judgmental, such as:

- accounting estimates and related disclosures;
- going concern, particularly when evaluating management's plans for the future;
- related party relationships and transactions;
- consideration of laws and regulations; and
- the audit of significant unusual or highly complex transactions.

Audit scepticism should be clearly documented in working papers, particularly in relation to discussions with those charged with governance and where difficult or contentious issues have been discussed between members of the audit team or experts from others areas in the firm. Documentation needs to show, for example that where any doubts arose about an explanation provided, the audit team have questioned the entity appropriately and not just taken the client at their word.

Reviewers should also review with an open mind, not placing any reliance on, nor forming expectations based on the previous year's audit. Every review should be treated with the same sceptical attitude as if it were a new client.

23.9.4   The growing importance of scepticism

Changes in accounting requirements, particularly the increase in estimates involved in preparing financial statements in accordance with IFRS means that auditor scepticism is increasingly important in determining audit quality. Auditor scepticism should be directed at management, to challenge them about the appropriateness of accounting estimates, and also directed inward to the audit team to determine whether appropriate audit evidence has been obtained to support management's estimates.

The *Auditor Scepticism: Raising the Bar* paper suggested that findings from audit failures, as well as reports from audit regulators tended to show audit scepticism may have been lacking. The paper cites the following particular areas of concern:

* over reliance on management representations;
* failure to investigate conflicting explanations; and
* failure to obtain appropriate third party confirmations.

Judgments relating to the fair value of impairment of goodwill and other intangibles were noted as lacking, with audit firms tending to look for evidence to corroborate management's valuations rather than seeking to challenge them.

23.9.5   Difficulties for audit firms

The *Auditor Scepticism: Raising the Bar* paper notes the difficulties facing firms in today's markets where costs and profitability are increasingly under scrutiny and typically a sceptical approach may be more expensive in terms of both costs and time. This is of particular importance for listed clients who are likely to have set their reporting deadline prior to the commencement of the audit, and where delays caused by additional audit procedures may damage the client relationship. The paper does point out, however, that too little scepticism can lead to audit failures which can expose the firm to litigation and reputational damage in the long and medium term.

23.9.6   Improving auditor scepticism

Audit firms can improve audit scepticism by employing staff with the appropriate attitude (perhaps through the increased use of electronic screening of character traits) and by having effective training and development programmes.

However, classroom training can only be effective if it is reinforced through the culture of the firm. In part this will be through the firm's mentoring and compensation system, by rewarding those who demonstrate the required skills.

Auditors also need to be aware of the dangers of 'detachment' associated with highly complex but standardised audit methodologies, and their effect on scepticism. As audit firms take advantage of electronic working papers, checklists and schedules there is the danger that the auditor becomes distanced from observing and inspecting the company's operations, spending increasingly large proportions of time away from discussions with clients or review of client records, and focusing instead on sitting in the audit room completing electronic schedules. A return to asking more open questions of clients may improve the levels of audit scepticism, as well as providing audit juniors with invaluable experience which will make them more effective reviewers of work at a later date.

Teams should also be warned against asking clients to prepare too many schedules and analyses prior to the audit commencing as academic research suggests that, whilst reducing audit costs, such client co-operation arrangements may make the auditor over-trusting.

A useful summary of conditions which would help the auditor demonstrate scepticism was included in the Feedback paper issued by the APB in 2012 following comments received on the *Auditor Scepticism: Raising the Bar* paper. These are set out in **Table 6**.

TABLE 6: Conditions necessary for professional scepticism

The individual auditor

- develop a good understanding of the entity and its business;
- have a questioning mind and be willing to challenge management assertions;
- assess critically the information and explanations obtained in the course of his work and corroborate them;
- seek to understand management motivations for possible misstatement of the financial statements;
- investigate the nature and cause of deviations or misstatements identified and avoid jumping to conclusions without appropriate audit evidence;
- be alert for evidence that is inconsistent with other evidence obtained or calls into question the reliability of documents and responses to inquiries; and
- have the confidence to challenge management and the persistence to follow things through to a conclusion – even if predisposed to agree with management's assertion, the auditor should actively consider the alternative views and challenge management to demonstrate that they are not more appropriate.

Engagement teams

- have good business knowledge and experience;
- actively consider in what circumstances management numbers may be misstated, whether due to fraud or error, and the possible sources of misstatement, notwithstanding existing knowledge and relationships;
- develop a good understanding of the entity and its business in order to provide a basis for identifying unusual events or transactions and share information on a regular basis;
- partners and managers are actively involved in assessing risk and planning the audit procedures to be performed – they think about the changes that are taking place in the entity and its environment and plan audit tests that are responsive to them;
- partners and managers actively lead and participate in audit team planning meetings to discuss the susceptibility of the entity's financial statements to material misstatement including through fraud and the misuse of related parties;
- partners and managers are accessible to other staff during the audit and encourage them to consult with them on a timely basis;
- engagement teams document their key audit judgments and conclusions, especially those reported to the audit committee, in a way that clearly demonstrates that they have exercised an appropriate degree of challenge to management and professional scepticism. In particular, the reasons why the audit team concurs with management's assertions are clearly articulated in a way that, where appropriate, discusses the appropriateness of reasonably credible alternative views and the reasons why they have not been adopted; and
- partners and managers bring additional scepticism to the audit through taking the steps necessary to carry out, face to face where appropriate, a diligent challenge and review of the audit work performed, and the adequacy of the documentation prepared, by other members of the engagement team.

Audit firms

- the culture within the firm emphasises the importance of:
    - understanding and pursuing the perspective of the shareholders (and other stakeholders) of the audited entity in making audit judgments;
    - coaching less experienced staff to foster appropriate scepticism;
    - sharing experiences about difficult audit judgments within the firm;
    - consultation with others about difficult audit judgments; and
    - supporting audit partners when they need to take and communicate difficult audit judgments;
- scepticism is embedded in the firm's training and competency frameworks used for evaluating and rewarding partner and staff performance;
- the firm requires rigorous engagement quality control reviews that challenge engagement teams' judgments and conclusions; and

- firm methodologies and review processes emphasise the importance of, and provide practical support for the auditor in:

  - developing a thorough understanding of the entity's business and its environment, sufficient to enable the auditor to carry out a robust risk assessment through his own fresh eyes;
  - identifying issues early in the planning cycle to allow adequate time for them to be investigated and resolved;
  - rigorously taking such steps as are appropriate to the scale and complexity of the financial reporting systems, to identify unusual transactions;
  - changing risk assessments, materiality and the audit plan in response to audit findings;
  - documenting audit judgments in a conclusive rather than a conclusionary manner and therefore setting out not only the conclusion but also the rationale for the conclusion, relating it to the nature of the challenges raised in the underlying work and reviews, the strength of the evidence obtained and the perspective of shareholders (and other stakeholders);
  - raising matters with the Audit Committee (or those charged with governance) in relation to which the auditor believes the perspective of shareholders (and other stakeholders) about the treatment or disclosure of the matter in the financial statements or related narrative reports could well be different from that adopted by the entity; and
  - ensuring that the disclosures relating to such matters are carefully assessed to ensure that those of relevance to shareholders (and other stakeholders) are sufficient and appropriate in the circumstances, having regard to the auditor's consideration of the true and fair view.

The role of audit committees and management

Both the audit committee and management will also have an important role in influencing the scepticism the auditor is able to exhibit. The audit committee should:

- promote a culture which ensures staff respond constructively to challenges from the auditor;
- challenge whether the auditor has a sufficiently deep understanding of the entity and its environment to perform the risk assessment;
- ensure that contentious issues which have been resolved between management and auditor are brought to the attention of the audit committee; and
- understand whether the challenge made by the auditor was rational, whether alternative conclusions were considered and why the final judgment was considered to be the most appropriate of the alternatives.

24 BANK CONFIRMATIONS

24.1 Introduction

This chapter reviews the confirmations that the auditor may obtain from banks. These are generally of two types:

- bank reports for audit purposes, confirming balances, interest and other account information; and
- confirmations of ongoing facilities.

New electronic confirmation services are also being developed, see **24.5.8**.

24.2 Guidance

Practice Note 16 *Bank Reports for Audit Purposes* contains guidance on the form of the request letters and has been agreed with the British Bankers' Association (BBA). The current version of Practice Note 16 was issued in February 2011.

24.3 Authority

Customers have to give explicit authority to their banks before any information can be released to their auditor and the BBA has asked that, where possible, this takes the form of an ongoing standing authority rather than as a separate authority each time information is requested.

A single authority can cover several entities, for example in group situations, provided that each entity is specified, together with the relevant authorised signatures. An example of such a letter is shown in **Table 1** below.

TABLE 1: Example of authority to disclose letter

XYZ Bank plc

(Parent Company Ltd, Subsidiary 1 Ltd, Subsidiary 2 Ltd)

I/we authorise XYZ Bank plc, including all branches and subsidiaries to provide our auditor ABC & Co any information that they may request from you regarding all and any of our accounts and dealings with you.

Authorised signatory

The Practice Note clarifies that banks do not need a new authority to disclose information to the auditor each time they are asked for confirmation of bank details. However, the auditor is responsible for ensuring that standing authorities remain up to date, e.g. they cover all relevant entities or are amended if the auditor changes its name or status.

24.4   Disclaimers

The request letter indicates that the process of obtaining a confirmation does not create any contractual or other duty between the bank and the auditor. In addition, the bank may include a disclaimer stating that their response is given solely for the purposes of the audit and creates no responsibility to the auditor.

The Practice Note suggests that neither the statement in the request letter nor the disclaimer in the bank's reply significantly impairs the value of the confirmation. This is because the information supplied by a bank ought not to be regarded as inaccurate simply because legal action cannot be taken against the bank supplying it. Therefore, the auditor can rely on this evidence as long as it is not:

- clearly wrong;
- suspicious; or
- inconsistent in itself or in conflict with other evidence gathered in the course of the audit.

24.5   Bank confirmation process

The Practice Note suggests that as part of his planning process, the auditor considers the need for a bank report as part of his assessment of risk. Given the importance of cash and its susceptibility to fraud, it is likely that the auditor will conclude that sufficient audit evidence cannot be obtained without receiving a bank report. In some rare circumstances where banking transactions and relationships are very simple, the auditor may determine that sufficient evidence is available from other sources. Having decided to obtain a bank report, the auditor:

- determines the date by which the bank report is needed;
- determines whether confirmation is needed for additional information such as trade finance transactions and balances;
- decides what type of report to use (see **24.5.3** below);
- makes arrangements for obtaining the necessary information to be included in the request. This will include the main account sort code and number for each legal entity, and any other references required for additional information;

- checks that the relevant authorities to disclose information are valid; and
- ascertains where to send the request.

24.5.1 Timing of requests

The Practice Note recommends that the auditor submits his requests for information at least one month before the period end date, an increase from the 14-day timescale set out in the original Practice Note. Where this notice is provided, banks will endeavour to provide the information within one month of the confirmation date. However, where the auditor submits an Incomplete Information Request (see **24.5.3** below), the bank's response period may increase. The Practice Note also recommends that additional time is allowed at busy times of the year, i.e. for December or March year ends.

Where auditors of listed clients or other entities with a tight reporting deadline require a faster response, they should use the Fast Track Template set out in **Table 3** below.

24.5.2 Information required

The Practice Note asks the auditor to provide the names of all the entities covered by the request, together with the main account and sort code of the principal entity or the holding company. The aim of this is to aid the identification of the customer by the bank as entity names are often similar and identification is sometimes problematic. Banks will still be responsible for identifying all other relevant accounts.

Where account details are taken from bank statements, this is not considered to diminish the value of the evidence.

It notes that there are clients with more complex relationships with their bankers and that in such cases, the auditor may require supplementary information about trade finance or derivative and commodity trading transactions. The decision on whether supplementary information is necessary will be based on the auditor's knowledge of the business and discussions with directors and management.

Where such information is requested, the auditor is required to supply a sample facility account number.

24.5.3   Type of report

The Practice Note contains three alternative templates to reflect the auditor's planning decisions as to the nature and timing of the information sought.

The Standard (**Table 2**) and Fast Track (**Table 3**) templates specify:

- the names of all legal entities covered by the request, together with the main account sort code and number of each entity listed;
- reference to a sample facility account number for any additional information required. This will enable the bank to identify the units providing specialist services which need to be consulted. A full listing of all transactions or balances is not required;
- the date for which the auditor is requesting confirmation and the date at which the report request is made;
- a statement that neither the auditor's request or the bank's response will create a contractual relationship between the bank and the auditor; and
- the auditor's contact details.

The template for Fast Track Requests is the same as the Standard but it also allows the auditor to explain the need for such an approach and provide the date by which a reply is needed.

The Incomplete Information Request (**Table 4**) contains:

- the names of all legal entities covered by the request, together with the main account number and sort code of the parent company and of as many group entities as can be obtained by the auditor;
- the period end date for which the auditor is requesting confirmation;
- the date at which the report request is made;
- a statement that neither the auditor's request or the bank's response will create a contractual relationship between the bank and the auditor; and
- the auditor's contact details.

TABLE 2: Example Standard Request

Please note – Complete **section 6** only where additional information is required.

In accordance with the agreed practice for provision of information to auditors, please forward information on our mutual client(s) as detailed below on behalf of the bank, its branches and subsidiaries. This request and your response will not create any contractual or other duty with us.

1. BANK NAME AND ADDRESS

2. AUDITOR CONTACT DETAILS

Name and address of auditor

Contact Number

Contact Name

Email address

Period end date (DD/MM/YYYY)

Date of request (DD/MM/YYYY)

3. COMPANIES AND OTHER BUSINESS ENTITIES

Company	Main account sort code	Main account number

4. AUTHORITY TO DISCLOSE INFORMATION

Authority already held and dated   Or   Authority Attached
(DD/MM/YYYY)

5. ACKNOWLEDGEMENT

Please complete this section if an acknowledgement is required.

Acknowledgement required   By email   Reference number to be quoted

OR   By post   (template attached)

6. ADDITIONAL INFORMATION REQUIRED

Trade Finance   One of the facility account numbers

Derivative & Commodity Trading   One of the facility account numbers

TABLE 3: Example Fast Track Request

Please note – Complete **section 6** only where additional information is required.

In accordance with the agreed practice for provision of information to auditors, please forward information on our mutual client(s) as detailed below on behalf of the bank, its branches and subsidiaries. This request and your response will not create any contractual or other duty with us.

1. BANK NAME AND ADDRESS

2. AUDITOR CONTACT DETAILS

Name and address of auditor

Contact Number

Contact Name

Email address

Period end date (DD/MM/YYYY)

Date response required (DD/MM/YYYY)

Date of request (DD/MM/YYYY)

Reason for fast track request

3. COMPANIES AND OTHER BUSINESS ENTITIES

Company	Main account sort code	Main account number

4. AUTHORITY TO DISCLOSE INFORMATION

Authority already held and dated   Or   Authority Attached
(DD/MM/YYYY)

5. ACKNOWLEDGEMENT

Please complete this section if an acknowledgement is required.

Acknowledgement   By email   Reference
required   number to be
                                   quoted

OR   By post   (template
                                   attached)

6. ADDITIONAL INFORMATION REQUIRED

Trade Finance   One of the facility account numbers

Derivative & Commodity Trading   One of the facility account numbers

TABLE 4: Example Incomplete Information Request

Please note – Complete **section 6** only where additional information is required.

In accordance with the agreed practice for provision of information to auditors, please forward information on our mutual client(s) as detailed below on behalf of the bank, its branches and subsidiaries. This request and your response will not create any contractual or other duty with us.

1. BANK NAME AND ADDRESS

2. AUDITOR CONTACT DETAILS

Name and address of auditor

Contact Number

Contact Name

Email address

Period end date (DD/MM/YYYY)

Date response required (DD/MM/YYYY)

We confirm that there are exceptional circumstances that require us to ask for this request to be processed on the basis of incomplete account numbers, sort code and facility account numbers for all companies in the group and/or a facility account number for additional information. We understand that this may result in the search taking longer to complete than the standard request

3. COMPANIES AND OTHER BUSINESS ENTITIES

Company	Main account sort code	Main account number

4. AUTHORITY TO DISCLOSE INFORMATION

Authority already held and dated   Or   Authority Attached
(DD/MM/YYYY)

5. ACKNOWLEDGEMENT

Please complete this section if an acknowledgement is required.

Acknowledgement required   By email   Reference number to be quoted

OR   By post   (template attached)

6. ADDITIONAL INFORMATION REQUIRED

Trade Finance   One of the facility account numbers

Derivative & Commodity Trading   One of the facility account numbers

24.5.4 Where to send the request

To better reflect banks' working practices, the Practice Note states that requests for bank reports should be sent to regional centres, rather than to individual branches. Addresses for regional centres, to which bank requests should be sent, are published on the BBA website, www.bba.org.uk.

Also on the site are contact details or preferred contact methods for the auditor to follow up bank requests. This information may also be included in the acknowledgement letter sent by the bank (see **24.5.5**).

24.5.5   Acknowledgement letters

A section of each bank report request template allows the auditor to select if he wishes to receive an acknowledgement from the bank.

Such acknowledgements should be provided within five working days of receipt. A list of those banks which do not provide acknowledgements is posted on the BBA website, together with contact details for pursuing enquiries.

24.5.6   Other issues

Other issues highlighted by the Practice Note are:

- minor omissions or amendments to a bank report may be communicated by telephone or e-mail, although the auditor may request written confirmation of these changes; and
- a bank has the right to decline to give information about accrued interest or charges as this is not within the scope of the guidance agreed between the British Bankers' Authority and the Auditing Practices Board.

24.5.7   Non-BBA banks

Where banks are not members of the BBA, the auditor should follow the same procedures. A full list of BBA banks can be found on the BBA website www.bba. org.uk. If the auditor is not able to obtain a satisfactory reply, he should consider whether this leads to a limitation of scope.

24.5.8   Online confirmations

In December 2014, the BBA launched an online confirmations service, allowing the auditor to send requests to banks online rather than through the post. Although not all banks are currently using this particular service, the number is increasing and both UK and overseas banks are registered. Alternative online services are also being developed which may lead to the problem of auditors needing to subscribe to a variety of services to get coverage of all the banks used by their various clients.

24.6   Confirmation of ongoing facilities

As part of his consideration of 'going concern' (see **Chapter 11**), the auditor will carry out a review of the ability of ongoing bank facilities to meet the entity's future cash needs. Where he considers existing banking facilities to be critical to the continuing operation of the entity, he may need to obtain a letter from the bank as to their intentions.

24.6.1 Procedures

As part of the reply to the standard request for a bank report for audit purposes, the auditor will have received details of any overdrafts and loans repayable on demand, specifying agreed facilities and dates of review. Where such facilities are in the process of being reviewed or they are to be reviewed within the time frame of the 'foreseeable future', and where the auditor considers their renewal as critical to his opinion, he may have to enter into correspondence with bankers to obtain confirmation.

Such correspondence should always be within the framework set out above for supplementary requests. This should encourage the banks to use standard disclaimers, which do not significantly impair the value of a response as audit evidence.

Table 5 contains suggested wording for a letter from the auditor to the bank requesting comfort as to the continuation of facilities, while **Table 6** provides an example of a letter from the bank to the auditor indicating their intentions concerning the facilities. It is suggested that this wording constitutes the minimum level of comfort acceptable from the bank.

In both cases, it is important to ensure that the client is made aware that such confirmation is being sought.

TABLE 5: Comfort letter request

The Manager XYZ Bank Plc

Dear Sir

X Limited

We refer to your above named customer's instructions given in the authority .... already held by you and to your reply to our Standard Request for Bank Report for Audit Purposes dated ....

For the purpose of our audit, as part of a request for supplementary information, we would ask you to confirm that, based on the information provided to you by the company (specific documents should be listed) and subject to unforeseen circumstances, you see no reason why the company's facilities will not be renewed on existing terms when they fall due nor are you aware of any reason why such facilities will not continue to be made available (specify timing, e.g. six months after that date).

Yours faithfully

TABLE 6: Bank's response to comfort letter request

ABC & Co

Dear Sirs

X Limited

We refer to your letter of .... requesting confirmation as to continuing facilities.

The company's facilities are due for renewal on ..... No decision has been reached as to whether the facilities will be renewed and we will continue to monitor the situation in the light of information which is supplied to us. Renewal of the facility will be considered on the agreed renewal date.

Yours faithfully

24.6.2   *Level of reliance to be placed on reply*

A satisfactory reply from the bank does not absolve the auditor from properly considering the going concern position of a client company by reference to primary audit evidence. Further reference should be made to the matters discussed in **Chapter 11**.

25 ANALYTICAL PROCEDURES

25.1 Introduction

The current ISA (UK and Ireland) 520 *Analytical procedures* was issued in October 2009 and is effective for the audit of financial statements for periods ending on or after 15 December 2010. This ISA was not included in the final draft of revised ISAs issued by the FRC in April 2016, and as such, the 2009 version remains applicable. It covers the use of analytical procedures including:

- the nature and purpose of analytical procedures;
- use of analytical procedures in risk assessment;
- analytical procedures as substantive procedures;
- overall review at the end of the audit; and
- investigating unusual items.

25.2 What is meant by analytical procedures?

Analytical procedures may be applied at the planning, execution and overall review stages of an audit. Analytical procedures are the examination and comparison of the financial and non-financial information of a business with internal and external information, for both the current and different periods. This is usually achieved by calculating ratios and trends and investigating fluctuations and inconsistencies. It may be described as the process of reviewing the figures to see if they make sense. Methods used range from simple comparisons to complex analyses using advanced statistical techniques. Analytical procedures may be applied to consolidated financial statements, financial statements of components, such as subsidiaries or divisions, and individual elements of financial information.

As well as comparing the current year information with that of prior periods, analytical review also includes comparisons with:

- budgets;
- estimates prepared by the auditor, such as depreciation; and
- similar industry information.

It also includes the consideration of various relationships among elements of financial information that are expected to conform to a predictable pattern based on the entity's experience, such as gross profit margin percentages, and between financial information and relevant non-financial information, such as payroll costs to number of employees. An example of this is shown in **Table 1**.

TABLE 1: Variable relationships

A company had 50 employees last year with total wages of £420,000 and 50 employees this year with a wage bill of £525,000, an increase of 25%. It is known that the annual pay rise was 12% and the level of business has remained approximately constant.

At first sight, the figures do not appear to make sense because the increase is substantially greater than expected. There may, however, be satisfactory explanations. For example, there may have been a change in sales mix with previously bought-in goods being replaced by goods manufactured in-house, resulting in substantial authorised overtime. This could be verified by looking at the sales figures for different products as well as the payroll. Alternatively, there could have been a switch to more skilled, and hence more expensive, labour; this could be verified from payroll and production records.

If no such explanation is available, it is possible that the payroll has been inflated by, for example:

(a) misposting in the general ledger;
(b) 'dummy' employees on the payroll;
(c) unauthorised overtime being paid; or
(d) employees being paid at higher rates of pay than authorised.

The auditor may direct his substantive testing towards finding any errors of this nature.

Comparisons should also be made with other branches or divisions in the same line of business, which are part of the same company or group or with other companies within the same industry. It is often helpful to make comparisons on a monthly or quarterly basis where such figures are available. This can eliminate any distorting effects of seasonal trade and may enable the auditor to distinguish genuine seasonal fluctuations from window dressing around the year end.

25.3 Problems in practice

Although analytical procedures are a useful source of evidence, there are certain pitfalls in relying on conclusions drawn from such comparisons. In particular, care must be taken that:

- *they are computed on a consistent basis for each period or location under review*. Where there is a change in the basis of the calculation of a ratio or in the relationships which make up the ratio, comparability may be lost. The ratio for the prior year may be restated to obtain a meaningful comparison. For example, if stock turnover is calculated using average stocks for the previous period, there is little point trying to make a comparison with a ratio for this year using year end stocks. Major changes in pricing policy and product lines may also render past relationships inconsistent with current results;

- *there ought to be a meaningful relationship between the items being compared.* For example, there is little point in comparing head office overheads with sales since there is unlikely to be any connection between them. Similarly, there is little point in examining the relationship between sales and gross profit if stocks are valued by reference to a fixed gross profit ratio;

- *results and balance sheet values are not distorted by the effects of changing price levels.* For example, under historical cost accounting, assets acquired at different times are stated at different price levels. This means that any ratio involving fixed assets is affected by when the assets were purchased. Hence, ratios such as return on capital employed and fixed asset turnover can be distorted and comparisons between different companies made meaningless unless they are carried out on a current cost basis;
- *they are not distorted by unusual items.* Such items are often first detected by means of analytical review procedures and once detected, they should be investigated separately and their effects removed from any ratios and trends;
- *they are not distorted by changes in accounting policy or accounting estimates.* It is necessary to adjust the figures for the prior year in order that comparisons can be made. It may also be useful to calculate the figures or ratios using the old accounting policy or estimate; this is not always possible but, if it is, it may give some indication of the effect, if any, of the change.

25.4 Use of analytical procedures in risk assessment

Guidance relating to the use of analytical procedures as risk assessment procedures is set out in ISA (UK and Ireland) 315 (Revised June 2016) *Identifying and assessing risks of material misstatement through understanding the entity and its environment.* That ISA requires that the auditor 'applies analytical procedures to assist in planning the nature, timing and extent of other audit procedures', including obtaining 'an understanding of the entity and its environment'.

The use of analytical procedures at the planning stage may also indicate aspects of the business of which the auditor is unaware but which he should take into account in planning his audit.

Analytical procedures at the planning stage are usually based on interim financial information, budgets and management accounts. For smaller entities such management information is often not extensive, and performance is monitored and controlled by less formal means. In such cases, it is suggested that the auditor extracts information from the existing accounting records, such as VAT returns and bank statements, as well as any draft financial statements and then discusses variations with management.

25.5 Analytical procedures as a substantive procedure

There is no requirement for analytical procedures to be used as substantive procedures, and the decision whether to use them, and the extent of such use is a matter for the auditor's professional judgment. Guidance on the nature, timing and extent of audit procedures in relation to assessed risks can be found in ISA (UK and Ireland) 330 (Revised June 2016) (see **Chapter 21**).

The auditor should consider whether sufficient reliable information is available to apply analytical procedures and the results of any similar procedures already performed by the entity. In addition, when designing and performing analytical procedures, the auditor should consider:

- the suitability of using substantive analytical procedures;
- the reliability of the data, whether internal or external, from which the expectation of recorded amounts or ratios is developed;
- whether the expected results are precise enough to show when a material misstatement has occurred; and
- the difference between expected and actual results which would be acceptable to the auditor.

Each item is considered in more detail below.

25.5.1 Suitability of using analytical procedures

Substantive analytical procedures are most effective when directed at high volumes of transactions that tend to be predictable over time. Where a financial statements amount is a result of few transactions, year-on-year comparisons are unlikely to be a useful source of evidence, as the components of the balance are likely to be different year on year.

In addition, if the auditor notes weak controls over an area, analytical procedures may be less conclusive than extensive detailed substantive tests. Similarly, an area with a historical problem of high error levels may be best tested using tests of detail as analytical procedures may show little or no trends for comparison purposes.

The ISA notes that where material balances occur the auditor would not rely on analytical procedures alone, instead coupling them with tests of detail. Tests of detail will also be required if a significant risk has been identified over a financial statements area or assertion at the planning stage.

25.5.2 Reliability of data

The reliability of data will depend on its nature, source and how it was obtained, i.e. direct from a third party or via the client. The auditor should consider:

- the source of the information available: information is normally more reliable when it is obtained from a source outside the entity;
- comparability of the information available: general industry data may need to be supplemented when the particular client deals only in a specialised area within the industry;
- nature and relevance of the information available: does the entity set attainable budgets, therefore making them a good benchmark for analytical procedures;
- controls over the preparation of the information: are budgets amended during the period to bring them closer in line to actual results? If so, this will lessen their use for comparative purposes;
- prior year knowledge and understanding: what data has been previously reliable and useful;
- whether the information has been produced internally: as noted above this will be less reliable than external information, but its reliability is enhanced if it is produced independently of the accounting system or there are adequate controls over its preparation; and
- whether controls over the preparation of the data are reliable.

25.5.3 Precision of expected results

The auditor must consider whether he can determine what the expected results of the analytical procedure will be with suitable precision before the test is performed. Precise expectations are required to allow the auditor to determine when results indicate that a material misstatement has occurred. The auditor should consider:

- the accuracy with which the expected result can be determined. Some results can be more easily predicted than others, such as gross margins compared to discretionary expense payments;
- the degree to which information can be disaggregated. Results may be more easily predicted for individual sections of an operation;
- the availability of information; and
- the frequency with which a relationship is observed.

25.5.4 Acceptable differences

The amount of difference from expectation that the auditor may accept without further investigation depends on the materiality of the item and the level of assurance he wishes to derive from the procedure.

25.6 Analytical procedures in the overall review at the end of the audit

ISA (UK and Ireland) 520 requires that the auditor should also apply analytical procedures at or near the end of the audit when forming an overall conclusion as to whether the financial statements as a whole are consistent with the auditor's knowledge of the entity's business.

The results from this review should corroborate the results of the detailed audit testing, both in individual areas and in forming the final conclusion. They may also indicate areas where further work needs to be carried out.

The auditor should consider the following when carrying out such procedures:

- whether the financial statements adequately reflect the information and explanations previously obtained and conclusions previously reached during the course of the audit;
- whether the procedures reveal any new factors that may affect the presentation of, or disclosures in, the financial statements;
- whether analytical procedures applied when completing the audit, such as comparing the information in the financial statements with other pertinent data, produce results which support the overall conclusion that the financial statements as a whole are consistent with his knowledge of the entity's business;
- whether the presentation adopted in the financial statements may have been unduly influenced by the desire of those charged with governance to present matters in a favourable or unfavourable light; and
- the potential impact on the financial statements of the aggregate of uncorrected misstatements (including those arising from bias in making accounting estimates) identified during the course of the audit and the preceding period's audit, if any.

25.7 Investigating unusual items

ISA (UK and Ireland) 520 requires that, when analytical procedures identify fluctuations or relationships that are inconsistent with other relevant information or that differ from expected values by a significant amount, the auditor should investigate and obtain adequate explanations and appropriate corroborative audit evidence.

Unexpected results may occur as a result of:

- actions of the client of which the auditor is unaware when he performs the review;
- external factors not controllable by the client of which the auditor is unaware when he carries out his review; or
- errors or omissions.

The investigation of unusual fluctuations will usually involve discussion between the client and the auditor. The auditor will then corroborate management's explanations by:

- comparing them with his existing knowledge of the business, either from previous years or obtained during the audit; or
- performing extra audit procedures to confirm the explanations received.

Where management are unable to offer any explanation the auditor should carry out additional work to identify the cause of the inconsistency.

Not all explanations are capable of verification; nevertheless, the auditor may be able to decide on the reasonableness of those offered. For example, if a decrease in sales is attributed to a fall in demand, it may not be possible to verify this explanation directly nor quantify its effect (unless there are total market figures published and available in time for the audit). If the decrease is in line with the auditor's knowledge of the industry and prevailing market conditions, he may accept it as being reasonable. If the explanation cannot be verified, he must rely on other sources of evidence to satisfy himself in this area.

25.8   Recording

Although the ISA does not cover this area, there was a section in the APC Guideline 417 *Analytical Review*. This provides useful guidance on how analytical procedures should be recorded.

The recording of analytical procedures will normally contain:

- the information examined, the sources thereof and the factors considered in establishing its reliability;
- the extent and nature of material variations found;
- the sources and level of management from which explanations for material unexpected variations have been obtained;
- the verification of those explanations;
- any further action taken; and
- the conclusions drawn by the auditor.

It may also be helpful to compile a client profile in permanent working papers detailing key ratios and trends from year to year. This allows the auditor to establish a base of financial and non-financial information for use in subsequent years.

26   AUDIT SAMPLING

26.1   Introduction

The current ISA (UK and Ireland) 530 *Audit sampling* was issued in October 2009 and is effective for the audit of financial statements for periods ending on or after 15 December 2010. This ISA was not included in the final draft of revised ISAs issued by the FRC in April 2016, and as such, the 2009 version remains applicable. It covers:

- use of sampling;
- risk assessment;
- design of the sample;
- sample size;
- selecting the sample;
- performing audit procedures;
- errors; and
- evaluating results.

26.2   Use of sampling

> When designing an audit sample, the auditor's consideration includes the specific purpose to be achieved and the combination of audit procedures that is likely to best achieve that purpose. *ISA (UK and Ireland) 530.*

The ISA recognises that the auditor does not normally examine all of the information available but reaches conclusions on, for example, account balances using audit sampling.

In the ISA, audit sampling is defined as 'the application of audit procedures to less than 100% of items within a population of audit relevance such that all sampling units have a chance of selection in order to provide the auditor with a reasonable basis on which to draw conclusions about the entire population'. It does not include procedures where individual items which have a particular significance are examined, e.g. all items over £10,000, as here the auditor is testing part of the population in its entirety and cannot use the results to draw conclusions about the rest of the population. Similarly, procedures such as walk-through tests are not sampling.

The auditor may use either tests of controls or substantive procedures in his work. When performing tests of controls, the auditor identifies a characteristic or attribute which indicates that a control has been implemented. This may be the signing of a purchase order or the completion of a credit check for new customers. The presence or absence of these attributes is then tested by the auditor. Audit sampling for tests of controls is generally appropriate when application of the control leaves audit evidence of performance, such as an approval stamp or the initials of an authorised person.

Substantive procedures can be broken down into substantive analytical procedures and tests of detail. Audit sampling will only relate to tests of detail.

26.3   Risk assessment

ISA (UK and Ireland) 530 states that 'the auditor should use professional judgment to assess the risk of material misstatement ... and design further audit procedures to ensure that this risk is reduced to an acceptably low level'.

A population will have a risk of material misstatement as assessed by the auditor at the planning stage. The level of risk of material misstatement will have a direct bearing on the sample size used. Where there is a high risk of material misstatement, the number of items tested from the population will be greater than in situations where the risk of material misstatement has been assessed as low. A higher sample size will result in lower sampling risk, increasing the auditor's confidence levels that the population does not contain a material misstatement. Other factors will also affect sample sizes (see **26.5** below).

26.3.1   Sampling risk

Where sampling is used, the auditor must accept a risk that the sample is not representative of the population from which it is drawn and that he may draw the wrong conclusion from the test.

Sampling risk may result in:

- a population such as a file of reconciliations, which is acceptable, being rejected because the sample happens to pick a large proportion of the items in error. This normally results in additional, unnecessary audit work but should not affect the validity of the final audit conclusion; or
- a population, which contains a material error, being accepted as satisfactory because the sample happens not to select any of the items that contain errors. This risk is more serious because there is the possibility that an unqualified audit report is issued when the financial statements contain material misstatement (although the auditor should organise his other audit procedures so that it is, in fact, unlikely that such an error escapes detection).

Sampling risk does not only affect substantive procedures; tests of controls may result in:

- too high an assessment of control risk, because the error in the sample is greater than that in the population; or

- too low an assessment of control risk, because the error in the sample is less than the error in the population as a whole.

Sampling risk may be reduced by using a rational (possibly a statistical) basis for planning, selecting and testing the sample and for evaluating the results. This will ensure that the auditor has adequate assurance that the sample is representative of the population from which it is drawn.

26.3.2   Non-sampling risk

Non-sampling risk arises from factors that cause the auditor to reach an incorrect conclusion and is not related to the size of the sample. For example, the auditor may plan unsuitable audit procedures or misinterpret audit evidence and fail to recognise an error.

26.4   Design of the sample

26.4.1   Deciding whether to sample

When designing audit procedures, the auditor must decide whether to:

- select all items in a population (100% examination);
- select specific items;
- use audit sampling; or
- use a combination of specific items and sampling.

Selecting all items

This is most appropriate for tests of detail, for example where the population constitutes a small number of large value items or where CAATs are used to test or reperform all the transactions in the period.

Selecting specific items

The decision to select specific items from a population will be based on the auditor's knowledge of the client, the assessed risk of material misstatement and the characteristics of the population itself. Items selected may include:

- high value or key items (i.e. those which are themselves material, or have some other characteristic);
- all items over a certain amount;
- items to obtain information; and
- items to test control activities.

Audit sampling

Audit sampling may be applied to a class of transactions or account balances. Either non-statistical or statistical approaches may be used (see **26.10**).

26.4.2   Designing the sample

When designing an audit sample, the auditor should consider the objectives of the audit procedure and the attributes of the population from which the sample will be drawn.

When designing an audit sample, the auditor should also consider the sampling and selection methods. *ISA (UK and Ireland) 530.*

Objectives

The auditor chooses the audit procedures that are most likely to achieve the stated audit objectives. Once the procedures have been decided, he designs the most appropriate form of sampling. This involves identifying conditions that are to be regarded as errors. For example, in a test of controls operating over purchases, non-compliance with the approval procedures may be assessed as an error. By contrast, the types of errors on a substantive test on sales invoices might be arithmetical inaccuracy and/or a failure to reflect them properly in the books of account.

Population

The auditor needs to ensure that he is extracting the sample from the appropriate population to test the specific audit objectives. This is more difficult when the audit objective is testing for understatement, such as the understatement of creditors, as the sample is chosen from a related population. The relevant population for such a test of understatement might be suppliers' statements, post-period payments or a list of all suppliers during the period, rather than unpaid invoices. In these cases, the auditor needs to take steps to ensure that the chosen population is complete, such as choosing suppliers' statements from a list taken from the purchase ledger.

The sampling unit is any of the individual items that make up the population and will vary according to the nature of the audit test. The auditor defines the sampling unit in order to obtain an efficient and effective sample to achieve his audit objective. For example, when testing the validity of debtors the sampling unit is the individual customer balances or invoices.

Stratification

By dividing a population into discrete sub-populations, sample sizes can be reduced without increasing sampling risk. Populations are often subdivided by monetary value, meaning greater audit effort can be directed to larger value items.

However, the results of audit procedures performed on a stratified population can only be projected to items in the same stratum; other items will have to be tested separately.

Value-weighted selection

When sampling for tests of details, the auditor may define the sampling unit as the monetary unit that makes up the population, e.g. each £1 of the balance. The auditor will then test the balance containing the £1 sampling unit. This means that larger balances have more chance of being selected for testing than smaller ones.

26.5   Sample size

In determining the sample size, the auditor should consider whether sampling risk is reduced to an acceptably low level.

Sample size is affected by the level of sampling risk that the auditor is willing to accept. The lower the acceptable risk, the greater the sample size will need to be.

Examples of some factors affecting sample sizes, taken from the ISA, are shown in **Table 1** and **Table 2**.

TABLE 1: Some factors influencing sample size for substantive tests

Factor	*Impact on sample size*
Inherent risk[1]	The higher the assessment of inherent risk, the more audit evidence is required to support the auditor's conclusion.
Control risk[2]	The higher the assessment of control risk, the greater the reliance on audit evidence obtained from substantive procedures.
	A high control risk assessment may result in the decision not to perform tests of controls and place reliance entirely on substantive procedures.
Detection risk[3]	Sampling risk for substantive tests is one form of detection risk. The lower the sampling risk the auditor is willing to accept, the larger the sample size.
	Other substantive procedures may provide audit evidence regarding the same financial statement assertions and reduce detection risk. This may reduce the extent of the auditor's reliance on the results of the substantive procedure using audit sampling.

	The lower the reliance on the results of a substantive procedure using audit sampling, the higher the sampling risk the auditor is willing to accept, and, consequently, the smaller the sample size.
Tolerable error rate	The higher monetary value of the tolerable error rate, the smaller the sample size and vice versa.
Expected error rate	If errors are expected, a larger sample usually needs to be examined to confirm that the actual error rate is less than the tolerable error rate.
Population value	The less material the monetary value of the population to the financial statements, the smaller the sample size that may be required.
Numbers of items in population	Virtually no effect on sample size unless population is small.
Stratification	If it is appropriate to stratify the population this may lead to a smaller sample size.

[1] Inherent risk is the susceptibility of an account balance or class of transactions to material misstatement, either individually or when aggregated with misstatements in other balances or classes, irrespective of related internal controls (see **Chapter 21**).

[2] Control risk is the risk that a misstatement could occur in an account balance or class of transactions. The misstatement could be material, either individually or when aggregated with misstatements in other balances or classes, and would not be prevented, or detected and corrected on a timely basis, by the accounting and internal control systems (see **Chapter 21**).

[3] Detection risk is the risk that the auditor's substantive procedures do not detect a misstatement that exists in an account balance or class of transactions, which could be material, either individually or when aggregated with misstatements in other balances or classes (see **Chapter 21**).

TABLE 2: Some factors influencing sample size for tests of controls

Factor	*Impact on sample size*
Sampling risk	The greater the reliance on the results of a test of controls using audit sampling, the lower the sampling risk the auditor is willing to accept and, consequently, the larger the sample size.
	The lower the assessment of control risk, the more likely the auditor is to place reliance on audit evidence from tests of controls.
Control risk	A high control risk assessment may result in a decision not to perform tests of controls.
Tolerable error rate	The higher the tolerable rate the lower the sample size and vice versa.

Expected error rate	If errors are expected, a larger sample usually needs to be examined to confirm that the actual error rate is less than the tolerable error rate.
	High expected error rates may result in a decision not to perform tests of controls.
Number of items in population	Virtually no effect on sample size unless population is small.

26.6 Selecting the sample

ISA (UK and Ireland) 530 requires the auditor to select items for the sample with the expectation that all sampling units in the population have a chance of selection. In other words, all items in the population must have an opportunity of being selected although this need not be equal. For example, the auditor will often choose samples so as to give higher value items a greater chance of selection.

The three most common methods of selecting a sample are:

- random selection, where each item has an equal chance of selection, using random number tables or CAATs;
- systematic selection, using a constant interval between selections and a randomly selected starting point. Where this method is being used, it is important that the population is not structured in such a way that the sampling interval used corresponds to a particular pattern in the population; and
- haphazard selection, so long as there is no bias in the selection.

26.7 Performing audit procedures

The auditor performs the planned procedures on each item in the sample. If any item selected is not appropriate a replacement item should be chosen. However, the auditor should consider whether the unsatisfactory item indicates an error. If procedures cannot be completed on a sample item, for example the supporting documentation has been lost, alternative audit procedures should be considered for that item. If no alternative procedures are possible, the item should be considered to be an error.

26.8 Errors

ISA (UK and Ireland) 530 requires the auditor to consider the sample results, the nature and cause of any errors identified, and their possible effect on the particular audit objective and other areas of the audit.

Before evaluating the results of a sample, the auditor needs to establish whether a matter detected is an error. There may be instances where such a matter does not meet the criteria for an error that were set in the planning of the test. For example, a substantive test of the validity of debtors may indicate that there has been a misposting between customer accounts. This does not lead to a misstatement of the total trade debtor balance; therefore in evaluating the sample it may be inappropriate to consider that this is an error. However, there may be implications for other areas of the audit, such as the recoverability of debtors.

The qualitative aspects of the error also need to be considered, particularly the nature and cause of the error, as they may have implications for other audit areas. It may be that all the errors fall within a particular time period or are at one location, in which case, it may be possible to identify the extent of the error in the rest of the population. For example, if the member of staff who inputs the sales invoices on to the system was away from work for a month and the replacement was entering the net amount of the invoice instead of the gross amount, an exercise could be undertaken to quantify the extent of the error by comparing the total of that month's gross and net sales.

26.8.1 Tolerable misstatement

This is the maximum error that is acceptable to the auditor, if he is to conclude that his audit objectives have been achieved. This is not necessarily the same as materiality, which relates to the financial statements as a whole rather than a particular balance or class of transactions, although it is the application of performance materiality in the case of substantive testing (see **Chapter 15**). The tolerable misstatement may be the same amount or an amount lower than performance materiality. Where tests of controls are being performed, the tolerable level of error will be the maximum rate of failure of an internal control that the auditor is prepared to accept.

26.8.2 Expected error

Before a test is performed, an error may already be expected. Here, a larger number of items may need to be tested to conclude that the actual error in the population is not greater than the planned tolerable error. This may be the case where previous years' audit tests have produced errors or the review of the internal controls indicates this.

26.8.3 Projecting errors

For tests of details, the auditor should project monetary errors found in the sample to the population, and should consider the effect of the projected error on the particular audit objective and on other areas of the audit.

When projecting errors found in the sample for tests of detail to the population from which it was drawn, the method used must be consistent with that used to select the sample. Projection commonly involves extrapolating the errors in the sample and estimating any further error not detected due to the imprecision of the methods used.

To assess whether errors in the population might exceed the tolerable error, the projected population error (net of adjustments made by the entity) should be compared with the tolerable error, taking into account the results of other audit procedures relevant to that financial statement assertion.

Where the projected errors exceed the tolerable error, the auditor reassesses sampling risk and if he concludes that it is unacceptable (for example, he has insufficient confidence in the results of the sample), he should consider:

- extending his own audit procedures; or
- performing alternative procedures (which may involve reviewing a client's exercise to investigate errors).

This will enable him to conclude on the test and may result in identifying the need for an adjustment to the financial statements.

Anomalous errors, i.e. errors which arise from an isolated event that has not recurred other than on a specifically identifiable occasion, may be excluded when projecting errors to the population. This is because anomalous errors will not be representative of the population as a whole. However, their effect still needs to be considered in addition to the projection of non-anomalous errors.

Projection of errors is not appropriate for tests of controls. On discovering errors in a test of controls, the auditor should consider whether the error is indicative of a general weakness in the control system.

26.9   Evaluating results

The auditor should assess the results of the sample tested to determine if the objectives of the test have been met.

For tests of controls, a high incidence of errors may lead the auditor to increase his assessment of the risk of material misstatement. For tests of detail, high error rates may indicate that a class of transactions or an account balance is materially misstated.

The auditor should use judgment where the projected error in a sample, plus any anomalous error which was not subject to projection, is close to his assessment of tolerable error. The auditor should be aware that sampling risk may mean that selection of a different sample may have provided an error which was greater than tolerable error. The auditor should consider the results of other audit procedures when assessing whether an adjustment to the financial statements is required.

If the auditor determines that test objectives have not been met, he may:

- request those charged with governance to investigate identified errors and the potential for further errors and to make any necessary adjustments; and/or
- modify the nature, timing and extent of further audit procedures. For example, in the case of tests of controls, the auditor might extend the sample size, test an alternative control or modify related substantive procedures; and/or
- consider the effect on the audit report.

26.10   Statistical and non-statistical sampling

There are several similarities between statistical and non-statistical sampling. Both:

- examine less than the total population to reach a conclusion about the population;
- involve sampling risk;
- provide approximate, not exact, knowledge about the population;
- perform the same audit steps; and
- require audit judgment.

One major difference between statistical and non-statistical methods is that a statistical sample must be selected using an appropriate statistical basis from the population while, although desirable, this is not essential for non-statistical methods.

Not every audit sample is worth performing on a rigorous statistical basis. Non-statistical sampling may be used whenever the auditor concludes that the additional costs of statistical sampling, such as set-up time, are in excess of the benefits to be obtained, for example, objectivity of sample selection and evaluation. Non-statistical sampling may be preferable in situations where the statistical selection is difficult to make because the records are not readily accessible or are in a form that makes it difficult to make a valid statistical selection. For example, at the physical stocktaking, when selecting items for test counting from floor to stock sheet there is no list of the population from which a statistical sample can be taken. In these cases, statistical sample sizes can still be used to get an idea of an appropriate sample size.

When using non-statistical methods, the auditor also needs to be satisfied that the selection is appropriate to obtain a reasonable conclusion and that he has not used these methods to exclude difficult items. Non-statistical sampling does not automatically solve problems or turn documents with errors into correct documents. Every item selected should be audited (and not replaced if not found). For example, a missing invoice should be investigated rather than inspecting the next available invoice. A conclusion about the population should be drawn from the sample evidence.

Approximate sample sizes should be generated for a population whether statistical or non-statistical methods are used. The sample size will depend on a number of factors such as population size, materiality and identified risk, and these will remain identical whichever sampling approach is used.

Statistical sampling is more likely to be used whenever the auditor concludes that the benefits are greater than the costs. Examples of this include situations where:

- the set-up time and selection time are reasonable in relation to the time required to test the selected items and follow up on discrepancies (more likely to be true for larger tests than for smaller ones);
- the most extensive part of the test is a representative selection, not the selection of material or unusual items;
- records of the entire population are reasonably accessible for the purpose of making the selection (although even if they are not readily accessible, statistical sampling could be desirable if it is likely that a non-statistical selection would yield an inappropriate conclusion because of a failure to include inconvenient records in the selection); and
- the selection of the statistical sample can be effected easily, perhaps with the aid of computer-assisted techniques.

Even where the approach adopted does not meet the criteria for statistical sampling, elements of the statistical approach may still be used, for example, the use of random selection of items to be tested using computer-generated random numbers.

27 AUDIT OF ACCOUNTING ESTIMATES

27.1 Introduction

This chapter has been updated to reflect the changes contained in final draft ISAs issued by the FRC in April 2016. Subject to legislative changes in progress at the time of writing, it is expected that ISA (UK and Ireland) 540 (Revised June 2016) *Auditing accounting estimates, including fair value accounting estimates, and related disclosures* will take effect for the audit of financial statements for periods commencing on or after 17 June 2016. For earlier periods, the version of ISA (UK and Ireland) 540 issued in October 2009 is applicable. The ISA includes issues relating to the audit of fair values and these are covered in **Chapter 28**.

The 2016 version of ISA (UK and Ireland) 540 (Revised June 2016) includes changes as a result of the Audit Directive and Audit Regulation. Most of the changes relate to the application material and are covered by **Chapter 21** and **Chapter 10**, and the only change in the body of the ISA is detailed in **27.7**.

27.2 Accounting estimates

ISA (UK and Ireland) 540 (Revised June 2016) requires that the auditor should obtain an understanding, assess the risk and then obtain sufficient appropriate audit evidence regarding the accounting estimates material to the financial statements on which to base his audit opinion.

Accounting estimates are approximations which are deemed necessary because there is no precise means of measurement for a particular item in the financial statements. Commonly encountered examples, other than fair value estimates, include:

- stock provisions;
- bad debt provisions;
- depreciation;
- accrued revenue;
- deferred taxation provisions;
- provision for costs arising from a lawsuit;
- profits or losses on construction contracts in progress; and
- warranty provisions.

The estimates in the financial statements are the responsibility of management and result from uncertainties regarding the outcome of events that have occurred, or are likely to occur. They involve the use of judgment and consequently the audit evidence available is less conclusive than with other items. When faced with estimates, the auditor must use his judgment in assessing the sufficiency and appropriateness of the evidence.

The processes involved in determining the estimate will depend on the nature of the item. For example, establishing an accrual for rent will involve taking the quarterly rental and apportioning it over the period concerned. On the other hand, establishing a provision for a slow moving stock item involves examining sales of the item over the period and since the year end, the costs associated with selling the item and the estimated selling price. In some cases, specialist knowledge may be required to make an estimate, such as the amount of damages payable in a legal case.

27.3   Risk relating to the use of audit estimates

When determining the risk assessment relating to audit estimates, ISA (UK and Ireland) 540 (Revised June 2016) requires the auditor to consider the:

- requirements of the financial reporting framework relating to the relevant accounting estimates;
- processes used by management to identify accounting estimates; and
- procedures management uses to quantify accounting estimates, including:
  - the method, and where applicable, the model used to determine the value of the estimate;
  - relevant controls;
  - whether an expert has been used;
  - the assumptions underlying the estimate;
  - whether there has been, or ought to have been, a change from the prior period in the methods used by management; and
  - whether, and if so how, management has assessed the effect of estimation uncertainty (i.e. the susceptibility of the estimate to an inherent lack of precision in its measurement).

In considering management's assessment of estimation uncertainty, the auditor may determine:

- whether management has considered alternative assumptions or outcomes by performing a sensitivity analysis to determine the effect of changes in the assumptions on an accounting estimate;
- how management quantifies the estimate when the sensitivity analysis suggests alternative outcomes; and
- whether management monitors prior period's accounting estimates and responds appropriately to their findings.

As part of the risk assessment, the ISA requires the auditor to reconsider accounting estimates made in the prior period and determine whether their accuracy, or otherwise, compared to actual results may indicate a risk of material misstatement.

In addition to assessing whether management have considered estimation uncertainty, the auditor is also required by the ISA to perform his own evaluation of estimation uncertainty. Where any accounting estimates are deemed to have a high level of estimation uncertainty, the auditor should consider whether these give rise to significant risks.

27.4 Audit procedures

The ISA requires that the auditor should obtain sufficient audit evidence as to whether an accounting estimate is reasonable in the circumstances and when required, is appropriately disclosed. To this end, the auditor should adopt one, or a combination, of the following approaches in the audit of an accounting estimate:

(a) review and test the process used by management to develop the estimate;
(b) test the operating effectiveness of the controls over how management made the accounting estimate together with appropriate substantive procedures;
(c) develop his own estimate to compare to the estimate generated by management; or
(d) review subsequent events which confirm the estimate made.

The review of subsequent events may remove the need for the auditor to obtain other evidence to support an accounting estimate. For example, if an estimate is made concerning an insurance claim for loss of profits after a fire and is provisionally settled during the audit, this will provide evidence on the estimate and means that the auditor may reduce the attention he gives to the process by which management derive the estimate. An estimate may become an accrual where it is fully supported by the subsequent evidence, for example, an estimate in respect of legal fees incurred before the year end becomes an accrual when those fees are rendered.

27.4.1 Significant risks

Where accounting estimates give rise to significant risks, the auditor should evaluate:

● whether the significant assumptions used by management are reasonable;
● whether management intend and are able to carry out any courses of action required by those assumptions; and
● how management have considered alternative assumptions and why they have been rejected.

The ISA also requires the auditor to obtain evidence concerning management's decision whether or not to recognise the estimate in the financial statements and if the measurement basis used for that estimate is in accordance with the requirements of the applicable financial reporting framework.

27.4.2 *Testing management's methods*

Testing management's methods and models for determining accounting estimates may be an effective audit tool when:

- the estimate is derived from a routine processing of data by the entity's accounting system;
- previous experience of similar estimates has shown that management's processes have been effective; and
- the accounting estimate is based on a large population of items of a similar nature, which individually are not significant.

Testing how management made the accounting estimate may involve:

- testing the reliability, accuracy, completeness and relevance of the data on which the estimate is based. This may be internal or external data supplied by experts;
- recalculating the estimate or assessing the validity of the model used (see **Table 1**);
- considering the process used to assess or review the calculated amount before approving it for use in the financial statements.

Where a model is used to determine the accounting estimate, the auditor may consider the procedures in **Table 1**.

TABLE 1: Audit procedures to assess the validity of models used to determine accounting estimates

The auditor may test whether:

- the model is validated prior to use, with periodic ongoing reviews. This should include evaluation of:
    - the theoretical soundness and mathematical integrity of the model;
    - the consistency and completeness of the model's inputs with market practices; and
    - the model's output as compared to actual transactions;
- appropriate change control policies and procedures exist to eliminate the risk of unauthorised changes being made;
- the model is periodically calibrated and tested for validity;

- necessary adjustments are made to the output of the model to reflect changing assumptions in the market place; and
- the model is adequately documented including its applications and limitations, key parameters, required inputs and results of any validation analysis performed.

In addition, if the financial reporting framework does not set out a fixed method for determining a particular accounting estimate, the auditor may consider:

- management's rationale for selecting the method used;
- whether management have applied any criteria set out in the financial reporting framework when selecting the chosen method;
- if the method is appropriate given the nature of the asset or liability being estimated; and
- if the method is appropriate in relation to the business, industry and environment in which the entity operates.

27.5   Evaluation of results

The ISA requires that the auditor should make a final assessment of the reasonableness of the accounting estimate based on the auditor's knowledge of the entity and its industry and whether it is consistent with other evidence obtained during the audit and subsequent events.

If the auditor believes management's estimate to be unreasonable and management refuses to revise its estimate, the difference between management's estimate and the auditor's estimate must be considered with all other misstatements in assessing whether the effect on the financial statements is material.

27.6   Disclosure

The auditor is required to obtain sufficient evidence as to whether disclosure of the accounting estimate in the financial statements is in accordance with the applicable financial reporting framework.

Where accounting estimates give rise to significant risks, the ISA also requires the auditor to evaluate the adequacy of the disclosure of the estimation uncertainty. In some situations, the auditor may consider it appropriate to encourage management to provide additional information regarding estimation uncertainty in the notes to the financial statements.

27.7   Indicators of possible management bias

The auditor is required to review the decisions and judgments made by management in making their estimates and identify whether there are any

461

indicators of possible management bias. Indicators of possible management bias do not themselves constitute misstatements, however, where identified the auditor should consider whether they affect his risk assessment and the implications for the rest of his audit. Examples of possible management bias include:

- changes in accounting estimate, or the method for making it, where management has made a subjective assessment that there has been a change in circumstances;
- use of an entity's own assumptions for fair value estimates when they are inconsistent with observable marketplace assumptions;
- selection of significant assumptions that yield a point estimate favourable for management objectives; and
- selection of a point estimate that may indicate a pattern of optimism or pessimism.

ISAs also require the auditor to maintain professional scepticism throughout the audit and in particular, when reviewing management estimates relating to fair values, the impairment of assets, provisions, and future cash flow relevant to the entity's ability to continue as a going concern. Scepticism is an essential feature of any audit and the subject is discussed further in **23.9**.

27.8 Written representations

The auditor is required to obtain written representations from management, and where appropriate those charged with governance, whether they believe significant assumptions used in making their accounting estimates are reasonable.

27.9 Documentation

The auditor is required to include in his documentation:

- the basis for his conclusions about the reasonableness of the accounting estimates and their disclosure that give rise to significant risks; and
- indicators, if any, of possible management bias.

27.10 International developments

The IAASB is currently engaged in a project to update ISA 540 and is aiming to issue a revised standard prior to the implementation date for IFRS 9 *Financial Instruments*. As part of the project, the IAASB is considering how to strengthen auditor scepticism in relation to accounting estimates and ensure that adequate consideration is given to the possibility of management bias, whether intentional or unintentional.

28 AUDITING FAIR VALUE

28.1 Introduction

Certain financial assets and financial liabilities may be presented or disclosed at fair value in the financial statements. The fair value used may arise from the initial recording of that asset or liability or from a subsequent change in its value. The use and determination of fair values is governed by the applicable financial reporting framework.

The measurement of fair value can be simple, for example, if assets are bought and sold in an active and open market, or more complex. Examples of fair values that can be difficult to determine include investment properties or complex financial derivatives. In these cases, an estimation of fair value may be achieved by using the work of an expert valuer or a valuation model.

This chapter builds on the guidance in **Chapter 27**.

28.2 Guidance

This chapter has been updated to reflect the changes contained in final draft ISAs issued by the FRC in April 2016. Subject to legislative changes in progress at the time of writing, it is expected that ISA (UK and Ireland) 540 (Revised June 2016) *Auditing accounting estimates, including fair value accounting estimates, and related disclosures* will take effect for the audit of financial statements for periods commencing on or after 17 June 2016. For earlier periods, the version of ISA (UK and Ireland) 540 issued in October 2009 is applicable.

The 2016 version of ISA (UK and Ireland) 540 (Revised June 2016) includes changes as a result of the Audit Directive and Audit Regulation. Most of the changes relate to the application material and are covered by **Chapter 21** and **Chapter 10**. The only change to the requirements of the ISA is a requirement for the auditor to maintain professional scepticism particularly when reviewing estimates relating to fair values, and other matters as detailed in **27.7**.

Further guidance is contained in Practice Note 23 *Special considerations in auditing financial instruments*. The current version of this was issued by the FRC in July 2013. It supersedes a number of previous and interim versions of Practice Note 23 and is based on International Auditing Practice Note (IAPN) 1000, *Special Considerations in Auditing Financial Instruments*, supplemented with further UK guidance.

The Practice Note is intended to assist auditors in understanding the nature of, and risks associated with, financial instruments, the different valuation techniques and types of controls that may be used by entities in relation to them, and identifies the important audit considerations.

Practice Note 23 supplements APB Bulletin 2008/1 *Audit Issues when Financial Market Conditions are Difficult and Credit Facilities may be Restricted* and is detailed in **28.9** below.

28.3 Understanding the entity's process

It is the responsibility of those charged with governance to establish procedures to allow the determination of fair values as necessary. This determination of procedures is often delegated to the entity's management, although responsibility remains with those charged with governance. This process may be simple, such as consulting published price quotations, or more complex involving assumptions and uncertainty.

In accordance with ISA (UK and Ireland) 315 (Revised June 2016) *Identifying and assessing risks of material misstatement through understanding the entity and its environment*, the auditor is required to gain an understanding of the process adopted by management and the related control activities in order to assess the risk of material misstatement (see **Chapter 21**). The risk of material misstatement should be assessed at the assertion level to allow the auditor to determine the nature, extent and timing of his audit tests.

When obtaining an understanding of the entity's fair value process, the auditor may consider the areas set out in **Table 1**.

TABLE 1: Areas to consider when gaining an understanding of an entity's fair value process

- the relevant control activities over the process used to determine fair value measurements, including, for example, controls over data and the segregation of duties between those committing the entity to the underlying transactions and those responsible for the valuation;
- the expertise and experience of those persons determining the fair value measurements;
- the role that information technology has in the process;
- the types of accounts or transactions requiring fair value measurements or disclosures (e.g. whether the accounts arise from the recording of routine and recurring transactions or whether they arise from non-routine or unusual transactions);
- the extent to which the entity's process relies on a service organisation to provide fair value measurements or the data that supports the measurement. When an entity uses a service organisation, the auditor should refer to ISA (UK and Ireland) 402 *Audit considerations relating to entities using service organisations* (see **Chapter 22**);

- the extent to which the entity uses the work of experts in determining fair value measurements and disclosures;
- the significant management assumptions used in determining fair value;
- the documentation supporting management's assumptions;
- the methods used to develop and apply management assumptions and to monitor changes in those assumptions;
- the integrity of change controls and security procedures for valuation models and relevant information systems, including approval processes; and
- the controls over the consistency, timeliness and reliability of the data used in valuation models.

If the auditor considers that the risk of material misstatement identified is a significant risk that requires special audit consideration, he should refer to ISA (UK and Ireland) 315 (Revised June 2016).

There may only be limited control activities that can be effective in relation to fair value as fair value determinations often involve subjective judgments by management. As fair value measurements become more complex, the likelihood of effective controls decreases whilst the risk of material misstatement increases.

28.4   Evaluating the entity's approach

The auditor uses his knowledge of the business and financial reporting requirements to assess whether the fair value approach used by the entity is appropriate and consistently applied. For example, knowledge of a client's business and future plans will assist with assessing the valuation applied to research and development work.

The auditor should pay particular attention to management's intentions, for example, whether the intentions relied upon as part of the fair value process are realistic and relevant. The auditor may:

- consider management's past history of carrying out its stated intentions with respect to assets or liabilities;
- review written plans and other documentation, including budgets and minutes as appropriate;
- consider management's stated reasons for choosing a particular course of action;
- consider management's ability to carry out a particular course of action given the entity's economic circumstances, including the implications of any contractual commitments; and
- consider whether the course of action is allowed by UK or International Accounting Standards as relevant.

When a valuation method is not determined by statute or accounting standards, the auditor should consider whether management's reasons for selecting a particular valuation method are appropriate. He should consider whether:

- management has sufficiently evaluated and appropriately applied any criteria that have been provided in accounting standards to support the selected method;
- the valuation method is appropriate to the item being valued; and
- the valuation method is appropriate for the business, industry and environment in which the entity operates.

The selected valuation method should be applied consistently, both for like assets and year on year. Where the valuation method has been changed in the period, the auditor considers whether the change is justified either as a result of a change to the financial reporting rules or a change in the entity's circumstances, and whether the new method of valuation is more appropriate.

28.5   Using the work of an expert

Where valuation methods are complex or specialised, the auditor may require the assistance of an expert when assessing the entity's methods and procedures. Where an expert is used, the auditor should refer to ISA (UK and Ireland) 620 (Revised June 2016), *Using the work of an auditor's expert* (see **Chapter 31**).

In accordance with the ISA, the auditor should assess the expert's work. This will involve obtaining an understanding of the significant assumptions and methods used, and considering whether they are appropriate, complete and reasonable given the auditor's knowledge of the business and the results of other audit procedures.

28.6   Audit procedures

Once the risk of material misstatement has been assessed, the auditor should plan and perform his audit procedures. Procedures are likely to vary widely as a result of the many different types of fair value measurements that may occur. The three main types of procedure are:

- testing the entity's assumptions, the valuation model and the underlying data;
- developing independent fair value estimates to corroborate the entity's valuation; and
- considering the effect of subsequent events.

For some valuations, it may merely be a case of consulting the same third party pricing data that the entity has used; for other areas, the work performed will be more complex.

Whatever procedure is used, the auditor should consider the results of his testing in relation to the rest of the evidence gained during the audit, for example is the discount rate used reasonable given the interest rates on borrowings by the entity.

28.6.1   Testing the entity's assumptions, model and data

When assessing an entity's fair value measurements, the auditor may evaluate whether:

- the assumptions used by management are reasonable;
- the fair value measurement was determined using an appropriate model; and
- management used relevant information that was reasonably available at the time.

Assumptions

The auditor assesses whether the assumptions used by the entity provide a reasonable basis for the fair value measurements and disclosures in the financial statements. To provide a reasonable basis, the assumptions must be relevant, reliable, neutral, understandable and complete.

The assumptions will vary depending on the asset or liability being valued and the valuation method used, for example, where discounted cash flows are used assumptions will be required about the level of cash flows, the period over which they are measured and the discount rate applied.

The auditor should concentrate on significant assumptions, i.e. those that cover matters that materially affect the fair value measurement, and this will typically include those which are:

- sensitive to variation or uncertainty, such as long-term interest rates; and
- susceptible to misapplication or bias.

The auditor should encourage the entity to perform a sensitivity analysis on their fair value measurements, and should consider performing the analysis himself if it is not completed by the entity.

Assumptions are often interdependent and should be assessed both individually and in conjunction with each other. Sometimes assumptions which appear reasonable on their own may not be consistent with others used in the same valuation. Assumptions should be consistent with:

- the general economic environment and the entity's economic circumstances;
- the plans of the entity;
- assumptions made in prior periods, if appropriate;
- past experience of the entity, although past experience may not be indicative of future conditions or events;
- other matters relating to the financial statements, for example, assumptions used by management in other accounting estimates, whether fair value or not; and
- if applicable, the risk associated with the cash flows.

The auditor should obtain written confirmation of representations made by management or those charged with governance regarding the reasonableness of significant assumptions.

Model

Where a valuation model is used, the auditor reviews the model and evaluates whether it is appropriate and the assumptions used are reasonable.

Data

The auditor should plan and perform audit procedures to determine whether the data used in deriving the fair value measurement is accurate, complete and relevant. He should also consider whether the fair value measurement has been properly calculated using that data and the entity's assumptions.

Typical audit procedures will include:

- verifying the source of the data;
- mathematical recalculation of the valuation; and
- reviewing the information for internal consistency.

28.6.2   Independent fair value estimates

Instead of testing the assumptions, model and data as stated above, the auditor may choose to attempt to corroborate the entity's fair value measurement by using his own model to generate a valuation. Typically, he would use the entity's assumptions and data in this model, and would, therefore, be required to plan and perform procedures to verify these as discussed in **28.6.1** above.

Alternatively, the auditor could use his own model and assumptions, but he would still be required to understand the assumptions applied by the entity in order to consider how his valuation differs from that prepared by the entity.

28.6.3   Subsequent events

Transactions and events that appear after the period end, but before the completion of the audit, may provide evidence about fair value measurements. An example would be the sale of an investment property after the period end. Care should be taken, however, that the post balance sheet events may no longer reflect events at the balance sheet date, e.g. a property value may vary considerably month on month in a time of volatile markets.

28.7   Disclosures

The auditor is required to consider whether the disclosures made about fair values are in accordance with the requirements of statute and financial reporting standards. This will include considering whether any additional information given voluntarily is appropriate and not misleading.

The auditor must also ensure that, where a change in valuation methods has occurred in the period, the details and reasons for this change have been properly disclosed.

28.8 Communication with those charged with governance

As the assumptions used in fair value measurement can often have significant effects on the financial statements, the auditor may choose to include details of the assumptions, the degree of subjectivity involved in their formulation and the relative materiality of items measured at fair value in his communications with those charged with governance.

28.9 Complex financial instruments

28.9.1 Background

Practice Note 23 *Special considerations in auditing financial instruments* gives a large amount of detailed guidance which should be read when dealing with complex financial instruments.

28.9.2 General considerations

New financial instrument products are being developed all the time, but typical examples are derivatives (including option contracts, futures and swaps) and notes or security instruments involving:

- contracts with one or more optional or conditional characteristic embedded within them; and/or
- underlying risk exposures which are not apparent from the form of the financial instrument (sometimes described as a 'host contract').

Values of complex financial instruments can be volatile and this increases their risk. There is often further risk due to the complex nature of the activities, which management sometimes do not fully understand.

However, the use of complex financial instruments can reduce some risks such as exposure to exchange rates, interest rates and commodity prices, by leveraging risks or providing a hedge to compensate for losses.

The guidance in the Practice Note ('the PN') is intended to be helpful for audits of entities with different levels of use of complex financial instruments, ranging from banks with high levels of trading to entities with a low number of foreign currency transactions.

The guidance on valuation in the PN is likely to be more relevant for financial instruments measured or disclosed at fair value, while the guidance on areas other than valuation applies equally to financial instruments either measured at fair value or amortised cost. The PN is also applicable to both financial assets and financial liabilities. The PN does not deal with instruments such as:

- the simplest financial instruments such as cash, simple loans, trade accounts receivable and trade accounts payable;
- investments in unlisted equity instruments; or
- insurance contracts.

Also, the PN does not deal with specific accounting issues relevant to financial instruments, such as hedge accounting, profit or loss on inception (often known as 'Day 1' profit or loss), offsetting, risk transfers or impairment, including loan loss provisioning. Although these subject matters can relate to an entity's accounting for financial instruments, a discussion of the auditor's consideration regarding how to address specific accounting requirements is beyond the scope of the PN.

28.9.3   Responsibilities

Management and those charged with governance are responsible for establishing a suitable control environment over complex financial instruments to ensure that they are able to make the relevant assertions about the existence, completeness and value of those financial instruments in their financial statements. Auditors are responsible for obtaining sufficient audit evidence to satisfy themselves that management's assertions give a true and fair view and are prepared in accordance with the applicable financial reporting framework.

The auditor may need special skills or knowledge to plan and perform auditing procedures for certain assertions about complex financial instruments and this may require the assistance of an expert from within or external to the firm. Difficult areas include the:

- operating characteristics and risk profile of the industry;
- instruments used by the entity and their characteristics;
- methods of valuing the complex financial instruments; and
- requirements of relevant legislation, regulations and applicable accounting standards.

The audit team may need to make use of the experience of an expert, from within or external to the firm, with the necessary skills or knowledge to help plan and perform the audit procedures. In periods of economic uncertainty, use of an expert may be required where previously it was not considered necessary (e.g. where valuation methods have moved away from observable market prices and have become more complex).

The requirements of ISQC (UK and Ireland) 1 (Revised June 2016) and ISA (UK and Ireland) 220 (Revised June 2016) require that an engagement quality control reviewer is appointed for all audits of financial statements of listed entities and those other audits that fall within the procedures laid down by the firm. Typically other audits where the appointment of an engagement quality control reviewer is required would include those with unusual circumstances or risks. The auditor should consider whether the complex financial instruments or the market conditions surrounding the financial instruments would require such a review to take place.

28.9.4 Understanding the entity

The auditor must understand the type of financial instruments the entity is using and its objectives and strategies for using them, for example, to eliminate risk or maximise income. The entity may use service organisations such as asset managers to initiate the purchase or sale of complex financial instruments. If so, the auditor should have regard to ISA (UK and Ireland) 402 (see **Chapter 22**).

ISA (UK and Ireland) 315 (Revised June 2016) requires that the auditor obtains an understanding of internal control relevant to the audit. Internal control will consist of:

- the control environment, in relation to complex financial instruments, of particular relevance are:
  - the level of knowledge and experience of management and those charged with governance;
  - strength, or lack, of direction from management and those charged with governance;
  - segregation of duties and the assignment of personnel; and
  - whether or not the general control environment has been extended to those responsible for complex financial instrument activities;

- the entity's risk assessment process, including the assessment of operational risk, valuation risk, market risk, credit risk and settlement risk;
- the information system relevant to financial reporting and communication, particularly whether it is sophisticated enough to handle complex financial instruments with minimal manual intervention;
- control activities, including whether the entity's control activities remain capable of preventing, detecting and correcting material misstatements, even at times when the entity may have changed the way it uses financial instruments or the market conditions have deteriorated, leading to an increase in risk; and

- monitoring of controls, including ensuring that dealers are properly authorised and prices are independently verified.

As part of assessing internal control, the auditor may consider the role of internal audit and whether they have sufficient knowledge and skill to cover complex financial instruments. Skills in this area are typically quite different to those required in other parts of the business.

When considering the risk of material misstatement in relation to complex financial instruments, the auditor should consider:

- the business purpose of the entity's financial instrument activities;
- the complexity and features of the financial instruments used;
- whether the transaction involves the exchange of cash;
- the entity's experience in the field of complex financial instruments;
- whether the financial instrument includes an embedded derivative;
- whether risk is affected by external factors such as a declining market;
- whether the complex financial instrument is traded nationally or across borders; and
- the strength of the entity's control environment.

The nature and use of some complex financial instruments may increase the likelihood of fraud risk factors related to them, and this may be more marked when financial market conditions are difficult. Incentives to engage in fraudulent financial reporting may include protection of personal bonuses, hiding management error, avoiding breaching borrowing limits or avoiding reporting catastrophic losses.

28.9.5 Reliance on controls

Where the auditor's assessment of risk includes an expectation that controls are operating effectively, he is required to perform tests of those controls. In determining the level of testing required in relation to complex financial instruments, the auditor should consider the:

- importance of the complex financial instrument activities to the entity;
- nature, frequency and volume of complex financial instrument transactions;
- potential effect of any identified weaknesses in control procedures;
- types of control activities being tested;
- frequency of performance of these control activities;
- evidence of performance.

Key areas for evaluation are listed in **Table 2**.

TABLE 2: Key areas to be evaluated as part of testing control activities

Procedures may include evaluating whether:

- complex financial instruments have been used in accordance with the agreed policies, guidelines and within authority limits;
- appropriate decision-making processes have been applied and the reasons behind entering into selected transactions are clearly understandable;
- the transactions undertaken were within the policies for complex financial instrument transactions, including terms and limits and transactions with foreign or related parties;
- the transactions were undertaken with counterparties with appropriate credit risk;
- complex financial instruments are subject to appropriate timely measurement, and reporting of risk exposure, independent of the dealer, including regular review and challenge of the valuation of transactions, the appropriateness of valuation models and variations in profit and loss;
- counterparty confirmations have been sent;
- incoming confirmation from counterparties have been properly matched and reconciled;
- early termination and extension of transactions are subject to the same controls as new transactions;
- designations, including any subsequent changes in designations, are properly authorised;
- designations, including any subsequent changes in designations, as hedging are properly authorised;
- transactions have been properly recorded and are entered completely and accurately in the accounting records, and correctly processed in any subsidiary ledger through to the financial statements; and
- adequate security has been maintained over passwords necessary for electronic fund transfers.

28.9.6 Audit procedures

The auditor is required to perform substantive procedures for each material class of transaction, account balance and disclosure. In addition, when a significant risk has been identified, he is required to perform substantive procedures that are specifically responsive to that risk.

Materiality may be difficult to determine for complex financial instruments where their impact on the balance sheet is small, but their relative risk is high, and will vary depending on the complexity of the financial instruments entered into.

In addition, the auditor may have difficulty in assessing materiality for an entity using complex financial instruments, particularly if their valuation is likely to be volatile. Some assets may become liabilities between the initial assessment of materiality and the year end date. Where the auditor becomes aware of information during the course of his audit which would have caused him to assess materiality differently, he should revise his assessment of materiality accordingly.

The auditor may need to make use of management representations to gain appropriate evidence in relation to some aspects of complex financial instrument transactions, including management's objective in entering into such transactions and whether all such transactions have been disclosed, conducted at arm's length and at market value.

In designing substantive procedures, the auditor considers:

- the appropriateness of the accounting treatment;
- the involvement of a service organisation;
- interim audit procedures performed and market movements since the date at which they were performed;
- routine and non-routine transactions; and
- procedures performed in other audit areas such as cash receipts and payments.

The use of analytical procedures may be difficult as the complex interplay of the factors from which these instruments are derived often masks any unusual trends that might arise. Volatile markets also make meaningful comparisons difficult.

Existence, rights and obligations

In relation to existence and rights and obligations, substantive tests are likely to involve obtaining confirmations from the holder of, or counterparty to, the financial instrument and inspecting the underlying agreement.

Completeness

Substantive tests for completeness may include:

- sending zero balance confirmations to potential holders or counterparties to complex financial instruments;
- reviewing brokers' statements for the existence of complex financial instruments;
- reviewing unresolved reconciliation items; and
- inspecting other documentation, such as loan or equity agreements or sales contracts for embedded derivatives.

Valuation

It is management's responsibility to estimate the value of the financial instrument and the auditor is required to test the valuation model used. Where quoted market prices are available, these are generally considered to provide sufficient evidence. Otherwise the auditor is required to assess the valuation, and may:

- assess the reasonableness and appropriateness of the model used by the entity, including whether the variables and assumptions used are reasonable and consistently applied;
- recalculate the value using his own or a third party model;
- compare the value with recent transactions;
- consider the sensitivity of the valuation to changes in variables and assumptions; and
- inspect supporting documentation for subsequent realisation or settlement of the instrument after the balance sheet date.

It would not normally be sufficient to rely on a broker quote obtained from the institution that initially sold the instrument without further verifying that quote. This may be done by supplementing the quote with quotes from other brokers or from pricing services.

If management obtain valuations of complex financial instruments directly from third parties such as banks and other financial institutions, the auditor should consider the:

- competence and objectivity of the third party, and their independence from the audited entity; and
- appropriateness of the valuation, the model used and its sensitivities.

Disclosure

The auditor considers whether complex financial instruments are presented in conformity with relevant legislation, regulations and the applicable financial reporting framework. His judgment will be based on whether, in his opinion:

- the accounting policies selected and applied are in keeping with the relevant financial reporting framework;
- disclosure is adequate to ensure that the entity is in full compliance with the current disclosure requirements;
- the information presented in the financial statements is classified and summarised in an appropriate and meaningful manner; and
- the financial statements show a true and fair view.

The auditor is also required to consider whether information in the Directors' report relating to the use of financial instruments by the company is consistent with his knowledge of the client and their activities.

28.9.7 Evaluating audit evidence

The assertions relating to the audit of complex financial instruments may be based on highly subjective assumptions or be particularly sensitive to changes in underlying assumptions. This can make the evaluation of audit evidence challenging and management bias, whether intentional or unintentional, can be difficult to detect. Examples of indicators of possible management bias with respect to accounting estimates relating to financial instruments include:

- changes in accounting estimate, or the method for making it, where management has made a subjective assessment that there has been a change in circumstances;
- use of an entity's own assumptions for fair value accounting estimates when they are inconsistent with observable market place assumptions;
- selection or construction of significant assumptions that yield a point estimate favourable for management objectives; and
- selection of a point estimate that may indicate a pattern of optimism or pessimism.

28.9.8   Management representations

Depending on the volume and complexity of financial instrument activities, management representations sought to support other evidence obtained by the auditor may include:

- management objectives with respect to complex financial instruments, for example, whether they are used for hedging, asset/liability management or investment purposes;
- those about the appropriateness of presentation of the financial statements, for example, the recording of financial instrument transactions as sales or financing transactions;
- those relating to the financial statements disclosures concerning financial instruments, for example that:

  - the records reflect all complex financial instrument transactions;
  - the assumptions and methodologies used in the complex financial instrument valuation models are reasonable;
  - all embedded derivative instruments have been identified;

- whether all transactions have been conducted at arm's length and at market value;
- the terms of transactions;
- the appropriateness of the valuations of financial instruments;
- whether there are any side agreements associated with any complex financial instruments;
- whether the entity has entered into any written options;
- management's intent and ability to carry out certain actions; and
- whether subsequent events require adjustment to the valuations and disclosures included in the financial statements.

28.9.9 *Considerations in difficult market conditions*

When financial market conditions are difficult, it can lead to the severe curtailment or even cessation of trading in certain complex financial instruments. This makes valuation of such instruments difficult because:

- values may fluctuate rapidly; and
- there is no ready market to obtain valuations from.

In such situations, the degree of estimation increases, and this leads to an increased risk of material misstatement.

Even where a market remains, in times of economic difficulty it is important for management and the auditor to examine the continuing appropriateness of models and assumptions, which may have been determined when markets were healthier.

In such difficult times, there may also be an increased risk in relation to fraudulent financial reporting. Market instability may lead to unexpected losses, and financial difficulties may create pressures on management who are concerned about the solvency of the business. This may lead to fraudulent activities to protect personal bonuses, hide management error, avoid breaching borrowing limits or avoid reporting catastrophic losses.

In auditing fair value accounting estimates, the auditor may therefore need to consider whether the circumstances give risk to increased fraud risks.

29 THE AUDIT OF RETIREMENT BENEFITS

29.1 Introduction

Both UK and international accounting frameworks contain standards for accounting for retirement benefits and dealing with the related disclosures. Although the standards are similar, the requirements may vary slightly in some areas and the auditor needs to be aware of those differences and of which reporting regime is being applied to each of his clients.

Whichever framework is applicable will deal with accounting by companies for the defined benefit and defined contribution schemes which provide pensions for their employees and cover such areas as:

- requirements to value scheme assets and liabilities using specified methods;
- the recognition by the reporting entity of the surplus or deficit as an asset or liability;
- how the change in the defined benefit asset or liability (other than that arising from contributions to the scheme) is analysed into specified components and recognised in the profit and loss account or other components of equity; and
- which other additional disclosures are made in the reporting entity's financial statements.

The recognition of pension fund assets and liabilities in companies' balance sheets or even in the notes to the balance sheet presents the auditor with a number of problems. These include, for example, access to records and how far to rely on actuaries' valuations.

29.2 Guidance

In November 2001, the APB issued Practice Note 22 *The Auditors' Consideration of FRS 17 Retirement Benefits – Defined Benefit Schemes* ('the Practice Note').

This was followed in February 2002 by the issue of Technical Release Audit 1/02 *Practical Points for Auditors in Connection with the Implementation of FRS 17 'Retirement Benefits' – Defined Benefit Schemes* ('the Technical Release') by the Audit and Assurance Faculty of the ICAEW.

Although the Practice Note and Technical Release were issued prior to the issue of ISAs (UK and Ireland), some of the guidance within them remains relevant under the new regime. Where the guidance refers to the old SASs, this commentary also includes references to the relevant ISA (UK and Ireland).

Although the Practice Note and Bulletin deal specifically with FRS 17, as it was the published guidance at that time, many of the principles are still relevant in the context of updated standards and other frameworks. ISA (UK and Ireland) 500 *Audit Evidence* contains standards and guidance relating to the use of management's experts and is considered in **23.3**.

29.3 Respective responsibilities

The Practice Note makes clear that it is the directors' responsibility to develop procedures to enable the entity to comply with accounting requirements. As directors may not have immediate access to the records of scheme assets, and are unlikely to possess the expertise to value the scheme liabilities, they may need to involve others in the process:

- the scheme trustees to value the scheme assets; and
- a qualified actuary to value the scheme liabilities.

The auditor's objectives are to consider the appropriateness of the steps taken by directors to satisfy themselves that the amounts and disclosures made in the financial statements are sufficiently reliable. Auditors need to consider whether directors have devoted sufficient resources to this process.

The Practice Note emphasises that it is not the auditor's role to 'second guess' actuaries' work in valuing scheme liabilities. The auditor should, however, assess whether the procedures taken by directors are appropriate and whether the accounting entries and disclosures are consistent with his knowledge of the reporting entity. See **Chapter 31** for further guidance on relying on the work of others.

The Practice Note stresses the need for the auditor to satisfy himself that he is independent and objective when the audit firm provides other services to a client. This is especially important when such services directly affect the client's financial statements. Where an audit firm provides actuarial services to a client, this could constitute a threat to the auditor's objectivity and independence. Where the audit firm concludes that it cannot adopt safeguards to address this problem, the firm would be unable to accept both engagements.

29.4 Planning

When planning, the auditor should assess the process by which directors intend to comply with the relevant accounting framework in preparing their financial statements. The auditor's discussions with directors are likely to cover:

- who is responsible for the process;
- the arrangements to identify the schemes where the accounting framework may present significant issues;

- who is valuing the scheme assets;
- the arrangements to identify significant matters affecting the actuarial valuation;
- who is valuing the scheme liabilities;
- how the actuarial assumptions are to be developed and approved;
- whether there is a realistic coordinated timetable (allowing time for the auditor to complete his work on retirement benefits); and
- whether procedures exist to enable effective communication between all parties.

29.4.1   Risks of material misstatement

The auditor and directors should also discuss the risk of material misstatement in the financial statements arising from the requirements of the accounting framework. Some examples of risks are given in **Table 1**.

TABLE 1: Examples of risks of material misstatement in relation to accounting for retirement benefits

The risks below may not necessarily exist in every case, nor is this table intended to be an exhaustive list of all possible risks.

General

- directors may not have allocated sufficient resources to the compliance process.

Completeness of retirement benefit arrangements

- directors may not be aware of all schemes (for example, information about overseas schemes may not be well documented).

Subsidiaries

- directors of subsidiary entities may not fully understand the accounting requirements.

Scheme changes

- scheme actuaries may not have been advised of important changes to schemes (for example, changes in benefit structures).

Consistency

- the treatment of scheme assets and liabilities related to bulk transfers may be inconsistent (leading to cut-off errors).

Actuarial assumptions

- key assumptions may be inconsistent (for example, the discount rate and the expected return on assets) or may be inappropriate (for example, benefit improvements).

Timetable

- the timetable for valuing scheme assets and liabilities may not be compatible with the entity's reporting timetable.

Surpluses

- directors may not have considered the recoverability of a surplus or may argue that it will be used for future benefit improvements (and therefore should not be accounted for in full).

Deficits

- the entity may be in breach of loan covenants when the deficit is taken into account and this may bring the entity's going concern into question.

Distributable profits

- the impact of any deficits in the group on distributable profits may not have been considered.

Actuarial updates

- changes since the most recent full actuarial valuation may give rise to imprecise liability calculations.

Source data

- actuaries may use incomplete or inaccurate source data (for example, in respect of membership records).

Asset values

- a timely, appropriate report on scheme assets may not be provided by trustees (for example, investments may be incomplete).

Multi-employer schemes

- it may be possible to allocate assets and liabilities to an individual reporting entity within the scheme and this may not have been identified.

Measurement and disclosure

- there may be a misallocation between the profit and loss account and other changes in equity.

Deferred taxation

- directors may have failed to consider the allocation of deferred tax between the profit and loss account and the STRGL.

29.4.2   Communication

Effective communication between all the parties involved in compliance with the accounting framework is essential to ensure a common understanding of what has to be done by each party and the timetable for its completion.

With the permission of directors, the auditor communicates with actuaries at the audit planning stage to:

- inform actuaries of his intention to use their work as audit evidence;
- discuss the scope of their work, for example:

    - steps to produce the valuation within the reporting timescale;
    - procedures to establish the validity and completeness of the source data used in the valuation;
    - the possible variation in the liability and costs estimated by actuaries;
    - the impact of any significant events on the valuation;
    - the extent to which a fuller or more recent valuation may be required;

- ascertain the form and content of any reports to be issued in respect of retirement benefits;
- confirm that actuaries:

    - will follow the relevant accounting requirements and their own professional guidance;
    - will include all the retirement benefits payable under schemes they have been engaged to advise upon;
    - understand the timetable for the preparation and audit of the financial statements;
    - will advise the auditor of any matters occurring between the reporting entity's balance sheet date and the completion date of the valuation which would have a material effect on the valuation of scheme liabilities;
    - are content for directors to supply the auditor with copies of the actuaries' draft or final reports.

Although actuaries are not professionally obliged to agree an engagement letter with directors, any terms of reference for their work may assist the auditor in understanding the scope of their work.

For most accounting purposes, actuaries can often update the most recent scheme valuation to reflect current conditions. Where significant changes have taken place, however, they may lead to material changes in the value of liabilities (for example, the impact of large bulk transfers or major new early retirement programmes). In such cases, the auditor has to discuss the issues with directors and actuaries to determine whether actuaries need to carry out any additional work.

The entity auditor may also contact the scheme auditor, fund managers or investment custodians who may be valuing the scheme assets.

Where the reporting entity prepares consolidated financial statements, there may be a large number of schemes. This may therefore involve a number of different trustees and actuaries with whom the auditor may have to communicate. In practice, some responsibility passes to the subsidiary auditor, although it is important to establish that he is familiar with the relevant accounting requirements (especially in the case of overseas subsidiaries). The reporting entity may appoint a lead actuary to communicate with the actuaries of the various schemes and collate information.

The Technical Release identifies a number of steps which the auditor may take in respect of overseas schemes. These are shown in **Table 2**.

TABLE 2: Steps in respect of overseas schemes

- consider how, if at all, the principles of the relevant accounting framework apply to the overseas schemes (for example, pension schemes being state run);
- review the year end reporting timetable;
- determine whether overseas accounts staff are familiar with the relevant accounting framework and its requirements;
- enquire if it is possible to communicate with overseas actuaries; and
- assess whether there are material schemes within overseas joint ventures or associates.

29.5   Audit evidence

29.5.1   Understanding the schemes involved

Given the potential material impact which accounting for retirement benefits could have on an entity's financial statements, it is important for the auditor to understand which schemes are involved and the general nature of their provisions.

The auditor should therefore obtain from directors an understanding of the scheme rules which could have a significant influence on the entity's compliance with accounting requirements (for example, the details of obligations to pay retirement benefits).

There could, however, be other benefits payable not covered in the scheme rules, for example:

- legal obligations to pay retirement benefits arising from informal agreements rather than formal contracts; and
- statutory requirements overriding the original scheme provisions.

The auditor should also take care to ensure that he receives the most up-to-date copy of the scheme rules.

The auditor may perform other procedures during his work which may help identify obligations to pay retirement benefits (for example, the review of board minutes or communications with employees).

29.5.2   Scheme assets

Scheme assets normally comprise one or more of the following:

- quoted securities;
- unquoted securities;
- unitised securities;
- insurance policies;
- loans and debt instruments; and
- freehold and leasehold properties.

The auditor may be able to obtain satisfactory evidence in respect of scheme assets without carrying out procedures on scheme asset records. Where there is a short period between the most recent scheme year end and the reporting entity's year end, and audited scheme financial statements are available, the auditor may be able to obtain sufficient audit evidence by:

- asking directors to reconcile the scheme assets valuation at the scheme year end date with the assets valuation at the reporting entity's date being used for accounting purposes;
- obtaining direct confirmation of the scheme assets from the investment custodian; and
- examining the key reconciling items (for example, contributions paid, benefits paid and estimated investment returns).

29.5.3   *Using the work of the scheme auditor*

Where the above reconciliation is not possible, it may be necessary to carry out procedures directly on the records of scheme assets. Although the entity auditor could perform this work himself (with the permission of directors and the scheme trustees), it may be more cost-effective to ask directors to arrange with the scheme trustees for the scheme auditor to carry it out, because of his familiarity with the scheme assets and accounting records.

The scheme auditor needs to perform additional procedures to those carried out in the audit of the scheme financial statements if:

- the scheme and reporting entity have different accounting periods. This could involve additional procedures to update his work on the audit of the scheme to the reporting entity's balance sheet date. Where the period between the different period ends is short and the scheme period end precedes that of the entity, the entity auditor may be able to obtain sufficient appropriate audit evidence of the scheme assets at the entity period end by reviewing major movements in scheme assets since the scheme period end; and
- the scheme and reporting entity have the same accounting period but the scheme financial statements will be audited at a date later than that of the reporting entity. Arrangements may be necessary to supply the entity auditor with the evidence he requires on a timely basis.

The entity auditor, with the permission of directors and scheme trustees, also needs to communicate with the scheme auditor at the planning stage of the audit to:

- confirm in writing the nature and extent of the scheme auditor's work;
- agree the materiality to be applied;
- agree a timetable for the scheme auditor to report to the entity auditor and the manner in which he is to report (the entity auditor, where practicable, requires the scheme auditor to provide a report of factual findings resulting from the specified procedures).

29.5.4   *Multi-employer schemes*

A multi-employer scheme is one where a number of employers participate in a single defined benefit scheme. Sometimes there is no clear allocation of scheme assets to specific employers and it may be difficult to attribute a reasonable share of the assets and liabilities to each employer. Different accounting frameworks have different rules as to how such schemes should be treated. The auditor needs to be careful to ensure that such schemes are appropriately classified for this purpose.

The auditor should ask directors and others (for example, actuaries) about how they concluded that the scheme was a multi-employer arrangement in which the entity's share of assets and liabilities cannot be identified. Where, for example, different employers within the scheme contribute at different rates this may suggest that a reasonable allocation of assets and liabilities is possible.

The auditor should also understand the principal provisions of these schemes and those circumstances (for example, wind up of the scheme) which could cause a scheme deficit and:

- a liability or contingent liability for the reporting entity; or
- possible going concern problems for the entity.

29.5.5   Scheme liabilities

The Practice Note covers the actuaries' role in determining scheme liabilities either by a full actuarial valuation (see **Chapter 44**) or an annual update. The auditor will need to use the work of actuaries as audit evidence. For this purpose, the actuary will normally be regarded as acting in the role of management's expert and the auditor will need to evaluate the actuary and his work in accordance with ISA (UK and Ireland) 500 *Audit evidence*. The role of management's experts is dealt with more fully in **23.3**.

29.5.6   Competence and objectivity of the actuary

The auditor should consider whether actuaries are members of an appropriate professional body. Where a foreign actuary is involved in work on retirement benefits, a UK professional body, such as the Institute of Actuaries or Faculty of Actuaries, can advise on the acceptability of the standards of overseas actuarial professional bodies.

Actuaries' objectivity should also be evaluated, particularly where they are employees of, or related to, the reporting entity.

29.5.7   The actuary's work as audit evidence

The auditor needs to consider a number of matters to evaluate the appropriateness of actuaries' work for his purposes, including:

- the source data used;
- the assumptions and methods used; and
- the results of actuaries' work in the light of the auditor's knowledge of the business and results of other audit procedures.

Actuarial source data is likely to include:

- scheme member data (for example, classes of member and contribution details); and
- scheme asset information (for example, values and income and expenditure items).

Directors are responsible for the source data used by actuaries. The auditor should discuss with directors and actuaries what has been done to establish that the data is relevant, reliable and sufficient. Where the auditor has concerns over the scope of such procedures, he may wish to perform his own procedures.

The nature, timing and extent of any additional procedures depends on:

- the nature of the data and its sensitivity to the actuarial valuation;
- the source of the data and the extent to which it has already been subjected to audit procedures (for example, by the entity auditor or the internal audit function); and
- actuaries' approach to verify the completeness and validity of the data.

29.5.8 Actuarial assumptions

Actuarial assumptions are estimates of future events that will affect the valuation of the scheme liabilities and the reporting entity's costs of retirement benefits (for example, mortality rates, termination rates, retirement age and changes in salary and benefit levels). Accounting frameworks generally state that the assumptions are the ultimate responsibility of directors but should be set upon advice given by actuaries.

The auditor will not have the same expertise as actuaries and is unlikely to be able to challenge the appropriateness and reasonableness of the assumptions. The auditor can, however, through discussion with directors and actuaries:

- obtain a general understanding of the assumptions and review the process used to develop them;
- compare the assumptions with those which directors have used in prior years;
- consider whether, based on his knowledge of the reporting entity and the scheme, and on the results of other audit procedures, the assumptions appear to be reasonable and compatible with those used elsewhere in the preparation of the entity's financial statements;
- consider whether estimates are consistent with those used by other entities in similar circumstances; and
- consider whether there is an indication of management bias in the selection of assumptions.

Depending on the significance to the entity's financial statements, the auditor may choose to obtain independent actuarial advice to provide additional assurance in respect of assumptions made and the calculation of pension liabilities.

29.5.9 *Assessing the results of the actuary's work*

There is no prescribed form for actuaries' reports on the results of their work. The pensions scheme figures required by the relevant accounting framework are normally provided in a letter or written report. Actuaries may also provide a commentary on other matters, such as:

- the movements since the previous valuation in the figures required for inclusion in the balance sheet and the profit and loss account;
- the possible variation in the valuation of the scheme liabilities and the implications for the financial statements and the audit; and
- the sensitivity of the results, funding level, scheme maturity and investments to variations in the source data and assumptions.

The auditor should obtain copies of all written communications from actuaries to directors concerning the findings of their work.

The auditor should also discuss with directors whether actuaries have indicated that:

- any matters have occurred in the period from the reporting entity's balance sheet date up to the date on which the valuation was completed that would have a material effect on the valuation; or
- there was a departure from relevant professional requirements or guidance issued by their professional body.

The auditor may request actuaries to:

- provide specific confirmation on the above points;
- comment on the degree of precision attaching to the valuation and factors giving rise to potential material misstatement;
- indicate whether the amounts and disclosures in the financial statements adequately reflect the results of their work.

Where the results of actuaries' work is inconsistent with other audit evidence, the auditor should discuss the inconsistency with the directors and actuaries. Additional procedures, such as requesting directors to obtain evidence from another actuary, may assist in resolving the inconsistency.

29.5.10 *Valuation of scheme liabilities and materiality*

The defined benefit asset (or liability) is based on the surplus (or deficit) of the value of the scheme assets over the value of scheme liabilities.

Generally, accepted actuarial techniques may give a range of acceptable values. The auditor may be faced with a large range arising from an unusual event (for example, the outcome of a recent court case, which could potentially have a significant effect on the scheme, cannot be established with certainty before the approval of the financial statements).

Both the Practice Note and the Technical Release stress the need for the auditor to check that financial statements contain sufficient disclosures about the actuarial assumptions. The auditor may, in exceptional circumstances, consider an explanatory paragraph in his report where the uncertainty caused by the range is unusually large.

29.5.11 Disclosures

The Practice Note makes clear that, where the auditor has concerns regarding the disclosures in the financial statements, he should discuss his views with directors. If this does not lead to the matter being resolved, the auditor may decide to communicate his concerns to those charged with governance (in accordance with ISA (UK and Ireland) 260 (Revised June 2016) *Communication with those charged with governance*) and consider the effect on his audit opinion (see **Chapter 10**).

29.5.12 Going concern

When evaluating going concern, directors consider all relevant information of which they are aware at the time they approve the financial statements, including events known or expected to occur more than a year beyond the date on which they approve the financial statements (for example, a scheme is inadequately funded to a significant extent and the defined benefit liability to be recognised in the balance sheet may be material). In these circumstances, the auditor would:

- enquire into the expected timing of the cash flows likely to arise as a result of this liability and how directors would fund these payments; and
- consider whether the recognition of the defined benefit liability may cause the reporting entity to breach any existing loan covenant.

Under ISA (UK and Ireland) 570 (Revised June 2016) *Going concern*, the auditor should assess how directors have satisfied themselves that the going concern basis and any related disclosures are appropriate.

29.5.13 Distributable profits

The auditor should be aware of the potential problem arising where the individual financial statements of the reporting entity show a defined benefit liability so large that it reduces realised profits below that needed to cover any intended distribution.

ISA (UK and Ireland) 250 (Revised June 2016) Section A *Consideration of laws and regulations in an audit of financial statements* requires the auditor to obtain sufficient appropriate audit evidence about compliance with those laws and regulations relating directly to the preparation of, or the inclusion or disclosure of specific items in, the financial statements.

If the auditor becomes aware that there may be insufficient realised profits to make a proposed distribution, he normally discusses his concerns with directors and advises them of the potential consequences of making a potentially unlawful distribution. Directors and the auditor may wish to consult their respective legal advisers. If directors are unable to dispel the auditor's concerns and do not modify the proposed distribution, the auditor should consider the implications of this disagreement for his report. This may result in the auditor issuing a qualified or adverse opinion.

29.5.14   Management representations

ISA (UK and Ireland) 580 *Written representations* requires the auditor to obtain written confirmation of management representations on matters material to the financial statements when those representations are critical to obtaining sufficient appropriate audit evidence. Management representations cannot, however, be a substitute for other audit evidence.

Examples of typical representations which may be obtained by the entity auditor are shown in **Table 3**.

TABLE 3: Typical management representations

- actuarial assumptions underlying the valuation of scheme liabilities are consistent with the entity directors' knowledge of the business;
- all significant retirement benefits, including any arrangements that:
    - are statutory, contractual or implicit in the employer's actions;
    - arise in the UK and the Republic of Ireland or overseas;
    - are funded or unfunded;
    - are approved or unapproved;
    - have been identified and properly accounted for; and
- all settlements and curtailments have been identified and properly accounted for.

29.6   Smaller entities with insured schemes

The Practice Note is intended to apply to auditors of all reporting entities and all types and sizes of defined benefit scheme (although some of the guidance may be more relevant to auditors of entities with significant and complex retirement benefit arrangements). These entities usually have well-resourced actuaries available but are often also subject to tight reporting deadlines (for example, listed companies).

The situation for smaller reporting entities is often quite different. Their retirement benefit arrangements may often be less complex and they generally enjoy a more relaxed reporting timetable. This may allow more time for directors and actuaries to comply with the requirements of the accounting framework and allows the auditor more time to obtain the necessary audit evidence.

A smaller reporting entity's occupational pension scheme is, however, sometimes administered by an insurance company with the only scheme asset an insurance policy (a 'fully insured scheme'). Scheme actuaries will usually be an employee of the insurance company and directors will probably ask the insurance company and its in-house actuary to provide the information for compliance with the relevant accounting framework.

In such circumstances, the auditor should consider whether:

- the insurance company will be able to supply directors with values of the scheme assets and liabilities as at the entity balance sheet date, where it differs from the scheme year-end date;
- it will be appropriate for them to communicate with the insurance company's actuary;
- the basis to be used by the insurance company to value the insurance policies will represent 'the best approximation to fair value' under the relevant accounting framework: a surrender value will not be appropriate unless the trustees have decided to surrender the policy or wind up the scheme;
- 'earmarked' insurance policies (for example, deferred annuity policies), excluded from the accounts of the scheme in accordance with statutory exemptions, will have been valued and included in the fair value of scheme assets to comply with the relevant accounting framework; and
- evidence will be available to support the basis for valuing the insurance policy as at the entity balance sheet date.

Where the insurance company is unable to provide a valuation of an insurance policy as at the reporting entity balance sheet date, directors might decide to adjust the most recently obtained valuation for contributions received and benefits paid, also allowing for investment returns. The basis of this approach would need to be clearly disclosed in the notes to the financial statements.

The fact that the auditor is not able to discuss matters with actuaries does not of itself give rise to a need to qualify the auditor's opinion on the financial statements as the auditor may be able to obtain sufficient appropriate evidence by:

- discussing the matters with directors; and
- reviewing any correspondence between directors and actuaries.

30 AUDITS OF GROUP FINANCIAL STATEMENTS

30.1 Introduction

This chapter examines those situations where the auditor acts as auditor of a set of group financial statements and relies on audit work performed by other auditors on financial information of components of the group. The chapter does not cover reliance on internal audit functions or on experts, these are covered in **Chapter 31**.

30.2 Auditing standards and guidance

This chapter has been updated to reflect the changes contained in final draft ISAs issued by the FRC in April 2016. Subject to legislative changes in progress at the time of writing, it is expected that ISA (UK and Ireland) 600 (Revised June 2016) *Special considerations – audits of group financial statements (including the work of component auditors)* will take effect for periods commencing on or after 17 June 2016. For earlier periods, ending on or after 15 December 2010, the version of ISA (UK and Ireland) 600 *Special considerations – audits of group financial statements (including the work of component auditors)* issued in October 2009 applies.

Changes in the 2016 version include Audit Directive requirements regarding responsibilities of the group engagement team. These include specific requirements for confirming the component auditor's independence and for the component auditor transferring relevant documentation to the group engagement team. Both these issues are covered in **30.8**.

The ISA sets standards for auditors and provides guidance covering:

- responsibilities;
- acceptance and continuance as group engagement team;
- overall audit strategy and audit plan;
- understanding the group, its components and their environments;
- understanding the component auditor;
- materiality;
- responding to assessed risks;
- consolidation process;
- subsequent events;
- communication with the component auditor;
- evaluating the sufficiency and appropriateness of audit evidence obtained;

- communication with group management and those charged with governance of the group; and
- documentation.

In November 2013, the ICAEW issued *Auditing Groups: A Practical Guide*, replacing an earlier version issued in 2008. This guide draws on the experience of auditors who have acted as both group and component auditors to provide additional practical guidance on some of the more challenging aspects of ISA (UK and Ireland) 600 (Revised June 2016). Supplementary Material relating to the component auditor's report to the group engagement team was published in March 2014. Further details are set out in **30.17** below.

30.3 Definitions

A 'component' of a group is an entity or business unit for which financial information that should be included in the group accounts is prepared. A component may be a separate legal entity such as a subsidiary, joint venture or associate or it may be a branch or division of an entity which prepares financial information separately from the remainder of the entity.

A 'significant component' is a component determined by the group engagement team to be of such significance to the group, by virtue either of its size or its circumstances, that it is likely to include significant risks of material misstatement of the group financial statements.

A 'component auditor' is the person or firm who provides an audit opinion on the financial information of a component, on which reliance is placed by the group engagement team. This may be another firm (which may or may not be a member of the group engagement team's network) or may be another office or audit team from the auditor's own firm.

The 'group engagement team' is the partners, including the group engagement partner, and staff who formulate the overall group audit strategy and plan, communicate with component auditors as necessary and perform the work on the consolidation necessary to form an overall audit opinion on the group financial statements.

30.4 Responsibilities

ISA (UK and Ireland) 600 (Revised June 2016) sets out that although component auditors may perform work on the financial information of the components for the group audit, and as such are responsible for their overall findings, conclusions and opinions, it is the group engagement partner who is responsible for the direction, supervision and performance of the group audit and for the group audit opinion.

The ISA does not deal specifically with the situation where the group audit is carried out by two or more auditors acting as joint auditors.

30.5   Acceptance and continuance

ISA (UK and Ireland) 600 (Revised June 2016) requires that, before deciding to act for a particular organisation, the group engagement partner should consider whether sufficient appropriate audit evidence can reasonably be expected to be obtained in relation to the consolidation process and the financial information of the components on which to base the group opinion.

In order to do this, the auditor should consider:

- the group structure including how the financial reporting system is organised;
- the industry and the regulatory, economic and political environments in which the significant components' business activities take place;
- the use of service organisations;
- a description of group-wide controls;
- the complexity of the consolidation process;
- whether any of the component auditors are from outside the group engagement team's firm or network;
- whether the group engagement team will have unrestricted access to the management and those charged with governance of both the group and the components as well as the component auditors; and
- whether the group engagement team will be able to perform necessary work on the financial information of the components.

This is intended to ensure that the group engagement team is sufficiently involved with the component auditors to the extent necessary to obtain sufficient appropriate audit evidence. If they feel that they are not sufficiently involved, they should either not accept appointment or take appropriate action to ensure that they have sufficient involvement.

30.6   Overall audit strategy and audit plan

ISA (UK and Ireland) 600 (Revised June 2016) requires the group engagement team to formulate an overall audit strategy and audit plan for the group as a whole. This is to be reviewed by the group engagement partner.

In respect of any component considered to be a significant component, the plan should include an audit of the financial information relating to that component. In respect of components that are not significant components, the group engagement team should determine the nature and extent of work to be done in order to obtain sufficient appropriate evidence for group audit purposes. This may involve a full audit (for example where an audit is required for local statutory purposes anyway) or it may be limited in scope to relate only to those matters that are considered to be of greatest relevance to the group audit. For components that are individually and collectively material, it may be possible for the group engagement team to obtain sufficient evidence by performing review procedures and making enquiries without involving a component auditor.

It is important, when planning a group audit, to ensure that the involvement of component auditors and the role of the group audit team in directing their work is established and communicated at an early stage.

30.7   Understanding the group, its components and their environments

The auditor is required to identify and assess the risks of material misstatement through obtaining an understanding of the entity and its environment. The ISA requires the group engagement team to perform procedures to update its understanding of the group, its components and their environments, and also to obtain an understanding of management's consolidation process. This understanding should be sufficient to confirm, or revise, the group engagement team's initial identification of significant components and to assess the risks of material misstatement to the group financial statements. Areas requiring an understanding include:

* group-wide controls, including internal audit functions;
* the consolidation process, including:

    - the instructions issued by group management to components;
    - matters relating to the applicable financial reporting framework;
    - the group's processes for ensuring complete, accurate and timely financial reporting by the components;
    - the process for recording consolidation adjustments;
    - the consolidation adjustments required by the applicable financial reporting framework; and
    - procedures for monitoring, controlling, reconciling and eliminating intra-group transactions and unrealised profits, and intra-group account balances.

ISA (UK and Ireland) 240 (Revised June 2016) requires the key members of the engagement team to discuss the susceptibility of the entity's financial statements to material misstatement due to fraud. In a group audit, these discussions may include the component auditors. The group engagement partner determines who to include in these discussions based on a number of factors including his prior experience with the group.

From this work, the group engagement team should determine which components are likely to be significant and assess the risks of material misstatement in the group financial statements.

30.8   Understanding the component auditor

ISA (UK and Ireland) 600 (Revised June 2016) requires the group engagement team to consider the professional competence of the component auditor in the context of the assignment including whether they understand, and will comply with, the ethical requirements that are relevant to the group audit, and in particular is independent. The group engagement team also considers whether they will be able to be involved with the work of the component auditor to the extent necessary and whether the component auditor operates in a regulatory environment which actively oversees auditors.

If a component auditor does not meet the relevant independence requirements or the group engagement team has serious concerns about the other matters noted above, the group engagement team needs to obtain sufficient appropriate audit evidence relating to the financial information of the component without asking the component auditor to perform any work.

The component auditor is also asked to agree to transfer any relevant documentation to the group engagement team during the audit of the group financial statements. If this request is refused, the group engagement team will be unable to rely on the work of the component auditor.

There are various factors that affect the group engagement team's assessment of the component auditors, including:

- previous experience of their work;
- any affiliation of the other firm;
- membership of relevant professional bodies;
- the resources available to the component auditor to perform the necessary work; and
- discussions with the component auditors.

These factors are not mutually exclusive and the group engagement team considers them together when gaining his understanding of component auditors, as shown in the example below.

Example

The auditor of component A consistently applies quality control and monitoring policies and procedures and a methodology which are in common with the group engagement team's or he operates in the same jurisdiction as the group engagement team.

The auditor of component B does not have quality control and monitoring policies and procedures or a methodology which are the same as those of the group engagement team and/or he operates in a foreign jurisdiction.

The extent of the group engagement team's procedures to obtain an understanding of each component is likely to vary. The procedures for component A's auditor are likely to be less than those required to obtain an understanding of component B's auditor. The nature of the procedures performed in relation to each component is also likely to differ.

30.9 Materiality

ISA (UK and Ireland) 600 (Revised June 2016) requires the group engagement team to determine:

- the materiality level for the group financial statements as a whole;
- any materiality level to be applied to particular classes of transactions, account balances or disclosures which are lower than the general materiality level;
- materiality for individual components; and
- the threshold above which misstatements cannot be regarded as clearly trivial to the group financial statements. This will normally be the level at which the component auditor will be requested to report any identified misstatements to the group engagement team.

Where a component is also subject to a local statutory audit requirement it is likely that the component auditor will want to use a materiality level lower than that which the group engagement team considers to be appropriate for group purposes. This is generally not a problem. Problems may arise, however, where the group engagement team specifies a materiality level lower than that which would normally be used by the component auditor. In this case the matter needs to be resolved by discussion with the component auditor.

30.10 Responding to assessed risks

It is the role of the group engagement team to determine the type of work to be performed by the group engagement team, or the component auditors on its behalf. The group engagement team also needs to determine the nature, timing and extent of its involvement in the work of any component auditors. The type of audit procedures to be performed in relation to components and the level of involvement the group engagement team will have in the component auditor's work will depend on the:

- significance of the component;
- identified significant risks of material misstatement of the group financial statements;
- group engagement team's evaluation of the design of group-wide controls and determination of whether they have been implemented; and
- group engagement team's understanding of the component auditor.

Where individual components are not significant, either in terms of size or a significant risk of material misstatement, ISA (UK and Ireland) 600 (Revised June 2016) requires only that analytical procedures at group level need be performed. The group engagement team may supplement this as required with additional procedures relating to the component, performed either by the group engagement team or the component auditor on their behalf.

The diagram in **Table 1** shows how the significance of the component affects the group engagement team's determination of the type of work to be performed on the financial information of the component.

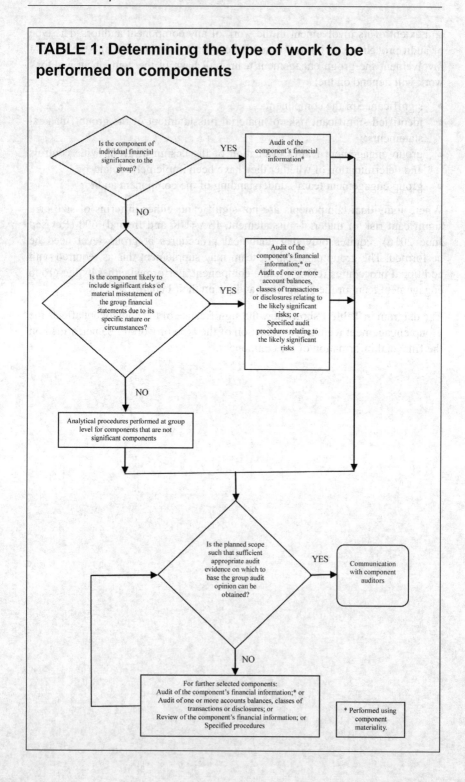

TABLE 1: Determining the type of work to be performed on components

Is the component of individual financial significance to the group?

YES → Audit of the component's financial information*

NO

Is the component likely to include significant risks of material misstatement of the group financial statements due to its specific nature or circumstances?

YES → Audit of the component's financial information;* or Audit of one or more account balances, classes of transactions or disclosures relating to the likely significant risks; or Specified audit procedures relating to the likely significant risks

NO

Analytical procedures performed at group level for components that are not significant components

Is the planned scope such that sufficient appropriate audit evidence on which to base the group audit opinion can be obtained?

YES → Communication with component auditors

NO

For further selected components:
Audit of the component's financial information;* or
Audit of one or more accounts balances, classes of transactions or disclosures; or
Review of the component's financial information; or
Specified procedures

* Performed using component materiality.

30.11   The consolidation process

The group engagement team is required by ISA (UK and Ireland) 600 (Revised June 2016) to design and perform further audit procedures to respond to the risk of material misstatement of the group financial statements arising from the consolidation process. The group engagement team's evaluation of the appropriateness, completeness and accuracy of the consolidation adjustments may include:

- evaluating whether significant adjustments appropriately reflect the events and transactions underlying them;
- determining whether significant adjustments have been correctly calculated, processed and authorised by group management and, where applicable, component management;
- determining whether significant adjustments are properly supported by documentation; and
- checking reconciliations and eliminations of intra-group transactions and balances.

30.12   Subsequent events

ISA (UK and Ireland) 600 (Revised June 2016) requires either the group engagement team or the component auditors to identify any events that occur between the dates on which they reported on the financial information of the components and the date of the auditor's report on the group financial statements, where those events may require adjustment to, or disclosure in, the group financial statements.

30.13   Communication with the component auditor

The group engagement team should communicate with the component auditor on a timely basis, setting out the work to be performed, what use is to be made of that work and what form reports back to the group engagement team should take. The ISA states that the group audit team should:

- request that the component auditor confirms that he will cooperate with the group engagement team;
- set out the ethical requirements[1] that are relevant to the group audit;
- set out relevant materiality levels and reporting thresholds;
- identify risks of material misstatement to the group financial statements that are relevant to the component auditor; and

---

[1] For UK entities, the relevant ethical requirements will be the FRC's Ethical Standards and the ICAEW's Code of Ethics. Where component audits are carried out overseas, it may be appropriate to ask component auditors to confirm compliance with IESBA's Code of Ethics.

- provide a list of related parties prepared by group management, and any other related parties of which the group engagement team is aware.

The group engagement team should request that the component auditor communicates the following matters back to the group engagement team:

- whether he has complied with ethical requirements that are relevant to the group audit, including independence and professional competence;
- whether he has complied with the group engagement team's requirements;
- identification of the financial information of the component on which the component auditor is reporting;
- information on instances of non-compliance with laws and regulations that could give rise to a material misstatement of the group financial statements;
- a list of uncorrected misstatements of the financial information of the component (the list does not need to include those misstatements below the level of 'clearly trivial' communicated to the component auditor by the group engagement team);
- indicators of possible management bias;
- any identified significant deficiencies in internal control at component level;
- other significant matters that the component auditor has, or expects to, communicate to those charged with governance;
- any other matters relevant to the group audit, including exceptions noted in the written representations from component management; and
- the component auditor's overall conclusion or opinion.

If effective two-way communication between the group and component auditors does not happen, there is a risk that the group engagement team may not obtain sufficient appropriate audit evidence on which to base the group's audit opinion.

In addition to two-way communication, cooperation between auditors is also needed.

For UK subsidiaries (of a UK group), the component auditors have a statutory duty to communicate such information and explanations as may be reasonably required by the group engagement team. Where there is no such obligation, the component auditors should obtain the permission of the component's management before giving such assistance.

Where the component auditors have been unable to conclude on a matter, or feel that there is something that should be brought to the attention of the group engagement team, they should do so bearing in mind their statutory obligation as noted above.

There is no complementary obligation, but the group engagement team may inform component auditors of such matters if they consider it appropriate after due consultation with those charged with governance at the parent entity.

30.14 Evaluating the sufficiency and appropriateness of audit evidence

The group engagement team should consider the communication with the component auditor (in **30.13** above) and discuss significant findings arising from that evaluation with the component auditor, component management or group management, as appropriate. They also consider whether it is necessary to review other relevant parts of the component auditor's audit documentation.

If the group engagement team concludes the work of the component auditor is insufficient, the group engagement team determines what additional procedures are necessary, and whether they are to be performed by the group engagement team or the component auditors.

The Audit Directive specifically requires that for audits of group financial statements, the group engagement team shall:

(a) evaluate the audit work performed by the component auditor for the purpose of the group audit; and

(b) either:

    (i) review the audit work performed by the component auditor for the purpose of the group audit; or

    (ii) where the group engagement team is unable to do such a review, the group engagement team takes appropriate measures and informs the relevant competent authority[2]. Such measures shall, as appropriate, include carrying out additional audit work, either directly or by outsourcing such tasks, in the relevant component.

30.15 Communication with those charged with governance of the group

The group engagement team needs to determine which identified deficiencies in internal control to communicate to those charged with governance and group management. In making this decision, the group engagement team will consider deficiencies in internal control:

- identified by the group engagement team that affect the whole group;
- identified by the group engagement team that affect components; and
- identified by component auditors that affect components.

If fraud has been identified by the group engagement team or informed to the group engagement team by any of the component auditors, this should be reported to management of the group on a timely basis.

---

[2] The competent authority is the FRC although for non-public interest audits certain regulatory tasks may be delegated to the auditor's Recognised Supervisory Body.

In addition to those items required by ISA (UK and Ireland) 260 (Revised June 2016) and detailed in **Chapter 10**, ISA (UK and Ireland) 600 (Revised June 2016) requires the group engagement team to communicate the following to those charged with governance of the group:

- an overview of the type of work to be performed on the financial information of the components;
- an overview of the nature of the group engagement team's planned involvement in the work to be performed by the component auditors of significant components;
- instances where the group engagement team's evaluation of the work of a component auditor gave rise to a concern about the quality of that auditor's work;
- any limitations on the group audit, for example, where the group engagement team's access to information may have been restricted; and
- fraud or suspected fraud involving group management, component management, employees who have significant roles in group-wide controls or others where the fraud resulted in a material misstatement of the group financial statements.

The revised ISA specifically notes that for group financial statements, the group engagement partner's firm bears the full responsibility for the additional report to the audit committee as required by ISA (UK and Ireland) 260 (Revised June 2016) and covered in **10.7.2**.

30.15.1   Public interest entities

For public interest entities, there is certain information regarding the component audits that the group engagement team is also required to include in the additional report to the audit committee as detailed in **10.7.2**.

30.16   Documentation

ISA (UK and Ireland) 600 (Revised June 2016) requires the group engagement team to include the following in their audit documentation:

- an analysis of components, indicating those that are significant, and the type of work performed on the financial information of the components;
- the nature, timing and extent of the group engagement team's involvement in the work performed by the component auditors on significant components including, where applicable, the group engagement team's review of relevant parts of the component auditors' audit documentation and conclusions thereon;
- sufficient and appropriate documentation to enable a competent authority to review the work of the auditor of the group financial statements; and
- written communications between the group engagement team and the component auditors about the group engagement team's requirements.

Where the group engagement team is subject to a quality assurance review or an investigation concerning the group audit and the competent authority is unable to obtain documentation of the work carried out by a component auditor from a non-EEA member state and then requests such additional documentation of the work performed by that component auditor for the purpose of the group audit, the group engagement team shall, in order to comply with this request, either:

(a) keep copies of the documentation of the work carried out by the component auditor for the purpose of the group audit (including the component auditor's working papers relevant to the group audit);

(b) obtain the agreement of the component auditor that the group engagement team shall have unrestricted access to such documentation on request;

(c) retain documentation to show that the group engagement team has undertaken appropriate procedures to gain access to the audit documentation, together with evidence supporting the existence of any impediments to such access; or

(d) take any other appropriate action.

Table 2, below, also provides some examples of documentation that may be sent to component auditors.

TABLE 2: Possible documentation to send to component auditors

This is not a definitive list and should be tailored to the circumstances of the individual group.

Referral instructions

Including:

- timetable for the work;
- details of component(s) to be audited together with required scope of work, arrangements for coordination of work at the planning stage and during the audit, including the group engagement team's involvement in their work;
- any other known related parties;
- level of materiality and threshold for 'clearly trivial' misstatements;
- details of specific risks and areas of focus for the group audit, including fraud risks and specific procedures required including work to be done on intra-group transactions and balances and the work to be done on subsequent events;
- description of any group-wide controls including any testing by the group engagement team relevant to the work of other auditors, work by the internal audit function; and
- details of the applicable financial reporting framework, auditing standards and any other statutory reporting responsibilities, including group accounting policies and applicable laws and regulations.

Letter from other auditor acknowledging instructions

Including:

- the use that will be made of their work and that they will perform the work required;
- confirmation of independence and, for unrelated firms, of whether the quality control system complies with ISQC (UK and Ireland) 1[1] and any relevant issues noted in recent monitoring reports;
- confirmation of understanding of the applicable financial reporting framework and auditing standards.

Specimen reports to the group engagement team

Including:

- template for planning memorandum to describe proposed audit approach;
- template for clearance memos, summary memoranda and/or questionnaires to report findings including significant accounting, financial reporting and auditing matters including accounting estimates and related judgments, going concern matters;
- template for specimen management letter/report to those charged with governance of components including details of any significant deficiencies in internal control and/or for reporting such issues to the group engagement team;
- template for reporting uncorrected misstatements;
- template for reporting any actual fraud or information obtained that indicates a fraud may exist, including any suspected or alleged fraud affecting the component and any instances of non-compliance with laws and regulations that may have a material effect on the group financial statements;
- template for reporting audit component auditor's opinion on financial information of the component;
- subsequent events review sign-off; and
- confirmation of independence including details of fees for non-audit services.

[1] For component auditors based outside the UK, it may be appropriate to refer instead to ISQC 1 as issued by the IAASB.

30.17   ICAEW practical guidance

In November 2013, the Audit and Assurance Faculty of the ICAEW published *Auditing Groups: A Practical Guide,* to provide practical guidance on some of the more challenging aspects of group audits. The guidance was based on the experience of auditors who have acted as both group and component auditors and replaces previous guidance documents on group audits issued by the ICAEW. It does not, however, address all the requirements of ISA (UK and Ireland) 600 (Revised June 2016) and is not a substitute for the ISA in any way. Supplementary material dealing with the component auditor's report to the group engagement team was issued in March 2014.

The guide is split into sections which are then divided further as follows:

- Section 1: Planning

  - Part A – Planning: scoping and materiality

    - Overview and summary: scoping and materiality
    - Evaluating component auditor competence and independence and the standards they apply
    - Determining the coverage of components and the work to be performed
    - Materiality
    - Group engagement team's involvement in the work of component auditors
    - The appropriate level of work effort and evaluating component auditors and their work

  - Part B – Planning: communications and group audit instructions

    - Overview and summary: communications
    - Two-way communications between group and component auditors
    - The component auditors' view
    - Communications between group engagement team and group management and those charged with governance

  - Part C – Planning: logistics

    - Overview and summary: logistics
    - Documentation
    - Logistics proper
    - Timelines
    - Budgets and the cost of work on associates
    - Access to working papers and component auditor reports to the group engagement team

- Section 2: Execution

  - Part A – Execution: auditing the consolidation

    - Overview and summary: auditing the consolidation
    - Obtaining an understanding
    - Group instructions
    - Testing the consolidation process
    - Consolidation adjustments
    - Different accounting policies

  - Part B – Execution: review of component auditor work

    - Visits to component auditors
    - Documentation
    - Suggestions for reviewing component auditor documentation

- Part C – Execution: shared service centres

  - Understanding the use of shared service centres
  - Obtaining evidence regarding the operations of service centres

- Section 3: Completion and reporting

  - Reporting by component auditors and other completion procedures

    - Overview and summary: reporting by component auditors
    - Component auditor audit reports to the group engagement team
    - Component auditor reports on specified procedures
    - Memoranda of work performed and group audit questionnaires
    - Representation letters
    - Subsequent events
    - Evaluating evidence obtained
    - Archiving and retaining component auditor documentation

- Section 4: Specific issues

  - Non-conterminous year ends, inconsistent accounting policies, 'letterbox' companies, subsidiary audit exemption

    - Overview and summary: specific issues
    - Non-conterminous year ends
    - Aligning inconsistent accounting policies
    - 'Letterbox' companies
    - Subsidiary audit exemption

- Supplementary material

  - Component auditor reports to the group engagement team for group audit purposes: matters for consideration and illustrative reports

30.18 International developments

In 2014, the IAASB set up a project with the aim of looking at issues relating to group audits, including feedback from inspection reports of regulators.

A Staff Practice Alert *Responsibilities of the Engagement Partner in Circumstances when the Engagement Partner Is Not Located Where the Majority of the Audit Work is Performed* was issued in March 2015. Whilst this provides useful reading, it is not a substitute for the ISA.

This paper aims to address concerns related to the performance of audits when the engagement partner is not located where the majority of the audit work is performed, for example, when an entity is structured such that the entity is legally registered in one jurisdiction and the majority of the general and financial management, business activities and transaction processing are undertaken in a different jurisdiction. In these circumstances, the group engagement partner and group engagement team may be located where the entity is legally registered, with the majority of the audit work being performed in the other jurisdiction(s). Because the engagement partner is not physically located where the audit work is being performed, meeting the objectives of the ISAs can pose different challenges than in situations when the engagement partner is located where the majority of the work is performed. In particular, concerns have been raised about how the engagement partner has taken responsibility for the direction, supervision, performance and review of the work, the adequacy of the audit documentation and whether, and how, the engagement partner has become satisfied that sufficient appropriate audit evidence has been obtained to enable the engagement partner to take responsibility for the auditor's report in these circumstances.

The project is now working on the broader aspects of group audits and a document entitled *Enhancing Audit Quality in the Public Interest* was issued for comment in December 2015. Responses to this document will shape the future output of the project.

31 RELIANCE ON OTHERS

31.1 Introduction

This chapter examines situations where the auditor relies on others for part of the audit evidence. It examines reliance on:

- the internal audit function; and
- experts.

The chapter does not cover the audit of group financial statements and reliance on component auditors, these are covered in **Chapter 30**. Nor does it cover the situation where the auditor relies on work performed by an expert appointed by management ('management's expert'); this is covered in **Chapter 23**.

31.2 Internal audit function

31.2.1 Auditing Standards

The latest version of ISA (UK and Ireland) 610 (Revised June 2013) *Using the work of internal auditors* was issued in June 2013 and is effective for the audit of financial statements for periods ending on or after 15 June 2014. This ISA was not included in the final draft of revised ISAs issued by the FRC in April 2016, and as such, the 2013 version remains applicable.

The ISA covers:

- determining whether, in which areas, and to what extent the work of the internal audit function can be used;
- using the work of the internal audit function; and
- documentation.

The ISA also covers determining whether, in which areas, and to what extent an internal auditor can be used to provide direct assistance and then further detail on using the internal auditor to provide the direct assistance. However, this is prohibited under ISAs (UK and Ireland) as explained in **31.2.5**.

31.2.2 Understanding the internal audit function

Even where the entity has an internal audit function, the auditor is not required to use its work to modify the nature or timing, or reduce the extent of audit procedures to be performed directly by the external auditor. Use of the internal audit function remains a decision of the auditor in establishing his overall audit strategy.

However, where an internal audit function exists, in accordance with ISA (UK and Ireland) 315 (Revised June 2016), the auditor must make inquiries of appropriate individuals within the internal audit function as part of his risk assessment. In addition, regardless of whether he plans to use the work of internal audit, he must obtain an understanding of the nature of the function's responsibilities, its organisational status, and the activities performed, or to be performed. The auditor should document his inquiries and understanding of the internal audit function as part of his understanding of the entity and its environment, and his identification and assessment of risks of material misstatement (see **Chapter 21**).

The objectives and scope of an internal audit function, the nature of its responsibilities and its status within the entity, all vary widely from entity to entity. These matters depend on the size and structure of the entity and the requirements of management and those charged with governance. Depending on the responsibilities of the internal audit function, it may play an important role in the entity's monitoring of internal control over financial reporting. Equally, however, its responsibilities may be more focused on evaluating the efficiency and effectiveness of operations and if so, its work may not relate directly to the entity's financial reporting.

The auditor's inquiries of appropriate individuals within the internal audit function help him to obtain an understanding of the nature of the internal audit function's responsibilities. If he determines that the function's responsibilities are related to the entity's financial reporting, he may obtain further understanding of the activities performed, or to be performed, by the internal audit function and may then determine whether to use this work (see **31.2.3**).

Establishing communications with the appropriate individuals within an entity's internal audit function early in the engagement, and maintaining such communications throughout the engagement, can facilitate effective sharing of information. It creates an environment in which the auditor can be informed of significant matters that may come to the attention of the internal audit function when such matters may affect the work of the auditor.

31.2.3   Use of the work of the internal audit function

The internal audit function is defined by the ISA as 'a function of an entity that performs assurance and consulting activities designed to evaluate and improve the effectiveness of the entity's governance, risk management and internal control processes'. It requires that the external auditor considers the activities of this function and their effect, if any, on external audit procedures, although it does not relieve him of any of his responsibilities.

The activities of an internal audit function may include:

- assessment of the governance process in its accomplishment of objectives on ethics and values, performance management and accountability;

- identifying and evaluating significant exposures to risk and contributing to the improvement of risk management and internal control;
- performing procedures to assist the entity in the detection of fraud;
- reviewing controls, evaluating their operation and recommending improvements;
- examination of financial and operating information;
- review of the economy, efficiency and effectiveness of operations; and
- review of the compliance with laws, regulations and other external requirements and with management policies and directives.

Some of these activities will concern non-financial information and as such will not generally be of direct relevance to the external auditor. The level of precision that an internal auditor works to, may also be higher than that of the external auditor who is primarily concerned with material misstatement in the financial statements, but some of the methods used will be common.

Some entities will sub-contract the internal audit function to a third party but as this is still within the control of the entity, the external auditor may consider its impact on his own procedures.

Where the entity has an internal audit function and the external auditor expects to use the work of that function to modify the nature or timing, or reduce the extent, of audit procedures to be performed directly by the external auditor, the external auditor must:

(a) determine whether the work of the internal audit function can be used, and if so, in which areas and to what extent; and having made that determination:

(b) if using the work of the internal audit function, determine whether that work is adequate for purposes of the audit.

The external auditor should obtain a sufficient understanding of the activities of the internal audit function to identify and assess the risks of material misstatement of the financial statements and to design and perform further audit procedures.

Where an internal audit function is effective, the external auditor may be able to reduce the extent of his own testing. However, he will not be able to rely solely on the work of the internal audit function to the extent of performing no additional testing himself. Additionally, if the internal audit function is effective this may be a consideration in the external auditor's assessment of the entity's control environment and risk assessment.

Evaluating the internal audit function

In order to determine whether, and to what extent the work of the internal audit function can be used, the external auditor needs to firstly evaluate the internal audit function.

The ISA sets out the criteria the auditor should use to make this evaluation. The external auditor should concentrate on the:

- extent to which the function's organisational status and relevant policies and procedures support the objectivity of the internal audit function;
- technical competence of the persons performing the work; and
- application of a systematic and disciplined approach to planning, performing, supervising, reviewing and documenting the work of the internal audit function.

The external auditor's evaluation of these criteria may indicate that the risks to the quality of the work of the function are too significant and that it is therefore not appropriate to use any of the work of the function as audit evidence.

In making this evaluation, it is important to consider the factors in aggregate since an individual factor may in itself not lead the auditor to the same conclusion as if that factor were considered in the light of others.

Determining the nature and extent of work of the internal audit function that can be used

Having determined that the work of the internal audit function can be used for purposes of the audit, the external auditor should consider whether the planned nature and scope of the internal audit function's work is relevant to his overall audit strategy and audit plan.

Examples of work of the internal audit function that may be used by the auditor include:

- testing of the operating effectiveness of controls;
- substantive procedures involving limited judgment;
- observations of inventory counts;
- tracing transactions through the information system relevant to financial reporting;
- testing of compliance with regulatory requirements; and
- in some circumstances, audits or reviews of the financial information of subsidiaries that are not significant components to the group.

Even where using the work of the internal audit function, the external auditor must still make all the significant judgments in the engagement and should therefore plan to perform more of the work himself in areas where:

- more judgment is involved, for example, in evaluating significant accounting estimates;
- he considers there to be a higher risk of material misstatement or where significant risks have been identified;
- the level of competence of the internal audit function is lower; and
- the organisational status and relevant policies and procedures of the function support their objectivity to a lesser degree.

Of course, in the latter two situations, the auditor would need to consider carefully whether any reliance on the internal audit function was appropriate.

The auditor also needs to evaluate whether, in aggregate, using the work of the internal audit function to the extent planned would still result in him being sufficiently involved in the audit, given his sole responsibility for the audit opinion. In addition, the external auditor needs to include in his communication with those charged with governance how he has planned to use the work of the internal audit function.

31.2.4   Using the work of the internal audit function

Where the external auditor plans to use the work of the internal audit function, he needs to:

- agree the timing, nature, extent of the work with the internal audit function as well as discussing materiality, sample methods, documentation and review and reporting procedures;
- read the reports of the internal audit function that relate to the work the auditor plans to use to obtain an understanding of the nature and extent of the audit procedures performed by the internal audit function and the related findings;
- perform sufficient audit procedures on the internal audit function's work to determine its adequacy for purposes of the audit;
- reperform some of the internal audit function's work; and
- determine whether his initial evaluation of the internal audit function and the appropriateness of their work to the audit remains valid.

Coordination of the timing of the two auditors' work is best achieved by regular meetings throughout the year. This will normally ensure that the external auditor is made aware of any relevant matters as they come to light. The process also works in reverse, particularly at the end of the external audit when there may be matters in the report to management which are of concern to the internal audit function.

Table 1 gives examples of two scenarios and details the reliance that may be placed on the work of an internal audit function in each situation.

If the external auditor concludes that the internal audit function's work is not adequate for his purposes, he should consider what additional procedures of his own are necessary in order to have sufficient appropriate evidence to form an opinion.

TABLE 1: Evaluating the work of the internal audit function

Case A

An internal audit function is staffed by a number of qualified accountants. Reports go to the audit committee. Their programme of work consists of, among other things, systems checks and periodic audits of branch returns. The external auditor receives reports as and when produced.

Case B

Internal audits are carried out on a part-time basis by the controller of one subsidiary. Work is mainly of an ad hoc nature, looking at problem areas both in terms of control and efficiency and producing reports for the finance director.

Extent of reliance

Based upon the facts set out above, the possible extent of reliance in Case A would appear to be far greater than in Case B. The auditor may seek to rely on work performed on the internal control systems by the internal audit function together with some of the checks carried out during the audits of branch returns.

In contrast, in Case B, the opportunities for reliance on the internal audit function would be greatly reduced. Some reliance may be possible in areas reported on which have relevance to the external audit. However, because of the status of the internal audit function and its method of operation, there would probably be less reliance and a greater level of procedures in the relevant area.

31.2.5 Direct assistance

Direct assistance is defined as the use of an internal auditor to perform audit procedures under the direction, supervision and review of the external auditor. Under the IAASB's ISA 610, direct assistance is permitted subject to certain restrictions.

However, the FRC has concluded that it is not appropriate to allow the use of direct assistance in audits under ISA (UK and Ireland) 610 (Revised June 2013). This is because those individuals providing the direct assistance would not be independent of the audited entity under the Ethical Standards, which would seem to compromise the independence of the audit engagement team employed by the audit firm. Further, the risk to audit quality is heightened by the use of direct assistance since the individual providing direct assistance would not be familiar with the external auditor's processes, including those for quality control.

Therefore, the FRC has concluded that direct assistance should be prohibited for audits conducted in accordance with ISAs (UK and Ireland) and that this should be extended in a group audit to any component auditor whose work is relied upon by the group auditor, including for overseas components. This does not represent a divergence from the IAASB's ISA 610, since the IAASB makes clear that its requirements in this area will not be applicable in jurisdictions where direct assistance is prohibited.

31.2.6   Documentation

When the auditor uses the work of the internal audit function, his documentation needs to include:

(1)   an evaluation of:

    (a)   whether the function's organisational status and relevant policies and procedures adequately support the objectivity of the internal auditor;

    (b)   the level of competence of the function; and

    (c)   whether the function applies a systematic and disciplined approach, including quality control;

(2)   the nature and extent of the work used and the basis for that decision; and

(3)   the audit procedures performed by the external auditor to evaluate the adequacy of the work used.

Where the auditor decides not to use the work of the internal audit function, he should nevertheless document his understanding of the internal audit function's responsibilities, its organisational status and the activities to be performed and the implications for his risk assessment.

31.3   Experts

31.3.1   Auditing standards

This chapter has been updated to reflect the changes contained in final draft ISAs issued by the FRC in April 2016. Subject to legislative changes in progress at the time of writing, it is expected that ISA (UK and Ireland) 620 (Revised June 2016) *Using the work of an auditor's expert* will take effect for the audit of financial statements for periods commencing on or after 17 June 2016. For earlier periods, ending on or after 15 December 2010, the version of ISA (UK and Ireland) 620 issued in October 2009 applies.

The ISA covers:

- determining the need for an auditor's expert;
- the nature, timing and extent of audit procedures;
- the competence, capabilities and objectivity of the expert;
- obtaining an understanding of the field of expertise of the expert;

- agreement with the expert;
- evaluating the adequacy of the expert's work; and
- reference to the expert in the audit report.

Changes in the 2016 version include Audit Regulation requirements for public interest entities (see **31.3.5**) and Audit Directive requirements for statutory audits regarding documentation (see paragraph **31.3.10**).

Situations where the engagement team includes a member, or consults with an individual or organisation, with expertise in a specialised area of accounting and auditing are covered in **3.2**.

Where the auditor makes use of the work of a management's expert, i.e. an expert in a field other than accounting and auditing whose work has been used by the entity in preparing the financial statements, this is covered in **Chapter 23**.

31.3.2   Definition of an expert

An auditor's expert is an individual, or organisation, possessing expertise in a field other than accounting and auditing, whose work in that field is used by the auditor to assist him in obtaining sufficient appropriate audit evidence. The auditor's expert may be either an auditor's internal expert (who belongs to the auditor's firm or network) or an auditor's external expert. They are often members of another profession such as surveyors, actuaries or engineers.

The types of evidence that the auditor may obtain from experts will usually be a report, opinion or valuation, such as:

- valuation of an asset, for example property;
- determination of the quantity of an asset, for example minerals;
- determination of amounts using specialised techniques, for example actuarial valuation;
- measurement of work completed on contracts in progress; and
- legal opinions on interpretations of agreements.

Although the work of an expert may be used, the auditor retains sole responsibility for the audit opinion.

31.3.3   Determining the need for an auditor's expert

The auditor is required to determine whether it is necessary to use an auditor's expert to assist in obtaining appropriate audit evidence. The auditor may consider the following, when deciding whether or not to use an expert:

- whether those charged with governance have used an expert (management's expert) in preparing the financial statements;
- the nature and significance of the matter, including its complexity;

- the risks of material misstatement in the matter; and
- the expected nature of audit procedures planned to respond to identified risks.

31.3.4 The nature, timing and extent of audit procedures

The nature, timing and extent of audit procedures with respect to the expert will vary depending on the circumstances. In determining the nature, timing and extent of those procedures, however, the auditor considers the following matters:

- the nature of the matter to which the expert's work relates, i.e. whether it relates to an area involving subjective and complex judgments;
- the risks of material misstatement in the matter;
- the significance of the expert's work in the context of the audit;
- the auditor's knowledge of and experience with work performed previously by that expert; and
- whether the expert is subject to the auditor's firm's quality control policies and procedures.

31.3.5 Competence, capabilities and objectivity of the expert

When planning to use the work of an expert, the auditor should assess the competence, capabilities and objectivity of the expert. This assessment may use information from a number of sources, including:

- personal experience with previous work of that expert;
- discussions with the expert;
- discussions with others who are familiar with the work of that expert;
- knowledge of that expert's qualifications and membership of professional bodies; and
- the audit firm's quality control policies and procedures.

The objectivity of the expert will be impaired if he is either employed by the entity or related to it in some way (for example, they are a shareholder). The ISA states that where 'a proposed auditor's expert is an individual who has played a significant role in preparing the information that is being audited, that is, if the auditor's expert is a management's expert', there are no safeguards that can be applied to reduce the threats to objectivity to an acceptable level.

Where the expert is an employee of the auditor or his firm, the auditor will still need to assess aspects of the expert's work and results as if the expert was a third party, although he may not need to consider the expert's skills and competence for each assignment. The auditor, however, needs to have regard to the related ethical guidance when deciding if he can use employees of his firm as experts on an audit assignment. He must ensure that their objectivity and independence is not impaired, which would be the case where 'in house' experts have performed a valuation of an asset or liability of the client for inclusion in its balance sheet.

Public interest entities

For public interest entities, where the auditor has used the work of an auditor's external expert, he needs to obtain a confirmation from that external expert regarding his independence. In addition, ISA (UK and Ireland) 260 (Revised June 2016), see **Chapter 10**, requires the auditor to communicate in the additional report to the audit committee when he has used the work of an external expert and to confirm that he has obtained confirmation from the external expert regarding his independence.

31.3.6   *Understanding the expert's field of expertise*

Before using the work of an expert, the auditor needs to obtain a sufficient understanding of the field of expertise of the expert to enable him to:

(1)   determine the nature, scope and objectivity of the expert's work for purposes of the audit; and

(2)   evaluate the adequacy of that work.

This includes understanding whether the expert's field has areas of speciality that are relevant to the audit, whether any professional, legal or regulatory requirements apply, what assumptions and methods will be used by the expert and whether they are generally accepted within the field and appropriate for financial reporting purposes.

31.3.7   *Agreement with the auditor's expert*

The nature, scope and objectives of the auditor's expert's work may vary considerably depending on the circumstances. Therefore, these matters should be agreed before the expert commences his work and may be best clarified in writing.

The letter of instruction should contain details of:

* the nature, scope and objectives of the expert's work;
* the respective roles and responsibilities of the auditor and the expert;
* the nature, timing and extent of communication between the expert and the auditor and the form of any report to be provided; and
* the need for the expert to observe confidentiality requirements.

The letter of instruction may also contain details regarding access to, and retention of, each other's working papers and the expected method and frequency of communication between the auditor and the expert.

31.3.8   Evaluating the adequacy of the expert's work

The auditor should assess the appropriateness of the expert's notes as audit evidence regarding the financial statement assertions being considered. This will involve assessment of:

- the relevance and reasonableness of the expert's findings and their consistency with other audit evidence;
- the assumptions and methods used and their relevance and reasonableness in the circumstances; and
- the source data used and its relevance, completeness and accuracy.

The auditor should ensure that the data used by the expert is sufficient, relevant and reliable and may consider reviewing or testing this data.

The expert's assumptions will not usually be challenged by the auditor as he does not have sufficient expertise, but he does need to understand the assumptions and consider whether they are reasonable given the auditor's knowledge of the business and the results of the other audit procedures.

Where the auditor determines that the work of the expert is not adequate for his purposes, he needs to agree with the expert on the nature and extent of further work to be performed by the expert or perform additional audit procedures himself.

31.3.9   Reference to the expert in the audit report

When the auditor is satisfied with the work of the expert, there is no need for him to refer to this in his report, unless specifically required by law or regulation. If the auditor needs to refer to the expert because such a reference is relevant to an understanding of a modification in the report, then the auditor has to make it clear in his report that the reference does not in any way reduce the auditor's responsibility for the opinion.

31.3.10   Documentation

The Audit Directive requires that for statutory audits of financial statements, when an auditor asks an auditor's expert for advice, the auditor needs to document the request made and the advice received.

32 MANAGEMENT REPRESENTATIONS

32.1 Introduction

ISA (UK and Ireland) 580 *Written representations* was issued in October 2009 and is effective for the audit of financial statements for periods ending on or after 15 December 2010. It covers the need to gain written confirmation of management representations and includes:

- acknowledgement of management's responsibilities;
- representations as audit evidence; and
- the auditor's response where appropriate written representations cannot be obtained.

Although ISA (UK and Ireland) 580 was included in the final draft of revised ISAs issued by the FRC in April 2016, it had no substantive changes made. As such, the 2009 version remains applicable, with some minor changes to the application material.

Certain specific representations from management are required to be requested by the auditor. Other ISAs also require written representation to be obtained on specific matters as set out in **32.4** below.

Additional guidance on written representations can be found in the ICAEW's technical release Audit 04/02, an Explanatory Note on *Management Representation Letters*, issued in November 2002. The aim of the Note is to help the auditor increase the usefulness of management representation letters as audit evidence by suggesting methods to ensure that representations are reliable. The Explanatory Note is detailed in **32.10** below.

32.2 Requirement to obtain written representations

Certain written representations are required by ISAs to be requested from management; in other cases, the auditor may seek written representations to confirm oral representations made by management during the course of the audit or in response to particular enquiries or in support of other audit evidence obtained by him.

References to 'management' in this context include references to those charged with governance as they have the primary responsibility for the financial statements. In the case of UK companies, written representations required by

ISAs will need to be obtained from the directors but the auditor may also seek representations on specific matters from other members of senior management.

Written representations must be obtained in the form of a representation letter addressed to the auditor and signed by one or more persons with the appropriate authority. Usually, the letter is signed by one or more directors on behalf of the board. In this case, the letter may be discussed by the board before it approves the financial statements to ensure that all members are aware of the representations on which the auditor intends to rely in expressing his opinion on those financial statements.

Written representations should be obtained as near as practicable to the date of the auditor's report. Where there is a significant delay in signing the auditor's report after receipt of the representation letter, the auditor may need to obtain an updated letter or written confirmation that the representations made in the original letter remain valid.

The auditor may discuss the representations with those responsible for providing the written confirmation before they sign it to reduce the possibility of misunderstanding.

An example of a management representation letter in the case of a single entity is shown in **Table 1** at **32.9**. It should be tailored for the circumstances of each client.

32.3 Acknowledgement of directors' responsibilities

ISA (UK and Ireland) 580 requires the auditor to request that those charged with governance provide a written representation that they have fulfilled their responsibility for the preparation of financial statements that give a true and fair view in accordance with the applicable financial reporting framework.

In addition, the auditor should request written representations from those charged with governance (and others as appropriate) that:

- they have provided the auditor with all relevant information and access agreed in the terms of the audit engagement; and
- all transactions have been recorded and are reflected in the financial statements.

This last representation may refer to a threshold amount agreed with the auditor or to state that all transactions that may have a material effect on the financial statements have been recorded.

The use of language to the effect that the representations are made to the best of management's knowledge and belief does not invalidate the representation as long as the auditor has found no evidence that the representations are incorrect.

In group situations, acknowledgement of the directors' responsibilities applies to the group financial statements as well as those of the parent undertaking.

32.4   Other written representations required by ISAs

Other ISAs also require that the auditor should obtain, in writing, from management or those charged with governance as appropriate:

ISA (UK and Ireland) 240 (Revised June 2016), The Auditor's Responsibilities Relating to Fraud in an Audit of Financial Statements:

- representations regarding their responsibility for the design, implementation and maintenance of internal control; disclosure of management's assessment of the risk that the financial statements may be materially misstated as a result of fraud; disclosure of their knowledge of fraud or suspected fraud affecting the entity; and disclosure of their knowledge of any allegations of fraud, or suspected fraud, affecting the entity's financial statements communicated by employees or others (see **16.7**).

ISA (UK and Ireland) 250 (Revised June 2016), Consideration of Laws and Regulations in an Audit of Financial Statements:

- representations regarding disclosure of all known instances of non-compliance or suspected non-compliance with laws and regulations where the consequences may affect the financial statements (see **17.5.1**).

ISA (UK and Ireland) 450 (Revised June 2016), Evaluation of Misstatements Identified during the Audit:

- representations that they believe the effects of uncorrected misstatements are immaterial, individually and in aggregate, to the financial statements as a whole. A summary of uncorrected misstatements must be included in or attached to the written representation (see **15.9**).

ISA (UK and Ireland) 501, Audit Evidence – Specific Considerations for Selected Items:

- representations that all known actual or possible litigation and claims which may affect the preparation of the financial statements have been disclosed to the auditor and treated in the financial statements in accordance with the applicable financial reporting framework (see **23.6.2**).

ISA (UK and Ireland) 540 (Revised June 2016), Auditing Accounting Estimates, Including Fair Value Accounting Estimates, and Related Disclosures:

- representations that they believe significant assumptions used in making accounting estimates are reasonable. For this purpose, an assumption used in making an accounting estimate is considered significant if a reasonable variation in the assumption would materially affect the measurement of the estimate (see **27.8**).

ISA (UK and Ireland) 550, Related Parties:

- representations that they have disclosed to the auditor the identity of the entity's related parties and all the related party relationships and transactions of which they are aware; and have appropriately accounted for and disclosed such relationships and transactions (see **20.8**).

ISA (UK and Ireland) 560, Subsequent Events:

- representations that all events occurring subsequent to the date of the financial statements and for adjustment or disclosure have been adjusted or disclosed where required in accordance with accounting standards (see **33.3**).

ISA (UK and Ireland) 570 (Revised June 2016), Going Concern:

- where events or conditions have been identified that may cast significant doubt on the entity's ability to continue as a going concern, representations regarding their plans for future action and the feasibility of these plans (see **11.9**).

ISA (UK and Ireland) 710, Comparative Information – Corresponding Figures and Comparative Financial Statements:

- a specific representation regarding any restatement made to correct a material misstatement in prior period financial statements that affects the comparative information (see **19.4**).

32.5   Additional written representations

The application material in ISA (UK and Ireland) 580 notes that the auditor may also consider it necessary to request:

- other written representations about the financial statements including whether the selection and application of accounting policies are appropriate;
- a written representation from management that it has communicated to the auditor all deficiencies in internal control of which it is aware; and
- written representations about specific assertions in the financial statements; in particular, to support an understanding that the auditor has obtained from other audit evidence of management's judgment or intent in relation to, or the completeness of, a specific assertion.

32.6 Representations by management as audit evidence

ISA (UK and Ireland) 580 asserts that, although written representations provide necessary audit evidence, they support other audit evidence obtained and do not on their own provide sufficient appropriate audit evidence about any of the matters with which they deal. Where no other evidence is available, it could lead to a qualification to the auditor's report because of a limitation of scope.

This also applies to cases where there is a genuine limitation of scope and the auditor does not expect any other evidence to be available. For example, where the auditor is appointed after the end of the reporting period and is unable to find any means of verifying material quantities of stock, management representations could never be considered sufficient evidence on their own to support quantities.

There will, however, be instances when no supporting evidence is available and cannot reasonably be expected to be available, and where written confirmation of the representation, when taken into consideration with other information of which the auditor is aware, will constitute sufficient evidence. For example, when auditing a deferred tax provision, the auditor may need to accept representations about management's intentions in regard to future capital spending. Similarly, the classification of financial instruments may depend on management's intentions regarding the use of the instrument. In such cases, the auditor should ensure that nothing conflicts with the representations and that they are consistent with other evidence obtained during the course of the audit regarding management's plans and intentions.

32.7 Reliability of representations

If the auditor has concerns about the integrity, competence or diligence of those from whom representations are sought, he needs to consider whether this affects the reliability of the written representations and their value as audit evidence.

Where there is an apparent contradiction between the representation and other audit evidence, the auditor should investigate the circumstances through discussions with management and other substantive procedures, and seek to resolve the difference.

Where the auditor concludes that representations are not reliable, he should consider the implications for the audit including the possible impact on the auditor's report. In particular, if the auditor concludes that the required representations regarding management's responsibilities (see **32.3**) are unreliable he should disclaim an opinion.

32.8   Refusal to provide written confirmation

Where management refuse to provide the auditor with written confirmation of representations, the auditor should re-evaluate the integrity of management and consider the implications for the reliability of other representations and audit evidence in general. He should also consider the implications for the auditor's report including whether this leads to a limitation of scope requiring either a qualified opinion or a disclaimer of opinion.

Where management refuse to provide the written representations requested in accordance with ISA (UK and Ireland) 580 acknowledging management's responsibilities for the financial statements (see **32.3**), the auditor should disclaim an opinion.

32.9   Example representation letter

Table 1 provides an example of a representation letter.

TABLE 1: Example letter of representation

ABC & Co 1 High Street London

Dear Sirs

Financial Statements for the year ended 31 March 20 ...

We confirm to the best of our knowledge and belief, and having made appropriate enquiries of other directors and officials of the company, the following representations given to you in connection with your audit of the company's financial statements for the year ended 31 March 20 ...

We acknowledge as directors our responsibility under the *Companies Act* 2006 for preparing the financial statements which give a true and fair view and have been prepared in accordance with the relevant accounting framework and applicable law. All the accounting records have been made available to you for the purpose of your audit and all the transactions undertaken by the company have been properly reflected and recorded in the accounting records. All other records and related information, including minutes of all management and shareholder's meetings have been made available to you.

Uncorrected misstatements

We confirm that we believe that the effects of the uncorrected misstatements listed in the attached schedule are not material to the financial statements, either individually or in aggregate.

Significant assumptions

We confirm that the following significant assumptions used in making accounting estimates, including those measured at fair value, are reasonable.

[Details ...]

Accounting policies

We confirm that the selection and application of the accounting policies used in the preparation of the financial statements are appropriate.

Plans or intentions

We have no plans or intentions that may materially alter the carrying value and, where relevant, the fair value measurements or classification of assets and liabilities reflected in the financial statements.

Litigation and claims

Either

We have disclosed to you the following actual or possible litigation and claims, the effects of which should be considered when preparing the financial statements and these have been accounted for and disclosed in accordance with the applicable financial reporting framework.

[Details ...]

Or

We confirm that there are no actual or possible litigation and claims affecting the company.

Related parties

Either

We have disclosed to you the identity of all related parties and all the related party relationships and transactions of which we are aware. We have appropriately accounted for and disclosed such relationships and transactions in accordance with the requirements of the applicable accounting framework.

Or

We confirm that there have been no material transactions with related parties [other than transactions with group undertakings which are not required to be disclosed].

Subsequent events

Either

We have disclosed to you the following events occurring subsequent to the date of the financial statements for which the applicable financial reporting framework requires adjustment or disclosure:

[Details …]

Or

There have been no events since the balance sheet date which necessitate revision of the figures included in the financial statements or inclusion of a note thereto. Should any material events occur, which may necessitate revision of the figures included in the financial statements or inclusion of a note thereto, we will advise you accordingly.

Going concern

Either

We confirm that we are satisfied that it is appropriate for the financial statements to have been drawn up on the going concern basis. In reaching this conclusion, we have taken into account all relevant matters of which we are aware, including the availability of working capital and have considered a future period of at least one year from the date on which the financial statements [were/will be] approved. [In particular, we have considered (give details of any matters relating to going concern on which specific representations are required, e.g. promises of support from other companies, negotiations with bankers or suppliers, etc.).]

Or

We confirm that we are satisfied that the use of the going concern assumption is inappropriate as the company will not continue in operational existence for the foreseeable future, and that, it is appropriate for the financial statements to have been drawn up on an alternative basis.

We have also considered the adequacy of the disclosures in the financial statements relating to going concern and are satisfied that sufficient disclosure has been made in order to give a true and fair view.

[Comparative information

We confirm that, in respect of the restatement to correct a material misstatement in prior period financial statements that affects the comparative information, [the adjustment relates to a change in accounting policy as we believe that the new accounting policy is more appropriate, and accordingly, to ensure the consistency of accounting treatment between periods, it is necessary to restate the current and corresponding periods on the basis of the new policy] [the adjustment relates to the correction of a fundamental error which has no bearing on the results of the current period, and accordingly, should be accounted for by restating prior periods].]

Internal control

We acknowledge our responsibility for the design, implementation and maintenance of internal control to prevent and detect fraud.

Either

We have disclosed to you the following deficiencies in internal control of which we are aware:

[Details ...]

Or

There have been no deficiencies in internal control of which we are aware.

Fraud

We have disclosed to you the results of our assessment of the risk that the financial statements may be materially misstated as a result of fraud.

Either

We have disclosed to you our knowledge of fraud or suspected fraud affecting the company, and of any allegations of fraud or suspected fraud affecting the financial statements communicated to us by employees, former employees, analysts, regulators or others, involving management, employees who have significant roles in internal control, or others.

Or

We are not aware of any fraud or suspected fraud affecting the company and no allegations of fraud or suspected fraud affecting the financial statements have been communicated to us by employees, former employees, analysts, regulators or others.

Compliance with laws and regulations

Either

We have disclosed to you the following instances of non-compliance or suspected non-compliance with laws and regulations, whose effects should be considered when preparing the financial statements, together with the actual or contingent consequences which may arise therefrom:

[Details ...]

Other than these matters, we are not aware of any actual or possible instances of non-compliance with laws or regulations whose effects should be considered when preparing financial statements of the company.

Or

We are not aware of any actual or possible instances of non-compliance with laws or regulations whose effects should be considered when preparing financial statements of the company.

Control

We confirm that the company is controlled by [...] and that the ultimate controlling party is [...].

Related parties

We confirm that we have disclosed to you the identity of all the company's related parties, related party relationships and transactions of which we are aware.

Liabilities, contingent liabilities or guarantees

There are no liabilities, contingent liabilities or guarantees to third parties other than those disclosed in the financial statements.

Title to assets

The company has satisfactory title to all assets and there are no liens or encumbrances on the assets except for those disclosed in the financial statements.

Contractual agreements

The company has complied with all aspects of contractual agreements that could have a material effect on the financial statements in the event of non-compliance.

[Additional matters

Any other matters relevant to the financial statements on which written representations are sought.]

Yours faithfully,

Signed on behalf of the board of directors

.... Date ....

32.10 Audit 4/02: Management Representation Letters

In November 2002, the Audit and Assurance Faculty of the ICAEW issued an Explanatory Note on *Management Representation Letters* (Audit 04/02). The guidance was issued following a High Court decision concerning the audit of Barings Futures (Singapore) Pte Ltd (BFS) by Deloitte & Touche (D&T).

32.10.1   The case

Following an audit by D&T, BFS collapsed as a result of losses arising from unauthorised trading activity by one of its employees. D&T faced a claim for damages and attempted to defend themselves by stating that management representations provided to them were recklessly fraudulent, as they were made by a director of BFS who had little knowledge of the employee's activities, despite being nominally his reporting superior.

However, the claim failed because D&T could not prove that the director signed the representation letter whilst:

- knowing that the statements were untrue; and
- knowing that he had no reasonable grounds for making the statements.

Despite D&T not winning their argument, the judge did state that if they had been successful, he would have held BFS vicariously liable for the director's actions.

32.10.2   Increasing the usefulness of representation letters

The Explanatory Note re-emphasises the requirement that the auditor should discuss the contents of the representation letter with management, so that they understand what they are being asked to sign. The auditor should also consider whether the person signing the letter is in a position to enable him to sign the letter in full knowledge of the matters contained therein.

The Note suggests adding the following statement to all management representation letters to focus the attention of those signing the letter on whether proper enquiries have been made:

> 'We confirm that the above representations are made on the basis of enquiries of management and staff with relevant knowledge and experience (and, where appropriate, of inspection of supporting documentation) sufficient to satisfy ourselves that we can properly make each of the above representations to you.'

The auditor may also ask signatories what enquiries have been made of management and staff and how they went about this process. Where signatories have themselves obtained written representations from others, for example in relation to complex or specialist areas such as financial instruments, these may be attached to the management representation letter itself and referred to in the letter. The auditor may also wish to impress upon his client that it is an offence under the *Companies Act* 2006, s. 501 to knowingly or recklessly make a misleading or false statement to the company's auditor.

33   SUBSEQUENT EVENTS

33.1   Introduction

The current version of ISA (UK and Ireland) 560 *Subsequent events* was issued in October 2009 and is effective for the audit of financial statements for periods ending on or after 15 December 2010. It covers:

- events between the period end and the date of the audit report;
- matters of which the auditor becomes aware after the date of the audit report but before the financial statements are issued; and
- matters of which the auditor becomes aware after the financial statements have been issued.

ISA (UK and Ireland) 560 does not deal with any matters relating to the auditor's responsibilities for other information obtained after the date of the auditor's report, these are covered in **Chapter 34**. However, it is worth noting that such other information may bring to light a matter which is within the scope of ISA (UK and Ireland) 560.

In April 2016, the FRC issued a final draft of a suite of revised ISAs (UK and Ireland). Although ISA (UK and Ireland) 560 does not include any changes to the requirements, and as such it is not 'revised' and the October 2009 version remains applicable, it does include some revised application material largely dealing with the implications of facts that become known to the auditor after the financial statements have been issued. Subject to legislative changes in progress at the time of writing, it is expected that the revised ISAs will take effect for periods commencing on or after 17 June 2016 and the chapter has been updated to reflect the revisions.

33.2   Subsequent events

ISA (UK and Ireland) 560 states that 'the auditor should consider the effect of subsequent events on the financial statements and on the auditor's report'.

Subsequent events are those events (favourable or unfavourable) which occur between the balance sheet date and the date when the financial statements are authorised for issue.

Subsequent events are events occurring after the year end or matters that become known after the year end and either:

- provide additional evidence of conditions existing at the balance sheet date; or
- concern conditions which arose after the balance sheet date.

In forming his audit opinion, the auditor is required to consider the effects of events and transactions of which he becomes aware, occurring up to the date of his audit report. Such matters may directly affect the reported performance or financial position of the entity or may otherwise affect or require disclosure in the financial statements or the auditor's opinion thereon.

33.3   Before the date of the audit report

The auditor should perform audit procedures designed to obtain sufficient appropriate audit evidence that all events occurring between the date of the financial statements and the date of the auditor's report that require adjustment of, or disclosure in, the financial statements have been identified.

The nature and extent of procedures carried out by the auditor will depend on the circumstances and on the auditor's risk assessment. These may involve examination of accounting records or detailed consideration of particular transactions, in addition to work that would normally be carried out to confirm certain account balances, such as inventory cut-off or payments to creditors, although these procedures may themselves provide useful insights into subsequent events.

In any case the ISA requires that the following procedures be performed as near as practicable to the date of the audit report:

- enquiring into procedures that management has established to identify subsequent events;
- reviewing minutes of meetings of members, directors, and audit and executive committees held since the period end and enquiring about any matters discussed at meetings for which minutes are not available;
- reading the latest available information concerning the entity, including the accounting records and any management accounts;
- making enquiries of the entity's legal counsel concerning litigation and claims; and
- making enquiries of management as to whether any subsequent events have occurred which might affect the financial statements.

The extent of these procedures will depend on the length of the period between the balance sheet date and the date of the audit report and the records available.

Some examples of further specific enquiries that the auditor might make of management are provided in the guidance and include:

- the current status of items involving subjective judgment or which were accounted for on the basis of preliminary data – for example, litigation in progress;
- whether sales of fixed assets are planned or have occurred;
- whether new commitments, borrowings or guarantees have been entered into;

- whether the issue of new shares or debentures or an agreement to merge or liquidate has been made or is planned;
- whether any assets have been appropriated by government or destroyed, for example, by fire or flood;
- whether there have been developments regarding risk areas and contingencies;
- whether any unusual accounting adjustments have been made or are contemplated; and
- whether any events have occurred or are likely to occur which might bring into question the appropriateness of accounting policies used in the financial statements – for example, any that would bring the validity of the going concern basis of accounting into question.

One area which is the frequent subject of specific enquiries by the auditor is the appropriateness of the going concern basis of accounting and consideration of material uncertainties in relation thereto. This is considered in **Chapter 11**.

Under any circumstances, the auditor will request a written representation from those charged with governance, in accordance with ISA (UK and Ireland) 580 *Written representations*, that all events occurring subsequent to the date of the financial statements and which require adjustment or disclosure have been adjusted or disclosed.

In a group audit situation, the auditor should make arrangements to ensure that an appropriate review of subsequent events at component level is carried out either by the group engagement team or by component auditors (if any) up to the date of the audit opinion on the group accounts, and that the results are reported back to the group engagement team for consideration (**30.12**).

When the auditor becomes aware of an event which materially affects the financial statements, he should consider whether the events are properly accounted for and adequately disclosed in the financial statements.

33.4 Before the financial statements are issued

Once his report has been dated, the auditor has no responsibility to perform procedures to review subsequent events. However, if there is a delay between the issue of the auditor's report and the issue of the financial statements, the auditor may reasonably expect management to inform him of any events discovered which may affect the financial statements.

If the auditor becomes aware of subsequent events before the issue of the financial statements, he should establish whether the financial statements need amendment, and, if so, discuss the matter with the directors and consider the implications for his report.

33.4.1 *Directors make the required amendments*

Where the directors agree to make the necessary amendments to the financial statements, there are a number of possible scenarios:

(a) in the simplest case the financial statements are amended and re-approved by the directors, the auditor extends his subsequent review procedures to cover the period from the previous report date and issues a new report dated on or after the date of approval of the amended financial statements;

(b) the directors restrict the amendment of the financial statements to the effects of the subsequent event. In this case, the auditor may either reissue his audit report on a 'dual dated basis' or issue a new report with an appropriate emphasis of matter or other matter paragraph explaining that the auditor's procedures on the subsequent event were restricted to the amendment as described in the financial statements.

The version of ISA (UK and Ireland) 560 issued in October 2009, introduced the concept of dual dating where events occur subsequent to the signing of the audit report which require amendment to an element of the financial statements. This concept is not permitted by some laws, regulations or financial reporting frameworks covered by the International ISA, but the UK and Ireland specific guidance in the ISA (UK and Ireland) does not restrict its use.

An example of a dual dated report would be:

> [Date of auditor's report], except as to Note Y, which is as of [date of completion of audit procedures restricted to amendment described in Note Y].

33.4.2 *Failure to amend financial statements*

If the financial statements are not amended, the auditor should consider the implications for his report and issue a qualified report if the original report has not been issued to the entity. When the original report has been issued, the auditor should request management not to issue the financial statements; but if these are issued, the auditor needs to take action to prevent reliance on the audit report and may need to take legal advice.

33.5 Revising or withdrawing financial statements

In situations where the auditor becomes aware of events after the financial statements have been issued, if the facts would have led him to issue a different report he should consider whether the financial statements need amendment and consider the implications for his report. Where events have occurred after the date of the audit report, but before the financial statements have been issued there is no statutory procedure, but this normally involves attempting to have management withdraw the statements and, failing this, taking legal advice. This is a difficult area in which to give specific guidance, as much will depend on the circumstances.

In such circumstances, the auditor may wish to make use of his power under the *Companies Act* to address the general meeting at which the members consider the financial statements. The possibility of withdrawing his audit report is also one that is sometimes raised. However, it appears that this may not legally be effective.

34 THE AUDITOR'S RESPONSIBILITIES IN RELATION TO OTHER INFORMATION

34.1 Introduction

Companies often issue, because of legal requirement, custom or investor demand, other information as part of the annual report which contains the audited financial statements. This 'other information' may include both financial and non-financial information. An entity's annual report may be a single document or a combination of documents serving the same purpose. Under ISAs (UK and Ireland), the auditor has certain responsibilities in respect of this information.

In addition, in the UK the auditor has certain statutory responsibilities in respect of other information contained in, for example, the directors' report, strategic report, directors' remuneration report and other reports that may be required under applicable legislation. Further responsibilities are imposed by the Listing Rules of the FCA in respect of premium listed companies.

Annual reports may also include, or be accompanied by, other reports on which the auditor provides separate assurance, usually in the form of an assurance report separate from his report on the financial statements. Such additional assurance reports on, e.g. greenhouse gas emissions statements or corporate responsibility statements are becoming more popular with large companies but derive from separate assurance engagements outside the scope of a financial statements audit. See **Chapter 41** for further guidance on such reports.

The principal reason for the auditor's consideration of other information is that there may be information therein that is materially inconsistent with the auditor's knowledge which, in turn, may indicate the existence of matters that should be reflected in the financial statements or would otherwise affect the auditor's opinion. Alternatively, the other information may contain items that are materially incorrect or misleading and would inappropriately affect the economic decisions of users of the financial statements. Consideration of other information may also assist the auditor in complying with ethical requirements to avoid allowing himself to be associated with information that is false or misleading.

34.2 Auditing standards

This chapter has been updated to reflect the changes contained in final draft ISAs issued by the FRC in April 2016. Subject to legislative changes in progress at the time of writing, it is expected that ISA (UK and Ireland) 720

(Revised June 2016) *The auditor's responsibilities relating to other information* will take effect for periods commencing on or after 17 June 2016.

The revision of ISA (UK and Ireland) 720:

- reflects revisions made to the international standard in 2015 by the IAASB;
- updates the standard to reflect recent changes in UK company law;
- incorporates certain material, previously contained in ISA (UK and Ireland) 700 relating to entities applying the UK Corporate Governance Code; and
- incorporates amendments relating to the EU Audit Directive.

Prior to the revision of this standard, there were two applicable standards in the UK and Ireland. ISA (UK and Ireland) 720 Section A – *The auditor's responsibilities relating to other information in documents containing audited financial statements* imposed on the auditor a general responsibility to read other information in the annual report, and to consider the implications for his report in the event that the other information contained errors or inconsistencies. This standard was last updated in October 2012. ISA (UK and Ireland) 720 Section B *The auditor's statutory reporting responsibility in relation to directors' reports* covered the auditor's statutory responsibility in respect of the directors' report, and by extension the strategic report. These responsibilities are in the process of changing. This standard was last updated in October 2009.

34.3 The auditor's consideration of other information

34.3.1 Other information

'Other information' is defined in ISA (UK and Ireland) 720 (Revised June 2016) as the other financial and non-financial information, apart from the financial statements and the auditor's report on them, that is contained in an entity's 'annual report'. The 'annual report' in this context may be a single document or a combination of documents, the purpose of which is to provide stakeholders of the entity with information about the entity's operations, results and financial position. This is a widening of the definition compared with the previous version of the ISA and to some extent means that the determination of what constitutes other information may be a matter of judgment for the auditor.

The ISA also defines 'statutory other information' as being those documents or reports that are required to be produced and issued by the entity and on which the auditor is required to report in accordance with law or regulation. For UK companies, this will include the directors' report and strategic report, where required, and, if applicable, the separate governance statement for listed companies.

'Other information' includes at least any statutory other information that is required for the entity. In addition, it includes information that is incorporated by cross reference in, or distributed to shareholders with, statutory other information.

For example, if the entity decides to present a voluntary Operating and Financial Review (OFR) which includes some or all of the matters required for the business performance review section of the strategic report or the directors' report, then rather than duplicate the information, the entity may cross refer from the strategic report or the directors' report to the relevant information provided in the OFR. This information in the OFR would then be included in the definition of 'other information'.

The auditor's responsibilities relate to other information regardless of whether or not the information is obtained by the auditor prior to, or after, the date of his report. Confusingly, the ISA suggests that the auditor may issue his report on the financial statements before all other information has been obtained. However, the ISA does note that ISA UK and Ireland) 700 (Revised June 2016) does require that the auditor must obtain and examine all other information before he can sign or date his report.

34.3.2   The auditor's responsibility

ISA (UK and Ireland) 720 (Revised June 2016) states that the objectives of the auditor, having read the other information, are to:

- consider whether there is a material inconsistency between the other information and the financial statements;
- consider whether there is a material inconsistency between the other information and his knowledge gained during the course of performing the audit;
- respond appropriately where he believes such inconsistencies exist or where he becomes aware that other information appears to be materially misstated;
- report in accordance with the ISA (UK and Ireland); and
- form an opinion on whether the other information is consistent with the financial statements and the auditor's knowledge and report in accordance with applicable legal and regulatory requirements.

Except in respect of his responsibilities in respect of statutory other information, the auditor is not expressing assurance on the other information and is not required to obtain audit evidence beyond that which would be required to form an opinion on the financial statements.

34.3.3   Obtaining an understanding

As part of his obtaining an understanding of the entity and its environment (see **Chapter 21**), the auditor is also required to obtain an understanding of the legal and regulatory requirements applicable to the preparation of statutory other information by the entity, and how the entity is complying with those requirements.

34.3.4   Obtaining the other information

The auditor determines, through discussion with management, which documents are part of the annual report, when and how they will be issued and arranges to get copies of these, prior to the date of the audit report.

34.3.5   Reading and considering the other information

The auditor reads the other information and:

- considers whether there is a material inconsistency between the other information and the financial statements; and
- considers whether there is a material inconsistency between the other information and his knowledge obtained in the audit, in the context of audit evidence obtained and conclusions reached in the audit.

In order to consider whether there is a material inconsistency, the auditor selects specific amounts or items in the other information and compares them with the amounts in the financial statements to which they relate. For example, the auditor may compare a statement such as 'total research and development expense in 20X1 was £x' with the amounts shown in the financial statements.

The auditor is not expected to compare all amounts and items, and selecting the amounts to compare is a matter of professional judgment.

In considering whether there is a material inconsistency between the other information and the auditor's knowledge, the more experienced and the more familiar the auditor is with the key aspects of the audit, the more likely it is that his recollection of relevant matters will be sufficient. There may be instances, however, where he needs to refer to the audit documentation or to make enquiries of team members to determine whether an inconsistency exists. For example, if the other information describes important details of a lawsuit relevant to the audit, reference to the audit documentation will probably be necessary.

In reading and considering this other information, the auditor maintains professional scepticism and recognises that management may be overly optimistic as regards their future plans.

At the same time, he remains alert for any indications that the other information not related to the financial statements or his knowledge appears to be materially misstated.

Statutory other information

In addition to the above, when reading the statutory other information, the auditor considers, based on the work undertaken in the course of the audit, whether the statutory other information appears to be materially misstated in the context of his understanding of the applicable legal and regulatory framework. The auditor performs such procedures as are necessary, in his professional judgment, to determine whether such material misstatements exist.

Procedures

The ISA makes it clear that the determination of the nature and extent of procedures to be applied when checking for consistency in other information is a matter of judgment for the auditor. It is clear, however, that some procedures are required and that a quick casual glance will not suffice.

34.4   Responding to inconsistencies and misstatements

ISA (UK and Ireland) 720 (Revised June 2016) requires that if, as a result of his consideration of any 'other information', he identifies that a material inconsistency appears to exist (or becomes aware that the other information appears to be materially misstated), the auditor should discuss the matter with management and, if necessary, perform other procedures to conclude whether:

(a)   a material misstatement of the other information exists;

(b)   a material misstatement of the financial statements exists; or

(c)   the auditor's understanding of the entity and its environment needs to be updated.

34.4.1   *Responding when a material misstatement of the other information exists*

In situation (a) in **34.4**, if the auditor concludes that a material misstatement of the other information exists, he asks management to correct the other information. If they agree to make the correction, he checks that this has been done. If management refuse to make the correction, the auditor communicates with those charged with governance to ask that the correction be made.

Prior to the date of the audit report

If the auditor concludes that a material misstatement exists in other information obtained prior to the date of his report, and the other information is not corrected after communicating with those charged with governance, he needs to take appropriate action. This includes:

(a) considering the implications for his audit report and communicating with those charged with governance about how the auditor plans to address the material misstatement in his report; or

(b) withdrawing from the engagement, where withdrawal is possible under applicable law or regulation.

If the auditor considers that there are inconsistencies with the financial statements and/or with his knowledge obtained during the audit, and he cannot resolve the issues through discussion, he considers asking those charged with governance to consult with a third party, such as the entity's legal counsel.

Where the matter remains unresolved, the auditor may also use his right to be heard at the entity's general meeting.

After the date of the audit report

If he concludes that a material misstatement exists in other information obtained after the date of his report, the auditor shall:

(a) if the other information is corrected, perform procedures necessary to determine that the correction has been made and those already in receipt of the information, if already issued, have been informed of the correction; or

(b) if the other information is not corrected after communicating with those charged with governance, take appropriate action considering his legal rights and obligations, to seek to have the uncorrected material misstatement appropriately brought to the attention of users for whom the auditor's report is prepared.

Where a material misstatement remains uncorrected, the auditor's action requires professional judgment and may be affected by laws and regulation, though may include providing a new or amended auditor's report, communicating with a regulator or relevant professional body or withdrawing from the engagement.

34.4.2 Responding when a material misstatement in the financial statements exists or the auditor's understanding needs to be updated

If, as a result of performing the procedures in paragraphs **34.3.5**, the auditor concludes that a material misstatement in the financial statements exists or his understanding of the entity and its environment needs to be updated, the auditor responds appropriately. This may include:

- revising his risk assessment (see **Chapter 21**);
- evaluating the effect of misstatements on the audit and of uncorrected misstatements, if any, on the financial statements (see **Chapter 15**); and
- considering his responsibilities relating to subsequent events (see **Chapter 33**).

34.5 Timing

The auditor's reading of the 'other information' should be carried out in the final phase of the audit, once other evidence has been obtained. Such a review requires a person with 'appropriate levels of experience and skills'. As with other parts of the audit, the auditor considers materiality when performing this review. The review complements his other evidence and is not intended to be the only procedure that the auditor carries out in order to give his opinion.

The auditor should obtain the other information as soon as possible to allow time for any inconsistencies to be resolved.

34.6 Reporting

34.6.1 All entities

In the UK, the auditor is not permitted to sign, and hence date, his report earlier than the date on which all the other information has been approved by those charged with governance and the auditor has considered all necessary available evidence. As such, his report will always include a separate section headed 'Other Information', or other appropriate heading.

ISA 720 (UK and Ireland) (Revised June 2016) now contains specific detailed reporting requirements related to other information. As a result, the 'Other Information' section of the report will need to include:

- a statement that management is responsible for the identification of the other information;
- a statement that the auditor's opinion on the financial statements does not cover the other information and that (except where explicitly stated otherwise) the auditor does not express any assurance thereon;
- a description of the auditor's responsibilities; and
- a statement that the auditor has nothing to report or otherwise describes any uncorrected material misstatement of the other information.

(Note that inconsistencies do not get reported as they are supposed to be resolved and concluded on in accordance with **34.4** above.)

34.6.2 Directors' report and strategic report

For companies required to prepare a strategic report and/or directors' report, the *Companies Act* 2006, s. 496 requires the auditor to state in his report:[1]

---

[1] Applies for periods commencing on or after 1 January 2016 or earlier adoption of provisions of the *Companies, Partnerships and Groups (Accounts and Reports) Regulations* 2015 (SI 2015/980).

(a) whether, in his opinion, based on the work undertaken in the course of the audit:

    (i) the information given in the strategic report (if any) and the directors' report for the financial year for which the accounts are prepared is consistent with those accounts; and

    (ii) any such strategic report and the directors' report have been prepared in accordance with applicable legal requirements;

(b) whether, in the light of the knowledge and understanding of the company and its environment obtained in the course of the audit, he has identified material misstatements in the strategic report (if any) and the directors' report; and

(c) if applicable, give an indication of the nature of each of the misstatements referred to above.

34.6.3   Separate corporate governance statement

Where a company prepares a separate corporate governance statement[2] in respect of a financial year, the *Companies Act* 2006, s. 497A requires that the auditor must, in his report:[3]

(a) state whether, in his opinion, based on the work undertaken in the course of the audit, the information given in the statement in compliance with rules 7.2.5 and 7.2.6 in the Disclosure Rules and Transparency Rules sourcebook made by the Financial Conduct Authority (information about internal control and risk management systems in relation to financial reporting processes and about share capital structures):

    (i) is consistent with those accounts; and

    (ii) has been prepared in accordance with applicable legal requirements;

(b) state whether, in the light of the knowledge and understanding of the company and its environment obtained in the course of the audit, he has identified material misstatements in the information;

(c) if applicable, give an indication of the nature of each of the misstatements referred to above; and

(d) state whether, in his opinion, based on the work undertaken in the course of the audit, rules 7.2.2, 7.2.3 and 7.2.7 in the Disclosure Rules and Transparency Rules sourcebook made by the Financial Conduct Authority (information about the company's corporate governance code and practices and about its administrative, management and supervisory bodies and their committees) have been complied with, if applicable.

---

[2] A separate corporate governance statement is not required if the relevant information is included within the directors' report.

[3] Applies for periods commencing on or after 1 January 2016 or earlier adoption of provisions of the *Companies, Partnerships and Groups (Accounts and Reports) Regulations* 2015 (SI 2015/980).

34.7   UK Corporate Governance Code reporting

For entities that are required, and those that choose voluntarily, to report on how they have applied the UK Corporate Governance Code or to explain why they have not, the auditor shall specifically address each of the following elements of the other information:

(a)   the statement given by the directors that they consider the annual report and accounts taken as a whole is fair, balanced and understandable and provides the information necessary for shareholders to assess the entity's performance, business model and strategy, that is materially inconsistent with the auditor's knowledge obtained in the audit;

(b)   the section describing the work of the audit committee that does not appropriately address matters communicated by the auditor to the audit committee;

(c)   the explanation as to why the annual report does not include such a statement or section that is materially inconsistent with the auditor's knowledge obtained in the audit;

(d)   the parts of the directors' statement required under the Listing Rules relating to the entity's compliance with the UK Corporate Governance Code containing provisions specified for review by the auditor in accordance with Listing Rule 9.8.10R(2) that do not properly disclose a departure from a relevant provision of the UK Corporate Governance Code; and

(e)   the directors' statement relating to Going Concern required under the Listing Rules in accordance with Listing Rule 9.8.6R(3) that is materially inconsistent with the auditor's knowledge obtained in the audit.

In reporting on other information, the auditor shall describe the specific reporting responsibility relating to these matters and shall report on each of these matters.

34.7.1   Statement on the directors' assessment of the principal risks that would threaten the solvency or liquidity of the entity

For entities reporting on their application of the UK Corporate Governance Code, the auditor shall also give a statement as to whether he has anything material to add or draw attention to in respect of:

(a)   the directors' confirmation in the annual report that they have carried out a robust assessment of the principal risks facing the entity, including those that would threaten its business model, future performance, solvency or liquidity;

(b)   the disclosures in the annual report that describe those risks and explain how they are being managed or mitigated; and

(c)   the directors' explanation in the annual report as to how they have assessed the prospects of the entity, over what period they have done so and why they consider that period to be appropriate, and their statement as to whether they have a reasonable expectation that the entity will be able to continue in operation and meet its liabilities as they fall due over the period of their assessment, including any related disclosures drawing attention to any necessary qualifications or assumptions.

In reporting under paragraph 22, the description of the auditor's responsibilities in relation to the other information required by paragraph 22(d) shall also include the auditor's additional responsibilities under paragraph 18-2 of ISA (UK and Ireland) 570 (Revised June 2016) and the auditor's responsibility to report whether the auditor has anything material to add or draw attention to in relation to each of the above elements of the other information. In addition, where the auditor has identified anything material to add or draw attention to in respect of these elements of the other information, the auditor shall include in the auditor's report a statement that describes any other material information that the auditor considers it appropriate to add or draw attention to.

34.8 Modified audit reports

When the auditor's opinion on the financial statement is adverse or qualified he should consider whether the matter giving rise to the modification of the opinion has any implications for his conclusions he is reporting in relation to other information.

34.9 Documentation

The auditor must ensure that he fully documents the procedures he performed on 'other information' and that he includes in his file the final version of the 'other information' on which he has performed this work.

34.10 Electronic publication

The Electronic Communication provisions of the *Companies Act* 2006 allow companies to meet, subject to certain conditions, their statutory reporting obligations to shareholders by distributing their annual financial statements and certain other reports electronically, or to post their financial statements on their website and advise shareholders of this. The implications for the auditor's work and report are set out in section **4.20**.

35 AUDITING IN AN E-COMMERCE ENVIRONMENT

35.1 Introduction

E-commerce (electronic commerce) is now an established and fast evolving element of many businesses. This chapter was based on material that is now out of date and has been withdrawn. In depth guidance on cyber security is outside the scope of this publication. Auditors should ensure that they have an understanding of client's use of information technology and their cyber security environment and consider the potential implications for the audit, taking specialist advice where appropriate.

36 THE AUDIT OF SMALL BUSINESSES

36.1 Introduction

In 2015, the government confirmed its intention to increase the threshold for audit exemption in line with increases to small company size limits. As a result, an increasing number of small companies do not now require an annual audit.

In order to claim exemption from audit under the *Companies Act* 2006, s. 477, a company must qualify as a small company in relation to the financial year in question. A company qualifies as small in its first year if it satisfies two out of the following criteria: turnover, total assets, and employees.

In subsequent years, a small company will continue to qualify as small unless the criteria are not met for two successive years. The relevant criteria are shown in the table below:

	For periods beginning before 1 January 2016	For periods beginning on or after 1 January 2016
Turnover	Less than £6.5m	Less than £10.2m
Total assets	Less than £3.26m	Less than £5.1m
Employees (average monthly number)	Less than 50	Less than 50

The turnover and asset thresholds for small companies increased to £10.2m and £5.1m respectively for years commencing on or after 1 January 2016 as a result of the EU Accounting Directive. Small companies may apply the new limits shown for accounting purposes for periods commencing on or after 1 January 2015 but will not be able to use them to claim audit exemption for periods commencing before 1 January 2016 if they would not have otherwise been so entitled. This means that for periods commencing in 2015 there will be a mismatch between the limits for accounting and auditing purposes. For periods beginning on or after 1 January 2016, however, the limits will be lined up again.

Audit exemption is subject to the rights of members of the company to require an audit and is conditional on certain statements being made by the directors on the balance sheet. For years ended prior to 1 October 2012, companies also needed to satisfy both the turnover and asset criteria above. This is no longer the case.

Certain companies, such as public companies, banks and insurance companies will not qualify as small companies and will not be entitled to the exemption. Special rules also apply to companies that are members of a group. Dormant companies (including dormant public companies) may also be entitled to audit exemption under the *Companies Act* 2006, s. 480.

There are, however, many small businesses which still require an audit because they do not qualify for the exemptions and even some which fall within the exemptions but for which its shareholders or some third party, for example, a lender requests an audit. Whilst ISAs (UK and Ireland) apply equally to the audit of smaller entities as to larger ones, the standards applicable do, in some cases, contain some considerations for smaller entities.

For more guidance on the accounting framework for small and micro-entities, refer to the book *Preparing Company Accounts: Small and Micros* published by Wolters Kluwer and available on CCH Online.

36.2   Guidance

Guidance to assist the auditors of small businesses in applying the documentation requirements contained within the current ISAs (UK and Ireland) is contained in Practice Note 26, *Guidance on Smaller Entity Audit Documentation*. The current version of this was issued in December 2009 to incorporate documentation changes introduced by the clarified ISAs. It is detailed in **36.10** below.

Further guidance on considerations specific to smaller entities is contained within the application material sections of many of the ISAs.

36.3   Characteristics of small businesses

The definition of a 'small business' cannot be a solely quantitative one, i.e. by reference to some measure of the size such as turnover. It also depends more upon qualitative characteristics.

Practice Note 26 notes that smaller, simpler entities are typically those where:

(a)   ownership is concentrated in a small number of individuals (or one individual) who are actively involved in managing the business;

(b)   the operations are uncomplicated with few sources of income and activities;

(c)   business processes and accounting systems are simple; and

(d)   internal controls are relatively few and may be informal.

A restriction on the number of managers that an entity has may mean that there is only limited management time to devote to such matters as formal internal control procedures. However, this lack of formality may not necessarily mean an increased risk of fraud or error. Indeed, supervisory controls exercised on a day-to-day basis by the owner-manager may also have a significant beneficial effect.

On the other hand, owner-managers may have the ability to override controls, and this may have an adverse effect on the control environment and lead to an increased risk of misstatement. The auditor must assess this based upon his knowledge of the attitude and motives of the owner-manager. In auditing small businesses, as with any other audit, the auditor should not assume that management is dishonest, but likewise should not assume unquestioned honesty.

Where a business has few sources of income and simple record-keeping procedures, this may make it easier to acquire, record and maintain knowledge of the business. Accounting populations may be very easily analysed and many analytical review tests may be simple to perform, with easily corroborated explanations for any variations found. Analytical review procedures may, as a result, significantly reduce the amounts of tests of detail to be performed.

By contrast, small businesses may have very informal accounting systems and completeness of records may therefore be a specific audit risk.

36.4   The relationship between small businesses and their auditors

Because they do not employ many people, small businesses often engage the auditor to provide additional services such as accounting, advising on accounting and computer systems, taxation and other matters such as the preparation of budgets and forecasts and assisting with obtaining finance.

This in-depth involvement with a small business will allow the auditor to keep his knowledge of the business up to date and help him to plan and conduct the audit as efficiently as possible.

Where assistance with the keeping of accounting records and the preparation of financial statements is given, the auditor is able to use the information gained as audit evidence, which may reduce the need for separate audit procedures.

Note, however, that provision of other services must always be limited by the knowledge that the client value of an audit derives from its objectivity. The auditor must always strive therefore to ensure that his relationship with small business does not prejudice his ability to form an objective opinion. To maintain this independence, he must ensure that he does not take over the role of management. This is a particular problem where management are not aware of the nature and extent of their own responsibilities in certain areas (for example, choice of accounting policies and preparation of financial statements), which they may otherwise regard as part of the audit.

The Ethical Standard *Provisions available for small entities* (PASE) provides useful guidance to the auditor in managing the potential self-review threat arising from performing non-audit services for small entities.

36.5   Responsibilities

36.5.1   The auditor's responsibilities relating to fraud

The fact that small businesses are often controlled by a single individual makes them more susceptible to the risk of fraud and error described in ISA (UK and Ireland) 240 (Revised June 2016). The auditor's knowledge of the owner-manager's general attitude to control issues and the way they exercise supervisory control will have a significant influence on his approach.

Examples of conditions or events typical of, but not exclusive to, small businesses, which may increase the likelihood of fraud or error or be indicative that it is occurring include those set out in **Table 1** below:

TABLE 1: Conditions which may indicate fraud or error

- the owner-manager has a specific motive to distort the financial statements, and has the ability to do so;
- there is confusion between personal and business transactions;
- the owner-manager's lifestyle is inconsistent with his remuneration;
- the owner-manager has not taken any holiday for a long period;
- there have been frequent changes in professional advisers;
- the audit start date is repeatedly delayed;
- there are demands to complete the audit in an unreasonably short period of time;
- accounting records are unavailable or have been lost;
- significant level of cash transactions with inadequate documentation;
- numerous unexplained aspects of audit evidence (e.g. differences with third-party confirmations, etc.);
- inappropriate use of accounting estimates;
- unusual transactions around the year end with a material effect on profit;
- unusual related party transactions; and
- excessive fees for agents or consultants.

36.5.2   Consideration of laws and regulations

The laws and regulations governing small companies tend to be largely identical to those of larger entities. A possible difference though, is the fact that small businesses tend to have less complicated activities, and thus are subject to a less complex regulatory environment. However the auditor must assess each situation on its own merits.

36.5.3   Going concern

The same considerations apply to smaller entities as they do to larger ones, however, the forecasts and projections may be more informal and less detailed than those prepared by management of a larger entity. The auditor will need to consider whether the directors have given sufficient attention to going concern issues and the use of the going concern basis of accounting and matters affecting the entity's ability to continue as a going concern.

In many cases, management of smaller entities may not have prepared a detailed assessment of the entity's ability to continue as a going concern, but instead may rely on in-depth knowledge of the business and its future prospects. Nevertheless, the auditor needs to evaluate management's assessment and it may be appropriate to discuss the medium and long-term financing of the entity with management, provided their views can be corroborated. Continued financial support by owner-managers is often important to smaller entities' ability to continue as a going concern and the auditor may need to evaluate the owner-manager's ability to meet the obligations under the support arrangements.

Although smaller entities may be able to respond quickly to exploit opportunities, they may lack the reserves to sustain their operations in difficult times. The impact of the bank ceasing to support the entity, for example, or the loss of a principal supplier or customer may be greater than the impact on a larger entity.

Where the auditor assists an owner-manager with the assessment of going concern and the production of projections and budgets, he must ensure that the owner-manager is aware that he remains responsible for this information and the reasonableness of the assumptions on which the information is based.

36.5.4   Agreeing the terms of the engagement

One way of ensuring that owner-managers are aware of their responsibilities in areas such as going concern, as mentioned above, and their responsibilities for financial statements, even when these have been prepared by the auditor, is to ensure that this is stated in the engagement letter.

36.5.5   Subsequent events

Because of the lack of reporting deadlines often associated with small companies, the length of time to be considered in a subsequent events review will often be greater.

In addition, accounting records and minutes may not have been written up since the year end and the auditor may need to rely on representations from the owner-managers. Here a representation letter, dated when the financial statements are approved and which ensures that the entire period since the year end has been covered, becomes increasingly important.

36.6 Planning, controlling and recording

36.6.1 Planning an audit of financial statements

The basic considerations relating to planning are identical to entities of all sizes; however, planning the audit of a small business need not be a complex or time consuming exercise. With a smaller team, coordination of, and communication between, team members should be easier.

Where accountancy work is being performed, the planning process must be properly co-ordinated in order to gain the most benefit from effort and cost. Planning should also be reconsidered as the accountancy work progresses.

Planning the audits of smaller businesses may also be easier in that much of the information may be obtained from:

- discussion with the owner-manager; and
- the knowledge of the audit engagement partner who is often involved in the provision of other services and will have some first-hand knowledge.

There will be cases where an audit is carried out entirely by the engagement partner, meaning that the issue of direction and supervision of engagement team members and review of their work does not arise. In such cases, the engagement partner, having personally conducted all aspects of the work, will be aware of all material issues. This can present other issues, however, for example, the ability to form an objective view on the appropriateness of the judgments made in the course of the audit can present practical problems when the same individual also performs the entire audit. If particularly complex or unusual issues are involved, and the audit is performed by a sole practitioner, it may be desirable to consult with other suitably-experienced auditors or the auditor's professional body.

36.6.2 Identifying and assessing risks of material misstatement

Often the provision of other services to small businesses enables the auditor to gain additional information about the client's accounting system, activities, management style, plans for the future, etc. However, this information may be obtained incidentally, and therefore, it is important to document such findings so that they can be taken into account when planning and conducting the audit. Irrespective of the circumstances, inquiry about identified risks and how they are addressed by management is still necessary for the audit.

The documentation must be of a level sufficient to:

- facilitate proper planning of the audit; and
- enable any change of responsibility within the audit firm (either partner or staff) to occur smoothly.

Many smaller entities will not have interim or monthly financial information that can be used for purposes of analytical procedures. In these circumstances, although the auditor may be able to perform limited analytical procedures for planning the audit or obtain some information through inquiry, he may need to plan to perform analytical procedures to identify and assess the risks of material misstatement when an early draft of the entity's financial statements is available.

36.6.3   Materiality

The levels of materiality used for the preparation of financial statements by the auditor and the audit work itself are likely to be different as management will want to ensure that their accounting records are as accurate as possible, which involves a greater degree of accuracy than would be necessary to give an unqualified audit opinion.

In the case of small businesses, draft financial statements may not be available on which to assess planning materiality. Therefore, it is important for any initial judgments to be revisited once the final figures are available.

To focus the auditor's attention on the more significant financial statement items, while determining the audit strategy, materiality is generally assessed by reference to some measure of the size of the business. One method is to use a percentage of a figure in the financial statements, such as:

- profit or loss before tax (adjusted, if appropriate, for the effect of any abnormal levels of items of expenditure such as directors' remuneration);
- turnover; or
- balance sheet total.

If an entity is at or near 'break-even' point, as may more often be the case with small businesses, assessing materiality as a percentage of pre-tax results alone may be inappropriate and lead to excessive audit work.

36.7   Accounting systems and internal control

36.7.1   Identifying and assessing risks and the auditor's responses to them

The information system and related business processes relevant to financial reporting in small entities is likely to be less sophisticated than in larger

559

entities, but its role is just as significant. Small entities with active management involvement may not need extensive descriptions of accounting procedures, sophisticated accounting records, or written policies. Understanding the entity's information system relevant to financial reporting may therefore be easier in an audit of smaller entities, and may be more dependent on inquiry than on review of documentation. The need to obtain an understanding, however, remains important.

In applying ISAs to small entities, control risk is invariably assessed as high and therefore it is extremely unlikely that the audit of a small business will involve tests of controls. In many small businesses, there will be no formal system of internal control. This does not make such businesses 'unauditable' as it only raises the possibility of a risk of error. Such a risk may be offset by a number of factors and the absence of error may be established by reference to evidence obtained externally to the company. In fact, as explained above, a strong control environment will more often than not offset the potential problems that could result from lack of formal internal controls. Even where controls exist, they will not generally be ones that are easy to test. Thus, it is rarely cost-effective to plan to rely on them. In these circumstances, audit evidence may have to be obtained entirely through substantive procedures.

As small businesses tend to have few internal controls, the assessment of audit risk will often depend entirely on the assessment of inherent risk, as the risks identified here cannot be mitigated by a strong control environment. Therefore, it is important that the assessment of inherent risk is performed carefully and in possession of full knowledge of the client, its business and trading position.

In addition, the risks of small businesses are often mitigated by the auditor's providing of other services, such as accountancy, and this should also be taken into account.

The auditor needs to remember that although disclosures in financial statements of smaller entities may be less detailed or less complex, this does not relieve him of the responsibility to obtain an understanding of the entity and its environment, including internal control, as it relates to disclosures.

36.7.2   Service organisations

Smaller entities often make use of service organisations, for example, by using an external bookkeeping service which may do anything from the processing of certain transactions (for example, payment of payroll taxes) and maintenance of their accounting records to the preparation of their financial statements.

The use of such a service organisation for the preparation of its financial statements does not relieve management and, where appropriate, those charged with governance, of their responsibilities for the financial statements.

36.8   Evidence

36.8.1   Audit evidence and external confirmations

Although the ISAs recognise that audit evidence may be obtained from a number of sources (such as tests of controls and substantive procedures), where segregation of duties is limited and evidence of supervisory control is lacking, evidence may be obtained entirely from substantive procedures. This would often be the case for small businesses.

As mentioned above, gaining assurance from accountancy procedures may lead to a reduction in the level of other audit procedures. This assurance may be gained through:

- examining prime documentation which supports a transaction or balance;
- calculating a balance for inclusion in the financial statements; or
- posting entries in the accounting records.

While the work may not be performed by those directly involved with the audit, it is important to ensure that the accountancy work is planned with the needs of the audit in mind.

While some verification work may be undertaken in connection with accountancy services provided to the entity, there will always be a need for some additional audit procedures in areas where this does not on its own provide sufficient assurance, for example, on the recovery of debtors, the valuation and ownership of stock, the carrying value of fixed assets and investments and the completeness of creditors. For convenience, this work may be carried out at the same time as the accountancy work.

In the case of small businesses, the completeness assertion may cause the auditor particular problems. The two main reasons for this are:

- the owner-manager occupies a dominant position and may be able to ensure that some transactions are not recorded; and
- the business may not have internal control procedures that provide documentary evidence that all transactions are recorded.

With small entities, as with other audits, the auditor should plan and conduct the audit with an 'attitude of professional scepticism', and should not accept representations from management as a substitute for other audit evidence that would be expected to be available. However, unless the audit reveals evidence to the contrary, the auditor is entitled to accept representations as truthful and records as genuine.

36.8.2   Analytical procedures

The use of analytical review procedures when planning the audit of a small business may be limited due to lack of reliable information such as interim or monthly financial reports. Therefore, analytical procedures at the planning stage may be more worthwhile once some of the accountancy work is completed. In some cases, a brief review of the general ledger or discussions with the owner-manager may prove sufficient.

When the activities of a business are uncomplicated and the number of variables to be considered is limited, analytical procedures may often be a very cost-effective way of obtaining audit assurance.

Such analytical review may also provide effective evidence regarding completeness, where expected results can be predicted with a reasonable degree of precision and confidence.

All auditors are required to perform a final analytical review to assess whether the financial statements are consistent with their knowledge of the business. However, due to the relative simplicity of small businesses many of the procedures performed are very similar to those used as substantive procedures. These may include:

* comparison to prior year;
* comparison to budget or forecast;
* review of trends in ratios;
* consideration of whether any changes in business are adequately reflected; and
* enquiry into unusual and unexplained features of the financial statements.

36.8.3   Audit sampling

The smaller populations normally encountered in small businesses may occasionally make it feasible to test:

* the whole population; or
* some part of the population – for example, all items above a given amount – applying analytical procedures to the balance of the population, if it is material.

Where the auditor decides to sample a population, the same underlying principles apply to a small business as to a larger one.

36.8.4   Written representations

An important issue in respect of audit evidence in relation to the completeness assertion is that of acceptance of management representations. In many smaller businesses, the accounting system is often controlled by one or two individuals and the auditor may have difficulty in obtaining sufficient reliable evidence to assure himself of the completeness of populations. This is particularly the case with cash businesses but may also apply to service industries or in businesses where stock is not purchased for specific customers. The auditor may also need to rely on representations when establishing that all expenditure is a valid charge on the business, given the confusion between the company and the owner in many small companies.

On their own, representations as to the completeness and accuracy of the accounting records cannot be sufficient. They may only be used if they are supported by or support the results of substantive tests of transactions and analytical review of costs and margins (or possibly one of them).

36.8.5 Initial audit engagements and comparative information

A small business which is a limited company may find itself in the position where its comparatives are taken from preceding period financial statements which were covered by the exemption from audit conferred on small companies.

The auditor will still need to obtain sufficient assurance about the opening balances and comparatives. Some information may be easily available (such as cash and debtors), but where he is unable to obtain the required evidence, he must consider qualifying his audit report. This issue is discussed in more detail in **Chapter 19** where a suitable report for use in this situation is set out.

36.8.6 Estimates and fair values

In smaller entities, the circumstances requiring an accounting estimate often are such that the owner-manager is capable of making the required point estimate himself. In some cases, however, an expert will be needed. Discussion with the owner-manager early in the audit process about the nature of any accounting estimates, the completeness of such estimates, and the adequacy of the estimating process may assist the owner-manager in determining the need to use an expert.

The process for making accounting estimates is likely to be less structured than in larger entities. However, just because the entity has no formal established process, it does not mean that management is not able to provide a basis upon which the auditor can test the accounting estimate.

36.8.7 Related parties

Small businesses are as likely as larger businesses to enter into related party transactions, and the disclosures are identical.

Control activities in smaller entities are likely to be less formal and smaller entities may have no documented processes for dealing with related party relationships and transactions. An owner-manager may mitigate some of the risks arising from related party transactions, or potentially increase those risks, through active involvement in all the main aspects of the transactions. For such entities, the auditor may obtain an understanding of the related party relationships and transactions, and any relevant controls that exist, through inquiry of management combined with other procedures, such as observation of management's oversight and review activities, and inspection of available relevant documentation.

Equally, auditors of small businesses are more likely to be closely involved in the preparation of the financial statements, and may have a relatively detailed knowledge of the businesses' transactions, enabling them to identify those that are disclosable.

36.9   Reporting

36.9.1   The independent auditor's report on financial statements

The auditor's reports, including the auditor's report on a small company are discussed in **Chapter 4** (see **4.18**).

36.9.2   Communication with those charged with governance

In the case of smaller entities, the auditor may communicate in a less structured manner with those charged with governance than in the case of listed or larger entities. This is acceptable provided communication is still relevant and appropriate.

Small businesses will often have simple, informal accounting systems and the scope for detailed internal control procedures based on segregation of duties will be limited. This is not necessarily a weakness, as the accounting system in place may be suitable for the size and complexity of the business and the degree of owner-manager involvement. The auditor must, therefore, ensure that recommendations to management are relevant and realistic to their business.

In addition, if management has not acted upon points made in previous management letters as the suggestions are not practical or cost-effective, the auditor is likely to gain little from repeating the same recommendations again. However, he should continue to check that the recommendations remain valid.

While the concepts underlying control activities in smaller entities are likely to be similar to those in larger entities, they are likely to operate in a less formal manner.

Smaller entities may also find that certain types of control activities are not necessary because of controls applied by management. For example, management's sole authority for granting credit to customers and approving significant purchases can provide effective control over important account balances and transactions, lessening or removing the need for more detailed control activities.

This higher level of management involvement needs to be balanced against the greater potential for management override of controls.

36.10 Practice Note 26 and documentation

36.10.1 Background

Practice Note 26, *Guidance on Smaller Entity Audit Documentation* is aimed at auditors of companies that are exempt from audit, but have chosen to have a voluntary audit. It provides guidance on the application of the documentation requirements set out in the ISAs (UK and Ireland) for the audits of such entities.

Practice Note 26 provides examples of documentation where working papers have been prepared to meet the requirements of the ISAs, but without documenting the entirety of the auditor's understanding of the entity and matters related to it. The illustrative examples are not, however, mandatory.

It is also worth remembering that the auditor of a smaller entity may find it helpful and efficient to record various aspects of the audit together in a single document, with cross-references to supporting working papers as appropriate.

36.10.2 The purpose of audit documentation

ISA (UK and Ireland) 230 (Revised June 2016) requires auditors to prepare audit documentation that provides:

- a sufficient and appropriate record of the basis for the auditor's report; and
- evidence that the audit was performed in accordance with ISAs (UK and Ireland) and applicable legal and regulatory requirements.

In addition, good documentation serves a number of purposes, including:

- assisting the audit team to plan and perform the audit;
- assisting members of the audit team to fulfil their review responsibilities;
- enabling the audit team to be accountable for its work;

- retaining a record of matters of continuing significance to future audits; and
- enabling an experienced auditor to conduct quality control reviews or external inspections as required.

These points remain relevant irrespective of the size of the entity. However, the audit documentation for the audit of a smaller entity will generally be less extensive than that for the audit of a larger entity.

36.10.3 Special considerations for smaller entities

A number of factors will influence the nature and extent of documentation required for a small company:

- the qualitative indicators of a simple entity:
  - ownership is concentrated in a small number of individuals who are actively involved in managing the business;
  - the operations are uncomplicated;
  - business processes and accounting systems are simple; and
  - internal controls are relatively few and may be informal;
- the characteristics of a smaller entity audit team and the way they carry out their work, including:
  - the provision of accounting and business related advice;
  - relatively small team size; and
  - the use of proprietary audit systems.

Concentration of ownership and management

For small entities, there are often few owners who are typically involved in the day to day running of the company, and this means that documentation of ownership is typically brief. Particular care should be taken, however, when documenting family and other close relationships which may impact the auditor's risk assessment in respect of related parties.

Uncomplicated operations

Typically, smaller entities have a limited range of products or services and a limited number of locations. This means that documentation of the auditor's understanding of their operations is likely to be simple and relatively brief. Such documentation may be in free-form narrative notes or by completing a structured form.

Simple accounting systems

For small companies, accounting systems are typically uncomplicated, with few, if any, personnel solely engaged in record keeping. There are likely to be no documented descriptions of accounting policies and procedures and limited opportunities for segregation of duties.

Small entities will typically use well known accounting systems, and previous knowledge of that system can help the auditor focus on areas of risk.

Limited and informal controls

For the audit of smaller entities, most of the audit evidence will typically come from substantive tests of detail. However, there is still a requirement for the auditor to document his understanding of the entity's system of internal control relevant to the audit.

Both size and economic considerations mean that internal controls are usually limited in such operations, but the direct control that management is able to exert will be an important feature of the control environment. Therefore, the extent and nature of management's involvement is likely to be a key aspect of the auditor's documentation, including whether the dominant position of management may be abused, leading to an override of controls.

Professional relationship between auditors and small entity clients

It is common for audit firms to provide non-audit services to smaller clients. The provision of such services can help the auditor gain further understanding of the entity and keep his knowledge up to date. The auditor must keep in mind the need to maintain objectivity throughout his work.

The Practice Note lists the following considerations associated with providing non-audit services:

- to achieve completeness of audit documentation, information, gained as a result of the provision of other services, which is used as audit evidence needs to be incorporated or cross-referenced into the audit documentation;
- the auditor's assessment of his objectivity and independence is documented, including a description of the threats identified and the safeguards applied to eliminate or reduce the threats to an acceptable level; and
- the respective responsibilities of directors (or equivalent) and the auditor are documented in an engagement letter. This is particularly important where the audit firm is involved in the preparation of the financial statements.

Small audit team

Whatever the size of the audit team, even if it is an audit partner working alone, the documentation must be sufficient to enable an experienced auditor, having no previous connection with the audit, to understand the audit approach adopted, the audit evidence obtained, and the significant matters arising during the audit and the conclusions reached thereon.

If the audit team size increases, further documentation may be useful in enabling the team to obtain an appropriate understanding of the entity.

Use of proprietary audit system

Where the auditor of a small entity operates in a small practice, proprietary audit systems are likely to be used. Such systems are designed to deal with a wide variety of situations and must be tailored or adapted to meet each client's circumstances.

Sections of such systems relating to documenting the client, its operations and controls are usually checklists or blank spaces for narrative notes. Audit team members should be adequately trained before using such tools to ensure that they do not prepare excessive and, therefore, costly audit documentation.

36.10.4   Audit documentation requirements in the ISAs

The Practice Note lists the documentation requirements set out in each ISA on an ISA by ISA basis. The table is not reproduced here. The Practice Note, and hence the table, has not been updated since it was written in 2009. This means that the documentation requirements listed have not been updated for any amendments in the most recent revisions of ISAs (UK and Ireland).

36.10.5   Assembling the final audit file

Chapter 12 sets out the procedures for assembling the final file, including document retention requirements and how to deal with the situation where documentation requires amendment after the date of the auditor's report.

36.11   International guidance

IFAC has also issued a *Guide to Using ISAs in the Audits of Small- and Medium-Sized Entities*. The guide is based on ISAs; however, is still applicable to audits under ISAs (UK and Ireland) and is useful reading for auditors of smaller entities. The guide can be found on the IFAC website (www.ifac.org).

37   OTHER OPERATIONAL ISSUES

37.1   Introduction

This chapter covers various guidance issued by the ICAEW and FRC covering:

- the auditing implications of FRS 102;
- XBRL tagging of information in financial statements;
- computer assisted audit techniques;
- paid cheques; and
- auditing when financial market conditions are difficult.

37.2   The auditing implications of FRS 102

In recent years, the FRC fundamentally revised financial reporting standards in the UK and Ireland, replacing the extant standards with a suite of new Financial Reporting Standards. These new UK GAAP standards mostly took effect from 1 January 2015, except that small companies may continue to apply the FRSSE for periods prior to 1 January 2016 and thereafter apply the new Section 1A of FRS 102 or FRS 105.

Of most relevance to the auditor is FRS 102 *The Financial Reporting Standard applicable in the UK and Ireland*. It is effective for accounting periods beginning on or after 1 January 2015. This differs in a number of significant respects from previous accounting standards, giving rise to issues for both companies and their auditors.

The new UK GAAP standards and detailed guidance is available on CCH Online and Navigate GAAP as well as in various books published by Wolters Kluwer.

37.2.1   Guidance for auditors

In September 2014, the ICAEW published guidance for auditors in the form of Technical Release TECH 13/14AAF *Issues for auditors arising from the implementation of FRS 102, The Financial Reporting Standard applicable in the UK and Republic of Ireland*.

FRS 102 is to be applied by all entities which are neither required nor elect to apply EU-adopted IFRSs, FRS 101 *Reduced Disclosure Framework*, FRS 105 *The Financial Reporting Standard applicable to the Micro-entities Regime* or the FRSSE. It will, therefore be applied by the majority of large and medium-sized UK entities.

The FRSSE was also withdrawn on 1 January 2016 which will lead to more entities applying FRS 102 or FRS 105 in due course.

FRS 102 is based on the IASB standard IFRS for SMEs which means there are a number of key differences between previous UK GAAP and FRS 102, for example, in the areas of financial instruments, investment properties, business combinations, deferred tax and defined benefit pension schemes.

As the standard is effective for periods beginning on or after 1 January 2015, and comparatives will be required, companies and other entities should be considering the options available to them and the degree of change to their financial reporting. In many cases, this will mean significant work and challenges for these entities.

There are also significant implications for the auditors of the entities subject to this change and TECH 13/14AAF addresses the key issues of concern to those auditors. It covers the technical and process challenges arising for them and the risks that they will need to address, as well as ethical issues that may arise. Auditors should consider at an early stage both what they should expect their clients to be doing and also what they should be doing themselves. Auditors should take early action and advise their clients to start preparing for transition as early as possible, if they have not done so already.

There are a number of things the auditor should expect the entity to have considered. To ensure the client entity is appropriately prepared for the transition, the auditor may wish to have an early discussion with the client about their plans, including considering the following areas:

- clarifying the responsibilities of management;
- establishing a timeline for transition;
- communicating changes with stakeholders;
- assessing the need for any additional resources or training;
- identifying the differences between the entity's current accounting policies and FRS 102;
- identifying any changes in financial data and additional information needed to meet the revised requirements;
- identifying any impact on wider business issues, such as considering bank covenant arrangements;
- planning the transition process; and
- implementing the changes.

37.2.2   Ethical considerations

Many entities are likely to benefit from the support of their auditors in the transition process, however, the auditor needs to ensure he considers ethical matters before providing assistance to clients. For example, clients may ask the auditor to provide accounting assistance in the preparation of financial statements under FRS 102, or ask for advice on the tax consequences that might arise as a result of FRS 102, or assistance with valuations under FRS 102. In all of these situations, the auditor must carefully document the nature of the service and consider all threats and safeguards before concluding whether he is able to assist the client.

In providing such advice, the auditor needs to guard against giving bookkeeping advice or making specific accounting entries that go beyond those permitted by ES 5[1] *Non-audit services provided to audited entities*, i.e. beyond those considered to be of a technical, mechanical or informative nature (see **Chapter 2**). When considering the extent to which the auditor may provide advice to his clients on the transition to FRS 102, it should be clearly established that management retains full responsibility for all financial information, including the selection and application of appropriate accounting policies. Management cannot ask their auditor to make decisions about the preparation and presentation of financial statements under the new standard. Whilst the auditor can assist in identifying the choices that need to be made and discussing them with management, he cannot make any of these choices for management.

Similarly, the Ethical Standards contain strict prohibitions on the provision of valuations by the auditor. On transition to FRS 102, many entities will be required to carry more items at a valuation than under their previous GAAP. Where the entity is not familiar with valuation techniques for such items, they may ask the auditor for assistance. However, in accordance with the Ethical Standards, the auditor is not permitted to provide a valuation for a listed entity where the valuation is material, nor for any other entity where the valuation involves a significant degree of subjective judgment and has a material effect on the financial statements, either separately or in aggregate with other valuations provided.

TECH 13/14AAF provides further details of ethical considerations and scenarios.

37.2.3   Potential problem areas

With the adoption of FRS 102, **Table 1** shows some of the areas which may present problems for the client and/or auditor:

TABLE 1: Potential problem areas with the adoption of FRS 102

Audit team members and engagement partner	Do the audit team, and the engagement partner, themselves have the necessary skills and competence or do they themselves require additional training in FRS 102?
Ethical requirements	As noted above, there may be an increased likelihood of threats arising from the provision of non-audit services.
Fraud risk assessment	Changes to accounting systems may provide increased opportunity for aggressive earnings management and fraud.

---

1 The FRC proposes to replace the Ethical Standards with a single revised Ethical Standard for periods commencing 17 June 2016. Full details are in **Chapter 2**.

Comparatives	Comparatives have to be restated under FRS 102, i.e. for a year ending 31 December 2015, the comparatives would need to be restated for the year ended 31 December 2014 and an opening statement of balances at the date of transition also prepared. In this case, the date of transition would be 1 January 2014. There may be some items in the financial statements for which management may find it difficult to obtain historical valuations and such information should be gathered as soon as possible.
Transitional adjustments	Transitional adjustments may be permitted and/or required in certain areas, for example, property valuation, recognition of forex forward contracts, deferred tax provisions. Such adjustments may reduce reserves to such a level that they affect dividends already paid out for 2014 if not considered in good time.
Goodwill	FRS 102 has different requirements around the determination of a useful economic life for goodwill.
Fair values	FRS 102 generally requires, for example, investment properties to be revalued to fair value rather than market value. This may create problems in setting a fair value for the first time. The auditor will also need to ensure that exceptions granted by FRS 102 are not abused by client entities.
Pension schemes	Under FRS 102, for groups, the pension deficit will likely need to be recognised in at least one entity rather than just at a group level. This can impact on reserves and tax and the auditor should be aware of this when auditing the component entities.

TECH 13/14AAF contains detailed guidance on the implementation of FRS 102, and also contains a very helpful table in Appendix 1 highlighting some of the specific issues likely to arise during the period of implementing FRS 102.

37.3   XBRL tagging of information in financial statements

37.3.1   Background

In February 2010, the APB issued Bulletin 2010/1, *XBRL tagging of information in audited financial statements – guidance for auditors*. This was in response to the joint statement by HMRC and Companies House made in September 2009, that the Company Tax Return, including the supporting statutory accounts and tax computations showing the derivation from those accounts of the entries in the Company Tax Return, must be delivered electronically using the Inline XBRL (iXBRL) format. This requirement is mandatory for accounting periods ending on or after 31 March 2010 where the tax return is submitted to HMRC after 31 March 2011.

XBRL stands for Extensible Business Reporting Language and it is a computer-based language for the electronic communication of business data. It works by tagging individual items of information with machine-readable codes which are drawn from a library of codes referred to as a 'taxonomy'. The use of XBRL allows data to be more easily accessed, manipulated and reviewed. In line XBRL uses tags which can still be read by the human eye, for example, by hovering the computer mouse over the tagged item.

37.3.2   Auditor's involvement

Aspects of XBRL tagging can be automated, but there is likely to remain an element of judgment over which tag to map to which piece of data.

There is no requirement for an audit of the data or the XBRL tagging and the ISAs (UK and Ireland) do not impose a general requirement on the auditor to check the tagging. In addition, because the XBRL tag is just a machine-readable rendering of the data in the financial statements it does not constitute 'other information' as defined in ISA (UK and Ireland) 720 (Revised June 2016), and the requirement to read the other information with the purpose of identifying material inconsistencies or material misstatement is not invoked (see **Chapter 34**).

There is a possibility that regulators may impose a requirement for companies to obtain assurance from their auditor on XBRL-tagged data in the future.

However, some companies may wish to engage an audit or accountancy firm to:

- perform the tagging exercise;
- perform an agreed upon procedures engagement to provide assurance about the tagging process;
- provide advice on the selection of individual tags;
- supply accounts preparation software that automates the tagging; or
- train management in XBRL tagging.

If such non-audit services are provided by the company's auditor, he must consider whether any possible threats to independence and objectivity arise. Particular care must be taken not to take decisions that are the responsibility of the management of the entity and suitable safeguards should be put in place.

Although there is currently no audit requirement in relation to XBRL tagging, firms should carefully consider how services provided either to set up a system for XBRL tagging or to tag data on behalf of a client may become a self-review threat if an audit requirement is introduced in future years. If XBRL becomes integrated into accounting systems, it may be difficult to separate tagging from accounting services. In such situations, the prohibition in Ethical Standard 5 that auditors of listed companies (or significant affiliates of listed companies) cannot provide accounting services to those clients will apply (see **2.6.6**).

37.3.3   Technical Release AAF 04/10

In June 2011, the Audit and Assurance Faculty of the ICAEW issued Technical Release AAF 04/10 to provide guidance for practitioners who are requested to perform agreed upon procedures engagements in relation to XBRL-tagged data.

In order for iXBRL to be useful, the data included must be accurate and reliable. Businesses may request practitioners to perform additional procedures to address the accuracy, existence, completeness or consistency of XBRL tagged information included within financial statements.

Terms of engagement

As a company's tax return to HMRC is a private submission, the majority of such agreed upon procedures engagements will not involve a third party and the terms of engagement should be agreed between practitioners and management. Where a company's auditor is requested to perform the procedures, he should ensure that he has satisfied himself that there are no threats to independence that arise in relation to Ethical Standards (see **Chapter 2**). Particular attention should be applied to the management threat and the self-review threat.

The entity's management is responsible for selecting the XBRL tags to be used and for applying them to the financial information. The practitioner will provide a factual report on his findings and will provide no assurance or opinion. The report should be addressed solely to those who have agreed to the procedures being performed.

An example engagement letter is given in **Table 2**.

TABLE 2: Extracts from an example engagement letter for an agreed upon procedures engagement relating to the accuracy, existence, consistency and completeness of XBRL tagged data included within financial statements prepared in iXBRL format

This letter is to confirm our understanding of the arrangements for our performance of certain agreed-upon procedures to assist management and the audit committee of ABC Company in evaluating the accuracy, existence, consistency and completeness of XBRL tagged data included within financial statements prepared in an iXBRL format.

Financial statements prepared in iXBRL format contain XBRL-tagged data which is readable by computers and which is formatted in accordance with the human-readable financial statements used as the source document.

ABC Company's iXBRL financial statements are separate and distinct from the source statutory financial statements [to be] signed by the directors on [date], which [do not/will not] include XBRL tagged-data.

XBRL tags are drawn from published taxonomies. The relevant taxonomies for this engagement are the UK Common Data Set and [[the UK GAAP/UK-IFRS Taxonomies published by XBRL UK]/[the UK GAAP minimum tagging set/UK-IFRS minimum tagging set published by HMRC]].

Responsibilities

You are responsible for preparing iXBRL financial statements to accompany Company Tax Returns. Accordingly, you are responsible for selecting suitable XBRL taxonomies and applying XBRL tags to financial information to prepare iXBRL financial statements.

Our responsibility is to complete the procedures set out in the attachment to this letter and report our findings. These procedures are performed solely for your purposes. You are responsible for determining whether the scope of our work is sufficient for your purposes. Consequently, we make no representation regarding the sufficiency of the procedures described in Attachment A either for the purpose for which this report has been requested or for any other purpose.

We have no responsibility for the completeness, accuracy or consistency of the XBRL-tagged data included within the iXBRL financial statements provided to us for the purposes of our work.

Our work

We will conduct our engagement in accordance with ICAEW Technical Release 04/10: Performing agreed upon procedures engagements that address XBRL-tagged data included within financial statements prepared in an iXBRL format.

Our engagement to perform agreed-upon procedures will not constitute either an audit or review made in accordance with International Standards on Auditing (UK & Ireland) or the International Standard on Review Engagements (UK & Ireland).

Consequently, we will not express any assurance on the XBRL-tagged data included within the iXBRL financial statements. If we were to perform additional procedures or if we were to perform an audit or review, that would constitute a separate engagement.

Reporting

At the completion of our agreed-upon procedures, we will provide you with a report of our findings in the form that is attached to this letter [attach pro forma report], solely for your information. Our report is not to be used for any other purpose, recited or referred to in any document, copied or made available (in whole or in part) or disclosed to any other person without our prior written consent. We accept no duty, responsibility or liability to any other party in connection with the report or this engagement.

Planning

Practitioners must obtain a general understanding of the tags or taxonomies relevant to the engagement and should be mindful that taxonomies are subject to periodic revision and may not remain relevant year on year. If the engagement requires expertise beyond that possessed by the practitioner, an expert may be used to assist with the engagement (see **Chapter 31**).

Procedures

The extent of procedures performed will be agreed between the practitioner and management. The level of testing required will be determined by:

- the length of the financial statements and the number of taggable items contained therein;
- the relevant taxonomies used;
- the method of preparation of the financial statements and the controls over their preparation; and
- management's expectations of the competence and experience of those who performed the tagging.

Possible procedures may include checking:

- the consistency of the human-readable element of the iXBRL financial statements with the source signed financial statements which were previously approved by the directors;
- whether the correct taxonomies have been applied;
- the accuracy, existence, completeness and consistency of XBRL-tagged data; and
- any company-specific extensions to the relevant taxonomies.

Further possible procedures are provided in an appendix to the Technical Release.

Reporting

The report should be factual in nature and not give an opinion. An example report is given in **Table 3**.

TABLE 3: Illustrative report for an agreed upon procedures engagement that address the accuracy, existence, consistency and completeness of XBRL tagged data included within financial statements prepared in an iXBRL format

Report of factual findings in connection with agreed-upon procedures that address XBRL-tagged data included within financial statements prepared in an iXBRL format

To [those who engaged the practitioner]

We have performed the procedures set out in Attachment A [*not shown in this example*], solely to assist you in evaluating the accuracy, existence, completeness and consistency of XBRL-tagged data included within the iXBRL financial statements of ABC Company for the [year/period ended date].

Financial statements prepared in iXBRL format contain XBRL-tagged data which is readable by computers and which is formatted in accordance with the human-readable financial statements used as the source document. ABC Company's iXBRL financial statements are separate and distinct from the source statutory financial statements signed by the directors on [date], which do not include XBRL tagged-data.

Our engagement was undertaken in accordance with the ICAEW's Technical Release 04/10: *Performing agreed-upon procedures engagements that address XBRL-tagged data included within financial statements prepared in an iXBRL format.*

The sufficiency of the procedures is solely the responsibility of ABC Company's management. Consequently we make no representation regarding the sufficiency of the procedures described in Attachment A either for the purpose for which this report has been requested or for any other purpose.

The findings relating to the procedures are included in Attachment A.

Because the procedures do not constitute any type of assurance engagement, we do not express any assurance on the XBRL-tagged data included within the iXBRL financial statements.

Had we performed additional procedures or had we performed an audit or review, other matters might have come to our attention that would have been reported to you.

Our report is provided solely to you and solely for your information. Our report is not to be used for any other purpose, recited or referred to in any document, copied or made available (in whole or in part) or disclosed to any other person without our prior written consent. We accept no duty, responsibility or liability to any other party in connection with the report or this engagement.

[Name of Practitioner]

[Date]

[Address]

37.4   Computer-assisted audit techniques

ISAs (UK and Ireland) do not provide any detailed guidance on computer-assisted audit techniques (CAATs), but we provide some background on them below.

Auditors may use CAATs to:

- examine the entity's computer files (audit software); and
- check the processing of data (test data).

CAATs may in some cases be the only way to obtain some of the required audit evidence or may improve the efficiency of the audit.

The main type of CAAT is an audit enquiry package. These may take various forms, including separate software packages or audit functions embedded in the client's software. This can be used to perform substantive tests, compliance tests and analytical review procedures including:

- reperforming calculations and casts, such as payroll calculations, calculations of royalties payable, casts of debtor balances, etc.;
- selecting samples and checking the population for unusual conditions, such as duplicated items;
- testing items for certain conditions and printing out exceptions;
- comparing files at two points in time to detect records that have been added or deleted so that the reason and authority for these can be examined;
- creating information not otherwise available from or reported by the client's system; and
- proving certain figures in total by matching standing data with transaction data.

The choice between CAATs and manual audit techniques will depend on:

- whether there is any evidence of performance, as computers may not leave visible audit evidence, making manual testing impracticable;
- the cost-effectiveness of the CAAT and whether it can be used for other audit tests;
- whether the use of CAATs will be quicker and, if so, whether this is important;
- whether the relevant computer files are available, as some CAATs need to be carried out before ledgers for the relevant period are closed down;
- where CAATs are used by internal auditors, the extent that the external auditors are able to rely on them; and
- whether the data can be made available in a form capable of being interpreted by the IS auditors.

37.5   Paid cheques

Changes in legislation and audit practices have made it less important for the auditor to review paid cheques returned to entities by their clearing bank.

37.5.1 Existing guidance

Guidance in this area was updated in February 2009 with the publication of the ICAEW's Audit and Assurance Faculty Technical Release AAF 1/09 *Paid Cheques*. The guidance encourages the auditor to:

- consider using alternative procedures;
- advise his clients to adopt more rigorous controls over cheque payments; and
- use cost-effective methods of examining paid cheques where they consider it to be necessary.

The statement does not provide detailed procedural guidance.

37.5.2 Audit evidence

Where adequate controls exist over purchasing and cheque payments it may not be necessary to examine returned cheques. In cases where controls are weak, the auditor may want evidence that:

- there has been no fraudulent endorsement of cheques;
- cheques are properly recorded and controlled; and
- the cash book accurately reflects details of them.

With regard to purchase ledger items, other forms of evidence may be sufficient such as the reconciliation of supplier statements. Evidence on other items may be obtained from analytical review or examination of supporting evidence.

Additionally, the entity may use other forms of payment, such as electronic funds transfers, standing orders or direct debits.

37.5.3 Cheques Act 1992

Further controls against fraudulent endorsement comes from the *Cheques Act* 1992, which means that cheques crossed 'account payee' cannot be transferred by way of endorsement. Many banks now pre-print their cheques with this, which greatly reduces the risk and, in turn, the auditor's need to examine paid cheques.

37.5.4 Obtaining paid cheques

Where the auditor decides that he needs to review paid cheques, he should aim to choose the most cost-effective method of obtaining this evidence. Discussions with the client and their bank will normally be necessary as to the most appropriate method. Options include:

- returning all paid cheques to the client;
- providing the auditor with an agreed number of paid cheques directly, the selection being left to the bank;
- providing photocopies of paid cheques;
- extracting cheques before they are stored and forwarding them to the auditor directly; and
- providing specific paid cheques at the auditor's request.

Where paid cheques are to be sent to the auditor directly by the bank, authority will have to be provided by the client.

37.6   Auditing when financial market conditions are difficult

In January 2008, the APB issued Bulletin 2008/1 *Auditing issues when financial market conditions are difficult and credit facilities may be restricted* in response to developments in the financial markets commonly termed 'the credit crunch'.

As financial markets are characterised by difficult trading conditions made worse by a reduction in liquidity, entities with exposure to the financial markets through debt, equity, derivative and leveraged finance activities may experience a significant difficulty both trading in and valuing certain investments. This in turn will lead to an increased risk of material misstatement in the financial statements.

Even for those businesses outside the financial sector, the effect may be felt through:

- reduced liquidity making it expensive or impossible to replace finance arrangements that have expired, which may lead to going concern issues; and
- an increased difficulty in valuing investments where there has been a curtailment or cessation in market trading.

The Bulletin did not establish any new requirements, but pulled together guidance from the APB's other material into one place and provides useful guidance should such conditions be experienced again.

38 CHANGE OF AUDITOR

38.1 Introduction

There are three main ways in which an auditor can cease to hold office under the *Companies Act* 2006 ('the Act'):

- removal (s. 510–513), where the auditor is removed by the company by ordinary resolution at a general meeting;
- resignation (s. 516–518), where the auditor sends a notice in writing at the company's registered office; or
- failure to reappoint an auditor (s. 514–515), which occurs when a company proposes a resolution (either written or at a general meeting), the effect of which is to appoint a person as auditor in place of the outgoing auditor whose term of office has expired, or is due to expire.

Under the Act, each of these methods of ceasing to hold office require certain statements to be made by the auditor and the company. These are set out in **38.2** below.

For periods commencing on or after 1 October 2015, the *Deregulation Act* 2015, s. 18 and Sch. 5 amended the *Companies Act* 2006, s. 519–525 regarding statements to be made by the auditor when ceasing to hold appointment. The new rules distinguish between 'public interest companies' (companies with any securities listed in the UK or equity securities officially listed in an EEA state) and other companies and provide exemptions where the auditor ceases to hold office because the company becomes audit exempt, enters into insolvency proceedings or, in the case of a subsidiary, the audit is taken over by the group auditor. The main purpose of the changes to the rules was to simplify procedures and remove some of the duplication of reporting that existed previously, especially in situations where the change in appointment resulted from a change in the company's circumstances rather than a change in the relationship between auditor and client.

This edition of the book does not cover the previous rules for periods commencing prior to 1 October 2015, and an earlier edition should be referred to.

Once an auditor has been replaced, the incoming auditor may wish to use information gathered by the outgoing auditor. Under the Act, and for periods commencing on or after 6 April 2008, the outgoing auditor is required to provide access to relevant information where the newly appointed auditor makes a written request for such access. Guidance on obtaining this access is given in the ICAEW's Technical Release AAF 01/08 *Access to Information by Successor Auditors*. This is discussed in **38.3** below.

38.2 Procedures on cessation of office as auditor

38.2.1 The Companies Act 2006 requirements

The *Deregulation Act* 2015 made a number of changes to the provisions of the *Companies Act* 2006 dealing with auditor resignation and removal. The result is that new procedures apply where an auditor resigns in respect of a financial period commencing on or after 1 October 2015.

Slightly different procedures apply depending on whether or not:

- the company is a 'public interest company' (a company with any securities included in the Official List of the Financial Conduct Authority or equity securities officially listed in an EEA state);
- the auditor ceases to hold office at the end of his term of office;
- the reasons for the auditor ceasing to hold office are 'exempt' reasons; and
- there are matters which the auditor considers need to be brought to the attention of members or creditors.

38.2.2 All companies

The rules essentially require that:

- except in certain circumstances in the case of a non-public interest company, the outgoing auditor provides a statement of reasons for the change;
- where appropriate, the auditor will also provide a statement of matters that he considers should be brought to the attention of members and creditors;
- statements are filed by the auditor with the appropriate regulatory body (ICAEW or FRC);
- where the auditor ceases mid-term or where the reasons are not all exempt reasons the company is also required to file a statement with the appropriate audit authority;
- the company may apply to the court if it thinks that the auditor's statement is defamatory, otherwise it is obliged to send the auditor's statement to members (except in the case of non-public interest companies where there are no matters to be brought to the attention of members or creditors);
- for public interest entities and others where there are matters to be brought to the attention of members or creditors, statements are filed at Companies House.

38.2.3   Non-public interest companies

Auditor appointment ceases at end of term

Where, in the case of a private company, the auditor ceases to hold office at the end of a period for appointing auditors, or, in the case of a public company, at the end of an accounts meeting:

- the auditor notifies the company of ceasing to act; and
- no further actions are necessary.

This is the most straightforward situation, but unfortunately one which is least likely in practice as, in the case of private companies, it is not always easy to determine when the end of the period for appointing auditors is and in any case this may well not coincide with the timing of the company's decision to change auditor.

EXAMPLE

An auditor is appointed to perform the audit of a non-major private company for the year ended 30 April 2016. The period for appointing an auditor to perform the audit for the year ended 30 April 2017 ends on 27 February 2017 (i.e. filing deadline of 30 January 2017 plus 28 days) or, if earlier, 28 days after the April 2016 accounts are sent to members.

Note – the period for appointing auditors is a period of 28 days beginning with the end of the time allowed for sending out the annual report and accounts for the previous financial year or, if earlier, the date on which the annual report and accounts were actually sent out to members.

Auditor appointment ceases mid-term

The auditor has to consider first whether the reasons for his ceasing to hold office are all exempt reasons.

Exempt reasons are:

- the auditor is ceasing to carry out statutory audit work within the meaning of the *Companies Act* 2006, s. 1210;
- the company intends to take advantage of audit exemption under the *Companies Act* 2006;
- the company is a subsidiary of a UK company that prepares group accounts and the audit is to be carried out by the group auditor (provided that the group auditor is to take over the audit of all UK subsidiaries where an audit is required);
- the company is being wound up under the Insolvency Act or a petition for winding up has been presented and not withdrawn.

If all reasons are exempt reasons AND the auditor has no matters which he considers should be drawn to the attention of members or creditors, he simply needs to deposit a notice of resignation as above and no further actions are necessary.

If the reasons are not all exempt reasons, OR there are matters to be brought to the attention of members or creditors then the auditor is required to prepare and send to the company a statement of reasons for his ceasing to hold office (a 'section 519 statement').

38.2.4   Section 519 statement

Where a section 519 statement is required, this must be sent to the company's registered office and state:

- the auditor's name and address;
- the auditor's registered number (as entered in the register of auditors);
- the company's name and registered number;
- the auditor's reasons for ceasing to hold office;
- details of any matters connected with his ceasing to hold office which the auditor considers need to be brought to the attention of members or creditors of the company – or if there are none, a statement to that effect.

The section 519 statement must be sent as follows:

Reason for cessation of appointment	Timeframe for delivery of s. 519 statement to the company
Resignation	Must accompany the notice of resignation
Failure to seek reappointment	At least 14 days before the end of the time allowed for next appointing an auditor
Removal/not reappointed	Up to 14 days after ceasing to hold office

38.2.5   Notifications – non-public interest companies

Notification to ICAEW (auditor and company)

Where a section 519 statement has been prepared, the auditor, at the same time, sends a copy to the appropriate audit authority which will be the Recognised Supervisory Body ('RSB') with which he is registered. In the case of auditors registered with the ICAEW, notifications should be sent to:

Change of Auditor Notifications

Quality Assurance Department

ICAEW

Metropolitan House

321 Avebury Boulevard

Milton Keynes

MK9 2FZ

or by e-mail to auditorchange@icaew.com.

Under the *Companies Act* 2006, s. 523, the company is also required to notify the audit authority. This can be done by preparing a statement that the auditor is ceasing to hold office, including what the company believes are the reasons for the auditor ceasing to hold office and containing the auditor's name and registered number and the company's name and registered number. Alternatively, the company can simply endorse a copy of the section 519 statement and send that to the RSB. In either case, the notification should be sent within 28 days of the auditor ceasing to hold office.

Notification to members (by company)

Where circumstances are set out in the section 519 statement, the company may apply to the court if it believes the auditor is using the statement to secure needless publicity for a defamatory matter. The application to the court must be made by the company within 14 days of receiving the statement.

In other cases, the company must send the statement, within 14 days of receipt, to members and any other person who is entitled to receive copies of the accounts under the *Companies Act* 2006, s. 423.

Notification to registrar (by auditor)

Where the section 519 statement includes a statement to the effect that the auditor considers that none of the reasons for his ceasing to hold office and no matters (if any) connected with his ceasing to hold office need to be brought to the attention of members or creditors of the company, there is no need for either the auditor or the company to send a copy to the registrar.

Where the section 519 statement does include such matters then the auditor should send a copy to the registrar. In this situation, he should wait 21 days after depositing the statement with the company and, provided he has not, in that time, received notice from the company of an application to the court (as above) then he should send the statement to the registrar within a further seven days.

38.2.6   Public interest companies

In the case of a public interest company, the auditor must always prepare a section 519 statement, as above, regardless of the reasons for ceasing to hold office or circumstances connected with this. The auditor cannot, in this statement, say that there are no matters to bring to the attention of members or creditors as the statement in respect of a public interest entity will always be sent to the members and be filed at Companies House.

The auditor sends his section 519 statement to the company and, at the same time, to the appropriate audit authority, which for a public interest company is the FRC:

Change of Auditor Notifications
Financial Reporting Council
8th Floor, 125 London Wall
London
EC2Y 5AS

or by e-mail to auditorchange@frc.org.uk.

Notification to members (by company)

As above, the company may, within 14 days, apply to the court if it thinks that the auditor is using the statement to secure needless publicity for a defamatory matter. In all other cases, the company must, within 14 days send the statement to members and others entitled to receive the accounts of the company under the *Companies Act* 2006, s. 423.

Notification to registrar (by auditor)

In all cases, the auditor should send a copy of the section 519 statement to the registrar. In this situation, he should wait 21 days after depositing the statement with the company and, provided he has not, in that time, received notice from the company of an application to the court (as above) then he should send the statement to the registrar within a further seven days.

Auditor appointment ceases at end of term

A public interest company will always be a public company and the auditor's term of office will cease at the conclusion of the accounts meeting (the general meeting of the company at which accounts are laid before members) unless he is re-appointed.

For most public interest entities, the timing of issue of the section 519 statement is important as the company will generally want to send out the statement to members along with the notice of AGM. This will usually be at least 21 days in advance of the AGM date.

Auditor appointment ceases mid-term

Where the appointment ceases mid-term, the procedure is the same as for cessation at the end of term with one exception which is that if the auditor's reasons for ceasing to hold office are not all exempt reasons (as above) then the company should also send a statement to the FRC. As with a non-public interest company, this can be done by the company sending its own statement of reasons or endorsing and forwarding the auditor's section 519 statement.

38.2.7   *Legal advice*

In most situations, the reasons for the change in appointment are straightforward and uncontentious and there are no matters that the auditor considers need to be brought to the attention of members or creditors. However, auditors should be alert to the fact that where there are such matters, and in all cases for public interest entities, the section 519 statement will be on public record and may be considered sensitive. Auditors may wish to ensure that all section 519 statements are reviewed by someone with appropriate seniority in the firm before issue and in difficult cases seek legal advice.

TABLE 1: Auditor cessation – non-public interest company

Non-public interest company	Auditor notifies company of resignation or company notifies auditor of termination	Section 519 statement required				Company statement of reasons (s. 523)
		Auditor sends section 519 statement to company and audit authority (ICAEW)	Includes matters for attention of members/creditors OR statement that there are no such matters	Company sends to members or applies to court	Auditor waits 21 days then sends to registrar if no court application made	Company sends statement of reasons to audit authority (ICAEW)
Cessation at end of term – no action required						
Cessation mid term but all reasons are exempt reasons and no matters for attention of members/creditors	✓					
Other situations (non-exempt reasons and/or matters for attention of members/creditors)		✓	✓			✓ (but only if reasons are non-exempt)
If there are matters for attention of members or creditors				✓	✓	

TABLE 2: Auditor cessation – public interest company

Public interest company	Section 519 statement always required			Company statement of reasons (s. 523)
	Auditor sends section 519 statement to company and audit authority (FRC)	Company sends to members or applies to court.	Auditor waits 21 days then sends to registrar if no court application made	Company sends statement of reasons to audit authority (FRC)
In all cases	✓	✓	✓	
Where cessation is mid-term AND reasons are not all exempt reasons				✓

TABLE 3: Example section 519 statement for a non-public interest company

Statement under the *Companies Act* 2006, s. 519

To the Directors of [Company Name and Registered Number]

In accordance with section 519 of the Act, we set out the following reason[s] for ceasing to hold office as auditor of the company:

- [SPECIFY REASONS …]

These [are/are not] all considered to be exempt reasons as defined in section 519A of the Act.

Either:

We consider that the following matter(s) connected with our ceasing to hold office as auditors need to be brought to the attention of members or creditors of the company:

- [GIVE DETAILS …]

Or:

We consider that none of the reasons for us ceasing to hold office and no matters connected with our ceasing to hold office need to be brought to the attention of members or creditors of the company.

[Auditor name]

[Auditor registered number]

[Date]

TABLE 4: Example letter of resignation of auditors of a non-public interest company in circumstances where no section 519 statement required

The Directors

[Company]

[Address]

Dear Sirs

Cessation as auditors

If ceasing at end of term

As discussed, we confirm that we will cease to be auditors of the company when our term of office expires 28 days after the date you send the company's financial statements to members or the latest date on which they are due for filing at Companies House, if later.

We would like to take this opportunity to remind you of your obligation to appoint new auditors under Section 485 of the *Companies Act* 2006 ('the Act') unless you consider you will meet the conditions for exemption from audit under the Act.

OR

If ceasing mid term

We hereby resign as auditors of the company with effect from [date]. We consider that our reasons for ceasing to hold office are considered exempt reasons under Section 519A Part 3 of the *Companies Act* 2006 and we have no matters to bring to the attention of members or creditors.

Yours faithfully

Auditor

TABLE 5: Example letter of resignation of auditors of a non-public interest private company in non-exempt circumstances – section 519 statement required

The Directors

[Company]

[Address]

Dear Sirs

Cessation as auditors

We hereby resign as auditors of the company with effect from [date]. We consider that our reasons for ceasing to hold office are not all considered exempt reasons under Section 519A(3) of the *Companies Act* 2006 and accordingly, we enclose the statement required under Section 519 of the Act setting out the reasons for our ceasing to hold office.

As required under the Companies Act, we have sent a copy of the statement to the ICAEW as the appropriate audit authority. You are also required to notify the ICAEW of the reasons for our ceasing to hold office. If you agree with our statement, you may do this simply by endorsing a copy of the statement indicating your agreement and sending it to:

> Change of Auditor Notifications
>
> Quality Assurance Department
>
> ICAEW
>
> Metropolitan House
>
> 321 Avebury Boulevard
>
> Milton Keynes
>
> MK9 2FZ
>
> or by e-mail to auditorchange@icaew.com.

If you do not agree, you should write separately to ICAEW setting out what you consider the reasons to be. In either case the Act provides that your notification should be sent within 28 days from the date on which we cease to hold office.

[If the statement contains matters to be brought to the attention of members or creditors

The statement also sets out matters we consider need to be brought to the attention of members or creditors of the company. You are required, within 14 days of receipt, either to send a copy of the statement to members of the company and all others entitled to receive copies of the company's annual report and accounts, or to apply to the Court for a direction. If you apply to the court, you should let us know. If we do not receive notification that you have applied to the Court, we will send a copy of the statement to the registrar of companies for filing.]

Yours faithfully

Auditor

TABLE 6: Example letter of resignation of auditors of a public interest company

The Directors

[Company]

[Address]

Dear Sirs

Cessation as auditors

Either

We hereby resign as auditors of the company with effect from [date] and enclose the statement required under Section 519 of the *Companies Act* 2006 setting out the reasons for our ceasing to hold office.

Or

Our term of office as auditor of the company expires at the conclusion of the next accounts meeting and we will not be seeking re-appointment. Accordingly, we enclose the statement required under Section 519 of the *Companies Act* 2006 setting out the reasons for our ceasing to hold office.

You are required, within 14 days of receipt, either to send a copy of the statement to members of the company and all others entitled to receive copies of the company's annual report and accounts, or to apply to the Court for a direction. If you apply to the court, you should let us know. If we do not receive notification that you have applied to the Court, we will send a copy of the statement to the registrar of companies for filing.

As required under the Companies Act, we have also sent a copy of the statement to the FRC as the appropriate audit authority. [You are also required to notify the FRC of the reasons for our ceasing to hold office. If you agree with our statement, you may do this simply by endorsing a copy of the statement indicating your agreement and sending it to:

Change of Auditor Notifications

Financial Reporting Council

8th Floor

125 London Wall

London

EC2Y 5AS

By e-mail to auditorchange@frc.org.uk.]

If you do not agree, you should write separately to the FRC setting out what you consider the reasons to be. In either case the Act provides that your notification should be sent within 28 days from the date on which we cease to hold office.][1]

Yours faithfully

Auditor

[1] Omit this section if cessation is at end of term or if all reasons are exempt reasons.

38.3 Access to information by a successor auditor

38.3.1 Changes introduced by the Act

Prior to 2008, it was unusual for a predecessor auditor to share audit working papers with his successors, due mainly to liability concerns. However, the European Union's Statutory Audit Directive states that:

> where a statutory auditor or audit firm is replaced by another statutory auditor or audit firm, the former statutory auditor or audit firm shall provide the incoming statutory auditor or audit firm with access to all relevant information concerning the audited entity.

As a result, the Recognised Supervisory Bodies were required under the *Companies Act* 2006 to introduce rules to give effect to this requirement which are now incorporated into Audit Regulation 3.09 as follows:

> When a Registered Auditor (the "predecessor") ceases to hold an audit appointment and another Registered Auditor (the "successor") is appointed the predecessor must, if required in writing by the successor, allow the successor access to all relevant information held by the predecessor in respect of its audit work … Any information obtained by the successor is for the purposes of its audit and must not be disclosed to a third party unless the successor is required to do so by a legal or professional obligation.

The aim of the Audit Regulation is to maintain the effectiveness, including cost effectiveness, and efficiency of the audit process and to reduce the actual or perceived risk of changing auditor.

The Regulation is effective for the audits of financial periods commencing on or after 6 April 2008.

38.3.2   Technical Release AAF 01/08

The Audit and Assurance Faculty of the ICAEW issued Technical Release AAF 01/08, *Access to Information by Successor Auditors*. AAF 01/08 provides practical guidance on the application of Audit Regulation 3.09 and accompanying guidance.

Information requested

As well as the current year's audit working papers, information requested by a successor auditor may include permanent information on any standing or systems audit file as well as prior year audit papers if these are relevant. AAF 01/08 suggests that the successor auditor asks for the most recent audit working papers in the first instance and then, if his review suggests it is necessary, ask for older papers in another request.

As well as the papers relating to the standard audit, the following are set out in the 2006 Act as areas where a registered auditor may be required to perform specific functions, and therefore, for which access to working papers can be requested:

- a company applying to re-register as a public company (s. 92);
- a statement on summary financial statements issued by a quoted company (s. 428);
- abbreviated accounts (s. 449);
- when a private company makes a payment out of capital for the redemption or purchase of its own shares (s. 714);
- when a distribution is to be made by a company and the audit report was qualified (s. 837); and
- when initial accounts are prepared for a proposed distribution by a public company (s. 838).

There is no requirement for a successor auditor to make a request to see working papers from the predecessor auditor and he must, as part of his planning process, decide if such access is required and the areas to cover and amount of information to request.

There are specific references to reviewing a predecessor's audit work in ISA 510 (Revised June 2016) (opening balances), ISA 710 (comparatives) and ISA 300 (Revised June 2016) (planning), and information is likely to be necessary in these areas. This includes, for public interest entities, the Audit Regulation imposing a requirement on a predecessor auditor to grant the incoming auditor access to the additional report to the audit committee from previous years.

An example request letter from successor to predecessor is set out in **Table 7**.

TABLE 7: Specimen letter from the successor requesting access

[Predecessor firm]

[Address]

For the attention of [Name of Senior Statutory Auditor]

Dear Sirs

Provision of information pursuant to Audit Regulation 3.09 relating to the audit of [audit client]

This firm was duly appointed statutory auditor (as defined by the *Companies Act* 2006, s. 1210 ('the Act')) on [date] to [company] ('the Company') [and its UK subsidiaries as listed in the schedule to this letter (together 'the Companies')].

Pursuant to para. 9(3) of Sch. 10 to the *Companies Act* 2006 and Audit Regulation 3.09, and in accordance with Technical Release AAF 01/08 issued by the Institute of Chartered Accountants in England and Wales, we request for the purposes of our audit work, access to the following information:

[*Set out information necessary at this stage, noting the guidance under Audit Regulation 3.09 that wherever possible a request framed simply as a request for 'all relevant information held by the predecessor and concerning the audited entity' or 'all relevant information held by the predecessor in relation to the office of auditor' should be avoided. The successor should strive to identify the information required, or the type of information required, as precisely as possible.*]

[*Where the request is for access to audit working papers and subsequent interim review working papers, insert where applicable*:

[The working papers in respect of your audit report on the financial statements of the [Company/Companies] relating to [insert period between the beginning of the last financial statements on which the predecessor reported and the date of cessation of the predecessor's appointment]].

[Where in your capacity as auditor you conducted a review of interim financial information subsequent to the audit report referred to above, this request includes a request for access to the working papers relating to that review also.]

We may also request explanations from you in connection with our consideration of the above information, and on the same basis.

[We/the Company will meet reasonable costs that you will incur in giving access/ providing copies, provided that a maximum amount is agreed first.]

We look forward to receiving your confirmation letter in response to this request, which should be addressed for the attention of [name of successor engagement partner].

Yours faithfully

[Successor]

[Schedule of UK subsidiaries to which this letter applies in addition to the Company

Company 2 Limited

Company 3 Limited

…]

Audit files may contain information in a number of formats such as text, electronic file, sound or image and they may be kept in hard copy or electronic format, or a mixture of the two. Allowing another auditor access to information may mean that the successor auditor may gain access to the proprietary audit software of the outgoing auditor. If this is the case the successor cannot use the intellectual property or copyright of the software in any way. The predecessor auditor may prefer to make paper copies of working papers for the incoming auditor to review.

Care should also be taken where audit files also contain other documents relating to the client such as tax working papers. Papers to which the successor auditor has no right of access should be removed from the file before the successor auditor commences his review.

Where successors require access to tax papers, the Technical Release suggests that this would be best done directly from the client.

Relevant period

The period for which relevant information is normally requested would be in respect of any audit report relating to a period falling between the beginning of the last financial statement on which the predecessor reported and the date of cessation of the predecessor's audit appointment.

Example: An auditor resigns from an audit on 1 March 2010. The last accounting period for which he acted as auditor was the year ended 31 December 2009. The successor auditor can request access to relevant working papers for any reports prepared by the predecessor in the period 1 January 2009 to 1 March 2010.

The request for information can be made by the immediate successor only.

Liability

In order to ensure that there is no involvement of one auditor in liability for the other's work an exchange of letters as set out in **Tables 7** and **8**, should be undertaken. These letters should also be copied to the audit client.

Copying

There is no obligation to allow a successor auditor to copy working papers, but it would be usual to allow extracts of the papers to be copied. The predecessor and successor should come to an agreement about what it is reasonable to copy prior to the meeting. Typically this would include documents such as the breakdown of analyses of financial statements figures and documentation of the client's systems and processes.

The Technical Release suggests that predecessors check through any document that the successor asks to copy and to keep a log of documents that have been copied on the audit file.

Timing

A request for relevant information may be made by a successor once the successor has formally been appointed to the audit client and will typically be made soon after appointment when the incoming auditor commences his planning.

Access should be granted by the predecessor on a timely basis, with regard to:

- the point at which the predecessor's audit file will be complete as ISA (UK and Ireland) 230 (Revised June 2016) allows up to 60 days from the date of the audit report for the audit file to be completed; and
- the successor's reporting timetable.

The predecessor should also provide oral or written explanations in response to any further questions by the successor following the review of the working papers on a timely basis.

In providing such explanations, the predecessor should remember that:

- its obligation does not extend beyond relevant information;
- explanation should be given a factual or evidential reference point; and
- an internal written note or record of the request made and the explanation given should be put on file.

Location

The location where access is to be granted will be decided by the predecessor and will usually be his premises. The predecessor should be mindful of the confidentiality of other clients' information where access is granted at the predecessor's office.

Costs

Some recovery of the predecessor's costs of providing access may be reasonably recovered, but the legislation is silent on this point. Excessive charging may, however, be seen as a barrier to competition and choice, and it would not be reasonable to include an element of profit.

It may be reasonable to charge the successor auditor for the cost of:

- copying documents;
- paying someone to make the copies;
- retrieving documents from archive sources; and
- paying someone to attend to such retrieval and to provide documents for inspection by the successor.

Confidentiality

The predecessor is not breaching client confidentiality by allowing the successor access to its working papers. However, as a matter of courtesy a letter would be sent by the predecessor to the successor prior to granting access, in line with the example in **Table 8**.

TABLE 8: Specimen letter from predecessor responding to the successor's request for access

[Successor firm]

[Address]

Dear Sir

Provision of information pursuant to Audit Regulation 3.09 relating to the audit of [audit client]

We refer to your letter dated [date] following your appointment as statutory auditor of [company] ('the Company') [and its UK subsidiaries listed in the schedule to your letter (together 'the Companies')].

We confirm we will provide access to the information requested, namely:

[This should reflect the information set out in the successor's request letter. The successor should have identified the information required, or the type of information required, as precisely as possible.]

We understand that you may also request explanations from us in connection with your consideration of the above information, and on the same basis.

In accordance with the guidance under Audit Regulation 3.09 and Technical Release AAF 01/08 issued by the Institute of Chartered Accountants in England and Wales this letter sets out the basis on which the information and explanations (if any) are to be provided. Should you request or we provide any supplementary information to that set out above, such provision will be made on the same basis.

This access is provided to you:

(a) solely in your capacity as duly appointed statutory auditor (as defined by the *Companies Act* 2006, s. 1210 ('the Act')) of the [Company/Companies];

(b) solely because we are required to give you access to information pursuant to para. 9(3) of Sch. 10 to the Act and Audit Regulation 3.09.

The provision of access does not and will not alter any responsibility that we may have accepted or assumed to the [Company/Companies] or the [Company's/respective Companies'] members as a body, in accordance with the statutory requirements for audit, for our audit work, for our audit report or for the opinions we have formed in the course of our work as auditor.

To the fullest extent permitted by law we do not accept or assume responsibility to you or to anyone else:

(a)   as a result of the access given;

(b)   for the information to which we provide access;

(c)   for any explanation given to you;

(d)   in respect of any audit work you may undertake, any audit you may complete, and audit report you may issue, or any audit opinion you may give.

Where access is provided to audit [and interim review] working papers, those papers were not created or prepared for, and should not be treated as suitable for, any purpose other than the statutory audit that was the subject of our audit report [and respectively the interim review we carried out]. The statutory audit was planned and undertaken solely for the purpose of forming and giving the audit opinion required by the relevant statutory provision to the persons contemplated by that statutory provision. [The interim review was planned and undertaken solely for the purpose of meeting the requirements of the relevant standard.] The statutory audit [and the interim review] [was/were] not planned or undertaken, and the working papers were not prepared in contemplation of your appointment as statutory auditor or for the purpose of assisting you in carrying out your appointment as statutory auditor.

Neither you nor anyone else should rely on the information to which access is provided or any explanations given in relation to that information. The information cannot in any way serve as a substitute for the enquiries and procedures you should undertake and the judgments that you must make for any purpose in connection with the audit for which you are solely responsible as the auditor.

If notwithstanding this letter you rely on the information for any purpose and to any degree, you will do so entirely at your own risk.

[We will remove/have removed from the audit working papers all material in respect of which legal professional privilege is asserted.]

[Thank you for your confirmation that you/the Company will meet the reasonable costs that we will incur in giving access. [As already agreed] these will not exceed £x.]

In accordance with the guidance issued under Audit Regulation 3.09:

(a)   you should refuse to accept an additional engagement, such as to act as an expert witness or to review the quality of our audit work, where the engagement would involve the use of the information obtained by you under the Regulation;

(b)   you should not comment on the quality of our audit work unless required to do so by a legal or professional obligation; and

(c)   the information should not be disclosed beyond persons who have a need to access the information where to do so is a necessary part of your audit work, nor should the information be disclosed to a third party including the [Company/Companies] (although this does not prevent you discussing the information with the [Company/Companies] where to do so is a necessary part of your audit work, or providing information to any third party if that is required of you by a legal or professional obligation).

In the event that access to information involves your having access to any intellectual property of ours or any material in which we have copyright, we do not grant permission to you to use or exploit that intellectual property or copyright and you must respect the same at all times.

When in this letter we refer to ourselves, we include [any person or organisation associated with this firm through membership of the international association of professional service firms to which this firm belongs,] our [and their] partners, directors, members, employees and agents. This letter is for the benefit of all those referred to in the previous sentence and each of them may rely on and enforce in their own right all of the terms of this letter.

Yours faithfully

[Predecessor]

cc The Company/Companies

Money laundering

In accordance with the Anti-Money Laundering Guidance for the Accountancy Sector issued by the CCAB (see **Chapter 18**):

- any money laundering report and papers recording the predecessor's consideration of apparently suspicious activities should not be provided to the successor unless the predecessor has clear advice that it would be lawful to do so; and
- if any information provided to the successor causes the successor to conclude that there are money laundering suspicions that need to be reported to the Authorities, he should make that report whether or not he is aware of any report already made by the predecessor.

39 REVIEW OF INTERIM FINANCIAL INFORMATION

39.1 Introduction

With some limited exceptions, a company whose shares or debt securities are listed on the London Stock Exchange must issue a half-yearly financial report covering the first six months of each financial year. This is sometimes referred to as an interim report. Rules governing the preparation of half-yearly reports are contained in the Disclosure and Transparency Rules (DTR) of the Financial Conduct Authority (FCA), which are derived from the EU's Transparency Directive (2004/109/EC).

The half-yearly financial report must include:

- a condensed set of financial statements;
- an interim management report; and
- responsibility statements.

If the company is required to prepare consolidated accounts, the condensed set of financial statements must be prepared in accordance with IAS 34 *Interim Financial Reporting*, as adopted by the European Union.

If the company is not required to prepare consolidated accounts, the condensed set of financial statements should be prepared in accordance with IAS 34, FRS 104 *Interim Financial Reporting* or (for periods commencing prior to 1 January 2015) the Accounting Standards Board's (ASB) Reporting Statement *Half-Yearly Financial Reports* issued in 2007, depending on the accounting framework used for the annual accounts.

Companies may choose to have the half-yearly report audited or reviewed by their auditor. If the half-yearly financial report has been audited or reviewed by the auditor pursuant to the APB's guidance (see **39.2** below), the audit report or review report must be reproduced in full. If the half-yearly financial report has not been audited or reviewed by the auditor pursuant to the APB's guidance, the company must make a statement to this effect in its report.

AIM companies must also prepare half-yearly reports in accordance with the AIM Rules for Companies issued by the London Stock Exchange (AIM Rules).

The information contained in a half-yearly report for an AIM company must include at least a balance sheet, an income statement, a cash flow statement and must contain comparative figures for the corresponding period in the preceding financial year. Additionally, the half-yearly report must be presented and prepared in a form consistent with that which will be adopted in the company's annual accounts, having regard to the accounting standards applicable to such annual accounts. Half-yearly reports for AIM companies are not required to comply with IAS 34, FRS 104 or the ASB's Reporting Statement although companies may choose to do so.

Guidance notes contained in the AIM Rules state that where the half-yearly report of an AIM company has been audited it must contain a statement to this effect. AIM Rules do not require publication of review reports.

In practice, whilst reviews of half-yearly reports are common it is rare for such reports to be audited.

39.2   Guidance for the auditor

The APB issued standards on these engagements in International Standard on Review Engagements (UK and Ireland) 2410, *Review of interim financial information performed by the independent auditor of the entity*. As with the ISAs, the ISRE is the text of the international version, supplemented by UK and Ireland specific guidance. The ISRE is effective for the reviews of interim financial information for periods ending on or after 20 September 2007.

39.3   General principles

Although a review engagement is different in scope to a full audit, the auditor should comply with the ethical requirements relevant to the audit of the entity's annual financial statements and implement the same relevant quality control procedures such as leadership responsibilities, acceptance arrangements and monitoring. The same attitude of professional scepticism should be applied to an interim review as to a full annual audit.

39.4   Assurance provided

The interim financial information may be significantly less in scope than that included in the annual financial statements. The work performed does not provide a basis for expressing a true and fair opinion or that the interim financial information is free from material misstatement. The procedures are designed so that the auditor can give an opinion that the interim financial information has been prepared in accordance with the applicable financial reporting framework. The review will not generally include:

- inspection, observation or confirmation of accounting records;
- obtaining corroborative evidence in response to enquiries; or
- other typical audit tests such as tests of controls or verification of assets and liabilities.

Where the auditor has not audited the latest annual financial statements or has not reviewed the corresponding financial information in the preceding year, additional review procedures are likely to be necessary.

Additional guidance on cases where there are changes of auditor is given in **39.6** below.

39.5 Engagement letters

An engagement letter for the review, or a separate section in the main audit engagement letter, confirms the auditor's acceptance of the appointment and helps to avoid misunderstandings about the level of assurance provided by the review. It also clarifies the extent of the auditor's responsibilities for the review.

An illustrative engagement letter is shown in **Table 1** below.

TABLE 1: Example engagement letter for interim review report

Board of Directors XYZ PLC

Date

Dear Sirs

XYZ Plc Financial information for the six months ended 30 June 20 ...

We are providing this letter to confirm our understanding of the terms and objectives of our engagement to review the entity's interim balance sheet as at 30 June 20.. and the related statements of income, changes in equity and cash flows for the six-month period then ended.

As directors of XYZ plc, you are responsible under the *Companies Act* 2006 for keeping adequate accounting records. You are also responsible for presenting the half-yearly financial report in accordance with [International Accounting Standard 34, 'Interim Financial Reporting', as adopted by the European Union] [FRS 104 'Interim Financial Reporting'] and the requirements of the Disclosure and Transparency Rules of the Financial Services Authority. *[The second sentence identifies the applicable financial reporting framework for the entity and should be amended as necessary.]*

For the purpose of our review, you will make available to us all of the company's accounting records and all other related information, including minutes of directors', shareholders' and audit committee meetings and of all relevant management meetings that we consider necessary.

Our review will be conducted in accordance with International Standard on Review Engagements (UK and Ireland) 2410, 'Review of Interim Financial Information Performed by the Independent Auditor of the Entity' issued by the Auditing Practices Board with the objective of providing us with a basis for reporting whether anything has come to our attention that causes us to believe that the interim financial information is not prepared, in all material respects, in accordance with the [indicate applicable

---

financial reporting framework, including a reference to the jurisdiction or county of origin of the financial reporting framework when the financial reporting framework used is not International Financial Reporting Standards]. Such a review consists of making inquiries, primarily of persons responsible for financial and accounting matters, and applying analytical and other review procedures and does not, ordinarily, require corroboration of the information obtained. The scope of a review of interim financial information is substantially less than the scope of an audit conducted in accordance with International Standards on Auditing (UK and Ireland) whose objective is the expression of an opinion regarding the financial statements and, accordingly we shall express no such opinion.

We expect to report on the interim financial information as follows:

[include text of sample report]

Responsibility for the interim financial information, including adequate disclosure, is that of management of the entity. This includes designing, implementing and maintaining internal control relevant to the preparation and presentation of interim financial information that is free from material misstatement, whether due to fraud or error; selecting and applying appropriate accounting policies; and making accounting estimates that are reasonable in the circumstances. As part of our review, we will request written representations from management concerning assertions made in connection with the review. We will also request that where any document containing interim financial information indicates that the interim financial information has been reviewed, our report will also be included in the document.

A review of interim financial information does not provide assurance that we will become aware of all significant matters that might be identified in an audit. Further, our engagement cannot be relied upon to disclose whether fraud or errors, or illegal acts exist. However, we will inform you of any material matters that come to our attention.

[Insert additional information regarding fee arrangements and billings, as appropriate.]

This letter will be effective for future years unless it is terminated, amended or superseded (if applicable).

Please sign and return the attached copy of this letter to indicate that it is in accordance with your understanding of the arrangements for our review of the financial statements.

39.6 Planning

As with any other engagement, the auditor should plan his review so that it is carried out effectively. The planning process, which should focus on areas of potential risk of material misstatement, will include:

- updating the auditor's knowledge of the business;
- consideration of the company's organisation, accounting and control systems and operating characteristics; and
- consideration of the nature of its assets, liabilities, revenues and expenses.

The auditor's understanding of the entity and its environment should be sufficient to allow him to identify potential material misstatement and consider the likelihood of it occurring and to select the review procedures required.

Where the auditor has previously been engaged to report on the most recent full financial statements, it will be sufficient for him to update his existing understanding of the business. Typical procedures implemented to do this are listed in **Table 2**.

TABLE 2: Example procedures to update the auditor's understanding of the entity and its environment

- reading the documentation, to the extent necessary, of the preceding year's audit and reviews of prior interim period(s) of the current year and corresponding interim period(s) of the prior year, to enable the auditor to identify matters that may affect the current period interim financial information;
- considering any significant risks, including the risk of management override of controls, that were identified in the audit of the prior year's financial statements;
- reading the most recent annual and comparable prior period interim financial information;
- considering materiality with reference to the applicable financial reporting framework as it relates to interim financial information to assist in determining the nature and extent of the procedures to be performed and evaluating the effect of misstatements;
- considering the nature of any corrected material misstatements and any identified uncorrected immaterial misstatements in the prior year's financial statements;
- considering significant financial accounting and reporting matters that may be of continuing significance, such as significant deficiencies in internal control;
- considering the results of any audit procedures performed with respect to the current year's financial statements;
- considering the results of any internal audit performed and the subsequent actions taken by management;
- reading management accounts and commentaries for the period;
- considering any findings from prior periods relating to the quality and reliability of management accounts;
- inquiring of management about the results of management's assessment of the risk that the interim financial information may be materially misstated as a result of fraud;
- inquiring of management about the effect of changes in the entity's business activities;
- inquiring of management about significant changes in internal control and the potential effect of any such changes on the preparation of interim financial information; and
- inquiring of management of the process by which the interim financial information has been prepared and the reliability of the underlying accounting records to which the interim financial information is agreed or reconciled.

Where the auditor has not previously been involved with the audit of the full year financial statements, he will have to perform more rigorous procedures, particularly in relation to:

- knowledge of the business;
- assessment of inherent risk;
- understanding the accounting systems; and
- verification of opening balances.

However, any work performed at the interim stage will reduce the year-end workload.

The planning exercise should determine the extent of the review work required, if any, for the different parts of the business, such as divisions, subsidiaries and associates or joint ventures. The following factors will influence this decision:

- the materiality of, and risk of misstatement in, the financial information associated with each part of the business;
- the extent to which management control is centralised within the group, and therefore the degree to which central management have a detailed understanding of operations and financial information in those parts of the business; and
- the strength of the control environment including the group accounting and reporting processes.

Where other auditors are involved, the principal auditor should ensure that the work of the other auditors is adequate for the purposes of the review.

39.7   Procedures and evidence

The auditor's evidence will be obtained primarily through enquiry and analytical review procedures. In the context of the review of interim financial information, analytical procedures are:

- comparison with comparable information for the prior period – both interim and full;
- evaluation of the information by consideration of plausible relationships between financial data and also between non-financial and financial data elements; and
- comparison of amounts and ratios with the auditor's expectations, based on his knowledge of the business.

The extent of the procedures necessary will be based on the auditor's assessment of the risk of material misstatement. In determining the procedures necessary, the auditor should consider:

- the financial position and trading conditions of the company;
- his knowledge of the business derived through previous audits;
- his knowledge of the company's accounting systems;

- the extent to which an item is affected by management judgment;
- management's own assessment of risks and the controls in place; and
- the materiality of transactions and account balances.

The ISRE suggests various procedures that the auditor may use as part of his review. These include:

- reviewing prior year matters which may have a material effect on the financial information;
- considering whether the financial information is prepared on a basis which is consistent with the previous period and with the stated accounting policies;
- reviewing significant consolidation adjustments for consistency with the previous period;
- reading the financial information and considering it in the light of matters which have come to his attention during the course of his review work, and reading the rest of the interim report to ensure there are no inconsistencies or misstatements;
- considering the disclosures;
- considering the going concern status of the entity and the disclosures of any significant uncertainties;
- obtaining management representations (see **39.12** below); and
- ascertaining whether the financial information has been approved by the directors and the audit committee.

Where the auditor considers that there is a high risk of material misstatement, he should carry out additional procedures in order to be able to issue an unmodified review report.

In addition, the ISRE requires the auditor to obtain evidence that the interim financial information agrees or reconciles to the underlying accounting records. For consolidated group accounts, it is sufficient to agree the financial information of group components to the consolidation working papers.

The auditor may perform many of the review procedures before or simultaneously with the entity's preparation of the interim financial information. In addition, for convenience, some of the procedures required for the full period audit may also be performed at the interim stage, for example, reading minutes or procedures relating to unusual transactions in the period.

39.8   Documentation

The auditor should record in his working papers:

- details of the planning of the engagement;
- the nature, timing and extent of the procedures performed and his conclusions; and
- his reasoning and conclusions on all significant matters which require the exercise of judgment.

39.9   Subsequent events

To ensure that any relevant subsequent events are properly dealt with in the financial information, the auditor should make enquiries about events up to the date of the approval of the financial information.

39.10   Going concern

At the interim period end, directors should undertake a review of the going concern assessment they made at the previous full year end. In the light of the directors' review, the auditor should consider whether any significant factors identified at the previous audit have changed to such an extent as to affect the appropriateness of the going concern basis of accounting. Particular attention should be paid to the period since the sign off of the full financial statements.

Where the auditor does not have significant concerns, he should limit his enquiries to discussions with management about changes to cash flow and banking arrangements.

Where there are significant concerns, the ISRE notes that additional procedures will be necessary and the auditor should consider whether adequate disclosure has been made.

39.11   Comparative periods

Where comparative financial information is presented, the auditor should consider whether the accounting policies used for the comparative interim report are consistent with those used for the current period. Where this is not the case, appropriate adjustments and disclosures should be made. The auditor should also check that the comparatives used have been correctly extracted from the prior year's interim report.

Extra review procedures will be required where the auditor did not review the corresponding prior year interim financial information. The Listing Rules require comparatives to be given and readers will have expectations that these comparatives have been reviewed on the same basis as the prior period figures. If the auditor is unable to perform additional procedures on the comparatives, he should modify his report to indicate that the comparative figures have not been reviewed.

39.12   Management representations

As with the year end audit, the auditor may obtain from directors written representations to confirm matters arising throughout the review. The confirmation should include an acknowledgement of the limited scope of the review and of the directors' responsibilities for the interim report and the completeness of the financial records and minutes.

An example representation letter is included in the ISRE and this is shown in **Table 3** below, which should be tailored to suit the circumstances of the review engagement.

TABLE 3: Illustrative management representation letter for review of interim financial information

[Entity Letterhead]

[To auditor]   [Date]

This representation letter is provided in connection with your review of the balance sheet of ABC Entity as of 31 March 20X1 and the related statements of income, changes in equity and cash flows for the three-month period then ended and a summary of the significant accounting policies and other explanatory notes for the purposes of expressing a conclusion whether anything has come to your attention that causes you to believe that the interim financial information does not give a true and fair view of (*or 'does not present fairly, in all material respects,'*) the financial position of ABC Entity as at 31 March 20X1, and of its financial performance and its cash flows in accordance with [IAS 34 as adopted by the European Union/FRS 104] and the Disclosure and transparency Rules of the Financial Conduct Authority.

We acknowledge our responsibility for the fair presentation of the interim financial information in accordance with [indicate applicable financial reporting framework].

We confirm, to the best of our knowledge and belief, the following representations:

- The interim financial information referred to above has been prepared and presented in accordance with [indicate applicable financial reporting framework].
- We have made available to you all books of account and supporting documentation, and all minutes of meetings of shareholders and the board of directors (namely those held on [insert applicable dates]).
- There are no material transactions that have not been properly recorded in the accounting records underlying the interim financial information.
- There has been no known actual or possible non-compliance with laws and regulations that could have a material effect on the interim financial information in the event of non-compliance.
- We acknowledge responsibility for the design and implementation of internal control to prevent and detect fraud and error.
- We have disclosed to you all significant facts relating to any known frauds or suspected frauds that may have affected the entity.
- We have disclosed to you the results of our assessment of the risk that the interim financial information may be materially misstated as the result of fraud.
- We believe the effects of uncorrected misstatements summarised in the accompanying schedule are immaterial, both individually and in the aggregate, to the interim financial information taken as a whole.

- We confirm the completeness of the information provided to you regarding the identification of related parties.
- The following have been properly recorded, and when appropriate, adequately disclosed in the interim financial information:

  - Related party transactions, including sales, purchases, loans, transfers, leasing arrangements and guarantees, and amounts receivable from or payable to related parties;
  - Guarantees, whether written or oral, under which the entity is contingently liable; and
  - Agreements and options to buy back assets previously sold.

- The presentation and disclosure of the fair value measurements of assets and liabilities are in accordance with [indicate applicable financial reporting framework]. The assumptions used reflect our intent and ability to carry out specific courses of action on behalf of the entity, where relevant to the fair value measurements or disclosure.
- We have no plans or intentions that may materially affect the carrying value or classification of assets and liabilities reflected in the interim financial information.
- We have no plans to abandon lines of product or other plans or intentions that will result in any excess or obsolete inventory, and no inventory is stated at an amount in excess of realisable value.
- The entity has satisfactory title to all assets and there are no liens or encumbrances on the entity's assets.
- We have recorded or disclosed, as appropriate, all liabilities, both actual and contingent.
- [Add any additional representations related to new accounting standards that are being implemented for the first time and consider any additional representations required by a new International Standard on Auditing (UK and Ireland) that are relevant to interim financial information.]

To the best of our knowledge and belief, no events have occurred subsequent to the balance sheet date and through the date of this letter that may require adjustment to or disclosure in the aforementioned interim financial information.

—

(Senior Executive Officer)

—

(Senior Financial Officer)

39.13   Other information

The other information in the interim report will often include:

- the management commentary;
- prospective information; and
- a chairman's statement.

The auditor should read any information to be published with the interim financial information and consider whether it is materially inconsistent with the interim financial information or his knowledge of the client and its circumstances. The auditor should only allow his review report to be included where he considers that the additional information is not in conflict with his report and that it is not misleading. Where there is an apparent misstatement or a material inconsistency between the other information and the financial information which cannot be resolved through discussion with the directors, the ISRE suggests that the auditor should consider taking legal advice and that he is likely to make reference to the matter in his review report.

39.14   Evaluating misstatements

The ISRE requires the auditor to assess misstatements individually and in aggregate to determine whether a material adjustment is required to the interim financial information. He is not required to aggregate any misstatements that are 'clearly trivial'.

39.15   Communication

The auditor should report matters which will necessitate a material adjustment to the interim financial information to the relevant level of management as soon as possible. If management does not respond adequately, the matter should be escalated to those charged with governance. If those charged with governance do not make the relevant changes to the interim financial information, the auditor considers:

- whether to modify his report;
- the possibility of withdrawing from the engagement; and
- the possibility of resigning from the full audit.

If matters come to the attention of the auditor which suggest that fraudulent activity has taken place, it should be reported to the appropriate level of management, unless management are involved in the fraud, and then the matter should be reported directly to those charged with governance.

39.16   Reporting

The auditor should issue a written report at the end of his work, and **Table 4** gives the example report taken from the ISRE.

TABLE 4: Unmodified review report

Independent review report to XYZ plc

Introduction

We have been engaged by the company to review the condensed set of financial statements in the half-yearly financial report for the six months ended [date] which comprises [specify the primary financial statements and the related explanatory notes that have been reviewed].

We have read the other information contained in the half-yearly financial report and considered whether it contains any apparent misstatements or material inconsistencies with the information in the condensed set of financial statements.

Directors' responsibilities

The half-yearly report is the responsibility of, and has been approved by the directors. The directors are responsible for preparing the half-yearly financial report in accordance with the Disclosure and Transparency Rules of the United Kingdom's Financial Services Authority.

As disclosed in note X, the annual financial statements of the [group/company] are prepared in accordance with IFRSs as adopted by the European Union. The condensed set of financial statements included in this half-yearly financial report has been prepared in accordance with International Accounting Standard 34, 'Interim Financial Reporting', as adopted by the European Union.

Our responsibility

Our responsibility is to express to the Company a conclusion on the condensed set of financial statements in the half-yearly financial report based on our review.

Scope of review

We conducted our review in accordance with International Standard on Reporting Engagements (UK and Ireland) 2410, 'Review of Interim Financial Information Performed by the Independent Auditor of the Entity' issued by the Auditing Practices Board for use in the United Kingdom. A review of interim financial information consists of making enquiries, primarily of persons responsible for financial and accounting matters, and applying analytical and other review procedures. A review is substantially less in scope than an audit conducted in accordance with International Standards on Auditing (UK and Ireland) and consequently does not enable us to obtain assurance that we would become aware of all significant matters that might be identified in an audit. Accordingly, we do not express an audit opinion.

Conclusion

Based on our review, nothing has come to our attention that causes us to believe that the condensed set of financial statements in the half-yearly financial report for the six months ended … is not prepared, in all material respects, in accordance with International Accounting Standard 34 as adopted by the European Union and the Disclosure and Transparency Rules of the United Kingdom's Financial Services Authority.

Auditor

Address

Date

39.16.1 Modification of the review report

The auditor's review report will be modified if he considers that there is or has been:

- a departure from the applicable financial reporting framework;
- a limitation on scope; or
- going concern or significant uncertainties.

Departure from applicable financial reporting framework

Where the auditor concludes that the interim financial information has not been prepared in accordance with the applicable financial reporting framework and a material adjustment is required, he should issue a qualified or adverse opinion, depending on the severity of the departure.

Limitation on scope

Where the auditor cannot finish his review because of a limitation on scope, he should write to the appropriate level of management or those charged with governance to set out the reasons why. He should also consider the implications for his report.

The auditor should not accept an engagement to review the interim financial information if he is aware that a limitation on scope would be imposed by management. If the limitation is imposed after the auditor has accepted the engagement, and management refuse all requests to remove the limitation, he would ordinarily issue a disclaimer of opinion and ensure that his report outlines the reasons for issuing such a report.

Going concern or significant uncertainties

If there are going concern issues, and these are adequately disclosed in the interim financial information, the auditor does not qualify his report, but instead should add an emphasis of matter paragraph to highlight the material uncertainty relating to going concern. An example of such a report is given in **Table 5**.

If there is not adequate disclosure of any going concern issue in the interim financial information, the auditor will issue a qualified or adverse conclusion.

Emphasis of matter paragraphs should also be used for other significant uncertainties which are disclosed in the interim financial information. An example is given in **Table 6**.

TABLE 5: Extract from review report with emphasis of matter relating to going concern

Review work performed

...

Emphasis of matter – going concern

In arriving at our review conclusion, we have considered the adequacy of disclosures made in the condensed set of financial statements concerning the company's ability to continue as a going concern. The company incurred a loss of £x during the period to 30 June 20 ... and at that date its liabilities exceeded its assets by £y. These conditions, along with the other matters explained in note x to the financial information, indicate the existence of a material uncertainty that may cast significant doubt about the company's ability to continue as a going concern. The financial information does not include the adjustments that would result if the company was unable to continue as a going concern.

Review conclusion

On the basis of our review, we are not aware of any material modifications that should be made to the condensed set of financial statements as presented for the six months ended 30 June 20.. .

TABLE 6: Extract from review report with significant uncertainty

Review work performed

...

Emphasis of matter – possible outcome of litigation

In arriving at our review conclusion, we have considered the adequacy of disclosures made in the note ... concerning the possible outcome of litigation against B Limited, a subsidiary undertaking of the company, for an alleged breach of environmental regulations. The future settlement of this litigation could result in additional liabilities and the closure of B's business, whose net assets included in the summarised balance sheet total £y and whose profit before tax for the year is £z. Details of the circumstances relating to this significant uncertainty are described in note x.

Review conclusion

On the basis of our review we are not aware of any material modifications that should be made to the condensed set of financial statements as presented for the six months ended 30 June 20.. .

39.16.2 Prior period modifications

Where the prior period review report was modified or the audit report on the most recent financial statements was qualified and the matter has not been resolved, the review report should refer to the earlier modification or qualification and discuss the current status of the matter.

39.16.3 Date of review report

The date the auditor signs his report should not be earlier than the date on which the directors approve the financial information.

39.17 Complete set of interim financial information

The Listing Rules of the UK and Irish Stock Exchanges require condensed half yearly financial reports to be prepared. However, on some occasions where the company is not listed on the UK or Irish Stock Exchanges, the interim financial information may comprise a complete set of general purpose financial statements prepared in accordance with a financial reporting framework designed to achieve fair presentation. The appendices to the ISRE provide example engagement letter paragraphs, representation letter paragraphs, review reports and modified review reports for such circumstances.

39.18 Requests to discontinue an interim review engagement

As a review of the interim statement is not mandatory, directors may request the auditor to discontinue his review engagement if it becomes clear that a modified review report will be given.

If this is the case, the auditor must inform the Audit Committee of this in writing. If, in the auditor's opinion, the company does not take appropriate action to address his concerns about the interim financial information, the auditor may request the directors discuss the issue with the company's brokers. The directors and brokers should then consider whether the matter should be reported to the Stock Exchange.

In such a case, the auditor should also consider whether as a result he should resign as the company's auditor. The ISRE suggests that he may consider taking legal advice in these circumstances. If the auditor decides to resign, the details of the issue should be included, after taking appropriate legal advice, in his statement to shareholders (see **Chapter 38**).

40 REPORTS FOR SPECIAL PURPOSES AND TO THIRD PARTIES

40.1 Introduction

Managing the auditor's own risk has become increasingly important, and one major area of concern is reliance by parties other than those with whom the auditor has contractual relations. For example, where loans and other facilities are made available to businesses, the extent to which the auditor is responsible to the lender is often ambiguous. This becomes more difficult and potentially more dangerous where the auditor has an obligation to report to other third parties, for example, regulatory authorities. Managing the terms under which third parties can, or more importantly cannot, place reliance on reports is an area in which increasing guidance has been produced. This chapter provides an overview of this guidance and covers a number of areas where it is likely to happen. The chapter covers:

- an overview of applicable guidance (**40.2** and **40.3**);
- auditor's duties to lenders (**40.4**);
- covenants in loan agreements (**40.5**);
- engagements to report on covenant compliance (**40.6**);
- reports on internal controls of service organisations (**40.7**);
- reports to other third parties (**40.8**); and
- discussion of examples of claims by third parties (**40.9**).

Chapter 41 covers the following related areas:

- reviews of historical financial statements (**41.2**);
- assurance on non-financial information (**41.5**);
- reports on special purpose financial statements (**41.4**); and
- agreed upon procedures engagements (**41.3**).

Reporting to regulators of regulated entities is covered in **Chapter 49**. Reporting on grant claims is covered in **Chapter 48**. Compilation engagements are covered in **Chapter 8**.

40.2 Development of guidance

In November 2000, the Consultative Committee of Accountancy Bodies (CCAB) issued a Statement which contains guidance aimed at helping all parties involved in financing arrangements. This addresses issues such as the appropriate form of report, firms' duties of care and reporting in connection with covenants in loan agreements and other facilities.

The Statement was reissued by the Audit and Assurance Faculty of the ICAEW as Technical Release 4/00 *Firms' reports and duties to lenders in connection with loans and other facilities to clients and related covenants.*

The guidance also deals with reports on client's compliance with loan covenants, including the scope of work to be performed and the format of the report to be given.

Since 2001, a number of further publications have been issued addressing various aspects of liability to third parties. The main additional guidance is contained in:

- ICAEW Technical Release TECH 10/12AAF: *Reporting to third parties* (see **40.8** below);
- ICAEW Technical Release Audit 2/01: *Requests for references on clients' financial status and their ability to service loans* (see **40.8** below);
- ICAEW Technical Release AAF 01/06: *Assurance reports on internal controls of service organisations made available to third parties* (see **40.7** below); and
- ICAEW TECH 09/13 AAF: *Assurance review engagements on historical financial statements* (see **Chapter 41**).

In addition, ICAEW Technical Release AAF 02/07 *A framework for assurance reports on third party operations* is intended to provide high-level yet practical guidance for practitioners who provide assurance services on operations or arrangements agreed between two or more organisations (third party operations). TECH 04/13AAF, *Assurance reporting on relevant trustees* is a supplement to AAF 02/07. Although not specifically detailed in this chapter, the reader should be aware of the existence of these pieces of guidance.

Further guidance has been issued by the ICAEW to develop the guidance in TECH 10/12AAF for specific circumstances:

- TECH 09/16AAF (previously TECH 07/12AAF): *Revised arrangements for ATOL reporting accountants reporting to the Civil Aviation Authority*[1];
- AAF 01/11: *Reporting to the Audit Bureau of Circulations limited (ABC)*;
- AAF 01/07: *Independent accountants report on packaging waste*; and
- AAF 04/06: *Assurance Engagements: Management of Risk and Liability*, see **40.3**.

A study of the legal cases involving claims by third parties against auditors was completed by the Audit and Assurance Faculty in 2005, in conjunction with the law firm Simmons & Simmons. The review, *Audit liability: Claims by third parties*, summarises the key matters arising from the relevant cases and is considered in **40.9** below.

---

[1] From 1 April 2016, auditors carrying out ATOL reporting work must be individually licensed under the ATOL Reporting Accountants Scheme administered by the CAA and professional accountancy bodies including the ICAEW. Details of the scheme can be found on the ICAEW's website or in CAA's revised Guidance Note 10 which includes details of the licensing process, reporting requirements for ATOL holders and their ATOL Reporting Accountants and the purpose for which the ATOL holders' reports are used by the CAA and the ATT.

40.3 General guidance

AAF 04/06, *Assurance Engagements: Management of Risk and Liability* provides principles for reporting accountants to consider in relation to managing their risk and liability when agreeing to undertake assurance engagements and providing assurance reports to third parties. It does not seek to provide detailed advice on the planning and conduct of the work involved in such engagements or how to manage risk and liability in particular circumstances. Such detail will be provided in other technical releases which will cross-refer to this over arching guidance.

Additional general guidance on these issues is also given in TECH 09/15BL (previously TECH 02/11), *Managing the professional liability of accountants.*

40.3.1 Accepting an engagement

Reporting accountants should have appropriate engagement acceptance procedures to assess the risks associated with taking on a particular engagement. Reporting accountants should consider the:

- purpose for which the work is being sought;
- party or parties seeking to benefit from the work, whether they are directly party to the engagement or not yet identified;
- use that will be made of the work; and
- professional competence of the engagement team.

40.3.2 Managing professional liability

AAF 04/06 outlines the following arrangements into which reporting accountants may enter:

- a tri-partite or multi-partite engagement contract with the client and the third parties, accepting that they owe a duty of care not only to the client but also to those third parties. Provisions to limit liability may be appropriate;
- an engagement with the client, with the option for third parties to join the duty of care if they accept the relevant terms of the engagement letter. Again, liability may be limited;
- an engagement with the client alone, but allowing access to the audit report for third parties as long as they:

  - acknowledge in writing that the reporting accountant owes them no duty of care; and
  - agree in writing that no claims will be brought against the reporting accountant in relation to the assurance report; and

- an engagement with the client alone, disclaiming any liability or duty to others by notice in the assurance report. This may be in conjunction with the client indemnifying the reporting accountant if a third party makes a claim against the reporting accountant, although such indemnities may not be commercially attractive or reliable if the client is not financially stable.

Alternatively, if the risks are too high or reporting accountants are unable to reach acceptable terms with the client or third parties, reporting accountants may decline to accept the engagement.

40.3.3   Agreeing the terms of the engagement

Reporting accountants must manage their relationship with the client and any third party, and clarify that any assurance engagements are separate from statutory audit engagements. Depending on the type of contractual arrangement agreed upon (see **40.3.2**), reporting accountants will need to agree specific terms with all parties to the engagement and record them in writing in the engagement letter. The engagement letter should include details of the purpose of the report to be issued, its agreed use and any accompanying disclosure restrictions setting out the extent to which, the context in which, and the basis on which the report may be made available by the client to the third parties.

It is often useful to include a draft pro forma report as an appendix to the engagement letter.

40.4   Duties to lenders

As set out above, the position of the auditor in relation to the provider of loans and other facilities can be ambiguous. Technical Release 4/00 *Firms' reports and duties to lenders in connection with loans and other facilities to clients and related covenants* provides guidance in relation to various aspects of the relationship of auditors with providers of finance to their clients.

40.4.1   Case law

The guidance issued in Technical Release 4/00 is based on case law. In his judgment in the case of *Caparo Industries plc v Dickman* (1990) 2 WLR 353, Lord Bridge stated that a duty of care to a third party will exist if the person who owes the duty of care is aware:

- of the transaction to be undertaken by the third party;
- that the advice given will be passed to the third party, either directly or indirectly; and
- that it is likely that the third party will rely on that information in deciding whether to enter into the transaction.

Since this judgment, banks and other lenders have sought to document a direct and sufficient relationship between themselves and their customer's auditor so as to be able to rely on statutory audit reports.

40.4.2 Duties of care for the statutory audit report

An auditor's duty of care in respect of his audit report would not normally be expected to extend beyond that owed to his client. However, the general trend of authorities since *Caparo* makes it clear that, unless there is an effective disclaimer, an auditor may owe a duty of care to a lender or other third party. The test is whether the auditor, in making the statements in his audit report, assumed a responsibility to a lender who may subsequently be given a copy of those statements. The important issue is not whether the auditor in question intended to assume the responsibility towards the third party, but rather whether a reasonable auditor would have assumed the responsibility in those circumstances.

Therefore, the auditor must be aware that he may inadvertently accept responsibility unless steps are taken to limit his exposure. The auditor may assume responsibility without his knowledge by the client having discussions with the lender, or the lender being passed a set of the most recent audited financial statements, if it is deemed that a reasonable auditor would assume such responsibility.

The use of a *'Bannerman'* paragraph in the auditor's report to clarify the auditor's responsibilities is discussed in **4.22**.

Lenders will often seek to establish a relationship with the auditor. In this regard, certain banks have included a clause in the conditions attached to a loan, which requires the auditor of the borrower to provide written acknowledgement to the bank that the bank may rely on the audited financial statements of the borrower in connection with the facilities offered. Where the auditor is aware, or is in receipt, of a request to provide acknowledgement, he should not let it go unanswered.

In addition, banks may write directly to auditors stating that they do intend to rely on audited financial statements in connection with a proposed transaction. In this situation, a duty of care will be created unless the auditor vigorously denies it. A firm should normally disclaim all responsibility in this situation in writing. Where the auditor has included a *'Bannerman'* style paragraph in his auditor's report on the financial statements, it may also be appropriate to refer to this in any separate disclaimer issued to lenders or others. See paragraph **4.22** for further details of *Bannerman* paragraphs.

40.4.3   Draft accounts

The courts have held that reliance on draft audited accounts was not actionable, since a reasonable auditor would not intend such reliance to occur. However, there may be circumstances in which a duty of care may arise and care must be taken, therefore, when circulating draft audited accounts. The status of the accounts must be clearly stated and the giving of assurances or representations about the reliability of the accounts (or whether the final position is likely to differ greatly from that shown in the draft) should be avoided.

40.4.4   Disclaimer of responsibility

Disclaimers of responsibility can only be relied upon if they pass the reasonableness test set out in the *Unfair Contract Terms Act* 1977, s. 2. If the disclaimer is not reasonable, it will be void.

Disclaimers can be worded to pass the reasonableness test and are therefore an effective way of limiting an auditor's liability to lenders and other third parties who seek to claim reliance on a report. They may also be useful in avoiding any doubt that a firm does not have a duty of care to a lender or third party to whom a report is shown or a reference to a report is made.

However, it is important to note that a disclaimer of responsibility does not exempt an auditor or an accountant issuing a review report from carrying out his work in accordance with auditing standards or other applicable standards.

40.4.5   The Contracts (Rights of Third Parties) Act 1999

The *Contracts (Rights of Third Parties) Act* 1999 came into force on 11 November 1999 and applies to all contracts entered into after 10 May 2000. Under the Act, a third party to a contract has the right to enforce a term of that contract if it confers a benefit or right to the third party. This equates to a partial abolition of the concept of 'privity of contract', which has been a central feature of the English law of contract for more than 100 years. Therefore, if a reference is made to the provision of a set of financial statements to a lender, or to a lender requiring the financial statements for a specific purpose, within a contract between an auditor and his client, a benefit may have been conferred upon the lender.

Audit engagement letters should state clearly that they do not confer any rights on any third party and that, for the avoidance of doubt, any rights conferred on third parties pursuant to the *Contracts (Rights of Third Parties) Act* 1999 shall be excluded.

The Act does not apply to Scotland, which has long recognised the concept of *ius quaesitum tertio*, a right vested in and secured to a third party in and by a contract between two parties. Accordingly, a third party has the right to enforce a contract between two parties if the intention to confer a benefit on that third party can be gathered from the terms of the document.

40.4.6   Separate engagements to provide specific assurances to lenders

If a firm decides that it is able to provide specific assurances to a lender, it should be the subject of a separate engagement between the firm, the client and the lender. There should be a separate engagement letter in place for this work, normally the subject of separate financial arrangements.

A firm should also consider whether entering into such an agreement with both client and lender could present it with a conflict of interest. Reference should be made to the ethical guidance of the Institute which governs the firm.

40.5   Covenants in agreement for loans and other facilities

Agreements for certain financing arrangements often contain a number of covenants with which the borrower is expected to comply. Typically, the directors of the borrower are required to prepare a periodic statement or report, a 'Statement of Covenant Compliance', to confirm continuing compliance with the covenant terms agreed when arranging the finance.

Imposed covenants will be either financial or non-financial. Non-financial covenants tend to be more common and take the form of commitments by the borrower as to its future actions. Financial covenants may also need to be maintained by the borrower. These will often be financial statement ratios, the intention of which is to provide the lender with some assurance as to the continuing financial condition of the business.

40.5.1   Common financial and non-financial covenants

A list of common financial and non-financial covenants is given in **Table 1**. In specialised industries, lenders may require the maintenance of industry key performance indicators (KPIs), which are derived from management information outside the financial statements, such as room occupancy rates for hotels or pollution levels for heavy industry.

TABLE 1: Common covenants for borrowings

Financial

- cash flow to total debt service;
- dividend cover;
- minimum share capital and reserves;
- PBIT-based interest cover;
- gearing;
- cash flow-based interest cover;
- net current assets/borrowings;
- proportion of debtors below certain days outstanding;
- current ratio;
- quick asset ratio;
- EBITDA;
- gross profit margin;
- rent roll ratios.

Non-financial

- first charge over specified assets;
- audited annual accounts within a specified period;
- cross default clauses;
- monthly management accounts within a specified period;
- restrictions on changes to ownership;
- restrictions on additional borrowings (from other sources);
- maintenance of adequate fire, theft and other insurances;
- restrictions in mergers/acquisitions;
- restrictions on asset disposals;
- no capital expenditure beyond certain limits without approval;
- compliance with environmental laws and regulations;
- compliance with other laws and regulations;
- no redemption of preference shares while loans outstanding;
- charges over key-man insurance;
- key-man critical illness policy;
- limits on directors' remuneration.

40.5.2 The lender's requirement for evidence of covenant compliance

The lender will require from the directors of the borrower, a written confirmation that they have complied with all covenants for the period under review. This confirmation should set out the computation of the relevant financial covenants for the applicable accounting date. Simple calculations of gearing and interest cover are often self-evident and can easily be reperformed by the lender to ensure compliance. However, where information for covenants is not readily available to the lender, or it is not contained in the borrower's financial statements, the lender may require a report from the borrower's auditors.

The auditor is not compelled to accept such an engagement, as he cannot be bound to comply with the terms of an agreement to which he is not party. Therefore, if the auditor becomes aware that a client is negotiating a loan or other facility, it is good practice to enquire whether the draft loan agreement seeks to place any reporting obligations on him.

Where a requirement to report is found, the auditor should write to the lender to clarify the basis of preparation. This is particularly important if the lender approaches the auditor directly, rather than through the borrower. An example letter for this purpose is set out in **Table 2**.

TABLE 2: Example letter to lender setting out basis on which reports under a loan agreement will be provided

[Lender plc]

Dear Sirs

XYZ plc – [Loan Agreement Reference]

XYZ plc has provided us with a copy of [and you have written to us in connection with], the Loan Agreement referred to above, Clause X of which contemplates that reports will periodically be provided to you by the auditors of XYZ plc in connections with XYZ plc's compliance with certain covenants.

As auditors of XYZ plc, we confirm that, provided that XYZ plc authorises us to do so and you sign an engagement letter with us substantially in the attached form, we will report to you on the following matters:

- whether the financial information contained in the Statement of Covenant Compliance prepared by the directors of XYZ plc has been accurately extracted from the sources identified therein and, where applicable, agrees with the underlying accounting records;
- whether the calculations shown in the Statement, made in accordance with Clause X of the loan agreement, are arithmetically accurate; and
- where the elements and composition of the financial information contained in the Statement are the subject of objective accounting definition in the Loan Agreement, or have subsequently been agreed by Lender plc and XYZ plc, whether the financial information is presented in compliance with the relevant definitions and agreement.

As regards our audit work on XYZ plc's financial statements for future periods, our work will be carried out in accordance with our statutory and professional obligations and will not be planned or conducted in contemplation of your requirements or any matters which might be set out in the Loan Agreement. In particular, the scope of our audit work will be set and judgments made by reference to our assessment of materiality in the context of the audited accounts taken as a whole, rather than in the context of your needs. For this reason, our work will not necessarily address or reflect matters in which you may be primarily interested as lenders. Therefore, we cannot accept any responsibility to you in relation to our audit opinions and disclaim all liability to you in connection therewith.

Yours faithfully

cc. XYZ plc

Enc. Form of engagement letter [see **Table 3**]

40.5.3 The firm's duty of care

Auditors accepting an engagement to report on compliance with covenants acknowledge a duty of care to the lender. Firms will use their established risk management techniques to control this duty. One key method of achieving this is to issue an engagement letter which limits the use of the report to the intended addressee of the report, includes a disclaimer of responsibility to all other parties and specifies liability limits.

In addition, an engagement letter normally includes an exclusion of liability to the lender in respect of their normal audit or review report. This ensures that no responsibility to lenders is assumed for these reports.

Firms must consider whether the engagement is between themselves and the lender, or if it is a separate engagement between themselves and their client. In either case, a separate engagement letter is sent. An example wording is set out in **Table 3**.

The example wording also includes clauses excluding liability in respect of any loss or damage caused by, or arising from, fraudulent acts, misrepresentation or concealment on the part of the client entity, its directors, employees or agents, and excluding all liability to third parties.

TABLE 3: Example engagement letter

[Lender plc]

[Other addressees as provided for in the second paragraph of the letter]

Dear Sirs

XYZ plc – [Loan Agreement reference]

Under the terms of Clause [X] of the agreement dated [date] between XYZ plc and Lender plc ('the Loan Agreement'), the Directors of XYZ plc are required to procure that their auditors report to you in connection with the Directors' Statement of Covenant Compliance ('the Statement'), prepared in accordance with Clause [X] of the Loan Agreement. At the request of the Directors of XYZ plc, we are writing to set out our understanding of the work you wish us to perform and the terms and conditions upon which we are prepared to provide such a report for your use. A copy of this letter is being sent to the Directors of XYZ plc to confirm their authorisation and understanding of the basis on which we will report to you.

[This engagement letter is addressed to Lender plc, as lead manager/arranger of the facility/syndication agreement, and to each of the other lenders participating in the facility/syndication agreement whose names, as set out in Attachment 1, have been notified to us by Lender plc as having validly authorised it to accept this engagement letter on their behalf. By signing and accepting the terms of this engagement letter, Lender plc confirms that it will ensure that it receives prima facie authority from each other lender identified in Attachment 1, as participating in the facility/syndication agreement authorising it to enter into this engagement letter on the relevant lender's behalf.]

Respective responsibilities of directors and auditors

The Directors of XYZ plc are responsible for ensuring that XYZ plc complies with all of the terms and conditions of the Loan Agreement including each of the Covenants set out in Clauses [X] to [X] thereof. Under Clause [X] thereof, the Directors are responsible for preparing their Statement of Covenant Compliance. Our responsibility is to prepare a report to you on the computation of those financial covenants which pertain to accounting matters as identified below.

We are auditors of XYZ plc and have audited the annual accounts of XYZ plc ('the audited accounts') and reported to its members in accordance with our responsibilities under the Companies Act on [date]. Our audit of the accounts of XYZ plc was not intended to address compliance with financial covenants or other matters in which the addressees of this letter may be primarily interested. In particular, the scope of our audit work was set and our judgments made by reference to our assessment of materiality in the context of the audited accounts taken as a whole, rather than in the context of the report contemplated in this letter. Accordingly, we do not acknowledge any responsibility, and deny any liability, to the addressees of this letter in relation to the audited accounts.

Basis of report

Our work will be conducted in accordance with the framework for reporting in connection with loan covenants set out in guidance issued by the Consultative Committee of Accountancy Bodies and published as Audit Technical Release 4/00 by the Institute of Chartered Accountants in England and Wales [*or alternative CCAB member*]. We will read the Statement prepared by the Directors. Our work will be based on obtaining an understanding of the compilation of the Statement and by enquiry of management, reference to the Loan Agreement, comparison of the financial information in the Statement to the sources from which it was obtained and re-computation of the calculations in the Statement. [The specific procedures that we have agreed to conduct are set out in the Appendix to this letter.] Other than as set out herein, we will not carry out any work by way of audit, review or verification of the financial information nor of the management accounts, accounting records or other sources from which that information is to be extracted for the purpose of providing you with our report.

Use of report

Our report will be provided solely for your use in connection with the Loan Agreement and should not be made available to any other party without our written consent. The report is confidential to you and will be provided only for the purpose of your assessment of XYZ plc's compliance with the terms of Clause [X] of the Loan Agreement. We accept no liability to any other party who is shown or gains access to our report.

Obligations and liabilities

We undertake that we will exercise reasonable professional skill and care in the performance of our work as set out in this letter in accordance with applicable professional standards. This engagement is undertaken subject to certain terms excluding liability where information is or has been misrepresented to us, or withheld or concealed from us, and providing for our aggregate liability to the addressees of this letter and XYZ plc to be limited to a maximum aggregate amount of £[X] and subject to that cap, to the part of any loss suffered which is proportional to our responsibility.

It is agreed that the allocation between addressees of the limit of liability specified above will be entirely a matter for the addressees, who shall be under no obligation to inform us of it, provided always that if (for whatever reason) no such allocation is agreed, no addressee shall dispute the validity, enforceability or operation of the limit of liability on the ground that no such allocation was agreed.

Our detailed Terms of Business are set out in the attachment to this letter which shall apply as if set out in full herein.

Acknowledgement and acceptance

We will be grateful if, having considered the provisions of this letter together with the attachments and having concluded that they are reasonable in the context of all the factors relating to our proposed engagement, you will indicate your agreement to these arrangements by signing and returning to us the enclosed copy of this letter.

Yours faithfully

The terms and conditions contained in this letter and the attached Terms of Business are agreed and accepted on behalf of Lender plc by:

.... (authorised person)

Authorised and accepted on behalf of XYZ plc by:

.... (authorised person)

40.5.4 The firm's consideration of acceptance of the engagement

Before accepting the engagement the auditor must ensure that the respective responsibilities of the borrower and the auditor are clearly defined. It is the responsibility of the directors of the borrower to prepare the financial information and the Statement of Covenant Compliance, and the auditor's responsibility is to report on that information to the extent that it relates to financial and accounting matters.

The Statement of Covenant Compliance will normally set out the calculations of financial ratios, etc., as provided for under the loan agreement. The loan agreement will usually require the borrower to comply with the covenants at all times during the period being reported upon, but the auditor's report will only refer to compliance at specific dates. A firm would not normally accept an engagement which requires confirmation of compliance with covenants over an extended period of time, or for which confirmation that the borrower will comply with covenants in the future based on prospective information is required.

Firms should also consider carefully the implications of accepting an engagement to report on a Statement of Covenant Compliance based on financial covenants whose terms are imprecise.

40.6 Engagements to report on covenant compliance

40.6.1 Scope of work performed

The scope of work will vary from engagement to engagement and should be agreed with both the client and the lender. Typical procedures will include:

- reading the relevant clauses of the loan agreement and gaining an understanding of the operation of the covenants;
- reading the directors' Statement of Covenant Compliance;
- agreeing the financial information in the Statement to the sources from which it has been extracted;
- re-computing the calculations and ratios set out in the Statement in order to ascertain their arithmetical accuracy; and
- obtaining a representation from the client as to the completeness of disclosure in the Statement.

Firms will not undertake procedures to confirm the reliability of the financial information in the Statement nor of the sources from which the data has been extracted. In addition, they will not report on non-financial information in the Statement, such as directors' judgments on future business trends.

An example representation letter is provided in **Table 4**.

TABLE 4: Example representation letter

[Auditor's name and address]

Dear Sirs

[Loan Agreement Reference]

In connection with your proposed report in accordance with the arrangements set out in your letter of [date], we are writing to confirm to the best of our knowledge and belief the following representations we have made to you and on which you need to rely in providing your report on the Statement of Covenant Compliance ('the Statement') to Lender plc.

We are responsible for preparing the Statement, accurately reflecting the matters contained therein at the relevant dates.

The Statement is complete and accurate and reflects all matters of significance relating to Lender plc's assessment of XYZ plc's compliance with the Covenants set out therein as at the relevant dates and all significant matters relevant to that assessment have been brought to your attention.

Throughout the period since [date], the Company has at all times been in compliance with the terms of the Loan Agreement or, if not, all such instances of non-compliance have been notified to Lender plc in accordance with the terms of the Loan Agreement. Copies of such notifications have been made available to you.

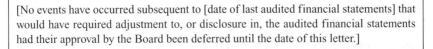

[No events have occurred subsequent to [date of last audited financial statements] that would have required adjustment to, or disclosure in, the audited financial statements had their approval by the Board been deferred until the date of this letter.]

Yours faithfully

.... (signature of authorised person on behalf of XYZ plc)

40.6.2   The report

The report should be prepared in accordance with the engagement letter. The report will:

- identify the addressees who can rely on it;
- contain a statement concerning the scope of the report and the respective responsibilities of the directors and the auditor;
- refer to the Statement of Covenant Compliance;
- set out the basis for the report;
- provide a description of the procedures undertaken (either in the body of the report or in an appendix);
- report on the arithmetical accuracy of the extraction and calculation of the financial information within the Statement; and
- where the elements and composition of the financial information in the Statement are the subject of objective accounting definition in the loan agreement, or have been subsequently agreed by the parties, report whether the financial information is presented in compliance with the relevant definitions and agreement.

An illustrative form of report is given in **Table 5**.

TABLE 5: Example report

[Lender plc]

[Other addressees as provided for in the engagement letter]

Dear Sirs

XYZ plc – [Loan Agreement reference]

We refer to the above-mentioned agreement ('the Loan Agreement'). Under the terms of Clause [X] thereof, XYZ plc is required to comply with specified financial covenants and to supply the addressees of this letter with information in connection therewith reported upon by its auditors.

The directors of XYZ plc have prepared a Statement of Covenant Compliance ('the Statement'), a copy of which is appended to this letter.

This report letter is provided pursuant to, and must be read in conjunction with, our engagement letter dated [date] and is subject to the terms and limitations set out therein.

Basis of report

Our work was conducted in accordance with the framework for reporting in connection with loan covenants set out in guidance issued by the Consultative Committee of Accountancy Bodies [and published as Audit Technical Release 4/00 by the Institute of Chartered Accountants in England and Wales, *or alternative CCAB member*]. We have read the attached Statement prepared by the Directors. Our work was based on obtaining an understanding of the compilation of the Statement by enquiry of management, reference to the Loan Agreement, comparison of the financial information in the Statement to the sources from which it was obtained and recomputation of the calculations in the Statement. [The specific procedures we performed are set out in the Appendix to this letter.] For the purpose of providing you with this letter, other than as set out herein, we have not carried out any work by way of audit, review or verification of the financial information nor of the management accounts, accounting records or other sources from which that information has been extracted.

Report

Based solely on the procedures described above, we confirm that:

- the financial information contained in the accompanying Statement has been accurately extracted from the sources identified therein and, where applicable, agrees with the underlying accounting records;
- the calculations shown in the Statement made in accordance with Clause [X] of the Loan Agreement are arithmetically accurate; and
- the financial information in the Statement is presented in compliance with the relevant accounting definitions as to its elements and composition set out in Clause [X] of the Loan Agreement [and as agreed between Lender plc and XYZ plc and confirmed to us in a letter dated [date]].

Our report as set out herein is confidential to the addressees of this letter and should not be made available to any other party without our written consent. It is provided solely for the purpose of your assessment of XYZ plc's compliance with the terms of [Clause [X] of] the Loan Agreement. We accept no liability to any other party who is shown or gains access to this letter.

Yours faithfully

cc. XYZ plc

40.7 Reports on internal controls of service organisations

40.7.1 Background

Many entities use service organisations to perform various tasks for them. These services may vary from performing a certain task, such as preparing the payroll, to replacing entire business units. Many of the functions undertaken by service organisations affect an entity's financial statements and so the auditor may seek information about the control procedures put in place by the service organisation.

Reporting accountants may be asked by service organisations to provide a report on their internal controls which they can supply to their customers and the customers' auditor.

In June 2006, the Audit and Assurance Faculty of the ICAEW issued AAF 01/06 *Assurance reports on internal controls of service organisations made available to third parties* specifically in relation to financial service activities, including:

- custody;
- investment management;
- pension administration;
- property management;
- fund accounting; and
- transfer agency.

The guidance may be applied to other areas, such as payroll processing, but further considerations may be required.

AAF 01/06 replaced guidance previously issued as FRAG 21/94 and Audit 4/97. AAF 01/06 was updated in 2010 by the inclusion of a new Appendix 8 to reflect the issue by the IAASB of ISAE 3402, *Assurance Reports on Controls at a Third Party Service Organisation*. It was further updated in March 2011 by the inclusion of a Stewardship supplement, which was further revised in November 2012, covering assurance reporting on principles of the UK Stewardship Code for institutional investors.

Guidance on using reports on service organisations when conducting the audit of an entity is covered in **Chapter 22**.

40.7.2   Responsibilities of the service organisation

The directors of the service organisation are required to identify control objectives and the control procedures which they consider appropriate to ensure that these control objectives are met. Their key responsibilities are:

- accepting responsibility for internal control;
- evaluating the effectiveness of the service organisation's control procedures using suitable criteria;
- supporting their evaluation with sufficient evidence, including documentation; and
- providing a written report of the effectiveness of those control procedures for the relevant period.

The appendices to AAF 01/06 include a list of detailed control objectives for the financial services activities listed in **40.7.1** above. The list is not exhaustive and the directors of the service organisation are responsible for considering whether the objectives are sufficient for their organisation. The directors are required to make a statement in their report that they have referred to the examples in the appendices.

Service organisations are also responsible for:

- providing the reporting accountants with access to appropriate service organisation resources, such as service organisation personnel, systems documentation, contracts and minutes of management or audit committee meetings;
- disclosing to the reporting accountants any significant changes in control procedures that have occurred since the service organisation's last examination or within the last 12 months if the service organisation has not previously engaged reporting accountants to issue an assurance report;
- disclosing to the reporting accountants and the affected customers any illegal acts, fraud, or uncorrected errors attributable to the service organisation's management or employees that may affect its customers and the entity's whistle-blowing arrangements;
- disclosing to the reporting accountants any relevant design deficiencies in control procedures of which it is aware, including those for which the directors believe the cost of corrective action may exceed the benefits;
- disclosing to the reporting accountants all significant instances of which it is aware when control procedures have not operated with sufficient effectiveness to achieve the specified control objectives; and
- providing the reporting accountants with a letter of representation.

40.7.3   Accepting the engagement

As with other reports where third parties may be seeking to place reliance on their report, reporting accountants may:

- accept that they owe a duty of care to the third parties and enter into a tri-partite or multi-partite engagement contract with the client and the third parties. Provisions to limit liability may be appropriate. A multi-partite engagement contract may be difficult where the service organisation has numerous customers;
- engage with the service organisation with the ability for its customers to be afforded the same duty of care agreed between the reporting accountant and the service organisation if they subsequently accept the relevant terms of the engagement letter, including any limitations on liability;
- proceed with an engagement with the client alone, but allowing access to the report for third parties as long as they:
  - acknowledge in writing that the reporting accountant owes them no duty of care; and
  - agree in writing that no claims will be brought against the reporting accountant in relation to the assurance report;

- engage with the client alone, disclaiming any liability or duty to others by notice in the assurance report. This may be in conjunction with the client indemnifying the reporting accountant if a third party makes a claim against the reporting accountant; or
- decline to accept the engagement.

Reporting accountants will always disclaim liability to the auditor of the service organisation's customers, as the auditor will have responsibility for his own audit report.

Example extract terms of engagement are shown in **Table 6**.

Reporting accountants may become aware of third parties other than the service organisation's customers who may request sight of the report. In such cases, accountants may decline the request, or access may be agreed if the third party acknowledges in writing that they owe the accountant no duty of care.

TABLE 6: Extracts of example engagement letter paragraphs for assurance reports on internal controls of service organisations

Responsibilities of directors

The Board of Directors ('the Directors') of [entity name] in relation to which the reporting accountant's assurance report is to be provided ('the Organisation') are and shall be responsible for the design, implementation and operation of control procedures that provide adequate level of control over customer's assets and related transactions. The Directors' responsibilities are and shall include:

- acceptance of responsibility for internal controls;
- evaluation of the effectiveness of the service organisation's control procedures using suitable criteria;
- supporting their evaluation with sufficient evidence including documentation; and
- providing a written report ('Directors' Report') of the effectiveness of the service organisation's internal controls for the relevant financial period.

In drafting this report, the Directors have regard to, as a minimum, the criteria specified within the Technical Release AAF 01/06 issued by the Institute of Chartered Accountants in England & Wales ('the Institute') but they may add to these to the extent that this is considered appropriate in order to meet customers' expectations.

Responsibilities of reporting accountants

It is our responsibility to form an independent conclusion, based on the work carried out in relation to the control procedures of the Organisation's [ ] function carried out at the specified business units of the Organisation [located at [ ]] as described in the Directors' Report and report this to the Directors.

Scope of the reporting accountants' work

We conduct our work in accordance with the procedures set out in AAF 01/06, issued by the Institute. Our work will include enquiries of management, together with tests of certain specific control procedures which will be set out in an appendix to our report.

In reaching our conclusion, the criteria against which the control procedures are to be evaluated are the internal control objectives developed for service organisations as set out within the AAF 01/06 issued by the Institute.

Any work already performed in connection with this engagement before the date of this letter will also be governed by the terms and conditions of this letter.

We may seek written representations from the Directors in relation to matters on which independent corroboration is not available. We shall seek confirmation from the Directors that any significant matters of which we should be aware have been brought to our attention.

Inherent limitations

The Directors acknowledge that control procedures designed to address specified control objectives are subject to inherent limitations and, accordingly, errors or irregularities may occur and not be detected. Such procedures cannot guarantee protection against fraudulent collusion especially on the part of those holding positions of authority or trust. Furthermore, the opinion set out in our report will be based on historical information and the projection of any information or conclusion in our report to any future periods will be inappropriate.

Use of our report

Our report will, subject to the permitted disclosures set out in this letter, be made solely for the use of the Directors of the Organisation, and solely for the purpose of reporting on the internal controls of the Organisation, in accordance with these terms of our engagement.

Our work will be undertaken so that we might report to the Directors those matters that we have agreed to state to them in our report and for no other purpose.

Our report will be issued on the basis that it must not be recited or referred to or disclosed, in whole or in part, in any other document or to any other party, without the express prior written permission of the reporting accountants. We permit the disclosure of our report, in full only, to customers [of the Organisation using the Organisation's [financial services] ('customers') [(as defined in appendix [ ] to this letter,] and to the auditors of such customers, to enable customers and their auditors to verify that a report by reporting accountants has been commissioned by the Directors of the Organisation and issued in connection with the internal controls of the Organisation without assuming or accepting any responsibility or liability to them on our part.

To the fullest extent permitted by law, we do not and will not accept or assume responsibility to anyone other than the Directors as a body and the Organisation for our work, for our report or for the opinions we will have formed.

Liability provisions

We will perform the engagement with reasonable skill and care and acknowledge that we will be liable to the Directors as a body and Organisation for losses, damages, costs or expenses ('losses') suffered by the Directors as a body and the Organisation as a result of our breach of contract, negligence, fraud or other deliberate breach of duty. Our liability shall be subject to the following provisions:

- we will not be so liable if such losses are due to the provision of false, misleading or incomplete information or documentation or due to the acts or omissions of any person other than us, except where, on the basis of the enquiries normally undertaken by us within the scope set out in these terms of engagement, it would have been reasonable for us to discover such defects;
- we accept liability without limit for the consequences of our own fraud or other deliberate breach of duty and for any other liability which it is not permitted by law to limit or exclude;
- subject to the previous provisions of this Liability paragraph, our total aggregate liability, whether in contract, tort (including negligence) or otherwise, to the Directors as a body and the Organisation, arising from or in connection with the work which is the subject of these terms (including any addition or variation to the work), shall not exceed the amount of [to be discussed and negotiated].

To the fullest extent permitted by law, the Organisation agrees to indemnify and hold harmless [name of reporting accountants] and its partners and staff against all actions, proceedings and claims brought or threatened against [name of reporting accountants] or against any of its partners and staff by any persons other than the Directors as a body and the Organisation, and all loss, damage and expense (including legal expenses) relating thereto, where any such action, proceeding or claim in any way relates to or concerns or is connected with any of [name of reporting accountant]'s work under this engagement letter.

The Directors as a body and the Organisation agree that they will not bring any claims or proceedings against any of our individual partners, members, directors or employees. This clause is intended to benefit such partners, members, directors and employees who may enforce this clause pursuant to the *Contracts (Right of Third Parties) Act* 1999 ('the Act'). Notwithstanding any benefits or rights conferred by this agreement on such partners, members, directors or employees by virtue of the Act, we and the Directors as a body may together agree in writing to vary or rescind the agreement set out in this letter without the consent of any such partners, members, directors or employees. Other than as expressly provided in this paragraph, the provision of the Act are excluded.

Any claims, whether in contract, negligence or otherwise, must be formally commenced within [years] after the party bringing the claim become aware (or ought reasonably to have become aware) of the facts which give rise to the action and in any event no later than [years] after any alleged breach of contract, negligence or other cause of action. This expressly overrides any statutory provision which would otherwise apply.

This engagement is separate from, and unrelated to, our audit work on the financial statements of the Organisation for the purposes of the *Companies Act* 2006 (or its successor) or other legislation and nothing herein creates obligations or liabilities regarding our statutory audit work, which would not otherwise exist.

[*Appendix*

List of customers to whom the assurance report may be made available.]

40.7.4   Reporting accountant's procedures

Reporting accountants will read the directors' description of the control procedures and undertake procedures to determine whether that description is a fair presentation. Procedures may include:

- discussing aspects of the control framework and relevant control procedures with management and other personnel;
- determining who the customers are and how the services provided by the service organisation are likely to affect the customers;
- reviewing standard terms of contracts with the customers to gain an understanding of the service organisation's contractual obligations;
- observing the procedures performed by the service organisation's personnel;
- reviewing the service organisation's policy and procedure manual and other systems documentation; and
- performing walkthrough tests on selected transactions and control procedures.

Reporting accountants should consider whether the control procedures are suitably designed. Their assessment may include:

- considering the linkage between the control procedure and the associated control objectives;
- considering the ability of the control procedures to prevent or detect errors; and
- performing further procedures such as enquiries of personnel, inspection of documentation and observation of control procedures to determine whether they are adequately designed and operated as prescribed.

Where reporting accountants become aware that the control objectives are incomplete or inappropriate, they discuss their findings with the directors and request that the directors amend their report accordingly. If the directors refuse to make suitable amendments, reporting accountants will highlight this fact in their report.

40.7.5   Reporting

The engagement performed by the reporting accountant is a reasonable assurance engagement, that is sufficient evidence is obtained to allow them to express a positive conclusion on the directors' report.

The report concludes on the fairness of the description and the design and operating effectiveness of control procedures over a specified period. An example report is given in **Table 7**.

TABLE 7: Example report on internal controls of service organisations

To the directors of [name of entity]

Use of report

This report is made solely for the use of the directors, as a body, of [name of entity], and solely for the purpose of reporting on the internal controls of [name of entity], in accordance with the terms of our engagement letter dated [date] [and attached as appendix [ ]].

Our work has been undertaken so that we might report to the directors those matters that we have agreed to state to them in this report and for no other purpose. Our report must not be recited or referred to in whole or in part in any other document nor made available, copied or recited to any other party, in any circumstances, without our express prior written permission.

We permit the disclosure of this report, in full only, by the directors at their discretion to customers [of [name of entity] using [name of entity]'s [financial services] ('customers'),] and to the auditors of such customers, to enable customers and their auditors to verify that a report by reporting accountants has been commissioned by the directors of [name of entity] and issued in connection with the internal controls of [name of entity], and without assuming or accepting any responsibility or liability to customers or their auditors on our part.

To the fullest extent permitted by law, we do not accept or assume responsibility to anyone other than the directors as a body and [name of entity] for our work, for this report or for the conclusions we have formed.

Subject matter

This report covers solely the internal controls of [name of entity] as described in your report as at [date]. Internal controls are processes designed to provide reasonable assurance regarding the level of control over customers' assets and related transactions achieved by [name of entity] in the provision of [outsourced activities] by [name of entity].

Respective responsibilities

The directors' responsibilities and assertions are set out on page [ ] of your report. Our responsibility is to form an independent conclusion, based on the work carried out in relation to the control procedures of [name of entity]'s [ ] function carried out at the specified business units of [name of entity] [located at [ ]] as described in your report and report this to you as the directors of [name of entity].

Criteria and scope

We conducted our engagement in accordance with International Standard on Assurance Engagement (ISAE) 3000 and the Institute of Chartered Accountants in England & Wales Technical Release AAF 01/06. The criteria against which the control procedures were evaluated are the internal control objectives developed for service organisations as set out within the Technical Release AAF 01/06 and identified by the directors as relevant control objective relating to the level of control over customers' assets and related transactions in the provision of [outsourced activities]. Our work was based upon obtaining an understanding of the control procedures as described on page [ ] to [ ] in the report by the directors, and evaluating the directors' assertions as described on page [ ] to [ ] in the same report to obtain reasonable assurance so as to form our conclusion. Our work also included tests of specific control procedures, to obtain evidence about their effectiveness in meeting the related control objectives. The nature, timing and extent of the tests we applied are detailed on pages [ ] to [ ].

Our tests are related to [name of entity] as a whole rather than performed to meet the needs of any or any particular customer.

Inherent limitations

Control procedures designed to address specific control objectives are subject to inherent limitations and, accordingly, errors or irregularities may occur and not be detected. Such control procedures cannot guarantee protection against (among other things) fraudulent collusion especially on the part of those holding positions of authority or trust. Furthermore, our conclusion is based on historical information and the projection of any information or conclusions in this report to any future periods would be inappropriate.

Conclusion

In our opinion, in all material respects:

- the accompanying report by the directors describes fairly the control procedures that relate to the control objectives referred to above which were in place as at [date];
- the control procedures described on pages [ ] to [ ] were suitably designed such that there is reasonable, but not absolute assurance that the specified control objective would have been achieved if the described control procedures were complied with satisfactorily [and customers applied the control procedures contemplated]; and
- the control procedures that were tested, as set out in the attachment to this report, were operating with sufficient effectiveness for us to obtain reasonable, but not absolute, assurance that the related control objectives were achieved in the period [x] to [y].

Name of firm

Chartered Accountants

Location

Date

40.8   Reports to other third parties

40.8.1   Introduction

The Audit and Assurance Faculty increased the scope of the original guidance on reporting to lenders to other third parties by publishing two further Technical Releases: Audit 1/01, *Reporting to third parties* and 2/01 *Requests for references on clients' financial status and their ability to service loans*.

Audit 1/01 was revised in 2012 and released as TECH 10/12AAF. The main changes relate to updating references to reflect current guidance, revising technical terms in line with current guidance and adopting the ICAEW's current presentational style. The substance of the guidance did not change.

The aim of TECH 10/12AAF is to establish the same type of approach as set out in Audit 4/00 for all special reporting engagements. Firms should be on their guard to avoid circumstances that may result in a duty of care for the statutory audit report becoming established with a third party without sufficient disclaimers being put in place.

The guidance in Audit 2/01 is only appropriate where there is no need to perform any work, research or investigation to produce the reference. If further work is required, then a formal engagement should be agreed under TECH 10/12AAF.

40.8.2   TECH 10/12AAF: Reporting to third parties

Accountants have no obligation to sign reports requested by third parties such as trade bodies or regulators, but may wish to do so in order to assist their clients. Accountants should endeavour to become familiar with third parties' demands for customised reports as early as possible in the relationship with their client so that appropriate engagement terms can be negotiated.

Technical Release TECH 10/12AAF aims to help accountants to manage their risk in relation to providing such reports. However, it does not cover corporate finance engagements, reports made under UK company legislation, which will be covered by Practice Note 8, reports relating to public sector entities or requests for references, which are covered by Audit 2/01.

The Technical Release sets out, under a number of headings, the process accountants should follow in response to requests from third parties. The process is illustrated by the flowchart in **Table 8**.

TABLE 8: Process for responding to requests from third parties

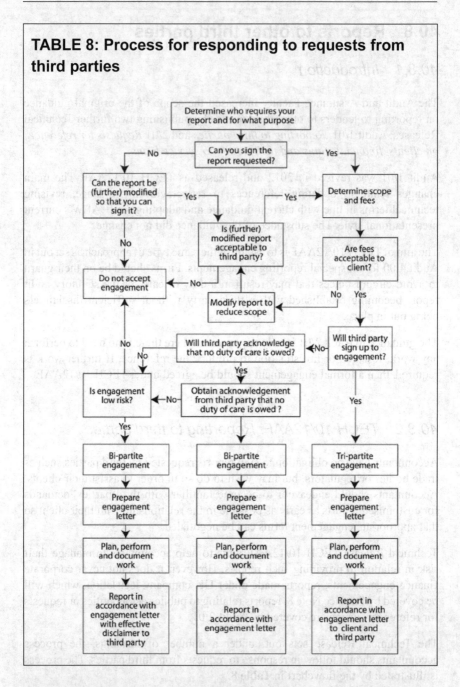

Determine who will rely on the accountants' work and for what purpose

When accountants become aware that a report has been requested, and will be relied upon, by a third party there is a risk that the accountant will owe that third party a duty of care unless an effective disclaimer is put in place. Therefore, the accountant must determine the identity of the third party and details of the reliance they wish to place on the report, as well assessing the extent of loss the third party could suffer if they relied on the report and it proved to be misleading.

Once accountants have an understanding of the risks involved, they can decide whether to:

- contract with the third party for the engagement and accept that they have a duty of care to the third party and limit liability if appropriate;
- contract with their client for the engagement and ensure that the third party confirms in writing that no duty of care exists before allowing them access to the report;
- contract with their client but disclaim or limit liability or duty to the third party in their report; or
- not accept the engagement.

If accountants regard a report as high risk, they should only agree to provide the report if the third party either is a party to the engagement contract or has acknowledged that the accountants owe no duty of care to them in writing. Accountants should not allow their reports to be provided to third parties unless the extent of their liability to that party is clear and agreed.

Consider the form of the report requested by the third party

Accountants are not bound by any form of report agreed between the client and the third party without the accountants' consent. The form of report requested by the third party may not be appropriate for the accountant, and the accountant should not accept arguments that the form of the report cannot be changed (even where the report is of a 'standard' format in a pre-printed form).

Accountants should be wary of the following:

- wording giving an opinion on a matter as a statement of fact when that matter, by its nature, is inherently uncertain or a matter of judgment;
- the use of the term 'true and fair' when financial information is not prepared under an acceptable financial reporting framework (e.g. Financial Reporting Standards or International Financial Reporting Standards);
- 'fair and reasonable' opinions, which are usually associated with investment banks making recommendations to shareholders in respect of transactions;
- wording that might suggest that the third party is able to rely on the statutory audit of the client;
- opinions that are open-ended or otherwise cannot be supported by the work carried out by the accountants;
- opinions which accountants do not have the necessary competence to provide such as actuarial opinions or property valuations;
- opinions on matters beyond the accountants' knowledge and experience, particularly in relation to the detailed and specific operational circumstances of the client;
- wording that is open to interpretation;

- reports on internal controls where there are inadequate criteria for a sound control system;
- reports without addressees;
- reports on financial information which is not explicitly approved by the client;
- modifications or qualifications in covering letters only; and
- opinions which would impair the accountants' independence.

Accountants must only sign reports if they have performed sufficient work to support the statements they are asked to make. In some circumstances, such as reports on future solvency or performance of the client, statements cannot be supported by any amount of work, and accountants should refuse to sign such reports. Instead an agreed upon procedures form of report may be given, see below.

Agree the work to be performed and the form of the report to be given

In agreeing the work to be performed and form of report, accountants must make clear to clients and third parties that these engagements are separate from the statutory audit engagement and will be subject to separate terms and a separate fee. The terms for the report to third parties may include a limitation of liability.

The accountant must agree the form of report that is appropriate and the timescale in which it is to be delivered. The timescale must be realistic in relation to the amount of work the accountant will need to perform to provide the required opinion.

No UK auditing standards cover the forms of report which may be given, though some guidance is available in international standards. International standards break the types of report down into four types:

- *reasonable assurance*, where a conclusion is expressed in positive terms;
- *limited assurance*, requiring performance of limited procedures and possibly involving the provision of negative assurance in the style of 'nothing has come to our attention …';
- *agreed upon procedures,* which involves performing certain defined procedures on factual information and reporting findings without any form of opinion on the implications of the work done; and
- *compilation engagements*, which involve preparing financial information on behalf of clients.

Where reports are to be given to third parties an agreed upon procedures report is usually most suited to the requirements of the client and the third party. Accountants must consider the level of risk of giving the type of report requested by the third party (even after appropriate liability limits are set) and consider whether the engagement should be accepted.

Agree appropriate terms of agreement

The accountant should agree terms of engagement in writing with both the client and third party. If the third party refuses to sign an engagement letter, the accountant should either refuse to provide a report, or do so only subject to a disclaimer of liability to the third party. Disclaimers must be reasonable to be effective. An example disclaimer notice is given in **Table 9**.

TABLE 9: Example disclaimer notices

Where the third party does not sign the engagement letter:

Our report is prepared solely for the confidential use of [client's name] and solely for the purpose of [details]. It may not be relied upon by [client's name] for any other purpose whatsoever. Our Report must not be recited or referred to in whole or in part in any other document. Our report must not be made available, copied or recited to any other party [without our express permission]. [Accountant's name] neither owes nor accepts any duty to any other party and shall not be liable for any loss, damage or expense of whatsoever nature which is caused by their reliance on our report.

Where the third party signs the engagement letter:

Our report is prepared solely for the confidential use of [client's name] and [name of third party], and solely for the purpose of [details]. It may not be relied upon by [client's name] or [name of third party] for any other purpose whatsoever. Our report must not be recited or referred to in whole or in part in any other document. Our report must not be made available, copied or recited to any other party [without our express written permission]. [Accountant's name] neither owes nor accepts any duty to any other party and shall not be liable for any loss, damage or expense of whatsoever nature which is caused by their reliance on our Report.

Example engagement letter extracts for an agreed upon procedures engagement are set out in **Table 10**.

TABLE 10: Example extracts from an engagement letter for an agreed upon procedures engagement

Services to be provided

We will complete the specified limited scope procedures set out below:

(Describe the nature, timing and extent of the procedures to be performed, including specific reference, where applicable, to the identity of the documents and records to be read, individuals to be contacted and parties from whom confirmations will be obtained.)

The above procedures will be performed solely for your purposes. You are responsible for determining whether the scope of our work specified above is sufficient for your purposes.

Upon completion of the procedures we will provide you with a report of our findings in the form of that attached to this letter, solely for your information. Our report is not to be used for any other purpose or disclosed to any other third party without our consent. [We consent to the report being released to [third party name] provided that [third party name] acknowledges in writing that we owe no duty of care to [third party name] and we will not be liable to [third party name] for any reliance it chooses to place on the report.]

We have agreed that, under this engagement, we will not perform any verification procedures other than those which are specified in the scope section above. [If we were to perform additional procedures or if we were to perform an audit or any more limited review, other matters might come to our attention that would be reported to you.] Our report will not extend to any financial statements of the Company taken as a whole.

Audit work

Our audit work on the financial statements of the Company is carried out in accordance with our statutory obligations and is subject to a separate engagement letter. Our audit report is intended for the sole benefit of the Company's shareholders as a body, to whom it is addressed, to enable them to exercise their rights in general meeting. Our audits of the Company's financial statements are not planned or conducted to address or reflect matters in which anyone other than such shareholders as a body may be interested.

We do not, and will not, by virtue of this report or otherwise, assume any responsibility whether in contract, negligence or otherwise in relation to our audits of the Company's financial statements; we and our employees shall have no liability whether in contract, negligence or otherwise to [third party name if addressee to this letter, or to] any [other] third parties in relation to our audits of the Company's financial statements.

Timetable

We will be able to commence our limited scope procedures on [date] and we expect our work to be completed by [date]. Our work will depend upon receiving without undue delay full cooperation from all relevant officials of the Company and their disclosure to us of all [the accounting records of the Company and all other] records and related information (including certain representations) we may need for the purpose of our work.

Staffing

[X] will be the partner in charge of the engagement. [Y] will act as manager.

Scope of our work

The scope of our work and the procedures we shall carry out in preparing our report, together with the limitations inherent therein, are outlined above. If the scope and procedures do not meet your requirements, please tell us so that we can discuss a different scope or additional or alternative procedures. [You should understand that there is no guarantee that these procedures will result in the identification of all matters which may be of interest to you.]

Our work will be based primarily on internal management information and will be carried out on the assumption that information provided to us by the management of the Company is reliable and, in all material respects, accurate and complete. We will not subject the information contained in our reports and letters to checking or verification procedures except to the extent expressly stated. This is normal practice when carrying out such limited scope procedures, but contrasts significantly with, for example, an audit. Even audit work provides no guarantee that fraud will be detected. You will therefore understand that the Services are not designed to and are not likely to reveal fraud or misrepresentation by the management of the Company. Accordingly, we cannot accept responsibility for detecting fraud (whether by management or by external parties) or misrepresentation by the management of the Company.

Any engagement letter should include the following:

- an unambiguous description of the scope of work and form of report to be given;
- a description of the client's obligations and responsibilities;
- a statement that the engagement is separate from the statutory audit and that no duty of care will arise in relation to the statutory audit;
- if agreed, an appropriate liability cap;
- details of the addressee for the report, together with details of restrictions on who is entitled to see and rely on the report; and
- a copy of the report that will be provided.

Example wording for a liability cap is set out in **Table 11**.

TABLE 11: Example liability cap

The aggregate liability, whether to [client's name] or [third party name] or any other party, of whatever nature, whether in contract, tort or otherwise, of [Accountant's name] for any losses whatsoever and howsoever caused arising from or in any way connected with this engagement [and this transaction] shall not exceed [amount] (including interest).

Perform the work

The work for a third party report is separate to that for the statutory audit, and the audit team should put together a separate working paper file for this engagement.

Report

The report should reflect the terms set out in the engagement letter, and should not include undefined terms such as 'review' without specifying what the terms mean.

Accountants should not modify the wording of their reports at the client's or third party's request unless the modification is appropriate and they have the opportunity to perform any additional work that is required to support the change in wording. If a different form of report is required to that set out in the engagement letter, the accountants should either reissue their terms of engagement or refuse to report, giving their reasons in writing.

Illustrative contents of a report of factual findings for an agreed upon procedures engagement are set out in **Table 12**.

TABLE 12: Illustrative contents of a report of factual findings for an agreed upon procedures engagement

These include:

- addressee;
- identification of the applicable engagement letter and specific information to which the agreed upon procedures have been applied;
- a statement that the procedures performed were those agreed with the client (and third party, if applicable);
- identification of the purpose for which the agreed upon procedures were performed;
- a listing of the specific procedures performed;
- a description of the accountants' factual findings, including sufficient details of errors and exceptions found;
- a statement that the procedures performed do not constitute either an audit or a review;
- a statement that had the accountants performed additional procedures, an audit or a review, other matters might have come to light that would have been reported;
- a statement that the report is restricted to those parties that have agreed to the procedures performed;
- a statement that the report relates only to the matters specified and that it does not extend to the entity's financial statements taken as a whole; and
- the date of the report.

40.8.3   Requests for references on clients' financial status

Accountants may be asked to provide references to banks, building societies and a range of other bodies about their clients' financial position, ability to pay debts as they fall due or service a loan. This is particularly relevant for individuals or small businesses that may not have audited accounts. Audit 2/01 *Requests for references on clients' financial status and their ability to service loans* provides guidance on how reporting accountants can manage their risks effectively when asked to perform such procedures.

The guidance is only appropriate where the accountant does not have to perform any additional work, research or investigation to give the reference. Where extra procedures have to be performed the guidance in TECH 10/12AAF should be followed.

The main issues

Third parties would like accountants to confirm that their client will have sufficient future income to service a loan or other commitment. However, no amount of enquiry can provide accountants with the assurance required to give such a confirmation.

Reporting on the present solvency of a client is only possible if the accountant is engaged to report on accounts, computations and projections as at a stated date. It is likely that the costs involved in producing such a report will be prohibitive to any third party.

References covered by Audit 2/01 require no extra work, and therefore incur no fee. This avoids the possibility of an implied contract. The fact that no extra work has been performed is stated in the reference.

Accountants may legitimately refuse to give a reference if they think the risks of doing so are too high, e.g. if the amounts involved are judged to be too large.

Unincorporated entities

Lenders who are entering into agreements with individuals and other unincorporated small borrowers, will not have audited reports to consider when making their lending decision. Accountants can, however, supply information that might be useful to a lender. This will include:

- the length of time the accountant has acted for the client;
- the net income or profits declared to HMRC; and
- a statement that the accountant has no reason to suppose that the client would have entered into a commitment which they would not expect to fulfil.

The third item above is a matter of judgment and will be based on the accountants' past experience of the client and the client's attitude to commercial obligations. Where accountants have insufficient knowledge of their client (for example, they have only just started to act) or there is any doubt about the judgment, they can decline to comment.

If the accountants' knowledge of the client is out of date, this will also be noted in the report.

Reporting

Accountants should report in a manner suitable for the particular circumstances. Third parties may provide a standard form of report, but accountants should amend the wording if necessary to reflect any limitations to the information requested.

651

Accountants should ensure that all technical terms are sufficiently defined, and should refer the third party to information provided directly by the client if this is more appropriate.

An example report is given in **Table 13**.

TABLE 13: Example of an accountants' reference in connection with a lending application made by an individual or other small borrower

Without responsibility

[Name of lender]

[Address]

Dear Sirs

REFERENCE IN CONNECTION WITH THE LENDING APPLICATION MADE BY [name of client and application reference, as appropriate]

Our above named client has approached us for a reference in connection with the proposed loan by you of [amount] [repayable by monthly instalments of amount over number years].

We have acted in connection with our client's [personal/business/corporate tax] affairs since [date]. However, it should be noted that our knowledge of our client's affairs may not be fully up to date. In addition, we have not carried out any specific work with regard to this statement.

Our client's net income [insert definition] declared by our client to HMRC as at [date] amounted to [amount]. (To be adapted for borrowers who are not individuals.)

(Income/profits for previous years and identification of those agreed with HMRC may be added.)

Whilst we have no reason to believe that our client would enter into a commitment such as that proposed which our client did not expect to be able to fulfil, we can make no assessment of our client's continuing income or future outgoings.

Whilst the information provided above is believed to be true, it is provided without acceptance by [Accountant's name] of any responsibility whatsoever, and any use you wish to make of the information is, therefore, entirely at your own risk.

Yours faithfully

Signed ....

Dated ....

40.9   Audit liability: Claims by third parties

In June 2005, the Audit and Assurance Faculty of the ICAEW, in conjunction with the law firm Simmons & Simmons, published a review of the legal cases involving claims by third parties against auditors. It sets out the key matters arising from the cases of which auditors in practice should take note.

All the cases have in common an institution seeking assurance or reassurance from a company's auditor as to that company's financial strengths at a particular point in time, whether by reference to its audited accounts or by means of some other independent confirmation from the auditor that the company is financially sound.

As stated in **40.4** above, the case law surrounding the auditor's duty of care was set out in the *Caparo v Dickman* judgment. That case set out that there would only be sufficient grounds to establish a duty of care to a third party where:

- the work produced was required for a purpose made known to the auditor; and
- the auditor knew, or should have known, that its work would be communicated to the non-client party for that purpose; and
- the auditor, knew or should have known, that its work would be likely to be relied upon by that third party for that purpose, without independent enquiry.

The main categories of cases where the application of these principles has been considered in the paper are:

- potential investors;
- creditors and lenders;
- regulators and trade bodies; and
- affiliates/associates of the audit client.

40.9.1   Potential investors

A duty of care to potential investors may occur other than in written form. In *ADT v Binder Hamlyn*, ADT, the potential investor, argued that a duty of care had been created when the audit partner made a comment in a meeting that the firm stood by its earlier unmodified audit opinion. ADT stated that they made further investment in Britannia Securities Group plc as a result of this affirmation and therefore sought damages from Binder Hamlyn when that investment lost money. By orally restating the true and fair opinion to the potential investor, the audit partner had assumed a duty of care to ADT which did not exist from the earlier audit report itself, as this had been prepared only with the shareholders of Britannia in mind.

An important element of the *Caparo* decision is whether the third party would have had another way of obtaining the assurance it sought from the auditor. In *Barker v Grant Thornton*, where potential investors sued the auditor, no duty of care was found to exist as it was reasoned that it would have been practical for the investor to have instructed investigating accountants to obtain the necessary assurance for them rather than rely on the statutory audit report. In addition, Grant Thornton had already specifically disclaimed responsibility to the investor.

In *Yorkshire Enterprises Ltd v Robson Rhodes*, however, as the auditor was aware that he was completing the audit promptly because the financial statements were to be passed on to venture capitalists, it was not judged reasonable to require the investors to instruct their own investigating accountants. In addition, Robson Rhodes had not specifically disclaimed responsibility to Yorkshire Enterprises.

Two other cases set out in the study, *Electra Private Equity Partners v KPMG* and *Man Nutzfahrzeuge Aktiengesellschaft v Ernst & Young* demonstrate that the auditor may have a duty of care to a third party arising not from what he said or did when auditing the financial statements, but merely on the basis of what he was told during the audit, for example, that the audited financial statements were to be relied upon as the basis of a proposed sale.

Another case where actuaries were sued by a potential investor in a client highlights the need for caution when the auditor or other professional advisors are asked to provide copies of their reports to third parties. Although the courts eventually found for the actuaries, the absence of a statement clarifying that no responsibility was being assumed to the third party in providing a copy of the report caused a lengthy protraction of the case.

40.9.2   Creditors and lenders

The same principles apply to those that lend money rather than invest in a company. In the case of *Royal Bank of Scotland v Bannerman Johnstone Maclay*, it was sufficient that the auditor should have been aware that a lender would rely on audited financial statements to create a duty of care. This case is discussed in **Chapter 4**.

40.9.3   Regulators and trade bodies

In a similar manner, in *Andrew v Kounnis Freeman*, the auditor ought to have known that the audited financial statements which they forwarded to the Civil Aviation Authority (CAA) would be relied upon by the CAA in determining whether to renew a company's ATOL licence, and by sending the audited financial statements, they assumed a duty of care.

In another case, audited financial statements were forwarded by the client to ABTA and IATA. In addition, they were sent to the provider of bond facilities to the travel agent. A travel agent is required to hold such bonds in order to be a member of ABTA and IATA. A duty of care was found to exist between the auditor and the bond provider, despite the auditor not knowing who would be providing the bond facilities. In this situation, it was sufficient that the auditor, with experience of clients in the travel business, should be aware that a bond provider would be required and that this provider would need sight of the audited financial statements.

40.9.4   Affiliates or associates of the audit client

As well as separate third parties pursuing claims against auditors, there are situations where a claim is made by entities affiliated or associated with the audit client. In *Barings plc (in administration) v Coopers & Lybrand*, Barings sought damages from the auditor of one of its own indirect subsidiaries. It was judged that Coopers & Lybrand knew that their audit report on the subsidiary would be required to allow directors of the parent company to prepare group financial statements which showed a true and fair view. In addition, the auditor of the subsidiary had liaised directly with the auditor of the parent company, reporting to them any matters of significance so that they could inform the parent company management. Both these matters created a duty of care between the subsidiary auditor and the parent company, independent of the duty of care the subsidiary auditor had to his own client.

41 OTHER ENGAGEMENTS

41.1 Introduction

Increases in audit exemption limits in recent years have led to an increasing number of companies being entitled to take advantage of audit exemption. The thresholds for audit exemption are set out in **36.1**. Whilst many such companies still choose, or are required for other reasons, to have their financial statements audited, this has created an expanding market for services that add credibility to financial statements, without being a full audit. In summary, the options available are:

- A limited assurance review engagement in which the accountant carries out procedures and enquiries that are limited in scope and do not constitute a full audit, in order to provide a basis for his conclusion. International Standard for Review Engagements (ISRE) 2400 (Revised) *Engagements to Review Historical Financial Statements* issued by the IAASB and effective for periods ending on or after 31 December 2013 sets standards and provides guidance on the conduct of such a review. In the UK, ISRE 2400 is supplemented by ICAEW technical release TECH 09/13 AAF *Assurance review engagements on historical financial statements*. See **41.2** below.
- Agreed-upon procedures, which result in a report of purely factual findings relating to procedures carried out. The user is left to draw his own conclusions, but will have increased confidence as these conclusions will be based on facts that have been checked by an independent accountant. More information can be found in the International Standard for Related Services (ISRS) 4400 *Agreed-upon procedures regarding financial information*, and in the ICAEW technical release TECH10/12 AAF *Reporting to third parties* (see **40.8** and **41.3**).
- A compilation engagement, where the accountant is engaged to prepare the financial statements from accounting records provided by a company's directors but without carrying out any verification of those records. Guidance can be found in technical releases TECH 07/16AAF (incorporated entities) and TECH 08/16AAF (unincorporated entities) (see **Chapter 8**). IFAC has also issued further guidance on these engagements, in its *Guide to Compilation Engagements* published in September 2015. Although based on the International Standard on Related Services 4410 (Revised) *Compilation Engagements*, it provides useful guidance applicable to the UK.

The differences between these different types of engagement are illustrated in **Table 1**.

TABLE 1: Rules of engagement

Type of engagement	Assurance engagement		Agreed upon procedures engagement	Compilation engagement
	Reasonable assurance	**Limited assurance ('review')**		
Example	Audit in accordance with ISAs (UK and Ireland)	Review in accordance with ISRE 2400/TECH 09/13 AAF		
Type of conclusion	Positive opinion, e.g. 'true and fair'.	Negative opinion, e.g. 'nothing has come to our attention'	Factual report of results of procedures, no conclusion given	Confirm facts of compilation only, no conclusion given

Other assurance engagements include:

- engagements to report on special purpose financial statements under ISA 800, *Special Considerations – Audits of Financial Statements Prepared in Accordance with Special Purpose Frameworks* and ISA 805, *Special Considerations – Audits of Single Financial Statements and Specific Elements, Accounts or Items of a Financial Statement*. These are covered in **41.4**;
- engagements to provide assurance on non-financial information, using guidance in ISAE 3000 *Assurance Engagements other than Audits or Reviews of Historical Financial Information*. These are covered in **41.5**.

41.2 Review engagements

41.2.1 Guidance

Guidance on this is given in TECH 09/13 AAF *Assurance review engagements on historical financial statements* which is based on the IAASB's International Standard on Review Engagements (ISRE) 2400 (Revised) *Engagements to Review Historical Financial Statements*, issued in September 2012.

In an assurance engagement, the accountant expresses a conclusion on the financial statements. In those review engagements covered by TECH 09/13 AAF the accountant gives a negative form of conclusion on the unaudited financial statements. This is known as a limited assurance engagement, as opposed to a reasonable assurance engagement where positive assurance is given, usually in terms of a true and fair view.

International Standard on Review Engagements (ISRE) 2400 (Revised), *Engagements to Review Historical Financial Statements* applies when a practitioner who is not the auditor of an entity undertakes an engagement to review financial statements. The principles contained therein may also be applied to reviews of other historical information. ISRE 2400 (Revised) helps practitioners performing review engagements to follow a globally accepted benchmark for undertaking such engagements, and aims to promote clarity for users about the nature of a review.

TECH 09/13 AAF issued by the ICAEW aims to provide guidance to assist with compliance with ISRE 2400 and includes example letters and reports to support these engagements and is discussed further below.

41.2.2 Features of a review engagement

The IAASB believes that an engagement performed under the revised standard should:

- enhance users' degree of confidence in the entity's financial statements, by reporting on them in a manner commensurate with the limited assurance obtained by the practitioner;
- be able to be performed on a cost-effective basis; and
- be clearly distinguishable from an audit of financial statements.

The ISRE sets out guidance in the following areas:

- conduct of a review engagement in accordance with the ISRE;
- ethical requirements;
- professional scepticism and judgment;
- engagement level quality control;
- acceptance and continuance of review engagements;
- communication with management and those charged with governance;
- performing the engagement;
- subsequent events;
- written representations;
- evaluating evidence;
- forming a conclusion on the financial statements;
- reporting; and
- documentation.

41.2.3 Accepting the engagement

The terms of the engagement should be agreed in writing. Example engagement letter wording is given in **Table 2**. The assurance report may be received by people not party to the engagement and the accountant should assess the risks of litigation arising from third parties prior to accepting the engagement. The engagement letter should be suitably worded to ensure that no liability is assumed to any third party.

TABLE 2: Example extracts from an engagement letter for a limited assurance review engagement for an audit exempt company

Your responsibilities as directors

As directors of the company, you are responsible for preparing financial statements which give a true and fair view and which have been prepared in accordance with the *Companies Act* 2006 (the Act). As directors, you must not approve the financial statements unless you are satisfied that they give a true and fair view of the assets, liabilities, financial position and profit or loss of the company.

In preparing the financial statements, you are required to:

- select suitable accounting policies and then apply them consistently;
- make judgments and estimates that are reasonable and prudent; and
- prepare the financial statements on the going concern basis unless it is inappropriate to presume that the company will continue in business.

You are responsible for keeping adequate accounting records that set out with reasonable accuracy at any time the company's financial position, and for ensuring that the financial statements comply with United Kingdom Generally Accepted Accounting Practice (UK GAAP) and with the *Companies Act* 2006 and give a true and fair view.

You are also responsible for such internal control as you determine is necessary to enable the preparation of financial statements that are free from material misstatement whether due to fraud or error.

You are also responsible for safeguarding the assets of the company and hence for taking reasonable steps to prevent and detect fraud and other irregularities.

You are responsible for ensuring that the company complies with laws and regulations that apply to its activities, and for preventing non-compliance and detecting any that occurs.

You have undertaken to make available to us, as and when required, all the company's accounting records and related financial information, including minutes of management and shareholders' and directors' meetings, that we need to do our work.

Our responsibilities when carrying out a review

Our review will be conducted with the objective of expressing our conclusion on the financial statements. Our conclusion, if unmodified, will be in the form:

'Based on our review, nothing has come to our attention that causes us to believe that the financial statements have not been prepared:

- so as to give a true and fair view of the state of the company's affairs as at [date], and of its profit [loss] for the year then ended;
- in accordance with United Kingdom Generally Accepted Accounting Practice [applicable to Smaller Entities]; and
- in accordance with the requirements of the *Companies Act* 2006.'

We will conduct our review in accordance with International Standard on Review Engagements (ISRE) 2400 (Revised) *Engagements to Review Historical Financial Statements* and ICAEW Technical Release TECH 09/13AAF *Assurance review engagements on historical financial statements*. ISRE 2400 (Revised) requires us to conclude whether anything has come to our attention that causes us to believe that the financial statements, taken as a whole, are not prepared in all material respects in accordance with the applicable financial reporting framework. ISRE 2400 also requires us to comply with relevant ethical requirements.

A review of financial statements in accordance with ISRE 2400 (Revised) is a limited assurance engagement. We will perform procedures, primarily consisting of making enquiries of management and others within the entity, as appropriate, applying analytical procedures, and evaluating the evidence obtained. We will also perform additional procedures if we become aware of matters that cause us to believe the financial statements as a whole may be materially misstated. These procedures are performed to enable us to express our conclusion on the financial statements in accordance with ISRE 2400 (Revised). The procedures selected will depend on what we consider necessary applying our professional judgment, based on our understanding of the company and its environment, and our understanding of UK GAAP and its application in the context of your company.

A review is not an audit of the financial statements, therefore:

(a)　there is a commensurate higher risk than there would be in an audit, that any material misstatements that exist in the financial statements reviewed may not be revealed by the review, even though the review is properly performed in accordance with ISRE 2400 (Revised);

(b)　in expressing our conclusion from the review of the financial statements, our report on the financial statements will expressly disclaim any audit opinion on the financial statements.

Our report will be made solely to the company's directors, as a body, in accordance with the terms of this engagement letter. Our work will be undertaken so that we might state to the directors those matters that we have agreed to state to them in a review report and for no other purpose. To the fullest extent permitted by law, we will not accept or assume responsibility to anyone other than the Company and the Company's directors as a body for our work, for our report or the conclusions we form.

> We have discussed with you the extent of our liability to you in respect of the professional services described within this engagement letter (the professional services). Having considered both your circumstances and our own, we have reached a mutual agreement that £ … represents a fair maximum limit to our liability.
>
> In reaching this agreement, it is also agreed that:
>
> (a) in the event of any claim for loss or damage arising from the professional services, you have agreed that the sum of £ … represents the maximum total liability to you in respect of the firm, [its] [principals] [directors] [members] [and staff]. This maximum total liability applies to any and all claims made on any basis and therefore includes any claims in respect of breaches of contract, tort (including negligence) or otherwise in respect of the professional services and shall also include interest;
>
> (b) we confirm that the limit in respect of our total aggregate liability will not apply to any acts, omissions or representations that are in any way criminal, dishonest or fraudulent on the part of the firm, [its] [principals] [directors] [members] [or employees]; and
>
> (c) you have agreed that you will not bring any claim of a kind that is included within the subject of the limit against any of our [principals] [directors] [members] [or employees]; on a personal basis.

As part of their risk management process, accountants should consider whether there are third parties who may seek to rely on their report. Depending on circumstances, and similar to the general guidance for managing professional liability set out in **40.3.2**, accountants may:

- accept that they owe a duty of care to the third parties and enter into a tri-partite or multi-partite engagement contract with the client and the third parties. Provisions to limit liability may be appropriate;
- proceed with an engagement with the client alone, but allowing access to the report for third parties as long as they:
  - acknowledge in writing that the reporting accountant owes them no duty of care; and
  - agree in writing that no claims will be brought against the reporting accountant in relation to the assurance report;
- engage with the client alone, disclaiming any liability or duty to others by notice in the assurance report. This may be in conjunction with the client indemnifying the reporting accountant if a third party makes a claim against the reporting accountant; or
- decline to accept the engagement.

41.2.4   Reliance by third parties

During the performance of the engagement, or after the report has been issued, the accountant may become aware of third parties, such as banks or lenders, who may request sight of the report. In such cases, the accountant may decline the request, or access may be agreed if the third party acknowledges in writing that they owe the accountant no duty of care.

When the accountant becomes aware that a third party has obtained a copy of his report, he should consider writing to the third party informing them that he did not undertake the work for the use of third parties and that he does not accept any responsibility to them and that all liability is denied.

It is likely that most assurance review reports will relate to general purpose financial statements, including statutory financial statements for audit exempt companies. These may become widely available, for example, they may be filed at Companies House although there is no obligation on the company to do so. This will make it impossible to restrict who has access to them, and it may therefore not be possible for the accountant to limit liability purely by means of a contract. An assurance review report appended to general financial statements may, however, include a paragraph disclaiming liabilities to third parties. The illustrative report in **Table 3** includes a paragraph to this effect, which is equivalent to the 'Bannerman' paragraph used in audit reports, and relies on the same legal precedent (see **4.22**).

41.2.5   Performing the engagement

Further guidance on performing the engagement is given in the ISRE. In particular, the accountant should be aware that he is still subject to the *Money Laundering Regulations* 2007 and the requirements of the *Proceeds of Crime Act* 2002. In addition, although the depth of work carried out on going concern will be less than that for an audit, the accountant will still need to consider the disclosures in this area in accordance with the applicable accounting framework and the FRC guidance for directors.

An emphasis of matter paragraph is required when the accountant considers a matter to be of such importance that it is fundamental to users' understanding of the financial statements. This will include situations where there is material uncertainty related to events or conditions that may cast significant doubt on the entity's ability to continue as a going concern.

41.2.6   Written representations

Written representations are still required from management and example wording is given in TECH 09/13.

41.2.7   Reporting

The accountant's report helps addressees derive comfort from the involvement of an independent accountant. It also assists in clarifying the scope of the engagement and ensuring that readers are aware that a full audit has not taken place. **Table 3** includes an example report to directors.

TABLE 3: Example accountant's report to directors

Independent Chartered Accountant's review report to the directors of [entity name]

To the Board of Directors of [entity name] ('the Company')

We have reviewed the financial statements of XYZ Limited for the year ended [date], which comprise the [Profit and Loss Account, the Balance Sheet, the Cash Flow Statement, the Statement of Total Recognised Gains and Losses,] and the related notes 1 to [X]. The financial reporting framework that has been applied in their preparation is applicable law and the Financial Reporting Standard for Smaller Entities (effective January 2015) (United Kingdom Generally Accepted Accounting Practice applicable to Smaller Entities).

This report is made solely to the Company's directors, as a body, in accordance with the terms of our engagement letter dated [date]. Our review has been undertaken so that we may state to the company's directors those matters we have agreed with them in our engagement letter and for no other purpose. To the fullest extent permitted by law, we do not accept or assume responsibility to anyone other than the Company and the Company's directors as a body for our work, for this report or the conclusions we have formed.

Directors' Responsibility for the Financial Statements

As explained more fully in the Directors' Responsibilities Statement [set out on pages …], the directors are responsible for the preparation of the financial statements and for being satisfied that they give a true and fair view.

Accountants' Responsibility

Our responsibility is to express a conclusion based on our review of the financial statements. We conducted our review in accordance with International Standard on Review Engagements (ISRE) 2400 (Revised), *Engagements to review historical financial statements* and ICAEW Technical Release TECH 09/13AAF *Assurance review engagements on historical financial statements*. ISRE 2400 also requires us to comply with the ICAEW Code of Ethics.

Scope of the Assurance Review

A review of financial statements in accordance with ISRE 2400 (Revised) is a limited assurance engagement. We have performed additional procedures to those required under a compilation engagement. These primarily consist of making enquiries of management and others within the entity, as appropriate, applying analytical procedures and evaluating the evidence obtained. The procedures performed in a review are substantially less than those performed in an audit conducted in accordance with International Standards on Auditing (UK and Ireland). Accordingly, we do not express an audit opinion on these financial statements.

Conclusion

Based on our review, nothing has come to our attention that causes us to believe that the financial statements have not been prepared:

- so as to give a true and fair view of the state of the company's affairs as at [date], and of its profit [loss] for the year then ended;
- in accordance with United Kingdom Generally Accepted Accounting Practice [applicable to Smaller Entities]; and
- in accordance with the requirements of the *Companies Act* 2006.

[Accountant's signature – name of individual or firm]

[Firm name] Chartered Accountants [Address]

[Date]

41.3   Agreed upon procedures

Guidance in the area of agreed upon procedures reports to third parties is provided by International Standard on Related Services (ISRS) 4400, *Engagements to Perform Agreed-Upon Procedures Regarding Financial Information*. ISRS 4400 sets out the general principles and standards to be applied by the accountant when an engagement to perform agreed-upon procedures is undertaken.

In an agreed-upon procedures engagement, the accountant will carry out procedures of an audit nature on which he and the entity, together with any relevant third parties, have agreed, and report on his findings.

As the accountant simply provides a report of the factual findings of agreed-upon procedures, no assurance is expressed. Instead, users of the report assess for themselves the procedures and findings reported by the accountant and draw their own conclusions from the results of the work performed. Under ISRS 4400, the accountant's report is restricted to those parties that have agreed to the procedures to be performed since others, unaware of the reasons for the procedures, may misinterpret the results.

ISRS 4400 contains detailed guidance on:

- defining the terms of the engagement;
- planning;
- documentation;
- procedures and evidence; and
- reporting.

Further matters to consider and example engagement letters and reports in respect of an agreed upon procedures engagement are further discussed in **40.8**.

41.4 Auditor's reports on special purpose financial statements

Guidance covering reports by the auditor on special purpose financial statements is given in ISA 800 (Revised), *Special Considerations – Audits of Financial Statements Prepared in Accordance with Special Purpose Frameworks* and ISA 805, *Special Considerations – Audits of Single Financial Statements and Specific Elements, Accounts or Items of a Financial Statement*. As there are no direct UK equivalents of these ISAs, the international versions are being increasingly referred to by UK auditors. These standards are not appropriate for engagements to report on statutory accounts of UK companies which will need to comply with a recognised framework.

The current version of both ISA 800 (Revised) and ISA 805 (Revised) were issued in January 2016 and are effective for audits of financial statements for periods ending on or after December 15, 2016.

These latest versions include limited amendments to provide clarity about how the new and revised audit reporting standards issued by the IAASB apply in the context of special purpose financial statements, but the changes do not substantively change the underlying premise of these engagements.

41.4.1 Special purpose frameworks

ISA 800 is applicable where an audit opinion (i.e reasonable rather than limited assurance) is given on a complete set of financial statements but the financial statements have been prepared in accordance with a special purpose framework rather than a generally accepted one. A special purpose framework is one designed to meet the financial information needs of specific users and will usually be based on a generally accepted framework but deviate from it in one or more material respects because the information required by the framework is either inappropriate or irrelevant for the special purpose for which the financial statements are prepared. Examples of such frameworks include:

- a tax basis of accounting for a set of financial statements accompanying an entity's tax return;
- cash receipts and payments basis of accounting for cash flow information that an entity may be requested to prepare for creditors;
- the financial reporting provisions established by a regulator to meet the requirements of that regulator; and
- the financial reporting provisions of a contract, such as a bond indenture, loan agreement, or a project grant.

ISA 800 deals with special considerations in the application of ISAs to an audit of financial statements prepared in accordance with a special purpose framework and in particular sets standards and provides guidance on accepting the engagement, planning and performing procedures and forming an opinion and reporting. An example audit report is given in **Table 4** below:

TABLE 4: Example of an audit report in accordance with ISA 800[1]

Independent Auditor's Report to [Appropriate Addressee]

We have audited the accompanying financial statements of ABC Company, which comprise the balance sheet as at December 31, 20X1, and the income statement, statement of changes in equity and cash flow statement for the year then ended, and a summary of significant accounting policies and other explanatory information. The financial statements have been prepared by management of ABC Company based on the financial reporting provisions of Section Z of the contract dated January 1, 20X1 between ABC Company and DEF Company ('the contract').

Management's Responsibility for the Financial Statements

Management is responsible for the preparation of these financial statements in accordance with the financial reporting provisions of Section Z of the contract, and for such internal control as management determines is necessary to enable the preparation of financial statements that are free from material misstatement, whether due to fraud or error.

Auditor's Responsibility

Our responsibility is to express an opinion on these financial statements based on our audit. We conducted our audit in accordance with International Standards on Auditing. Those standards require that we comply with ethical requirements and plan and perform the audit to obtain reasonable assurance about whether the financial statements are free from material misstatement.

An audit involves performing procedures to obtain audit evidence about the amounts and disclosures in the financial statements. The procedures selected depend on the auditor's judgment, including the assessment of the risks of material misstatement of the financial statements, whether due to fraud or error. In making those risk assessments, the auditor considers internal control relevant to the entity's preparation of the financial statements in order to design audit procedures that are appropriate in the circumstances, but not for the purpose of expressing an opinion on the effectiveness of the entity's internal control. An audit also includes evaluating the appropriateness of accounting policies used and the reasonableness of accounting estimates made by management, as well as evaluating the overall presentation of the financial statements.

We believe that the audit evidence we have obtained is sufficient and appropriate to provide a basis for our audit opinion.

Opinion

In our opinion, the financial statements of ABC Company for the year ended December 31, 20X1 are prepared, in all material respects, in accordance with the financial reporting provisions of Section Z of the contract.

Basis of Accounting and Restriction on Distribution and Use

Without modifying our opinion, we draw attention to Note X to the financial statements, which describes the basis of accounting. The financial statements are prepared to assist ABC Company to comply with the financial reporting provisions of the contract referred to above. As a result, the financial statements may not be suitable for another purpose. Our report is intended solely for ABC Company and DEF Company and should not be distributed to or used by parties other than ABC Company or DEF Company.

[Auditor's signature]

[Date of the auditor's report]

[Auditor's address]

[1] This example is based on the IAASB's version of ISA 800 and does not include any UK specific amendments.

41.4.2 Reports on specific elements

ISA 805 deals with special considerations in the application of ISAs to an audit of a single financial statement or of a specific element, account or item of a financial statement. The single financial statement or the specific element, account or item of a financial statement may be prepared in accordance with a general or special purpose framework. If prepared in accordance with a special purpose framework, ISA 800 also applies to the audit.

41.5   Assurance on non-financial information

41.5.1   Non-financial information

There are a number of areas where entities currently report on non-financial information, and these include:

- statements and information contained in the annual report, such as the enhanced business review, corporate governance statements and information on risk management policies, internal controls or wider operating data;
- corporate responsibility reporting on environmental, economic and social performance;
- reports to Regulators on matters such as risk exposures, pricing policies or compliance with regulatory requirements; and
- reporting on public interest concerns, for example, quality of service provision, carbon emissions or the conduct of public competitions.

Demand for credible information in these areas is growing, and therefore, there has been an increasing requirement for practitioners to provide assurance reports.

41.5.2   Current practices and guidance

The current version of the International Standard on Assurance Engagements (ISAE) 3000 *Assurance Engagements other than Audits or Reviews of Historical Financial Information*, published by the IAASB, was issued in December 2013 and is effective for assurance reports dated on or after 15 December 2015. It covers all aspects of assurance engagements including:

- engagement acceptance;
- agreeing the terms of engagement;
- planning and performing the engagement;
- using the work of experts;
- obtaining evidence;
- considering subsequent events;
- documentation; and
- preparing the external assurance report.

Reference may be made to this standard where an assurance engagement is being conducted which is not an audit, or a review of historical financial information.

This standard is increasingly being used in the UK by accountants who are engaged to provide assurance on non-financial information produced by entities such as greenhouse gas emissions statements or sustainability reports. Such statements may form part of a company's annual report to members or may be a separate report(s) published on a website or prepared specifically for use by third parties.

Corporate responsibility

Corporate responsibility reports provide non-financial information on the social, economic and environmental performance of an organisation. There is no generally accepted framework or standard for preparing a corporate responsibility report, however, the sustainability reporting guidelines issued by the Global Reporting Initiative (GRI) are the best-known global voluntary code for sustainability reporting.

Information in the annual reports and accounts

Non-financial information in the annual reports and accounts may be included in:

- the strategic report (where applicable) or directors' report;
- corporate governance statements;
- Chairman's statement or other statements or reports included in the annual report; and
- disclosures in the audited accounts.

There is no requirement for the disclosures in the strategic report or directors' report to be audited, but the auditor is required to report whether the information in these reports is consistent with the financial statements (see **Chapter 34**).

Under the Listing Rules, the auditor is only required to review certain of the statements relating to UK Corporate Governance Code provisions (see **Chapter 42**). Information relating to other aspects of compliance with the Code would be included in the 'other information' requirements set out in **Chapter 34**, which also apply to other statements/reports included in the annual report.

Qualitative or other non-financial information included in the accounts is covered by the auditor's opinion on the financial statements.

Regulatory reporting

Many regulatory bodies require information from the entities that they regulate in order to perform their duties, but the nature and volume of the information required varies significantly from Regulator to Regulator. Practitioners should ensure that they are fully conversant with the requirements of the relevant Regulator prior to accepting an engagement to provide assurance on such information.

Where Regulators request reports on non-financial information, the form of report made by the regulated entity and the nature of external assurance requirements will be set out by the Regulator.

Other reports

Other areas where practitioners may be asked to report on non-financial information include:

- the application of quality assurance standards in relation to information security or customer service; and
- the administration of public competitions and telephone voting.

There is no external framework of guidance to assist practitioners with this type of engagement, but ISAE 3000 should be helpful, and ISO 9000 may also provide some useful guidance on quality assurance.

41.5.3   Considerations for practitioners

By providing external assurance reports, practitioners are enhancing the credibility of non-financial information by:

- following rigorous ethical standards covering independence;
- following a defined framework and standards which cover the whole assurance engagement; and
- having the relevant skills and experience in carrying out assurance engagements, following professional standards, complying with CPD and training requirements and having internal quality control procedures in place.

When accepting such an engagement, practitioners should:

- consider the motivations and purpose behind the request to ensure that they are able to meet this need;
- understand the needs of the users of the non-financial information;
- be clear about what the information is that they are reporting on and why it is needed;
- have agreed criteria by which they can measure the information; and
- clearly communicate these considerations in their report to help to avoid any expectation gap.

Skills

Practitioners' auditing experience may be valuable when carrying out assurance engagements on non-financial information. They are used to applying professional judgment and are familiar with assessing materiality, understanding the business and obtaining sufficient appropriate evidence.

Specialists can be consulted or a multi-disciplinary team can be used where practitioners have less experience in assessing qualitative, rather than quantitative, information or have a lack of in-depth technical knowledge, such as in engineering or surveying.

Subjective information

Compared to financial information, established measurement conventions do not exist for non-financial information. In such situations, it may not be possible to establish consistent measurement criteria that are acceptable to all interested parties, and practitioners must consider whether the criteria used are relevant to the needs of the intended users of the information.

A reference to the measurement criteria used should be made in the external assurance report so that the basis of the practitioners' conclusion is clear.

Information from third parties

Reported non-financial information may include data sourced from third parties, such as retail statistics, average market prices, etc. In line with the requirements of ISA (UK and Ireland) 402, *Audit considerations relating to entities using service organisations* (see **Chapter 22**), practitioners should consider whether the bodies producing this information have suitable controls and procedures in place to ensure that the information produced is accurate. This assurance may be in the form of an external assurance report on their operations (see **40.7**). If any such evidence is lacking, practitioners may exclude the associated data from the scope of their assurance report.

Evidence

Practitioners need to be aware that non-financial information is often qualitative, and therefore, it is often difficult to determine criteria against which to measure the information. Evidence may also be harder to obtain as there is likely to be less documentation to support disclosure and third-party verification is likely to be less readily available. In addition, determining materiality can be difficult in areas which are less quantitative in nature.

Control environment

Internal controls related to non-financial business activities and operations are not always well monitored or documented and may not be as robust as those related to financial reporting. Therefore, at the planning stage of the engagement, practitioners consider how they will obtain evidence that the information is robust enough to express an opinion on.

42 CORPORATE GOVERNANCE

42.1 Background

42.1.1 Corporate governance framework

Corporate governance has been developed over many years since the early 1990s and over that time a number of committees and reports (for example, The Cadbury Report, the Greenbury Report and the Combined Code) have been developed, resulting in today's governance framework.

The current relevant document is the *UK Corporate Governance Code*, referred to as 'the Code', issued by the FRC. This is supported by a number of FRC documents aimed at assisting boards and audit committees with the application of the Code. These include:

- *Guidance on Board Effectiveness*, published in 2011;
- *Guidance on Audit Committees*, updated in 2012 and considered in **42.8**;
- *Guidance on Risk Management, Internal Control and Related Financial and Business Reporting*, published in 2014 and consolidating and updating earlier guidance; and
- an *Audit Quality Practice Aid for audit committees*, issued in March 2015 and covered in **Chapter 3**.

The latest edition of the Code was issued in September 2014 and applies to reporting periods beginning on or after 1 October 2014. The 2014 version of the Code included a requirement for boards to include a 'viability statement' in the strategic report to investors. This provides an improved and broader assessment of long-term solvency and liquidity and is expected to look forward for a period significantly longer than 12 months. Further guidance in this area is contained in *Guidance on Risk Management, Internal Control and Related Financial and Business Reporting*.

In April 2016, a revision to the Code was issued, updating section C.3 on audit committees and auditors. The changes to the Code have been kept to the minimum required to align with the Audit Regulation and Directive and to limit the regulatory burden. The changes relate to the tenure of the auditor where the 2012 Code change introducing ten-year retendering is now redundant; and to changes in the composition and role of the audit committee.

The Code is not mandatory but is intended to be applied on a 'comply or explain' basis under which entities applying the Code will make a statement of compliance in which they identify those provisions of the Code with which they have not complied and provide an explanation for their non-compliance.

The Code contains broad principles and more specific provisions. All companies with a Premium Listing of equity shares in the UK are required under the Listing

Rules to report in their annual report and accounts on how they have applied the main principles of the Code, and either to confirm that they have complied throughout the reporting period with all relevant provisions of the Code or, where they have not, to provide an explanation. The relevant section of the Listing Rules can be found at www.fshandbook.info/FS/html/handbook/LR/9/8. Auditors of such companies are required to review this statement of compliance, but only insofar as it relates to certain specified provisions of the Code.

These requirements do not apply to companies with a Standard Listing only.

42.1.2   *Directors' remuneration*

Directors' remuneration remains a key issue for corporate governance and the 2014 revisions to the Code included changing:

- Main Principle D.1 so that it refers to the design of remuneration to promote the long-term success of the company; and
- Provision D.1.1 to recommend that provisions are put in place to recover and/ or withhold remuneration when appropriate.

Under the *Companies Act* 2006, quoted companies are required to prepare a separate Directors' Remuneration Report. Some, but not all of the information in the Directors' Remuneration Report is required to be examined and reported on by the auditor.

The detailed requirements relating to the Directors' Remuneration Report are set out in the *Large and Medium-Sized Companies and Groups (Accounts and Reports) Regulations* 2008 (SI 2008/410), Sch. 8. A new Sch. 8 was substituted for financial years ending on or after 30 September 2013 by the *Large and Medium-sized Companies and Groups (Accounts and reports) (Amendment) Regulations* 2013 (SI 2013/1981).

The requirement to prepare a Directors' Remuneration Report applies not only to premium listed companies but to any 'quoted' company which is defined as a company incorporated under the *Companies Act* 2006:

- whose equity share capital has been included in the official list; or
- is officially listed in an European Economic Area (EEA) state; or
- is admitted to dealing on either the New York Stock Exchange or the exchange known as Nasdaq.

The definition includes companies with standard listed equity shares but does not include companies traded on the Alternative Investment Market (AIM) or entities with standard listed debt or non-equity shares only.

42.1.3 Disclosure and transparency rules

With effect for financial years beginning on or after 29 June 2008, certain disclosures relating to corporate governance, and auditors' responsibilities in relation thereto, came into effect as a result of the European Union directives. The requirements were incorporated into the Disclosure Rules and Transparency Rules (now part of the FCA Handbook) and the *Companies Act* 2006. These included a requirement for listed companies to produce a Corporate Governance Statement and to include in it a description of the main features of their internal control and risk management systems in relation to the financial reporting process. Details of requirements relating to the Corporate Governance Statement are set out in **42.7.1** below.

42.2 Guidance

42.2.1 FRC – companies and investors

In addition to the UK Corporate Governance Code, the FRC publishes a series of guidance notes intended to assist companies address specific aspects of governance and accountability. Currently, these cover:

- board effectiveness;
- the role of audit committees; and
- risk management, internal control and assessing and reporting on whether the business is a going concern.

The FRC also publishes the UK Stewardship Code which sets standards for investors for monitoring and engaging with companies. The Stewardship Code sets out a number of areas of good practice to which the FRC believes institutional investors should aspire and also operates on a 'comply or explain' basis. The FCA requires UK authorised asset managers to report on whether or not they apply the Code.

The FRC publication *UK Approach to Corporate Governance* explains the code-based approach, and how it fits into the UK's regulatory regime.

42.2.2 FRC – auditors

In September 2006, the APB issued Bulletin 2006/5, *The combined code on corporate governance: requirements of auditors under the Listing Rules of the Financial Services Authority and the Irish Stock Exchange* to update guidance for auditors when reviewing a company's statement made in relation to the Combined Code (now the UK Corporate Governance Code).

Additionally, in December 2009, the APB issued Bulletin 2009/4 *Developments in corporate governance affecting the responsibilities of auditors of UK companies.* This new bulletin:

- updated and superseded guidance in paragraphs 68 to 72 of Bulletin 2006/5 relating to the requirement for the auditor to review the directors' statement on going concern (see **42.6.4**);
- provided guidance in relation to the corporate governance statements required by the Disclosure Rules and Transparency Rules of the Financial Conduct Authority (see **42.7.1**); and
- provided guidance for reporting on 'standard listed companies' (see **42.7.2**).

For auditors of companies incorporated in Ireland, the appropriate Bulletin is 2011/1 *Developments in corporate governance affecting the responsibilities of auditors of companies incorporated in Ireland*.

The FRC now seeks to maintain standards and guidance for auditors in parallel with its guidance for companies and recent developments in the UK Corporate Governance Code have been accompanied, where applicable, by changes to ISAs (UK and Ireland).

The 2016 version of ISA (UK and Ireland) 720 (Revised June 2016) *The auditor's responsibilities relating to other information* contains a number of requirements and associated guidance applicable only to those entities that are required, or choose voluntarily to report on how they have applied the Code.

Previously, these requirements were covered in ISA (UK and Ireland) 700 *The independent auditor's report on financial statements*. The latest version of this standard containing these requirements was issued in September 2014 and applies for periods commencing on or after 1 October 2014.

Bulletin 4: *Recent developments in company law, the Listing Rules and Auditing Standards that affect United Kingdom Auditor's Reports*, which was revised by the FRC in June 2015, contains examples of how these requirements of ISA 700 might be applied in an auditor's report, although at the time of writing the examples in the Bulletin did not cover the requirements of paragraph 22C of the ISA regarding the auditor's views on the various statements made by the directors relating to risk, going concern and viability.

The implications for the auditor's report of compliance with the Code and the Listing Rules are considered in **Chapter 4**.

ISA (UK and Ireland) 260 (Revised June 2016) *Communication with those charged with governance* contains specific requirements applicable to auditors of entities that report on application of the Code and sets out the matters that should be communicated by the auditor to the audit committee in connection with the responsibilities of those charged with governance under the Code.

ISA (UK and Ireland) 570 (Revised June 2016) *Going concern* contains specific requirements relating to the auditor's responsibility in relation to statements and disclosures made by the directors in the annual report in relation to risk, going concern and longer term viability.

42.3 Terms of engagement

Bulletin 2006/5 recommended that for premium listed companies, in order to clarify the auditor's responsibilities:

- the engagement letter explains the scope of the auditor's review of the directors' statement of compliance with the Code; and
- the auditor discusses the findings of his review with those charged with governance, prior to the publication of his report.

The Bulletin contains an example of suitable paragraphs to include in an engagement letter with respect to the company's compliance with the Listing Rule (LR) 9.8.10R.

The example terms of engagement also include paragraphs relating to the auditor's responsibilities in relation to the Directors' Remuneration Report, where applicable.

42.4 Auditor's responsibilities for the 'Comply or Explain' statement

The Listing Rules require listed companies to include a two-part statement in their annual report relating to the Code:

- *Part one*: explaining how the company has applied the main principles of the UK Corporate Governance Code, in a manner that would enable shareholders to evaluate how the principles have been applied;
- *Part two*: either:

  - *Comply* – include 'a statement as to whether it has complied throughout the accounting period with all relevant provisions set out in the UK Corporate Governance Code'; or
  - *Explain* – include 'a statement as to whether it has not complied throughout the accounting period with all relevant provisions set out in the UK Corporate Governance Code' and if so, set out:

    (i)   those provisions, it has not complied with;
    (ii) in the case of provisions whose requirements are of a continuing nature, the period within which, if any, it did not comply with some or all of those provisions; and
    (iii) the company's reasons for any non-compliance.

Auditors have no responsibility to assess and comment upon a company's decision to depart from the provisions of the Code. The auditor is, however, required by LR 9.8.10R(2), to review the parts of the statement that relate to certain of the objectively verifiable Code provisions as set out in **Table 1**.

In February 2012, the FRC published a paper titled *What Constitutes an Explanation under 'Comply or Explain'?* which was based on discussion meetings between senior investors and companies and identified a number of features of a meaningful explanation. These included, for example, providing a clear rationale for the action taken and describing any mitigating actions and ensuring that explanations – and corporate governance reporting generally – are specific to the company's position, not generic or off-the-shelf.

42.5   Provisions of the UK Corporate Governance Code

The Listing Rules require that the auditor reviews compliance with a number of provisions of the Code and the relevant provisions are set out in **Table 1**.

TABLE 1: Provisions of the UK Corporate Governance Code which the auditor is required to review

C.1.1

The directors should explain in the annual report their responsibility for preparing the annual report and accounts, and state that they consider the annual report and accounts, taken as a whole, is fair, balanced and understandable and provides the information necessary for shareholders to assess the company's performance, business model and strategy. There should be a statement by the auditor about their reporting responsibilities.

C.2.1

The directors should confirm in the annual report that they have carried out a robust assessment of the principal risks facing the company, including those that would threaten its business model, future performance, solvency or liquidity. The directors should describe those risks and explain how they are being managed or mitigated.

C.2.3

The board should monitor the company's risk management and internal control systems and, at least annually, carry out a review of their effectiveness, and report on that review in the annual report. The monitoring and review should cover all material controls, including financial, operational and compliance controls.

C.3.1

The board should establish an audit committee of at least three, or in the case of smaller companies two, independent non-executive directors. In smaller companies, the company chairman may be a member of, but not chair, the committee in addition to the independent non-executive directors, provided he or she was considered independent on appointment as chairman. The board should satisfy itself that at least one member of the audit committee has recent and relevant financial experience. The audit committee as a whole shall have competence relevant to the sector in which the company operates.

C.3.2

The main role and responsibilities of the audit committee should be set out in written terms of reference and should include:

- to monitor the integrity of the financial statements of the company, and any formal announcements relating to the company's financial performance, reviewing significant financial reporting judgments contained in them;
- to review the company's internal financial control and, unless expressly addressed by a separate board risk committee composed of independent directors, or by the board itself, to review the company's internal control and risk management systems;
- to monitor and review the effectiveness of the company's internal audit function;
- to make recommendations to the board, for it to put to the shareholders for their approval in general meeting, in relation to the appointment, reappointment and removal of the external auditor and to approve the remuneration and terms of engagement of the external auditor;
- to review and monitor the external auditor's independence and objectivity and the effectiveness of the audit process, taking into consideration relevant UK professional and regulatory requirements;
- to develop and implement policy on the engagement of the external auditor to supply non-audit services, taking into account relevant ethical guidance regarding the provision of non-audit services by the external audit firm; and to report to the board, identifying any matters in respect of which it considers that action or improvement is needed and making recommendations as to the steps to be taken; and
- to report to the board on how it has discharged its responsibilities.

C.3.3

The terms of reference of the audit committee, including its role and the authority delegated to it by the board, should be made available.

C.3.4

Where requested by the board, the audit committee should provide advice on whether the annual report and accounts, taken as a whole, is fair, balanced and understandable and provides the information necessary for shareholders to assess the company's position and performance, business model and strategy.

C.3.5

The audit committee should review arrangements by which staff of the company may, in confidence, raise concerns about possible improprieties in matters of financial reporting or other matters. The audit committee's objective should be to ensure that arrangements are in place for the proportionate and independent investigation of such matters and for appropriate follow-up action.

C.3.6

The audit committee should monitor and review the effectiveness of the internal audit activities. Where there is no internal audit function, the audit committee should consider annually whether there is a need for an internal audit function and make a recommendation to the board, and the reasons for the absence of such a function should be explained in the relevant section of the annual report.

C.3.7

The audit committee should have primary responsibility for making a recommendation on the appointment, reappointment and removal of the external auditors. If the board does not accept the audit committee's recommendation, it should include in the annual report, and in any papers recommending appointment or reappointment, a statement from the audit committee explaining the recommendation and should set out reasons why the board has taken a different position.

C.3.8

A separate section of the annual report should describe the work of the committee in discharging its responsibilities. The report should include:

- the significant issues that the committee considered in relation to the financial statements, and how these issues were addressed;
- an explanation of how it has assessed the effectiveness of the external audit process and the approach taken to the appointment or reappointment of the external auditor, and information on the length of tenure of the current audit firm and when a tender was last conducted and advance notice of retendering plans; and
- if the external auditor provides non-audit services, an explanation of how the auditor's objectivity and independence is safeguarded.

The Listing Rules also require that the going concern statement and longer term viability statement made by the directors should undergo auditor review (Listing Rule 9.8.10R).

42.6 Procedures

Bulletin 2006/5 sets out a number of general procedures relating to the auditor's review of the statement of compliance, and specific procedures relating to each Code provision that is to be reviewed. Code provisions are numbered according to the 2014 Code, which in some cases differ from Bulletin 2006/5 and auditors should bear in mind that both the Code and business and reporting practices have evolved since the Bulletin was issued.

42.6.1   General procedures

For the code provisions within the scope of his review, the auditor should obtain appropriate evidence to support the compliance statement made by the company. Procedures he may undertake include:

- reviewing board and relevant committee meeting minutes (e.g. audit or risk management committees);
- review of supporting documents prepared for the board or committees;
- making enquiries of the directors or company secretary about the procedures used by the company to implement the Code provisions;
- attending meetings of the audit committee at which the annual report and accounts, including the statement of compliance, are considered and approved for submission to the board of directors; and
- requesting written confirmation of representations made by directors during the review.

42.6.2   Specific procedures – the verifiable code provisions

Responsibilities of directors and the auditor (Code provision C.1.1)

Directors' responsibilities

The auditor should ensure that the directors' responsibility for preparing the accounts is explained in the annual report. This is usually contained within the directors' report or in separate statement of responsibilities.

Auditor's responsibilities

The auditor has responsibilities to audit, review or read different parts of the annual report. These should be clarified by inclusion of a statement of auditor's responsibilities in the audit report or as a separate statement and by inclusion of a paragraph in the engagement letter. In practice, the standard form of audit report used by the FRC in its published examples deals adequately with the auditor's responsibilities and a separate statement is rare.

Directors' assessment of risks (Code provision C.2.1)

Not covered by the Bulletin.

Monitoring of risk management and internal control (Code provision C.2.3)

Directors' responsibilities

Under the FRC's guidance on internal control issued in October 2005, boards were recommended to 'confirm that necessary actions have been or are being taken to remedy any significant failings or weaknesses identified from [their review of the effectiveness of the system of internal control]' in their statement on internal control. In addition, FCA Rule DTR 7.2.5 R requires companies to describe the main features of the internal control and risk management systems in relation to the financial reporting process.

Auditor's responsibilities with respect to the directors' narrative statement

The annual report will contain a narrative statement about how the company has applied Code principle C.2.1. This should, as a minimum, disclose that there is an ongoing process for identifying, evaluating and managing the significant risks faced by the company that is regularly reviewed by the Board. This statement is likely to vary significantly from company to company.

The auditor has no responsibility to review this narrative statement, but is expected to read it in line with the requirements of ISA (UK and Ireland) 720 (Revised June 2016).

However, in relation to the additional recommendation that the Board should confirm that actions have been or are being taken to remedy significant weaknesses, Bulletin 2006/5 recommends that the auditor:

- review the documentation prepared to support the Board's statement in relation to any significant failings or weaknesses and consider whether or not this documentation provides sound support for the Board's statement;
- discuss actions already taken or about to be taken with directors; and
- consider the statement made in relation to his knowledge of the company obtained during the audit of the financial statements. This would include whether the directors have considered any significant deficiencies in internal control reported to those charged with governance in accordance with ISA (UK and Ireland) 260 (Revised June 2016) (see **Chapter 10**).

The auditor is not required, however, to assess the Board's decision as to what constitutes a 'significant' failing or weakness or whether the actions taken or planned will actually remedy the failure identified.

Auditor's review of compliance

The auditor is, as part of his review, required to assess whether the summary of the process given by the board is supported by documentation and reflects the actual process that took place. The auditor's procedures will include:

- discussing the process used with the directors and comparing the understanding this provides with the statement made in the annual report;
- reviewing the documentation connected with the process and considering whether it supports the statement; and
- considering whether the statement is reasonable given the knowledge gained about the company during the audit of the financial statements.

The auditor should also consider whether the directors' statement covers the year under review and the period to the date of approval of the annual report and accounts.

As his knowledge of the client is narrower than the directors', the auditor is not expected to assess whether all risks and controls have been addressed or that risks are satisfactorily addressed by internal controls. However, if the auditor discovers a significant deficiency in internal control as part of his audit work, he should report it to those charged with governance as soon as possible so that it can be considered as part of the statement on internal control.

Significant problems in the annual report

The FRC's internal control guidance recommended that the internal control aspects of any 'significant problems' disclosed in the annual report and accounts are discussed in the Board's statement. Unfortunately, the term 'significant problem' is not defined, and in practice this is likely to be highly subjective and include both financial and non-financial items.

Auditors have a responsibility to:

- discuss the steps the directors have taken to identify 'significant problems' disclosed in the annual report and accounts; and
- assess whether the narrative disclosure of the process applied to deal with any internal control aspects of these problems is an appropriate reflection of the actual process undertaken.

If the auditor is aware of a significant problem in the annual report and accounts which has not been considered in the statement, this should be brought to the attention of the directors. If the matter cannot be resolved, the auditor should consider whether there is an impact on his report.

Groups of companies

The review of effectiveness of internal control should be from a group perspective and where material joint ventures and associated companies have been excluded, this fact should be disclosed. Using his knowledge of the client, the auditor should assess whether any material joint ventures or associated companies have been excluded.

Non-executive Directors (Code provision C.3.1)

Bulletin 2006/5 recommends that the auditor should:

- check the number of members of the audit committee complies with the Code requirements (at least three members, or two for smaller companies);
- obtain an understanding of the process used by the Board to determine:
  - if the audit committee are all independent non-executive directors; and
  - that at least one member of the audit committee has recent and relevant financial experience; and

- review evidence, such as minutes and other documentation, to support the above.

The auditor is not responsible for determining whether the directors are independent or whether a particular audit committee member has the relevant financial experience. However, if he has doubts over either of these areas, they should be communicated to the audit committee and board.

Audit Committee (Code provision C.3.2)

The Bulletin recommends that the auditor should obtain a copy of the terms of reference of the audit committee and review whether the roles and responsibilities described therein reflect the recommendations of Code provision C3.2.

The auditor is not responsible for considering whether the audit committee has fulfilled its roles and responsibilities.

Audit Committee Terms of Reference (Code provision C.3.3)

The auditor should review whether the terms of reference for the audit committee are posted on the company's website or otherwise made readily available.

Audit Committee Advice on Annual Report (Code provision C.3.4)

The Bulletin does not provide guidance for the auditor in respect of this Code provision.

Raising Staff Concerns (Code provision C.3.5)

The auditor should review:

- supporting documentation to determine whether there is evidence that the audit committee has reviewed the arrangements and discuss the review with staff as necessary; and
- documentation supporting the company's arrangements for 'proportionate and independent' investigations.

The auditor is not responsible for considering whether the arrangements do allow 'proportionate and independent' investigations or whether follow-up action is appropriate, but rather should review the process undertaken to assure the audit committee that this is the case.

Internal Audit (Code provision C.3.6)

The Bulletin states that the auditor should perform the following procedures:

- hold discussions with the audit committee chairman and review supporting documentation to establish that the effectiveness of any internal audit function has been monitored and reviewed;

- where no internal audit function exists, review whether:

    - the audit committee has considered the need for an internal audit function;
    - there is documentation that this recommendation has been made to the Board; and
    - the reasons for not having an internal audit function are included in the relevant section of the annual report.

The auditor is not responsible for considering whether the internal audit function is effective or whether the reasons disclosed in the annual report for not having an internal audit function are reasonable.

Appointment, Reappointment and Removal of the External Auditor (Code provision C.3.7)

The auditor should:

- review the terms of reference of the audit committee, or other documentation, to ensure that the audit committee has primary responsibility for making a recommendation on the appointment, reappointment and removal of the auditor;
- review documentation of the audit committee's recommendation to the board;
- where the board has not accepted the audit committee's recommendation, review the annual report and any papers recommending appointment or reappointment of the auditor, to ensure inclusion of:

    - a statement from the audit committee explaining its recommendation; and
    - a statement from the board setting out reasons why they have taken a different position from that recommended by the audit committee.

Non-audit services (Code provision C.3.8)

The auditor should review whether a description of the work performed by the audit committee is included in a separate section of the annual report, and is not materially inconsistent with the information that the auditor has obtained in the course of his audit work.

The auditor should review whether the annual report includes a statement explaining how the objectivity and independence of the auditor is safeguarded where non-audit services are also provided. He should consider this statement and:

- notify the audit committee and board if the audit committee has not fulfilled its responsibilities to review and monitor the independence and objectivity of the external auditor and to develop and implement policy on the engagement of the external auditor to supply non-audit services; and
- consider the requirements of ISA (UK and Ireland) 720 (Revised June 2016) in relation to other information issued with audited financial statements if

they believe the explanation is misleading. This will involve attempting to resolve differences with the board, and considering the implications for his report if they are not able to do so.

42.6.3   Non-compliance with the Code

Where the auditor discovers a non-compliance with a Code provision that is within the scope of his review, he should ascertain whether adequate disclosure has been made in the directors' statement of compliance. He need not perform any additional procedures in this respect, and as long as the non-compliance has been adequately disclosed, he need not refer to it in his audit report.

If the non-compliance is not adequately disclosed, the auditor should report this in the 'Matters on which we are required to report by exception' section of his report. This does not affect the opinion on the financial statements.

42.6.4   Going concern

The Listing Rules (LR 9.8.6R (3)) require the directors of all UK companies with a premium listing to include in the annual report a statement on:

(a)   the appropriateness of adopting the going concern basis of accounting (containing the information set out in provision C.1.3 of the *UK Corporate Governance Code*); and

(b)   their assessment of the prospects of the company (containing the information set out in provision C.2.2 of the *UK Corporate Governance Code*);

prepared in accordance with the *Guidance on Risk Management, Internal Control and Related Financial and Business Reporting* published by the Financial Reporting Council in September 2014.

Auditor's procedures

The Listing Rules require a UK company with a premium listing to ensure that the auditor reviews the going concern and longer term viability statements prior to publication of the annual financial report (LR 9.8.10R).

The guidance in the Bulletin is out of date in this respect as it has been overtaken by changes to the Code requirement, changes to ISA (UK and Ireland) 570 (Revised June 2016) and changes to the auditor's reporting responsibilities as set out in ISA (UK and Ireland) 700 (Revised June 2016) and ISA (UK and Ireland) 720 (Revised June 2016).

Whereas previously auditors reviewed the directors' statement and reported only by exception, ISAs now explicitly require the auditor to make a statement as to whether he has anything material to add or to draw attention to in relation to:

(a) the directors' confirmation in the annual report that they have carried out a robust assessment of the principal risks facing the entity, including those that would threaten its business model, future performance, solvency or liquidity;

(b) the disclosures in the annual report that describe those risks and explain how they are being managed or mitigated;

(c) the directors' statement in the financial statements about whether they considered it appropriate to adopt the going concern basis of accounting in preparing them, and their identification of any material uncertainties to the entity's ability to continue to do so over a period of at least twelve months from the date of approval of the financial statements; and

(d) the director's explanation in the annual report as to how they have assessed the prospects of the entity, over what period they have done so and why they consider that period to be appropriate, and their statement as to whether they have a reasonable expectation that the entity will be able to continue in operation and meet its liabilities as they fall due over the period of their assessment, including any related disclosures drawing attention to any necessary qualifications or assumptions.

This statement should be made by the auditor:

- having regard to the work performed by him in accordance with ISA (UK and Ireland) 570 (Revised June 2016); and
- having read and considered the directors' statements and disclosures in the annual report in the light of the knowledge he has acquired during the audit, including that acquired in the evaluation of management's assessment of the entity's ability to continue as a going concern.

Matters that the auditor considers should include:

- whether the auditor is aware of information that would indicate that the annual report and accounts taken as a whole are not fair, balanced and understandable in relation to the principal risks facing the entity including those that would threaten its business model, future performance, solvency or liquidity; and
- matters relating to the robustness of the directors' assessment of the principal risks facing the entity and its outcome, including the related disclosures in the annual report and accounts, that the auditor communicated to the audit committee and that are not appropriately addressed in the section of the annual report that describes the work of the audit committee.

42.7 Other disclosures and reporting requirements

42.7.1 Disclosures under the 'Disclosure Rules and Transparency Rules'

European Directive 2006/46 requires that listed companies include a Corporate Governance Statement in the annual report. This includes all issuers with a Premium or Standard listing. In the UK, this has been implemented through:

- section 7.2 of the *Disclosure Rules and Transparency Rules* (DTR) of the FCA; and
- various amendments to the *Companies Act* 2006.

The disclosure requirements set out in the DTR may be fulfilled by including the Corporate Governance Statement:

- as a separate section of the directors' report; or
- in a separate report, which is either:
    - published together with the annual report; or
    - available on the company's website with its location cross-referenced in the director's report.

Wherever the disclosure is made, the auditor is responsible for forming an opinion on whether the information in the Statement is consistent with the financial statements and contains the information it is supposed to contain.

Where the required disclosures are made in the directors' report, the auditor is not required to make specific reference to them in his report as this is covered by his review of consistency of the directors' report and compliance with relevant legislation.

When there is no Corporate Governance Statement in the directors' report, CA 2006, s. 498A requires the auditor to ascertain whether or not such a statement has been prepared. If no statement has been prepared, this must be stated in the auditor's report.

If the disclosure is made in a separate Corporate Governance Statement, the auditor is required by CA 2006, s. 497A to review the Statement and report certain matters in his audit report on the annual financial statements. These matters will usually be included within the 'other matters' section of the report. Section 497A was amended by the *Companies, Partnerships and Groups (Accounts and Reports) Regulations* 2015 (SI 2015/980):

The auditor is required to state:

- whether, in his opinion, based on the work undertaken in the course of the audit, the information given in the statement in compliance with rules 7.2.5 and 7.2.6 in the *Disclosure Rules and Transparency Rules* sourcebook made by the Financial Conduct Authority (information about internal control and risk management systems in relation to financial reporting processes and about capital structures) is consistent with the financial statements;

Additionally, for periods commencing on or after 1 January 2016 or for earlier periods where the company has applied the provisions of the *Companies, Partnerships and Groups (Accounts and Reports) Regulations* 2015 (SI 2015/980):

- whether the separate corporate governance statement has been prepared in accordance with applicable legal requirements. The auditor shall also state whether, in the light of the knowledge and understanding of the company and its environment obtained in the course of the audit, he has identified any material misstatements in the statement and, if applicable, give an indication of the nature of each of the misstatements; and
- the auditor must also state whether in his opinion, based on the work undertaken in the course of the audit, rules 7.2.2, 7.2.3 and 7.2.7 in the *Disclosure Rules and Transparency Rules* sourcebook made by the Financial Conduct Authority (information about the company's corporate governance code and practices and about its administrative, management and supervisory bodies and committees) have been complied with, if applicable.

An example extract from an auditor's report where a listed company has produced a separate corporate governance statement is given in **Table 2**.

In addition, if the separate Corporate Governance Statement is included within the annual report, the requirements of ISA (UK and Ireland) 720 (Revised June 2016) apply (see **Chapter 34**).

TABLE 2: Example auditor's report[1] extract where the Corporate Governance Statement is a separate report rather than being included in the directors' report

- *Company is a listed company required to comply with Disclosure and Transparency Rules*
- *Company is a quoted company preparing a directors' remuneration report*
- *Report is for a period commencing on or after 1 January 2016 or an earlier application of the Companies, Partnerships and Groups (Accounts and Reports) Regulations 2015*

Opinion on other matters prescribed by the Companies Act 2006

In our opinion:

- the part of the Directors' Remuneration Report to be audited has been properly prepared in accordance with the *Companies Act* 2006;

- based on the work undertaken in the course of the audit, the information given in the Strategic Report and the Directors' Report for the financial year for which the financial statements are prepared is consistent with the financial statements and the Strategic Report and Directors' Report have been prepared in accordance with applicable legal requirements. We have not identified any material misstatements in these reports; and

- based on the work undertaken in the course of the audit, the information given in the Corporate Governance Statement set out [on pages] [in *describe document*] [at *include web-address*] in compliance with rules 7.2.5 and 7.2.6 in the Disclosure Rules and Transparency Rules sourcebook made by the Financial Conduct Authority (information about internal control and risk management systems in relation to financial reporting processes and about share capital structures) is consistent with the financial statements and has been prepared in accordance with applicable legal requirements. We have not identified any material misstatements in this information; and

- based on the work undertaken in the course of the audit, rules 7.2.2, 7.2.3 and 7.2.7 in the Disclosure Rules and Transparency Rules sourcebook made by the Financial Conduct Authority (information about the company's corporate governance code and practices and about its administrative, management and supervisory bodies and committees) have been complied with.

Matters on which we are required to report by exception

We have nothing to report in respect of the following:

Under the ISAs (UK and Ireland), we are required to report to you if, in our opinion, information in the annual report is:

- materially inconsistent with the information in the audited financial statements;
- apparently materially incorrect based on, or materially inconsistent with, our knowledge of the Group acquired in the course of performing our audit; or
- is otherwise misleading.

In particular, we are required to consider whether we have identified any inconsistencies between our knowledge acquired during the audit and the directors' statement that they consider the annual report is fair, balanced and understandable and whether the annual report appropriately discloses those matters that we communicated to the audit committee which we consider should have been disclosed.

Under the *Companies Act* 2006, we are required to report to you if, in our opinion:

- adequate accounting records have not been kept, or returns adequate for our audit have not been received from branches not visited by us;
- the financial statements and the part of the Directors' Remuneration Report to be audited are not in agreement with the accounting records and returns;
- certain disclosures of directors' remuneration specified by law are not made;
- we have not received all the information and explanations we require for our audit; or
- a Corporate Governance Statement has not been prepared by the company.

Under the Listing Rules, we are required to review:

- the directors' statements, [set out [on page ...]], in relation to going concern and [set out [on page ...]] longer term viability; and
- the part of the Corporate Governance Statement relating to the company's compliance with the provisions of the UK Corporate Governance Code specified for our review.

[Signature]

[name] (Senior Statutory Auditor)

For and on behalf of ABC LLP, Statutory Auditor

[Address]

[Date]

¹ This example is based on existing ISAs and has not been updated to reflect changes to audit reporting ISAs which will take effect for periods commencing 17 June 2016.

42.7.2   Standard listed companies

Companies with only a Standard Listing of securities are not required to make the going concern statement required by Listing Rule 9.8.6R(3) or the corporate governance statement required by Listing Rule 9.8.6R(6). The section of the auditor's report dealing with matters set out by the Listing Rules to be reported on by exception does not therefore apply to such companies. However, should such companies choose voluntarily to make a statement of compliance with the UK Corporate Governance Code, this will bring them within the scope of the enhanced audit reporting requirements applicable to such companies and the auditor's statement in relation to risk, going concern and viability described in **42.6.4** will be applicable.

Standard listed companies are required to comply with the DTR requirements. Elements of the auditor's report referring to these requirements will be applicable in such cases.

42.8   Audit committees and the external auditor

42.8.1   Role and responsibilities of the audit committee

The roles and responsibilities of audit committees have been clarified and reinforced over recent years and there are now a number of publications available to audit committees to assist with their role.

The principal source of guidance is the FRC's *Guidance on Audit Committees* which was last revised in 2012 although a final draft of revised guidance was published in April 2016 along with final drafts of the FRC's proposed changes to the Code, ISAs and ethical standards. Key aspects of the guidance insofar as it relates to relationships with the external auditor are discussed below.

In February 2012, the FRC published jointly with the Institute of Chartered Accountants of Scotland and the Institute of Chartered Accountants in Australia *Walk the Line: Discussions and insights with leading audit committee members*, a report summarising discussions with the audit committee chairs of leading companies in the UK, Australian and other markets. The report covers issues such as the role and composition of the audit committee and its relationship and communications with the board, management and the external auditor.

In November 2014, the Quoted Companies Alliance published an *Audit Committee Guide for Small and Mid-Size Quoted Companies* to assist audit committee members to be effective in their roles, meeting the expectations of investors and complying with best regulatory best practice for small and mid-size quoted companies. It covers the operational aspects of the committee; the roles and responsibilities of those on the committee and those that work with the committee; the internal focus of the committee on risk management and internal control; the external focus of the committee on the corporate reporting cycle; and the audit committee report in the annual reports and accounts.

Earlier guidance which is now a bit dated but may nevertheless contain some useful information includes:

- *The Power of Three: Understanding the roles and relationships of internal and external auditors and audit committees* published in 2003;
- the ICAEW series of seven booklets published in 2003 and 2004 covering:

  - *Working with your auditor;*
  - *Company reporting and audit requirements;*
  - *Reviewing auditor independence;*
  - *Evaluating your auditor;*
  - *Monitoring the integrity of financial statements;*
  - *The internal audit function; and*
  - *Whistleblowing arrangements.*

42.8.2 FRC guidance on audit committees

In respect of the external audit process, the guidance states that the audit committee is the body responsible for overseeing the company's relations with the external auditor. It recommends the following:

Appointment and tendering

- The audit committee should have primary responsibility for making a recommendation on the appointment, reappointment and removal of the external auditor. This includes negotiating the fee and scope of the audit and influencing the selection of the engagement partner.
- Where it recommends considering the selection of a possible new auditor, the committee should be responsible for and oversee the selection process.
- The audit committee should annually assess, and report to the board on, the qualification, expertise and resources, and independence of the external auditors and the effectiveness of the audit process and make a recommendation regarding reappointment of the auditor. This assessment will involve the audit committee obtaining a report on the auditor's own internal quality control procedure and their annual transparency report.
- If the external auditor resigns, the audit committee should investigate the issues giving rise to such resignation and consider whether any action is required.
- The audit committee should evaluate risks to audit quality and the effectiveness of the financial reporting process.

Terms and remuneration

- The audit committee should approve the terms of engagement and the remuneration to be paid to the external auditor in respect of audit services provided.
- The committee should review and agree the engagement letter issued by the external auditor at the start of each audit and should satisfy itself as to the adequacy of the scope of the external audit proposed by the auditor.
- The committee should satisfy itself that the fee payable in respect of the audit is appropriate and that an effective, high quality, audit can be conducted for such a fee.

Annual audit cycle

- At the start of each annual audit cycle, the audit committee should ensure that appropriate plans are in place for the audit. The committee should consider whether the auditor's overall work plan, including planned levels of materiality, and proposed resources available is consistent with the proposed scope of the audit, having regard also to the seniority, expertise and experience of the audit team.
- The audit committee should review, with the external auditors, the findings of their work and should:
  - discuss with the auditor any major issues, both resolved and unresolved, that arose during the audit;
  - key accounting and audit judgments; and
  - errors identified during the audit.

- The audit committee should review and monitor management's responsiveness to the auditor's findings and recommendations. It should also review audit representation letters before signature and give particular consideration to matters where representation has been requested that relate to non-standard issues. It should consider whether the information provided is complete and appropriate based on its own knowledge.
- As part of the ongoing monitoring process, the audit committee should review the management letter (or equivalent) and monitor management's responsiveness to the external auditor's findings and recommendations.
- The audit committee should assess the effectiveness of the audit process. This includes consideration of mind-set, culture, skills, knowledge and judgment including the robustness of the auditor in dealing with key judgments and their assessment of internal control;
- The audit committee should:

    - ask the auditor to explain the risks to audit quality, and how they have been addressed. This should include consideration of firms and network controls over audit quality and the results of internal and external monitoring;
    - understand the reasons for any changes to the audit plan, including changes in perceived audit risks and the work undertaken by the external auditors to address those risks;
    - consider the robustness and perceptiveness of the auditors in their handling of the key accounting and audit judgments identified and in responding to questions from the audit committee;
    - obtain feedback about the conduct of the audit from key people involved; and
    - review and monitor the content of the auditor's management letter.

Independence, including the provision of non-audit services

The audit committee should:

- assess the independence and objectivity of the external auditor annually, including consideration of all relationships between the company and the audit firm, including throughout the group and with the audit firm's network firms, and any safeguards established by the external auditor;
- develop and recommend to the board the company's policy in relation to the provision of non-audit services by the auditor, and keep the policy under review;
- set and apply a formal policy specifying the types of non-audit service (if any) for which the use of the external auditor is pre-approved (but this should only apply to matters that are clearly trivial);
- develop and monitor the application of the company's policy for the employment of former employees of the external auditor, taking into account the *Ethical Standards* for auditors and paying particular attention to the policy regarding former employees of the audit firm who were part of the audit team and moved directly to the company; and

- monitor the external audit firm's compliance with the *Ethical Standards* for auditors relating to the rotation of audit partners, the level of fees that the company pays in proportion to the overall fee income of the firm, or relevant part of it, and other related regulatory requirements.

42.8.3 Communication between the auditor and the audit committee

ISA 260 (Revised June 2016) includes a number of matters which are included in an additional report to the audit committee; this is covered in **Chapter 10**. It requires that, in the case of companies reporting compliance with the Code, the auditor shall communicate to the audit committee the information that the auditor believes will be relevant to the board (in the context of fulfilling its responsibilities under Code provisions C.1.1, C.1.3, C.2.1, C.2.2 and C.2.3) and the audit committee (in the context of fulfilling its responsibilities under Code provision C.3.4) and to the audit committee (in the context of fulfilling its responsibilities under Code provision C.3.2).

This information includes the auditor's views:

(a)   on business risks relevant to financial reporting, the application of materiality and the consequent implications for the overall audit strategy, the audit plan and the evaluation of misstatements;

(b)   on significant accounting policies (both individually and in aggregate);

(c)   on management's valuations of the entity's material assets and liabilities and the related disclosures;

(d)   without expressing an opinion on the effectiveness of the entity's system of internal control as a whole, and based solely on the audit procedures performed in the audit of the financial statements, about:

   (i)   the effectiveness of the entity's system of internal control relevant to risks that may affect financial reporting; and

   (ii)   other risks arising from the entity's business model and the effectiveness of related internal controls;

(e)   about the robustness of the directors' assessment of the principal risks facing the entity, including those that would threaten its business model, future performance, solvency or liquidity and its outcome, including the related disclosures in the annual report confirming that they have carried out such an assessment and describing those risks and explaining how they are being managed or mitigated (in accordance with Code provision C.2.1);

(f)   about the directors' explanation in the annual report as to how they have assessed the prospects of the entity, over what period they have done so and why they consider that period to be appropriate (in accordance with Code provision C.2.2), and their statements:

   (i)   in the financial statements, as to whether they considered it appropriate to adopt the going concern basis of accounting in preparing them, including any related disclosures identifying any material uncertainties to the entity's ability to continue to do so over a period of at least 12 months from the date of approval of the financial statements (in accordance with Code provision C.1.3); and

 (ii) in the annual report as to whether they have a reasonable expectation that the entity will be able to continue in operation and meet its liabilities as they fall due over the period of their assessment, including any related disclosures drawing attention to any necessary qualifications or assumptions (in accordance with Code provision C.2.2); and

(g) on any other matters identified in the course of the audit that the auditor believes will be relevant to the board or the audit committee in the context of fulfilling their responsibilities referred to above.

42.9 Monitoring

Since 2011, the FRC has published an annual report on the impact and implementation of the UK Corporate Governance Code and its Stewardship Code for institutional investors. The latest report is *Developments in Corporate Governance and Stewardship 2015* which is available from the FRC's website.

43 CHARITIES

43.1 Legal background

There are a number of different regulators with responsibility for charities throughout the UK. The Charity Commission regulates charities in England and Wales, the Office of the Scottish Charity Regulator ('the OSCR') regulates charities registered in Scotland and also, to some extent, English or Welsh charities operating in Scotland. Northern Ireland has recently established its own Charity Commission. This chapter mainly addresses the regime governing English and Welsh charities.

The main laws that relate to a charity's financial statements and audit are:

All charitable companies	*Companies Act* 2006
Registered charities in England and Wales	*Charities Act* 2011
All charities registered in Scotland with the Office of the Scottish Charity Regulator (OSCR)	*Charities and Trustee Investment (Scotland) Act* 2005
Non-company charities in Northern Ireland	*Charities Act (Northern Ireland)* 2008 and the *Charities Act (Northern Ireland)* 1964 (to the extent this has not been superseded by the *Charities Act (Northern Ireland)* 2008)

By virtue of an order under the *Charities Act* 2011, s. 144 and 147, the audit regimes of companies and non-company charities are identical if the company elects for exemption from audit under the *Companies Act*. (The option to elect for audit exemption is only available to charitable companies whose income is under £6.5m and gross assets are under £3.26m.) Larger company audits continue to be performed under the Companies Act regime. Charitable companies (if they elect for exemption from the Companies Act audit requirement) are subject to the same independent examination and audit regime, depending upon their gross income and gross assets, as non-company charities.

By virtue of the *Charities Act* 2011, charitable parent companies of small groups are required to prepare accounts and be audited under both the *Companies Act* 2006 and the *Charities Act* 2011. As a result, the audit requirement and trustees' responsibilities need to reflect the legal requirements of both pieces of legislation.

Charities that are subject to alternative legislative requirements to the Charities Act (such as the Companies Act for larger charities that are limited companies), or alternative SORPs to the Charities' SORP (for example, Registered Providers of Social Housing) should follow the accounting and auditing requirements in the alternative legislation or SORP. For charities which are limited companies, the Department for Business, Innovation and Skills considers the FRS 102 Charities SORP ('the FRS 102 SORP') to be indicative of the accounting practices necessary for charities to produce financial statements which show a true and fair view. This chapter deals mainly with charities applying the FRS 102 SORP or subject to the *Charities Act* 2011 accounting and auditing requirement. While academies prepare their accounts in accordance with the FRS 102 SORP, there are additional requirements for auditors as set by the Department for Education. Auditors of academies should refer to the DfE website for details of these requirements.

In charitable companies, the directors are also the charity trustees and the term 'trustees' has been used throughout to refer to both.

Furthermore, charities established in Scotland register separately as Scottish charities and charities registered in Northern Ireland are now being called forward by the regulator to register separately as Northern Irish charities.

Dual registered charities (i.e. registered with the Charity Commission and with the OSCR and/or with the Charity Commission for Northern Ireland) need to comply with the FRS 102 SORP, but the audit requirement, annual report, and trustees' responsibilities need to reflect the legal requirements of all countries in which they are registered.

It should be noted that there are currently two charity SORPs in existence – the FRS 102 SORP as well as a SORP in line with the Financial Reporting Standard for Smaller Entities ('the FRSSE SORP') which charities within the *Companies Act* 2006 definition of small companies can elect to adopt. However, the FRSSE SORP will be withdrawn for accounting periods beginning on or after 1 January 2016 and all charities preparing accruals accounts will have to follow the FRS 102 SORP from this date (although reduced disclosures are available within the FRS 102 SORP for small charities).

The legislation, SORPs and further accounting guidance can be found on CCH Online and in the Wolters Kluwer publication *Preparing Charity Accounts*. In addition, CCH has produced a separate industry guide *Charities: A CCH Industry Tax, Accounting and Auditing Guide* which covers the material in this chapter in greater detail.

43.1.1 General

The *Charities (Accounts and Reports) Regulations* 2008 continue to set out the requirements for preparation of accounts in respect of English and Welsh charities. Whilst all charities must prepare accounts, the impact of these regulations depends on the threshold requirements as set out in the 2011 Act and on whether the charity is registered or not. These requirements can be summarised as follows:

- registered charities with gross income and total expenditure of £25,000 or less, and charities which are not registered, are not required to submit annual reports or accounts to the Charity Commission, unless requested to do so. All registered charities must prepare an annual report, even if they are not requested to submit it to the Charity Commission;
- non-company charities with gross income of £250,000 or less may prepare a receipts and payments account and a statement of assets and liabilities; and
- all charitable companies and non-company charities that exceed this £250,000 threshold must prepare accounts on an accruals basis to give a true and fair view. Certain additional disclosure requirements are placed on charities whose gross income exceeds the audit exemption threshold.

The audit or examination requirements for charitable companies and non-company charities are as follows:

- gross income does not exceed £25,000 – no statutory requirement for either an audit or an independent examination;
- gross income does not exceed £250,000 – an election may be made for the accounts to be independently examined;
- gross income does not exceed £1,000,000 in the year and gross assets do not exceed £3.26m – an election may be made for the accounts to be independently examined but the examiner must be a member of a specified body (note – for charities registered with OSCR, the income limit is £500,000); and
- gross income exceeds £1,000,000 in the year (£500,000 for charities registered with OSCR), or gross income exceeds £250,000 and gross assets exceed £3.26m – a statutory audit is required.

An audit can only be undertaken by a registered auditor, unless the Charity Commission gives a dispensation.

As noted above, where the charity is a company and has not elected for exemption from the Companies Act audit requirement then the audit is conducted under the *Companies Act*.

43.1.2   Independent examination

An independent examination for a charity below the thresholds discussed above, does not have to be carried out by a professionally qualified individual but should be by a person suitable to the circumstances of the charity. The examiner must be 'an independent person who is reasonably believed by the trustees to have the requisite ability and practical experience to carry out a competent examination of the accounts'.

The independent examiner's report to the charity's trustees is intended to provide a moderate level of assurance (negative assurance) and should:

- specify that it is a report in respect of an examination carried out under the Charities Act and in accordance with any directions given by the Commissioners which are applicable;

- state whether or not any matter has come to the examiner's attention which gives him reasonable cause to believe that in any material respect:

  - accounting records have not been kept in accordance with the Act;
  - the accounts do not accord with the records; or
  - the accounts do not comply with the regulations;

- state whether or not any matter has come to his attention which should be drawn to the attention of the trustees;
- disclose any material expenditure or action which appears not to be in accordance with the trusts of the charity; and
- disclose any information or explanation provided or any information in the accounts which is materially inconsistent with the trustees' report.

The duties of an examiner are set out in CC32 issued by the Charity Commission, which is available from the Commission's website. This is subject to revision during 2016.

43.1.3 Whistle-blowing duties for auditors and examiners

The *Charities Act* 2011 imposes the same duties on auditors and independent examiners of all charities, whether or not they are limited companies.[1] Under this whistle-blowing requirement, they have to report in writing, under s. 156 (Duty of auditors, etc. to report matters to the Commission) of the 2011 Act, any matters which may be of material significance to the Charity Commission's function as a regulator, which came to light as a result of their work.[1]

The charity audit Practice Note provides additional guidance in this area.

43.2 Audit guidance

The major source of guidance for auditors is Practice Note 11 *The Audit of Charities*, which is designed to provide guidance on the application of the various ISAs to charities.

In April 2016, the FRC issued a suite of revised ISAs (UK and Ireland) (see **1.6.4**). At the time of writing, however, Practice Note 11 had not been updated and still referred to the previous version of ISAs. References to ISAs within this chapter have, however, been updated to the most recent version where applicable.

In March 2012, the APB issued Bulletin 2010/2 (Revised), *Compendium of illustrative auditor's reports on United Kingdom private sector financial statements for periods ended on or after 15 December 2010*. The Bulletin details

---

[1] 'Exempt' charities are excluded from the CCEW's supervision and monitoring, and consequently, the auditor is not required to report matters of material significance to CCEW. Instead, the auditor of an exempt charity reports such matters to the charity's principal regulator. There is, however, no disapplication of the reporting duty for exempt company charities.

changes to auditor's reports for charities following earlier revisions to ISA (UK and Ireland) 700 but has not been updated for the most recent revisions to ISAs (see **Chapter 4**)[2].

It should be noted that at the time of writing, the Financial Reporting Council has indicated that the contents of Practice Note 11 will be updated to address the new factors auditors will need to consider under the new accounting framework of FRS 102. However, until the revised guidance is available, the auditor will need to use his judgment in determining how to apply the concepts in Practice Note 11 to financial statements prepared in accordance with FRS 102. Particular areas which may need consideration include the audit of donated second hand goods, the audit of intangible assets arising on business combinations between two charities and the audit of legacy income.[2]

43.3 Background

The Practice Note only covers audits of charities and considers independent examinations as a different type of engagement. It points to the problems presented by charities given:

- the complex regulatory regime involving different Regulators in different countries;
- the diversity of accounting requirements which depend on size and corporate status;
- the whistle-blowing regime;
- its governing document and the extent of its objects and powers;
- the fact that they may be responsible for public money;
- the wide public interest in them; and
- their special features, such as voluntary income, restricted funds and charitable status.

It should also be noted that the Charity Commission and HMRC guidance is being updated continually. Therefore, auditors should have regard for the latest guidance issued by these bodies, particularly HMRC guidance on fit and proper persons and overseas expenditure.

43.4 Overall conduct of an audit in accordance with ISAs

Practitioners should not undertake the audit of a charity unless they are satisfied that they have, or can obtain, the necessary level of competence. The auditor's

---

[2] It should be noted that if charities voluntarily choose to apply the UK Corporate Governance Code, then the requirements of the relevant version of ISA (UK and Ireland) 700, depending on year end date, will also need to be taken into account.

responsibilities in this respect are not related to the level of fee charged for the audit.

Auditors also need to comply with relevant ethical requirements relating to audit engagements. Particular issues relating to charities include:

- self interest – the auditor needs to be aware of other interests in the charity which may affect the conduct or outcome of the audit. The auditor therefore ensures that none of the audit team is in any way dependent upon the charity or provide significant support to the charity;
- self review – auditors will be often asked to provide additional help and advice, often on a pro-bono basis. The provision of this service is regarded in the same way as other non-audit services in assessing whether there is a threat to objectivity.

43.5   Agreeing the terms of audit engagements

Engagement letters will normally be sent to the trustees although they may be sent to a different appointing authority. The engagement may cover reports on other funds or on the disposition of local authority grants. The auditor will need to check documentation relating to funds received by the charity for consideration requiring special reports. Where trustees are not involved in the day-to-day running of the charity, the Practice Note suggests that the auditor may send an additional copy to the chief executive or person responsible for that day-to-day management.

43.6   Quality control for an audit of financial statements

As well as ensuring that the engagement team has an appropriate level of knowledge of the charity sector, the engagement partner also satisfies himself that the members of the engagement team have sufficient knowledge, commensurate with their roles in the engagement, of:

- the Charities SORP (FRS 102 SORP or FRSSE SORP, depending on which is being applied);
- the governing document of the charity;
- the legal responsibilities and duties of charity trustees; and
- the regulatory framework within which charities operate

to identify situations which may give them reasonable cause to believe that a matter should be reported to a charity regulator.

The audit also considers if an engagement quality control review is required based on the nature of the engagement, including the extent to which it involves a matter of public interest. What is a matter of public interest is difficult to define: factors that may apply to a charity include:

- the size of the charity;
- its national or local profile; and
- its source of funds, including the extent to which the charity receives public funds.

43.7   The auditor's responsibilities relating to fraud

In applying ISA (UK and Ireland) 240 (Revised June 2016) to charities, the auditor must be aware that the trustees are responsible for the prevention or detection of fraud in relation to the charity. However, the planning process of the audit must include an assessment of the possibility of fraud being committed by any of the people involved in the operation of the charity as well as by third parties. Certain features of charities may increase the risk of fraud, namely:

- the limited involvement of trustees in key decision making or monitoring transactions, and limited engagement with charity staff;
- widespread branches or operations, such as those established in response to emergency appeals in countries where there is no effective system of law and order;
- reliance on management and staff with limited management or supervision and a lack of segregation and rotation of duties;
- transactions often undertaken in cash;
- unpredictable patterns of giving by members of the public, both in terms of timing and point of donation;
- informal banking or cash transfer methods used in areas remote from conventional banking systems;
- inconsistent regulation across international borders; and
- international transfer of funds.

Auditors are required by ISA (UK and Ireland) 240 (Revised June 2016) to consider whether one or more fraud risk factors are present and to investigate whether unusual or unexpected relationships may indicate risks of material misstatement due to fraud.

The Practice Note lists the various authorities which regulate charities as being the proper authorities to which reports of frauds in the public interest should be made. For example, for charities established in England and Wales, except where exempt, the proper authority is the Charity Commission as well as the National Crime Agency (NCA).

43.8   Consideration of laws and regulations

Because there are laws and regulations specifically made to cover charities and their activities, including laws which affect charities which undertake fundraising, auditors must have an understanding of applicable law and regulation. Auditors must be aware of the risk of money laundering given the relatively large sums of cash which many charities receive.

As in ISAs, the Practice Note examines this area from the point of view:

- of laws relating directly to the preparation of financial statements; and
- those which provide a legal framework within which the entity conducts its business.

43.8.1   Laws relating directly to the preparation of financial statements

Auditors here must be aware of, in particular, the 2008 *Accounts and Reports Regulations, the Charities Accounts (Scotland) Regulations* 2006 and the relevant Charities SORP. In addition, charities may also be subject to *Companies Act* requirements and those which relate to housing associations.

Auditors should also check whether the charity's governing document contains any special disclosure or reporting requirements.

43.8.2   Laws central to a charity's conduct of business

Guidance is given on the interpretation of 'central' in the context of charities. Laws and regulations are seen to be central by the Practice Note where:

- compliance is a pre-requisite of obtaining a licence to operate; or
- non-compliance may reasonably be expected to result in the entity ceasing operations, or call into question the entity's status as a going concern.

These laws will to a large extent be dependent on the charity's activities. They may be subject to:

- Charities Act requirements relating to fundraising, property and borrowing transaction;
- laws on raising funds through lotteries;
- laws relating to house to house or street collections;
- Trustee Act;
- Children Act requirements;
- Registered Homes Act;
- Environmental Protection Act; and
- food safety and hygiene regulations.

The auditor must be aware of the objects of the charity and the fact that the Charity Commission has powers to suspend or remove trustees, officers, agents or employees and to freeze the property and appoint a receiver and manager if they consider that the charity's property requires protection.

The auditor must also be aware of tax, as although most activities of a charity do not attract taxation, trading other than directly or indirectly in furtherance of the charity's objects may well give rise to a tax liability. In addition, the VAT position is different to that relating to corporation tax as exemptions do not generally apply.

Furthermore, charities often receive donations tax effectively, through gift aid, payroll giving, and gifts of land and shares. For most tax effective schemes, and especially for gift aid, there are detailed requirements relating to the procedures to be followed by donors and recipient charities, as well as detailed rules designed to prevent abuse.

Similar considerations to those for other companies apply where breaches of law and regulations are found.

The Practice Note points out that even where fraud has been reported to the trustees, the audit report must include details of any fundamental uncertainty or disagreement over disclosure of a suspected or actual instance of fraud or error.

43.9   The auditor's right and duty to report to regulators

Although the title of ISA (UK and Ireland) 250 Section B (Revised June 2016) refers to reports to regulators in the financial sector, the principles and essential procedures included in this ISA apply in respect of the statutory duty and the discretionary right to report to charity regulators in England and Wales and Scotland.

Auditors should refer to appendix five within Practice Note 11, which sets out the Charity Commission's and OSCR's guidance on whistle-blowing. This includes the list of eight topics which are always considered to be of material significance and hence reportable (this includes items such as fraud, significant loss of funds, money laundering and beneficiaries being mistreated).

The auditor does not need to perform additional work as a result of the statutory duty although he will need to make members of the audit team aware of reportable matters which are likely to be encountered.

The auditor must report matters which he has reasonable cause to believe are, or are likely to be, of material significance in relation to the Commissioners power to institute enquiries or to act for the protection of charities.

Additionally, where the auditor ceases to hold office, for any reason, he is required to make a statement as to whether there are any matters concerning his ceasing to hold office which should be brought to the attention of the trustees. A copy of this statement should be sent to the Charity Commission if there are such matters.

'Material significance' does not have the same meaning as 'material' in the context of the audit of financial statements. For example, dishonesty by a trustee may not be significant in financial terms but would have a significant effect on the commissioner's consideration of whether the person concerned should be allowed to continue to act as a charity trustee.

For dual registered charities, the auditor's duty to report is to both the Charity Commission and OSCR (although at present there is no requirement to report to the Charity Commission for Northern Ireland).

43.10 Communication with those charged with governance

Any breaches of duties relevant to the administration of the charity imposed by law on the trustees or managers should be notified to trustees regardless of whether the matter gave rise to a statutory duty to report to the charity regulators. The only exception is where notification would cause non-compliance with legislation relating to 'tipping off'.

43.11 Communicating deficiencies in internal control

The Practice Note suggests that the auditor's work on the charity's system of internal control may identify information on these systems which would assist the trustees in seeking to establish and maintain effective and efficient systems. Even if management letters are addressed to the executives responsible for the day-to-day running of the charity, a copy of the report should be sent to the trustees.

43.12 Planning an audit of financial statements

Particular issues the auditor considers at the planning stage include:

- the applicable reporting framework including:
    - the legislative requirements, e.g. the *Companies Act* 2006 or, in England and Wales the *Charities Act* 2011 or, in Scotland the *Charities and Trustee Investment (Scotland) Act* 2005;
    - the relevant Charities SORP (or sector specific SORP where one applies);

- the governing document for the charity, which may also include specific reporting requirements;
- governance arrangements, including planning with the trustees the form and timing of communications;
- operating structures, branches and overseas operations including:
  - the extent to which the charity's activities (either of a fundraising or a charitable nature) are undertaken through branches or overseas activities and the impact this has on the auditor's required knowledge of the business (for example taxation and employment law), the auditor's risk assessments and sources of audit evidence; and
  - the structure and management of any related or connected entities, in particular the degree to which the entities are managed and controlled by the trustees and management of the charity;
- the charity's activities in the context of its stated objects and powers, including any limitations within the charity's governing document, or terms and restrictions placed on material gifts or donations received;
- the likely impact on the financial statements of the charity of the activities of any related or connected entities (for example, a separate limited company set up to undertake commercial activities for the charity);
- the statutory duty to report matters to the charity regulators including whether members of the audit team have sufficient understanding (in the context of their role) to enable them to identify situations which may give reasonable cause to believe that a matter should be reported to the regulator; and
- whether other auditors' reports are required – for example, special reports to funders of the charity, grant donors or EU agencies.

43.13   Identifying and assessing risks of material misstatement

The auditor will need knowledge of the special features of charity audits, and in planning, he will need to be aware of the following:

- the existence of special regulations governing the conduct of charities;
- sources of income which may include grants from public authorities or funds held on trust. Breaches of the conditions relating to the use of such income can have serious implications to the charity;
- tax relief dependent upon a charity complying with the governing document submitted to HMRC;
- activities of the charity which bring it within the scope of other regulations, as well as those relating to charities;
- the level of involvement in the administration of the charity which can be expected of trustees; and
- the way in which the charity is managed on a day-to-day basis.

In terms of the regulatory framework, the factors considered under ISA (UK and Ireland) 250 Section A (Revised June 2016) above will apply (section **43.8** above).

The auditor must be aware of the way in which the charity conducts its operations, whether through:

- groups of distinct legal entities;
- associated undertakings;
- what are effectively branches; or
- by subcontracting to non-controlled organisations.

Depending on the structure, the accounting requirements will be different.

Overseas operations can also present difficulty as there is a wide range of structures which charities can adopt. The auditor must determine the legal status and decide whether their accounts need to be incorporated within the main accounts of the charity.

The source of much information about a charity will be its officers and trustees together with its governing document. For larger charities, sources of information may include specialist publications and umbrella organisations which provide statistics and industry norms. ISA (UK and Ireland) 315 (Revised June 2016) requires the auditor to use his understanding of the entity and its environment to assess the risk of material misstatement in the financial statements and gives details of the areas that auditors of charities should consider.

ISA (UK and Ireland) 315 (Revised June 2016) requires the auditor to obtain an understanding of the accounting and internal control systems sufficient to plan the audit and develop an effective audit approach. There is a wide variation between different charities in terms of size, activity and organisation so that there can be no standard approach to internal control and risk. Even large national charities with sophisticated control systems may have local branches that are run by voluntary staff on an informal basis.

43.13.1   Risk of misstatement

Factors which may affect the auditor's assessment of the risk of misstatement include:

- the significance of donations and cash receipts;
- fundraising by non-controlled bodies;
- the valuation of donations in kind;
- uncertainty over completeness of income;
- operational limitations imposed by governing documents;
- restricted funds;
- difficulties in identifying and quantifying liabilities arising from constructive obligations;

- sensitivity of key statistics, such as the proportion of resources used for administration purposes;
- trading activities; and
- complexities of tax rules relating to charities.

43.13.2   Control environment

The auditor must assess the adequacy of controls in relation to the circumstances of each charity. Here, the attitude rather than involvement of the trustees is likely to be fundamental.

The features of a sound control environment – for example, clearly defined authority, segregation of duties, competent staff, budgetary controls – are similar to those that apply in commercial organisations.

The auditor may also need to ensure that there is control over grants made to other bodies.

The Practice Note provides details of factors that the auditor should consider when assessing the control environment of a charity. These include:

- the amount of time committed by trustees to the charity's affairs;
- the skills and qualifications of individual trustees;
- the trustees' understanding of the charity and its legal and regulatory environment;
- the regularity and effectiveness of trustee meetings and the level of attendance at these meetings;
- the independence of trustees from each other;
- the policies and processes for managing trustee conflicts of interest;
- the supervision by the trustees of relatively informal working arrangements which are common when using volunteers;
- the degree of involvement, by the trustees, in key decision making or monitoring transactions and engagement with charity staff;
- the attitude of trustees to previously identified control deficiencies;
- the level of delegation by trustees to senior management and the formality of this delegation; and
- the committee structure of the organisation.

In addition, the auditor should review any risk register maintained by the charity to ascertain what the trustees determine to be the business risks faced by the charity and what control systems they have established to mitigate those risks. The auditor's assessment of related business processes, in line with the requirements of ISA (UK and Ireland) 315 (Revised June 2016), should include ensuring that systems accurately capture details of restrictions on income.

43.13.3   Control activities

The Charity Commission has produced guidance on control activities in its publication 'CC8 – Internal financial controls for charities'. This includes some of the control activities which may be applicable to charities and of which the auditor should gain an understanding to enable him to assess the risk of material misstatement at the assertion level and design further audit procedures responsive to those assessed risks. The auditor may also consider how the trustees have met the Charity Commission requirement to conduct an annual review of the effectiveness of the charity's internal controls.

In accordance with ISA (UK and Ireland) 315 (Revised June 2016), the auditor is required to assess the risk of material misstatement at the financial statements level, for classes of transactions, account balances and transactions. There are many factors which may affect the risk of material misstatement in charities including the:

- complexity and extent of regulation;
- valuation of donations in kind;
- uncertainty of future income; and
- special consideration that must be made of restricted funds.

Further examples are provided in the Practice Note. The auditor must then consider whether any of these risks are significant risks for which special audit consideration must be given, including the evaluation of related controls and the planning and performance of related procedures.

43.13.4   Accounting policies

The auditor must review accounting policies and ensure these are in line with the Charities SORPs and other accounting standards. Policies that may require particularly careful consideration include those for the recognition of:

- legacies receivable;
- grants receivable as voluntary income;
- grants receivable or payable on performance related conditions;
- liabilities resulting from constructive obligations;
- gifts in kind and donated services; and
- heritage assets.

43.14   Materiality in planning and performing an audit

Materiality should be considered with regard to the applicable laws and regulations and any additional reports the auditor is required to make – for example, in respect to restricted funds. The general principles underlying the consideration of materiality apply to audits of charities in a similar way to other entities.

Many charities receive funds subject to specific trusts, which must be accounted for separately in accordance with the relevant Charities SORP. There is no presumption that the auditor will set a different monetary materiality level for such funds. However, ISA (UK and Ireland) 320 (Revised June 2016) provides guidance on the factors that may indicate that lower amounts than materiality could reasonably be expected to influence the economic decisions of users and which may result in different materiality considerations being applied to particular aspects of the financial statements.

43.15   The auditor's responses to assessed risks

ISA (UK and Ireland) 330 (Revised June 2016) requires the auditor to plan and perform specific audit procedures where he has identified a significant risk of material misstatement. Common areas for the risk of material misstatement for charities are:

- ensuring completeness of incoming resources;
- overseas operations; and
- restricted funds.

43.15.1   Completeness of income

Typically, income from charities comes from a number of different sources, such as grants and public donations, and its amount and timing is often difficult to predict. Trustees cannot be expected to have responsibility for funds until they are, or should be, within the control of the charity, but as soon as this happens, trustees should implement procedures to ensure appropriate recording and safeguarding of the funds.

The Practice Note suggests possible substantive procedures for completeness of incoming resources, including the following:

- to check for a loss of incoming resources through fraud, the auditor can assess and test the sorts of controls described in section **43.13.3** for appeals and 'non-routine' sources, and compare donations actually received to past results for similar appeals and statistics for response rates for charities in general;
- check the arrangements for the transferral of funds from branches, associates or subsidiaries to the main charity, to determine when funds are recognised;
- review correspondence with solicitors to determine when legacy income is reasonably certain, its value can be measured and it can therefore be recorded. These criteria will normally be met following probate and once

the executor of the estate has established that there are sufficient assets, after settling liabilities, to pay the legacy. Certainty and measurability may also be affected by events such as valuations and disputes. The Auditor therefore reviews information up to when the accounts are approved for evidence relating to legacies receivable existing at the balance sheet date; and

- examination of grant applications and correspondence to determine completeness of grant income, including direct confirmation about the amounts receivable from the grant provider.

Substantive procedures may be limited by the uncertainty affecting donations, but they may be of use to corroborate other evidence.

43.15.2   Overseas operations

Where overseas operations exist, the auditor will be required to obtain evidence of material expenditure overseas and gain an understanding of when overseas expenditure has occurred. Where the overseas operations are part of the charity, the expenditure will not be incurred when money is transferred to the overseas branch, but when the expenditure is actually made by that branch.

The Practice Note suggests the following procedures:

- consideration of internal control procedures put in place by the charity, and how adherence to procedures is monitored;
- obtaining evidence from field officers' reports as to work undertaken;
- comparison of accounting returns of expenditure with field reports and plans for consistency and reasonableness;
- analytical review of accounting returns received from overseas branches or local agents;
- consideration of any inspection or internal control visit reports undertaken by any internal audit function;
- consideration of audit work undertaken by local auditors, and consideration of any audit reports carried out on behalf of international donors, for example, government departments; and
- evidence from the audit work of another audit firm.

Where material assets are held or material funds are applied by overseas operations, the Practice Note suggests that the auditor may seek observational evidence by way of site visit.

Where a charity makes a grant to an autonomous overseas charity, the auditor ensures:

- receipt of the funding; and
- that the charity has exercised reasonable diligence in ensuring that the funds are used for charitable purposes in order that adverse tax consequences are not suffered.

43.15.3   Restricted funds

Restricted funds which are subject to specific rules about their application may give rise to a significant risk of material misstatement. The auditor should consider:

- the terms or conditions attached to the restricted funds;
- any funds in deficit;
- any income funds held in illiquid assets, preventing application of the fund; and
- capital being expended without authority.

The Practice Note suggests the following audit procedures:

- consideration of internal control procedures put in place by the charity to identify restricted funds;
- consideration of the methods used in cost allocation;
- comparison of expenditure with the terms of the restricted funds;
- consideration of the future funding to recover negative balances;
- consideration of the validity of the transfer between funds;
- consideration of the ability of the fund to meets its obligations in view of its underlying assets; and
- consideration of whether the capital of an endowed fund has been expended without express authority.

43.16   Audit considerations relating to an entity using a service organisation

The requirements for the auditor to review arrangements between charities and their service organisations does not vary from that which exists where a company is audited.

The use of service organisations by charities is not uncommon and includes services provided to the charity such as:

- maintenance of accounting records and payroll services;
- fundraising; and
- custodianship of assets, and investment management services.

43.17   External confirmations

Some charities will have bank accounts in overseas locations. In this situation, the auditor considers the format of the request for information to ensure it will be fully understood by the bank.

The auditor should also assess the implications of failures of overseas banks to reply to requests for information, and whether these should be reported to those charged with governance.

43.18   Initial audit engagements – opening balances

Because of the possibility that charities will qualify by reason of size for an audit where previously they were exempt, cases will arise where charities will not have had opening balances audited and the receipts and payments basis of accounting may have been used.

Where there has been a change in the basis of accounting, procedures may include checking bank statements, reviewing receipts and payments after the year end and physically checking any tangible fixed assets. For analytical review procedures, the auditor is likely to need to adjust the prior year management information prepared on a receipts and payments basis to enable a proper comparison.

43.19   Analytical procedures

The Practice Note sets out certain analytical procedures which the auditor may find useful. These include:

- comparison of actual income and expenditure to prior year figures and trends;
- comparison of actual to budgeted results;
- comparison of actual income to successful bids, legacy notifications and potential legacies reported in the minutes;
- comparison of actual expenditure to the auditor's own estimate of expenditure;
- comparison of results of an individual branch to those of similar branches of the main charity; and
- checking charity shop sales revenue between different periods and to other shops operating in similar locations.

43.20   Auditing accounting estimates, including fair value accounting estimates, and related disclosures

Common areas of charity financial statements which are affected by accounting estimates or fair value adjustments include:

- the valuation of defined benefit pension schemes. Charities also have the specific complexities of allocating pension deficits/assets between funds and the effect of these deficits/assets on their free reserves;

- the need to recognise material grant commitments at their present value in the balance sheet;
- the basis of the valuation of investments, whether financial, programme-related investments or mixed motive investments[3];
- the option to recognise tangible fixed assets and heritage assets at valuation and the valuation methods used;
- the need to fair value the assets and liabilities acquired where acquisition accounting is applied (in this situation, the due diligence process may only provide limited information on the fair value of some assets such as land and buildings and heritage assets);
- the need to recognise gifts in kind (apart from second-hand goods donated for resale) at a reasonable estimate of their gross value to the charity and donated services and facilities at a reasonable estimate of the value to the charity of the service or facility received;
- the accrual of income in relation to legacy income;
- the allocation of costs between different expenditure categories in the Statement of Financial Activities.

The different Charities SORPs provide detailed guidance on appropriate accounting policies and measurement bases. In particular, certain valuations can be undertaken by the trustees or employees of a charity provided that, in the case of property valuations, they are suitably qualified. In this situation, the auditor assesses the individual's relevant experience in accordance with ISA (UK and Ireland) 500.

The auditor will ensure that techniques selected by the trustees enable the financial statements to give a true and fair view and that the financial statements disclose a description of the estimation techniques used, in order to comply with UK GAAP and the relevant Charities SORP.

On occasion, evidence obtained from post balance sheet review and observation may be insufficiently conclusive. Where such estimates are likely to be material, the auditor reviews the process by which the estimate was arrived at and considers the basis of the calculation in terms of its reasonableness, justifiability and consistency. In so doing, the auditor will draw heavily on its knowledge of the charity in testing the consistency of principles adopted. Estimates of this nature may include:

- the quantification of future charitable commitments and constructive liabilities;
- valuations of gifts in kind, particularly property;
- valuation of assets received for onwards distribution;
- valuation of fixed asset investments where no market price exists;
- valuation of heritage assets;
- valuation of intangible income derived from donated services or use of facilities;
- estimates of ongoing service potential of fixed assets, in the absence of a cash flow, in an impairment review;

---

[3] Mixed motive investments are not covered by Practice Note 11. However, this is an emerging concept and further guidance on this is given in the FRS 102 SORP, FRSSE SORP and CC14 issued by the Charity Commission. This is also subject to new legislation expected to become law during 2016.

- impairment of programme-related investments made in furtherance of a charity's objectives, rather than for financial return; and
- recoverability of loans made to beneficiaries in the furtherance of a charity's objects.[3]

43.21 Related parties

It is a fundamental principle of trust law that a trustee should not benefit directly or indirectly from his or her trust. Neither charity trustees nor persons connected with them should obtain benefit from the charity unless expressly permitted by the charities governing document or an appropriate authority. There are also disclosure requirements in the relevant Charities SORP and in the regulations.

The auditor needs to understand the controls management have put in place to authorise and approve significant transactions.

43.22 Subsequent events

The determination after the balance sheet date of the amount of a gift aid payment to a parent charity by a subsidiary undertaking, if the subsidiary had a present legal or constructive obligation at the balance sheet date, is an adjusting post balance sheet event.

43.23 Going concern

This can be a difficult area in the audit of charities as many charities have an apparent financial weakness which is often compounded by the uncertainty of future income. Their ability to raise revenue will often be outside their direct control, and be dependent on such matters as the voting of grants and spending of the public.

It may also be difficult for a charity to cut back on a project or grant funding in the event of a liquidity problem, and although it may have an apparently large bank balance, it may be unable to meet general liabilities because the balance in question belongs to a restricted fund.

The Practice Note provides examples of conditions which may indicate that the charity is not a going concern. These include:

- inability to finance its operations from its own resources or unrestricted funds;
- decision by the trustees to curtail or cease activities;
- transfer to, or take-over by, another entity of the charity's activities;

- loss of essential resources or key staff;
- existence of tax liabilities which cannot be met from existing resources;
- deficits on unrestricted funds;
- loss of clients, for example, where a public authority ends a practice or contract to refer (and pay for) clients to the charity;
- loss of operating licence;
- significant changes in strategy of major funders and significant decline in donations by the public;
- investigation by a charity regulator;
- loans made to subsidiaries which cannot be repaid;
- claw-back of grant received and gift aid refunds; and
- failure to meet reserves policy targets.

Similar considerations apply to charities as to commercial entities. The auditor must assess whether there is sufficient disclosure of relevant circumstances to enable financial statements to give a true and fair view on this issue. The trustees' report may also contain disclosures giving indications of factors such as future expected income based on past donations or patterns of giving.

The going concern concept does not apply to the preparation of financial statements on a receipts and payments basis (allowed for small non limited company charities in England and Wales which are within the income thresholds defined by legislation). In these circumstances, the auditor should consider whether there are matters that affect the charities' ability to continue in operational existence for the foreseeable future. The auditor should not issue his report unless he is satisfied with explanations received from trustees concerning future funding arrangements. If he is not satisfied, he may find it appropriate to include an explanatory paragraph in his report. He will not qualify his report on the proper presentation of the receipts and payments account.

43.24   Written representations

A representation letter in respect of the financial statements of the charity is normally signed by the trustees who are responsible for the contents and presentation of the financial statements.

Where day to day management of the charity is delegated to senior management by trustees and representations are taken from those staff, the auditor should ensure that the staff involved have the necessary authority and all such representations are considered and approved by the trustees.

In addition to representation required by ISAs (UK and Ireland), the auditor of a charity also considers obtaining confirmation that:

- all income has been recorded;
- the restricted funds have been properly applied;
- constructive obligations for grants have been recognised;

- all correspondence with regulators has been made available to the auditor including, in England and Wales, any serious incident reports; and
- the trustees consider there to be appropriate controls in place to ensure overseas payments are applied for charitable purposes.

43.25   Audits of group financial statements

Where other auditors are used because they act for local branches, subsidiaries or other units, the group auditor must assess the degree of reliance he intends to place on the other auditors' work. Where the charity is a limited company, there is a statutory obligation on the component auditors of any subsidiary undertaking that is a company to communicate such information and explanations as may be reasonably required by the group auditor. Where the charity is unincorporated, the auditor has rights under s. 15 of the 2011 Act of access to books, documents and records which relate to the charity. This extends beyond those actually in the ownership of the charity.

Where charitable groups have components overseas, there are added complications for the group auditor to ensure the results of the components are appropriately consolidated into the group financial statements. The group auditor:

- obtains an understanding of the component business;
- obtains an understanding of the accounting framework under which the component accounts will be prepared;
- considers the need to get the component auditors to review the charity's conversion of the component financial statements into UK GAAP format;
- considers the need for the component auditors to comment on UK GAAP specific areas. Depending on the local accounting framework, this may require details of the accounting requirements under the Charities SORP to be explained to the component auditors.

Chapter 30 provides further guidance on group audit situations, including consideration of overseas components.

43.26   The auditor's report on financial statements

The 2008 Regulations determine that audit reports should be addressed to the trustees unless the auditor has been appointed by the Charity Commission. Companies and Friendly Societies statutes require audit reports to be addressed to the members. Scottish law requires company audit reports to be addressed to trustees and members.

The trustees' responsibilities may vary depending upon the constitution and size of the particular charity. The Companies Act and the Co-operative and

Community Benefit Societies Act establish duties under law. Where a charity is not subject to other regulation, appendix four of the Practice Note recommends the form of words to be used in the statement of trustees' responsibilities within the financial statements.

The Charities SORPs have been developed and issued under the code of practice established by the Financial Reporting Council for the production and issue of SORPs. They are authoritative guidance on the application of accounting standards to charities.

As the 2011 Act requires trustees to state whether financial statements have been prepared in accordance with SORP, this provision, taken with the general status of the SORPs, implies a strong presumption that the financial statements will need to follow the relevant SORP in order to give a true and fair view.

In addition, UK GAAP and the SORP indicate that it is necessary for a reporting entity to prepare consolidated financial statements in certain circumstances.

Bulletin 2010/2 (revised) was issued by the APB to provide examples of certain opinions for accounting periods ending on or after 23 March 2011. The auditor should refer to the bulletin when drafting his audit report but should note that the examples have not been updated for recent changes to company legislation and ISA 700. In particular:

- where the 'scope' paragraph does not refer to the FRC's website, it should be replaced by the relevant paragraph specified in the appropriate version of ISA 700. See **Chapter 4** for appropriate wording;
- for corporate charities, the opinion on consistency of 'the information in the directors' report' with the financial statements should refer instead to the consistency of 'the information given in the strategic report and directors' report', unless the charity is a small company for which no strategic report is prepared;
- where no strategic report is prepared, the matters on which we report by exception paragraph should include, in the bullet relating to entitlement to small company exemptions, the phrase 'and take advantage of the small companies exemption from the requirement to prepare a strategic report'.

In addition, where a charity has chosen to include in its annual report a statement about how it has complied with the provisions of the UK Corporate Governance Code, additional reporting requirements apply and the auditor should refer to the appropriate version of ISA 700 and the example in the FRC's Bulletin 4. Note, however, that at the time of writing, Bulletin 4 had not been updated for changes to reporting requirements arising from the adoption of the 2014 edition of the Code and reflected in ISA 700 (revised September 2014).

Further, none of the examples reflect the new requirements of ISA (UK and Ireland) 700 (Revised June 2016) which is expected to come into effect for periods commencing on or after 17 June 2016.

43.27   Other information

The Practice Note lists the types of other information that may be in documents containing audited financial statements.

The Charities SORPs require trustees of charities which are subject to audit under charity law (see section **43.1.1**)[4] to state in their report that the major identified risks to which the charity is exposed have been reviewed and that systems have been put in place to manage such risks. Smaller charities are not required to give this information, but it is considered good practice to make a statement about risk assessment and management. The Charity Commission is also encouraging larger charities to give expanded details on their risk management processes. Whilst the auditor is not expected to verify any risk management statement made by trustees, he should consider the disclosures made in relation to his knowledge of the charity's circumstances and systems.

The auditor of charitable companies must disclose in his report if, in his opinion, the trustees' report and strategic review is consistent with the financial statements. The auditor of non-company charities only needs to report where, in his opinion, the trustees' report is not consistent with the financial statements.

43.28   Summarised financial statements

The Practice Note contains guidance on auditor's reports on summarised financial statements produced by charities. Where summarised accounts were produced, the 2005 Charities SORP required that they be accompanied by a report from the auditor.

For periods commencing on or after 1 January 2015, where a charity continues to produce summarised financial statements, there is no requirement for a report by the auditor. However, should the charity wish such a report to be produced the auditor may continue to do so. In this case, the auditor will need to decide whether to continue to refer to Bulletin 2008/3 or to refer to other guidance such as the IAASB's ISA 810 *Engagements to Report on Summary Financial Statements*. A revised version of ISA 810 was issued in March 2016.

---

[4] For those charities operating in jurisdictions where there is no charity law audit requirement, the reference to larger charities is construed as applying to those charities with a gross income exceeding £500,000 (UK) or €500,000 (Republic of Ireland) in the reporting period.

44 PENSION SCHEMES

44.1 Introduction

Pension schemes operate in a complex legal environment and specific guidance to auditors of schemes is provided in Practice Note 15 *The audit of occupational pension schemes in the United Kingdom,* most recently revised in January 2011.

This chapter is intended to guide auditors of pension schemes to the key items addressed in PN15 and to provide details of where other relevant information can be obtained.

In April 2016, the FRC issued final drafts of a suite of ISAs. Subject to legislative changes in progress at the time of writing it is expected that these ISAs will take effect for the audit of financial statements for periods commencing on or after 17 June 2016, as set out in **1.6.4**. Practice Note 15 has not yet been updated for these revisions, however, references within this chapter to individual ISAs have been updated to the revised versions.

44.2 Legal background

ISA (UK and Ireland) 250 (Revised June 2016) *Section A – Consideration of laws and regulations in an audit of financial statements* sets out the auditor's responsibility to consider laws and regulations. The legislative framework for pension schemes is dominated by the *Pension Schemes Act* 1993, the *Pensions Act* 1995 ('PA 1995'), the *Pensions Act* 2004 ('PA 2004') and Regulations that accompany them. The subsequent *Pensions Act* 2007 ('PA 2007'), *Pensions Act* 2008 ('PA 2008'), *Pensions Act* 2011 ('PA 2011'), *Pensions Act* 2014 ('PA 2014') and *Pensions Schemes Act* 2015 ('PSA 2015') are also relevant for background knowledge but with less direct impact on pension scheme auditors.

The *Pensions Schemes Act* 1993 is consolidating legislation addressing the contracting out of the additional element of the state scheme (currently the State Second Pension) and the protection of members through the disclosure of information to them and by placing restrictions on employer-related investment.

The *Pensions Act* 2007 is primarily concerned with the provision of state pensions including the change in state pension age, increasing from 65–68 over the period 2019–46.

The *Pensions Act* 2008 introduced the requirement on employers to auto-enrol all eligible employees into qualifying workplace pension schemes.

The *Pensions Act* 2011 puts into law changes to the state pension age timetable established under PA 2007 and, together with associated Regulations, implements the automatic enrolment and related provisions first set out in PA 2008.

The *Pensions Act* 2014 introduces the single-tier state pension from 6 April 2016, with consequent withdrawal of contracting out of NICs.

The *Pension Schemes Act* 2015 introduces collective benefit schemes and details the 'pension flexibilities' which allow greater access to pension benefits to those aged 55 and above.

The *Pensions Act* 1995 and PA 2004 are both reforming legislation and primarily enabling Acts with detailed requirements set out in Regulations made under them. The principal Regulations that pension scheme auditors need to be aware of are:

- The *Occupational Pension Schemes (Disclosure of Information) Regulations* 1996 ('the Disclosure Regulations');
- The *Occupational Pension Schemes (Scheme Administration) Regulations* 1996 ('the Administration Regulations');
- The *Occupational Pension Schemes (Requirement to obtain Audited Accounts and a Statement from the Auditor) Regulations* 1996 ('the Audited Accounts Regulations'); and
- The *Occupational Pension Schemes (Investment) Regulations* 2005 ('the Investment Regulations').

The Pension Acts and the Regulations referred to above have received numerous amendments inserted subsequently, and care should be taken to review the latest amended versions.

The *Pensions Act* 1995, PA 2004 and the Regulations set out the basis on which auditors are appointed, auditors' responsibilities and the form and content of pension scheme financial statements and annual reports. They also set out responsibilities for trustees such as obtaining the annual report and financial statements and the establishment and operation of internal controls.

The *Pensions Act* 2004 also introduced the Pensions Regulator ('the Regulator'). The Regulator replaced the Occupational Pensions Regulatory Authority ('OPRA') from April 2005.

The Regulator, which is sometimes abbreviated to 'TPR' or 'tPR', has a range of powers, which include issuing:

- codes of practice, as explained further below, and other regulatory guidance;
- improvement notices: the ability to prevent those responsible for a scheme contravening pensions legislation;
- third party notices: the ability to take action against a third party who is preventing a person from complying with the law;
- contribution notices: to order contributions from parties attempting to avoid employer debt to a defined benefit scheme; and
- financial support directions: to secure financial support from a party associated with the principal employer if the employer is either a service organisation or insufficiently funded.

Codes of practice are primarily directed at trustees. They are not statements of law, but are an indication of what is considered to be best practice. Any departure from them should, therefore, be justifiable and not be in breach of any underlying legal requirements. All professionals involved with pension schemes should be aware of the codes of practice and should refer regularly to the Pension Regulator's website (www.thepensionsregulator.gov.uk), which also provides guidance related to each code of practice. There have been 14 codes of practice issued to date. Those which are particularly relevant to the responsibilities and work of a pension scheme auditor are:

01   Reporting breaches of the law

03   Funding defined benefits

05   Reporting late payment of contributions to occupational pension schemes

07   Trustee knowledge and understanding

09   Internal controls

13   Governance and administration of occupational defined contribution trust-based schemes*

14   Governance and administration of public service pension schemes

* Code 13 is currently being significantly updated and a revised code is expected to be issued in 2016.

The codes of practice referred to above are explained in more detail in the relevant parts of this chapter.

The Pensions Regulator also issues guidance to help understand what the law requires with regard to regulating pension provision.

In explaining the legal environment in which pension schemes operate, code of practice 01 refers to 'enactments or rule of law', which are broadly defined to include the *Theft Act* 1968, the *Trustee Act* 2000 and other trust law and common law. Auditors of pension schemes must, therefore, maintain an understanding of many legal requirements. In addition, there must also be familiarity with the scheme's own rules and regulations which are set out in its trust deed and rules.

44.3   Accounting guidance

The accounting guidance for pension schemes is contained in the Statement of Recommended Practice *Financial Reports of Pension Schemes* ('the SORP'). The SORP is issued by the Pensions Research Accountants Group ('PRAG') who also issue other guidance for the accounting and governance of pension schemes. Auditors of pension schemes should refer to the PRAG website (www.prag.org.uk) for details of the latest guidance.

The current version of the SORP was issued in November 2014 and applies to accounting periods commencing on or after 1 January 2015. It implements the requirements of FRS 102 for pension scheme accounts. Compared to the previous version, the 2014 SORP requires significantly more disclosures in the financial statements relating to investments, and particularly about the risks attached to investments, with both qualitative and quantitative disclosures. This poses an additional challenge for auditors in gathering sufficient, appropriate, reliable evidence.

In March 2016, the Financial Reporting Council published a change to FRS 102 allowing financial institutions and retirement benefit plans to use the investment fair value hierarchy required by International Financial Reporting Standards rather than that currently required by FRS 102 and incorporated in the 2014 SORP. This change can be early adopted and thus effectively applied retrospectively. The guidance and further details can be found on CCH Online.

Auditors are required by reg. 3 of the *Audited Accounts Regulations* to report whether the financial statements contain the information specified in the Schedule to those Regulations. The Schedule sets out the format in which the financial information should be presented and certain disclosures that need to be made. One disclosure is whether the financial statements have been prepared in accordance with the SORP and if not, an indication of material departures.

PN15 explains that it is normally necessary to follow the guidance in the SORP in order for pension scheme accounts to show a true and fair view. Auditors must, therefore, be familiar with the requirements of the SORP and be prepared to refer to any material non-compliance with it in the audit opinion.

It should be noted that pension scheme financial statements do not include the scheme's liabilities to pay pensions and other benefits that fall due after the end of the scheme year. A net assets statement is required instead of a balance sheet.

44.4 Schemes exempt from audit

A number of categories of scheme are exempt under the Administration Regulations from the requirement to appoint an auditor. The principal exemptions relate to:

- occupational pension schemes with fewer than two members;
- certain public sector schemes;
- occupational money purchase small schemes (prior to *Finance Act* 2004, these were known as Small Self Administered Schemes or 'SSASs') meeting specified criteria in respect of unanimous decision making and membership of the trustee board;
- schemes not registered under *Finance Act* 2004; and
- unfunded occupational schemes.

Any of the above schemes may be audited on a 'voluntary basis', for example, where the trustees request an audit to be performed or where the scheme rules require an audit.

In addition, money-purchase schemes which invest only in one or more insurance policies which specifically allocate benefits to individual members ('ear-marked' schemes) only require an auditor's statement about contributions, not audited accounts.

44.5   Appointment and resignation

To be effective, the appointment of a scheme auditor must be made in accordance with the Administration Regulations. The trustees or managers of the scheme must forward a notice of appointment to the auditor which specifies the effective date of appointment, to whom the auditor is to report, and from whom the auditor will take instructions. For the appointment to be effective, PA 1995 requires the auditor to acknowledge receipt of the notice of appointment within one month of receipt. It also requires the auditor to state that he will notify the trustees immediately he becomes aware of the existence of any conflict of interest.

PN15 provides examples of a notice of appointment and an acknowledgement of appointment as well as example paragraphs for the relevant engagement letter. PN15 also details the matters that the auditor should consider before accepting the appointment.

On resignation, the Administration Regulations require the auditor to provide a written notice of resignation to the trustees. This must contain either a statement specifying any circumstances connected with the resignation which, in his opinion, significantly affect the interests of the members or prospective members of, or beneficiaries under, the scheme or a declaration that there are no such circumstances.

44.6   Considerations of fraud

Although PN15 comments that the risk of fraudulent financial reporting is low given the nature of pension schemes, it also states that the potential for fraud cannot be ignored. The most likely risk is the misappropriation of assets and PN15 explains that, even if activities are delegated, the trustees retain responsibility for the prevention and detection of fraud.

Examples of the type of fraud that may occur in a pension scheme are:

- misappropriation of assets;
- deliberate non-payment of employee and/or employer contributions to the scheme;
- use of assets of the scheme either directly or as collateral for borrowing by either the employer or an associate of the employer;
- misapplication of the assets of a scheme to meet the obligations and expenses of either another scheme or of the sponsoring employer;

- dealing in scheme assets by the investment manager without the required mandate or authorisation;
- lending of scheme assets by the custodian without authorisation;
- exchange of assets without sufficient valuable consideration (for example, selling assets such as property at below market value);
- assets of the scheme used for the personal preferment of the trustees or used for the personal preferment of an individual scheme member;
- benefit claims by members or their beneficiaries to which they are not entitled (for example, failure to notify a scheme of the death of a member or other beneficiary); and
- creation of fictitious scheme records by the administrator (for example, dummy beneficiary records).

PN15 indicates that auditors may rebut the presumption that revenue recognition gives rise to a risk of material misstatement due to fraud. This is due to the nature of the income, the not-for-profit nature of a pension scheme and the limited scope for revenue manipulation.

There are circumstances that increase the risk of fraud and the auditor needs to be aware of these when planning the audit. These include:

- failure by the trustees to establish and operate adequate internal control mechanisms;
- trustees or scheme management displaying a significant disregard for the various regulatory authorities;
- trustees or scheme management having little or no involvement in the day-to-day administration of the scheme;
- trustees or scheme management having ready access to the scheme's assets and an ability to override any internal controls;
- trustees or scheme management failing to put in place arrangements to monitor activities undertaken by third parties, including the employer;
- trustees or scheme management displaying a lack of candour in dealings with members, the actuary or the auditor on significant matters affecting scheme assets;
- the sponsoring employer operating in an industry with increasing business failures, or itself having financial difficulties;
- significant levels, or unusual types, of related-party transactions (including employer-related investments) involving unaudited entities or entities audited by other firms; and
- opaque investment arrangements where the flow of information to the trustees is restricted and therefore it is more difficult to control and monitor the investment.

To properly assess the above circumstances, scheme auditors should be communicating with the trustees and those responsible for the management of the scheme, which may include the sponsoring employer, its directors or staff and third parties to whom the trustees have delegated the conduct of scheme activities. Scheme auditors should also conduct analytical procedures and hold a fraud brain-storming discussion. As with all entities, an appropriate response to identified fraud risks should be determined and management representation sought on fraud.

44.7   Control activities

ISA (UK and Ireland) 315 (Revised June 2016) *Identifying and assessing risks of material misstatement through understanding the entity and its environment* requires the auditor to understand the systems and controls of entities being audited. PN15 sets out the features of an effective control environment, examples of control activities and the factors that increase the risk of material misstatement. In considering the risk of material misstatement, the auditor should refer to the appendices of PN15 which explain the risks which apply to different benefit structures.

Auditors should also consider the ability of the trustees and in doing so reference should be made to code of practice 07 'Trustee Knowledge and Understanding'. The Regulator intends that trustees should, amongst other areas, be familiar with their powers and the manner in which their scheme operates. The code of practice explains how trustees might approach the task of determining the elements of knowledge and understanding which are appropriate for them and how they might acquire the knowledge and understanding needed. This is, therefore, a part of the assessment of the environment. Many pension schemes delegate activities, most commonly administration and investment management, to third parties. Of particular relevance to pension scheme auditors is, therefore, ISA (UK and Ireland) 402 *Audit considerations relating to entities using a service organisation*. The responsibility for the operation of the scheme does, however, remain with the trustees when they have outsourced activities and they are responsible for ensuring that scheme has appropriate procedures and controls. Any weaknesses or gaps in the controls operated by trustees may lead to additional audit risk. In such circumstances, the auditor will need to design audit procedures to address that risk.

It must be emphasised that the systems and control activities that need to be understood are those operated by the trustees and which are under their direct control. The *Pensions Act* 2004, s. 249A and the *Occupational Pension Schemes (Internal Controls) Regulations* 2005 impose on trustees a statutory obligation to operate internal controls and in considering the internal controls the auditor should refer to the Regulator's code of practice 09 Internal Controls and associated guidance. The PRAG publication 'Outsourcing for Trustees' is also a useful reference.

It is necessary for scheme auditors to gain an understanding of how the scheme's use of a service organisation affects the scheme's internal control. The following should, therefore, be documented and understood:

- the nature and significance of services provided;
- the nature and materiality of transactions processed or accounts processes affected;
- the nature of the relationship including contractual terms;
- interaction of the control systems of the scheme and the service organisation;
- the scheme's controls relevant to the service organisation and how risks are identified and controlled;
- the trustees' assessment procedures covering the capability of the service organisation; and
- information available to the trustees in respect of the service organisation's operations including general and IT controls.

The directors of the service organisation may provide information to the trustees by producing an 'internal control report' in accordance with *AAF 01/06 Assurance reports on internal controls of service organisations made available to third parties* ('AAF 01/06') (see **Chapter 40**).

The essential content of an internal control report under AAF 01/06 is for the service organisation to explain how control procedures achieve control objectives. Control objectives are set by the management of the service organisation, but AAF 01/06 provides mandatory objectives for pension scheme administrators, custodians and investment managers. An internal control report produced under AAF 01/06 will also contain a report from a Reporting Accountant providing an opinion on the fairness of the description and the design and operating effectiveness of control procedures.

Service organisations with an international clientele may alternatively produce an internal control report in accordance with the International Auditing and Assurance Standards Board standard ISAE 3402 *Assurance reports on controls at a service organisation* which has similar objectives to AAF 01/06.

Trustees should seek to obtain such reports from service providers and incorporate an assessment of them into their control procedures.

Having gained an understanding of the service organisation's controls, it may be concluded that these controls do not impact on the overall assessment of the audit risk in respect of the scheme. This could, for example, be because either the activities are not significant to the audit of the scheme or because the trustees have appropriate controls in place over their use of the service organisation.

If, however, the activities of the service organisation do result in audit risk, appropriate audit procedures will need to be designed. The nature of the procedures will be specific to each scheme and are dependent upon the service and the risks that have been assessed. Access to the service organisation will not always be necessary as the trustees may either hold sufficient documentation, or the service organisation provides periodic reports which contain adequate information. The internal control reports provided to trustees may also provide useful information to the scheme auditor.

44.8   Communication with trustees

Scheme auditors must ensure that there is interaction with those charged with governance at various stages of the audit. For pension schemes, those charged with governance will normally be the trustees, or the directors of the corporate trustee. As well as being a requirement of ISA (UK and Ireland) 260 (Revised June 2016) *Communication with those charged with governance*, it is fundamental to the planning of the audit and compliance with ISA (UK and Ireland) 315 (Revised June 2016) *Identifying and assessing risks of material misstatement through understanding the entity and its environment.*

Auditors will communicate with the trustees on a range of matters including:

- the responsibilities of the auditor;
- independence;
- scope of the audit, the audit plan and any additional procedures;
- timetable;
- fees;
- access to third parties and information;
- fraud;
- procedures, controls and internal audit;
- changes to the scheme;
- issues arising from a review of the minutes;
- unadjusted errors other than those that are clearly trivial; and
- communication with the Regulator.

As part of their assessment and communication of matters concerning their independence, scheme auditors should also consider services provided to the sponsoring employer of the scheme. Regulatory guidance issued by the Regulator in 2008 highlights trustees' responsibilities to assess and manage conflicts of interest, including advisor conflicts.

At the end of the audit process, the auditor will also communicate with trustees. ISA (UK and Ireland) 265 *Communicating deficiencies in internal control to those charged with governance and management* requires the auditor to report deficiencies to the extent that the auditor considers that they warrant the trustees' attention. In making that assessment, the auditor should have regard to factors such as:

- the significance and nature of the risk(s) to the scheme that are not being addressed as a result of the deficiency;
- the possible impact on scheme assets;
- the possible impact on member benefits;
- the extent to which the operation of controls is formal and documented or otherwise;
- whether alternative preventative controls are operating; and
- whether other parties such as third-party administrators compensate for the deficiencies.

Trustees should be notified of all breaches of duties relevant to the administration of the scheme discovered in the course of the audit work. These duties include those imposed by any enactment or rule of law on the trustees or managers, the employer, any professional adviser or any prescribed person acting in connection with the scheme. The notification to the trustees should be made, regardless of whether the matter gave rise to a statutory duty to report to the Regulator. If there are no matters that need to be notified, the trustees should be advised in writing accordingly.

44.9   Reporting

The form and content of auditor's reports on the financial statements of pension schemes follow the requirements established by ISA (UK and Ireland) 700 (Revised June 2016) *Forming an opinion and reporting on financial statements*, supplemented by the particular detailed requirements of the *Audited Accounts Regulations*. Those regulations require the trustees of a scheme to obtain audited financial statements and so it is to the trustees that the auditor's report is addressed, although other parties may be added if required by the trust deed or other applicable rules.

A statement of trustees' responsibilities, usually included within the trustees' report, assists in meeting the requirement to distinguish between the auditor's responsibilities and the responsibilities of those charged with governance (in the case of a pension scheme, its trustees). The responsibilities of the trustees may vary according to the constitution of the particular pension scheme. Example trustee responsibility statements are set out in the appendix to Practice Note 15.

The *Audited Accounts Regulations* set out the requirements of the auditor to report on whether, in their opinion, the financial statements:

- show a true and fair view of the financial transactions of the scheme during the year, and of the amount and disposition at its year-end of its assets and liabilities, other than the liabilities to pay pensions and benefits after the end of the year; and
- contain the information specified in reg. 3 of, and the Schedule to, the *Occupational Pension Schemes (Requirement to Obtain Audited Accounts and a Statement from the Auditor) Regulations* 1996, made under the *Pensions Act* 1995.

United Kingdom Generally Accepted Accounting Practice requires, among other things, compliance with the SORP. Any material departure therefrom is required to be noted in the financial statements, and the auditor should consider their opinion in the light of any such departure.

An example of an unmodified audit report on the financial statements of a pension scheme is set out in **Table 1** below. Note that this example does not include the auditor's separate statement on contributions which is often given as a separate report (see **44.10**).

TABLE 1: Unqualified audit opinion[1]

INDEPENDENT AUDITOR'S REPORT TO THE TRUSTEES OF THE XYZ PENSION SCHEME

We have audited the financial statements of [name of pension scheme] for the year ended [...] which comprise the fund account, the net assets statement and the related notes. The financial reporting framework that has been applied in their preparation is applicable law and United Kingdom Accounting Standards (United Kingdom Generally Accepted Accounting Practice).

Respective responsibilities of trustees and auditor

As explained more fully in the Trustees' Responsibilities Statement [set out on page ...], the scheme's trustees are responsible for the preparation of financial statements which show a true and fair view. Our responsibility is to audit and express an opinion on the financial statements in accordance with applicable law and International Standards on Auditing (UK and Ireland). Those standards require us to comply with the Financial Reporting Council's [(FRC's)] Ethical Standards for Auditors.

Scope of the audit of the financial statements

Either:

A description of the scope of an audit of financial statements is [provided on the FRC's website at www.frc.org.uk/auditscopeukprivate]/[set out [on page ...] of the Trustees' Annual Report].

Or:

An audit involves obtaining evidence about the amounts and disclosures in the financial statements sufficient to give reasonable assurance that the financial statements are free from material misstatement, whether caused by fraud or error. This includes an assessment of: whether the accounting policies are appropriate to the scheme's circumstances and have been consistently applied and adequately disclosed; the reasonableness of significant accounting estimates made by the trustees; and the overall presentation of the financial statements. In addition, we read all the financial and non-financial information in the [describe the annual report] to identify material inconsistencies with the audited financial statements and to identify any information that is apparently materially incorrect based on, or materially inconsistent with, the knowledge acquired by us in the course of performing the audit. If we become aware of any apparent material misstatements or inconsistencies we consider the implications for our report.

731

Opinion on financial statements

In our opinion the financial statements:

- show a true and fair view of the financial transactions of the scheme during the year ended [...], and of the amount and disposition at that date of its assets and liabilities, other than the liabilities to pay pensions and benefits after the end of the year;
- have been properly prepared in accordance with United Kingdom Generally Accepted Accounting Practice; and
- contain the information specified in reg. 3 of, and the Schedule to, the *Occupational Pension Schemes (Requirement to obtain Audited Accounts and a Statement from the Auditor) Regulations* 1996, made under the *Pensions Act* 1995.

Statutory Auditor

Address

Date

¹ This example is based on existing ISAs and has not been updated to reflect changes to audit reporting ISAs which will take effect for periods commencing 17 June 2016.

44.10 Contributions

Scheme auditors are required by the Audited Accounts Regulations to make a statement about contributions. This is separate to the opinion that is given on the financial statements. The statement is whether contributions have, in all material respects, been paid at least in accordance with the payment schedule or the schedule of contributions.

Auditors need to understand the basis under which contributions are paid to the scheme by the employer. Money purchase schemes are required to have a payment schedule under PA 1995, s. 87 and defined benefit schemes are required to have a schedule of contributions under PA 2004, s. 227 ('the schedule(s)').

Pension scheme auditors need to be familiar with the form and content of the schedule relevant to the scheme. Since 2005, contributions to defined benefit schemes come under the 'scheme specific funding' regime, which replaced the previous minimum funding requirements.

The schedule of contributions must be prepared in accordance with the *Occupational Pension Schemes (Scheme Funding) Regulations* 2005 and is required to show separately any deficit funding and 'other' contributions due from the employer. It must also be signed by the trustees and the employer.

Auditors need to ascertain when a schedule becomes effective. PN15 provides guidance on the issues that need to be considered, but it is important to be aware that a schedule of contributions cannot be effective until it is certified by the actuary and that it cannot be backdated.

Code of practice 03 'Funding defined benefits' and code of practice 05 'Reporting late payment of contributions to occupational pension schemes' provide guidance for trustees on the monitoring of contributions and the reporting responsibilities in the event of late or incorrect payments being made.

In order to make his statement about contributions, the auditor must obtain the schedule and undertake procedures to obtain sufficient appropriate evidence to conclude whether or not contributions payable have, in all material respects, been paid at least for the amounts and within the timeframe set out in the schedule.

The auditor needs to consider a range of issues, including:

- changes in rates of contributions payable and the extent to which these have been included in the schedule;
- changes in the definition of salary on which the contributions are based;
- whether the schedule is sufficiently clear;
- whether the schedule complies with legal requirements and guidance issued by the Regulator;
- whether there have been any member complaints about incorrect contributions;
- the scheme's systems for recording and monitoring contributions; and
- any reports to the Regulator of late or inaccurate contributions.

As the statement about contributions is separate to the audit opinion, PN15 indicates that it should be a separate report. PN15 also recommends that a summary of contributions paid during the scheme year under the schedule is produced by the trustees and included with the annual report ('the summary').

The summary shows details of contributions payable during the year together with a reconciliation to the contributions shown in the fund account. The significance of the summary is that it enables the reader of the annual report and financial statements to identify which contributions the auditor's statement refers to.

As the schedule refers to both the quantum and the timing of the payment of contributions, materiality must be considered in terms of both value and time. It is normal to apply materiality to values and the pension scheme auditor should consider this in the same manner as for any other transaction stream. The application of materiality to timing is more complex.

The application of materiality is a matter of judgment for individual pension scheme auditors and the only guidance provided by PN15 is that there should be regard to the nature and frequency of the breaches and the cumulative, as well as the individual, impact of the breaches.

In considering the application of materiality to timing, there are, however, some salient factors which may be considered:

- the statement about contributions is on an aggregate basis and so materiality should not be applied based on the perception of a single member's contribution;
- late contributions are usually more significant in a money purchase arrangement; and

- the manner of the monitoring of contributions, the identification of any late contributions and the timeliness of such identification should be considered.

Example wording of the auditor's statement about contributions and guidance on the wording of qualified statements about contributions is given below. **Table 2** provides an example of an unmodified statement and **Table 3** gives a qualified statement.

TABLE 2: Example of an Unmodified Auditor's Statement about Contributions

INDEPENDENT AUDITOR'S STATEMENT ABOUT CONTRIBUTIONS TO THE TRUSTEES OF THE XYZ PENSION SCHEME

We have examined the summary of contributions to the [name of scheme] for the scheme year ended [...] [to which this statement is attached/which is set out in the Trustees' Report on page x].

Respective responsibilities of Trustees and the auditor

As explained more fully in the Statement of Trustees' Responsibilities, the scheme's Trustees are responsible for ensuring that there is prepared, maintained and from time to time revised a [schedule of contributions/payment schedule] showing the rates and due dates of certain contributions payable towards the scheme by or on behalf of the employer and the active members of the scheme. The Trustees are also responsible for keeping records in respect of contributions received in respect of active members of the scheme and for monitoring whether contributions are made to the scheme by the employer in accordance with the [schedule of contributions/payment schedule].

It is our responsibility to provide a Statement about Contributions paid under the [schedule of contributions/payment schedule] and to report our opinion to you.

Scope of work on Statement about Contributions

Our examination involves obtaining evidence sufficient to give reasonable assurance that contributions reported in the [attached] summary of contributions have in all material respects been paid at least in accordance with the [schedule of contributions/ payment schedule]. This includes an examination, on a test basis, of evidence relevant to the amounts of contributions payable to the scheme and the timing of those payments under the [schedule of contributions/payment schedule].

Statement about Contributions payable under the [schedule of contributions]/[payment schedule]

In our opinion, contributions for the scheme year ended [...] as reported in the summary of contributions and payable under the [schedule of contributions]/[payment schedule] have in all material respects been paid at least in accordance with the [schedule of contributions certified by the scheme actuary on [date]/payment schedule dated [...]].

Statutory Auditor

Address

Date

TABLE 3: Extract from a Modified Auditor's Statement about Contributions

Basis for statement about contributions

As explained on page [...], [give brief details of the departure from the schedule including an indication of the frequency of late payments, and quantification of the amounts involved – e.g. 'during the year, three months' contributions amounting in total to £X were paid [specify timing of payment] later than the due date set out in the schedule of contributions'].

Qualified statement about contributions payable under the [schedule of contributions]/[payment schedule]

In our opinion, except for the effects of the departure from the schedule of contributions, contributions for the scheme year ended [...] as reported in the summary of contributions and payable under the [schedule of contributions]/[payment schedule] have in all material respects been paid at least in accordance with the [schedule of contributions certified by the scheme actuary on [date ...]/payment schedule dated [...]].

In the event that the auditor's statement about contributions is qualified, trustees should have already considered the need to report to the Regulator because of their responsibility to monitor the receipt of contributions. In such circumstances, the auditor will need to consider the following:

- if a report has been made by the trustees, did it contain all relevant information that the Regulator would expect?
- if the trustees were aware of the issue giving rise to the qualification, have they documented why a report was not made to the Regulator and is the conclusion reasonable?
- if the trustees were not aware of the issue, are their monitoring procedures insufficient and are there wider implications?

Depending upon the results of the above, it may be necessary for a report to be made to the Regulator by either the trustees or the auditor. Further guidance on the necessity of a report to the Regulator is provided in the Regulator's Code of Practice 05 *Reporting late payment of contributions to occupational pension schemes*. A qualified statement about contributions does not automatically result in a report to the Regulator. A report by the trustees to the Regulator on the timing of contributions is, however, more likely to result in a qualified statement about contributions, but the pension scheme auditor should give the matter proper consideration.

The requirement for an auditor's statement about contributions applies to all schemes that are required to appoint an auditor, irrespective of the size or nature of the scheme. Practical difficulties have arisen for auditors in relation to large, multi-employer 'master-trust' pensions schemes, many of which have been set up in response to the requirement on all employers to establish a pension arrangement for their eligible workers. The Department for Work and Pensions has proposed that multi-employer schemes with at least 20 unconnected participating employers be exempt from the requirement to obtain an auditor's statement about contributions. It is anticipated that a change in regulations will be made during 2016.

44.11 Schemes in the process of winding up

Schemes in winding up are not exempt from the requirement to produce an annual report and audited financial statements until the wind up is complete. The Administration Regulations do not require the appointment of an auditor if the membership is less than two, so potentially, the statutory requirement for an audit can cease before the wind up is finalised. However, trust law and best practice indicate that financial statements should still be prepared. In these circumstances, the audit becomes non-statutory and the auditor needs to consider whether the existing engagement terms remain appropriate.

A schedule of contributions is no longer required once the wind up of a defined benefit pension scheme commences and the auditor should only express an opinion in his statement about contributions on compliance with the schedule of contributions up to the date the wind up commences. In relation to subsequent periods, the statement concerns compliance with the scheme rules and, where appropriate, the recommendations of the actuary.

For a money purchase scheme, the payment schedule is still required during the wind up period. Trustees should revise the payment schedule to reflect the basis on which contributions are payable from the start of winding up, which is normally nil. The auditor expresses an opinion on the payment schedule in force up to the commencement of winding up and thereafter on the revised schedule if one has been produced.

Once winding up is formally concluded the auditor's appointment automatically lapses without the need for formal resignation. Evidence of winding up should be obtained, but, if no such evidence is available, the auditor should consider formal resignation. Where no audit work has been performed for several months, it may be appropriate for the auditor to include in the statement on resignation that he is not able to know of any circumstances which might affect members' interests.

44.12 Other reporting situations

There are situations when audited financial statements are required for periods other than the usual agreed accounting reference date. These will normally coincide with the requirement for an actuarial valuation in circumstances such as:

- the present recovery plan being significantly inadequate;
- a claim against an employer under PA 1995, s. 75 due to an employer ceasing to participate in a multi-employer scheme;
- following a bulk transfer into or out of a scheme and/or a significant change in membership; and
- for the purpose of the Pension Protection Fund following the entry of the scheme into the assessment period.

The financial statements in all of these situations should be prepared in accordance with the Audited Accounts Regulations. A trustee report is not usually required, although a statement of trustee responsibilities should be included, and the notes to the financial statements should specify the purpose for which the financial statements have been prepared. The auditor will report on the financial statements in the usual manner, again specifying the purpose for which they have been prepared. There is not usually a requirement to give a separate statement about contributions. PN15 provides detailed guidance and examples of reports. In each of these situations, it is likely that the auditor will need to issue a revised engagement letter to recognise the altered scope and purpose of the engagement compared with a normal annual audit.

44.13 Whistle-blowing responsibilities

The *Pensions Act* 2004, s. 70 imposes on the auditor (and virtually everyone associated with the running of a scheme) a duty to report to the Regulator any breaches of the law that are likely to be of material significance to the Regulator. PN15 provides comprehensive information on the auditor's considerations leading to such a report and the manner in which this should be undertaken.

The Regulator's code of practice 01 explains the 'whistle-blowing' requirements and this, together with further guidance issued by the Regulator, should be understood by the scheme auditor. The duty to report to the Regulator arises where the trustees or others associated with the scheme have failed to comply with their legal duties. The Regulator has, however, indicated that it expects most reporting to be by trustees and, if a report has already been made, the auditor should only report if there is additional information to be provided. Note that the auditor is only required to report matters that are of 'material significance to the Regulator', not all breaches of regulations or law. The auditor is not required to undertake any additional work other than to fulfil his responsibilities.

45 SOLICITORS' ACCOUNTS RULES

45.1 Background

The rules dealing with solicitors' accounts are contained in the SRA Accounts Rules 2011 ('the Rules'). The Solicitors Regulation Authority (SRA) is the independent regulatory body for solicitors in England and Wales.

The Rules, together with the SRA Authorisation Rules 2011 and the SRA Indemnity Rules 2012 can be found in the SRA Handbook, version 15 of which was issued on 1 November 2015. Further details and guidance can be found in the CCH publications *Client Money Programmes* and the *Solicitor's Industry Accounting and Auditing Guide,* available on CCH Online.

45.1.1 Changes to the Accountant's Report and removal of Rule 39

All practising solicitors who, at any time during an accounting period, held or received client money, or operated a client's own account as signatory, must obtain an accountant's report for that accounting period within six months of the end of the accounting period. If the report has been qualified, the solicitor is responsible for delivering it to the SRA within six months of the end of the accounting period.

Prior to November 2015, the solicitor was required to deliver the accountant's report to the SRA only when it included qualifying breaches of the SRA Accounts Rules. From November 2015, the nature of the work required to be carried out by the reporting accountant changed and an accountant's report is now only deemed to be qualified where the reporting accountant forms the judgment that the rules have not been complied with such that the safety of client money is at risk.

In November 2014, the Rules were changed to require submission of accountants' reports to the SRA only where they contained qualifications. Part of the drive by the SRA for this initial change was simply to reduce the burden and costs of administration resulting from receiving unqualified reports. The change was also consistent with the Outcomes Focused Regulation (OFR) regime being implemented by the SRA; that is law firms take responsibility for complying with the need for the accountant's report to be prepared without the requirement for formal submission to the SRA in the case where there were no non-compliance matters to report.

A further change became effective for reporting periods ending on or after 1 November 2015 including:

- a change in the report format;
- qualification of the report only being required for material breaches and/or significant weaknesses in the firm's systems and controls for compliance with the Accounts Rules; and
- removal of Rule 39 which covered defined procedures that should be undertaken.

The changes to the accountant's report and the removal of Rule 39 are primarily a further step by the SRA to reinforce the OFR regime for law firms in respect of client money and from a practical viewpoint to further reduce the level of resource it invests in reviewing the accountant's reports.

The SRA has issued its own guidance related to the changes *SRA's Guidance to Reporting Accountants and firms on planning and completion of the annual Accountant's Reports, under Rule 32 of the SRA Accounts Rules 2011*. The ICAEW have also issued a Technical Release, TECH 16/15AAF *Solicitors Regulation Authority (SRA) Accounts Rules: interim guidance for reporting accountants following changes to the accountant's report requirements*.

The changes are discussed in more detail below.

45.1.2   Compliance with the Rules

Ten high level Principles overlay the Rules. These are mandatory and underpin all aspects of regulation, including the Rules.

A firm's first point of reference when considering compliance with the Rules must always be the principles set out in **Table 1**.

TABLE 1: High level principles

- uphold the rule of law and the proper administration of justice;
- act with integrity;
- not allow your independence to be compromised;
- act in the best interests of each client;
- provide a proper standard of service to your clients;
- behave in a way that maintains the trust the public places in you and in the provision of legal services;
- comply with your legal and regulatory obligations and deal with your regulators and ombudsman in an open, timely and cooperative manner;
- run your business or carry out your role in the business effectively and in accordance with proper governance and sound financial and risk management principles;
- run your business or carry out your role in the business in a way that encourages equality of opportunity and respect for diversity; and
- protect client money and assets.

The Rules apply to 'you' (as defined in Rule 2) and include ABSs (licensed bodies), and their managers and employees, as well as if you are a solicitor, a registered European lawyer (REL), a registered foreign lawyer (RFL), a recognised body or a licensed body. There are additional categories and detailed definitions contained in Rule 4. The Rules apply to all those who carry on or work in a firm and to the firm itself. In relation to multi-disciplinary practices (MDPs), the Rules apply only in respect of those activities for which the practice is regulated by the SRA.

Solicitors who practise outside England and Wales are governed by Part 7 of the Rules. These are similar to the rules governing those who practice in England and Wales, but are less detailed and less onerous in their requirements.

All practising solicitors (subject to the exemptions below) who handle clients' money are required to obtain a report confirming their compliance with the Rules within six months of the solicitor's firm's year end. This must be given by an authorised reporting accountant. Firms are not required to submit a report if:

- all of the client money held or received during an accounting period is money held or received from the Legal Aid Agency or in the circumstances set out in rule 19.3; or
- in the accounting period, the statement or passbook balance of client money you have held or received does not exceed:

    (i)   an average of £10,000; and
    (ii)   a maximum of £250,000,

    or the equivalent in foreign currency.

The report is only required to be submitted to the SRA if it contains qualifications. The responsibility for delivery is that of the firm and not the reporting accountant. A clean accountant's report must be retained by the law firm and also the reporting accountant for a period of six years, for inspection on request by the SRA.

45.1.3   Objective

The purpose of the Rules is to keep client money safe. More specifically, as stated in Rule 1, 'you' must:

- keep other people's money separate from money belonging to you or your firm, safely in a bank or building society account identifiable as a client account; ensure that each client's money is used for that client's matters only;
- ensure that money held as trustee of a trust is used for the purposes of that trust only;
- establish and maintain proper accounting systems, proper internal controls over those systems, and proper accounting records to ensure compliance with the rules and accurately show the position with regard to the money held for each client or trust;
- account for interest on other people's money in accordance with the rules;

- cooperate with the SRA in checking compliance; and
- obtain annual accountant's reports as required by the rules.

All the principals in a practice must ensure compliance with the rules both by themselves and by everyone employed in the practice. This duty also extends to the directors of a recognised body or a licensed body which is a company, or to the members of a recognised body which is an LLP. The Rules also extend this duty to the Compliance Officer for Finance and Administration (COFA) of a firm (whether the COFA is a manager or non-manager). Under r. 8.5(e) of the SRA Authorisation Rules 2011, the COFA must keep a record of any failure to comply with the Rules for production to the SRA on request, and also report any breaches to the SRA.

Breaches of the Rules must be rectified promptly upon discovery, including the replacement of money improperly withheld or withdrawn from a client account. The duty to remedy breaches rests not only on the person causing or discovering the breach but also on all the principals. This duty extends to replacing missing client money from principals' own resources, even if the money has been misappropriated by an employee or another principal and whether or not a claim is made on the solicitors' indemnity or the Compensation Fund.

The basic principle is that any money received from a client by a solicitor must be paid into a client account unless it is received in respect of a bill rendered to the client for time costs or disbursements that have already been paid by the solicitor. Money may only be withdrawn from a client account in accordance with the client's instructions, or to settle a solicitor's fee after a fee invoice has been given to the client. The money earmarked for costs in the office account becomes office money and must be transferred out of the client account within 14 days of the fee invoice being raised. There are more specific and prescriptive rules/definitions regarding the receipt and transfer of costs in r. 17.

The books of account maintained by the solicitor must show the current balance on each client's ledger and balances must be reconciled with the cash books and the bank statements every five weeks. The records must be kept for a period of six years and any bank statements must be kept as issued and printed by the bank. Further details are contained in r. 29.

45.2 Engagement letter

There is a formal requirement for engagement letters to be issued to and agreed with solicitors by the reporting accountant and both parties must keep these for six years after termination of the retainer. Rule 35 details a number of terms which need to be incorporated into the engagement letter. An example of suitable paragraphs for inclusion in the engagement letter is shown in **Table 2** below.

TABLE 2: Paragraphs to include in an engagement letter concerning whistle-blowing and other matters

In accordance with r. 35 of the SRA Accounts Rules 2011, we are instructed as follows:

(a)   I/this firm/this company/this limited liability partnership recognises that, if during the course of preparing an accountant's report:

    (i)   we discover evidence of fraud or theft in relation to money:

        (A)   held by a solicitor (or registered European lawyer, or registered foreign lawyer, or recognised body, or licensed body, or employee of a solicitor or registered European lawyer, or manager or employee of a recognised body or licensed body) for a client or any other person (including money held on trust); or

        (B)   held in an account of a client, or an account of another person, which is operated by a solicitor (or registered European lawyer, registered foreign lawyer, recognised body, licensed body, employee of a solicitor or registered European lawyer, or manager or employee of a recognised body); or

    (ii)   we obtain information which we have reasonable cause to believe is likely to be of material significance in determining whether a solicitor (or registered European lawyer, or registered foreign lawyer, or recognised body, or licensed body, or employee of a solicitor or registered European lawyer, or manager or employee of a recognised body) is a fit and proper person:

        (A)   to hold money for clients or other persons (including money held on trust); or

        (B)   to operate an account of a client or an account of another person,

    (iii)   we discover a failure by the firm to submit a qualified accountant's report to the Solicitors Regulation Authority, as required by these rules,

we must immediately give a report of the matter to the Solicitors Regulation Authority if required to do so under the *Solicitors Act* 1974, s. 34(9) or the *Legal Services Act 2007 (Designation as a Licensing Authority) (No. 2) Order* 2011, art. 3(1) as appropriate;

(b)   we may, and are encouraged to, make that report without prior reference to you;

(c)   we are to report directly to the Solicitors Regulation Authority should our appointment be terminated following the issue of, or indication of intention to issue, a qualified accountant's report, or following the raising of concerns prior to the preparation of an accountant's report;

(d)   we are to deliver to you our report which you should retain for at least six years from the date of its signature and to produce the copy to the Solicitors Regulation Authority on request;

(e)   you are to retain these terms of engagement for at least six years after the termination of the retainer and to produce them to the Solicitors Regulation Authority on request; and

(f)   following any direct report made to the Solicitors Regulation Authority under (a) or (c) above, we are to provide to the Solicitors Regulation Authority on request any further relevant information in our possession or in the possession of our firm.

To the extent necessary to enable us to comply with (a) to (f) above, you waive your right of confidentiality. This waiver extends to any report made, document produced or information disclosed to the Solicitors Regulation Authority in good faith pursuant to these instructions, even though it may subsequently transpire that we were mistaken in our belief that there was cause for concern.

45.2.1   'Whistle-blowing'

In addition to the accountant's obligations under money laundering regulations (see **Chapter 18**), the reporting accountant has a mandatory whistle-blowing duty if he discovers evidence of fraud or theft in relation to money:

- held by a solicitor (or registered European lawyer, registered foreign lawyer, recognised body, or licensed body, or employee of a solicitor or registered European lawyer, or manager or employee of a recognised body or licensed body) for a client or any other person (including money held on trust); or
- held in an account of a client, or an account of another person, which is operated by a solicitor (or registered European lawyer, registered foreign lawyer, recognised body, or licensed body, employee of a solicitor or registered European lawyer, or manager or employee of a recognised body or licensed body).

The mandatory whistle-blowing duty also applies if he obtains information which gives reasonable cause to believe it is likely to be of material significance in determining whether a solicitor is a fit and proper person to hold money for clients or other persons (including money held on trust), or to operate an account of a client or an account of another person.

The reporting accountant is encouraged to report directly to the SRA, without reference to the solicitors.

Matters which may indicate a requirement on the reporting accountant to report to the SRA include:

- false accounting, theft or misappropriation by any solicitor in the firm;
- evidence of theft or misappropriation by any employee, fee-earner, consultant or third party not reported to the police authorities;
- evidence leading to concerns about honesty or integrity of any solicitor;
- evidence of attempted tax evasion (either direct or indirect taxes);
- failure to properly control client money;
- failure to keep proper accounting records under the Accounts Rules which is so significant that the reporting accountant is unable to express an opinion in his report;

- failure to take professional advice without due consideration;
- evidence of indifference or recklessness in connection with client money or operation of a client's own account as signatory; or
- any other matters or indications of fraud or theft in connection with client money or operation of a client's own account as signatory.

Please note that the above indicators were taken from the Solicitor's Accounts Rules 1998 and not the SRA Accounts Rules 2011, but they are still considered to be good indicators of when a whistle-blowing obligation might arise.

45.2.2   Termination of appointment

The reporting accountant is also required to communicate with the SRA on the termination of his appointment where this has arisen from the issue of, or an indication of the intention to issue, a qualified accountant's report or following the raising of concerns prior to the preparation of an accountant's report.

45.2.3   Independence

Reporting Accountants must document any possible connections with the solicitors that may influence their independence.

Typical factors that should be considered include whether the reporting accountant, his principals, directors, members or employees of the accountancy practice:

- are related to the solicitor;
- normally maintain the solicitor's client accounts;
- place substantial reliance on the solicitor for referral of clients;
- are clients or former clients of the solicitor; and
- whether there are any other circumstances which may affect the reporting accountant's independence.

45.3   Procedures

As noted above, the SRA has made significant changes to the format of the accountant's report and to the Rules under which it is prepared.

SRA Accounts Rule 39, which previously included a wide range of prescriptive testing that a reporting accountant was required to undertake in order to provide the accountant's report, has been removed. A requirement has also been introduced for the reporting accountant to:

- determine for themselves what is the correct type and level of work to be performed for each particular law firm – based on their professional assessment of risk, the size of the law firm and the range of services provided; and
- qualify the report only in respect of 'material breaches of the Accounts Rules and/or significant weaknesses in the firm's systems and controls for compliance with the Accounts Rules'.

To replace SRA Accounts Rule 39, a new Rule 43A has been issued which states:

'43A.1 The accountant should exercise his or her professional judgement in determining the work required for the firm they are instructed to obtain the report on in order to assess risks to client money arising from compliance with these rules. This should cover the work that the accountant considers is appropriate to enable completion of the report required by the SRA at the date the report is commissioned.'

The most notable impact from the new Rule 43A is that it now falls to the reporting accountant, to decide on the actual work and to report based explicitly on risk assessment and judgment. Previously, this was determined (to a large extent) by the prescriptive requirements under Rule 39.

The latest accountant's report (AR1) together with guidance notes prepared by the SRA can be located at www.sra.org.uk/AR1.

Accountants should closely consider both the contents of the new form and the guidance notes and examples of what are considered likely to be qualifications contained therein prior to completing SRA Accounts Rules engagements for periods ending on or after 1 November 2015.

The SRA has emphasised that the examples in the guidance are intended to be helpful but are not definitive nor prescriptive, and the reporting accountant is expected to exercise professional judgment in completing the AR1 accountant's report form, whether qualified or not.

In practice, reporting accountants will need to be more focused on the systems and controls and documenting their methodology to support both the type of work they are undertaking and the volume in the context of the risk profile of their client.

Under the new Rule 43A, more time will be required at the planning stage in tailoring any work programmes used to match the specific law firm involved. This will be important to ensure that the work is directed in the most appropriate areas for the law firm concerned and its specific risk profile. It will also be important in terms of being able to justify to the SRA the sufficiency of the work undertaken.

Holding a planning meeting with the COLP (Compliance Officer for Legal Practice), COFA (Compliance Officer for Finance and Administration) and/or the firm's finance team is perhaps a useful source of information at the planning stage to identify and discuss risks with the client.

Under Rule 43A, there is an expectation that the Reporting Accountant will consider the control systems and procedures that a law firm has in place. This involves some consideration and work being directed to:

- documenting the control systems (both IT and non-IT controls);
- assessing their adequacy/effectiveness for their intended purpose; and
- testing the application of the control systems.

The SRA has confirmed that there is no intention within the new guidance to drive the work of the reporting accountant towards a controls-based approach. The SRA expects the reporting accountant to undertake a risk-based approach towards planning the work and expects substantive testing to form a significant element of the reporting accountants work.

The SRA require reporting accountants to assess compliance with the provisions of certain elements of the Accounts Rules. Work programmes will need to be modified to take these into account. These are specified in the new accountant's report. These provisions are:

- Rule 1 The overarching objective and underlying principles
- Rule 7 Duty to remedy breaches
- Rule 13 Client accounts
- Rule 14 Uses of a client account
- Rule 17 Receipt and transfer of costs
- Rule 18 Receipt of mixed payments
- Rule 20 Withdrawals from a client account
- Rule 21 Method of and authority for withdrawal from a client account
- Rule 27 Restrictions on transfers between clients
- Rule 29 Accounting records for client accounts.

If the circumstances outlined in Rule(s) 8, 9, 10,15, 16 and 19 are applicable, the accountant is required to assess compliance accordingly.

It will be for the reporting accountant to assess the nature and amount of work they should perform given the risk profile of the client. However, it seems likely that areas of work where historically few breaches have arisen would be considered low risk and therefore not reviewed in as much detail or depth as a high risk area. This will vary firm by firm and should be documented in the planning sections of the file.

The ICAEW technical circular provides some useful guidance on possible reduced areas of work and also where new work might need to be focused. For areas of work where historically few breaches have arisen, and hence which could be deemed low risk, less work may be required. Examples might include:

- checking transactions from the bank statements to transaction records or nominal ledger;
- detailed testing of bills of costs to transaction records;
- paid cheque testing;
- detailed transactional testing work at reconciliation dates; and
- reliance on bank audit letters at the two selected dates.

Conversely, more work may be required in the following areas:

- review of monthly client funds three way reconciliations across the year;
- greater focus on the office account and office account reconciliations as a source of breaches;
- review of client funds reconciliation to look for shortfalls/differences compared to the bank balances and how these are managed and dealt with (as opposed to the current regime of examining two specific dates in detail);
- reviewing instances of suspense accounts being used and compliance of their use with the SRA Accounts Rules; and
- testing treatment of old residual balances – specifically for sweeping up, acting as banker and charging of inappropriate expenses.

45.3.1   The role of the reporting accountant

In the vast majority of cases, reporting accountants will, when they carry out their work under the new regime, find the same sort of issues they have found in the past. There is also no reason to suggest that reporting accountants will start to identify different types of risks to client money or serious breaches.

If the reporting accountant had uncovered serious breaches previously, they would have been deemed reportable. The majority of issues identified by reporting accountants in the future will most likely be the same as have been found in the past – the key difference is that there is now guidance from the SRA, referred to above, to help reporting accountants conclude on which of the breaches/weaknesses they identify are material/significant and reportable to the SRA on revised AR1 accountant's report form, and which are reportable only to the law firm by way of management letter or discussions with the COFA and/or COLP. As noted in section **45.1.1**, the ICAEW has also issued a technical release TECH 16/15 AAF. This includes an appendix covering examples of material breaches and significant weaknesses in systems/controls. A further appendix discusses some of the most common, and in some cases potentially more serious, breaches of the Rules, with examples of potential conclusions on the qualification of an accountant's report.

As noted above, the most notable impact from the new regime is that it falls to the reporting accountant, under Rule 43A, to decide on the actual work and to report based explicitly on risk assessment and judgment. Previously, this was determined (to a large extent) by the prescriptive requirements.

A fundamental challenge for reporting accountants is that their perceived risk and exposure to the SRA will be deemed to be reduced if they qualify the accountant's report under the new regime. On the other hand, the reporting accountant may also come under pressure from law firms not to qualify the accountant's report and may not come to the same conclusion about whether a breach/weakness is considered material/significant or not.

In a situation where there was an adverse client fund issue with a law firm where no qualification had been issued in the accountant's report by the reporting accountant, the ICAEW have provided guidance which states that if the reporting accountant can demonstrate:

- a reasonable understanding of the systems, procedures, transactions and control systems that the law firm has in place and were operative in the relevant period;
- that they have planned and undertaken an appropriate level of work in completing the accountant's report; and
- that they have formed reasonable and well-supported conclusions based upon the information received and matters of concern identified,

the SRA would not take the view that the work they have performed nor conclusions reached were inadequate in the event that the law firm or the SRA subsequently identifies a risk to or actual loss of client funds in the law firm concerned.

45.4   Common breaches

The reporting accountant should ensure that he is aware of the following areas as part of his knowledge of the business, as they are the common areas in which solicitors breach the Rules. The ICAEW technical release referred to above provides other useful examples.

45.4.1   Debit balances

No client account may go into debit in the solicitor's ledger. Each client should be treated in isolation and it is not permissible to net off debits and credits on the client ledger. This would indicate a shortage of funds that should be disclosed.

The SRA does not allow debit balances to be offset against credit balances when stating the liabilities to clients as shown by the ledgers on the accountant's report form.

45.4.2   Client confidentiality

Solicitors may refuse to allow the accountant access to certain documents (privileged documents) on the grounds of client confidentiality (or privilege) and where this is the case the accountant should qualify the report, setting out the circumstances.

45.4.3 *'Without delay'*

'Without delay' is defined in the Rules as meaning, in normal circumstances, the day of receipt or the next working day. This means that solicitors must have procedures to ensure that cheque receipts are banked 'without delay'. Any cheques that are not banked within this time period will constitute a breach of the Rules.

45.4.4 *Receipt and transfer of costs – the '14 day rule'*

Rule 17.2 states that a bill of costs or other written notification of costs must be sent to the client if payment of the solicitors' fees is required from money held in a client account. Once Rule 17.2 is complied with (i.e. the bill or notification has been sent), the money earmarked for costs becomes office money and must be transferred out of the client account within 14 days.

Guidance note (vii) to r. 17 gives an example of when costs are 'properly' due under r. 17.2 and should be transferred out of the client account. Guidance note (viii) explains what is meant by 'earmarking' in r. 17.3, and deals with the issue where the firm wants to obtain clients' prior approval of its costs.

45.4.5 *Reconciliations*

Rule 29.12 states that a three-way reconciliation between the client cash account, statement/passbook and the client ledger account of the liabilities to clients must be undertaken at least once every five weeks.

45.4.6 *Prompt return of client money and residual balances*

Rule 14.3 states that client money must be returned to the client (or other person on whose behalf the money is held) promptly, as soon as there is no longer any proper reason to retain those funds. Rule 14.4 goes on to state that the client must be informed in writing of the amount of any client money retained at the end of a matter (or the substantial conclusion of a matter), and the reason for that retention. This also needs to be done in writing at least once every 12 months thereafter, again covering off the amount of client money still held and the reason for the retention.

The reporting accountant should be aware of the above and, if considered a particular risk at planning, should design procedures beyond just sample examination of files/matters. As well as discussing the firm's systems and controls to deal with this requirement, the reporting accountant might consider checking exception reports of residual client balances. It is likely the firm's system will be able to generate reports showing residual balances or client balances where no time has been charged for a certain period of time.

45.4.7 Providing bank facilities

Rule 14.5 states that banking facilities should not be provided through a client account. Payments into, and transfers or withdrawals from, a client account must be in respect of instructions relating to an underlying transaction or to a service forming part of normal regulated activities provided to clients. During testing, the reporting accountant should be alert to transactions not involving normal legal activities, such as payment of school fees on a conveyancing matter or banking of cheques on behalf of a client. It is likely that any such instances identified by the reporting accountant will lead to a qualification as firms are strictly prohibited from providing banking facilities.

45.5 Reporting

The accountant's report has to be prepared by an accountant who is a member of one of the Institutes listed in Rule 34.1(a) who is also a registered auditor, and strict rules for its compilation are set out in Part 6 of the Rules.

Although it is called an accountant's report, many of the procedures involved are of an auditing nature. The procedures in Rule 39 previously made the work slightly less judgmental as the reporting accountant was obliged to carry out a number of prescribed tests. However, with the removal of this rule, the work is now even more akin to an audit with a higher degree of judgment in both the type of work to be undertaken and the classification of any breaches identified as material or not. The work is still restricted to an examination of both client and office ledgers and the related bank accounts, and it does not involve the audit of a profit and loss account and balance sheet of the practice. No accounts have to be filed with the SRA.

The reporting accountant is no longer required to check that the solicitor's practice holds professional indemnity insurance for the period covered by the report.

The reporting accountant is also no longer required to complete a checklist covering the results of test checks, as prescribed by Rule 43. Along with Rule 39, as noted above, this rule has been removed.

The accountant's report requires details of:

- firm details – the names used by the firm or in-house practice from the offices covered by this report. This must include the registered name of a recognised body/licensed body which is an LLP or company, and the name under which a partnership or sole practitioner is recognised;
- the period covered by the report;

- firm COFA;
- any qualification; and
- matters of significance.

There is a box in section 2 of the accountant's report form to include details of material breaches of the Accounts Rules and or significant weaknesses in the firm's systems and controls identified by the reporting accountant. The details given should be sufficient to enable the SRA to understand the nature of the breach and will have a section for client comments on the breaches.

45.6　Future developments

Although there are no open consultations, the SRA has still said that it is working on a programme of reforming the rules. At the time of writing, no further details on future reforms have been issued by the SRA.

46 INVESTMENT BUSINESSES

46.1 Introduction

This chapter covers the audit considerations in respect of the financial statements for investment businesses. The guidance is taken from Practice Note 21 (Revised) *The audit of investment businesses in the United Kingdom* which was issued in December 2007. Paragraphs 180-263, Appendix 1 and Appendix 2 of Practice Note 21 were superseded by Bulletin 2011/2 *Providing assurance on client assets to the Financial Services Authority* although Bulletin 2011/2 has been superseded itself by the FRC's Assurance Standard *Providing Assurance on Client Assets to the Financial Conduct Authority* issued in November 2015 and effective for reporting periods commencing on or after 1 January 2016.

Practice Note 21 also covers auditors' reports to the regulator, which are covered in **Chapter 9** 'Reports to regulators in the financial sector'.

Other than as noted above, Practice Note 21 has not been updated for the revisions to ISAs following the IAASB's clarification project or subsequently, or for any other changes that have taken place in this industry since 2007. This should be borne in mind when referring to guidance in the Practice Note. References to ISAs within this chapter have, however, been updated to the most recent version.

The *Financial Services Act* 2012 abolished the Financial Services Authority (FSA) with effect from 1 April 2013 and split its responsibilities between the Prudential Regulation Authority (PRA) and the Financial Conduct Authority (FCA).

46.2 Rules and reporting requirements

Investment businesses incorporated in United Kingdom are subject to the same requirements of the Companies Act for a statutory audit of financial statements as any other company. The scope of the audit is no different, but some regulated businesses are not able to take advantage of the exemptions available for small and medium-sized entities.

In addition to the requirements for a statutory audit, investment businesses are governed by:

- the *Financial Services and Markets Act* 2000 (FSMA 2000), which sets out regulatory objectives covering:
  - market confidence;
  - public awareness;
  - the protection of consumers; and
  - the reduction of financial crime;

- various European Directives including:

  - Markets in Financial Instruments Directive (MiFID) which allows cross border trading across EEA member states without obtaining separate authorisation in each country;
  - Capital Requirements Directive which sets out the minimum amounts of regulatory capital which must be maintained by member firms;
  - Undertakings for Collective Investment in Transferable Securities Directive (UCITS) which allows firms to sell UCITS schemes in other EEA member states without registering in those jurisdictions; and
  - Alternative Investment Fund Managers Directive which regulates fund managers that manage alternative investment funds (essentially hedge funds and private equity funds) ('AIFs').

Under FSMA 2000, Pt. X, the FSA had the power to make rules, the primary objective of which is investor protection. The main categories of the FSA Rules which have now been adopted by the FCA and PRA are:

- High Level Standards to ensure that firms follow the regulator's Principles for Business and meet Threshold Conditions as well as ensuring that those within the firm performing Controlled Functions meet the requirement of the Approved Persons regime;
- Prudential Standards consisting of financial rules, designed to ensure that the business is financially sound, has appropriate controls and is able to meet its commitments;
- Business Standards consisting of:

  - Client Assets rules, requiring segregation of money and investments held for clients and also covering arrangements for custody;
  - Conduct of Business rules, to ensure that the business deals fairly, honestly and with due skill, care and honesty with its clients;
  - Market Conduct rules, containing the code of market conduct, price stabilising rules, interprofessional conduct and endorsement of the takeover code;

- Regulatory Process rules, containing details of the authorisation, supervision, enforcement and decision making processes; and
- Redress rules, covering dispute resolution, compensation and complaints against the business.

Compliance with the regulator's Rules is monitored in a number of ways, the principal ones being:

- internally, by the business itself;
- by submitting regular returns to the regulator;
- by monitoring and inspection by the regulator;
- reports to the regulator by the business' auditor.

Auditors constitute an important part of the system of supervision; as well as reporting on the financial statements which are submitted to the Regulator, they issue reports in relation to:

- whether the entity has complied with the rules concerning client assets; and
- interim profits for capital adequacy purposes.

The Practice Note splits these reports into three types:

- the audit of financial statements;
- review reports on interim profits; and
- reports to the regulator.

The audit of financial statements and the review of interim profits are discussed further in this chapter. **Chapter 9** contains details about reporting to the FCA in relation to client assets, in addition to guidance on ad hoc reporting to the regulator as set out in Section B of ISA (UK and Ireland) 250 (Revised June 2016).

The use of the CREST system of online share settlement means that auditors of investment businesses which are CREST users, such as stockbrokers, fund managers or custodians, need to understand the nature of the system. Guidance for auditors was originally provided by Audit 2/96 *Guidance for auditors of CREST users*, issued by the Audit Faculty of the Institute of Chartered Accountants in England and Wales. Although this guidance is no longer extant, the issues it raised are still relevant to the auditor and are discussed in **46.6** below.

46.3 The audit of financial statements

The Practice Note sets out guidance for the audit of financial statements on an ISA-by-ISA basis. This chapter sets out some of the major areas of which to be aware when auditing an investment business.

46.3.1 Overall objectives of the auditor and the conduct of an audit in accordance with ISAs

In addition to the ethical guidance issued by auditor's professional bodies, there are additional independence rules laid down by the regulator. Therefore, auditors should be aware of the increased threat to their independence and review these prior to accepting any regulated audit engagement.

46.3.2 Agreeing the terms of the engagement

The regulators' Rules have various requirements in relation to accepting engagements. There is no requirement for the auditor to be approved before he can be appointed. However, investment businesses must take reasonable steps to ensure that the auditor it is planning to appoint or has appointed, has suitable skills, experience and independence with the nature, scale and complexity of the firm's business and the requirements and standards under the regulatory system to which the business is subject.

To enable the business to assess the ability of an auditor, the regulator may seek information about the auditor's relevant experience and skills. They will normally seek such information by letter from an auditor who has not previously audited any regulated firm. The auditor should reply fully to the letter and the regulated firm should not appoint any auditor who does not reply to the regulator. The regulator may also seek further information on a continuing basis from auditors as it deems necessary.

Auditors should notify the regulator when they cease to hold office as auditor of an authorised firm.

The engagement letter may cover both the terms of engagement for:

- the client assets reports to the regulator; and
- the statutory audit.

If this is the case, it should be clear that the client assets report will be addressed to the regulator, not the directors to whom the engagement letter is addressed.

46.3.3   The auditor's responsibilities relating to fraud

Key indicators of potential fraud and error particularly relevant to investment businesses will include:

- backlogs in key reconciliations;
- inadequate segregation of duties between back, middle and front office staff;
- inadequate management understanding of complex products;
- inadequate definition of responsibilities and supervision of staff;
- inadequate whistle-blowing arrangements;
- high management and staff turnover;
- ineffective oversight of offshore operations;
- lack of an effective audit committee;
- ineffective personnel practices and policies;
- inadequate communication of information to management;
- scope for inappropriate revenue recognition or concealment of trading losses;
- ineffective regulatory compliance monitoring; and
- elements of remuneration packages linked to revenue or profits.

46.3.4   Consideration of laws and regulations

ISA (UK and Ireland) 250 Section A (Revised June 2016) – *Consideration of laws and regulations in an audit of financial statements* requires the auditor to perform procedures that identify possible or actual non-compliance with regulations which are central to the entity's ability to conduct its operations.

The ISA defines laws and regulations which are central to the entity's ability to conduct its business as those where either compliance is required to obtain a licence to operate, or where non-compliance could be reasonably expected to result in the entity ceasing to operate.

The Practice Note suggests the following procedures to help identify such possible or actual breaches of non-compliance for an investment business:

- obtain a general understanding of the legal and regulatory framework applicable to the entity and industry, and of the procedures followed to ensure compliance with the framework;
- inspect correspondence with the relevant regulators;
- review the business's Scope of Part IV Permission (a document which sets out the regulated activities that the firm is permitted to engage in, together with any limitations and requirements imposed on those activities);
- enquire of the directors whether they are on notice of any possible instances of non-compliance with law or regulations;
- include in the representation letter confirmation that the directors have disclosed to the auditor all those events of which they are aware which involve possible non-compliance, together with the actual or contingent consequences arising therefrom;
- hold discussions with the investment business's Compliance Officer and other personnel responsible for compliance; and
- review any work on compliance matters carried out by internal audit.

Two types of regulation are central to the investment businesses:

- prudential rules; and
- conduct of business rules.

The aim of the prudential rules is to ensure that regulated firms are adequately capitalised and to establish the minimum amount of such capital that must be held for the protection of clients. Typical procedures auditors may carry out include:

- enquiring how management ensure that the capital resources calculations are properly prepared and submitted on time;
- enquiring how management ensure that the firm complies with the capital resources requirements;
- examining the returns to see whether they show that the firm/group has a reasonable surplus of regulatory capital. This should include the period being audited and the future period as part of work on going concern; and
- reviewing relevant correspondence with the regulator.

The auditor has no direct reporting responsibility in respect of the conduct of business rules. However, any breaches of the rules may:

- lead to material fines and/or claims by investor; and
- cause the investment business to have its authorisation restricted or withdrawn, which will threaten its existence as a going concern.

Therefore, the auditor should be alert to any indications that management and staff are not monitoring compliance with these rules or that business is being conducted outside the scope of the company's authorisation.

46.3.5   Planning an audit of financial statements

The auditor will usually complete his work on the annual accounts at the same time as any other work required to report to the regulator, in an effort not to duplicate audit effort. The auditor must also ensure that his work is planned to meet the short timescales for reporting imposed by the regulator.

46.3.6   Identifying and assessing risks of material misstatement

The auditor must seek to understand the complex business and regulatory regime within which investment businesses operate. This will include:

- obtaining a general understanding of the applicable legal and regulatory framework and the procedures followed to ensure this framework is complied with;
- reviewing the firm's Scope and Permission Notice; and
- inspecting correspondence with regulators.

The Practice Note lists example procedures that the auditor may perform to assist him in understanding:

- the industry, regulatory and other external factors affecting the business, including the applicable financial reporting framework;
- the nature of the entity, e.g. the types of investment business undertaken, its risk management procedures, and the legal and operational structure of the entity;
- the selection and application of accounting policies;
- the entity's objectives and strategies and the related business risks;
- how the financial performance of the entity is measured and reviewed;
- how the entity has responded to risks arising from IT; and
- the control environment and control activities, so that they can assess the risk of material misstatement at the assertion level and design appropriate audit procedures.

Factors to be considered when assessing the control environment of an investment business are shown in **Table 1**.

TABLE 1: Factors to consider when assessing the control environment

- the nature and status of the investment business's clients and any changes in their status which may affect the application of investor protection requirements;
- a change in the market environment (e.g. an increase in competition);
- the introduction of new clients, products or marketing methods;
- claims made in promotional literature (particularly in relation to performance);
- the risk profile of the business undertaken by the entity;
- the complexity of products;
- the consistency, across geographical location, of products sold and methods used;
- the legal and operational structure of the investment business;
- financial and managerial support provided to and by any other group companies;
- the number of branches and sales offices;
- the use of appointed representatives;
- management's attitude towards control, regulation and investor protection;
- the roles and responsibilities allocated to the finance and compliance functions;
- the recruitment, training, competence and supervision of personnel; and
- the integrity, competence and experience of management.

Their understanding of the entity should then allow auditors to identify the risks of material misstatement at the financial statements and assertion levels, and to determine which risks are significant. Example risks which the auditor may conclude to be significant are:

- the valuation of investments, including derivatives, which could have a significant impact on the financial statements;
- breaches of the regulator's requirements;
- breaches of the terms of client mandates; and
- the calculation of performance fees to be paid by clients.

Investment businesses differ greatly in their size and the complexity of their operations, and therefore the reliance the auditor places on internal control systems varies. Where client assets exist, this is likely to be an area where detailed internal controls are relevant. Whilst client assets are not, in principle, part of the financial statements, any material deficiency could be indicative of poor control and may have an impact on the financial position of the business.

When the systems are designed, their dual purposes should be borne in mind. There are considerations both for the entity itself and for the protection of investors' interests. Detailed guidance on the requirements for the accounting records is included in each set of the regulators' Rules.

The auditor should not accept work that he is not competent to undertake and may consider using technical specialists for more involved areas – for example, when considering trades in complex products or for a business heavily involved in e-commerce. The use of specialists is particularly important in assessing valuations of particular derivative instruments for which there is no independent fair market valuation. Guidance on the use of specialists is given in section **31.3**.

46.3.7 The auditor's responses to assessed risks

In addition to tests of controls and general substantive tests, ISAs require that, where the auditor identifies significant risk of material misstatement, he should plan and perform specific substantive procedures to address that risk.

For investment businesses, significant risks may include:

- valuation of investments;
- liabilities for breaches of regulations, contract or mandate; and
- calculation of performance fees.

Valuation of investments

Year end positions may be valued by marking to market or at fair value. Where securities are traded openly their value can be ascertained with little judgment, and similarly where an unquoted security may be equated to an equivalent quoted security, its valuation can be easily verified.

However, other instruments which are more complex or do not have a readily ascertainable market value, may be valued using a complex model. In such cases, the auditor may require the input of an expert in such areas to determine whether the valuation is reasonable. Further details can be found in **Chapter 28**.

Liabilities for breaches

There are no substantive procedures that can identify breaches that the investment business or its advisors have not already identified. The auditor must rely on consistency of information from various sources, such as legal representatives, correspondence files, etc. and obtaining representations from management about the existence of any such liabilities.

Performance fees

The auditor should obtain an understanding of the investment business's systems and controls over performance fees. Tests of detail may include:

- confirming the basis of the performance fee calculation to the underlying agreement;
- agreeing the figures used in the performance fee calculation have been correctly extracted from the underlying records;
- reviewing the reasonableness of any estimates or underlying assumptions; and
- recalculating the performance fees.

Third party information may also be available to support the performance fee calculations.

46.3.8   Audit considerations relating to an entity using a service organisation

It is common for investment businesses to outsource some of their functions, including:

- safe custody of investments by a custodian;
- settlement or clearing of trades;
- maintenance of accounting records;
- product administration (such as unit trusts, savings schemes or ISAs); and
- investment management.

The auditor must consider where to obtain his audit evidence where activities are outsourced. Evidence may be obtained from the investment business itself, by contacting or visiting the third party, or by relying on the assurances of the third party's auditor. Investment business should take reasonable steps to ensure that, where applicable, each of its appointed representatives and material outsourcers give the auditor the same right of access to their accounting and other records as the firm itself is required to give to their own auditor. See further details on the auditor's consideration of the entity's use of service organisations in **Chapter 22**.

46.3.9   Analytical procedures

Analytical procedures for investment businesses may include comparison of:

- fees to funds under management and market indices; and
- commission income and expense to transaction volumes.

46.3.10   Auditing accounting estimates, including fair value accounting estimates, and related disclosures

Where independent fair market valuations are not available, accounting estimates are often used for valuation purposes. Where a mathematical model has been used, the auditor will review the process used to develop and test the model, as well as gaining an understanding of any assumptions used. The auditor should consider the reasonableness and consistency of the estimates, and also whether they conform with generally accepted practices.

Accounting estimates may also be used to establish liabilities for compensation payments to clients, for example, where funds have been priced incorrectly.

Further detail on the auditor's consideration of fair value accounting estimates is covered in **Chapter 28**.

46.3.11   Going concern

For investment businesses, the attitude of the regulator towards an entity and continuing authorisation of the entity are paramount to continuing as a going concern. Therefore, in considering matters related to going concern, the following items should also be considered:

- regulatory censures or fines;
- prudential capital shortages;
- non-routine visits from the regulator;
- reputation and other indicators; and
- general non-compliance with the regulator's Rules.

Any doubts about an entity's ability to continue as a going concern may be reportable to the regulator under the guidance in ISA (UK and Ireland) 250 Section B (Revised June 2016).

46.3.12   Written representations

ISAs require the auditor to obtain confirmation of the completeness of disclosure to the auditor of:

- all known actual or possible non-compliance with laws and regulations whose effects should be considered when preparing financial statements together with the actual or contingent consequences which may arise therefrom; and
- information provided regarding the identification of related parties and the adequacy of related party disclosures in the financial statements.

Possible additions to the standard management representation letter for investment businesses include:

- acknowledging management's responsibility for establishing and maintaining accounting records and systems of control in accordance with the regulator's Rules;
- confirming that management has made available to the auditor all correspondence and notes of meetings with the regulator relevant to the auditor's examination;
- that all complaints have been drawn to the attention of the auditor; and
- where applicable, representation that no client money or custody assets were held by the investment business.

46.4   High Level Standards and Conduct of Business Rules

Since 2013, investment businesses have been regulated by the FCA and subject to rules set out in the FCA's Handbook. This sets out High Level Standards and also contains Prudential Standards, Business Standards (Conduct of Business

Rules) and Specialist Sourcebooks applicable to different classes of investment business. Businesses that are subject also to regulation by the PRA must also comply with PRA rules.

The prime responsibility for ensuring compliance with, and reporting breaches of, the FCA's High Level Standards and Conduct of Business rules lies with the management of the investment business. The regulators perform periodic inspections of investment businesses to review compliance with the Rules.

The FCA's High Level Standards cover such matters as:

- Principles for Businesses;
- Senior Management Arrangements, Systems and Controls;
- Threshold Conditions;
- Statements of Principle and Code of Practice for Approved Persons;
- The Fit and Proper Test for Approved Persons;
- Financial Stability and Market Confidence;
- Training and Competence;
- General provisions; and
- Fees.

46.4.1   Impact on the audit

Auditors have no direct reporting responsibility in respect of the High Level Standards and Conduct of Business rules, although breaches of such rules may have implications for the financial statements of the investment business, other aspects of the annual reporting requirements, or ad hoc reports. Therefore some enquiry into possible breaches is called for. Examples of such situations are:

- rule breaches, which could give rise to fines or claims by investors; or
- a restriction or withdrawal of authorisation, which could threaten the business's viability as a going concern.

46.4.2   Audit approach

Staff involved in the audit should have a general understanding of the High Level Standards and Conduct of Business rules. They should assess the control environment that exists, considering such areas as:

- the adequacy of procedures and training to inform staff of the requirements of the FCA and to ensure that they meet those requirements;
- the adequacy of authorities and supervision;
- the review of compliance by senior management;
- procedures to ensure possible breaches are investigated by an appropriate person and are brought to the attention of senior management; and
- the authority of, and resources available to, the compliance officer.

Possible areas, outside client assets, where compliance problems commonly occur and may have an effect on the audit include:

- conducting business outside the scope of its authority: such action could result in fines, suspension or loss of authorisation;
- customer complaints: a significant level of complaints should put the auditor on guard;
- poor controls over appointed representatives: the business is liable for the acts of its representatives;
- personal dealings of its employees: the business could be liable if clients believe they are dealing with the business when in fact they are dealing with its employees;
- misclassification of customers as 'business' or 'private' investors: incorrect classification could result in claims;
- unauthorised deposit taking; and
- lack of or incomplete customer agreements.

It would normally be inappropriate to perform any direct testing for compliance with the High Level Standards and Conduct of Business rules, as it is beyond the auditor's responsibility. Ensuring compliance with such rules is part of the monitoring function of the regulator. However, the general steps that may be taken to assess the impact of any breaches on the auditor's report are:

- consideration of the investment business's compliance framework, including operational manuals and the documentation of its procedures and controls;
- review of the scope and results of the internal compliance monitoring and review;
- examination of the records maintained of any breaches and notifications to the regulator;
- examination of correspondence with the regulator and the results of the most recent inspection visit;
- review of the register of complaints from customers; and
- review of monitoring returns and questionnaires submitted to the regulator.

Where the auditor becomes aware of a possible breach of the High Level Standards or Conduct of Business rules, he should identify its cause and consider whether it imposes any reporting requirements on him.

The auditor should enquire of management and staff whether any breaches have occurred and obtain appropriate representations in writing from management.

46.5   Review reports on interim profits

All bodies subject to the Markets in Financial Instruments Directive are required to maintain adequate capital resources, as defined by the EC Capital Requirements Directive. The regulatory capital of an investment business is permitted to include interim profits as long as the interim profits have been verified. External auditors may be requested to perform this verification and report on interim profits for capital adequacy purposes. This verification is carried out under International

Standard on Review Engagements (UK and Ireland) 2410 – *Review of interim financial information performed by the Independent Auditor of the Entity*. Guidance on review of interim financial statements is given in **Chapter 39**.

An example review report is given in **Table 2**. This should be adapted where the entity is unincorporated, or a sole-trader, or where procedures have not been specified by the engagement letter.

TABLE 2: Example review report on interim profits for a regulated investment business

Review report by the independent auditors to directors of XXX ('the company')

Introduction

We have been instructed by the directors to carry out a review of the company's interim net profits report for the nine-month period ended 31 December 20XX.

This report has been prepared in accordance with our engagement letter dated [...] ('the Engagement Letter'). No person is entitled to rely on this report, unless such a person is a person entitled to rely upon this report by virtue of, and for the purpose of our terms of engagement, or has been expressly authorised to do so by our prior written consent. We do not accept responsibility to any other person or for any other purpose and we hereby expressly disclaim any and all such liability.

Directors' responsibilities

The interim net profit report is the responsibility of and has been approved by the Company's directors. The directors are responsible for preparing the interim net profit report in a form consistent with that adopted in the company's annual accounts having regard to the accounting standards applicable to such annual accounts.

Our responsibility

Our responsibility is to express to the directors a conclusion on the company's interim net profits for the nine-month period ended 31 December 20XX based on our review. We conducted our review in accordance with International Standard on Review Engagements (UK and Ireland) 2410, *Review of Interim Financial Information Performed by the Independent Auditor of the Entity*, issued by the Auditing Practices Board for use in the United Kingdom, and having regard to Practice Note 21 *The audit of investment businesses in the UK (Revised)*.

Scope of our Review

A review of interim financial information consists of making enquiries, primarily of persons responsible for financial and accounting matters, and applying analytical and other review procedures. A review is substantially less in scope than an audit conducted in accordance with International Standards on Auditing (UK and Ireland) and consequently does not enable us to obtain assurance that we would become aware of all significant matters that might be identified in an audit. Accordingly, we do not express an audit opinion.

> **Review conclusion**
>
> Based on our review, nothing has come to our attention that causes us to believe that:
>
> - the interim net profits have not been calculated on the basis of the accounting policies adopted by the company in drawing up its annual financial statements for the year ended 20YY;
> - those accounting policies differ in any material respect from the principles set out in International Financial Reporting Standards as adopted by the European Union; and
> - the interim net profits after tax amounting to £XXXk for the nine-month period ended 31 December 20XX (before dividends payable and share repurchases) are not reasonably stated.
>
> [Auditor]
>
> [Date]

46.6   CREST

CREST is the most commonly used commercial settlement system, however, the following considerations may apply to other settlement systems.

Auditors of entities which use CREST need to obtain an understanding of the nature of the processing system and the controls necessary to ensure that custody assets are properly safeguarded. They also have to be reasonably satisfied as to the assets' existence and ownership and year end balances for their statutory reports and those to the regulator concerning the keeping of adequate books and records.

The main areas where CREST may impact on the audit approach are:

- understanding the business; and
- evaluating internal controls.

46.6.1   Understanding the business

The following matters may need to be considered in seeking to comply with ISA (UK and Ireland) 315 (Revised June 2016) where CREST is used:

- the extent of the interaction between the entity and CREST, including:
  - whether securities are held as principal by the entity or whether the organisation conducts investment business on behalf of other clients as agents;
  - the volume and value of transactions settled;
  - the materiality of unsettled transactions and balances relative to the entity's financial position; and
  - its relationship with other parties within CREST;

- the manner in which the entity interacts with CREST, including:

  - the entity's status within CREST as a user, member or registrar;
  - the structure of the member's accounts that 'contain' the entity's investments;
  - details of the connection to CREST, such as gateway and network provider; and
  - the systems used to interact with CREST, whether standard interface, bespoke or off-the-shelf in-house systems.

Specialists, such as computer audit staff, may need to be involved to assess the systems in the first year that CREST is used by the entity, and the effort required is likely to be greater when in-house systems are used. Once the systems have been ascertained and documented, the guidance in ISA (UK and Ireland) 315 (Revised June 2016) (see **Chapter 21**) should be followed to develop an appropriate audit approach.

46.6.2 Evaluating internal controls

The types of internal controls which need to be considered in relation to CREST include:

- access and authorisation controls with regard to the CREST computer systems;
- adequate audit trail controls which identify CREST transactions;
- other IT controls such as security, disaster planning and authorised upgrading of the system;
- organisational and segregational controls over CREST transactions; and
- management controls such as reconciliations and follow-up of exception reports.

Auditors will need to consider controls at CREST as well as the procedures within the entity being audited in accordance with ISA (UK and Ireland) 402 *Audit considerations relating to an entity using a service organisation*. More reliance will need to be placed on CREST systems where the entity's records or systems are unreliable.

47 REGISTERED PROVIDERS OF SOCIAL HOUSING

The term Registered Providers of Social Housing (or Registered Provider) was introduced by the *Housing and Regeneration Act* 2008. The previous term, 'Registered Social Landlord' (RSL) was introduced by the *Housing Act* 1996. Registered Providers can now come from the profit-making sector as well as the traditional non-profit making sector. They can include housing associations, local housing companies, registered housing charitable trusts and housing care and support agencies. Local authorities managing social housing were within the regulatory framework for the first time from 1 April 2010. From 1 April 2010, a broader range of providers, such as profit-making organisations, were able to become registered providers. The entry of new forms of provider was intended to create greater competition and encourage innovation and the delivery of greater value for money by existing providers.

The *Housing and Regeneration Act* 2008 brought about a fundamental change to the way that housing and regeneration are regulated and funded, including the formation of the Homes and Communities Agency (HCA), the national housing and regeneration agency in England. Similar agencies exist for Wales, Scotland and Northern Ireland, with similar statutory objects to those applicable in England.

The HCA provides investment for new affordable housing and for improvements to existing social housing, as well as for regenerating land. The HCA is also the regulator for social housing providers in England. The focus of regulatory activity is on governance, financial viability and financial value for money as the basis for robust economic regulation. The HCA also sets consumer standards and can intervene in cases of serious detriment that have caused, or are likely to cause, harm. The HCA operates throughout England, including a regulatory role in London. However, responsibility for housing and regeneration activity in London lies with the Greater London Authority.

The statutory objects of the HCA, as listed in the *Housing and Regeneration Act* 2008 are to:

- improve the supply and quality of housing in England;
- secure the regeneration or development of land or infrastructure in England;
- support in other ways the creation, regeneration or development of communities in England or their continued well-being; and
- contribute to the achievement of sustainable development and good design in England, with a view to meeting the needs of people living in England.

The HCA has the power to do anything it considers appropriate for the purposes of its objectives or for purposes incidental to those purposes. It also has a wide range of specific powers relating to the provision, facilitation and acquisition of housing and infrastructure. Much of its work is focused on proactive risk-based economic regulation, i.e. governance and financial viability alongside an increased onus on value for money. While the HCA continues to set consumer standards, the primary responsibility for resolving issues now rests with social housing providers and their tenants at a local level. The *Localism Act* 2011 limits the HCA to a reactive role, only intervening in cases of serious detriment that have caused, or are likely to cause, harm. All the regulatory standards are set out in the *Regulatory Framework Requirements* which can be found at *www.gov.uk/ government/collections/regulatory-framework-requirements*.

These are important documents for auditors of Registered Providers of social housing to be familiar with, covering:

- regulatory requirements – what registered providers need to comply with;
- codes of practice – to amplify any economic standard to assist registered providers in understanding how compliance might be achieved;
- regulatory guidance – provides further explanatory information on the regulatory requirements and includes how the regulator will carry out its role of regulating the requirements.

The regulatory requirements include:

- Economic standards:
  - governance and financial viability (accompanied by a Code of Practice);
  - value for money;
  - rent;
- Consumer standards:
  - tenant involvement and empowerment;
  - home;
  - tenancy;
  - neighbourhood and community;
- Registration requirements;
- De-registration requirements;
- Information submission requirements;
- The accounting direction for private registered providers of social housing from April 2015;
- Disposal Proceeds Fund requirements;
- Requirement to obtain regulator's consent to disposals;
- Requirement to obtain regulator's consent to changes to constitutions.

Each standard sets out the high-level outcome that landlords should achieve, followed by a series of 'specific requirements' related to that outcome.

There is also regulatory guidance as follows:

- Regulating the standards;
- Rent standard guidance (part of) and associated guidance documents;
- Registration guidance and application form guidance notes;
- De-registration guidance;
- NROSH+ guidance documents;

- Guidance on intervention, enforcement and use of powers;
- Guidance for constitutional consents, restructuring and dissolution;
- Disposal Proceeds Fund guidance;
- Disposing of Land, and application form guidance notes;
- Procedural guidance notes for constitutional changes.

The approach of the HCA continues to be one of 'co-regulation' which means an expectation of robust self-regulation by the boards and councillors of registered providers who govern the delivery of housing services, incorporating effective tenant involvement.

Of particular note are requirements in relation to:

- records of assets and liabilities – particularly those liabilities that may have recourse to social housing assets;
- risk flows in group structures;
- stress testing of business plans against identified risks and combinations of risks across a range of scenarios;
- certification of compliance with the Governance and Financial Viability Standard within the annual report; and
- a Code of Practice designed to amplify the requirements in the Governance and Financial Viability Standard.

The above is not a comprehensive list of all new requirements and so, auditors should obtain a copy of relevant regulatory documents from the HCA's website.

47.1   Existing audit guidance

47.1.1   Practice Note 14

On 30 January 2014, the Financial Reporting Council issued *Practice Note 14 The audit of housing associations in the United Kingdom*. This provides guidance for auditors on the audit of housing associations in the light of the landscape in which the social housing sector now operates. Guidance for auditors was previously issued in 2006 and withdrawn in 2012 pending this revision.

The latest Practice Note contains the following four principal sections:

- background information about the social housing sector to provide context for the other three sections below;
- a description of the four devolved regulatory regimes, focusing on the interface between the regulator and the auditor and the regulators' viability assessments. Four appendices summarise the regulatory background relating to each regulator;
- a description of generic business risks that could adversely affect a housing association from achieving its objectives or successfully executing strategies. These are also risks which may give rise to a risk of material misstatement in a housing association's financial statements; and

- a discussion of audit risks, primarily arising from the above generic business risks, which the auditor is likely to need to pay particular attention to. This section is written in the context of special considerations relating to the audit of housing associations which arise from those ISAs (UK and Ireland) which are listed in the contents of the Practice Note. The Practice Note does not provide any material where there are no special considerations arising from an ISA.

In April 2016, the FRC issued a suite of revised ISAs (UK and Ireland) (see **1.6.4**). At the time of writing, however, Practice Note 14 had not been updated and still referred to the previous version of ISAs. References to ISAs within this chapter have, however, been updated to the most recent version where applicable.

47.1.2   Regulatory Circulars and Good Practice Notes

From 1 April 2010, changes to the regulatory framework for social housing in England resulted in the withdrawal of the majority of Circulars and Good Practice Notes that the sector had been accustomed to following.

Regulatory guidance which was applicable to the audit of Registered Providers in England included:

- Good Practice Note 7, *External audit of housing associations* – (GPN 7);
- Circular 04/07: *Requirement to submit external audit management letters and responses*;
- Circular 07/07: *Internal Controls Assurance*; and
- Good Practice Note 15: *Demonstrating internal controls assurance in housing associations* – (GPN 15),

all of which are now withdrawn. The Regulator has indicated that the above Circulars and Good Practice Notes will be subject to appropriate archiving provisions and they will continue to be available on request or through an online archive. Therefore, whilst they no longer have a place within the regulatory framework, they will continue to be useful sources of reference for good practice in the short to medium term.

Social housing providers in Wales, Scotland and Northern Ireland will have similar guidance in respect of external audit and internal controls assurance.

47.2   Background

47.2.1   The nature of Registered Providers of Social Housing

Most existing Registered Providers are not-for-profit housing associations, managed under the oversight of a board or committee of management, independently from local and central government. They provide social housing accommodation (usually made available at less than market rents and allocated to applicants in greatest housing need) and other related services. Councils managing social housing are also registered providers as are profit-making organisations where they are managing social housing.

Registered Providers operate under a variety of legal frameworks, including co-operative and community benefit societies, limited companies and charitable trusts. They are required, under legislation, to have an annual independent audit, although the specific auditing requirements will vary depending on the legal status. For example, some may be eligible to apply exemptions applicable to small companies, charities and co-operative and community benefit societies. For community benefit societies, for example, the *Co-operative and Community Benefit Societies Act* 2014 sets out criteria to disapply the requirements for appointment of auditors depending on certain financial thresholds and other factors. Advantage of these exemptions is only possible if permitted under the Rules under which they are incorporated.

Auditors of Registered Providers must be registered auditors, i.e. eligible under the *Companies Act* and registered with a supervisory body recognised under companies legislation.

Registered Providers undertake new building, refurbishment of existing property, acquisition of existing satisfactory properties or regeneration activities, with the aim of providing affordable, low cost rented accommodation. Some provide more specialised housing, including care and support, student accommodation and key worker accommodation. Under certain conditions such housing may be sold to tenants (e.g. right to buy, right to acquire and shared ownership). Increasingly, larger Registered Providers are involved in commercial development for outright sale and the private rented sector.

Registered Providers which are housing associations may be constituted in various ways, for example, as:

- co-operative and community benefit societies (either as exempt charities or non-charitable); or
- limited companies (either as registered charities or non-charitable).

As a result, auditors must understand the statutory framework of their social housing clients as this will affect audit reporting requirements. This does differ slightly between England, Wales, Scotland and Northern Ireland. The majority of Registered Providers in the United Kingdom are registered with the HCA under the *Housing and Regeneration Act* 2008 and the term given to that body is the 'Regulator'. Under certain pieces of legislation, the Regulator has the power to determine the accounting requirements of Registered Providers which will be important for the auditor to understand.

The constitution of Registered Providers or the legal rules under which they are incorporated usually prohibit them from distributing any surpluses or assets to shareholding members, even if they are non-charitable. Non-profit making organisations that are registered providers are required to have within their objects:

- the provision of social housing;
- not-for-profit status; and
- non-distribution of assets to members.

The majority of Registered Providers are co-operative and community benefit societies and most reference is made to a consolidating piece of legislation, the *Co-operative and Community Benefit Societies Act* 2014. As co-operative and community benefit societies, they fall under the administrative jurisdiction of the mutual societies division of the Financial Conduct Authority (FCA). This means that their constitution comprises 'Rules' which must be registered with the FCA. They will be governed by a board which is appointed by the members. The *Co-operative and Community Benefit Societies Act* 2014 contains some basic requirements for the accounts and audit. It requires proper financial records to be kept and that all financial statements agree with those records, that there is a satisfactory system of internal control over transactions and that the financial statements show a true and fair view of the social housing provider's financial position. Co-operative and community benefit societies which are charitable are known as exempt charities which means that they are subject to the *Charities Act* but are not regulated by the Charity Commission.

Co-operative and Community Benefit Societies Act 2014

The above Act was introduced as a Bill in the House of Lords on 19 December 2013 with the aim of consolidating the legislation relating to co-operative and community benefit societies (previously known as industrial and provident societies). The Bill became law in May 2014 and came into force on 1 August 2014 as the *Co-operative and Community Benefit Societies Act* 2014.

The law on co-operative and community benefit societies is complex and had become out of date. The previous *Industrial and Provident Societies Act* 1965 was a consolidation of earlier legislation and had been amended and supplemented by other Acts and secondary legislation. The new 2014 Act consolidates the 1965 Act and subsequent legislation to modernise and simplify the language of earlier legislation. It also omits provisions that no longer have any practical effect.

The outcome of the above is that registered providers of social housing which were previously industrial and provident societies have now become community benefit societies. Many Acts which govern these entities were consolidated into one Act. The changes introduce increases in the cap per member for withdrawable share capital, allow for troubled societies to enter insolvency rescue proceedings, gives the FCA additional powers to investigate societies and makes electronic submission of documents simpler.

Registered Providers which are limited companies are incorporated under the Companies Act and are generally companies limited by guarantee without share capital. They will therefore need to comply with the *Companies Act* 2006 but also the accounting directions issued by the relevant regulator, e.g. the HCA. Registered Providers that are charitable companies are also regulated by the Charity Commission but as Registered Providers, the Statement of Recommended Practice in the social housing sector takes precedence over the Charity SORP.

47.2.2   Responsibilities of the Board or the Committee of Management

Although day-to-day management of the Registered Provider may be delegated to subcommittees or staff, the board retains full responsibility for seeing that those functions are properly carried out.

The roles and responsibilities of the board normally include:

- defining and monitoring compliance with the governing documents, values and objectives of the Registered Provider;
- establishing plans to achieve those objectives;
- approving each year's budget and financial statements prior to publication;
- establishing and overseeing an appropriate framework of delegation and effective systems of control;
- taking key decisions on matters that will, or might, create significant risks for the Registered Provider;
- monitoring the performance of the Registered Provider in relation to these plans, budgets and decisions;
- appointing and, if necessary, dismissing the chief executive and being represented in the appointment of key second tier managers;
- appointing and agreeing the remuneration of the auditor;
- satisfying themselves that the affairs of the Registered Provider are conducted lawfully and in accordance with performance standards set by the Regulators; and
- overseeing the Registered Provider's relationship with its regulatory body.

Useful guidance is available through various representative bodies, such as the National Housing Federation (NHF) in England (www.housing.org.uk). The mission of the NHF is to support and promote the work that housing associations do and campaign for better housing and neighbourhoods. Examples of guidance for those charged with governance include:

- *Code of governance – Promoting board excellence for housing associations (2015 edition)*;
- *Board members' resource pack*; and
- *Leadership and control: a governance manual for board members.*

The NHF produces many other publications for housing associations covering:

- finance;
- assurance;

- development and regeneration;
- housing management;
- care and support;
- legislation;
- asset management and maintenance; and
- equality and diversity.

47.2.3 Responsibilities of audit committees

Whilst formally withdrawn on 1 April 2010 as a result of the changes to the regulatory framework, the October 2004 Housing Corporation publication *'Improving the Effectiveness of Audit Committees: a Good Practice Guide'* is still helpful. This publication addresses how audit committees can operate effectively and contribute to good governance in housing associations. It is also useful guidance for external auditors covering areas such as:

- understanding what goes into external audit management letters;
- assessing auditor performance and effectiveness;
- the independence of the auditor; and
- the audit committee's role with regard to accounting policies;

The guidance covers many other areas regarding good governance and internal audit arrangements.

47.2.4 Financial reporting requirements

Law and regulations

The financial statements of Registered Providers are prepared in accordance with the requirements of applicable law and regulations contained in accounting directions issued under the relevant statutes. The precise nature of the requirements is determined by two factors:

- how the Registered Provider is constituted (for example, as a registered charity, co-operative and community benefit society, or non-profit making company); and
- whether the Registered Provider is registered with a relevant regulatory body.

The *Housing and Regeneration Act* 2008 sets out the requirements for accounts and audit in s. 127–143.

Generally, each Registered Provider is required to prepare financial statements which give a true and fair view and hence should comply with applicable accounting standards. For example, the *Accounting Direction for Private Registered Providers of Social Housing from 2015*, issued in September 2015, sets out the accounting requirements that must be followed by English registered providers of social housing when preparing their annual accounts.

The 2015 accounting direction is essential reading for auditors and was updated in readiness for the switch over to FRS 102 financial reporting.

New UK GAAP

FRS 102 *The Financial Reporting Standard applicable in the UK and Republic of Ireland* has replaced pre-existing UK accounting standards and is applicable to registered providers of social housing.

A new Housing SORP was published in September 2014 in readiness for the changeover to new UK GAAP for financial years beginning on or after 1 January 2015. It is called *Housing SORP 2014 Statement of Recommended Practice for social housing providers*. Housing SORP 2014 is available from the National Housing Federation (www.housing.org.uk) and is essential reading for auditors of registered providers of social housing, especially in the context of new UK GAAP.

The changes introduced by FRS 102 and Housing SORP 2014 result in some of the biggest changes in financial accounting for registered providers in several decades. Many of these changes affect financial planning in the sector and potentially will have an impact on covenants contained in agreements with lenders. Examples of the more significant changes affecting registered providers are as follows.

- Categorising financial instruments into 'basic' or 'other'. This mostly affects those housing associations with complex debt instruments, especially standalone derivatives which require year end fair values to be recorded along with movements in fair value. Significant volatility through profit or loss could result with the outcome on reported results being influenced by the effectiveness of hedge instruments, including appropriate documentation.
- Social Housing Grant – historically, this grant has been shown on the face of the balance sheet as a deduction from the associated fixed asset housing property cost. Accounting for government grants under FRS 102 does not permit this accounting treatment. Housing associations have to consider whether certain performance conditions have been met and also the expected recommended practice for releasing such grant to income under a performance model or accrual model. Significant adjustments to opening reserves are expected from this change and likewise the impact on annual income and annual depreciation charges. Recycling of social housing grant will also have an impact on annual results which is not present under current UK GAAP.
- Fixed asset housing properties have to be separated into those which are held for social benefit and therefore categorised as property, plant and equipment and those which represent commercial lettings (e.g. shops, market rented accommodation) which will be shown at fair value. Any movement in fair value will be shown through profit and loss which is a change from current UK GAAP.

- Most registered providers are members of multi-employer defined benefit pension schemes, primarily the Social Housing Pension Scheme (SHPS). As a result, most have set up deficit funding plans which, under FRS 102, will require provisions for contributions payable to be carried on the balance sheet.
- New criteria for assessing and measuring impairment of fixed asset housing properties, including consideration of the service potential of these assets and alternative measures for value in use.
- Transitional reliefs available, most notably the use of 'deemed cost' for fixed asset housing properties and the impact on revaluation reserves, revenue reserves and accounting for related social housing grants. This in turn introduces decision-making regarding how much of a 'deemed cost' valuation is represented by non-depreciable land.

The above are just a handful of the changes along with new formats for the statutory accounts which the social housing regulator has prescribed in the *Accounting Direction for Private Registered Providers of Social Housing from 2015,* which takes into consideration the changes under FRS 102 and the new Housing SORP 2014.

47.2.5 Responsibilities of the auditor

Although Registered Providers may be subject to different legislation, the statutory duties of their auditor are similar. The auditor is required to:

- express an opinion as to whether the financial statements give a true and fair view and have been properly prepared in accordance with the appropriate statutory requirements; and
- state in the auditor's report:
    - where proper books of account have not been kept;
    - where a satisfactory system of control over transactions has not been maintained; and
    - if the financial statements are not in agreement with the books and records of the Registered Provider.

There may also be a requirement imposed by the relevant regulatory body to report to them on certain returns of Registered Providers, e.g. as requested by the HCA. Similarly with regard to funders, loan covenants may include the need for the auditor to report on compliance with financial covenants.

47.2.6   Features of social housing audits

Internal controls

Registered Providers are in receipt of substantial amounts of public funding in the form of grants and legislation requires the auditor to state in his report on the financial statements if the Registered Provider has failed to maintain a satisfactory system of internal control.

Other guidance

There are housing federations which represent the best interests of Registered Providers in the United Kingdom. Auditors should be aware of guidance issued by these federations, for example, codes of governance and finance updates.

The various UK regulators of registered providers of social housing also publish regular sector risk profiles. These focus on the financial risks that may cause a provider to fail to comply with economic standards, in particular, the viability element of the Governance and Financial Viability standard in England. The key message running through these sector risk profiles relates to the role and responsibility of boards to ensure effective governance and risk management is at the heart of their business. They highlight the importance of boards and executives in the co-regulatory environment. The same regulators often publish quarterly survey reports on the state of the social housing sector. These cover financial indicators for the sector as a whole covering areas such as income, rent arrears, void levels, asset sale values, borrowing headroom and capacity, development completions and exposure to standalone derivatives.

These sector risk profiles and quarterly surveys are essential reading for auditors to obtain an understanding of the wider operating environment in which registered providers operate.

The long-term nature of the business

The main income source, rents, is fairly predictable, and thus analytical procedures are often a useful audit tool.

Substantial debt financing

It is common for Registered Providers to have significant amounts of borrowing. Therefore, it is important for Registered Providers and their auditor to assess their medium-term financial forecasts to ensure that the going concern basis remains appropriate. Such debt financing brings with it loan covenant compliance requirements which are usually certified by the statutory auditor.

The Auditing Practices Board (APB) Bulletin 2008/1, *Audit issues when financial market conditions are difficult and credit facilities may be restricted* and the update in APB Bulletin 2008/10, is particularly relevant to Registered Providers (see **Chapter 37**). Both were triggered by the development in the financial markets commonly known as the 'credit crunch' and the worsening economic climate and were written to apply more generally to all entities with a focus on the possible risks of misstatement to the financial statements arising from:

- the possibility of the reduced availability of finance; and
- difficulties with valuing some assets for balance sheet purposes, especially those that are required to be measured at 'fair value'.

Concerns for Registered Providers stem from the impact of significant trading difficulties in the financial markets compounded by a reduction in liquidity plus the risks of developing properties for sale (both shared ownership and commercial outright sale), which in turn could impact on loan covenant requirements. Registered Providers with HCA development partnering status and hence large property development commitments will be dependent on facilities from their lenders and may still have further facilities to negotiate when the auditor is considering the going concern basis.

Complex direct tax, indirect tax and employee tax rules

Registered Providers are heavily involved in property transactions and this brings with it complex corporation tax and VAT requirements. As many Registered Providers are charitable housing associations, they need to be aware of their primary purpose when considering property development contracts involving mixed tenure (e.g. developments where a scheme may include an element of commercial units and units for outright sale). Other examples of complexities include:

- group structures and most often the inability to be considered a group for tax purposes, i.e. group relief;
- conflicts between social housing accounting requirements under accounting standards, and the social housing SORP and the tax treatment, e.g. first tranche shared ownership sales;
- transfer pricing, loan relationships and gift aid which can add complexity;
- partial exemption treatment for VAT purposes;
- the use of development company subsidiaries outside the VAT group to maximise the recovery of VAT on professional fees;
- tax risks associated with joint ventures and the use of special purpose vehicles for acquiring land or undertaking property construction;
- potential difficulties for stock transfer associations in claiming input VAT on certain property refurbishment costs;
- the effect of employee tax for employees transferring from local authorities and tax deduction requirements on payments made to overseas landlords, e.g. under temporary leasing arrangements;
- construction industry scheme administration; and
- self-employed tax rules when using consultants, especially in busy property development departments.

Auditors should be aware of joint guidance issued in May 2009 by HMRC, the Charity Commission and the Homes and Communities Agency titled *Affordable*

Home Ownership – Charitable Status and Tax. This guidance was issued because Registered Providers increasingly venture into commercial activities which may not always fit with their 'primary purpose' or charitable status. The guidance sets out the authorities' understanding of what may or may not qualify as covered by the charitable tax exemptions and considers the question of whether particular individual families would be suitable beneficiaries. Registered Providers with home ownership activities such as shared ownership will be affected by this as will those developing residential property for outright sale. The guidance can be found on the Charity Commission's website at www.charity-commission.gov.uk and HMRC's website at www.hmrc.gov.uk.

There is also a Technical Note from the ICAEW on the payment of Gift Aid to charitable entities by subsidiary trading companies which could affect registered providers of social housing. The Technical Note addresses situations where the Gift Aid exceeds distributable profits of the trading subsidiary and could potentially lead to adjustments for prior incorrect payments. More information on this can be found on the ICAEW website at www.icaew.com/en/technical/charity-and-voluntary-sector/law-and-regulation/charity-commission/charity-commission-guidance-changed-for-payment-of-gift-aid-by-charity-subsidiary-companies.

Supported housing

Registered Providers involved in supported housing and providing care services have access to various sources of funding, e.g. in England, 'Supporting People'. A large amount of this funding is available through contracts with local authorities. These contracts can be complex and the available funding may not always be sufficient to deliver the service.

Housing properties

A significant number of Registered Providers including many established by means of Large Scale Voluntary Transfers, carry their housing properties at an existing use valuation. A professional valuation is obtained and, as set out in ISA (UK and Ireland) 620 (Revised June 2016) *Using the work of an auditor's expert*, the auditor considers the proper inclusion of the valuation in the accounts, the information on which the valuer has relied and the reasons for any changes in the valuation from the previous period.

Judgment is needed on the depreciation policy to be adopted in respect of housing properties. This covers the useful economic lives of housing properties which for most Registered Providers can cover long periods depending on property type, location and construction method. Determining the amount of cost attributable to land (which is not depreciated) and to buildings can be difficult where the properties have been in ownership for many years and records may not provide the split.

Capitalisation of works to existing properties

The principles within accounting standards are followed and further guidance is given in the social housing SORP. The SORP recommends that works which result in an increase in the net rental income stream should be capitalised as improvements. This may arise from works carried out to existing properties, through a combination of increased rents, reduction in future maintenance costs or a significant extension to the life of the property. It is often difficult to demonstrate that any enhancement of the economic benefits of tangible fixed assets is in excess of the previously assessed standard of performance anticipated when the assets were first acquired, constructed, last replaced or revalued and should be capitalised. Registered Providers also adopt component accounting but this has implications for record keeping. Component accounting requirements are clarified in the Housing SORP 2014.

Impairment

Accounting standards relevant to impairment are important considerations in social housing audits. Impairments can be triggered under many circumstances for a registered provider. There are quite different accounting considerations under old and new UK GAAP which have to be understood by auditors of social housing providers as these can result in material adjustments to the financial statements.

For old UK GAAP, impairment is clarified in the SORP Update 2010, and a supplementary Technical Note. For new UK GAAP under FRS 102, the new Housing SORP 2014 is relevant reading.

47.2.7   The auditor's relationship with the Regulators

The *Housing and Regeneration Act* 2008 sets out the general requirements in respect of accounts and audit. Section 127 of this Act sets out the powers of the Regulator to issue accounts directions for Registered Providers. Section 143 concerns the disclosure of information by the auditor to the relevant authority.

This section applies to information that a person has received while acting as auditor or as a reporting accountant of a registered provider. Such persons may disclose the information to the regulator for a purpose connected with the regulator's functions:

- despite any duty of confidentiality; and
- whether or not the regulator requests the information.

The reference to disclosing information includes expressing an opinion on it.

47.3   Audit engagement letters

Audit engagement letters are covered by ISA (UK and Ireland) 210 (Revised June 2016) *Agreeing the Terms of Audit Engagements*. Engagement letters should set out additional auditor responsibilities in relation to Registered Providers, which may arise:

- under statute – such as additional returns to be reviewed;
- from recommendations issued to Registered Providers within the various codes and other recommendations from the relevant regulatory body or relevant housing federation; or
- by agreement with the Registered Provider.

Statutory requirements may also result in additional returns which a Registered Provider may require its auditor to review or sign, such as service charge summaries under the *Landlord and Tenant Act* 1985. The recommendations made to Registered Providers by their regulatory bodies are not themselves binding on auditors, but Registered Providers and their auditor will generally agree to increase the scope of the auditor's work to ensure that the Registered Provider complies with best practice.

An example of an audit engagement letter is shown in **Table 1**.

TABLE 1: Extract from an example engagement letter for Registered Providers – drafted for a Community Benefit Society and should be amended for other types of constitution

To the Board of [name of Registered Provider]

The purpose of this letter is to set out the basis on which we are to act as auditors of the association and the respective areas of responsibility of the Board, comprising of those charged with governance of the association, and of ourselves.

Financial statements, accounting records and internal controls

As members of the Board of the association, you are responsible for maintaining adequate accounting records and an appropriate system of internal control for the association. You are also responsible for preparing the annual report and the financial statements which give a true and fair view and have been prepared in accordance with applicable accounting standards; the *Co-operative and Community Benefit Societies Act* 2014 and, where the society is the parent of a group, the *Co-operative and Community Benefit Societies (Group Accounts) Regulations* 2014; the *Housing and*

Regeneration Act 2008; and the most recent applicable Accounting Determinations and/ or Accounting Directions as periodically issued. Failure to fulfil these requirements can result in your disqualification from the office of director, a fine or imprisonment.

In preparing the financial statements, you are required to:

- select suitable accounting policies and then apply them consistently;
- make judgments and estimates that are reasonable and prudent; and
- prepare the financial statements on the going concern basis unless it is inappropriate to presume that the association will continue in business.

You are responsible for keeping adequate accounting records that:

- show and explain the association's transactions;
- disclose with reasonable accuracy at any time the association's financial position; and
- enable you to ensure that the financial statements comply with the *Co-operative and Community Benefit Societies Act* 2014 and, where the society is the parent of a group, the *Co-operative and Community Benefit Societies (Group Accounts) Regulations* 2014; the *Housing and Regeneration Act* 2008; and the most recent applicable Accounting Directions as periodically issued.

You are also responsible for safeguarding the assets of the association and hence for taking reasonable steps to prevent and detect fraud and other irregularities.

As the board, you have a duty to prepare a board report for each financial year. You should have regard to the relevant Statements of Recommended Practice and Accounting Direction.

It is usual for a statement of your responsibilities to be included in the board report or elsewhere in the annual report. If no such statement is made, we are required to include one in our report.

You are responsible for filing the financial statements with the registrar and with other regulators within the requisite time limits. Failure to do so can result in action being taken against yourself and the association.

You are responsible for ensuring that the association complies with laws and regulations that apply to its activities, and for preventing non-compliance and detecting any that occurs.

You are required by law to make available to us, as and when required, all the association's accounting records and related financial information, including minutes of management and board meetings, that we need to do our work. We are entitled to require from the officers of the association such information and explanations we think necessary for the performance of our audit. We are also entitled to attend all general meetings of the association and to receive all notices of, and other communications relating to such meetings.

In addition, we ask that you provide high-speed internet access to our engagement team, if practicable, while working on the association's premises. This provision will serve to facilitate the progress of our work and minimise costs to you by enabling the audit partner and other team members to collaborate and share information efficiently.

Disclosure of information to auditors

You agree that the members of the board, having made enquiries of fellow members of the board and the association's auditors, will state in the board report that:

- so far as they are aware, there is no relevant audit information of which the association's auditors are unaware; and
- they have taken all reasonable steps they ought to have taken as board members in order to make themselves aware of any relevant audit information and to establish that the association's auditors are aware of that information.

Electronic publication

We recognise that you may wish to publish your financial statements and our audit report on your website or distribute them by means such as e-mail. If you choose to do so, it is your responsibility to ensure that such publication properly presents the financial information and any auditors' report.

You agree to advise us of any intended electronic publication before it occurs, and we reserve the right to withhold consent to the electronic publication of our audit report if we assess the audited financial statements or our report to be published in an inappropriate manner.

The members of the board are responsible for the controls over, and security of, the website used for this purpose, and examination of these controls is beyond the scope of our audit of the financial statements. You are also responsible for establishing and controlling the process for electronically distributing Annual Reports and other financial information to members.

If you choose to publish our audit report electronically, the following wording must also be published:

> *'Financial statements are published on the association's website in accordance with legislation in the United Kingdom governing the preparation and dissemination of financial statements, which may vary from legislation in other jurisdictions. The maintenance and integrity of the association's website is the responsibility of the members of the board. The responsibility of the members of the board also extends to the ongoing integrity of the financial statements contained therein.'*

Access to audit working papers

Our working papers and other internal documentation created for the purpose of carrying out our duties as auditors belong solely to Example Firm LLP and will not be provided to you. We may however be required to give access to our audit working papers for regulatory purposes or because of other statutory obligations.

Where consolidated financial statements are produced, the Financial Reporting Council's staff may request access to audit working papers produced in relation to other affiliated or subsidiary parts of your group. This includes those entities located overseas, whether or not Example Firm LLP has acted as auditor. Where relevant, you agree to take all steps considered reasonable and necessary to ensure that your overseas affiliated and subsidiary entities comply with such requests.

Our responsibilities as auditors

Audit under the Co-operative and Community Benefit Societies Act 2014

The responsibility for safeguarding the assets of the association and for the prevention and detection of fraud, error and non-compliance with law or regulations rests with yourselves. However, we shall endeavour to plan our audit so that we have a reasonable expectation of detecting material misstatements in the financial statements or accounting records (including those resulting from fraud, error or non-compliance with law or regulations), but our examination should not be relied upon to disclose all such material misstatements or frauds, errors or instances of non-compliance as may exist.

Under the *Insolvency Act* 1986, you have a statutory duty of care to the creditors of the association. You must ensure that the association does not continue to trade if there is no reasonable prospect of avoiding insolvent liquidation. If during our audit, any factors come to our attention that indicate such a possibility we shall of course inform you. However, this will not relieve you of your statutory and other duties as members of the board.

The law requires us to report to the members of the association whether, in our opinion:

- the financial statements give a true and fair view of the state of the association's affairs and of its surplus or deficit for the year;
- the financial statements have been properly prepared in accordance with the relevant financial reporting framework; and
- the financial statements have been properly prepared in accordance with the *Co-operative and Community Benefit Societies Act* 2014 and, where the society is the parent of a group, the *Co-operative and Community Benefit Societies (Group Accounts) Regulations* 2014; the *Housing and Regeneration Act* 2008; and the most recent applicable Accounting Directions as periodically issued.

The law also requires us to consider whether:

- adequate accounting records have been kept by the association;
- the association has maintained a satisfactory system of control over its transactions;
- the association's individual accounts are in agreement with the accounting records and returns; and
- we have obtained all the information and explanations which we think are necessary for the purposes of our audit.

We will plan and perform our audit work to anticipate issuing an audit report in accordance with ISA (UK and Ireland) 700 and relevant auditing guidance as issued by the Financial Reporting Council from time to time. However, should we conclude it to be necessary, this audit report will be amended or modified in accordance with ISAs (UK and Ireland) 705 and 706 as appropriate.

We are required to read the other information issued with audited financial statements and to consider whether it is consistent with the financial statements. This other information would include, where applicable, a chairman's statement, operating and financial review, financial highlights, corporate governance statement, the board's statement on internal control, etc. If we become aware of any apparent misstatements or material inconsistencies with the financial statements, we draw these to your attention. We also draw to your attention any apparent misstatements of which we become aware during the work that we carry out to enable us to report that the information given in the board's report is consistent with the financial statements.

We also have a professional responsibility to refer in our report to instances of material non-compliance with applicable accounting standards. We do not need to refer in our report to those areas where, in our opinion, the non-compliance is necessary for the financial statements to show a true and fair view and is adequately disclosed.

Scope of audit

Our audit will be conducted in accordance with International Standards on Auditing (UK and Ireland) and will have particular regard to the FRC's Practice Note applicable to registered providers of social housing. It will include such tests of transactions and of the existence, ownership and valuation of assets and liabilities as we consider necessary. We shall obtain an understanding of the accounting and internal control systems in order to assess their adequacy as a basis for the preparation of the financial statements and to establish whether adequate accounting records have been maintained by the association. We shall expect to obtain such appropriate evidence as we consider sufficient to enable us to draw reasonable conclusions therefrom.

The nature and extent of our procedures will vary according to our assessment of the association's accounting system and, where we wish to place reliance on it, the internal control system, and may cover any aspect of the business's operations that we consider appropriate.

Because of the test nature and other inherent limitations of an audit, together with the inherent limitations of any accounting and internal control system, there is an unavoidable risk that even some material misstatements may remain undiscovered.

Our audit is not designed to identify all significant weaknesses in the association's systems but, if such weaknesses come to our notice during the course of our audit which we think should be brought to your attention, we shall report them to you.

We shall request sight of all documents or statements which are due to be issued with the financial statements.

Note that as set out in the Auditing Practices Board's Bulletin 2010/1 *XBRL Tagging of Information in Audited Financial Statements – Guidance for Auditors*, HMRC have mandated that when filing a Company Tax Return for accounting periods ending after 31 March 2010 and submitted to HMRC after 31 March 2011, the Company Tax Return, including the supporting statutory accounts and tax computations showing the derivation from those accounts of the entries in the Company Tax Return, must be delivered electronically using the Inline XBRL (iXBRL) format. If requested, we are able to provide assurance over the XBRL tagging of the information submitted; however, this work is not part of the audit and therefore is not within the scope of the engagement.

Representations by management/board members

From time to time, we may have to rely on oral representations by management, which are uncorroborated by other audit evidence. Where they relate to matters which are material to the financial statements, we will request that you provide written confirmation of them. In particular, where misstatements in the financial statements that we bring to your attention are not adjusted, we are required to obtain your reasons in writing.

Use of reports

As noted above, our report will be made solely to the association's members, as a body, in accordance with the *Co-operative and Community Benefit Societies Act* 2014, s. 87 and the *Housing and Regeneration Act* 2008. Our audit work will be undertaken so that we might state to the association's members those matters we are required to state to them in an auditors' report and for no other purpose. In those circumstances, and to the fullest extent permitted by law, we will not accept or assume responsibility to anyone other than the association and the association's members as a body, for our audit work, for the audit report, or for the opinions we form.

We shall not be treated as having notice, for the purposes of our audit responsibilities, of information provided to members of our firm other than those engaged on the audit (for example, information provided in connection with accounting, taxation and other services).

Once we have issued our report, we have no further direct responsibility in relation to the financial statements for that financial year. However, where a general meeting is held at which the financial statements are laid, we expect that you will inform us of any material event occurring between the date of our report and the date of that meeting.

Communication with those charged with governance

We will communicate certain information to you, including:

- any matters relevant to the firm's independence and the integrity and objectivity of the audit engagement partner and audit staff;
- an outline of the nature and scope of the work that we propose to undertake;
- our views about the qualitative aspects of the association's accounting practices and financial reporting;

- uncorrected misstatements other than those that are clearly trivial; and
- material weaknesses in internal control identified during the audit.

Such communication may be oral or in writing. However, we will report in writing any findings from the audit that we consider to be significant or to confirm that there are no matters that we wish to report in writing. Any such report may not be disclosed to third parties without our prior written consent. Such consent will be granted only on the basis that such reports are not prepared with the interests of anyone other than the association in mind and that we accept no duty or responsibility to any other party as concerns the reports.

Communication

In carrying out the engagement, it may be necessary for us to communicate with auditors of divisions and subsidiary, associated or joint undertakings and to arrange for them to perform such work as we consider necessary. As part of this process, we may request you to communicate with directors or management of divisions and subsidiary, associated or joint undertakings in order to explain and expedite the necessary procedures.

If the association operates any pension or post-retirement benefit schemes, it may be necessary for us to communicate with the association's actuary in connection with accounting entries and disclosures in the financial statements relating to such schemes. You hereby give us permission to communicate directly with the actuary in order to establish the basis and reliability of the figures and information in the financial statements on which we are required to report.

47.4   Quality control

ISA (UK and Ireland) 220 (Revised June 2016) *Quality Control for an Audit of Financial Statements* requires the engagement partner to be satisfied that the engagement team collectively has the appropriate capabilities, competence and time to perform the audit engagement in accordance with professional standards and regulatory and legal requirements, and to enable an auditor's report that is appropriate in the circumstances to be issued. For a registered provider of social housing, this should include:

- the scope and nature of the activities of the Registered Provider;
- the most significant parts of the relevant regulator's guidance; and
- the relevant general principles of the social housing SORP.

47.5   Responsibilities relating to fraud

ISA (UK and Ireland) 240 (Revised June 2016) *The Auditor's Responsibilities Relating to Fraud in an Audit of Financial Statements* is of relevance to social housing due to the nature of the sector's assets and activities. Registered Providers have been encouraged by their respective regulatory bodies to establish adequate internal controls and to report frauds over a certain limit to their regulator. All frauds should be recorded in a fraud register.

As part of his risk assessment, the auditor should review any disclosures to the regulator and enquire whether the regulatory body has responded.

Various external issues could influence a Registered Provider's objectives and strategies. The auditor should be aware of the increase in consolidation within the sector, the increased focus on efficiency and cost control, and the desire to become or remain a HCA development partner. The strategies being adopted by Registered Providers to manage these issues may result in an incentive for material misstatement of the financial statements. Registered Providers often also have significant borrowings with covenants attached (generally interest cover and gearing covenants). This may create pressures on the entity that, in turn, may motivate management to take action to improve the reported business performance, boost reserves for gearing purposes or to misstate the financial statements.

Where the auditor suspects that there may be any matters which he believes should be included in the fraud register, he should document his findings and, subject to any requirement to report them directly to a third party, raise them with senior management or a board member as soon as possible. He should also consider reporting the matter to the board and audit committee once he is aware of all the circumstances. When considering the appropriate person to discuss these matters with the auditor should bear in mind the management structure of the Registered Provider.

There is no requirement for the auditor to report suspected instances of fraud to a regulatory body unless he considers it a matter of public interest or, in the case of an unincorporated, non-exempt charity, he believes it would be a matter of material significance in the exercise of the Charity Commission's functions. Section **47.2.7** above on the auditor's relationship with the Regulators sets out the implications of reporting matters to the Regulator.

47.6   Laws and regulations

47.6.1   ISA (UK and Ireland) 250 Section A (Revised June 2016) – Consideration of Laws and Regulations in an Audit of Financial Statements

Section A is applicable due to the many types of law applicable in the social housing sector. The law relating to a specific Registered Provider depends on:

- whether the Registered Provider is constituted as a registered charity, a society registered under the *Co-operative and Community Benefit Societies Act* 2014 or as a non-profit making company; and
- which regulatory body has granted registration to the Registered Provider.

Although, as noted above, the regulations imply that the financial statements of a Registered Provider should be prepared in accordance with the social housing SORP, consideration must also be given to any specific requirements of its governing document.

The auditor should perform further audit procedures to help identify instances of non-compliance with those laws and regulations where non-compliance should be considered when preparing financial statements, specifically:

(a) inquiring of management as to whether the entity is in compliance with such laws and regulations;

(b) inspecting correspondence with the relevant licensing or regulatory authorities, e.g. the HCA; and

(c) enquiring of those charged with governance as to whether they are on notice of any such possible instances of non-compliance with law or regulations.

In the UK and Ireland, the auditor's procedures should be designed to help identify possible or actual instances of non-compliance with those laws and regulations which provide a legal framework within which the Registered Provider conducts its business and which are central to its ability to conduct its business and hence to its financial statements.

Laws and regulations which are likely to be central to a Registered Provider are those where a breach would have any of the following consequences:

- intervention by the regulatory body to direct the affairs of the Registered Provider – for example, non-compliance with the various laws relating to fraud and corruption under which the regulatory body possesses various powers of intervention;
- loss of necessary licences to continue a major element of the Registered Provider's work – primarily laws and regulations applicable to building and planning regulations or contaminated land, or health and safety regulations in relation to homes in multiple occupation; or
- financial effects resulting in liabilities which are likely to exceed the available resources of the Registered Provider – for example, expenditure or activities outside grant conditions imposed by the regulatory body which may lead to disallowance and repayment of grant.

Auditors of Registered Providers other than unincorporated charities have no statutory duty to report suspected or actual instances of non-compliance with the law or regulations to an appropriate authority, unless they believe it should be reported in the public interest.

In accordance with Practice Note 11, the auditors of unincorporated charities have a statutory duty to report actual or suspected significant instances of non-compliance to the Charities Commission (see **Chapter 43**).

Given the significant cash flows involved in the purchase and development of land, all Registered Providers should be aware of the risk of money laundering occurring. Regard should be given to the Money Laundering Regulations and Practice Note 12 (revised) (see **Chapter 18**).

Instances of non-compliance identified by the auditor should be reported to the appropriate level of management. However, if management are involved in the breach, the auditor may consider it appropriate to communicate with the Board.

47.6.2   ISA (UK and Ireland) 250 Section B (Revised June 2016)

Where a Registered Provider of Social Housing is regulated by the Financial Conduct Authority (FCA), it falls within the scope of Section B of ISA 250 *The auditor's statutory right and duty to report to regulators of public interest entities and regulators of other entities in the financial sector.*

The FCA took over regulation of consumer credit from the Office of Fair Trading (OFT) in April 2014. Many registered providers (or 'firms' as they are referred to by the FCA) held an OFT licence and following the change, registered for interim permission with the FCA. These firms are being invited to apply to the FCA for authorisation to continue carrying on regulated consumer credit activities. Firms must be authorised by the FCA, or have interim permission, to offer consumer credit.

The status of any firm can be checked, together with the permissions they hold, by searching the Financial Services Register.

Activities that meet the definition of regulated activities in a registered provider are wide and varied. This is a specialist area where legal advice is often sought by the registered provider when determining whether they plan to carry out regulated activities.

Not-for-profit bodies may be able to apply for the limited permission regime for the full range of their consumer credit regulated, which may reduce the requirements that a regulated firm is required to comply with.

Registered providers should be alert to the requirement to provide special reports to the FCA on a routine basis, if required, as set out in the FCA Handbook.

Section B of ISA 250 deals with the auditor's duty to report directly to a regulator information which comes to the auditor's attention in the course of work undertaken in their capacity as auditor of the regulated entity which might be of material significance to the regulator. This can relate to work undertaken in providing an audit opinion or other reports specified by the regulator or legislation.

Auditors are not required to actively perform additional procedures to identify such matters, however, they must remain alert to the possibility of such matters when performing audit work.

Auditors of registered providers should consider any additional terms to be added to standard terms of engagement to describe both auditor and board responsibilities in respect of the FCA regulation, alongside the internal policies of the audit firm in undertaking such work, for example, review of this area by an auditor specialising in Financial Services.

Further guidance on ISA (UK and Ireland) 250 Section B (Revised June 2016) is in **Chapter 9**.

47.7   Communication with those charged with governance

ISA (UK and Ireland) 260 (Revised June 2016) *Communication with those Charged with Governance* needs to be understood due to the governance structures within social housing providers. As responsibilities in Registered Providers are delegated by the Board to the management team, the auditor needs to consider to whom it would be most appropriate to address his reports. Whilst the management team may play a central role in the management of the Registered Provider, their powers come from the Board, and therefore, it is to the Board that the auditor will normally address his management letters.

The ISA sets out examples of areas to consider when communicating to those charged with governance:

- expected modifications to the auditor's report;
- unadjusted misstatements;
- significant deficiencies in the accounting and internal control systems;
- views about the qualitative aspects of the Registered Provider's accounting practices and financial reporting;
- matters specifically required by other ISAs to be communicated to those charged with governance, such as fraud and error; and
- any other relevant matters relating to the audit.

All UK social housing regulators required Registered Providers to send them copies of auditor's management letters, together with management's response although this requirement no longer appears to be mandatory under the *Regulatory framework for social housing in England from April 2015*. It is recognised that the management letter addresses only those matters which have come to the attention of the auditor in the course of his audit.

47.8   Planning an audit

Under ISA (UK and Ireland) 300 (Revised June 2016) *Planning an Audit of Financial Statements*, the auditor should obtain an understanding of the accounting principles and their impact on the audit, and the auditor should make use of internal controls, internal audit and reporting arrangements in place at the Registered Provider. At the planning stage, the auditor should be aware of any additional reporting requirements that he may have and plan his work accordingly.

At the planning stage, the auditor should identify any additional procedures or evidence which may be necessary for work on other reports, for example, on service charges and loan covenants.

The auditor should develop an audit plan for the audit in order to reduce audit risk to an acceptably low level and should also document the overall audit strategy and the audit plan, including any significant changes made during the audit engagement.

47.9 Identifying and assessing risks of material misstatement

Under ISA (UK and Ireland) 315 (Revised June 2016) *Identifying and Assessing Risks of Material Misstatement through Understanding the Entity and its Environment*, the auditor should obtain an understanding of relevant industry, regulatory, and other external factors including the applicable financial reporting framework for Registered Providers including:

- the Constitution of Registered Providers, regulation and financial reporting requirements;
- obtaining an understanding of the nature of the entity including the overall structure, regulated and un-regulated activities, finances, guarantees and governance of the Registered Provider;
- complex projects such as schemes developed under the Private Finance Initiative (PFI) and the accounting for such schemes in accordance with accounting standards;
- the development of social housing, housing for outright sale and market rented property, sometimes as part of the same overall scheme. Under such arrangements, surpluses generated on the sale of properties may be used to subsidise other social housing which may be developed without recourse to social housing grant or with lower levels of grant than would normally be the case;
- understanding a Registered Provider's selection and application of accounting policies and considering whether they are appropriate for its business and consistent with the applicable financial reporting framework and accounting policies used in the relevant industry, especially in relation to depreciation, capitalisation of works to existing properties and impairment;
- understanding a Registered Provider's objectives and strategies, and the related business risks that may result in material misstatement of the financial statements;
- measurement and review of a Registered Provider's financial performance given the considerable external benchmarking and performance review

including, for example, participation in benchmarking clubs, other comparative information published by the HCA and various league tables in the housing press;

- understanding of internal control relevant to the audit including the statutory requirement to report if the Registered Provider has not maintained a satisfactory system of control; the expectation (in Wales, the requirement) that the management letter will be passed on to the regulatory body; and any additional procedures that have been agreed with the client;
- requirements of the auditor in relation to control systems;
- the control environment including considering and understanding the entity's process for identifying business risks relevant to financial reporting objectives and deciding about actions to address those risks, and the results thereof;
- control activities which are of particular significance to Registered Providers; and
- assessing the risks of material misstatement relevant to Registered Providers.

47.10   Materiality

With regard to ISA (UK and Ireland) 320 (Revised June 2016) *Materiality in Planning and Performing an Audit*, consideration of materiality for Registered Providers does not differ fundamentally from that for other entities. However, the auditor should be aware that particular disclosures or expenditure categories may be sensitive and warrant extra attention, for example, directors' remuneration, restricted funds and bad debt provisions. There can be arguments for setting a specific materiality that is lower than financial statement materiality due to the hybrid nature of activity in a registered provider. This could include one specific lower level of materiality for income and expenditure account items and a higher financial statement materiality for fixed asset housing properties due to the magnitude of construction costs in the larger developing housing associations.

47.11   Responses to assessed risks

In accordance with ISA (UK and Ireland) 330 (Revised June 2016) *The Auditor's Responses to Assessed Risks*, when the auditor has determined that it is not possible to reduce the risks of material misstatement at the assertion level to an acceptably low level with audit evidence obtained only from substantive procedures, the auditor should perform tests of relevant controls to obtain audit evidence about their operating effectiveness. Many social housing activities involve a large number of small transactions, e.g. rental income. Auditors seek evidence to determine the completeness and accuracy of rental income. Where the auditor is satisfied, through evaluation and testing, that there are appropriate and effective controls, including, for example, the effective reconciliation of housing management and finance systems, he can use the results of this internal control testing as a source of audit evidence about the completeness and accuracy of recorded transactions.

When the auditor has determined that an assessed risk of material misstatement at the assertion level is a significant risk, the auditor should perform substantive procedures that are specifically responsive to that risk. Examples of significant business risks in the sector that could result in material misstatements can be found in Practice Note 14. In respect of a significant risk arising from capitalisation, the auditor considers whether the Registered Provider's policy, for example, on the types of works to be capitalised, as well as the approach to the capitalisation of internal development costs and interest, is in compliance with applicable accounting standards and the detailed interpretation set out in the social housing SORP. The auditor will then carry out detailed checks to ensure compliance with the policy.

Auditors of Registered Providers also need to consider the risks surrounding significant and complex transactions and other factors such as:

- property development work including:
    - incorrect allocation of costs to schemes;
    - cost overruns due to poor budgeting or unauthorised expenditure leading to costs in excess of the original project appraisal;
    - fraud risks arising from purchasing frauds, such as payment for services not supplied; or
    - collusion;
- lack of experience of the Registered Provider's staff in carrying out non-core activities;
- the complexity of the transactions, e.g. legal structures, guarantees, tax, accounting and complex funding arrangements;
- involvement of, and reliance on, third parties;
- viability arising from cost overruns, reductions in government support, over reliance on property sales, etc.; and
- issues relating to the vires of the Registered Provider.

47.12 Using a service organisation

Under ISA (UK and Ireland) 402 *Audit Considerations Relating to an Entity Using a Service Organisation*, where a Registered Provider makes use of a service organisation it does not alter the ultimate responsibility of the board or the audit committee to meet their legal responsibilities, neither does it diminish the auditor's responsibilities when reporting on financial statements.

Examples of activities undertaken by a service organisation may include:

- maintenance of the Registered Provider's accounting records;
- processing of the payroll;

- other financial functions which involve establishing the carrying value of items in financial statements;
- management of assets, including outsourcing of repairs, maintenance and development work;
- management of agency schemes;
- internal audit; and
- undertaking or making arrangements for transactions as agents of the user entity, e.g. property management contracts.

47.13 Audit evidence

In order for the auditor to obtain reliable audit evidence under ISA (UK and Ireland) 500 *Audit Evidence*, the information upon which the audit procedures are based needs to be sufficiently complete and accurate. For example, in auditing rental income and bad debt provisions, the auditor considers the accuracy of the ageing of rental debtors derived from the housing management system. Obtaining audit evidence about the completeness and accuracy of the information produced by the housing management system may be performed concurrently with the actual audit procedure applied to the information when obtaining such audit evidence is an integral part of the audit procedure itself.

In other situations, the auditor may have obtained audit evidence of the accuracy and completeness of such information by testing controls over the production and maintenance of the information. However, in some situations the auditor may determine that additional audit procedures are needed. For example, these additional procedures may include using computer-assisted audit techniques (CAATs) to recalculate the information.

Given the large number of housing properties owned and managed by Registered Providers, physical inspection is unlikely to be an appropriate means of testing existence. The auditor views or obtains confirmation of documents of title from solicitors or the Land Registry. Such tests do not establish that the valuation of properties is appropriate.

47.14 External confirmations

With regard to ISA (UK and Ireland) 505 *External Confirmations*, situations in which external confirmations may be used by Registered Provider auditors may include:

- bank balances and other information from bankers;
- loan balances and terms and conditions;
- balances with local authorities, agencies and other partners;
- property title deeds held by lawyers.

Confirmations are unlikely to be appropriate as a means of checking balances with tenants and leaseholders given the volume and size of individual balances.

47.15   Analytical procedures

When applying ISA (UK and Ireland) 520 *Analytical Procedures*, the income and expenditure of Registered Providers, and in particular, the levels of capital and maintenance expenditure, interest payable and rental income, are predictable. This facilitates comparisons with budgets, with other organisations in the sector and proof in total tests.

In addition, as Registered Providers are required to submit a number of returns to their Regulator, many publish a comprehensive range of information and data, which may assist the auditor by indicating trends and current ratios.

Examples of items to consider and features of data are detailed in **Table 2**.

TABLE 2: Analytical procedures

Capital and repairs and maintenance expenditure:

- movements and unexpected or unusual relationships between current and prior year capital programme, allocations, budgeted amounts and cash planning targets for acquisitions and disposals;
- comparison of the level of development department activity and professional fees with recorded additions to housing properties;
- major repairs grants and repairs costs in comparison to budget and previous years' costs;
- the ratio of repairs and maintenance to the cost of housing, land and buildings;
- comparison against prior year and expected amounts for construction costs per property;
- comparison of actual expenditure against costs in stock condition surveys;
- for special need housing, comparison of the ratio of care staff to the number of bed spaces;
- review of amount of grant as a percentage of development cost;
- movements on any suspense or construction in progress accounts;
- comparison of interest and overheads capitalised with prior years;
- comparison with external benchmark indicators.

Rental income:

- the relationship between the number of housing units available for occupation, the incidence of empty units and rents receivable;
- movements, and any unexpected or unusual relationships, between current and prior year budgets for rent received or service charges;
- movements, and unexpected or unusual relationships, between current year, prior year and budget for voids and bad debts as a percentage of rents;
- rents and service charges for each month.

> *Other income and administrative expenses:*
>
> - amounts are usually related to comparable information for prior periods;
> - amounts are usually directly comparable to other Registered Providers of similar size and nature;
> - some amounts are closely related to non-financial information such as the number of units, the number of employees and the size of office buildings.

47.16 Auditing accounting estimates

In applying ISA (UK and Ireland) 540 (Revised June 2016) *Auditing Accounting Estimates, Including Fair Value Accounting Estimates, and Related Disclosures*, the main areas where estimates are likely to be involved in the audit of Registered Providers are:

- depreciation of housing properties, and especially the estimated useful economic life;
- the level of bad and doubtful debt provisions against tenant arrears; and
- impairment provisions, including situations where existing use valuations are below net cost but the Registered Provider assesses the net realisable value of the property, after deducting any grants that would need to be repaid or recycled, to be higher than net cost. Further judgments may be required in order to determine whether an alternative measure of service potential may be more appropriate where assets are held for social purposes.

Fair value measurements and disclosures are most likely to apply to those Registered Providers who hold fixed assets at valuation but under FRS 102 also those with complex financial instruments and investment properties.

Under acquisition accounting, the identifiable assets and liabilities of the Registered Provider acquired should be included in the acquirer's balance sheet at their fair value at the date of acquisition. The auditor ensures that the valuation method and amount adopted is appropriately supported and properly reflected in the financial statements.

In principle the fair value of housing properties is the Existing Use Value Social Housing (EUV-SH) of these properties. The fair value of other assets and liabilities can be assessed in accordance with the requirements of FRS 102. The auditor considers whether the information provided is consistent with the financial records subject to audit.

47.17 Related parties

Under ISA (UK and Ireland) 550 *Related Parties*, the principles and procedures apply to the audit of Registered Providers as for other entities. In addition, those Registered Providers that are companies need to comply with relevant sections of the Companies Acts.

Subject to certain exemptions, members of the board and those associated with them, and those associated with senior managers, are not allowed to benefit financially from their connection with the Registered Provider. If there is any evidence of the existence of such related party transactions, then both ISA (UK and Ireland) 550 and ISA (UK and Ireland) 250 – Section A (Revised June 2016) – *Consideration of laws and regulations in an audit of financial statements* applies.

In England, auditors may take account of the results of any examination of related party transactions undertaken by the Regulator's review teams. However, such examinations do not remove the requirement for the auditor to obtain sufficient and appropriate audit evidence that material, identified related party transactions are properly recorded and disclosed.

The auditor considers in particular whether appropriate disclosure, as required by accounting standards, is made in the financial statements of transactions between the Registered Provider and board members. The provisions of accounting standards in the context of related parties and the Registered Provider's management, are applied to all members of 'key management' not just members of the board. Key management may be taken to include those persons having authority and responsibility for planning, directing and controlling the activities of the Registered Provider, directly or indirectly, including any director (whether executive or otherwise) or officer of that Registered Provider.

47.18   Subsequent events

Under ISA (UK and Ireland) 560 *Subsequent Events*, the requirements for the auditor to consider subsequent events do not differ for Registered Providers compared to other entities. Auditors should be aware, however, that in most Registered Providers, the non-executive board plays a crucial role in approving the financial statements. This may be a significant time after the formal audit clearance meeting has taken place.

47.19   Going concern

Registered Providers should normally prepare accounts on a going concern basis.

Under ISA (UK and Ireland) 570 (Revised June 2016) *Going Concern*, auditors should consider the circumstances in which Registered Providers may cease to continue in operational existence. This takes the same form as for other entities. The board has primary responsibility to make an assessment as to whether the going concern concept is applicable.

As Registered Providers have a relatively long business cycle, the board may need to consider a longer period than normal. This is likely to involve an assessment of the extent to which there may be adverse variations or uncertainties, and because of this, it may be appropriate for the auditor to obtain representations from the board on these. Where there are uncertainties, confirmation of particular sources of funds or revenues of the Registered Provider may need to be obtained by the auditor in the same way as confirmation of facilities may be required for a company.

Factors which may indicate a potential going concern problem are listed in **Table 3** below.

TABLE 3: Factors indicating potential going concern problems

- transfers of the entire housing stock, or a significant proportion of it;
- potential action from the regulatory body;
- for a transferee Registered Provider, transfers of housing stock where the acquisition cost or carrying value is not covered by the long-term projected net rental income;
- onerous contract terms;
- inability to service interest payments;
- a significant amount of variable interest rate borrowings at a time when interest rates are rising or are predicted to rise;
- a significant short-term repair liability that the Registered Provider will have difficulty in meeting from its own resources;
- loan repayments or refinancing which cannot be met from the Registered Provider's own resources;
- housing property development commitments which cannot be met from available Social Housing Grant, available loan facilities and property sales proceeds;
- breach of loan covenants; and
- significant loans to subsidiaries involved in activities such as shared ownership or developments for sale.

In assessing going concern, the board considers the extent to which there may be adverse variations from anticipated funding or revenue, or additional unexpected costs, and any uncertainties as to whether or not the Registered Provider can continue in operational existence for the foreseeable future. Typically, Registered Providers acquire properties with the assistance of grants or long-term borrowings. This method of financing leads to predictable cash flows in that loan repayments can be predicted and, accordingly, the Registered Provider should be able to plan to meet its obligations from available resources. Registered Providers have a relatively long business cycle and, in preparing its medium term financial forecasts, the board may consider a longer period of time than for other entities.

If there are any indications that a particular source of funds or revenue may need to be renewed or renegotiated, the auditor may elect to request the Registered Provider to contact the source of such funds for confirmation that the facility, or grant, will continue to be made available to the Registered Provider. Where there continues to be uncertainty, it may be necessary for the board to disclose the circumstances in the financial statements and for the auditor to draw attention to the matter within their report.

47.20　Written representations

In accordance with ISA (UK and Ireland) 580 *Written Representations*, the auditor may include in his representation letters confirmation that all minutes and correspondence with the regulatory body have been made available to him.

47.21　Using the work of internal auditors

ISA (UK and Ireland) 610 (Revised June 2013) *Using the Work of Internal Auditors* applies to auditors making use of any internal audit function in place at the Registered Provider. Larger Registered Providers are required to determine what is an appropriate internal audit function.

Although liaison with internal audit may reduce the extent of the external auditor's procedures, this is a matter for his professional judgment which should take account of the particular circumstances of the Registered Provider and the auditor's assessment of the internal audit function.

Auditors should also be aware of the ICAEW's Audit and Assurance Faculty guidance '*The Power of Three, Understanding the roles and relationships of internal and external auditors and audit committees*' which was published in May 2003.

47.22　Using the work of an auditor's expert

ISA (UK and Ireland) 620 (Revised June 2016) *Using the Work of an Auditor's Expert*, alongside ISA (UK and Ireland) 540 (Revised June 2016) *Auditing accounting estimates, including fair value accounting estimates and related disclosures* are likely to be relevant where properties are shown at a valuation. The SORP requires that valuations of social housing rented properties should be on the 'existing use value social housing' basis, and any departure from this basis should be disclosed in the accounts. Normal auditing considerations apply and these are dealt with in **Chapter 28**.

Another area where the auditor may rely on the work of an expert is where information is supplied by an actuary about the surpluses or deficits on defined benefit pension schemes.

With the introduction of FRS 102, financial instruments are likely to involve fair value accounting, and where these are complex such as in the case of derivatives, the auditor may rely on the work of a specialist treasury adviser appointed by the housing association.

47.23   The auditor's report on financial statements

An example unqualified report and responsibility statement in accordance with ISA (UK and Ireland) 700 *The Auditor's Report on Financial Statements* are shown in **Tables 4** and **5** respectively.

TABLE 4: Audit report for single entity registered provider of social housing that is a community benefit society[1]

Independent auditor's report to the members of Example Housing Association

We have audited the financial statements of (name of entity) for the year ended [...] which comprise [specify the primary statements such as the Statement of Financial Position, the Statement of Comprehensive Income, the Statement of Cash Flows, the Statement of Changes in Equity] and the related notes. The financial reporting framework that has been applied in their preparation is an applicable law and United Kingdom Accounting Standards (United Kingdom Generally Accepted Accounting Practice).

This report is made solely to the company's members, as a body, in accordance with the *Housing and Regeneration Act* 2008 and the *Co-operative and Community Benefit Societies Act* 2014. Our audit work has been undertaken so that we might state to the company's members those matters we are required to state to them in an auditor's report and for no other purpose. To the fullest extent permitted by law, we do not accept or assume responsibility to anyone other than the Association and the Association's members as a body, for our audit work, for this report, or for the opinions we have formed.[2]

Respective responsibilities of the board and auditors

As explained more fully in the statement of board responsibilities, the board is responsible for the preparation of the financial statements and for being satisfied that they give a true and fair view. Our responsibility is to audit and express an opinion on the financial statements in accordance with applicable law and International Standards on Auditing (UK and Ireland). Those standards require us to comply with the Financial Reporting Council's (FRC's) Ethical Standards for Auditors.

Scope of the audit of the financial statements

A description of the scope of an audit of financial statements is provided on the FRC's website at www.frc.org.uk/auditscopeukprivate.

Opinion on financial statements

In our opinion, the financial statements:

- give a true and fair view of the state of the Association's affairs as at [...] and of its surplus for the year then ended;
- have been properly prepared in accordance with United Kingdom Generally Accepted Accounting Practice; and
- have been prepared in accordance with the requirements of the *Co-operative and Community Benefit Societies Act* 2014, the *Housing and Regeneration Act* 2008 and the *Accounting Direction for Private Registered Providers of Social Housing* 2015.

Matters on which we are required to report by exception

We have nothing to report in respect of the following matters where we are required to report to you if, in our opinion:

- the information given in the Report of the Board for the financial year for which the financial statements are prepared is not consistent with the financial statements;
- adequate accounting records have not been kept by the Association, or returns adequate for our audit have not been received from branches not visited by us;
- the Association's financial statements are not in agreement with the accounting records and returns;
- certain disclosures of directors' remuneration specified by law are not made; or
- we have not received all the information and explanations we require for our audit.

XYZ LLP, statutory auditor

Town,

United Kingdom

Date

---

[1] This example is based on existing ISAs and has not been updated to reflect changes to audit reporting ISAs which will take effect for periods commencing 17 June 2016.
[2] This Bannerman paragraph is optional and the use of such a paragraph is further discussed in **4.22.**

TABLE 5: Example responsibility statement for Registered Provider board

The board members are responsible for preparing the report of the board and the financial statements in accordance with applicable law and regulations.

Community and Co-operative Benefit Society law and social housing legislation require the board members to prepare financial statements for each financial year in accordance with United Kingdom Generally Accepted Accounting Practice (United Kingdom Accounting Standards and applicable law). The board must not approve the financial statements unless they are satisfied that they give a true and fair view of the state of affairs of the Association and of the surplus or deficit of the Association for that period.

In preparing these financial statements, the board members are required to:

- select suitable accounting policies and then apply them consistently;
- make judgments and accounting estimates that are reasonable and prudent;
- state whether applicable UK Accounting Standards and Statement of Recommended Practice have been followed, subject to any material departures disclosed and explained in the financial statements; and
- prepare the financial statements on the going concern basis unless it is inappropriate to presume that the Association will continue in business.

The board members are responsible for keeping adequate accounting records that are sufficient to show and explain the Association's transactions and disclose with reasonable accuracy at any time the financial position of the association and enable them to ensure that the financial statements comply with the *Co-operative and Community Benefit Societies Act* 2014, the *Housing and Regeneration Act* 2008 and the *Accounting Direction for Private Registered Providers of Social Housing* 2015. They are also responsible for safeguarding the assets of the Association and hence for taking reasonable steps for the prevention and detection of fraud and other irregularities.

The board is responsible for ensuring that the report of the board is prepared in accordance with the *Accounting Direction for Private Registered Providers of Social Housing* 2015 and the applicable Statement of Recommended Practice.

Financial statements are published on the Association's website in accordance with legislation in the United Kingdom governing the preparation and dissemination of financial statements, which may vary from legislation in other jurisdictions. The maintenance and integrity of the Association's website is the responsibility of the board members. The board members' responsibility also extends to the ongoing integrity of the financial statements contained therein.

ISA (UK and Ireland) 700 also requires auditor's reports to contain any further matters required by statute or other requirements applicable to the particular engagement. For Registered Providers, these matters may be set out in a number of areas, depending on the legal form and jurisdiction of the Registered Provider:

- the *Housing and Regeneration Act* 2008, together with any Statutory Instrument or Accounting Direction or Order issued under the Act;
- the *Co-operative and Community Benefit Societies Act* 2014;
- the *Companies Act* 2006;
- the *Charities Act* 2011;
- the trust deed.

Of particular note is the requirement for Registered Providers to maintain adequate books and records and satisfactory systems of internal control which vary depending on the legislation under which they are formed. Auditors are required to report if this is not the case, and consideration should also be given to a qualification on the grounds of limitation of scope.

47.23.1   UK Corporate Governance Code and enhanced audit reporting

Registered Providers of Social Housing are required to disclose in their financial statements the code of governance that has been adopted (*Accounting Direction for Private Registered Providers of Social Housing 2015*). Most choose to adopt the NHF's *Code of governance: promoting board excellence for housing associations* in which case there are no additional audit reporting requirements. However, some choose to voluntarily adopt all aspects of the UK Corporate Governance Code, which necessitates a requirement for enhanced audit reporting. Those that 'cherry pick' some aspects of the UK Corporate Governance Code and make it clear that they do not intend to fully comply and do not include a compliance statement are unlikely to require enhanced audit reporting.

47.24   Other information in documents containing audited financial statements

Although there may be no statutory requirement for the auditor to review other information in Registered Provider annual reports, it is noted that 'one of the fundamental principles set out in the FRC's *The Auditors' Code* is that auditors allow their reports to be included in documents containing other information only if they consider that the additional information is not in conflict with the matters covered by their report and they have no cause to believe it to be misleading'.

Examples of other information that may be included are:

- statements by the patron, president, chair or chief executive;
- an operating and financial review;
- a statement concerning arrangements for corporate governance;
- the board's statement on risks and internal control;
- a treasurer's report;
- financial summaries; and
- projections of future expenditure based on planned activity.

Where an inconsistency is identified between other information and corresponding or related amounts or disclosures in audited financial statements and conclude that the other information should be amended, they discuss the matter with management or the board of the Registered Provider with a view to appropriate amendments being made.

47.25   Miscellaneous reports

For many of the returns on which auditors are asked to report the guidance provided by ISA (UK and Ireland) 700 can be adapted to suit the specific circumstances.

There are many returns where auditors are asked to report which will vary from one Registered Provider to another. Due to the variety, it is impracticable to list them in this guidance. Auditors should refer to guidance contained in ISA (UK and Ireland) 700 which can be adapted to such returns and also the ICAEW's Technical Release Audit 03/03 *Public Sector Special Reporting Engagements – Grant Claims* (see **Chapter 48**).

47.26   Service charge audits

The *Housing and Regeneration Act* 2008 updates the requirements for the provision of information to leaseholders and in respect of monies held for service charges in designated accounts. It effectively replaces certain sections of the *Commonhold and Leasehold Reform Act* 2002.

On 25 October 2011, the ICAEW published a Technical Release: Tech 03/11, *Residential service charge accounts – guidance on accounting and reporting in relation to service charge accounts for residential properties on which variable service charges are paid in accordance with a lease or tenancy agreement.*

The introduction to Tech 03/11 includes a section covering the scope of the guidance which states:

> 'Whatever the nature of the landlord entity (e.g. the landlord can be an individual, a partnership, a company or an industrial and provident society) [now community benefit society]), if that person is entitled under the terms of a lease to levy variable service charges on residential property, it is subject to the provisions of the *Landlord and Tenant Acts* (LTAs) 1985 and 1987 in relation to accounting for service charges. Therefore, this guidance is relevant to lessee-owned companies such as RMCs [residents' management company], as well as to large for profit companies and registered providers of social housing.'

The guidance covers the preparation of service charge accounts for issue to the tenants/leaseholders of residential properties and considerations for independent accountants' reports on service charge accounts. It sets out the alternative types of examination that may be undertaken by the independent accountant depending upon the terms of the lease. The type of engagement, which should be agreed between the accountant and the housing association, will depend on the terms of the lease and should be proportionate to the size and nature of the property/ scheme.

Section 3 of Tech 03/11 includes reporting guidance on service charge statements covering:

- audit;
- engagement to deliver a report of factual findings; and
- reporting under the *Landlord and Tenant Act* 1985, s. 21.

The appendices to the Technical Release provide further guidance on:

- comparison of audit to an engagement to report on factual findings;
- procedures for undertaking an audit of service charge accounts;
- work programme for making a factual report on service charge accounts;
- paragraphs for engagement letters;
- example paragraphs for a representation letter from landlord/managing agent to the reporting accountant; and
- example reports on service charge accounts covering:

  - audit report in accordance with ISA 800;
  - accountant's report of factual findings to the landlord.

48 PUBLIC SECTOR AUDITS

48.1 Introduction

In recent years, the accountability of central government departments and other public bodies has become a topic of increasing public interest. There has been continuing debate concerning their audit arrangements with increasingly more audits being carried out by private sector auditors.

In October 2010, the APB issued a further revision to Practice Note 10, *Audit of financial statements of public sector bodies in the United Kingdom*. The revised Practice Note replaces the previous revision from January 2006.

The October 2010 revision updated the guidance following the introduction of clarified ISAs (UK and Ireland) and also included legal and regulatory developments since January 2006.

As well as providing guidance on the application of each ISA (UK and Ireland) to public sector audits in the UK, the Practice Note also considers the role of the public sector auditor. Note, however, that the Practice Note has not been updated for revisions to ISAs since it was issued and does not reflect any changes to requirements arising from revisions to ISAs (UK and Ireland) that were issued in final draft form in April 2016 and that come into effect for periods commencing on or after 17 June 2016, see **1.6.4** for more details. In this chapter, references to ISAs (UK and Ireland) in guidance derived from the Practice Note have been updated where appropriate to reflect new names or changes to requirements.

Practice Note 10(I) (revised), *Audit of central government financial statements in the Republic of Ireland* was issued in 2011, updating and replacing guidance for public sector auditors in Ireland.

A number of earlier APB Bulletins relating specifically to public sector audits have now been withdrawn.

In 2010, the ICAEW issued Technical Release AAF01/10 *Framework Document for Accountants' Reports on Grant Claims* (see **48.27**). This guidance replaced Technical Release Audit 03/03 *Public Sector Special Reporting Engagements – Grant Claims*.

48.2 The role of the public sector auditor

Those responsible for public finance and for spending public money are accountable for ensuring that public business is conducted in accordance with proper standards and the law and that public money is safeguarded and properly accounted for. External auditors are an essential part of the process of accountability and make an important contribution to the stewardship of public money.

As part of this role, external auditors may be asked to give an independent opinion on the financial statements and may also review and report on aspects of the arrangements in place to ensure that resources are used economically, efficiently and effectively.

48.2.1   Auditor responsibilities

Public sector auditors are given authority to carry out their work by mandates which are embodied in legislation or set out in codes of audit practice. These mandates will vary according to the area of government being audited and geographical location.

Broadly, these mandates establish responsibilities in relation to:

- the financial statements;
- compliance with legislative and other authorities (also known as 'regularity');
- economy, efficiency and effectiveness ('value for money' or 'use of resources').

48.2.2   Financial statements

The legislative framework governing each public sector body sets out different requirements in relation to the preparation of financial statements. The requirements include:

- format of financial statements;
- period within which financial statements must be prepared;
- who the financial statements are reviewed by.

48.2.3   Regularity

For central government bodies in England, the external auditor has to report on whether transactions included in the financial statements conform with the legislation that authorises them. The Comptroller and Auditor General then satisfies himself that expenditure and income have been applied in accordance with Parliament's wishes and reports to Parliament accordingly. Similar requirements exist in Wales, Scotland and Northern Ireland.

A similar requirement also exists in England and Wales in relation to health authorities and other specified National Health Service entities which are consolidated respectively into the financial statements of the Department of

Health and the National Assembly for Wales. In Northern Ireland, this requirement exists for health and social service boards.

In other health entities and in local government, there is no requirement for the external auditor to report on regularity, but he should be alert to questions of legality and review the procedures in place to ensure the legality of transactions that might have a significant financial consequence. Any transactions or events of questionable legality coming to light as a result of this review should be reported to the appropriate authorities.

The auditor's responsibilities in relation to regularity are discharged at the same time as the audit of the financial statements and are covered in a separate part of the audit report.

Guidance on regularity for the auditor is set out in a separate section of the Practice Note. In particular, the section considers:

- understanding the regulatory framework;
- testing for regularity, including auditing compliance with European Union authorities; and
- regularity and reporting.

48.2.4 Other assignments

External auditors may also be asked to review and report on other information prepared by public bodies on aspects of their corporate governance and on their arrangements to secure economy, efficiency and effectiveness in their use of resources. This information may include:

- *performance information* – for central government, where external auditors are invited to report on such information by the Minister responsible;
- *grant claims* – external auditors act as agents of the Audit Commission when reporting on the extent to which a grant claim has been prepared in accordance with the requirements of the government entity and that the figures presented have been properly and fairly presented;
- *corporate governance* – most public sector bodies are required to include corporate governance statements in their financial statements;
- *best value* – auditors of local government in England and Wales are required to report on whether the public bodies' Best Value Performance Plans are prepared and published in accordance with legislation and statutory guidance;
- *economy, efficiency and effectiveness* – auditor's responsibilities vary between different parts of the public sector, and so auditors should review relevant legislation for details; and
- *standards of financial conduct* – public sector auditors are required to review and report on issues relating to standards of financial conduct in public bodies and aspects of the arrangements set in place by the audited body to ensure the proper conduct of its financial affairs.

48.3 Standards governing public sector audits

In most cases, public sector audits are carried out in accordance with ISAs (UK and Ireland), applied in accordance with guidance in PN 10 and PN 10(I) and supplemented by specific legislative requirements and guidance issued by national audit agencies.

The Practice Notes give auditors guidance on the application of each ISA to the audit of public sector financial statements.

48.4 Quality control

International Standard on Quality Control (UK and Ireland) 1 (Revised June 2016) (ISQC 1) is relevant in its entirety to the audit of financial statements of public sector entities. Practice Note 10 (Revised) provides additional guidance in relation to withdrawing from an engagement and threats to auditor independence.

In the public sector, under statute the auditor may not be able to withdraw from an engagement. In most cases, there is a duty to publicly report matters that would have otherwise caused withdrawal from the engagement.

If a national audit agency is appointed by statute, there is no option to withdraw from an engagement where threats to independence have been identified and other steps should be taken to reduce these threats. Where an audit firm has been appointed as an agent of a national audit agency, that agency will assess the firm's independence when it is appointed. The firm must comply with the requirements of ISQC 1 on independence when carrying out their work.

48.5 Overall objectives of the auditor and the conduct of an audit

The general principles of auditing are the same in both private and public entities, but auditors of public entities often have wider duties and further responsibilities laid down in legislation, directives and codes of practice. For example, for auditors of central government bodies in England, specified health entities and Probation Trusts, there is a statutory requirement to obtain evidence on compliance with authorities. In recognition of the importance of regularity to the audit of these entities, the auditor's report includes an explicit opinion on the regularity of transactions.

48.6   Agreeing the terms of audit engagements

The terms of the engagement will depend on the type of body being audited and the government agency responsible for the oversight of such audits. For many central government assignments, the terms of engagement are set out in legislation and no engagement letter is necessary although the auditor may choose to set out his understanding in such a letter, sometimes called a letter of understanding.

Where the legislation does not prescribe the terms, these may be covered in a detailed letter of appointment from the relevant national audit agency, rather than in a letter from the auditor. If the auditor chooses to send a letter, this will not replace the agency's letter. The agency's letter normally covers all the terms contained in a standard audit engagement letter. These terms and the nature of the engagement cannot be changed by the auditor.

48.7   Quality control for an audit of financial statements

ISA (UK and Ireland) 220 (Revised June 2016) requires an engagement quality control review of the audit of listed entities and public interest entities. In the public sector, audit teams should consider whether such a review is necessary for each client. Reviews are likely to be appropriate for larger, more complex entities or those with a high profile.

48.8   Audit documentation

In addition to the documentation requirements of ISAs (UK and Ireland) (see **Chapter 12**), auditors of public sector entities may have additional responsibilities with regard to confidentiality or the retention of working papers. These may be imposed by Statute, such as the *Official Secrets Act* 1989 and the auditor should be aware of these.

48.9   The auditor's responsibilities relating to fraud

The Practice Note provides additional guidance on:

- responsibilities of the entity and the auditor;
- fraud in the context of the regularity assertion;
- consideration of fraud risk factors;

- the auditor's other responsibilities relating to fraud and corruption; and
- reporting to third parties.

48.9.1   Responsibilities of the entity and the auditor

For central government entities, the Accounting Officer is usually the permanent head or senior full-time official of the entity and directs its management. They are personally responsible for ensuring that:

- proper financial procedures are followed;
- assets and public funds are properly managed and safeguarded; and
- funds are applied to the extent and for the purposes authorised by Parliament.

The entity's management are generally responsible for developing and maintaining effective controls to prevent fraud and detecting it when it does occur.

In local government, an officer is appointed to have responsibility for the arrangements for the proper administration of financial affairs. For health entities in England and Wales, the Accounting Officer and other directors are responsible for ensuring that:

- systems are in place to produce reliable financial information and adequate accounting records;
- there are controls in place over the security of financial systems and data; and
- there is a fraud and corruption policy and response plan in place.

Responsibilities in Scotland and Northern Ireland are broadly similar to England and Wales.

Under ISAs (UK and Ireland), the auditor should plan, perform and evaluate his work so as to have a reasonable expectation of identifying the risk of material misstatement arising from fraud and error. These requirements apply to audits of public sector entities as well as private entities, but they are extended in the public sector context to ensure a reasonable expectation of detecting material breaches of regularity arising from fraud or error.

48.9.2   Fraud in the context of the regularity assertion

Fraudulent transactions cannot, by definition, be regular and where material fraud is proven a qualification on the regularity assertion is necessary. Where the auditor suspects fraud, the matter should be discussed with management to discover whether the transactions are in compliance with the authorities which govern them. If management do not accept the views of the auditor, it may be necessary to communicate the matter to higher authorities and to modify the audit report. In the case of central government, such matters may also need to be disclosed in the accounts as a loss and special payment, if a specified threshold is exceeded.

48.9.3   Consideration of fraud risk factors

When gaining an understanding of the public entity and its environment, including its internal controls, the auditor should consider whether fraud risk factors are present. The risk of external fraud may be high if the entity is making grants to the public or collecting tax revenues.

Internally, fraudulent financial reporting may occur where bodies are required to meet externally set targets, such as where financial results affect performance ratings by an inspectorate.

48.9.4   The auditor's other responsibilities

Public sector auditors are required to have a wider regard to fraud and corruption than just the potential impact on the financial statements as addressed by ISA (UK and Ireland) 240 (Revised June 2016). These additional responsibilities include consideration of the financial aspects of corporate governance arrangements for local government and health entities in England and Wales, and review of Treasury and other appropriate guidance on corporate governance for central government auditors.

If the auditor becomes aware of fraud when addressing these additional responsibilities, he should also ensure that he considers the impact of these findings on the financial statements in accordance with ISA (UK and Ireland) 240 (Revised June 2016).

ISA (UK and Ireland) 240 (Revised June 2016) recommends that where the auditor encounters circumstances arising from fraud or a suspected fraud which bring into question his ability to continue with the audit, he should consider resigning. For public sector clients, the auditor cannot decline or withdraw from an engagement if he has been appointed by statute. There is usually a statutory requirement to make a public report about any matter which would have caused withdrawal, had such action been permissible.

The ISA requires the auditor to presume that a risk of material misstatement due to fraud will exist in relation to revenue recognition. For many public sector entities, this will not apply, and as with other entities where this presumption can be rebutted, this conclusion must be clearly documented.

48.9.5   Reporting to third parties

When considering whether to report a suspected or actual fraud, the auditor must have regard to:

- the relevant provisions that set out management's responsibilities for reporting fraud or other irregularity;
- the duties to report to a third party set out in the auditor's terms of engagement.

When management is implicated in the fraud, or refuses to report a fraud themselves, the auditor has a duty to report to third parties depending on the type of public sector entity involved. The different entities are set out in **Table 1**.

TABLE 1: Third parties to whom fraud may be reported

Public sector type	*Fraud reportable to*
Central government departments in England and Wales	The Treasury
National Assembly for Wales and its sponsored public bodies	The Compliance Officer of the National Assembly for Wales
Central government departments in Scotland	The Auditor General for Scotland
Central government departments in Northern Ireland	The Department of Finance and Personnel
Non-departmental public bodies and executive agencies	The sponsor department
Local government entities	The relevant authority as set out in ISA (UK and Ireland) 240 (Revised June 2016)
Health entities	Counter Fraud and Security Management Service.

48.10   Consideration of laws and regulations

ISA (UK and Ireland) 250 Section A (Revised June 2016) is concerned with laws and regulations that, if not complied with, may materially affect the financial statements. These fall into two categories, those which set out the form or contents of the financial statements and those which set the provisions under which an entity is allowed to conduct its business. The auditor is required to obtain a general understanding of both categories of laws and regulations. Where the auditor is required to report on compliance with certain provisions of laws or regulations, for example, the regularity assertion for public entities, then as well as being familiar with the law itself, he must test the entity's compliance with its provisions.

Auditors of local government and health entities have separate statutory responsibilities when matters come to their attention that indicate that unlawful expenditure has been or will be incurred or that a financial loss or deficiency will arise. This is irrespective of the potential for material impact on the financial statements. In addition, the auditor must report on the elements of the local government or health entities' corporate governance arrangements that relate to the legality of transactions which might have a financial consequence.

48.11   Communication with those charged with governance

In addition to the requirements of ISA (UK and Ireland) 260 (Revised June 2016), the Practice Note stresses the importance of reports to management as a means of reporting non-compliance with:

- regularity;
- propriety; and
- other official guidance to Accounting Officers.

Where matters relating to other duties and responsibilities are reported to management in the same letter as matters arising from the audit of the financial statements, the auditor must be sure that the letter still meets the requirements of ISA (UK and Ireland) 260 (Revised June 2016).

The Practice Note sets out the correct addressee of the management report for each type of public sector entity.

Public sector bodies may be required to make public communications, such as an annual audit letter, between the auditor and those charged with governance. Even where this is not the case, reports to management may come into the possession of third parties and the auditor may wish to include a caveat in any such report to make it clear that the report was not intended for third party use and that it should not be relied on for any purpose other than that for which it was prepared.

48.12   Planning an audit of financial statements

With regard to the overall audit planning, the Practice Note covers the additional matters which should be considered, including:

- the auditor's other responsibilities laid down in Statute or in the letter of appointment; and
- planning the audit of regularity.

48.13   Understanding the entity and its environment and the auditor's responses to assessed risks

Under ISA (UK and Ireland) 315 (Revised June 2016) *Identifying and assessing risks of material misstatement through understanding the entity and its environment* and ISA (UK and Ireland) 330 (Revised June 2016) *The auditor's responses to assessed risks*, the auditor is required to obtain an understanding of the relevant financial reporting framework and regulatory factors and their impact on the audit. These include the financial reporting framework and other regulations set out in:

- the specific legislation that has established the audited entity and determines its activities;
- accounts directions;
- Managing Public Money and the Government Financial Reporting Manual (now based on IFRS);
- other HM Treasury guidance on the application of accounting standards, the *Companies Act* and the disclosure of information;
- manuals for accounts of NHS entities; and
- relevant SORPs.

An additional consideration for public sector auditors is the additional assertion of regularity. When assessing risk for reporting on the regularity assertion, the auditor should consider the following specific factors:

- the complexity of the regulations;
- the introduction of major new legislation or changes in existing regulations;
- services and programmes administered under European Union authorities, where the framework of authorities may be complex;
- services and programmes delivered through third parties; and
- payments and receipts made on the basis of claims or declarations.

ISA (UK and Ireland) 315 (Revised June 2016) requires the auditor to obtain an understanding of an entity's business objectives and strategies and assess any resulting business risks. Public sector entities may have a number of additional business risks as a result of their closely regulated regimes, public reporting process and typically high number of transactions processed. The Practice Note highlights the following as possible significant risks in the public sector:

- financial transactions entered into by the entity in the period do not conform to the authorities that govern them (i.e. regularity);
- organisations issuing grants have been subject to fraudulent grant claims;
- the financial statements have been manipulated to meet externally set targets; and
- Private Finance Initiative transactions have not been accounted for in accordance with UK GAAP and guidance issued by HM Treasury.

In addition, as set out in ISA (UK and Ireland) 240 (Revised June 2016), there will be a significant risk relating to management override of controls and a presumed risk of fraud in revenue recognition, as is the case in audits of private sector entities.

48.14 Materiality in planning and performing an audit

When assessing the qualitative aspects of materiality, the auditor should consider the interest of the body to whom the audit report is addressed. When considering materiality, the auditor should consider any higher body into whose financial statements the results of the audited entity is being consolidated, to be the addressee of the audit report. The auditor should also be aware of any special considerations applying to the reporting of certain classes of misstatement when assessing the materiality of uncorrected misstatements.

Where public sector auditors have a responsibility to report on matters that do not affect the opinion on the financial statements, they may adopt an appropriate level of materiality for these items which differs from the materiality level applied to the audit of the financial statements.

The concept of materiality applies to the audit of regularity as to any other assertions in the financial statements. Where required to report on regularity, auditors need only to obtain sufficient evidence to give an opinion on whether expenditure and income has been applied for the intended purposes 'in all material respects'. As with other financial statements assertions, the assessment of materiality will include both qualitative and quantitative judgments. Materiality for the purposes of regularity reporting may be set at a level lower than that which is applied to the financial statements as a whole.

48.15   Using a service organisation

The requirement for public sector auditors to give an opinion on the regularity of transactions may require inspection of records maintained by service organisations beyond that in other audits. ISA (UK and Ireland) 402 does not automatically secure access rights to this information, and so it is important that the contract terms between the public sector entity and its service provider allow sufficient access by the entity's auditor.

48.16   Audit evidence

When testing the regularity assertion, the auditor plans and performs procedures to confirm that the entity's expenditure and income comply with the specific authorities governing them. The principles and procedures applied are the same as those applied in the audit of any other financial statements assertion. However, there may be particular considerations in relation to the design of audit procedures as the auditor may encounter difficulties obtaining reliable audit evidence in relation to some aspects of regularity, such as the eligibility for grants. For example, the auditor may require access to the records of a third party who has received the grant, to ascertain whether conditions for its grant have been met.

48.17 Initial audit engagements – opening balances

The Practice Note sets out additional guidance which is reproduced in **Table 2**.

TABLE 2: Additional guidance on the audit of opening balances

Nature of opening balances	*Additional guidance*
Opening balance amounts are clearly identifiable from the preceding period's audited financial statements for the transferring entity.	The auditor adopts the requirements of paragraphs 6 and 7 of ISA (UK and Ireland) 510 (Revised June 2016).
Opening balance amounts are not identifiable from the preceding period's audited financial statements for another entity, but have been derived from balances contained in those statements.	If relevant, the auditor discusses with the auditor of the predecessor organisation whether information is available that would provide substantive evidence for the opening balances. In the absence of such evidence, the auditor carries out substantive testing of opening balances to confirm they have been brought forward appropriately in accordance with the terms of the transfer, at an appropriate valuation in line with the accounting policies of the receiving body.
Opening balances have been calculated as part of a separate disaggregation/ merger exercise, subject to a separate specific review and report by an auditor.	The auditor considers the scope and outcomes of that separate review, and considers whether the conclusions can be relied on in accordance with ISA (UK and Ireland) 500.
	Where the work from the separate specific review cannot be used, the auditor considers carrying out substantive testing of opening balances in line with the box above.
Opening balances have been calculated as part of a separate disaggregation/ merger exercise, but not subject to separate specific review and report.	The auditor considers carrying out substantive testing of opening balances. Completeness of assets and liabilities, together with appropriate valuation can be risks in a disaggregation exercise, and engagement with the audited body is made at an early stage.

In the public sector, the predecessor auditor is expected by the national audit agencies to adopt a co-operative approach in the interests of efficiency and reducing the audit burden.

48.18 Analytical procedures

In addition to the relationships set out in ISA (UK and Ireland) 520, public sector auditors also consider relationships in two classes:

- programme expenditure and income; and
- management costs.

Each class has certain features that will influence the type of analytical procedures performed.

48.18.1 *Programme expenditure and income*

Programme expenditure and income relate to the actual function of the entity, for example, grant payments and health care treatments. These are:

- usually closely related to non-financial information such as the number of bodies in receipt of grant or persons receiving hospital treatment;
- not always directly comparable to prior periods because of changes to eligibility rules and government policy; and
- often comparable to expenditure plans included in published departmental or entity strategy.

48.18.2 *Management costs*

Management costs relate to the running of the entity and can be distinguished from programme expenditure as they are:

- usually related to comparable information for the prior period and are less subject to change as a result of government policy changes;
- closely related to information such as number of employees, size of buildings, etc.; and
- directly comparable to other entities with similar establishment sizes.

48.19   Related parties

The Practice Note provides little specific guidance on the audit of related party transactions for public sector entities. It does note, however, that related parties of these entities are subject to specific restrictions on the nature and scope of the transactions that they enter with the entity. Guidance varies for each part of the public sector and auditors should be aware of these restrictions.

48.20   Subsequent events

For central government entities, the auditor must also consider matters arising from relevant parliamentary procedures as part of his subsequent events review. The auditor should consult relevant legislation to determine the dates the financial statements are deemed to be 'issued' and 'laid before members', as this varies for each central government entity.

For auditors of local government and health entities, the auditor is required to give both an audit opinion on the financial statements and to:

- discharge certain other statutory responsibilities and duties; and
- issue a certificate ('audit completion certificate') confirming that the audit and all related responsibilities and duties have been completed in accordance with the legislation.

The issue of the audit completion certificate marks the end of the auditor's duties.

There may be a significant delay between the auditor completing the work on the financial statements and him being in a position to issue the audit completion certificate. The auditor should consider whether these additional statutory duties are likely to give rise to matters which would have a material effect on the financial statements, and if so, the opinion on the financial statements should not be given until the additional statutory duties have been completed.

48.21   Going concern

The Practice Note gives guidance on the following areas:

- the auditor's other responsibilities relating to going concern;
- entities that prepare their financial statements on the going concern basis;
- circumstances affecting going concern;
- consideration of the foreseeable future;
- the auditor's responsibilities in considering going concern;
- written representations on going concern.

48.21.1   The auditor's other responsibilities relating to going concern

Auditors of local government and health entities in England and Wales must review and report on aspects of the entity's corporate governance arrangements as they relate to the ongoing financial standing of the entity. Similar requirements exist for local government in Scotland. In Northern Ireland, auditors are expected to assess the financial standing of the audited entity.

These requirements are outside the intended scope of ISA (UK and Ireland) 570 (Revised June 2016), but the auditor should ensure that when matters come to his attention through these additional responsibilities, he considers their impact on the financial statements in line with the requirements of the ISA.

48.21.2   Entities that prepare their financial statements on the going concern basis

The legislation determining the format of the financial statements will normally indicate whether the going concern basis should be adopted.

48.21.3   Circumstances affecting going concern

It is unlikely that a central government entity will cease to operate as a result of insolvency or inability to finance operations, unless they operate in a trading capacity at arm's length from the Government.

Cessation is most likely to result from a decision by the Government and may involve transferring the operations to another entity. In such cases, the individual circumstances should be considered when assessing whether the going concern basis is appropriate.

48.21.4   Consideration of the foreseeable future

Government policy is inherently subject to political uncertainty, but political decisions are no more uncertain than the risks faced by private entities. Therefore, the provisions in ISA (UK and Ireland) 570 (Revised June 2016) relating to 'foreseeable future' can be applied by the auditor of public sector entities.

48.21.5   The auditor's responsibilities in considering going concern

Public sector auditors should consider two factors:

- the risk associated with changes in policy direction (for example, where there is a change in Government); and
- the operational, or business, risk (for example, the entity has insufficient working capital).

Auditors need to obtain evidence concerning the Government's intentions in the particular area of policy that the entity operates in. This would include whether:

- they intend to review policy, for example, a manifesto commitment;
- a review has been announced;
- an efficiency review has concluded that rationalisation is necessary; or
- there is a known intention to privatise its activities.

Trading operations may also be subject to risks arising from changes in policy direction as well as operational and business risks.

48.21.6   Written representations on going concern

The Practice Note suggests that the receipt of written representations from the Accounting Officer about going concern may not be sufficient audit evidence as the officer may not be capable of making judgments about future conditions for support.

If the going concern assumption is only substantiated by written confirmation of support from the sponsoring department, the auditor should consider whether there is a need to refer to these confirmations in the financial statements.

Other evidence of the intention to continue the entity's activities could come from the most recent:

- public expenditure survey;
- supply estimates; and
- financial management and policy review.

The Practice Note contains example audit procedures in relation to going concern.

48.22   Written representations

Each type of public sector entity has a person or group of people with responsibility for the preparation and signing of the financial statements. The auditor should review relevant regulations to determine to whom this responsibility falls.

The responsible person signs letters of representation, including specific representations on the regularity assertion.

48.23 Audits of group financial statements (including the work of component auditors)

There are five situations where the auditor of a public sector entity is deemed to be the principal auditor:

- if the public sector entity consolidates the results of lower tier bodies into its own financial statements, the principal and other auditor relationship is identical to that within a group of companies;
- where the Comptroller and Auditor General audits the Whole of Government Accounts. This is a situation analogous to the audit of a group of companies;
- if the entity has pooled budgets or shared services audited by another auditor;
- where an entity has contracted out services to another party, a principal/other auditor relationship exists and the auditor applies the guidance in ISA (UK and Ireland) 402 accordingly; and
- where there is a duty to give an opinion on regularity and the auditor of the entity seeks to use the work of the grant recipient's auditor to reduce the extent of their own procedures.

Where the auditor is acting as group auditor and is relying on the work of one or more component auditors the considerations set out in ISA (UK and Ireland) 600 (Revised June 2016) will apply.

48.24 Using the work of internal auditors

The requirements of ISA (UK and Ireland) 610 (Revised June 2013) are as relevant to the audit of public sector entities as to private companies. The internal audit function is normally a mandatory element of a public sector entity's internal control framework, and auditors may have a responsibility to provide negative assurance on a Statement of Internal Control. An assessment of the internal control function is required even if it is not possible to rely on its work in relation to the financial statements.

48.25 The independent auditor's report on financial statements

When reporting on central government financial statements, the requirements of the auditor reporting ISAs (UK and Ireland) should be followed, bearing in mind any specific reporting requirements of the engagement, such as to whom the audit report is addressed.

The Practice Note gives additional guidance on responsibility statements which should draw attention to the responsibilities of the Accounting Officers or other financial officer with responsibility for the financial statements, separately from those of any other officers. **Table 3** sets out the expected disclosures in a public sector entity's Statement of Responsibilities.

TABLE 3: Expected disclosures in a public sector entity's Statement of Responsibilities

Responsibility for:

- proper accounting records that disclose with reasonable accuracy at any time the financial position of the entity and enable the entity to ensure that financial statements are prepared to comply with statutory requirements;
- safeguarding the assets of the entity and for taking reasonable steps for the prevention and detection of fraud and other irregularities;.
- preparation of financial statements for each financial year that give a true and fair view of/present fairly the state of affairs of the entity and its performance for that period;
- in preparing financial statements:
  - selecting suitable accounting policies and then applying them consistently;
  - making judgments and estimates that are reasonable and prudent;
  - stating whether applicable accounting standards have been followed, subject to any material departures disclosed and explained in the financial statements; and
  - preparing the financial statements on the going concern basis, unless it is inappropriate to presume that the entity will continue in business;
- the regularity of the public finances for which the Accounting/Accountable Officer is answerable, where a regularity opinion is given.

The wording of the audit opinion depends on the particular auditing framework. The opinion paragraph should clearly indicate the financial reporting framework used to prepare the financial statements and the statute which requires the financial statements to be audited. These vary from body to body.

Where the auditor is reporting on regularity, a separate and explicit opinion is given on the regularity of transactions in the entity's financial statements. In addition, the auditor may provide separate reports, other than through his audit opinions, on issues of regularity. Where the auditor gives a qualified opinion on regularity, this does not in itself lead to a qualification of the truth and fairness, fair presentation or proper presentation part of the opinion.

48.26   The auditor's responsibilities relating to other information in documents containing audited financial statements

Most public sector entities are required to include a foreword in the same document as the financial statements. The foreword usually contains the information which would be included in the directors' report in a set of Companies Act financial statements, and the auditor's opinion does not extend to the contents of the foreword.

Other information required will vary depending on the type of public sector entity.

48.27   Grant claims

Many organisations, both in the public and private sectors, receive grant in aid or other grants from government departments of other funding bodies, often requiring the recipient to obtain a report from their accountant or auditor regarding their eligibility for and/or use of the grant.

In 2003, the ICAEW issued Technical Release Audit 03/03 *Public Sector Special Reporting Engagement – Grant Claims* to provide guidance in situations where a grant paying body has awarded a grant for a special purpose and requires that a special accountant's report be produced. Audit 03/03 does not apply in situations where a grant paying body has awarded grant in aid or grants and requires a regularity opinion on the use of these funds.

The Technical Release, which was agreed with the Treasury, builds on the principles outlined in Audit 1/01 *Reporting to Third Parties* (see **Chapter 40**), and applied from September 2003 for grant arrangements entered into before 2010.

In March 2010, the ICAEW issued Technical Release AAF 01/10 *Framework Document for Accountants' Reports on Grant Claims*. This document sets out a new framework for reporting accountants, to be applied for new schemes developed from 1 April 2010. The framework is intended to be helpful to those involved in providing special reports on grants and returns and also to the grant paying bodies that receive and rely on such reports. The new framework was not intended to be applied to existing schemes whose terms and conditions were already in place, although the Technical Release notes that there is nothing to stop grant paying bodies considering the good practice principles in the framework for such schemes.

49 REGULATED ENTITIES

49.1 Introduction

Regulated entities, see **Table 1**, are often required to submit a large volume of financial information to their regulated body as part of the regulatory process and the exact requirements can vary significantly between industries. Regulators use this information in a number of ways, for example, in ensuring that costs and pricing are transparent, and the regulatory body often requires an independent accountant's report on elements of this information.

Guidance to assist accountants when reporting on regulatory information can be found in TECH 02/16AAF *Reporting to regulators on regulatory accounts* issued by the ICAEW. This technical release is an update to the one issued in October 2003, Audit 5/03 *Reporting to Regulators of Regulated Entities*.

The guidance in the technical release is based on TECH 10/12AAF *Reporting to Third Parties* (see **Chapter 40**), and was developed after discussion and consultation with a number of regulators. It does not apply to reporting to other regulatory bodies such as the Financial Conduct Authority (see **Chapter 9**).

TABLE 1: Regulatory bodies

The Government appointed regulatory bodies that oversee the activities of regulated entities for the purpose of TECH 02/16AAF are:

- Ofgem (Office of Gas and Electricity Markets);
- Ofwat (The Water Services Regulation Authority);
- CAA (Civil Aviation Authority);
- ORR (Office of Rail and Road);
- URegNI (Utility Regulator, Northern Ireland);
- Ofcom (Office of Communications).

49.2 Duty of care and engagement contracts

As noted in **Chapter 40**, when an accountant knows that a third party obtains and relies on his report, the accountant will owe that third party a duty of care unless an effective disclaimer is in place.

Regulatory returns and regulatory accounts are required by an individual regulator, who will specify what information they will contain and who uses that information as part of its overall role. The accountant will only accept a duty of care to the regulator if either a tri-partite or bi-partite engagement contract with a written notice is in place. If the regulator will not enter into a suitable engagement contract, the accountant will not accept a duty of care to the regulator and will make it clear in his report. However, the report will be addressed to the company and the regulator in order to meet the requirements of the regulatory licence.

The accountant will exclude a duty of care to any other third party by including a suitable disclaimer in his report. A third party may only rely on the report once they have become party to the engagement contract.

49.2.1 Tri-partite engagement contracts

A tri-partite engagement contract is a written engagement contract between the accountant, the regulated entity and the regulator. The contract will contain appropriate terms clarifying and limiting the scope and extent of the accountant's responsibilities and liability.

An example tri-partite engagement contract can be found in TECH 02/16AAF *Reporting to regulators on regulatory accounts*.

49.2.2 Bi-partite engagement contracts

A bi-partite engagement contract is a written engagement contract between the accountant and the regulated entity only. In order for the accountant to owe a duty of care to the regulator when a bi-partite engagement contract exists, there must be provision in that contract for the accountant to accept a responsibility to the regulator separately in a written notice. The contract will cap any financial liability to the regulator and regulated entity in aggregate to that which would have been paid to the regulated entity if no separate agreement had been made with the regulator.

A copy of the bi-partite engagement contract between the accountant and the regulated entity will be attached to the written notice. An example of both the bi-partite engagement contract and the written notice can be found in TECH 02/16AAF *Reporting to regulators on regulatory accounts*.

49.3 Reporting

Each regulator will stipulate in its regulatory licence the information to be included in reports it receives and state that the report should be accompanied by an independent accountant's report.

The report should follow the guidelines set out in ISA (UK and Ireland) 700 (Revised June 2016) *Forming an opinion and reporting on financial statements* (see **Chapter 4**). An example report is given in TECH 02/16AAF *Reporting to* *regulators on regulatory accounts*, which should be modified for the particular circumstances of the engagement.

The accountant should make clear in his report the regulatory information on which he is providing assurance, and that on which he is not. Where the regulatory information is part of a wider report or return, the material covered by the accountant's report should be clearly identified.

49.4   Materiality

Increasingly regulators are requiring entities to include a number of different analyses of their business segments or operations and for accountants to report on them. In order to do this, the accountant must use his professional judgment to assess materiality in the context of the regulatory accounts as a whole and in line with the principles outlined in ISA (UK and Ireland) 320 (Revised June 2016) *Materiality in planning and performing an audit*, see **Chapter 15**. His opinion should be on the regulatory accounts as a whole, not on the individual analyses.

If the regulator requires specific items to be reported on in detail, this should form the basis of a separate, 'agreed upon procedures' engagement, which is reported on separately to the opinion on the accounts. Guidance on agreed upon procedures engagements is given in **41.3**.

49.5   Working with independent experts

Accountants may need to rely on the work of independent experts when reporting on regulatory accounts and other regulatory information, such as technical or engineering experts to determine whether the cost of projects should be capitalised or expensed.

Where this is the case, the accountant would follow the guidance in ISA (UK and Ireland) 620 (Revised June 2016) *Using the work of an auditor's expert* (see **31.3**), and would not refer to the expert's work in his audit report. If an 'agreed upon procedures' engagement is undertaken and no opinion is given in the accountant's report, reference to the expert's work is likely. Consent should be obtained from the experts prior to issuing any report which refers to them or includes extracts of their work.

APPENDIX 1

EXISTING GUIDANCE AT 30 APRIL 2016

Table A sets out the Ethical Standards and other FRC pronouncements. Table B lists the ISAs (UK and Ireland). Table C sets out other Standards, Practice Notes, Bulletins. These are all issued by the FRC, or its predecessors. Items in Tables A and B shown as being issued in April 2016 are final drafts of revised standards due to be issued in June 2016.

Table D lists ICAEW Technical Releases extant on 30 April 2016.

TABLE A

FRC pronouncement	Date Issued
Scope and authority of audit and assurance pronouncements	March 2013
Glossary of terms (auditing and ethics) 2016	April 2016
Revised Ethical Standard 2016 (replaces Ethical Standards ES 1 to 5, provisions available for smaller entities and ethical standard for reporting accountants)	April 2016
ISQC 1 (Revised June 2016) Quality control for firms that perform audits and reviews of historical financial statements, and other assurance and related services engagements	April 2016

TABLE B

ISAs (UK and Ireland)	Date Issued
200 (Revised June 2016) Overall objectives of the independent auditor and the conduct of an audit in accordance with international standards on auditing (UK and Ireland)	April 2016
210 (Revised June 2016) Agreeing the terms of audit engagements	April 2016
220 (Revised June 2016) Quality control for an audit of financial statements	April 2016
230 (Revised June 2016) Audit documentation	April 2016
240 (Revised June 2016) The auditor's responsibilities relating to fraud in an audit of financial statements	April 2016
250 Section A (Revised June 2016) – Consideration of laws and regulations in an audit of financial statements	April 2016
250 Section B (Revised June 2016) – The auditor's statutory right and duty to report to regulators of public interest entities and regulators of other entities in the financial sector	April 2016

ISAs (UK and Ireland)	*Date Issued*
260 (Revised June 2016) Communication with those charged with governance	April 2016
265 Communicating deficiencies in internal control to those charged with governance and management	October 2009
300 (Revised June 2016) Planning an audit of financial statements	April 2016
315 (Revised June 2016) Identifying and assessing the risks of material misstatement through understanding of the entity and its environment	April 2016
320 (Revised June 2016) Materiality in planning and performing an audit	April 2016
330 (Revised June 2016) The auditor's responses to assessed risks	April 2016
402 Audit considerations relating to an entity using a service organisation	October 2009
450 (Revised June 2016) Evaluation of misstatements identified during the audit	April 2016
500 Audit evidence	October 2009
501 Audit evidence – specific considerations for selected items	October 2009
505 External confirmations	October 2009
510 (Revised June 2016) Initial audit engagements – opening balances	April 2016
520 Analytical procedures	October 2009
530 Audit sampling	October 2009
540 (Revised June 2016) Auditing accounting estimates, including fair value accounting estimates, and related disclosures	April 2016
550 Related parties	October 2009
560 Subsequent events	October 2009
570 (Revised June 2016) Going concern	April 2016
580 Written representations	October 2009
600 (Revised June 2016) Special considerations – audits of group financial statements (including the work of component auditors)	April 2016
610 (Revised June 2013) Using the work of internal auditors	June 2013
620 (Revised June 2016) Using the work of an auditor's expert	April 2016
700 (Revised June 2016) Forming an opinion and reporting on financial statements	April 2016
701 Communicating key audit matters in the independent auditor's report	April 2016
705 (Revised June 2016) Modifications to the opinion in the independent auditor's report	April 2016
706 (Revised June 2016) Emphasis of matter paragraphs and other matter paragraphs in the independent auditor's report	April 2016

ISAs (UK and Ireland)	*Date Issued*
710 Comparative information – corresponding figures and comparative financial statements	October 2009
720 (Revised June 2016) The auditor's responsibilities relating to other information	April 2016

TABLE C

	Date Issued
Standard: Providing assurance on client assets to the Financial Conduct Authority (replaces Bulletin 2011/2 and Bulletin 3)	November 2015
ISRE (UK and Ireland) 2410: Review of interim financial information performed by the independent auditor of the entity	July 2007
PN10 (Revised) Audit of financial statements of public sector bodies in the United Kingdom	October 2010
PN10(I) (Revised) Audit of central government financial statements in the Republic of Ireland	August 2011
PN11(Revised) The audit of charities in the United Kingdom	March 2012
PN12 (Revised) Money Laundering – Guidance for auditors on UK legislation	September 2010
PN14 The audit of housing associations in the United Kingdom	January 2014
PN15 (Revised) The audit of occupational pension schemes in the United Kingdom	January 2011
PN15(I) The audit of occupational pension schemes in Ireland	February 2010
PN16 (Revised) Bank reports for audit purposes in the United Kingdom	February 2011
PN19 (Revised) The audit of banks and building societies in the United Kingdom	March 2011
PN19(I) (Revised) The audit of banks in the Republic of Ireland	June 2008
PN20 (Revised) The audit of insurers in the United Kingdom	January 2011
PN21 The audit of investment business in the United Kingdom (Revised) (Paragraphs 180 to 263, Appendix 1.1 and Appendix 2 of PN21 are superseded by Bulletin 2011/12)	December 2007
PN22 The auditors' consideration of FRS17 'Retirement Benefits' – defined benefit schemes	April 2002
PN23 Special considerations in auditing financial instruments	July 2013
PN24 (Revised) The audit of friendly societies in the United Kingdom	July 2011
PN25 (Revised) Attendance at stocktaking	February 2011
PN26 (Revised) Guidance on smaller entity audit documentation (Revised)	December 2009

	Date Issued
PN27 (Revised) The audit of credit unions in the United Kingdom	May 2011
PN27(I) The audit of credit unions in the Republic of Ireland	December 2008
Bulletin 2006/4 Regulatory and legislative background to the application of Standards for Investment Reporting in the Republic of Ireland	April 2006
Bulletin 2006/5 The Combined Code on Corporate Governance: Requirements of auditors under the Listing Rules of the Financial Services Authority and the Irish Stock Exchange	September 2006
Bulletin 2007/2 The duty of auditors in the Republic of Ireland to report to the Director of Corporate Enforcement	March 2007
Bulletin 2008/1 Audit issues when financial market conditions are difficult and credit facilities may be restricted	January 2008
Bulletin 2008/2 The auditor's association with preliminary announcements made in accordance with the requirements of the UK and Irish Listing Rules	February 2008
Bulletin 2008/5 Auditor's reports on revised accounts and reports in the United Kingdom	April 2008
Bulletin 2008/6 The 'Senior Statutory Auditor' under the United Kingdom Companies Act 2006	April 2008
Bulletin 2008/9 Miscellaneous Reports by Auditors Required by the United Kingdom Companies Act 2006	October 2008
Bulletin 2008/10 Going Concern Issues During the Current Economic Conditions	December 2008
Bulletin 2009/4 Developments in Corporate Governance Affecting the Responsibilities of Auditors of UK Companies	December 2009
Bulletin 2010/1 XBRL Tagging of Information in Audited Financial Statements – Guidance for Auditors	February 2010
Bulletin 2010/2 (Revised) Compendium of illustrative auditor's reports on United Kingdom private sector financial statements for periods ended on or after 15 December 2010	March 2012
Bulletin 2011/1 Developments in Corporate Governance Affecting the Responsibilities of Auditors of Companies Incorporated in Ireland	May 2011
Bulletin 1(I): Compendium of Illustrative Auditor's Reports on Irish financial statements	October 2012
Bulletin 2: Guidance for Reporting Accountants of Stakeholder Pension Schemes in the United Kingdom	February 2013
Bulletin 4: Recent developments in Company Law, The Listing Rules and Auditing Standards that affect United Kingdom Auditor's Reports (Revised)	June 2015
ISRE (UK and Ireland) 2410: Review of interim financial information performed by the independent auditor of the entity	July 2007

TABLE D

ICAEW Technical Releases

AUDIT 04/00: Firm's reports and duties to lenders in connection with loans and other facilities to clients and related covenants

AUDIT 02/01: Requests for references on clients' financial status and their ability to service loans

AUDIT 01/02: Practical points for auditors in connection with the implementation of FRS 17 'Retirement Benefits' – defined benefit schemes

AUDIT 02/02: New arrangements for reporting to the ABTA

AUDIT 04/02: Management representation letters: Explanatory note

AUDIT 01/03: The audit report and auditor's duty of care to third parties

AUDIT 03/03: Public sector special reporting engagements – grant claims

AUDIT 04/03: Access to working papers by investigating accountants

AUDIT 03/04: Auditing implications of IFRS transition

AUDIT 02/05: Guidance on the implications of the *Freedom of Information Act* 2000

AAF 01/06 Assurance reports on internal controls of service organisations made available to third parties (Revised 2012)

AAF 02/06 Identifying and managing certain risks arising from the inclusion of reports from auditors and accountants in prospectuses (and certain other investment circulars)

AAF 04/06 Assurance engagements: management of risk and liability

AAF 01/07 Independent accountants report on packaging waste

AAF 02/07 A framework for assurance reports on third party operations

AAF 01/08 Access to information by successor auditors

AAF 01/09 Paid cheques

AAF 01/10 Framework document for accountants' reports on grant claims

AAF 04/10 Guidance for performing agreed-upon procedures engagements that address XBRL-tagged data included within financial statements prepared in an iXBRL format

AAF 01/11 Reporting to the Audit Bureau of Circulations Limited (ABC)

TECH 08/12AAF Regularity reporting for Academies 2011–12: Guidance

TECH 10/12AAF Reporting to third parties (superseded AUDIT 01/01)

TECH 04/13AAF Assurance reporting on relevant trustees

TECH 09/13 AAF Assurance review engagements on historical financial statements (supersedes AAF 03/06)

TECH 07/14 AAF Assurance reporting on master trusts (master trust supplement to AAF 02/07)

TECH 10/14 AAF Receipt of information in confidence by auditors (superseded AUDIT 02/99)

TECH 13/14 AAF Issues for auditors arising from the implementation of FRS 102 *The Financial Reporting Standard applicable in the UK and Republic of Ireland*

ICAEW Technical Releases

TECH 09/15 BL Managing the professional liability of accountants

TECH 16/15 AAF Solicitors Regulation Authority (SRA) Accounts Rules: interim guidance for reporting accountants following changes to the accountant's report requirements

TECH 02/16 AAF Reporting to regulators on regulatory accounts (supersedes AUDIT 05/03)

AAF 07/16 Chartered accountants' reports on the compilation of financial information of incorporated entities Revised March 2016 – updates AAF 02/10

AAF 08/16 Chartered accountants' reports on the compilation of historical financial information of unincorporated entities Revised March 2016 – updates AAF 03/10

TECH 09/16 AAF Revised arrangements for ATOL reporting accountants reporting to the Civil Aviation Authority (supersedes TECH 07/12AAF)

APPENDIX 2

SPECIFIC ISA REQUIREMENTS RELATING TO STATUTORY AUDITS OF PUBLIC INTEREST ENTITIES

The requirements listed below are those that apply specifically to public interest entities, PIEs[1]. These are in addition to requirements applicable to audits of listed companies (for example in ISQC1 and ISAs 220, 260, 700, 701 and 720) and entities that are required to or choose voluntarily to state how they have complied with the UK Corporate Governance Code (for example in ISAs 260, 570, 700, 701 720). Such entities may also be PIEs.

ISA	Paragraph Reference	Summary of requirement	Chapter reference
ISQC1	27R-2	Additional requirements before accepting or continuing an engagement	3.2.6
ISQC1	36R-2	Additional requirements about the EQCR	3.2.8
ISQC1	39R-1	Additional requirements about the need for an EQCR before the audit report is issued	3.2.8
ISQC1	43-R1	Resolving disagreements between the audit partner and EQCR	3.2.8
220	21R-1	Areas of consideration for an EQCR	3.3.6
220	25R-1	Documentation of the EQCR	3.3.8
220	25R-2	Documentation of the EQCR	3.3.8
240	41R-1	Suspicions about fraud or irregularities	16.8.1
240	43R-1	Informing the authorities when the entity does not investigate suspicions of fraud or irregularities	16.8.1
250A	22R-1	Suspicions about fraud or irregularities	17.8.4
250A	28R-1	Informing the authorities when the entity does not investigate suspicions	17.8.4
250B	13R-1	Reporting to regulators	9.7
260	11R-1	Report to the equivalent of the audit committee where none exists	10.2
260	16R-2	Additional report to the audit committee	10.7.2
260	17R-1	Confirmation and discussion of independence	10.6.5

---

[1] Public interest entities are defined in ISQC 1 as those whose transferable securities are admitted to trading on a regulated market, credit institutions and insurance undertakings. This includes fully listed entities in the UK, but not those listed on AIM.

ISA	Paragraph Reference	Summary of requirement	Chapter reference
260	20R-1	Requirements regarding the additional report to the audit committee	10.4.2
260	21R-1	Timing of additional report to audit committee	10.7.2
260	23D-1	Retention of documents relating to the additional report to the audit committee	10.4.2
330	19R-1	Requirement to assess the valuation methods used	21.4.2
510	8R-1	Obtaining an understanding of the predecessor auditor's methodology	19.3.3
600	49D-1	Responsibility for additional report to audit committee	30.15
620	9R-1	Confirmation of the external expert's independence	31.3.5
700	30-1	Reporting on key audit matters for those entities that apply the Code	4.3.3
700	45R-1	Requirements regarding the audit report	4.3.2
701	All	Requirements relating to key audit matters	4.3.3

Index

All indexing is to paragraph number